The Guide to the American Revolutionary War In South Carolina

The Guide to the American Revolutionary War In South Carolina

Battles, Raids, and Skirmishes

Norman Desmarais

Busca, Inc.
Ithaca, New York

Busca, Inc.
P.O. Box 854
Ithaca, NY 14851
Ph: 607-546-4247
Fax: 607-546-4248
E-mail: info@buscainc.com
www.buscainc.com

BUSCA = SEARCH

Copyright © 2012 by Norman Desmarais
All rights reserved. No part of this book may be reproduced or transmitted in any form or by any means, electronic or mechanical, including photocopying, recording, or by any information storage or retrieval system, without permission in writing from the copyright owner.

First Edition

Printed in the United States of America

ISBN: 978-1-934934-06-7

Publisher's Cataloging-In-Publication Data
(Prepared by The Donohue Group, Inc.)

Desmarais, Norman.
   The guide to the American Revolutionary War in South Carolina : battles, raids, and skirmishes / Norman Desmarais. -- 1st ed.

      p. : ill., maps ; cm. -- (Battlegrounds of freedom ; [6])

   Includes bibliographical references and index.
   ISBN: 978-1-934934-06-7

   1. United States--History--Revolution, 1775-1783--Battlefields--South Carolina. 2. South Carolina--History, Military--18th century. 3. United States--History--Revolution, 1775-1783--Campaigns--South Carolina. I. Title.

E230.5.S6 D47 2013
973.3/3

All state maps Copyright © 2012 DeLorme (www.delorme.com) Street Atlas USA®.
Reprinted with permission.

Photography: author unless otherwise noted

Composition: P.S. We Type ◆ Set ◆ Edit

The author has made every effort to ensure the accuracy of the information in this book. Neither the publisher nor the author is responsible for typographical mistakes, other errors, or information that has become outdated since the book went to press.

This volume is part of the BATTLEGROUNDS OF FREEDOM series.

To the men and women of our armed forces who go in harm's way to preserve the freedoms our ancestors have secured for us.

Contents

List of Illustrations xi

Acknowledgments xiii

Foreword by Mark Hurwitz...xv

Preface xvii
    Strategic Objectives xviii; Nomenclature xix; Conventions and Parts of This Book xxi

Introduction 1

1. Northeastern South Carolina 3
    McBee/Hem Branch 3; McPherson's Plantation/Jeffries Creek/Murphy's Defeat 3; Black Creek/Maple's Mill 5; Blair/Gibson's Meeting House or Mobley's Meeting House 6; Winnsboro 8; Lancaster/Battle of the Waxhaws (Buford's Defeat)/Near Waxhaws/Waxhaws Meeting House, near Lancaster/Waxhaws Presbyterian Church 9; Beckhamville/Gaither's Old Field/John Land's house/Beckhamville, Near Great Falls/Alexander's Old Field (Beckham's Old Field or the Battle of Beckhamville) 11; Great Falls/Fishing Creek Church/Fishing Creek Engagement/Catawba Ford 14; Union County and vicinity/Kelsey Creek/Fairforest/Love's Plantation/Brandon's Defeat/Bullock's Ford, Thicketty Creek/Bullock's Ford/Tyger River/Brandon's Camp/Stallion's (probably Sterling or Stalling)/Green Spring/Meador's Plantation 15; Greenville/Enoree River/Roebuck captures prisoners/Indian Creek/Fairforest Creek/Col. Hampton killed (Blasingame's house, Earle's Fort) 16; Heath Springs/Flat Rock and Hanging Rock/Rocky Creek/Rocky Creek Congregation/Flat Rock/Big Beaver Creek/Beaver Creek Ford/Hanging Rock skirmish 23; York County/Hill's Iron Works 27; Sumter/General Sumter's house burned, Sumter County/Bloody Savannah 28; Brattonsville/Williamson's plantation/Huck's defeat 29; Near Blenheim/Hunts Bluff/Three Creeks/Robert Gregg shot/Polk Swamp 31; Fort Thicketty/Fort Anderson (Thicketty Fort) 33; Great Falls vicinity/Caldwell's house/Rocky Mount engagement 35; Murray's Ferry 36; Rocky Creek 36; Mayesville/Capture of James Bradley/McCallum's Ferry 37; Kershaw County/Little Lynches Creek/Lynches River/Ratcliff's Bridge/Kershaw's Creek 38; Johnsonville/Williamsburg/Port's Ferry 41; Browns Creek/Hollingsworth Mill, Browns Creek/John Mayfield killed 42; Camden and vicinity/Camden/Wateree Ferry/Fort Carey/Carey's Fort/Ford of the Wateree/Battle of Wateree Ferry/Gum Swamp also known as Parker's Old Field, Saunder's Creek, Green Swamp and Sutton's Tavern/Antioch/Rugeley's Mill/Hermitage Mill/Major William Downes's house/Logtown/Near Camden/Hobkirk Hill 43; Kingstree/Mouzon's house burned/Lower Bridge 55; Hemingway/Pee Dee Swamp 57; Tearcoat Swamp/Blue Savannah, Little Pee Dee River/Black River/Black River/Lower Bridge 58; Black Mingo Creek/Shepherd's Ferry 61; Williamsburg Township/McGill's Plantation 62; Society Hill/Adam Cusack hanged/Darlington/Pine Log Bridge 64; Bigger's Ferry 64; Dillon/Rouse's Ferry/"Sweat Swamp" 65; York/Kings Mountain 65; Lake View/Bear Swamp 68; Manning/Ox Swamp 70; Carlisle/Fish Dam/Near Carlisle 71; Chester District 71; Chester/Jenkin's Cross Roads 72; Chester district/Broad River/Hopkins Place/

McKown's Mill/Love's Ford 72; Chester, Chester County/Lee's Creek 74; Brierly's Ferry or Ford 74; Sandy River 75; Near Rimini/Halfway Swamp/Singleton's Mill 76; Wallace/Cheraw, Great Pee Dee River 78; Ferry near Owen's Plantation/Brierly's Ferry 79; Lisles's Ford 79; Sharon/James Kirkpatrick killed 79; Amis's Mill/Hulin's Mill (Catfish Swamp)/The "Bull Pen"/Colonel Kolb killed/Mrs. Wilds robbed/Two Redcoats killed/Mulatto slave killed/Mr. Cotton killed/Courtney killed 80; Johnsonville/Snow Island/De Peyster's capture/Hasty Point (John Postell's plantation) 82; Cayce/The Congarees/Muddy Spring/Fort Granby/Friday's or Fridig's Ferry/ Hampton's Store/Vaudant's Old Field (Weaver's Old Field)/Ancrum's Plantation/ Eggleston's capture/Dreher Plantation 86; Orangeburg/Orangeburg County/Manigault's Ferry/Near Manigault's Ferry, Belleville/Belleville Plantation, Thomson's Plantation,/Big Savannah/Santee/Summerton/Fort Watson (Wright's Bluff)/Metts Crossroads/Moore's surprise/Rowe's Plantation/Richard Hampton's surprise/Saint Matthews/Calk brothers/Edisto River/Orangeburg/Fork of Edisto/Near Orangeburgh/McCord's Ferry 91; Edisto River, Battle of the Tory Camps, Bull Swamp/ Four Mile Branch/Below Orangeburg/Amelia Township close to Manigault's Ferry, Sharp's skirmish 92; Buckhead/Buckhead Creek, near Fort Motte/Fort Motte 101; Wiboo Swamp 101; Near Greeleyville/Mount Hope Swamp/Near Cantey's Plantation 102; Sampit/Sampit Bridge 103; Fairfield County/Dutchman's Creek 104; Florence County/Lynches River/Lynches River massacre/Witherspoon's Ferry 104; Conway/Bear Bluff 106; Heath Springs/Twitty's Mill/Beaver Creek 106; Lynchburg/Willow Grove 107; Cashua or Cashway Ferry/Brownsville Church 107; Prosperity/Camping Creek 108; Sawney's Creek 108; Bass's Mill 108; Leesville/ Hartley's Creek/Mount Willing/Lexington/Tarrar Spring/Clouds Creek (Carter's House, Carter's Old Field, Turner House Massacre, Big Lick, Lick Creek)/Lorick's Ferry 109; Near Salley/Dean Swamp/Battle of John Town 113; Bowling Green/ Burch's Mill/Black Lake 114; Bryan's Station 115

2. Charleston and Vicinity 116
Fort Johnson, James Island/Oohey River, Wallace's Road, James Island/James Island/ Horses captured/Dill's Bluff 116; Sullivan's Island/Fort Sullivan/Fort Moultrie/Ash's Plantation, Haddrell's Point/Haddrell's Point (Pest House) 123; Charleston/Hobcaw Magazine/Near Charleston/Old Race Track/Snider House 132; Charleston Harbor/Haddrell's Point/Charleston Bar/Rebellion Road/Bull's Inlet/Lemprière's Point 150; Sandy Point 154; Dewey's Inlet 154; Off Cummings Point/Tamar vs. 3 Canoes 155; Near Stono River/Mathews's Plantation (Massacre of the Beaufort Company)/Stono Inlet/13 Mile House, Stono Ferry/Stono River, mouth/Stono Ferry/Mathew's Ferry Stanyarne's and Eveleigh's Plantation/Rantowles Bridge/New Cut, Johns Island/Robert Gibbes's Plantation/William Gibbes's Plantation/Fenwick Hall/Folly Island/Chatham 156; Parker's Ferry/Charleston Road 165; Santee River/Charleston Road 165; Washington's Raid 166; Saint Andrews/Hammond's Plantation, Savage's Plantation or St. Andrews Church/Saint Andrews Creek (Armstrong's skirmish)/Drayton's Plantation/John Gibbes Plantation (Lowndes Grove Plantation) 166; Dorchester and vicinity/Dorchester Road/Fuller's Plantation (The Muck)/Horse Savannah/Cypress Swamp, Dorchester/Ashley River Church (Ashley River Baptist Church) 168; Near Summerville/Fort Dorchester/Dorchester (Fair Spring) 171; Ferguson's Plantation 175; Mouth of Wappoo Creek/Wappoo Cut/ Near Stan's Bridge 176; Wando River/Cainhoy/Colonel Maham's tour 177; Moncks Corner and vicinity/Moncks Corner/Fair Lawn/Moncks Corner Road/Biggin Bridge/Biggin Church 177; Berkeley County/Wadboo, Keithfield and Manigault's

Contents ix

Ferry/Keithfield Plantation (also known as Kitfield Plantation) 181; Lewisfield Plantation (also known as Little Landing) 182; Fair Lawn (also known as Fair Lawn Barony or Colleton House) 182; 15 Mile House and 10 Mile House/Goose Creek/Garden's Plantation/Head of Goose Creek 184; Charleston County/Ashley River/Ashley Ferry/Quarter House/Near Quarter House Tavern/Dewee's Tavern 185; Wappetaw Meeting House 187; Johns Island/Murder of Solomon Freer 188; Middleton Plantation, Ashley River 188; Huger/Wadboo/Biggin Church/Strawberry Ferry/Quinby Bridge and Shubrick's Plantation/Bull Head/Wells's Plantation 189; Berkeley County/Between Huger and Cainhoy/Videau's Bridge 194; Whitehall (Vanderhorst Plantation) 195

3. Southeastern South Carolina 196
Daufuskie Island/Bloody Point/Ash's Point, Port Royal River/Captain Martinangel killed 196; Atlantic Ocean off the South Carolina coast/East of Cape Romain 198; South Edisto Inlet/Edisto Island/Lacey vs. Landing Party 199; Beaufort and vicinity/Port Royal Harbor/Bull's Plantation/Port Royal Ferry/Port Royal Island/Battle of Halfway House/Fort Lyttleton/Hunting Island/Beaufort/Capers Creek 200; St. Helena Sound/Coosaw Island/Brigantine Dispatch 206; Beaufort County/Near Sheldon/Sheldon Church/Savannah River 206; Sheldon/Battle of Chehaw Point/Combahee Ferry 207; Georgetown Bar (snow lost)/Georgetown/Winyah Bay (brig *Peace & Harmony*)/White's Bridge/White's Plantation/Alston's Plantation/Waccamaw Neck/Waccamaw River/Avant's Ferry/Wragg's Ferry/Black River Road/Hanging of Loyalist Bradley/Black River Swamp 210; Purysburg/Savannah River south of Purysburg/Black Swamp/Yamasee Bluff/Congress and Lee/Harden's men search for boats/Near Purysburg/Hardeeville 220; Savannah River/Two Sisters Ferry/Mathew's Bluff/Wiggin's Hill/Wiggin's Plantation 222; Coosawhatchie/Coosawhatchie River/Black Swamp 224; General Barnwell repulsed 226; Yamassee, Hampton/Beaufort/Colleton Counties/Near Yemassee/McPherson's Plantation/Jacksonboro/Six Miles from McPherson's (Saltketcher Bridge)/Saltketcher River/Saltketcher Swamp 227; Pon Pon/Bee's Plantation 229; Jamestown/Ball's Plantation/Lenud's Ferry, Jamestown/Near McClellanville/Wambaw Creek/Tydiman's Plantation 230; Brier Creek/Tarleton Brown's father and 17 others 232; Silver Bluff, near Jackson/Fort Galphin/Fort Dreadnought 233; Eutawville/Great Savannah/Nelson's Ferry 234; Hilton Head/Hilton Head Island/British privateer *Vigilant/Ceres*/Charles Davant ambushed/Two Oaks Plantation (also known as Big Gate, Bear Island, Buckingham Landing) 235; Bear Island 237; Buckingham Landing/Richard Pendarvis killed 237; Colleton County/Saltketcher Bridge (Patterson's Bridge)/Four Holes Swamp/Barton's Post, Colleton City/Pocotaligo Road/Fort Balfour 238; Walterboro/Snipes's Plantation/Ford's Plantation/Ford's Horseshoe Plantation/Horseshoe/Parson's Plantation 240; Loyalists hanged by Captain Joseph Vince/Captain Vince wounded 243; Eutawville/Eutaw Springs/White Meeting House 243; Girard, Georgia/Stone's Ferry (modern Stoney Landing)/Colonel McGirth repulsed 245; Barnwell County/Vince's Fort 246; Barnwell County/Adam Wood killed/Mr. Collins killed 246; Blackville/Slaughter Field 247; Olar/Rush's Mill/Georges Creek 247; Greenland Swamp 248

4. Western South Carolina 249
Cranbury Inlet 164; Brigantine Beach 164; Egg Harbor 164; Tindall's Island/Bacon's Mount Carmel/Fort Charlotte 249; New Richmond 249; Congaree River/Mine Creek/Near Ninety Six 251; Gilbert/Lexington County/Ninety Six/Near Ninety Six/Road to Ninety Six/Middleton's (Mydelton's) Ambuscade (also known

as Juniper Spring, West's Old Field or Middleton's Defeat)/Old Man Palmer killed/Laurens County/Cunningham's Raid/Saluda River/Rawdon's/Cruger's baggage train captured 252; Pelzer/Golden Grove Creek 259; Near Simpsonville/ Great Cane Brake/Cane Brake/Snow Campaign 259; Landrum/Earle's Fort/Earlesville/Fair Forest Spring/Earle's Plantation/Near Wellford/Hampton Massacre/ Height's Blockhouse/Near Gowensville/Gowen's Fort/Fort Prince/McDowell's Camp/Shiloh Church/Earle's Ford 260; Middle Tyger River (Hampton Massacre)/ Woods Fort/Mountain Rest/Round Mountain (Howard's Gap) 264; Laurens/Fort Lindley (Lyndley) (Rayborn, Raeburns, Rabun's, Rabon or Creek) 266; Colonel Andrew Williamson's Indian Campaign/Cherokee Campaign/Seneca Old Town 266; Seneca (Esseneca)/Cherokee Town/Cherokee Indian Town (Seneca/Esseneca)/Keowee/Sugar Town/Jocassee/Oconee/Oconore/Estatoe/Tugaloo River/Brass Town/Tamassee (Tomassy, Ring Fight)/Cheowee/Eustaste (Eustustie, Oustestee)/ Chauga Quacoratchee (also known as Warachy, Tockorachee, Takwashua)/Oconee County/Indian Villages, Lower Settlements/Cherokee Villages/Oconee Creek or River/Keowee Town/Cherokee Campaign of 1782 267; Ustanali 267; Reedy River/Ridgeway's Fort 277; Edgefield County/Edgefield/Roger's Plantation/Turkey Creek/Stevens Creek 277; McGowan's Blockhouse 279; Fountain Inn/Kellett's Blockhouse 280; Iva/Wilson's Creek/Mr. Corruthers killed and Adam Files captured 281; Cedar Springs/Lawson's Fork/First Battle of Cedar Springs/Second Battle of Cedar Springs (the Peach Orchard Fight, The Old Iron Works Engagement or Wofford's Iron Works)/Clark's Ford/James Woods killed/Colonel John Woods killed/Hilliard Thomas killed/Duncan's Creek and Lawson's Fork/John Boyce's house 281; Green Spring/Wofford's Iron Works (Old Iron Works) (2nd Cedar Springs) 285; Cross Anchor/Musgrove Mill/Cross Anchor vicinity/Blackstock's Plantation/Tyger River 286; Saluda River/Rutledge's Ford/Hoil's Old Place 289; Near Troy/Long Cane/Near Ninety Six 290; Clinton/Hammond's Store/ Williams's Fort 292; Clinton/Hurricane Meeting House 293; Backcountry 293; Mann's Old Field 294; Gaffney/"Burr's" Mill/Bullock's Ford, Thicketty Creek 294; Chesnee/Dugan's Plantation (Indian Creek)/Cowpens 295; Newberry County/ Watkins 298; Laurens County/Williams's Fort (Mudlick, Battle of Mudlick Creek, near Fort Williams, Roebuck's Defeat) 299; Beattie's Mill/Little River/Dunlap's Defeat/Pratt's Mill 300; Horner's Creek or Corner/Hammond's Mill 301; Newberry County/Bush River 302; Aiken County/Beech Island 302; Backcountry 303; Near Vaughanville/Caldwell's house (Captain John Caldwell killed) 303; Greenwood County/Swancey's Ferry 303; Moore/Moore's Plantation 304; Clinton/Near Joanna/Hayes Station 304; Pine Wood House and White Hall 305; McCord Creek 305; Farrow's Station/Bryant's Mills 306; Pauline/Bryant's Mill 306

Notes 308

Glossary 357

Index..361

Please see the Busca website **www.buscainc.com** for more Resources on the volumes by Norman Desmarais including complete chronological and alphabetical lists of battles, raids, and skirmishes; a complete Bibliography for all sources used and cited in the creation of these volumes; and photos.

List of Illustrations

Maps

Northeastern South Carolina 4
Charleston and vicinity 117
Southeastern South Carolina 197
Western South Carolina 250

Photos

SC-1. Mobley's Mill 6
SC-2. General Cornwallis's headquarters, Winnsboro 8
SC-3. Beckhamville 12
SC-4. Hunts Bluff 32
SC-5. Blockhouse with loopholes 34
SC-6. Ratcliff's Bridge on Lynches River 39
SC-7. Open order 42
SC-8. Battle of Camden site 44
SC-9. Gum Swamp 45
SC-10. Kings Mountain 67
SC-11. Ferguson monument, Kings Mountain 69
SC-12. Snow Island 83
SC-13. Snow Island 83
SC-14. British grenadiers (Highlanders) 84
SC-15. Bastions 87
SC-16. Maham tower 89
SC-17. Grape shot 103
SC-18. Witherspoon's Ferry site 105
SC-19. Clubbed muskets 111
SC-20. Cannon gin 119
SC-21. Spontoon 123
SC-22. Fort Moultrie, palmetto logs 124
SC-23. Pettiauger 127
SC-24. Man-of-war (frigate) showing best bower 127
SC-25. Shots and shells 129
SC-26. Mortar 129
SC-27. Exchange and Provost dungeon, Charleston 132
SC-28. Remains of hornwork, Charleston 133
SC-29. Amusette or wall gun 137
SC-30. Hessian grenadiers 142
SC-31. Embrasure 145
SC-32. Swivel gun 152

SC-33. Fort Dorchester 172
SC-34. Biggin Church 178
SC-35. Beaufort arsenal 201
SC-36. Cannon and linstock with slow match 203
SC-37. Ruins of Sheldon Church 207
SC-38. British headquarters, Georgetown 211
SC-39. Marker commemorating Gabriel Marion, Georgetown 212
SC-40. Trunnions 219
SC-41. Fort Rutledge monument 268
SC-42. Fort Prince George 269
SC-43. Oconee Station 269
SC-44. Blunderbuss 280
SC-45. Musgrove Mill 286
SC-46. Blackstock's battlefield 287
SC-47. Long Cane Creek battlefield 290
SC-48. Cowpens 295

Acknowledgments

I would like to express my gratitude to Jack Montgomery, acquisitions librarian at the University of Western Kentucky, Bowling Green, for igniting the spark to write this book, for his encouragement through the project, and for introducing me to Connie Mills, the Kentucky Library Coordinator at the Kentucky Library and Museum. Michael Cooper, my publisher fanned the flame, nurtured the idea, and brought it to fruition.

I also wish to thank Providence College for providing research and faculty development funds as well as time to pursue research. That research began with one sabbatical and extended beyond two others. The staffs at the Phillips Memorial Library of Providence College and the other academic libraries in Rhode Island were very helpful in obtaining and providing much research material.

John C. Parker, author of *Parker's Guide to the Revolutionary War in South Carolina: Battles, Skirmishes and Murders*, is probably the most knowledgeable person alive for Revolutionary War actions in South Carolina. He spent many years traveling to the sites, walking the ground and interviewing people. I owe him a deep debt of gratitude for reading a draft of this volume and for his many suggestions, comments and recommendations. He was working on a second edition of his work at the same time I was working on this volume. He graciously shared the results of his research since the first edition and advised me about factors that caused him to change his mind about some of the locations.

David Loiterstein, Marketing Manager at Readex, also deserves my gratitude. He arranged for me to review the Early American Imprints Series I: Evans, 1639–1800 and the Early American Newspapers Series I, 1690–1876 and Series II, 1758–1900. The review periods coincided with important stages in my research. This undoubtedly made for better, more thorough, reviews; and it provided me with access to a wealth of primary sources that opened new avenues of research.

The members of the Brigade of the American Revolution (B.A.R.), the Continental Line, and the British Brigade generously give of themselves to help re-create the era of the American War for Independence. Some of these people work at musea or at historical sites. Some are members of their town historical societies or even historians for their city or town. Many are amateur historians who know a great deal about the Revolutionary War in their area. They provided enormous insight into events and the location of sites. Special thanks go to Bob Winowitch and David Clemens who guided me around Long Island to ensure that I visited all the relevant sites there. They also provided historical material and referred me to important sources for further information.

Other B.A.R. members, including Reinhard Batcher III, Todd Braisted, Todd Harburn, Thomas F. Kehr, Lawrence McDonald, Alan Morrison, Thaddeus J. Weaver, and VivianLea Solek read portions of the manuscript, suggested corrections and/or identified sources of additional information.

Many of the photographs were taken at various re-enactments. Without the efforts of the members of the B.A.R., these photos would not have been possible. Marshall Sloat, Scott Dermond, Daniel O'Connell, Todd Harburn, Paul Bazin, and Deborah Mulligan deserve credit for providing additional photographs.

There's a certain serendipity to research. During the 225th anniversary re-enactment of the march to Yorktown, Virginia, as the troops crossed the Hudson River in whale boats, I overheard B.A.R. member Daniel Hess talking about an engagement in which one of his ancestors had fought. I had been trying to locate documentation for that event; so I asked him about it after disembarking. He later sent me a copy of his ancestor's pension application which not only described the event which I had been trying to document but also identified two other events unknown to me.

DeLorme's Street Atlas USA software was very valuable in creating and annotating all the maps. GPS devices are useful for locating known places with addresses. They are not so useful for getting to a general location such as a particular hill or field. Maps are more useful for this purpose; but it takes a specially trained eye to identify changes in terrain that may cover earthworks or fortifications. The late Marshall Sloat had such an eye and I am grateful to him for accompanying me on some research trips, as both a companion and a navigator. He helped me locate landmarks, monuments, and other physical features that would elude the common person. He also helped document the visits with photographs.

Edward Ayres, Historian for the Jamestown-Yorktown Foundation, based at the Yorktown Victory Center in Yorktown, Virginia provided valuable assistance in locating Revolutionary War era maps.

John A. Robertson has done a yeoman's job in creating interactive maps to complement this series. The maps can be viewed as a Google or Yahoo cartographic or topographical map with cartographic, aerial or hybrid views. Google Earth maps can be zoomed to a variety of detail levels. Below an altitude of 200 feet, the maps turn to ground level view and allow taking a virtual tour of the landscape with a 360 degree view. One can toggle easily between aerial and ground level views. There's also a facility to add place marks or create polygons to modify the map to one's liking, add images, record a tour, or show sunlight across the landscape. A ruler makes it easy to measure distance between locations. Google Earth also has many photos that can be viewed with a single mouse click. These can sometimes provide a virtual tour of the better known sites.

Moving the cursor over each marker on the map displays the abbreviation for the state and the location name. Clicking on the marker reveals the dates of the action(s) there in mmddyy format along with an abbreviation for the volume which covers them and the page numbers. There's also an option to enter one's address or zip code to get driving directions. The maps can be accessed at **http://gaz.jrshelby.com/desmarais/**.

I wish to extend special thanks to my wife, Barbara, for her patience and support during the long periods of research and writing. She also accompanied me on many research trips and read maps and gave me directions as we drove to sites. She visited more forts and battlefields than she cares to remember.

Mark Hurwitz proofread the entire text and provided valuable feedback and suggestions. He also wrote the foreword. June Fritchman kindly offered some help with corrections and revisions of prior manuscripts in this series.

Foreword

by
Mark Hurwitz
Commander
Brigade of the American Revolution

To paraphrase Historian Geoffrey C. Ward, "the American War for Independence was fought from the walls of Quebec to the swamps of Florida, from Boston, to the Mississippi River." Now, if a shot was fired in anger, Norman Desmarais has documented it in this landmark study and guide, *The Guide to the American Revolutionary War*. It is a worthy successor to his *Battlegrounds of Freedom* (2005).

This comprehensive guide to the famous and unknown sites is groundbreaking. Beyond Lexington, Concord, Trenton, Brandywine, Saratoga, Monmouth, and Yorktown, Norman has fretted out the smaller actions and skirmishes which make up the eight year conflict, 1775–1783. Amazingly, Norman has found sites where settlers were scalped on the frontier to ships exchanging cannon fire on the high seas.

Norman Desmarais's passion for history comes as no surprise to me. After corresponding with Mr. Desmarais on an earlier multimedia CD-ROM project (*The American Revolution.*—American Journey: History in Your Hands series.—Woodbridge, CT: Primary Source Media, 1996), I finally got to meet him in November, 1995, when he attended a Brigade of the American Revolution (B.A.R.) event at Fort Lee Historic Park, Fort Lee, NJ. At that time, I had the opportunity to introduce him to Carl Becker, Commander of the 2nd Rhode Island Regiment, from his native state. Carl recruited him on the spot, and Norman, the academic historian, began his career as a re-enactor.

Becoming a "living historian" allows one to have laboratory to work in, wearing the uniforms, feeling the sweat, handling the weapons, experiencing the linear tactics, hearing the field music, smelling the smoke, which gives real perspective to the study of this period of history. This experience even goes beyond the "Staff Rides" of historic battlefields that the U.S. Army conducts with its officers.

The B.A.R. and the 2nd R.I. Regiment gave Norman the opportunity to visit many of the historic battle sites and get to see them "from the inside" and with the eye of a common soldier. This travel fueled his love for research and launched his encyclopedic study of Revolutionary War battle sites covering all of North America.

As a re-enactor, I have been studying the American War of Independence for nearly 35 years. Reading Desmarais's manuscript, I made discoveries both near and far.

- Being brought up and currently residing in my hometown of Springfield, NJ, I knew of the famous Battle of Springfield, June 23rd, 1780. Norman's research uncovered the following precursor, among many other actions there: "The militia killed and wounded 8 or 10 Waldeckers near Springfield on Sunday morning, January 19, 1777. They captured the rest of the party, 39 or 40, including 2 officers without suffering any casualties." (*The Pennsylvania Evening Post*, January 23, 1777)
- Meanwhile he found, west of the Mississippi: "St. Louis, Missouri—A small marker at 4th & Walnut Streets in downtown St. Louis which commemorates

the action that occurred on May 26, 1780." Desmarais's detailed entry then illuminates this unique action.
- Then at the end of the War for Independence, Savage Point, GA (Savage Point is located at a bend in the Ogeechee River at Richmond Hill State Park.): "Gen. Wayne suffered 5 men and horses killed and 8 wounded. He captured a British standard, 127 horses, and a number of packs." (*The Pennsylvania Packet or the General Advertiser.* 11:924 (August 15, 1782) p. 3)

I hope that readers can use this guide to find for themselves that history truly "happened here" as they travel the breadth of America and Canada.

Preface

The Guide to the American Revolutionary War in South Carolina: Battles, Raids, and Skirmishes is the fifth volume of a six-volume geographic history of the American War for Independence. The idea for the project came at a re-enactment of a 225th anniversary event when I overheard some of my fellow interpreters commenting about the several events on the calendar that summer that they knew nothing about. There had been no guidebooks published about the Revolutionary War since the nation's bicentennial in 1975. Moreover, those guidebooks and most of the history textbooks only cover the major, better known battles such as Lexington and Concord, Bunker Hill, Trenton and Princeton, Saratoga, Camden, Guilford Courthouse, and Yorktown.

Battlegrounds of Freedom: A Historical Guide to the Battlefields of the War of American Independence[1] served the purpose of an overview. It covered all the major battles and several of the minor ones, along with the winter encampments at Morristown and Valley Forge. It also included a chapter on re-enacting to make it distinctive from other guidebooks. The success of that volume encouraged me to continue the project.

This continuation of the *Battlegrounds of Freedom* series covers the battles and, much more specifically, the raids and skirmishes of the Revolutionary War, many of which do not get covered even in the most detailed history books. The series intends to provide comprehensive, if not exhaustive, coverage of the military engagements of the American War for Independence. It also aims to serve as a guide to the sites and the military engagements. It does not intend to cover specifically naval battles; but it does include naval actions in which one of the parties was land-based. British ships fired frequently on shore installations, ship-building industries, towns, houses, or troops on land. Such actions usually provoked a hostile response, even if a weak one. These minor clashes also illustrate the dangers faced by coastal residents and by troops moving within sight of enemy ships. Actions on inland lakes or bays are considered along with land actions as are attacks on enemy watering parties or other landing parties.

The work also covers engagements between French or Spanish troops and Crown forces as well as raids by Native Americans instigated or led either by British officers and agents or by Congressional forces. It does not attempt to cover raids on the cabins of western settlers that would have occurred regardless of the war, even though the residents retaliated.

Francis B. Heitman's *Historical Register of Officers of the Continental Army during the War of the Revolution, April 1775 to December 1783*[2] provides an alphabetical list of 420 engagements. This list seems to have been adopted as the U.S. Army's official list of battles and actions. Howard Henry Peckham's *The Toll of Independence: Engagements & Battle Casualties of the American Revolution*[3] expands this list to 1,330 military engagements and 220 naval engagements. He gives a brief description of the actions arranged chronologically, but his concern is primarily to tally the casualties. My research started with Peckham's work for the list of engagements, as his is comparatively the most extensive.

The multiple *Guide to the American Revolutionary War* volumes more than double the number of engagements (more than 3,000) found in Peckham. They correct some of the entries and provide documentary references. The lack of primary source materials makes some actions very difficult to discover and document. The problem is most evident in "neutral territory," such as Elizabethtown, New Jersey, and Staten Island, New York, where conflict pretty much became part of everyday life. Sometimes, military actions occurred in several places during the same expedition or as part of a multi-pronged effort. Rather than repeat a narrative in several different places, we refer the reader to the main or a related account through *See* and *See also* references. However, each volume of the series is intended to be self-contained as much as possible with respect to the others.

Mark Mayo Boatner's *Encyclopedia of the American Revolution*[4] and his *Landmarks of the American Revolution: A Guide to Locating and Knowing What Happened at the Sites of Independence*[5] have long been considered the Bible for Revolutionary War aficionados and re-enactors. These works appeared in a new edition in 2007.[6] This is an excellent source to begin research on the Revolutionary War together with *The Encyclopedia of the American Revolutionary War: A Political, Social, and Military History*.[7]

Each volume in the *Battlegrounds of Freedom* series covers its respective states affected by the war and each location where an engagement occurred. It follows a hybrid geographical/chronological approach to accommodate various audiences: readers interested in American history, re-enactors, tourists, and visitors. The states are arranged from north to south and east to west. Within each state, the engagements appear chronologically. Locations with multiple engagements also appear chronologically so readers can follow the text as a historical sequence or "story" of a site before proceeding to the next one. For example, the treatment of the events at Fairforest covers engagements dating from February 6, 1779; March 2, 1781; July 16, 1781 and August 29, 1782 before proceeding to Rocky Creek (June 12, 1780; August 3, 1780 and March 3, 1781). Cross references have been added as necessary.

The text identifies the location of the sites as best as can be determined, provides the historical background to understand what happened there, indicates what the visitor can expect to see there, and identifies any interpretive aids. It is not meant to replace the guides produced for specific sites and available at visitor centers. These guides usually provide more details about the features of a particular site. Also, monographs devoted to specific engagements or campaigns will be more detailed than what we can present here.

Strategic Objectives

The presence of large numbers of troops in an area gave residents cause for concern. The soldiers were always short of food and constantly searching for provisions. It took a lot of food to feed an army. While troops were allotted daily rations, they rarely received their full allocation.

A soldier's typical weekly ration would consist of:
- 7 pounds of beef or 4 pounds of pork
- 7 pounds of bread or flour sufficient to bake it
- 3 pints of peas or beans
- ½ pound of rice
- ¼ pound of butter[8]

This would translate to the following weekly rations for an army of 1,000 men:
- 3½ tons of beef or 2 tons of pork
- 3½ tons of bread or flour sufficient to bake it
- 94 bushels of peas or beans
- 1¾ tons of rice
- 250 pounds of butter

The threat of a foraging expedition caused residents to hide their cattle and the expedition usually elicited an attack from the enemy. As one side tried to obtain food and supplies, the other tried to prevent them from doing so or to re-capture the stolen goods along with the enemy's baggage and supplies. While most of these actions were militarily insignificant, they often had the effect of reducing both forces. Crown forces were harder to replace because they usually had to come from overseas.

Military objectives not only included the capture of enemy forts, strongholds, and armies but also the control of important crossroads, rivers, and ferries. The rivers were the 18th-century highways and made travel and transportation much quicker than the unpaved roads. Controlling these strategic points either facilitated or blocked troop movements and supply lines.

Nomenclature

The two sides in the American War for Independence are generally referred to as the British and the Americans. However, this is a gross oversimplification. While it is a convenient way to refer to both sides, it is often inaccurate, particularly when discussing engagements in the South where most of the actions were between militia units or armed mobs with very few, if any, regular soldiers. For example, Major Patrick Ferguson was the only British soldier at the Battle of Kings Mountain (South Carolina). Many actions in the South seem to have been occasions for people to settle grudges with their neighbors in feuds that resemble that between the Hatfields and the McCoys. In a sense, the war in the South was very much a civil war. In other areas, it took on the nature of a world war.

Moreover, the provincials were British citizens—at least until they declared their independence on July 4, 1776. Prior to that date, the provincials believed their grievances were with Parliament and not the King. Most of the citizens did not favor independence but rather hoped for redress of their grievances and the re-establishment of relations with Parliament. However, when King George III sided with Parliament and declared the colonies in rebellion on August 23, 1775, the provincials realized that their hopes were dashed. After the news reached the colonies on October 31, 1775, they began to see independence as their only recourse.

The Declaration of Independence made a definite break between England and her American colonies; but it took a while for those ideas to become widely accepted. In fact, it took 18 months after the outbreak of the war to enunciate that objective; and it took eight years to win the war that secured the independence of the United States of America. Even though England officially recognized the new country with the signing of the Treaty of Paris in 1783, it often continued to act as though it still controlled the colonies. This was one of the factors that led to the War of 1812.

While the provincials called themselves Americans, to refer only to those who favored independence as Americans is too broad, as they were less than a majority of the population. Although all the provincials were British citizens until the signing of the Declaration of Independence and their effective independence at the end of the war, to refer to them as Americans confuses a political position with hegemony. That would be comparable to referring to Republicans or Democrats as Americans, implying that the other party is not American. Similarly, to refer to them as Patriots implies that those who remained loyal to the King were less patriotic when they fought to maintain life as they knew it.

Consequently, we refer to the supporters of independence as Rebels, Whigs, or Congressional troops. We also distinguish between the local militias and the regular soldiers of the Continental Army ("Continentals") as narratives allow further distinction. We also refer to Allied forces to designate joint efforts by Congressional forces and their foreign allies, primarily French and Spanish.

Similarly, the "British" armies were more complex than just English troops. They certainly consisted of Irish, Scot, and Welsh troops. We sometimes refer to them by regiment, e.g. 71st Highlanders, Black Watch, Royal Welch Fusiliers, when individual regiments are prominent in an engagement. They are also referred to generically as Regulars or Redcoats. (Some derogatory references call them lobsterbacks or bloodybacks because of the flesh wounds from whipping—a common form of punishment at the time.)

While British troops are often called Redcoats, not all wore red coats. The artillerymen wore dark blue coats. While some of the dragoons wore red, others such as Tarleton's Legion, wore green coats. There are instances where the two sides confused each other because of the similarity of the coats. For example, Major General Henry "Light-Horse Harry" Lee (1756–1818) and his legion tried to surprise Lieutenant Colonel Banastre Tarleton (1744–1833) on the morning of February 25, 1781. The front of Lee's Legion encountered two mounted Loyalists who mistook them for Tarleton's Legion. The Loyalists were taken to General Lee who took advantage of their mistake by posing as Tarleton. He learned that Colonel John Pyle had recruited about 400 Loyalists and that they were on their way to join Tarleton. Lee and his men continued the ruse, surrounded the Loyalists, and captured them all, depriving General Charles Cornwallis of badly needed troops at Yorktown.

Loyalist troops were issued both red and green uniforms with a wide variety of facings. Those who wore the green coats were sometimes referred to as Green Coats or simply as the Greens. Some authors refer to the Loyalists as Tories, a term which has taken on derogatory significance.

Moreover, King George III, who was of German origin, arranged to reinforce his armies with large numbers of German troops. They wore coats of various shades of blue, as well as green with red facings. Many of these soldiers came from the provinces of Hesse Hanau and Hesse Kassel and became known as Hessians. Other regiments were known by their provinces of origin (e.g., Braunschweiger or Brunswick and Waldeck) or by the name of their commander (von Lossberg, von Donop, etc.).

We use the terms Crown forces, King's troops, Royal Navy to refer to these combined forces or the regiment name, commanding officer, or group designation (e.g. Hessians, Loyalists) to be more specific.

People of color fought on both sides. We use the currently politically correct terminology of African Americans, even though not all of them came from Africa, and Native Americans as the generic terms. We also use the specific tribal name, if known: Iroquois, Mohawk, Oneida, Cherokee, etc. Mulattoes referred to people of mixed race. Quotations retain the terminology used by the original writer.

The Native American tribes tended to support the Crown because they realized that the settlers coveted their land and presented a greater threat than the British Army. Great Britain had fewer troops in the West (west of the Appalachians) than in the East (along the East Coast and east of the Appalachians), so it needed their support. More than 1,200 Delawares, Shawnees, and Mingoes lived in the Ohio valley. North of them, 300 Wyandots, Hurons, and 600 Ottawas and thousands of Chippewas inhabited southern Michigan and the shores of Lake Erie. Several hundred Potawatomis extended toward the southern end of Lake Michigan. The area north and east of Fort Pitt was occupied by the Senecas, and several hundred Miamis lived along the Maumeee and upper Wabash rivers. The Weas, Piankeshaws, Kickapoos, and other tribes settled on the Wabash and west toward the Mississippi, while an unknown number of Foxes, Sauks, and Mascoutens lived beyond the Great Lakes.

The Native American tribes were unreliable and not great assets as combatants. Sometimes, they were even a liability. For example, the murder of Jane McCrea by her Native American escorts during the Saratoga campaign brought new recruits to the Congressional forces and deterred Loyalists from actively supporting the Crown troops. British commanders often found it impossible to determine whether the Native Americans would fight and for how long. When they did fight, they usually did so in small groups and for limited periods. They were also often divided by rivalries among themselves, easily frightened by any show of strength, and usually unwilling to leave their families for long campaigns. Without the support of the Native Americans, however, Crown forces had no hope of controlling the West. The Crown forces provided the tribes with gifts every year to insure their continued support. These gifts included a large supply of ammunition and clothing as well as gifts for the chief warriors.[9]

Nobody knows how many provincials remained loyal to King George III during the American War for Independence. Many history books credit John Adams with estimating that one-third of the population favored the Revolution, one-third were against it, and another third leaned to whichever side happened to control the area. The quotation reads:

> I should say that full one-third were averse to the revolution. These, retaining that overweening fondness, in which they had been educated, for the English, could not cordially like the French; indeed, they most heartily detested them. An opposite third conceived a hatred of the English, and gave themselves up to an enthusiastic gratitude to France. The middle third, composed principally of the yeomanry, the soundest part of the nation, and always averse to war, were rather lukewarm both to England and France.[10]

On another occasion, Mr. Adams noted that the colonies had been nearly "unanimous" in their opposition to the Stamp Act in 1765 but, by 1775, the British had "seduced and deluded nearly one third of the people of the colonies."[11]

In the first quotation, Ray Raphael[12] notes that Adams was writing about the political sentiments of Americans toward the conflict between England and France in 1797; but the two quotations somehow blended together in popular historiography to refer to the American War for Independence. So Adams has become the definitive contemporary source on the political allegiance of the period.

Conventions and Parts of This Book

Cognizant that one may begin a tour anywhere, the first occurrence of a person's name in a section identifies him or her as completely as possible with the full form of the name with birth and death dates, if known. Some readers will probably find this awkward or cumbersome as they read several sections. We hope that those who consult a specific section will find this helpful.

Most chapters begin with a map of the sites in that state to facilitate orientation, and additional maps face the beginning of their respective sections. Some chapters with many actions are subdivided north to south and east to west, and these divisions are reflected with references to their respective maps. These maps have pointers to engagement locations and are printed on regular paper like the photos.

Engagements are then listed chronologically within their subdivisions along with the corresponding map. Locations with multiple engagements group those events in chronological order under the same heading to provide a historical sequence or "story" of a site before proceeding to the next one. Cross references have been added as necessary.

Each site begins with the name of the city or town (or the most commonly known name of the engagement), and the name (and alternate names) of the battle or action. The location names are followed by the dates, in parentheses, of significant actions discussed in the text. Specially formatted text identifies the location of the site, indicates what the visitor can expect to see, and identifies any interpretive aids. Historical background to understand what happened at a site follows. In any case, this book does not mean to replace more-detailed tourist guides for specific sites that are available at visitor centers.

Events are marked with a bullet character (★) for easy identification and to dispel confusion.

Travelers should take care to map their route for most efficient travel as many sites are not along main roads. Sometimes, one must backtrack to visit a place thoroughly. Travelers should also be aware that some locations in a particular state may be farther than other locations in a neighboring state. Consulting maps allows the visitor to proceed from one location to another with the least amount of backtracking. It also offers options for side trips as desired. Consult the maps and the appendices at the publisher's web site (**www.buscainc.com**) to see how battle sites are grouped and keyed to major cities or locations. Interactive maps for this series are also available at **http://gaz.jrshelby.com/desmarais/**.

One of the appendices gives a chronological list of battles, actions, and skirmishes. History books often present events in purely chronological order. However, that is not a good approach for a guidebook to follow, as events can occur simultaneously great distances apart. For example, the powder alarm in Williamsburg, Virginia occurred on the same day as the battles of Lexington and Concord in Massachusetts. The web site also features a comprehensive state-by-state alphabetical list of locations where actions (battles, raids, or skirmishes) took place.

Other books take a thematic approach, covering campaigns or specific themes like the war on the frontier. This technique, while more focused, often ignores information relevant to a site that properly belongs to another theme. For example, a theme covering Major General John Burgoyne's (1722–1792) campaign of 1777 may not cover the capture of Fort Ticonderoga in 1775 or its role in the Seven Years War (also known as the French and Indian War).

The many photographs, with descriptive captions and keyed to the text, are important for identifying details of historic buildings, monuments, battlefields, and equipment. Many of the photos are of battle and event re-enactments. All photos, except otherwise identified, are by the author. Full-color photos of some of the images in this and other volumes are on the publisher's web site (**www.buscainc.com**).

Another feature that modern readers and visitors will find useful are URLs for web sites of various parks and tourist organizations. These URLs are correlated with various battle sites and sometimes events. Visitors may want to consult these web sites ahead of time for important, updated information on special events, hours, fees, etc. These URLs were active and accurate at the time this book went to press.

The Glossary provides definitions for some 18th-century military and historical terms. There are also scholarly reference Notes for sources used in this book and an Index. The full Bibliography of the sources consulted for the *Battlegrounds of Freedom* series is on the publisher's web site (**www.buscainc.com**).

Most of the sites described in this book are reconstructions or restorations. Many buildings were damaged during the War for Independence or fell into disrepair over the years. They were refurbished, for the most part, for the nation's bicentennial in 1975–1976. Battlefield fortifications were sometimes destroyed after a battle so they could not be re-used by the enemy at a later time. For example, the hornworks and siege trenches at Yorktown, Virginia were destroyed after the surrender of General Charles Cornwallis so the Crown forces could not re-use them for a subsequent assault. They were, however, rebuilt and used again during the War of Rebellion (Civil War). There are many houses and structures still standing that demonstrate what life was like in the 18th century. Only those related to the battles are covered.

Many of the sites have been obliterated by urban development and have nothing to see or visit. Houses and other construction have supplanted them. One battlefield is covered by a shopping mall; another has been submerged under a man-made lake; others were destroyed by high-rise apartment or office buildings. Many are remembered only with a roadside marker. Some don't even have that.

Many sites have little importance to the outcome of the war. Some actions were mere skirmishes or raids lasting only a few minutes. For example, some actions consisted of a single volley. After one of the forces fired, it fled. Yet, some important events, such as the capture of Fort Kaskaskia by George Rogers Clark in Illinois and the capture of Fort Ticonderoga by Benedict Arnold, Ethan Allen, and the Green Mountain Boys were effected without firing a single shot. The battle at Black Mingo Creek, South Carolina lasted only 15 minutes. Other engagements, particularly those involving Lieutenant Colonel Francis Marion, known as the Swamp Fox, were fought in the swamps of South Carolina and are hard to find.

Some sites remain undeveloped and virtually ignored. This is not necessarily bad. While erosion, neglect, and plant or tree growth slowly undermine earthworks, they do significantly less damage than the rapid deterioration resulting from bikers and walkers.

One cannot easily cover all the sites of the American War for Independence. However, one can visit all the sites and events that affected the outcome of the war. One can also visit enough locally significant spots to get an understanding of what the war was like for the people of that region. This book tries to cover the extant battle sites and hopes to serve as a companion on the voyage of discovery.

Norman Desmarais
normd@providence.edu

Introduction

South Carolinians were divided in their response to British taxation policies of the 1770s. They were more divided than most other colonists. That division was based primarily on geography. The plantation owners of the coastal low country were among the wealthiest men in the thirteen colonies and their social, cultural, and political interests centered on Charleston. Their wealth depended primarily on two crops, rice and indigo, which depended on British trade for their value. These plantation owners opposed any restrictions of that trade; and, although they accounted for less than 40% of the colony's population, they held 70% of the seats in the colonial assembly.

Settlers in the back country, mostly recent immigrants from the northern colonies, lacked proportional representation in the colonial assembly and had more grievances against the residents of the low country than they did against the British.

The river systems in South Carolina divide the terrain into districts. The rivers were the highways of the 18th century, allowing quick transportation of people and supplies to various locations—much easier than overland. Most of the rivers were bordered by swamps and had few, if any bridges. The only way to get across the swamps would be by boat, ferry or at a few fords. Unpredictable, torrential rains would raise the water level making a crossing difficult, hazardous, or impossible. Thus, the rivers and swamps controlled troop movements and often determined the outcome of campaigns.

General Henry Clinton (1730–1795) captured Charleston on May 12, 1780. He left General Charles Cornwallis (1738–1805) in charge when he returned to New York. Cornwallis established a series of forts from Charleston to Ninety Six, 29 miles from the Georgia border. He placed them at Camden, Rocky Mount, Hanging Rock, Fort Watson, Fort Motte, and Fort Granby.

Cornwallis defeated Major General Horatio Gates (1728–1806), commanding the Continental Army in the South, at Camden in August 1780. Major General Nathanael Greene (1742–1786) replaced Gates as commander in December 1780 and divided his army into several smaller groups. This forced Cornwallis to deal with many opposing units. Unable to risk a general engagement, Greene kept out of Cornwallis's reach.

The colonial assembly established two 750-man infantry regiments in the low country and a regiment of 450 mounted rangers in the back country. After the British captured Charleston, the political divisions resulted in some of the most bitter fighting of the war. Brigadier General Thomas Sumter (1734–1832) and Brigadier General Andrew Pickens (1739–1817) led partisan units that operated in the back country while Brigadier General Francis Marion's (1732–1795) forces operated in the low country. These partisan bands were mobile and flexible in numbers and engaged in hit-and-run raids that disrupted enemy supply lines and occupied the attention of large numbers of British and Loyalist militiamen.

More than 6,000 South Carolinians served in the Continental Army. Each of the state's 46 counties has Revolutionary War sites. A visitor cannot hope to see them all in a brief time. However, one can see enough significant local spots to understand how the people of South Carolina coped with the War for American Independence.

There are several significant books that cover many aspects of the American War for Independence in South Carolina. They include John C. Parker's *Parker's Guide to the Revolutionary War in South Carolina: battles, skirmishes and murders* (Patrick, S.C.: Hem Branch Publishing, 2009), Patrick O'Kelley's *Nothing But Blood and Slaughter* (Booklocker.com, 2004), John W. Gordon's *South Carolina and the American Revolution: a battlefield history* (University of South Carolina Press, 2003) and Daniel Barefoot's *Touring South Carolina's Revolutionary War Sites* (Winston-Salem: John F. Blair, 1999). *The South Carolina Highway Historical Marker Guide* (2nd Ed, Revised. Columbia, SC: South Carolina Department of Archives and History, 1998) provides information on individual historical markers. Updates and current information is available at **www.scaet.org/markers/**. The South Carolina Department of Parks, Recreation and Tourism (phone: 803-734-1700; website: **www.discoversouthcarolina.com**) is another good source for the state's Revolutionary War history as is the Department of Archives and History (8301 Parklane Road, Columbia, SC 29223; phone: 803-896-6100).

1
NORTHEASTERN SOUTH CAROLINA

See the map of northeastern South Carolina.

McBee, Chesterfield County
Hem Branch (1780–1782)

> Hem Branch is, a branch of Black Creek. The name evolved into Ham Creek on modern maps. The bridge over the Hem Branch [Ham Creek] is on Wire Road off Old Wire Road [Wire Road #4] in the National Wildlife Refuge northeast of McBee.

The Loyalists could plunder and ravage the property of the few Whigs in Chesterfield County without opposition until Captain Steven Jackson, Sr. (ca. 1750–1832), known as "Killing Stephen Jackson," and his men arrived. He fled to North Carolina after the battle of Camden but returned to South Carolina shortly afterward to pursue Loyalists between 1780 and 1782. He and his men engaged a party of Loyalists at a place called Hem Branch. They killed several Loyalists and dispersed the rest.[1]

McPherson's Plantation, Florence County (March 14, 1780)
Jeffries (Jefferies) Creek, Florence County
Murphy's Defeat (Nov. 8, 1780)

> McPherson's Plantation in Florence County should not be confused with McPherson's Plantation in Hampton County. It is about 3.5 miles south of route U.S. 301 and about 4.5 miles west of SC 327 (Francis Marion Road). It was on route S-21-57 (Claussen Road) about 3.8 miles east of its junction with route U.S. 52 (U.S. 301|South Irby Street) and about 0.7 miles south of Jeffries (Jefferies) Creek. The site is between McPherson Farm Road and Crepe Myrtle Road.
>
> The site of the skirmish was near the bridge over Jeffries (Jefferies) Creek on route S-21-57 (Old River Road) just south of Jefferies Creek Boulevard in Pamplico.

★ Colonel Francis Marion (1732–1795) received intelligence that the Loyalists were on the north side of the Pee Dee River on Tuesday, March 14, 1780 [some accounts date this in April 1781], and that they intended to join Colonel John Watson Tadwell Watson (1748–1826) in support of British operations. Colonel Peter Horry (1747–1815) crossed the Pee Dee with 70 dragoons. When he met a party of 30 foragers and a covering party of equal size at McPherson's plantation, he charged them on horseback, killed two and captured 13 British soldiers, two Loyalists, and two slaves without losing a single man.[2]

★ A band of about 90 Loyalists were believed to be organizing at Spike's Mill on Jeffries (Jefferies) Creek along the Georgetown to Cheraw road when Captain Thomas Delany and a force of South Carolina militiamen were sent to disperse them. Meanwhile Captains Morris [Maurice] Murphy [Murphey] (d. 1780) and Henry Council (1712–1784) and their companies patrolled the Pee Dee River area to keep the other Loyalists in check.

4 THE GUIDE TO THE AMERICAN REVOLUTIONARY WAR IN SOUTH CAROLINA

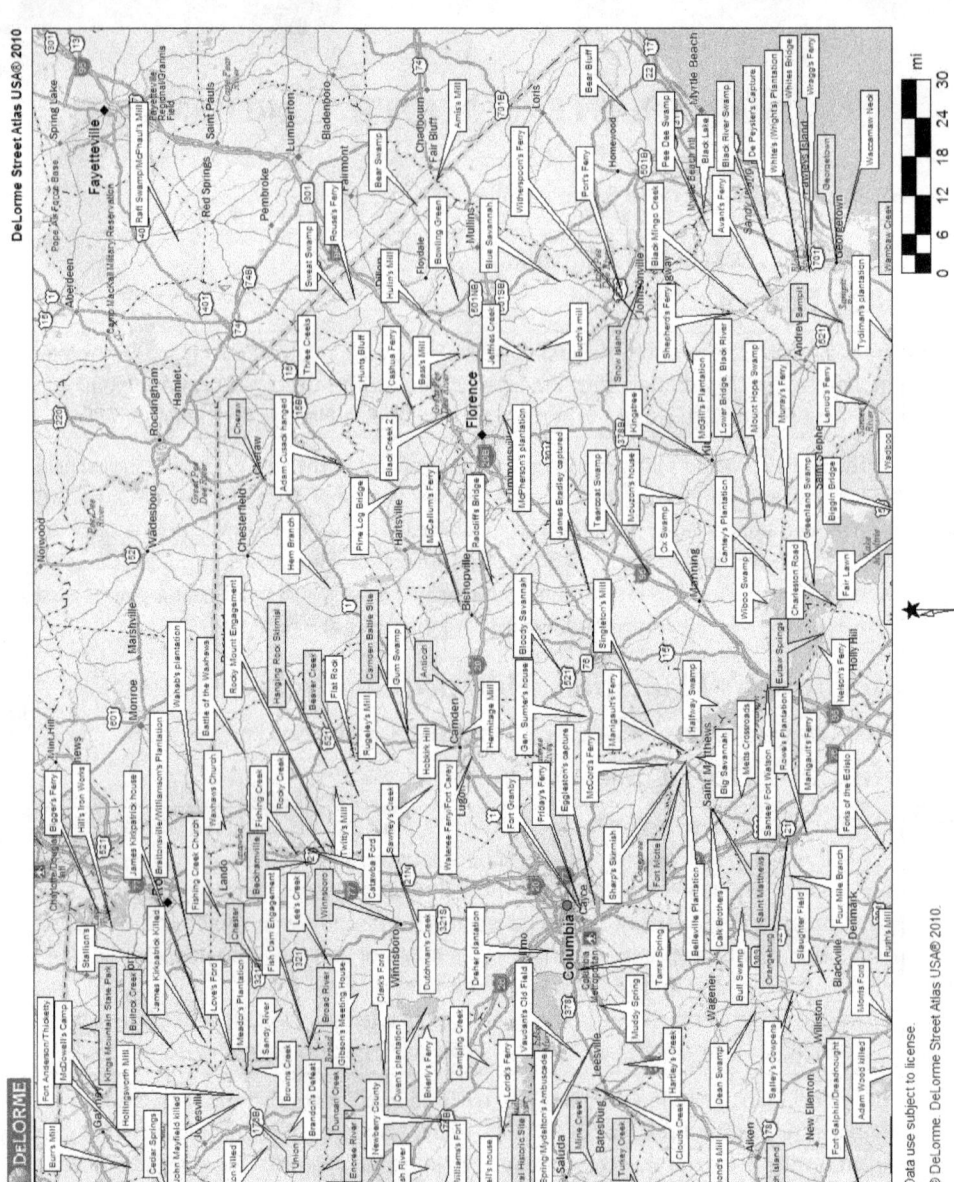

Northeastern South Carolina: Map for The Guide to the American Revolutionary War in South Carolina ©2012 DeLorme (www.delorme.com) Street Atlas USA®

At the same time, South Carolina Loyalist militia Major Jesse Barfield (1738–1780) roamed through the same countryside, plundering and killing at will. Captains Murphey's and Council's activities forced him to be more cautious. In one skirmish on Wednesday, November 8, 1780, Captain Murphey was killed and his company defeated. The Loyalists then withdrew to Georgetown.

North Carolina militia Colonel Thomas Brown (1744–1814) (not to be confused with the Loyalist officer in Georgia) recommended that the officers commanding the posts in the area meet him at Jonathan Miller's (1760–1849) which was near Barfield's location. The Whigs sent 162 men, about 45 of them mounted, in pursuit of Barfield to avenge Captain Murphey's defeat; but they were unsuccessful.[3]

Black Creek, Florence County (date unknown; late 1781 or early 1782)
Maple's Mill, Chesterfield County (date unknown)

Captain Stephen Jackson, Sr. lived about 2 miles north of Mount Croghan on the south side of Thompson Creek along the west side of Buddy Sellers Road. His house was just 7 miles from Maple's mill on Little Black Creek and about 10 miles from where route SC 265 crosses Black Creek northeast of Jefferson. The pension application that mentions this action locates it on Black Creek, but it could have occurred on Little Black Creek.
As mills were common meeting places for both sides during the war, Maple's mill on Little Black Creek seems another likely location for this skirmish. Other frequent locations for skirmishes are at meeting houses, intersections of two roads and where a road crosses a river or creek.
For this reason, another logical location for this action would be where route SC 265 crosses Black Creek about 4.75 miles east of Jefferson.
The most likely location would be about 400 yards south of the junction of routes SC 109 and S-13-138 (Bo Melton Loop|Woodward Mill Road) about 4 miles south of Ruby. There are remains of a trench about 12 feet wide and 50 feet long that parallels the old road about 300 yards away. There's also a spring nearby and the location is about 7.25 miles south of Captain Stephen Jackson, Sr.'s home.
The late 1781 or early 1782 action occurred on Roger's Bridge Road off Williston Road (SC 327) about a mile south of exit 170 off route I-95 northeast of Florence. It is the first road on the right after crossing the bridge over Black Creek.

Captain Stephen Jackson, Sr., of Lieutenant Colonel Lemuel Benton's (1754–1818) company, was known as "Killing Steve" because of the great number of men he killed in the war. He lived in the Thomson Creek region (modern Chesterfield County) where there were very few Whigs. The Loyalists could plunder and ravage the residents without opposition. Captain Jackson and his men intended to end this activity. They engaged the Loyalists in a skirmish on Black Creek and "killed a good number of them.[4]

★ Lieutenant Colonel Lemuel Benton (1754–1818) and a Captain Baker of Georgia joined forces to fight against the Loyalists. As Benton was sick, he requested that Baker take command. Their men were having breakfast when the Loyalists attacked them near the ferry over Black Creek on the Georgetown and Cheraw road near Pawley's Bridge in late 1781 or early 1782. The Loyalists threw them into confusion, but the Whigs rallied and forced the Loyalists to retreat. They pursued the Loyalists for some distance, killing several and wounding some too severely to escape.[5]

Blair, Fairfield County
Gibson's Meeting House or Mobley's Meeting House (May 26, 1780 or May 29, 1780 or June 8, 1780 or June 10, 1780; ca. April 23, 1781)

> A state historical marker for the Battle of Mobley's Mill (see Photo SC-1) is located about 2.75 miles north of the junction of routes SC 215 and S-20-18 (Ashford Ferry Road) at the junction with Chausey Circle. The marker says the battle occurred 1.5 miles east on the Little River. Jack Parker locates the battle site about 1.8 miles due southeast of the marker.
>
> Historians continue to debate whether the fight occurred at Mobley's Meeting House or at Gibson's Meeting House, a little to the south. Documentary evidence (Major Richard Winn's and some British accounts) indicates that the action took place at Gibson's Meeting House. Historians also disagree on the date. Accounts date the action as occurring on May 26 or 29, June 8, and June 10, 1780.

The British established a strong outpost at Shirer's (or Sherer's) Ferry on the east bank of the Broad River, opposite the Dutch Fork, in early June 1780. They summoned the inhabitants of the region to take the oath of allegiance to the king or be regarded as the King's enemies. The presence of the king's troops emboldened the Loyalists in the area to plunder Whig plantations.

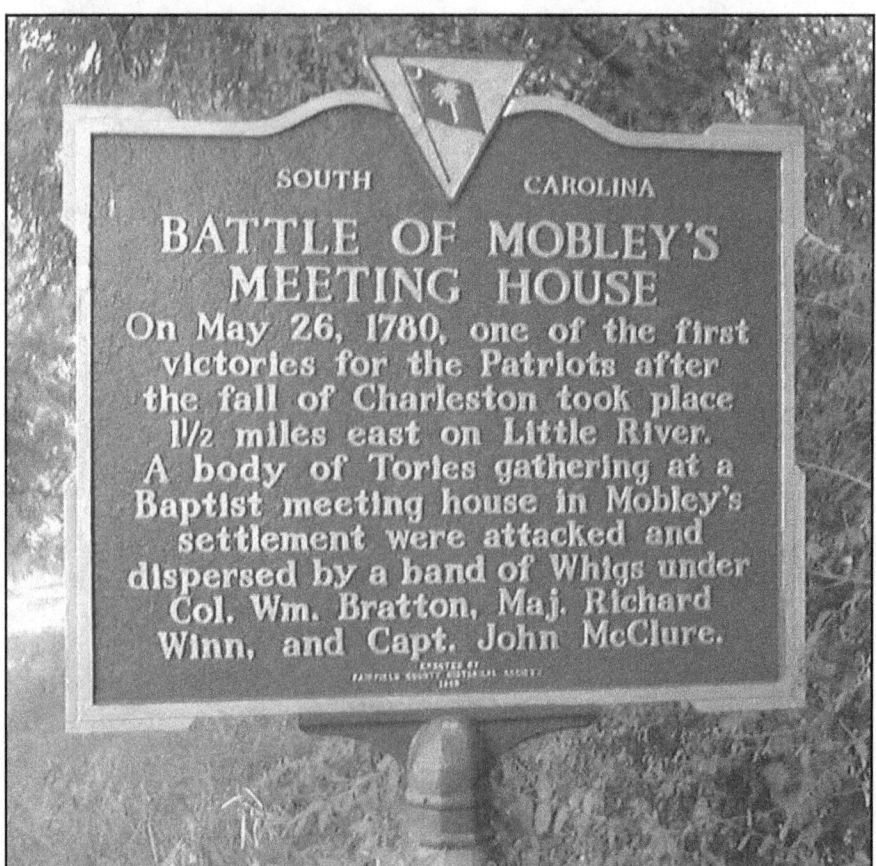

SC-1. Mobley's Mill roadside marker

Colonel Charles Coleman's Loyalists raided Captain John Hampton's (1745–1830) home and stole "thirty negroes, two or three wagons and teams and thirty valuable horses and a large quantity of household furniture." They arrested Captain John Hampton (1745–1830) and proceeded to his brother Henry Hampton's (1755–1826) plantation and plundered it also. They took both men prisoners and sent them to the British headquarters in Camden under a strong guard.

Major Richard Winn (1750–1818) learned that Colonel Coleman's Loyalists were going to meet at a meeting house near Little River. This site, known variously as Mobley's Meeting House or Gibson's Meeting House, was about 12 miles north of the British post at Shirer's Ferry, which Winn referred to as "Shiroe's Ferry." Major Winn set out immediately to rally the Whigs in his neighborhood. Unable to muster any men to oppose Colonel Coleman, Winn joined with Colonel William Bratton (1740–1815) and Captain John McClure (1730–1780) and the 100 militiamen they commanded.

The Whig militiamen rode until dark on Thursday, May 25, 1780, to put down Colonel Coleman's Loyalists. The militiamen "were directed to keep our horses with the saddles, lie down on our arms, and be ready when called." They rested a few hours and continued riding until just before sunrise. When they arrived at Gibson's Meeting House, Colonel Bratton sent out a reconnaissance party and learned that there were about 200 Loyalists gathered there. Many were "in a large log building, having three guards placed out—one in the yard and the other two at no great distance from each end of a long lane, through which the main road passed by the house."

Bratton's men moved slowly through the woods at dawn and surrounded the meeting house on three sides. The fourth side faced a steep bluff. The Whigs were confident that none of the enemy would try to escape out that side of the building. The sentries fired on the Whigs before they could get into position to attack, but they could not stop the attackers who rushed into the blockhouse yard and fired. Some of the Loyalists were cut down as they rushed out of the house. Others jumped out the windows on the unguarded side, leaving their weapons. Some accounts state that there were no casualties, but Winn wrote that the Loyalists were "totally defeated with a small loss of killed and wounded. The Whig party lost nothing."

James Potter Collins (1763–1844) wrote that "We took possession of most of their guns, which were stacked in the yard, and also took several of them prisoners; likewise, most of their ammunition, swords, and pistols. When all was over, we found that we had killed three of their best officers, and five others; sixteen were badly wounded." Samuel Walker (1760–post 1837) wrote in his pension application: "We attacked them and took 30 prisoners and sent them to Hillsborough." Bratton, Winn and McClure rode to Reverend John Simpson's (1740–1808) house and made camp after this skirmish.

This conflict, which lasted several minutes, was one of the first Whig victories after the surrender of Charleston, and was probably inspired by the alarm over Colonel Abraham Buford's (1749–1833) defeat at the Waxhaws. When local Loyalists learned that Winn had masterminded the raid on Gibson's Meeting House, they "had all his houses burnt to the ground, and every negro Plundered, together with every property he possessed in the world. His wife was plundered of her clothes and she was drove off with two infant children." The militiamen returned home after the battle. Winn's men recovered a great deal of loot the Loyalists had taken from the Whig plantations, including some 30 slaves, several wagons and teams, 30 horses and a large quantity of household furniture plundered from John and Henry Hampton.[6]

★ Brevet-Major John Coffin (1756–1838) raided the Waxhaws about Monday, April 9, 1781 (see **Waxhaws Meeting House** p. 11); so Brigadier General Thomas Sumter (1734–1832) sent some men about two weeks later (ca. April 23) to retaliate. They went to the Loyalists settlements of Sandy Run (Chester County) and Mobley (Fairfield County) to burn and kill. General Sumter wrote to Major General Nathanael Greene (1742–1786) on April 26: "As I found some delay unavoidable, marched into Mobley's and Sandy River settlements, with a view to harass the enemy, which has been effectually done, and will, I hope, in a great measure relieve our friends in that part of the country from the unnatural cruelties that were daily exercised over them. Some small skirmishes have happened, I have lost no men. Several of the enemy have fallen; and many others taken prisoners. Upon the whole, they have been pretty well scourged."[7]

Winnsboro, Fairfield County (May 29, 1780)

Winnsboro is in Fairfield County, 28 miles north of Columbia on route U.S. 321. It is an attractive town with about 50 places of historic interest. The most important ones date from the early 1800s, including the courthouse designed by Robert Mills (built 1823) and the famous Old Town Clock (installed in 1837 and still running).

The town was first settled around 1775. It is centrally located between Ninety Six and Camden and is the main line of communication down the Santee River to Charleston. The farm lands to the south were particularly rich for foraging.

General Charles Cornwallis is presumed to have stayed in the so-called Cornwallis House (see Photo SC-2) (private) at 8 Zion Street from late October 1780 to early January 1781. The original structure has massive masonry walls and partitions coated with a hard plaster. A wooden wing, added later, became the home of Captain John Buchanan, a Revolutionary soldier. His slave, Pompey Fortune, served

SC-2. General Cornwallis's headquarters, Winnsboro

> as Major General Marie Jean Paul Joseph du Motier Marquis de Lafayette's (1757–1834) servant during the war. Fortune Springs Garden, near Lafayette Heights in the northwestern portion of historic Winnsboro, commemorates his name.
>
> The Old Muster Ground, where Cornwallis's troops camped in 1780–1781, is near the Cornwallis House and opposite the site of the Mount Zion Academy or Institute.

The surrender of Charleston, on Friday, May 12, 1780, encouraged the South Carolina Loyalists to organize and join in repressing the Whigs. Colonel William Bratton (1740–1815) and Captain John McClure (1730–1780) led a party of Whig militiamen to defeat and disperse a party of Loyalists near Winnsboro on May 29, 1780.

Lord Cornwallis withdrew to Winnsboro with about half of his army after the defeat at Kings Mountain (Saturday, October 7, 1780) forced him to abandon his first attempt to invade North Carolina. He stayed in Winnsboro from late October 1780 to early January 1781. He received reinforcements and built his strength to about 4,000 troops before launching his second offensive into North Carolina.

Lancaster, Lancaster County
Battle of the Waxhaws (Buford's Defeat) (May 29, 1780; Sept. 22, 1780; Sept. 29, 1780; Oct. 31, 1780)
Near Waxhaws (May 31, 1780) see Camden p. 46
Waxhaws Meeting House, near Lancaster, Lancaster County (April 9, 1781)
Waxhaws Presbyterian Church

> The people who live in the vicinity commonly call the "Battle of the Waxhaws" "Buford's Defeat," "Buford's Massacre," or "Buford's Battleground." It is sometimes used as an alternative name for Wahab's (Wauchope's) plantation in North Carolina. The Waxhaws Presbyterian Meeting House on the Catawba River was the focal point of this predominantly Scotch-Irish Presbyterian community which stretched across both sides of the state line.
>
> The modern Waxhaws Presbyterian Church is on Old Hickory Road about 4.5 miles north of Lancaster. Founded in 1755, it was the first church in the upcountry. It was used as a hospital during the American War for Independence. Andrew Jackson's (1767–1845) father is buried in the churchyard as are Major William Richardson Davie and other soldiers of the war.
>
> There's a historical marker at the corner of West North Corner Road and Charlotte Highway (route U.S. 521) about 5.7 miles north of the junction of routes SC Highway 9 by-pass and Charlotte Highway. To get to the church, go to the end of West North Corner Road (about 1.3 miles); turn left onto Old Hickory Road and go about 1.5 miles to the Waxhaws Church on the left.
>
> The Battle of the Waxhaws site is near the intersection of routes SC 522 (Rocky River Road) and SC 9 (Pageland Highway), about 9 miles east of Lancaster. Colonel Buford's men are buried in a common grave in a grove alongside Rocky River Road. A 2-foot high wall of white rocks surrounds the grave and a 7-foot obelisk serves as the common headstone. The site looks like a little roadside park and is easy to ignore.

The British began to establish a ring of posts across the northern part of South Carolina after the fall of Charleston on Friday, May 12, 1780. The main one was at Camden, with others to the north, east, and west. Lieutenant Colonel Banastre Tarleton (1744–1833) and his cavalry eliminated the last organized resistance in the state at the Waxhaws, a district near the North Carolina border named after a Native American tribe that once lived in the area.

Colonel Abraham Buford (1749–1833) and 350 Virginians were moving north on the Camden-Salisbury road when Lieutenant Colonel Tarleton's 170 dragoons and 100 infantrymen (the infantrymen were mounted behind the cavalrymen) overtook him Monday afternoon, May 29, 1780. Tarleton sent a rider with a flag of truce to request Buford's surrender; but Buford declined and continued his march. Tarleton's vanguard attacked Buford's rear guard at 3 PM and routed them easily.

Tarleton formed his men on a nearby hill, only 300 yards away, in full view of Colonel Buford who formed a single line facing him. Even though Tarleton's men were exhausted after riding 105 miles in 54 hours, they attacked immediately in three groups, one on each flank and one at the center.

The Virginians obeyed Buford's strict orders to hold their fire until the dragoons were within 10 paces. Buford had several artillery pieces, but they were up front with the baggage and were never brought into action. As Buford's men opened fire at close range, they didn't have enough time to reload. The Crown infantry charged the center of the Congressional troops while Tarleton circled around their position with a cavalry unit. Tarleton's horse was shot from under him. Tarleton noted in his memoirs that a report spread through his cavalry that their commanding officer had been killed and "stimulated the soldiers to a vindictive asperity not easily restrained" and that the "slaughter was commenced before Lieutenant-colonel Tarleton could remount another horse."

A bayonet charge destroyed Buford's line and he decided to surrender. The ensign who raised the flag of truce was "instantly shot down." Tarleton's men slaughtered 113 and captured 203 (150 too badly wounded to be moved any great distance) of Buford's 350 Virginians. Tarleton reported losing only five men killed, 14 wounded and 31 horses dead or injured. The battle produced the phrase "Tarleton's quarter" meaning massacre of defenseless men. Robert Brownfield wrote:

> The demand for quarters, seldom refused to a vanquished foe was at once found to be in vain. Not a man was spared. . . . [Tarleton's dragoons] went over the ground plunging their bayonets into everyone that exhibited any signs of life, and some instances, where several had fallen over the others, these monsters were seen to throw off on the point of the bayonet the uppermost, to come at those underneath.[8]

On the other hand, Dr. Anthony Scotti, Jr. points out that "Under the rules of eighteenth-century warfare, an enemy force called upon to surrender which fails to do so forfeits its right to quarter in any upcoming combat."[8a] It has also become apparent, in recent years, that American history textbooks have consistently overlooked similar actions by Congressional commanders in similar situations such as at Hanging Rock, Hammond's Store, and Pyle's Massacre.

General Henry Clinton (1730–1795) returned to New York on June 8, leaving General Charles Cornwallis (1738–1805) in command in the South with about 8,300 British and Loyal American troops. Cornwallis established his main seaboard bases at Savannah, Beaufort, Charleston and Georgetown and, in the interior, extended his line of control along the Savannah River westward to Ninety Six and northward to Camden and Rocky Mount. However, his force was too small to police so large an area, even with the aid of the numerous Loyalists who took to the field.

Though no organized Continental force remained in the Carolinas and Georgia, Whig guerrillas, led by Brigadier Generals Thomas Sumter (1734–1832) and Andrew Pickens (1739–1817) and Lieutenant Colonel Francis Marion (1732–1795), began to harry British posts and lines of communication and to battle the bands of Loyalists. Whigs and Loyalists began to fight each other almost immediately after Clinton's departure. They engaged in frequent, bitter skirmishes through the rest of the summer rather than in battles between Continental and Crown troops. Neighbor fought against neighbor, sometimes taking an opportunity to settle grudges. Neither side took many prisoners. Any prisoners were usually executed soon afterward, especially if they had changed their loyalty. A bloody, ruthless, and confused civil war ensued, its character determined to a large extent by Tarleton's action at the Waxhaws.[9]

★ Colonel William Richardson Davie (1756–1820) and 116 cavalrymen and infantrymen surprised 100 Loyalists who were plundering the countryside near the Waxhaws on Friday morning, September 22, 1780. They engaged the Loyalists and defeated them 2 miles behind Loyalist lines. They killed 12 or 14 on the spot, "wounded near forty, and brought off fifty horses, and as many saddles, and a number of guns, without the loss of a man."[10]

★ Loyalist Major Dixon and a party of horsemen surprised a small enemy party at Mr. McCree's on Friday, September 29, 1780. They "took 17 prisoners, together with the old man, his sons, and Peter Johnston, who had taken paroles."[11]

★ Major John Coffin (1756–1838) commanded a Crown force of 150 troops, including a corps of light dragoons, a company of infantrymen, and a large number of Loyalist militiamen sent from Camden to help the local Loyalists intimidate the Whigs. Major Robert Crawford (1728–1801) mustered about 40 armed and mounted troops at Waxhaws Presbyterian Church on Monday, April 9, 1781. A party of Crown dragoons charged with drawn sabers, catching the Whigs by surprise. They killed or wounded an unknown number of militiamen and captured 14. The rest scattered. The raiders burned the Waxhaws Church, plundered the neighborhood, burning houses and taking prisoners.

The following morning, 14-year-old Andrew Jackson (1767–1845) was captured at the home of Lieutenant Thomas Crawford for refusing to clean a British officer's boots. Brigadier General Thomas Sumter (1734–1832) sent Colonel Thomas Taylor (1743–1833) and Colonel Henry Hampton (1755–1826) in pursuit, but they were unable to overtake the Crown force before it returned safely to Camden.[12]

Beckhamville, Chester County
Gaither's Old Field (June 1780)
John Land's house (June 2, 1780)
Beckhamville, Near Great Falls, Chester County (June 6 or 8, 1780)
Alexander's Old Field (Beckham's Old Field or the Battle of Beckhamville) (June 8, 1780)

> Gaither's Old Field was south of Rossville, which is about 5 miles west of Beckhamville.
>
> The skirmish at Alexander's Old Field is also known as Beckham's Old Field or the Battle of Beckhamville (see Photo SC-3). The exact date of this battle may never be known. It is sometimes indicated as May 1780. John Craig (d. 1837) told Lyman Copeland Draper (1815–1891) that it occurred on May 24th, two days before

SC-3. Beckhamville, probable site of the Battle of Beckhamville

> Mobley's Meeting House. Daniel Stinson claims it occurred on May 28th. Draper wrote that both Beckhamville and Mobley's Meeting House occurred between May 31st and June 11th. It most likely happened in June 1780, just after Colonel Abraham Buford's (1749–1833) defeat at the Waxhaws (May 29).
>
> A state historical marker for the Battle of Beckhamville (Alexander's Old Field or Beckham's Old Field) is at the junction of routes SC 97 and SC 99 in Beckhamville. A granite marker in the open field northeast of the junction marks the battle site.
>
> John Land's house was probably on Mountain Gap Road (SC 901) about 0.9 miles south of route SC 97 (Great Falls Highway) and about 120 yards north of its intersection with Dee Dee Lane in Blackstock. A marker commemorating the home of Justice John Gaston is on route SC 9, just west of the bridge over Fishing Creek in Chester County. The house was actually situated 2 miles south, at Cedar Shoals on the south side of Fishing Creek. All nine of his sons fought in the war and four died in service.

The last of the Continental troops in South Carolina were defeated at the Waxhaws (Lancaster, South Carolina) on May 29, 1780, but this did not eliminate opposition to the Crown forces. British authorities had summoned the people to gather at Alexander's Old Field to pledge their loyalty to the King.

Captain John Land (1740–1780) was mustering his company south of Rossville when Captain Daniel Muse and a party of 30 Loyalists headed to Captain Land's house on Friday, June 2, 1780. They captured two old men, a youth, and two boys who might communicate their presence to Land. When they got about 150 yards from his log house at midnight, the sentry at the door saw the Loyalists and fired on them. Captain Muse paused briefly to post a guard over his prisoners before charging the house. Captain Land and his seven companions received the Loyalists with a lively fire through the open spaces between the logs and repulsed them. Lieutenant Lewis Yarborough (d. 1780), the Loyalist second in command, was mortally wounded. The Loyalists retreated quickly through the woods toward Camden where they arrived about noon with the youth and the two boys they had captured. They left the old man and Lieutenant Yarborough along the way. Captain Land was captured later in the month and died in captivity. This action may also be known as Gaither's Old Fields. Other accounts say that a party of militiamen pursued and killed Land at the northwest corner of Richard Gaither's field in the woods. They also date this event as occurring on March 2, 1781 at Rocky Creek which is about 6 miles southeast of Rossville.[13]

★ Justice John Gaston (1700–1782), angry by the news of Lieutenant Colonel Banastre Tarleton's (1744–1833) massacre of Colonel Abraham Buford's (1749–1833) troops at the Waxhaws, gathered his nine sons, several nephews, and many of their friends together to oppose them. Justice Gaston's nephew, Captain John McClure (1730–1780) and 32 men "clad in hunting-shirts and moccasins, wool hats and deer-skin caps, each armed with a butcher-knife and a rifle" took a Native American path and quietly went to Alexander's Old Field/Beckham's Old Field as the sun began to rise Tuesday morning, June 6, 1780.

They agreed to attack the Loyalists immediately. They dismounted and the 32 militiamen spread out through the woods to surround the Loyalists. Captain Henry Houseman and a group of armed Loyalist militiamen were present to administer the oath of allegiance and sign up volunteers for the king's service. Many of the 200 people assembled had no real desire to take British protection but believed they had no choice. A number of them had already taken the oath of allegiance when McClure's company opened fire.

The Whigs, seeing their neighbors and friends present on the field, aimed with care, concentrating their fire on the armed Loyalists. Two young men, named Joe Wade and William Stroud Jr. (1752–1780), fell to the ground and "played dead" while the Whigs picked their targets. The attack was a complete surprise and a "general stampede took place," scattering in all directions. John Featherstone, who sported a large bushy shock of hair, ran off bareheaded, and a Whig named James Wylie took aim at Featherstone's head, determined to shoot him as he ran. Wylie was in such a hurry that he missed his shot and Featherstone escaped unharmed.

However some of the Loyalist militiamen stood their ground and returned the Whigs' fire before withdrawing from the field. In all, four Loyalists were killed and several more wounded. Two of the Whigs were also wounded: William McGarity was slightly injured in one arm, and Hugh McClure took a musket ball in his right arm above the elbow, which left the arm crippled for the rest of his life. The Whigs took nine prisoners. Several men, who had signed the oath of allegiance, including Wade and Stroud, renounced the declaration and immediately joined McClure's company. Wade and Stroud paid dearly for their decision later that summer when they fell into British hands. Stroud was hanged, and Wade was whipped almost to the point of death. According to family tradition, Joe Wade was captured as a spy, thrown in Camden prison and so irritated the British by his playing the tune "Yankee Doodle Dandy" with his chains that he was "whipped by the British a thousand lashes."[14]

Some accounts say that neither side had any casualties. One account says that the Loyalists lost four killed and that two of McClure's men were wounded. Joseph Gaston (1763–1836), Justice Gaston's youngest son, wrote that he lost two brothers in the fighting and that he was badly wounded when "one of the enemy, both raised their pieces at once and both fired the same instant and both fell, his antagonist shot through the heart." The ball that hit Gaston struck the bridge of his nose and passed under his left eye, "shattering the cheek bone and going out of the ear, partially impairing his sight and hearing."

The Loyalist commander sent some men to capture 80-year-old Justice John Gaston. "They found his dwelling deserted. His wife, concealed in some bushes near, saw them plunder the house of every thing, and carry off the stock from the plantation. Nothing was left but the family Bible."

McClure and his militiamen rode to join Brigadier General Thomas Sumter's (1734–1832) growing force. The Crown forces maintained an outpost at nearby Rocky Mount, but they found limited success in trying to enlist local Loyalists.[15]

Great Falls, Chester County
Fishing Creek Church (June 11, 1780)
Fishing Creek Engagement (Aug. 18, 1780)
Catawba Ford (July 15, 1780; Aug. 18, 1780)

> The Fishing Creek Church was at the intersection of routes SC 32 (Fishing Creek Church Road) and SC 50 (Steele Village Road), about 1.75 miles west of Interstate 77 in Chester.
> There was a ford near where Cedar Creek Road (SC 97) crosses the Fishing Creek Reservoir. The Catawbas used this ford since before recorded history. The location played a significant role in shaping military and economic events in the area. A state historical marker nearby notes that Nation Ford was located 2 miles downstream on the river. Colonial traders from Virginia used Nation Ford in the late 17th century. Brigadier General Thomas Sumter (1734–1832) camped at the Catawba ford with his army of 500 partisans in July 1780.
> The Fishing Creek engagement site is on route U.S. 21, about 1.75 miles north of the dam of the Fishing Creek Reservoir, near where Cedar Creek Road (SC 97) crosses the reservoir. The battle site itself is now covered by the Fishing Creek Reservoir. A SC historical marker on the east side of route U.S. 21, just south of Waterview Road and about 2 miles north of Great Falls tells the story. The British tend to refer to this action as Catawba Ford.

Lord Francis Rawdon (1754–1826) arrived at the Waxhaws on Saturday, June 10, 1780, to quell Whig attacks, promising protection to all who took the oath of allegiance to the King. General Andrew Williamson (ca. 1730–1786) who was recently paroled, ordered the Upper Ninety Six District Regiment to disband. Colonel Andrew Pickens (1739–1817) and Captain John Thomas, Sr. (1720–1811) took the British parole but Colonel John Thomas, Jr. (1751–1819) and his militiamen decided to continue fighting.

Captain Christian Huck (ca. 1748–1780) and his dragoons rode to the Fishing Creek Church on Sunday, June 11, 1780 expecting to find the militiamen, but they had already left. The dragoons raided the home of Janet Strong (1757–1833), a widow and Justice John Gaston's (1700–1782) sister, and plundered the house of everything. They found her son William Strong (1760–1780) reading a bible in the barn and shot him dead.

They then went to the church to burn it and to the house of Rev. John Simpson (1740–1808) who had joined the militia along with 80 of his congregation the day before. Mrs. Simpson heard the shot that killed Strong as she was having breakfast with her children and saw the dragoons coming. Forewarned of their intentions, she gathered a set of silver teaspoons and went out the back door with her four children and hid in the woods while Huck's men ransacked the house, took four feather beds into the yard and ripped them up. After plundering the house, they set it on fire along with the small outbuilding which was Reverend Simpson's library and study.

After the raiders rode away, Mrs. Simpson rushed into the burning study and carried out two aprons full of books but burned herself badly. She gathered enough feathers from the yard to fill one bed but all her possessions were in ruins, She went to live with one of her neighbors for a month and moved into a small outbuilding in the backyard; but the Loyalists still harassed her, threatening to bring her husband's scalp to her, and stealing her only milk cow. When she begged them to leave, they laughed at her and rode away.[16]

See also **Williamson's Plantation** (July 12, 1780) p. 29.

★ That same day, Sunday, June 11, 1780, two brothers named John and Richard Featherstone (Featherson, Fetherston or Fetherstone), members of a Loyalist family who lived on lower Rocky Creek, led a party of armed Loyalists to the plantations of several of their Whig neighbors, including David Leonard, George Wade (1747–1824), and Thomas McDaniels. They commandeered all the horses that were deemed fit for military service "in the name of the King." The Whigs saw this as another form of horse stealing.[17]

★ In August 1780, after his victory at Hanging Rock, British Lieutenant Colonel Banastre Tarleton (1744–1833) pursued Brigadier General Thomas Sumter (1734–1832). Sumter, on his way to support Major General Horatio Gates (1728–1806), learned of the defeat at Camden on August 16, so he chose to retreat. His exhausted troops camped along the west bank of the Wateree River near Rocky Mount on Thursday night, August 17. Tarleton, on the east bank of the river, could see the fires of Sumter's camp and forbade his troops to make fires or noise. He spent the night silently watching his prey.

The next day, Sumter continued his retreat across Fishing Creek where he set up a new camp. Tarleton crossed the Wateree River and reached Fishing Creek by noon of the same day, surprising Sumter's unprepared camp. They quickly took a position between most of Sumter's men and their weapons and slaughtered about 150, captured 300, and liberated 100 prisoners, while losing only 16 men. Sumter also lost two small artillery pieces, two ammunition wagons, 44 other wagons, and over 1,000 weapons.

Sumter leaped onto an unsaddled horse and narrowly escaped into the forest. Within a week, he gathered stragglers from the battle and new recruits and managed to reorganize his unit. Reports of this skirmish made Tarleton a national hero in England.

Union County and vicinity
Kelsey Creek, Spartanburg County (1779)
Fairforest (Feb. 6, 1779; March 2, 1781 July 16, 1781; Aug. 29, 1782)
Love's Plantation, York County (June 1780)
Brandon's Defeat (June 8, 1780)
Bullock's Ford, Thicketty Creek (June 1780)
Bullock's Ford, York County (June 24, 1780)
Tyger River (July 1780)
Brandon's Camp (July 12, 1780)
Stallion's (probably Sterling or Stalling), York County (July 12, 1780)
Green Spring (Aug. 8, 1780)
Meador's Plantation, Union County (Aug. 12, 1780)

Greenville
Enoree River (Aug. 20, 1780; Feb. 1781)
Roebuck captures prisoners, Spartanburg County (Nov. 1780)
Indian Creek, Newberry County (Dec. 14, 1780)
Fairforest Creek (March 1781; May 8, 1781)
Colonel Hampton killed (Blasingame's house, Earle's Fort) (Nov. 22, 1781)

> Fairforest Creek and Kelsey Creek meet about 15 miles northwest of Union. Captain John Thomas, Sr.'s house was located near this junction on Croft State Park Road in Croft State Park about 0.25 miles north of Foster Mill Circle and about 250 yards down the hill toward the creek on the right.
> Love's plantation was probably on Loves Creek about 0.4 miles north of its junction with Bullock Creek about 4.7 miles south of Hickory Grove. To get there, take route SC 97 south from Hickory Grove to Old Highway 97 Road and go about 0.4 miles. The site of Love's plantation is 0.25 miles ahead, on the right, on the west side of Loves Creek.
> There are two Bullock's Creek Fords. One is near "Burr's" Mill in Cherokee County west of the Broad River. The other is east of the Broad River in Hickory Grove, Sharon. The first is a branch of Thicketty Creek located in Cherokee County. It is near where Thicketty Creek and Bullock's Creek meet about 15 miles northeast of Union in Gaffney. This is where Lieutenant Alexander Chesney's militiamen defeated a band of Whigs attempting to cross the ford. The other is the site of the battle of the Stallions, discussed below p. 17.[18]
> Dr. Andrew Thompson's house on the Tyger River was on route S-42-231 (Morris Bridge Road) about 340 yards west of Miller Road and about 0.75 miles east of route I-26 where it crosses the North Tyger River in Roebuck. "Plundering Sam" Brown was killed here.
> The Enoree River is east of Greenville. Alexander Chesney's journal is the only source that mentions the skirmish that occurred here.
> The Roebuck Captures Prisoners site is where the bridge crosses over the Enoree River on route SC 56 close to Musgrove Mill. To get to the Roebuck vs. Frost site from the junction of routes U.S. 221 and SC 92 at Enoree, go south on U.S. 221 about 240 yards to the bridge over the Enoree River. The site is about 0.35 miles on the right. Note that the mouth of Beaverdam Creek is 12 miles from the SC 56 bridge over the Enoree River. While this fits the text, it is possible that the action took place in the vicinity of the route U.S. 221 bridge. This is about 11.6 miles from the SC 56 bridge over the Enoree River.
> Colonel Thomas Dugan's place on Indian Creek was about 8 miles south of Whitmire. Go south on route U.S. 176|SC 121 until SC 121 splits off. Continue south on route SC 121 for about 0.6 miles, then turn right onto Old Whitmire Highway. Go about 2.7 miles, then turn right onto Seymore Branch Road and go to its end. Turn right and go about 0.6 miles to the site of Colonel Dugan's Place about 315 yards ahead on the right. This action is commonly called Indian Creek, but it actually took place at Colonel Dugan's place on Gilder's Creek, a branch of Indian Creek.

Meador's plantation was located in the point formed by Old Ferry Road and River Road about 3.4 miles from the junction of Old Ferry Road and Main Street (SC 49) east of Union.

Colonel Thomas Brandon's (1741–1802) camp was near Fairforest Creek, 5 miles south of Union. The date of this action is disputed and is usually listed as occurring on June 8 or 10, 1780.

None of the primary sources gives an exact date for the battle of the Stallion's (probably a corruption of Sterling's or Stalling's); but it is generally accepted as occurring on July 12, 1780. There is also disagreement on the location. Major Joseph McJunkin, who lived in the area, places the site along Bullock's Creek which is a different stream from that referred to as "Bullock's Fork." It is 13.5 miles northeast of Union at its closest point to the city and on the east side of the Broad River. The creek empties into the Broad River just above its junction with the Pacolet River. This same point is only 4.75 miles north of Lockhart in Chester County and 3.5 miles south of where Thicketty Creek joins the Broad River.[19]

Most accounts, probably based on Major McJunkin's account, indicate that the Stallion's plantation was about 5 miles from Union. These indications, if correct, would correspond to today's Fairforest Creek in Buffalo, South Carolina, 5 miles west of Union. There's also a Buffalo Creek only 3 miles west of Union, also in Buffalo. If the Stallion's plantation was along one of these creeks, route SC 215 (Buffalo West Springs Highway) crosses both creeks, probably near the location of Brandon's camp on Fairforest Creek near route S-44-163 (Deepwater Road), about 1.7 miles west of route U.S. 176 (Whitmire Highway) in Union.

James Clinton, in his pension record (S2437), says he fought in the battle of the Stallions on Fishing Creek. Patrick O'Kelley and Michael C. Scoggins locate Stallion's plantation at the head of Fishing Creek. The South Fork of Fishing Creek is about 30 miles east of Union and the main branch of the creek is just a little farther east. If this account is accurate, the site of the plantation would probably be a little east of Williamson's plantation. Michael Scoggins identifies it as being in the "Derby Downs" development approximately 4 miles east of York and just south of the York Highway (SC 5) in the area bounded by Secretariat Drive, Blair Court, and Timberland Court. Jack Parker places it on the west side of Fishing Creek, near the intersection of route SC 1172 (Park Place) and Timberland Court. John Stalling, Sterling or Stallings (1730–1787), or "Stallions" as his neighbors knew him, purchased 470 acres of land here from Peter Kuykendall on June 6, 1768.[20]

Green Spring was on Fairforest Creek, 3.5 miles south of Spartanburg, about 1.5 miles west of route SC 56 and about 0.5 miles south of route SC 295.

The site of Leighton's House was probably at the end of an unnamed road in Sumter National Forest. From the intersection of routes U.S. 176 and SC 49, go south on route U.S. 176 for about 7.9 miles. The site is on the right about 0.8 miles on top of the ridge.

The site of Hayes's Defeat on May 8, 1781 is unknown. Fairforest Creek is about 30 miles long, spanning Union and Spartanburg counties; so the action could have occurred anywhere along the creek. Many Revolutionary War actions happened at the intersection of two roads or a road and a creek or river because the water slowed troop movement. Consequently, Union County is generally accepted as the location for this action. The site was probably about 5 miles west of Union where

> Mudbridge Road crosses Fairforest Creek, about 0.9 miles west of the intersection of Mudbridge Road and route SC 215 (Buffalo-West Springs Highway).
> Captain Thomas Blasingame's house was located about 200 yards west of the junction of Fairforest Creek and Sugar Creek, 4.8 miles west-southwest of Union.

Governor John Rutledge (1730–1800) sent a quantity of arms, gunpowder and lead to Captain John Thomas, Sr. (1720–1811) early in the war. Captain Thomas stored the supplies at his home near the junction of Fairforest and Kelsey creeks in Spartanburg. The house was fortified and guarded by 25 men. Captain Thomas learned that North Carolina Loyalist Lieutenant Colonel John Moore planned to capture the powder along with Captain Thomas and Lieutenant Colonel William Wofford (1728–1823). Captain Thomas decided to take as much of these military stores as the men could carry and leave the house, since the advancing force outnumbered them.

When Captain Thomas learned of Colonel Moore's plans, he sent his daughter for reinforcements. She rode 4 miles at night to report to Captain Matthew Patton (1728–1790). He mustered his men and arrived at the Thomas house about the same time as the Loyalists on Saturday, February 6, 1779. The Loyalists advanced and demanded the powder but were ordered to leave the premises. The Loyalists then opened fire and killed one of Captain Thomas's slaves.

Lieutenant Colonel Moore captured Wofford easily. Captains Thomas and Patton and most of Patton's men ran away after the first few volleys. Josiah Culbertson (1742–1839), Colonel Thomas's son-in-law, remained in the house and continued firing from the second floor of Thomas's house. Thomas's mother, wife (Jane Black Thomas) and 12-year-old son, William (1767–), stayed in the house with Culbertson who refused to leave them. The women and children joined him in firing whatever weapons they could find. The heavy logs of the house prevented the Loyalist musket fire from causing much injury but the occupants of the house inflicted serious injuries to the Loyalists.

Unaware that the militiamen had run away, Colonel Moore estimated the number of casualties he might suffer in taking the house were not worth it, so he decided to abandon the attack. The gunpowder in the house was later used at the battles of Rocky Mount and Hanging Rock in 1780.[21]

★ Colonel Thomas Brandon (1741–1802) joined forces with Colonel John Thomas, Sr. (1720–1811) and Lieutenant Colonel James Liles to keep the Loyalists in check and to prevent them from joining forces with the British. They established a camp near Fairforest Creek in June 1780 with 70 or 80 men. While waiting for Colonel John Thomas, Jr. (1751–1819) and Lieutenant Colonel James Liles to arrive with their militia regiments, Colonel Brandon's troops captured a Loyalist named Adam Steedham whom Major Thomas Young (1764–1848), one of Brandon's soldiers, called "as vile a tory as ever lived." Steedham escaped during the night and informed Captain William "Bloody Bill" Cunningham (d. 1787) of the location of the camp.

Captain Cunningham and his men rushed into the camp beside a steep ravine while 10 or 12 men were making breakfast and feeding the horses on Friday, June 8, 1780. They routed Brandon's men, many of whom escaped by jumping into the ravine where Cunningham's horses could not pursue them. Daniel McJunkin (1756–1825), Joseph's brother, "was ran through by a trooper with a bayonet entering between his shoulders and the point emerging through his heart, so he seized or clutched in agony with his hands. When the Loyalist trooper said, "Let go, my good fellow and I'll pull it out as carefully as possible." Putting one foot on McJunkin's back, he pulled it out and McJunkin fell to the ground. He was found later and nursed back to health.

Brandon lost five men killed. Captain Joseph McJunkin (1755–1846) wrote that "the rest of the whigs of Union District fled beyond the Broad River" to rendezvous at the Bullock's Meeting House. The pastor of the church, Reverend Doctor Alexander's "zeal for liberty and activity in exhorting his people to join in the cause of their country had made him so obnoxious to the British and Tories that he had been compelled to leave the State."

The men returned home to visit their families before joining Brigadier General Thomas Sumter (1734–1832) at Tuckasegee Ford on the Catawba River in North Carolina. Steedham went to Georgia where he stayed for several months until everything had calmed down. Brandon had men watching for his return. On the night Steedham returned home, Thomas Young and a group of Brandon's men captured him and hanged him from a tree to avenge the killing of Young's brother at Brandon's defeat.[22]

★ Alexander Chesney, a soldier in the 6th South Carolina Regiment, took the oath of allegiance after the surrender of Charleston (May 12, 1780) and was appointed a lieutenant in one of the new regiments being organized at Ninety Six. His company skirmished with some Whigs at Bullock's Creek in June 1780. (This may have been at what is now known as Little Thicketty Creek near Byce's Mill or Byas's Mill in Cherokee County, west of the Broad River or on Goucher Creek, a little west of Thickctty Creek). He wrote that the "Rebel Party was defeated in attempting to cross the ford; my father was present on this occasion, and hearing the bullets whistle without seeing by whom they were fired, asked me 'where are they, where are they?' I placed him near a tree until the affair was over, and resolved he should not be so exposed again."

According to Joseph McJunkin:

> Sumter [Brigadier General Thomas Sumter (1734–1832)] established his headquarters east of the Catawba River in the territory assigned to the nation of Indians of the same name. Here the whole of July was spent, but not in idleness. His men go out in quest of provisions, arms, and to rally their friends to take a stand under the standard of liberty.
>
> Provisions were obtained with great difficulty, for the want of current funds, so that their fare often consisted of barley meal without meat, salt or any other seasoning, and scarce at that. All the powder which could be obtained was collected. The good ladies in the region round about gave up their pewter vessels to be molded into bullets. Implements of husbandry were converted into swords. While engaged in these preparatory measures they were under the necessity of maintaining the strictest vigilance for the preservation of their lives. The Tories watched their movements, waylaid them and often fired upon them. An instance of this kind occurred to a small party led by Colonel Brandon [Colonel Thomas Brandon (1741–1802)], near Bullock's Creek. A captain by the name of Reed [Captain Davie Reid (d. 1780)] fell behind the party for some purpose or other and was killed by 2 Tories. His mother, having found out who his murderers were, followed Brandon to North Carolina and implored him to avenge the death of her son. Some of his men volunteered to go with him, and he hunted the Tories and killed them.[23]

★ Another version of the story says that Captain Hughes and Captain Davie Reid (d. 1780) pursued Loyalists William Sadler (d. 1780) and James Love (d. 1780) in retaliation for pillaging and burning Captain Hughes house. Captain Reid shot and killed James Love as he crossed the Broad River in June 1780.

★ Yet another version says that Captain Davie Reid (d. 1780) died on July 12, 1780 when he was visiting a neighbor's house in the York District. The landlady warned him that Loyalists William Sadler (d. 1780) and James Love (d. 1780) approached the house, warned him of the Loyalists advance and advised him to escape. Reid refused to go because he knew Love and Sadler all his life, as they had been his neighbors, and he thought he had nothing to fear from them. He walked out into the yard, offered them his hand and was killed on the spot.[24]

Captain Reid's mother traveled to Colonel Thomas Brandon's (1741–1802) camp in North Carolina. She arrived as the camp was turning out for the morning parade. She "came before us, leaning upon the arms of 2 officers. She drew from her bosom the bloody pocket-book of her son." Meanwhile, the friends of the murderers sought their own revenge and pursued Brandon with a considerable force. Brandon recruited his force and prepared to meet his pursuers. When he asked for volunteers to search for the Loyalists who had killed Captain Reid, "Twenty-five stepped out at once." They rode all night "halted in the day, kept watch in the woods, but slept not."

The next night, they arrived at old William Love's (also known as "English Bill") house. They attacked the house and broke down the door, knocking down Mr. Love and knocking out some of his teeth. At that moment, one of the Whigs yelled that the Loyalists were in the barn. Either William Sadler or James Love was killed when a shot was fired through the door. The other was killed in the ensuing skirmish. Thomas Love, who was sleeping in the barn, escaped through a briar patch.

A short time before Brandon overtook the Loyalists, he was joined by Captain James Love (1704|5–1781) who had encountered the Loyalists a short time before and killed two of them before escaping through an old field. Brandon soon learned that the Loyalists had stopped at the house of a man named John Sterling or Stalling for dinner. (The name has been corrupted to Stallion's.) Mrs. Sterling (d. 1780), one of Captain Love's sisters was a Whig and her husband a Loyalist.

Brandon divided his band of 50 men in two and advanced on the Loyalists in the fortified house before daybreak on Wednesday, July 12, 1780. Brandon sent Captain Love and 16 men to attack the front while he himself took the rest around the back to attack the rear and to capture anybody who tried to escape.

Mrs. Sterling ran out of the house to beg her brother not to fire on the house. She ran back to the house and was shot in the forehead by a ball coming through the opposite door as she crossed the doorstep. The Loyalists kept firing for some time, even though they were boxed in the front and rear. They eventually raised the flag to surrender. They lost two killed, four wounded, and 28 prisoners who were sent to Charlotte, North Carolina. Brandon lost only one man wounded, William Kennedy shot through the wrist and thigh. When he saw his son shot, Captain Thomas Kennedy, an excellent marksman, raised his rifle and killed one of the Loyalists trying to escape. One of Brandon's prisoners, Adam Steedham, escaped and notified the Loyalists of the position of his camp. A large body of Loyalists then attacked Brandon's camp and routed him and his 70 South Carolina militiamen. Major Thomas Young (1764–1848) recorded:

> One part of our company was to attack the house, another the barn. The house was attacked and the door broken down by a powerful man by the name of Maddox, who was afterwards killed at King's Mountain. In staving open the door he floored old Love and knocked some of his teeth out. At this moment a cry was raised that they were in the barn, and to the barn we all rushed. One of our men fired through the door and killed one of the murderers, the other was killed in the skirmish. What is most strange about the matter is, that another man was sleeping with them, and in the melee he escaped unhurt. We now felt that we had done all that was required of us and returned to our quarters in North Carolina.[25]

★ Loyalist Colonel George Turnbull (1752–1807) marched into the New Acquisition (York County) with the New York Volunteers and the militia under Captain Matthew Floyd (d. 1826) after the battle of Ramsour's Mill (North Carolina June 20, 1780). They joined Captain Christian Huck (ca. 1748–1780) and offered protection to anyone who would take the oath of allegiance to the King but only a few did. Captain Huck and Colonel James Ferguson (1740–1780) rode west to the Bullock's Creek and Turkey Creek area to quell the Whigs. They skirmished with a small band of Whigs, killing several and capturing several. They also killed a man at the ford on Bullock's Creek (where Wilson Chapel Road crosses Bullock's Creek) and proceeded about a mile north where they killed 70-year-old Mr. Robert Fleming (1710–1780) on or about Saturday, June 24, 1780 (the exact date is not given in sources).[26]

★ "Plundering Sam" Brown (d. 1780) lived with his mistress in a cave on Island Ford (near present-day Statesville) in North Carolina. He conducted illegal activities with his sister, Charity, before the war and increased his activity after the war arrived in the Carolinas. He and another Loyalist, known only as Captain Butler, rode into Fair Forest, in July 1780, to locate the home of Josiah Culbertson (1742–1839) who had been at the battle of Wofford's Iron Works. Culbertson's wife, Anne, refused to tell Brown where her husband was. Brown "became very provoked by this spirited woman, and retorted to much abusive and indecent language," threatening to come back in a few days to burn her house down and kill her husband. He headed back home to North Carolina that night.

When Josiah Culbertson learned of the abuse his wife endured, he gathered four friends and tracked "Plundering Sam" for 10 miles. As they were passing Dr. Andrew Thompson's (1767–1819) house on the Tyger River, they discovered Brown's and Butler's horses in the stable. They crept up to within rifle shot of the house and waited. When Brown walked outside in the early morning, Culbertson fired from 200 yards away and hit him between the shoulder blades, killing him instantly. Butler ran out of the house and fled into the woods.[27]

★ Josiah Culbertson (1742–1839) learned a short while later that another Loyalist threatened to kill him in revenge for killing "Plundering Sam" Brown. When the two men met at Green Spring on Tuesday, August 8, 1780, they both aimed their rifles and fired almost simultaneously. Culbertson's shot killed the Loyalist.[28]

★ Lieutenant Alexander Chesney (1755–1843) and a band of Loyalists routed Colonel Andrew Neal, Sr.'s New Acquisition Militia at Meador's plantation, near the mouth of Brown's Creek, on Saturday, August 12, 1780. They captured many prisoners, including Esaw [Esau] Smith. [Lieutenant Colonel Andrew Neal, Jr. (d. 1780) was killed at Rocky Mount, 12 days before this action.[29]

★ Loyalist militia Lieutenant Alexander Chesney (1755–1843) wrote that, after the defeat of the Continental Army at Camden, the "news made us happy as people in our position could possibly be." Colonel James Ferguson's (1740–1780) army marched quickly to intercept the Whig militiamen after the skirmish at Musgrove's Mill. Lieutenant Chesney commanded the rear guard as the army crossed the Enoree River. Some militiamen fired upon the Loyalists; but Chesney's men held them at bay throughout the night of Sunday, August 20, 1780. Colonel Ferguson arrived with the main body the next day "and the Americans retreated, on August 21st, after suffering some loss." Ferguson's army camped on the Enoree for a few days and then marched to Fair Forest.[30]

★ Lieutenant Alexander Chesney (1755–1843) "raised a company with great difficulty and joined a strong party at Col Williams's house on Little River, where there was a strong party under General Cunningham" in November 1780. Major Jonathan Frost (ca. 1745–1780) took command of Chesney's militia after Major Daniel Plummer (d. 1780) was killed at Kings Mountain. Major Frost ordered Chesney and his militiamen to "join him at an appointed place on the Enoree."

Lieutenant Colonel Benjamin Roebuck (1755–1788) learned about the rendezvous site and, when Chesney's militiamen arrived, he and his men captured the Loyalists, "immediately disarmed" them and marched them away. When Major Frost arrived at the rendezvous site and learned of Chesney's capture, he pursued Roebuck and his militiamen immediately. He caught up with them 12 miles up the river. Roebuck posted his men inside a cabin. Frost attacked the house and was killed. The rest of his men fled. Chesney and the other prisoners were paroled after the skirmish.[31]

★ Colonel Joseph Hayes (d. 1781), Captain Thomas Blasingame of Colonel Thomas Brandon's (1741–1802) regiment, Captain Christopher Case, Captain Ewing, Captain Harris and 40 or 50 militiamen attacked Major Moses Buffington's (d. 1782) 25 Loyalists posted at Colonel Thomas Dugan's place on Indian Creek on Thursday, December 14, 1780. They wounded Buffington and three of his men and captured seven or eight others. Some accounts say Buffington died of his wounds but he lived two more years after this skirmish.[32]

★ Captain Moses Shelby (1760–1828) made an attack along the Enoree River sometime after the battle of Cowpens, probably in February 1781. One of Shelby's militiamen named Smith told Lyman Copeland Draper (1815–1891):

> After Cowpens we got word of a company of Tories. We rallied what we could. Captain Shelby came along and joined up. There were other captains, Casey of Newberry, Elder, Berry from up Tyger. The command was given to Shelby. We went after the Tories. They had taken up the night at a house near Enoree where Odie lived. Shelby gave them a fire, which the Tories returned, but we retired as they were in a house. Robert Elder was shot. A rain came up and our Scout went to another house. When our party came back the Tories were gone.[33]

Odie is likely a local reference to O'Dell. The location could be O'Dell's Ford on the Enoree River in Whitmire, in the northeast corner of Laurens County, between Union and Laurens Counties. The action probably took place at John O'Dell's plantation about 0.3 miles southwest, near the end of route S-36-369 (Lakestone Drive) which runs north off route S-36-451 (Lovers Lane) about 2.5 miles west of Whitmire on route SC 72 (Clinton Highway).

★ Lieutenant John Jolly (1737–1781) led a patrol of eight militiamen in March 1781. As they rode near the mouth of Fairforest Creek, looking for signs of Loyalist activity, they stopped at the house of an old man named Leighton (or Layton) who "was of doubtful politics, with an inclination to the strongest side." Unaware that 100 Loyalists had also stopped at the house and were camped on the other side of the creek, Jolly and his men were caught by surprise when the Loyalists surrounded the house. William Sharp and William Giles(1749–1797) rode through the Loyalists and escaped when two of the Loyalists fired their weapons prematurely. Lieutenant Jolly and Charles Crane could not reach their horses, so they ran away on foot. Lieutenant Jolly was killed, but his companion escaped. The other four militiamen put up a fierce fight from inside the house. The fight continued until nightfall when the Whigs, outnumbered and running short of ammunition, surrendered. The Loyalists lost several men killed and wounded. They took their prisoners to the Ninety Six jail where two of the prisoners died. The other two escaped in August 1781.[34]

★ Major Joseph McJunkin (1755–1846) rode to Colonel Thomas Brandon's (1741–1802) camp on Friday, March 2, 1781 to report the fight at Williams's Fort. As he and

John Lawson approached a cabin at Fair Forest to determine if it was friendly or not, they did not see three Loyalists in the dark until they arrived at the front gate. It was too late to retreat; so both men raised their rifles and fired. Lawson killed one of the Loyalists, but McJunkin's rifle misfired due to damp powder. Lawson jumped off his horse and grabbed the dead Loyalist's musket and shot a second man and "passed his sword through his body." The man recovered from his wounds.

A powder flash ignited the latter Loyalist's shirt. He fled when McJunkin drew his sword but "His flight on horseback soon caused his shirt to burn like a candle." The flames frightened McJunkin's horse which would not pursue the man. McJunkin finally coaxed his horse forward and chased the Loyalist for a mile. When he approached close enough to strike the Loyalist with his sword, the man turned and fired a pistol at McJunkin, breaking his right arm. McJunkin quickly switched the sword to his left hand and struck. He swung at the Loyalist with a backhanded blow that killed him instantly.

The pain in McJunkin's arm "became so excruciating that some of his soldiers cut the ball out of his arm with a dull razor." His men later moved him to a safe location "into an unfrequented part of the country lying on Brown's Creek and his wants cared for in the midst of a dense thicket."[35]

★ Brigadier General Andrew Pickens (1739–1817) sent Colonel Joseph Hayes (d. 1781) to attack a large force of Loyalists on Fairforest Creek on Tuesday, May 8, 1781. Colonel Hayes was defeated and withdrew.[36]

★ Brigadier General Francis Marion (1732–1795) engaged Major Thomas Fraser (d. 1820) in several skirmishes in the Fair Forest area on Monday, July 16, 1781 and again on Thursday, August 29, 1782.

See **Fair Lawn** p. 182.

★ Colonel Edward Hampton (1746–1781) was on his way from the Congarees to Earle's plantation, to visit his father-in-law Baylis Earle (1734–1825). He stopped for breakfast at his friend's, Captain Thomas Blasingame's house, about Thursday, November 22, 1781 while his men camped at nearby Sugar Creek. Major William "Bloody Bill" Cunningham (d. 1787) rode to the house waiting for Colonel Hampton to come out. Hampton grabbed his pistols from the table to defend himself. Cunningham shot and killed him. This event is sometimes mistakenly attributed to happening at Earle's Fort.[37]

Heath Springs, Lancaster County
Flat Rock, Kershaw County and Hanging Rock, Lancaster County
Rocky Creek, Chester County (June 12, 1780; Aug. 3, 1780; March 3, 1781)
Rocky Creek Congregation (June 12, 1780)
Flat Rock, Kershaw County (July 20, 1780)
Big Beaver Creek
Beaver Creek Ford (July 21 or 22, 1780)
Hanging Rock skirmish (July 30, 1780; Aug. 6, 1780)

The Rocky Creek settlement was about 28 miles north-northwest of Camden. The Rocky Creek Congregation was located on route SC 97 about a mile east of exit 55 of Interstate-77. Rev. William Martin's house was probably located about 100 yards

> west of Mountain Gap Road (SC 901) about 0.9 miles north of its intersection with route SC 97 and about 0.5 miles east of the Rocky Creek Congregation. The Rocky Creek action of August 3, 1780 occurred near where Brooklyn Road (SC 141) now crosses the Catawba River in Great Falls.
>
> The site of the Hanging Rock Skirmish (website: **www.royalprovincial.com/history/battles/HangingRock1.shtml**) is along Flat Rock Road (S-29-15), 2 miles south of Heath Springs. To get to Hanging Rock, turn east on Hanging Rock Road (S-29-467). Proceed 0.6 miles to a dirt road on the right and take it to the site.
>
> Hanging Rock, so called because of a massive boulder 20 to 30 feet in diameter on the east bank of the Catawba River, was a British post between 1780 and 1781. One may walk the top of Hanging Rock and look across Hanging Rock Creek to where the Loyalist camp was situated. The Daughters of the American Revolution erected a stone monument at the foot of Hanging Rock. There's also a highway marker about 2.5 miles north, at the intersection of Flat Rock Road (S-29-15) and route U.S. 521 in Heath Springs.
>
> Flat Rock is on Flat Rock Road (S-29-15) about 4.5 miles south of Hanging Rock.
>
> Beaver Creek is about 4 miles south of Stoneboro. The best approach to the site, on the Kershaw County side of the creek, is to go north on routes U.S. 521 and 601 in Camden for about 2 miles, and then bear left onto Liberty Hill Road (SC 97). Go about 12.3 miles and turn right onto Running Fox Road. Running Fox Road will become River Road in about 1.3 miles. Continue on River Road for about 2.5 miles, then turn left onto Beaver Creek Cemetery Road and go about 1 mile to the road that leads to the Beaver Creek Cemetery. The creek and the washed-out bridge are about 0.6 miles beyond the cemetery road. The cemetery is about 0.5 miles south of where Beaver Creek Cemetery Road crosses Beaver Creek. While there is room to get off the main road at this location, the road can be rough and hard to turn around in places and there may be very deep washouts in the road.

After the Crown forces defeated Colonel Abraham Buford (1749–1833), some Loyalists told Colonel George Turnbull (1752–1807) in Camden that Rev. William Martin, pastor of the Rocky Creek Congregation, exhorted his congregation to ignore Lord Francis Rawdon's (1754–1826) proclamation and encouraged them to take up arms against the Crown.

Colonel Turnbull sent a party of dragoons to disperse them. The dragoons attacked the men of the congregation, who were organizing under Captain John Land (1740–1780), 7 miles north of Rocky Mount on Monday, June 12, 1780. They killed many militiamen, including Captain Land on their way to the meeting house. They then burned Rev. Martin's church and house. They arrested Rev. Martin at his house and took him to the Rocky Mount jail. The Crown dragoons then attacked another group of militiamen who were having their horses re-shod at a blacksmith shop 2 miles away. They killed one of the militiamen.[38]

★ Lord Francis Rawdon (1754–1826) established a post at Hanging Rock, about 24 miles north of Camden. Major William Richardson Davie (1756–1820), determined to interrupt the Crown communications between Charlotte, North Carolina and Camden, South Carolina. He surprised the escort, some dragoons and volunteers, and captured a convoy of provisions at Flat Rock on Thursday, July 20, 1780, without losing a single man. He had the wagons with the spirits and provisions destroyed. He mounted his prisoners on the captured horses and began to withdraw toward his camp at Waxhaw Creek at dusk. Worried that one of his stragglers would be captured and alert an enemy patrol, Davie took a less traveled route back. He passed by the left flank of Hanging Rock, under a full moon, to reach a plantation on Beaver Creek.

Major Davie expected Lord Rawdon to attempt to recover his booty and prisoners; so he took every precaution. Recognizing that the Beaver Creek ford, which crossed his route, would be a suitable place for an ambuscade and a good opportunity to rescue the prisoners, he sent Captain Charles Pettit (1736–1806) with an advance force to reconnoiter the lane, the ford of the creek, and the houses near it, and to secure everyone around to prevent any notice being given to the enemy.

Pettit returned and reported that he did not see anything suspicious, so Davie ordered the rest of his men to advance about 2 AM on Saturday, July 22, 1780. Captain Pettit led the column with guides and a few mounted infantrymen. Captain William Polk's (1758–1834) dragoons guarded the prisoners in the center, followed by the rear-guard. The rear-guard had just entered the lane when an officer discovered the Crown forces concealed under a fence in a corn field. They "hailed the enemy concealed under a fence and some standing corn; on challenging a second time he was answered by a discharge of Musquetry, which commenced on their right and passed like a running fire towards the rear of the Detachment." The advance force charged the Loyalists who fired a second volley. Davie hastened forward. He ordered the men to advance but they turned back.

Davie was compelled to repass the ambuscade under a heavy fire. He overtook his men retreating along the same road they had advanced, close to a panic. They were so shaken by the unexpected attack that Davie could not induce them to charge. His only option was to retreat. He rallied his men and halted them upon a hill overlooking the plantation. He ordered a retreat, leaving the mortally wounded prisoners on the hill as they rode off. Davie's guides having fled after the first shots, "a Tory who was taken from his bed and compelled to serve as guide enabled him to pass the enemys patroles and regain his camp the next day without any further reverse of fortune."

Davie's casualties were light, including some of the men guarding the prisoners: "Capt Petit and 2 men wounded and Lie^t [Elliott] killed; the fire fell principally among the prisoners, who were confined two upon a horse and mixed with the guard presented a larger object than a single dragoon; the advance guard with the prisoners nearly filled the lane, it was owing to these circumstances that the prisoners were all killed or wounded except 3 or 4."[39]

★ Brigadier General Thomas Sumter (1734–1832) asked Major William Richardson Davie (1756–1820) to create a diversionary attack on the British outpost at Hanging Rock on Sunday, July 30, 1780, while he attacked Rocky Mount. He had only 80 men and could not attack the fort which was garrisoned with 500 men. He learned that three companies of mounted Loyalist infantrymen were camped at a farmhouse near the fort. The farmhouse "was placed in the point of a right angle made by a lane of staked and ridered fence; the one end of which opened to the enemy's encampment, the other terminated in the woods."

Major Davie planned to surround the infantrymen, posing as a band of Loyalists. He sent forward Captain Samuel Flenniken's (Flennekin or Flanagan) (1746–1811) riflemen who looked like the Loyalist militiamen and would not arouse suspicion as they rode casually to the farmhouse. They rode past the sentries without being challenged, calmly dismounted and surprised a company of Loyalists camped outside the fortifications by opening fire. The Loyalists fled to the other end of a lane, where Davie's dragoons had circled around through the wood. The dragoons fired at the Loyalists and then rode through them. The Loyalists "all rushed against the angle of the fence where they were surrounded by the dragoons who had entered the field and literally cut to pieces." They took no prisoners because the farmhouse was so close to the fort. They did take 60 captured horses and 100 muskets and rifles which had just been issued to the Loyalist recruits. Davie lost only one man and there is no record of Loyalist losses; but the September 21, 1780 issue of the *Royal American Gazette* mentions that Captain Thomas Hewlett (d. 1780), of the New York Volunteers, died at Camden of wounds received at Hanging Rock. The action happened so quickly that the Crown forces inside the fortifications were unable to respond. In this little-known engagement, Major Davie's dragoon commander acted very similarly to British Lieutenant Colonel Banastre Tarleton at Waxhaws.

One of the youngest soldiers in this engagement was 13-year-old Andrew Jackson (1767–1845), who would later become President of the United States. He was there with his brother Robert and served Colonel Davie as a mounted orderly or messenger.[40]

★ After Brigadier General Thomas Sumter's (1734–1832) loss at the Battle of Rocky Mount on July 30, 1780, he withdrew his militia 3 miles north to the south bank of Rocky Creek. As the creek was flooded, he waited for it to subside. His men were foraging in the area when an alarm went out that Loyalist Major John Garden (d. 1783) was a mile away with two cannons. General Sumter sent Colonel Richard Winn (1750–1818) and 100 men to fight a delaying action as Sumter's men were in the open.

Colonel Winn wrote on Wednesday, August 2, 1780, that the garrison at Rocky Mount was reinforced with "eight hundred men and 2 field pieces." These troops were Major John Garden's Prince of Wales American Regiment which marched from Camden to reinforce Hanging Rock. The high water at Rocky Creek caused by all the rain prevented Brigadier General Thomas Sumter from moving his campsite until the 3rd. He crossed the creek with his army that afternoon and "turned out their horses and scattered about in search of roasting ears and green peaches."

While they foraged for food, an alarm was sounded. Garden's Loyalists were less than a mile away with two field pieces. The Loyalists stopped at Rocky Mount before proceeding to Hanging Rock. General Sumter, caught in the open, decided not to fight. He ordered Colonel Winn to take 100 men to delay the Loyalists until the militiamen could all withdraw. Winn sent Captain Richard Coleman (d. 1780) and Captain William Stroud Jr. (1752–1780) ahead to scout while the rest of the 100 men prepared their horses. The two scouts came too close to the Loyalists and were captured, "stript naked and immediately hung up by the side of the road."

Both sides exchanged long-range fire but did not get close enough to engage in a major skirmish. Colonel Andrew Neal (d. 1780) came too close to the fight and was shot out of his saddle when a bullet struck one hip and came out the other side. He died on the side of the road near the Loyalist forces. Another of Colonel Winn's men was wounded. Major Garden withdrew to Rocky Mount. Colonel Winn pursued at a distance but broke off as the Loyalists approached Rocky Mount. The following day, a burial party was sent under a flag of truce to bury Colonel Neal. They reported that they estimated the Loyalist dead at 12 to 14 men killed and wounded.[41]

★ Brigadier General Thomas Sumter (1734–1832) led 600 men against a Loyalist camp of 1,400 at Hanging Rock shortly after 6 AM on Sunday, August 6, 1780, as the

Loyalists finished breakfast and were engaged in morning chores. His riflemen fired into the camp, catching the Loyalists by surprise. The enemy's left flank broke and fled. The center held and formed a counterattack. They attempted several charges and were involved in savage hand-to-hand fighting. The marksmanship of well-positioned snipers took its toll. At one point, Major John Garden (d. 1783), in command of the Prince of Wales Regiment with only nine survivors, resigned his command on the spot in the heat of battle.

A small group of mounted infantrymen from the British Legion attempted an unsuccessful counterattack on Sumter's right. Sumter repelled the attack and advanced, driving the enemy's center into the right flank of their camp. After three hours of fighting and on the verge of a spectacular victory, the Congressional forces began to ransack the camp. This gave the Loyalists time to reorganize. They soon began firing at the looters. Sumter could not re-form his troops and retreated about noon.

The Battle of Hanging Rock was very savage with a high casualty rate. Sumter estimated enemy casualties of 250 and 70 prisoners. He lost 20 dead, 40 wounded, and 10 missing. Sumter himself was one of the wounded, having been shot in the leg.[42]

★ March 2, 1781 see **Gaither's Old Field** (June 1780) p. 13.

York County
Hill's Iron Works (June 18, 1780)

> Hill's Iron Works was located in York County where route SC 274 (Hands Mill Highway) crosses Allison Creek, now Lake Wylie near the North Carolina border. A historical marker is about 300 yards southwest of the site, across the bridge.

The New Acquisition Militia moved their camp to Hill's Iron Works when they learned that Captain Christian Huck's (ca. 1748–1780) Loyalist dragoons were looking for them. Lord Francis Rawdon (1754–1826) sent an officer to persuade them to lay down their arms and take the oath of allegiance to King George III (1738–1820). The militiamen refused the offer and the officer left quickly "for fear of the resentment of the audience."

The New Acquisition regiment elected Andrew Neal, Jr. (d. 1780) as their colonel and William Hill (1741–1816) as their lieutenant colonel. Men from Georgia and South Carolina came in a few days later, increasing their number. When Colonel Neal learned that Captain Matthew Floyd (d. 1826) was leading a group of Loyalists to Rocky Mount to form a militia, he took most of his men and rode out to intercept them. He left Lieutenant Colonel William Hill and 12 to 15 men to guard his iron works which consisted of a store, furnace and mills.

Loyalists came to Colonel George Turnbull's (1752–1807) headquarters at Rocky Mount to report that the New Acquisition Militia attacks were driving them out. Colonel Turnbull proposed to send troops to destroy Hill's Iron Works which was a major supplier of ammunition and guns for the Continental Army. He made Matthew Floyd a colonel when he arrived with his Loyalists and created the Upper District Loyalist Militia.

On Friday, June 16, 1780, Colonel Turnbull ordered Captain Huck to destroy the iron works. He took 60 men under Captain Abraham Floyd (1729–1833), Colonel Matthew Floyd's son. They forced Moses Ferguson (1762–1845), a representative in the legislature who lived on Little Allison Creek 2 miles south of Hill's Iron Works, to take them there.

Two of Colonel William Bratton's (1740–1815) militiamen arrived at the iron works on June 18th and warned the men there that 200 to 300 Loyalist dragoons and 60 militiamen were coming, but they didn't know which road they took. Colonel Hill only had a small garrison to defend the iron works. Huck's men approached from the south, forded Allison's Creek undetected, surprised the militiamen and fired. The militiamen thought that the small force of dragoons was the vanguard of the hundreds of troops they had been told about. Two of Colonel Hill's sons, Robert and William, Jr., procured a one-pound swivel gun manufactured at the iron works and set it up on a hill overlooking the south road. Huck outflanked them and circled around the iron works to attack from the north. The 12 to 15 defenders were caught completely by surprise.

The Whigs dismantled the bridge across the main branch of Little Allison Creek north of the iron works, hoping to slow or stop the dragoons. However the Loyalist militiamen quickly repaired the bridge and the Loyalists attacked the iron works. Both sides exchanged several volleys before the outnumbered Whigs mounted their horses and headed toward North Carolina. The Loyalist dragoons overtook them and killed seven. The rest fled except for four taken prisoners, including Colonel Hill's two sons who were later released. The Loyalists stripped the prisoners "of everything, even to the rings some of them wore on their fingers."

The Loyalists then plundered the camp of everything they could carry away. They then "burned the forge, furnace, grist and saw mills together with all other buildings even to the negro huts, & bore away about 90 negroes all which was done before Col. Niel returned with the army to camp." In addition to producing ammunition and guns, the iron works made agricultural implements which the farmers in the border area of the two Carolinas depended on. Many expected they would have to return to the wooden plough. Mrs. Hill and her family went to a neighbor's cabin for protection. The Loyalists then headed farther south in search of Whigs headquartered at White's Mill in southern York County.[43]

Sumter
General Sumter's house burned, Sumter County (ca. July 1780)
Bloody Savannah, Sumter County (July 1781)

> General Sumter's house was about 11 miles west-northwest of Sumter and about 2 miles west of Shaw Air Force Base. To get there, take route U.S. 76 (U.S. 378|Broad Street) to route SC 261 (North King's Highway). Go north about half a mile and turn right onto Deveaux Road. At the end, turn left onto Barnwell Road and go about 365 yards. The gated driveway on the right leads to the site which is private property. There's a marker on Meeting House Road, about 2.5 miles due north. Follow Barnwell Road north to its end, then turn right onto Raccoon Road and go about 1.5 miles. At the fork, bear left onto Hummingbird Road and go to its end. Turn left onto Fish Road and go about 370 yards, then turn left onto Acton Road and go to where it meets Meeting House Road. The General Sumter Historical Marker is straight ahead across the road. General Sumter's grave is at the end of Acton Road (about 0.3 miles from the marker). It's toward the back of the cemetery.
>
> Edgefield plantation is on the right about 67 yards from Edgehill Road which is off Raccoon Road, about 415 yards before it meets Hummingbird Road.
>
> The Loyalist hanging site is on route SC 261 (North King's Highway), 300 to 400 yards north of Deveaux Road. Holy Cross Church which replaces the Old St. Mark's

> Church is on the east side of the road. Across the highway and slightly to the north is a driveway that angles northwest from the road where the hanging site is in the yard.
>
> The area known as the "High Hills of Santee" served as a camp for both Crown and Congressional forces. The Whigs hanged a Loyalist from a large oak tree at the Borough House, a tavern, around July 1780. The oak stood until 1973 when a violent storm damaged it so badly that arborists advised cutting it down before it fell.
>
> Bloody Savannah was 6 miles northwest of present-day Sumter, south of Ardis Pond and about 1.5 miles east of route U.S. 521 (Thomas Sumter Highway).

General Charles Cornwallis (1738–1805) detached Lieutenant Colonel Banastre Tarleton (1744–1833) to chase Colonel Abraham Buford (1749–1833) after the fall of Charleston (May 12, 1780). Tarleton sent Captain Charles Campbell to burn Colonel Thomas Sumter's (1734–1832) home around July 1780. This enraged Sumter and brought the Continental officer out of retirement as the commander of the South Carolina militia. The house was rebuilt later and known as "The Ruins."[44]

★ Major John Singleton "with a small squad of Sumter's men . . . attacked a party of marauding Tories, eleven in number, at Bloody Savannah, ten miles distant" in July 1781. He "killed ten of the Loyal gentlemen, one of them making his escape by hiding behind a pile of rails."[45]

Brattonsville
Williamson's plantation (July 12, 1780)
Huck's defeat

> Williamson's plantation, the site of Huck's defeat, was on Percival Road, about 400 yards east of route S-46-165 (Brattonsville Road) 3.1 miles east of McConnells. The Daughters of the American Revolution erected a historical marker along Brattonsville Road near the site of Williamson's plantation to commemorate the engagement which occurred there.
>
> Colonel William Bratton's house still stands on the edge of some woods about 200 feet north of Williamson's plantation. Historic Brattonsville (website: **chmuseums.org/brattonsville/**) is at the corner of route S-46-165 (Brattonsville Road) and there's a historical marker on Brattonsville Road, about 0.5 miles north of Historic Brattonsville.

Loyalist Lieutenant Colonel George Turnbull (1752–1807), in camp at Rocky Mount, sent Captain Christian Huck (ca. 1748–1780) (also spelled Houk, Hauk, Huik, Huyck and, most frequently, Hook) with 30 or 40 dragoons, 20 mounted infantrymen of the New York Volunteers, and about 60 Loyalist militiamen, with orders to "collect all the royal militia on his march" and "push the rebels as far as he deemed convenient." With his force increased to about 400, Huck plundered the house of Captain John McClure (1730–1780) and took McClure's son, James (1740–1825), and son-in-law, Edward Martin (1758–1813), prisoners. Huck told them that he would hang them the next day.

Huck also looted Colonel William Bratton's (1740–1815) house while Bratton was away recruiting militiamen to fight Huck. He took three old men prisoner and forced Mrs. Bratton to feed his men. After eating, Huck moved 0.25 miles east to James Williamson's (1755–1836) plantation to camp for the night.

Mary Gaston McClure (1712–1802) brought the news to her father, Captain John McClure, and Colonel Bratton who were in camp with Brigadier General Thomas Sumter's (1734–1832) militia 30 miles away. They set out after Huck with 150 mounted volunteers. Militia officers Captain Edward Lacey, Jr. (1742–1813), Colonel William Hill (1741–1816), and Colonel Thomas Neal, Jr. (d. 1781) joined them with 350 other volunteers. This force had no organization and the officers had no authority. Their plan of action was decided by a vote of all the volunteers which resulted in the misunderstanding of orders.

As the militiamen advanced on Huck's position, they passed the house of Edward Lacey, Sr. His son, Captain Edward Lacey, Jr., was one of the militia officers, but the father was a staunch Loyalist. Captain Edward Lacey, Jr. "detailed four men to guard [his father] all night, and tie him, if necessary, so as to prevent him from going to the enemy and giving them notice of the intended surprise. Old Lacey, by some artifice, eluded the guard and started for Huck's camp, only two miles from his residence; fortunately, before he had gone two hundred yards, he was overtaken, brought back, and absolutely tied in his bed till morning."[46]

When the Whigs got about a mile and a half from Colonel Bratton's house, they dismounted and tied their horses in the woods. Colonel Lacey knew his brother Reuben, also a Loyalist, was with Huck's militiamen that night and would probably be returning to his home nearby before daylight. Reuben was blind in one eye and would have difficulty seeing in the dark, so Colonel Lacey and Lieutenant John Mills (1757–1795) waited for him about 20 paces off the road. When Reuben approached a short while later, Colonel Lacey disguised his voice and pretended to be a "friend of the King" who had fallen behind the main force and wanted to return to camp before reveille. Lacey and Mills learned that Huck was actually camped at Williamson's plantation and that there were only four sentries guarding the camp.

The militiamen were divided into two parties and attacked Huck's camp simultaneously from the front and rear at dawn (4:52 AM) on Wednesday, July 12, 1780. They got between the camp and the picketed horses, cutting off any avenue of escape. They fired from behind fences and overwhelmed any resistance. The Whigs jumped over the fences and charged the camp. Most of the Loyalist militiamen abandoned their horses and weapons and fled. The Whigs pursued them for about 12 miles, shooting many.

One of the Loyalist dead was Colonel James Ferguson (1740–1780) who was singled out to avenge the murder of William Strong (1760–1780) at Fishing Creek Church. Colonel Ferguson commanded the squad that killed him. Ferguson's clothing was blackened with gunpowder, indicating he had been shot at very close range.

Captain Matthew Floyd (d. 1826) and his slave, later known as Miller Sam, fled early in the conflict. Floyd dropped his saddlebag and ordered Sam to return to get it. Several Whigs mistook him for a Loyalist and aimed their weapons at him. Sam quickly removed his hat so they could see his face. He was taken prisoner along with other slaves accompanying the Loyalist soldiers.

The remaining Loyalist militiamen and New York Volunteers quickly surrendered. The Whigs put them under guard while the rest of their men attacked the Legion dragoons positioned around Williamson's house. Huck ran from the house and jumped on his horse to lead several ineffective charges. Huck and four other dragoons tried to escape to the main road near Bratton's house with a party of Whigs in hot pursuit. Two sharpshooters fired at the same time shooting Huck in the back of the head just above his neck. Huck clung to his saddle horn so tightly that he pulled off the saddle when he fell dead.

The Whigs lost only one man killed, one wounded and one captured. They also captured 100 horses with full equipment and liberated two men found tied up in a corncrib whom Huck had captured the day before and who were scheduled to be hanged that day. Most of Huck's 115-man command was eliminated: 30 to 40 killed and about 50 wounded and 29 captured.

This successful attack encouraged many men to join Brigadier General Thomas Sumter (1734–1832) at Mecklenburg, North Carolina, about 35 miles north of the South Carolina line. Loyalist Captain Abraham Floyd's (1729–1833) Rocky Mount Regiment switched sides, bringing all their horses and equipment with them. This increased Sumter's ranks to 600 men. He now led the only organized Congressional force in South Carolina, allowing him to attack Turnbull's post at Rocky Mount, the origin of Huck's expedition, on July 30. This engagement occurred just two months after the British captured Charleston on May 12.[47]

Near Blenheim, Marlboro County
Hunts Bluff, Marlboro County (July 25, 1780 or Aug. 1, 1780)
Three Creeks, Marlboro County (ca. April 12, 1781)
Robert Gregg shot, Florence County (Sept. 1782)
Polk Swamp

> Hunts Bluff (see Photo SC-4) overlooks the Great Pee Dee River at the end of Hunts Bluff Road (S-35-57), 5 miles west of Blenheim in Marlboro County. East of Blenheim, the road is numbered SC 381 (East High Street). Marlboro Road turns sharply to the right (north) at this point and there's a historical marker at this intersection. A dirt road continues straight ahead (west) a few hundred yards to the bluff.
>
> A state historical marker in the town of Blenheim near the intersection of routes SC 38 and S-35-49 indicates that the community was named for Blenheim Palace, near Oxford, England, which was the home of the duke of Marlborough, for whom Marlboro County was named. The Pee Dee River was an important commercial and military route in the 18th century. Some sources date this incident as having occurred on August 1, 1780 instead of July 25, 1780.
>
> Three Creeks is 0.25 miles east of Blenheim. Take East High Street (SC 381) east for 0.25 miles and turn south (right) on route S-35-603 (Spring Road). The site of the engagement is on the right about 100 yards down the road, just before it makes a sharp right turn. The Sparks house was located 0.6 miles north of the town, at the end of a road that branches off to the right of Blenheim Highway (SC 38).
>
> The site where Robert Gregg (1753–1813) was shot is about 8 miles east-southeast of Florence, northeast of the intersection of routes SC 327 (Francis Marion Road) and S-21-13 (East National Cemetery Road). Antique Circle intersects with route SC 327 (Francis Marion Road) about 0.3 miles north of route S-21-13 (East National Cemetery Road). The site is about 500 yards east of Antique Circle near the west bank of the Middle Branch.
>
> Polk Swamp is about 0.5 miles west of the intersection of routes SC 327 (Francis Marion Road) and S-21-13 (East National Cemetery Road).

The Crown forces abandoned many of their outposts to reinforce General Charles Cornwallis (1738–1805) at Camden. Colonel Archibald McArthur, commander of one

SC-4. Hunts Bluff overlooking the Great Pee Dee River

of these outposts at Cheraw, decided to take his sick and wounded troops to Georgetown to recuperate. Convinced that there were no enemies along the banks of the Pee Dee River, the convoy went by boat rather than take the difficult overland route.

Lieutenant John Nairne (1731–1802), of the 71st Highlanders, commanded the hospital flotilla. He was accompanied by a Loyalist escort commanded by Colonel William Henry Mills, a local physician who had been a Whig and served in the Provincial Congress in 1776 but became a Loyalist after the early victories of the Crown forces.

Whig militiamen learned of the voyage down the river and mustered under Captain James Gillespie (1746–1805) at Beding's Fields (later known as Irby's Mills), 3 miles from Cheraw. As they moved south, additional militiamen joined them, including Major Tristram Thomas (1752–1817) who took command of the unit. Hunts Bluff, about 25 miles south of Cheraw, was an excellent place to set up a battery of field guns to control the river. However, Thomas had no artillery, and muskets would not present much of a threat. He had his men chop down trees and cut the trunks to look like cannon. They fortified the bluff with a formidable arsenal of wood. When Mills's convoy, proceeding slowly down the river, came into sight on July 25 or 26, 1780, Thomas's men pretended to load their guns for firing.

They shouted for the convoy to surrender or be sunk. Colonel Mills acceded immediately and Thomas captured the entire convoy with 100 men aboard. Somehow, Mills escaped in the confusion. The militiamen also captured a supply boat that came by during the surrender. Some accounts say that the Loyalists were aware of the ambush and cooperated with the Whigs. Others say the Loyalist militiamen consisted of many Whigs who enlisted in Mills's force and knew of Captain Thomas's plan. They mutinied against Colonel Mills, forcing Lieutenant Nairne, with no allies, to surrender to a large force of Whigs.[48]

★ As the Continental Army and the British Army headed toward Guilford Courthouse, the Loyalists in the Cheraw area made frequent incursions on defenseless persons and property, concealing their plunder and themselves in the swamps. A band of Loyalists supposedly had a hiding place in the "Three Creeks." When the Whigs learned of it, South Carolina militia Colonel Abel Kolb (1750–1781) mustered the militiamen in the Cheraw district, determined to put an end to the raids.

The Whigs approached the edge of the swamp quietly but found no signs of the Loyalists. They were sure they were near the Loyalist camp, but they did not know its location and they had no guide. Harry Sparks (ca. 1750–1781), a young man noted for his activity and courage, volunteered to scout the area alone and report back soon. Sparks found the camp about Thursday, April 12, 1781, but the Loyalists had discovered and captured him. When he did not return, the Whigs followed his tracks. They located the deserted camp where they found Sparks's body hanging from a tree. They pursued the Loyalists far into North Carolina, killing two mulatto Loyalists while having only Mr. Cantey, wounded. The Loyalists now knew that a large force of Whigs was in the area and ceased their operations.

Captain Daniel Sparks (1740–1810), one of Harry's brothers, later captured one of the Loyalists who had hanged his brother. The man confessed and Daniel hanged him immediately.[49]

★ Andrew Hunter (1737–1823), one of Brigadier General Francis Marion's (1732–1795) scouts, was captured by Loyalist Colonel David Fanning (1755–1825) and was destined to be hanged. He managed to escape on Fanning's horse, Red Doe, with all of Fanning's equipment, pistols, papers, spurs, etc., by jumping the horse over Middle Branch.

On one of his expeditions to retrieve his horse, Fanning terrorized some Whigs along his route, including Robert Gregg (1753–1813), Captain James Gregg's (1752–1802) brother. As Fanning approached Gregg's house, Gregg fired at him but his musket misfired so he ran into nearby Polk Swamp in an attempt to escape. Fanning fired at Gregg and severely wounded him in the hip. Gregg fell and played dead so well that the Loyalists thought he was really dead and departed. The shot left Gregg crippled for the remainder of his life. Fanning, fearing Whig reprisals against him, went to the safety of British-occupied Charleston.[50]

Fort Thicketty (Thickety), Cherokee County (July 30, 1780)
Fort Anderson (Thicketty Fort), Cherokee County (July 30, 1780)

> Fort Thicketty or Thicketty Fort is also called Fort Anderson. It was probably located on Goucher Creek Road, 7 miles south-southwest of Gaffney, about one third of the way between Gaffney and Spartanburg, about 2.3 miles south of what is now the village of Thicketty named after the nearby Thicketty Mountain. The fort "had an upper line of loopholes [see Photo SC-5], and was surrounded by a very strong abatis; with only a small wicket to enter by." Dates for the action here vary between July 13 and 30, 1780, including July 26. McDowell's camp was very near the west side of Cherokee Ford used prior to the battle of Kings Mountain.

Captain William Johnston had captured Loyalist Captain Patrick Moore, the commander of Fort Anderson in early July 1780 but Moore managed to escape. When Brigadier General Thomas Sumter (1734–1832) learned that Major Patrick Ferguson's (1744–1780) force was moving beyond the Broad River, he directed Colonel Elijah

SC-5. Blockhouse at Fort Halifax in Winslow, Maine, the oldest blockhouse in the United States. Notice the loophole and the dovetail construction on the corners.

Clarke (1733–1799) to move his Georgia militiamen toward that area. Clarke joined Colonel Charles McDowell (1743–1815) at Cherokee Ford after which McDowell moved his camp near present-day Gaffney. His troop strength increased with arriving troops, including those of Colonel Isaac Shelby (1750–1826); so McDowell decided to eliminate the threat from Moore's Loyalists. He detached Colonel Shelby and 600 men to attack Fort Anderson.

Colonel Shelby, Colonel Elijah Clarke, Colonel Andrew Hampton (1716–1805), Major Charles Robertson (1740–1799) of Colonel John Sevier's (1745–1815) regiment, and 600 "mountain men" attacked the Loyalist post at Fort Anderson, or Thicketty Fort as it was more generally called. It was a strong fortress on Goucher Creek, a branch of the Pacolet River. It was surrounded by a strong abatis and was a good location for Loyalist raiders to plunder Whig families in the area.

The Whigs set out at sunset on Saturday, July 29, 1780 and surrounded the fort at sunrise the next day. Colonel Shelby sent Colonel William Cooke (1732–1804) to demand the surrender of the garrison. The commander replied that he would defend the place to the last extremity. As Shelby moved his men within musket range in preparation for an assault, Captain Moore, saw he was greatly outnumbered, relented and proposed to surrender on condition that the garrison be paroled. Shelby accepted the terms as he did not care to be encumbered with prisoners. The entire garrison of 93 Loyalists and one British sergeant-major surrendered without firing a single shot. Shelby and his men captured 250 stand of arms, all loaded with ball and buckshot. They were placed at the portholes in such a way that they could easily have repulsed double the number of attackers.

Shelby and his men returned to McDowell's camp near Cherokee Ford with their prisoners and spoils. A letter found after the battle of Kings Mountain states that the officer second-in-command of the garrison and all the other men wanted to defend the post. They charged the commander with cowardice and treachery.[51]

Great Falls vicinity, Fairfield County
Caldwell's house, Fairfield County (June 1780; Nov. 18, 1781)
Rocky Mount engagement (July 30, 1780)

> The site of Caldwell's house was in the southwest corner of the junction called Caldwell's Crossroads: Golf Course Road|Dewitt Road (SC 138) and Ross Dye Road|Old Winnsboro Road (SC 53) in Blackstock.
> To get to the site of the Rocky Mount outpost, take route U.S. 21 south from Great Falls. Proceed about 3 miles to Gibson End Road. Turn left (east) and go 1 mile, then turn left on Catawba Road and proceed another mile. A stone monument on the right of the road commemorates the action here. There are no remaining signs of the Rocky Mount outpost which was located about 0.3 miles further north on Catawba Road. Only the large rocks which protected the men who threw the torches remain. The stone monument is the only informational device located at this site. (The Fishing Creek Engagement site is also near Great Falls.)

Colonel John Phillips and some Loyalists were plundering in the York District in June 1780. Lieutenant Colonel James Hawthorne (1750–1809) and his New Acquisition (York County) militiamen pursued them and surrounded them at Caldwell's house. The Loyalists fled without presenting any opposition. "Colonel John Phillips, was found squatting in a briar patch, and dragged out a prisoner."[52]

★ After Loyalist militia Major William "Bloody Bill" Cunningham's (d. 1787) massacre at Clouds Creek (Lexington County) (see p. 109), he rode to Captain John Caldwell's (d. 1781) house which was only about 3.5 miles from Peach Hill, Brigadier General Robert Cunningham's (1741–1813) house. Cunningham had served under Caldwell in the South Carolina militia before he became disenchanted with the Whigs and changed sides. When Cunningham arrived at the gate, he greeted Caldwell who walked out to meet Cunningham. As Caldwell knew Cunningham, he did not fear him. However, Cunningham drew his pistol and killed Caldwell in front of his wife who fainted when her husband fell. He ordered the house set on fire before he left and crossed to the south side of the Saluda River and proceeded up the Cherokee Path.[53]

See **Hayes Station** p. 304.

★ Brigadier General Thomas Sumter (1734–1832) arrived near the British station at Rocky Mount with about 600 men early on Sunday, July 30, 1780. He camped outside the ditch and abatis surrounding the post just south of where Rocky Creek joins the Catawba River. Lieutenant Colonel George Turnbull (1752–1807), a Connecticut Loyalist, and about 150 New York Volunteers and some South Carolina militiamen occupied several log buildings inside the field fortifications.

When Turnbull refused his demand to surrender, General Sumter unsuccessfully attacked the post. Lacking artillery, he decided to burn the enemy out. He sent two men to throw torches at the buildings from behind large boulders. They set fire to one of the buildings which threatened the main structure. However, an unusually heavy rain began to fall and extinguished the flames. Sumter abandoned the attack in frustration after eight hours and withdrew "under as great mortification, as ever any number of men endured." He had lost three men killed, six wounded and two captured. Turnbull reported that he had only one officer killed, one wounded and 10 men killed or wounded.

Sumter had his men camp at Fishing Creek that night. The next day, Colonel Richard Winn (1750–1818) and 100 men rode along the road leading to Camden to determine if there were any reinforcements coming to help the British post. Winn's mounted men fell in "with a body of Tories," and dispersed them. General Sumter recorded: "I interrupted two parties going to reinforce that post." The Whigs captured several Loyalists and rescued the two men who were captured in the attack the day before. Both of the prisoners had been sentenced to be hanged in Camden for desertion when the Loyalists learned they had previously served with Colonel Turnbull. Colonel Winn returned to General Sumter's camp with "several prisoners, a great number of excellent horses, saddalles, guns, etc."[54]

Murray's Ferry (Aug. 2, 1780)

> Route U.S. 52 crosses the Santee River about mid-way between Moncks Corner and Kingstree. A long causeway goes over the Santee Swamp where a colonial road used to be. A modern bridge at the river marks the site of Murray's Ferry.

The Crown forces established a post at Murray's Ferry after they captured Charleston on May 12, 1780. Lieutenant Colonel Francis Marion's (1732–1795) part-time home, Belle Isle plantation, was about 7 miles from the ferry. Some sources say that he captured the post at Murray's Ferry on August 2, 1780.

Rocky Creek, Chester County (Aug. 3, 1780)

> The Rocky Creek action occurred near where Brooklyn Road (SC 141) now crosses the Catawba River in Great Falls.

Colonel Richard Winn (1750–1818) wrote on Wednesday, August 2, 1780, that the garrison at Rocky Mount was reinforced with "eight hundred men and 2 field pieces." These troops were Major John Garden's (d. 1783) Prince of Wales American Regiment, which marched from Camden to reinforce Hanging Rock. The high water at Rocky Creek caused by all the rain prevented Brigadier General Thomas Sumter (1734–1832) from moving his campsite until the 3rd. He crossed the creek with his army that afternoon and "turned out their horses and scattered about in search of roasting ears and green peaches."

While they foraged for food, an alarm was sounded. Garden's Loyalists were less than a mile away with two field pieces. The Loyalists stopped at Rocky Mount before proceeding to Hanging Rock. General Sumter, caught in the open, decided not to fight. He ordered Colonel Winn to take 100 men to delay the Loyalists until the militiamen could all withdraw. Winn sent Captain Samuel Coleman (1755–1804) and William Stroud Jr. (1752–1780) ahead to scout while the rest of the 100 men prepared their horses. The two scouts came too close to the Loyalists and were captured, "stript naked and immediately hung up by the side of the road."

Both sides exchanged long-range fire but did not get close enough to engage in a major skirmish. Colonel Andrew Neal (d. 1780) came too close to the fight and was shot out of his saddle when a bullet struck one hip and came out the other side. He died on the side of the road near the Loyalist forces. Another of Colonel Winn's men was wounded. Major Garden withdrew to Rocky Mount. Colonel Winn pursued at a distance but broke off as the Loyalists approached Rocky Mount. The following day, a burial party was sent under a flag of truce to bury Colonel Neal. They reported that they estimated the Loyalist dead at 12 to 14 men killed and wounded.[55]

Mayesville, Sumter County
Capture of James Bradley, Sumter County (Aug. 8, 1780)
McCallum's Ferry, Lee County (date unknown; Oct. 14, 1780)

> James Bradley (1752–1816) was a founder of the Salem Black River Presbyterian Church which is located on North Brick Church Road (SC 527) about 1.95 miles north of its intersection with route U.S. 378 (Myrtle Beach Highway) about 8.75 miles east of Sumter. Continue north on North Brick Church Road (SC 527) for about 1.4 miles, then turn left onto route SC 57 and go about 1.1 miles to the site of James Bradley's capture on the right just before the intersection with route SC 41.
>
> McCallum's Ferry was located about 10 miles northeast from the Salem Black River Church, 26 miles west of Florence and 3 miles northeast of Bishopville. It was on route U.S. 15 N (SC 34|Hartsville Highway) where the bridge crosses the Lynches River. A historical marker tells about the Dubose Ferry (see p. 38) and leads to confusion as to the location of McCallum's Ferry. It was at this site. Many of those killed in the vicinity of the ferry belonged to the Salem Black River Presbyterian Church and probably lived near the church. Their killers, the Harrisons, came from the McCallum's Ferry area.
>
> The site of the murder of Captain Robert Harrison was probably at Antioch, about 8.5 miles east of Camden. It was likely on the north (left) side of SC 34 (Bishopville Highway) just before Antioch Road bears to the left.

James Bradley (1752–1816), a founder of Salem Black River Presbyterian Church east of Sumter, suffered great cruelty inflicted on him at his house, in Salem, 30 miles northwest of Kingstree, due to the orders of British Lieutenant Colonel Banastre Tarleton (1744–1833). Tarleton dressed himself in the uniform of a Continental officer the day after destroying the houses of William and Edward Plowden (1744–1819). He visited James Bradley, saying he was Lieutenant Colonel William Washington (1752–1810) whose uniform was very similar to his own. He managed to get valuable information from Bradley and requested that Bradley guide him through the swamps to Camden. When Tarleton arrived at Camden on Tuesday, August 8, 1780, he ordered Bradley arrested and imprisoned with heavy irons around his legs. During his seven months in jail, Bradley was brought to the gallows frequently to witness the hanging of fellow Whigs. Mr. Bradley was promised freedom if he would swear allegiance to the King of England but each time he would refuse.[56]

Matthew Bradley (d. 1780), Thomas Bradley (1704–1780), and John Roberts (1731–1780), all respectable and upstanding citizens, who had remained neutral in the war, possibly along with some other members of the Salem Black River Presbyterian Church congregation were killed, in their own homes, by the Harrison brothers, Loyalists from Lynches Creek, in the vicinity of McCallum's Ferry. The minister feared for his life and returned to North Carolina until 1782 when he felt it was safe to return to the church.[57]

★ The Harrison brothers lived in a wretched log hut, next to the road near McCallum's Ferry and used the war as an excuse to plunder and murder the Whigs in the area. They proposed to General Charles Cornwallis (1738–1805) that they could raise a corps of 500 Loyalists in the area between the Pee Dee and Wateree Rivers. Cornwallis agreed to the proposal and commissioned John Harrison (ca. 1751–) as a major and his two brothers, Robert (d. 1780) and Samuel (1756–), as captains. "Harrison's Corps," sometimes called the "South Carolina Rangers," participated in Major James Wemyss's (1748–1833) campaign that burned homes and plantations in the Pee Dee area in September 1780. They were hated by all the Whigs in the area and even British Lieutenant Colonel Banastre Tarleton (1744–1833) called them men of fortune.

A Whig scouting party discovered that Robert Harrison (d. 1780) was home in bed, sick with smallpox. They burst into the house on Saturday, October 14, 1780, and shot him dead.[58]

Kershaw County
Little Lynches Creek (Aug. 8–11, 1780)
Lynches River (Lynch's Creek) (March 6, 1781)
Ratcliff's or Radcliff's Bridge, Lee County
Kershaw's Creek (also known as Keneshaw's Creek and Big Pine Tree Creek) (ca. April 13, 1781)

> The Little Lynches (Lynch's) River runs southeasterly and joins the Lynches River northeast of Camden and northwest of Florence.
> Kershaw's or Keneshaw's Creek (now known as Big Pine Tree Creek) is south of Camden near exit 98 off Interstate 20.
> Ratcliff's Bridge crossed the Lynches River (see Photo SC-6) near the end of route S-31-43 (Field Bridge Road East) about 1.2 miles due south of exit 123 off Interstate 20 in Lamar. A state historical marker near the intersection of routes U.S. 15 (Hartsville Highway), SC 341 (Main Street) and SC 34 (Church Street) in downtown Bishopville calls attention to the Battle of Ratcliff's Bridge, which took place 3.7 miles northeast of the marker on route U.S. 15|SC 34 just south of the bridge over the Lynches River. It also says that Brigadier General Thomas Sumter (1734–1832) retreated to Ratcliff's Bridge on the Lynches River. The action, which has never had a convenient name, started at the Stirrup Branch, now known as Bell's Branch, of the Lynches River. The stream was called Stirrup Branch in the 18th century because a broken stirrup was found in the branch after General Sumter's battle.
> Another state historical marker on route U.S. 15 (Hartsville Highway), near a bridge across the Lynches River about 3 miles northeast of Bishopville, commemorates Captain Peter Du Bose (1755–1846), one of Colonel Francis Marion's guerrillas. Du Bose's grave is located approximately 100 yards north of the marker in an old family cemetery. After the war, Du Bose lived near here and operated a river ferry, known as Du Bose's Crossing.

Lieutenant Colonel Francis Marion (1732–1795) and a band of about 20 "men and boys, some white, some black, and all mounted, but most of them miserably equipped" arrived in Major General Horatio Gates's (1728–1806) camp on Friday, August 4, 1780. General Gates sent them "towards the interior of South Carolina, with orders to watch the motions of the enemy and furnish intelligence."

SC-6. Site of Ratcliff's Bridge on the Lynches River

Lord Francis Rawdon (1754–1826) marched his army to the west branch of Lynches Creek toward Granny's Quarter after the battle at Hanging Rock, thinking that Brigadier General Thomas Sumter (1734–1832) had captured the post. He was aware that General Gates's army was approaching Camden, but he considered Sumter's mounted force a greater threat. When Rawdon learned the next morning that the British Legion infantry defeated Sumter at Hanging Rock and that the post was still in British hands, he hurried to occupy the bridge across the western branch of Lynches Creek.

General Gates rendezvoused with Brigadier General Richard Caswell's (1729–1789) 2,100 North Carolinians on August 7th and the army marched toward Lynches Creek the next day "encumbered with a great multitude of women and children, with immense amount of baggage." Major John Dean (d. 1781) was ordered to escort these women and children to Charlotte but there were no wagons to take them back.

General Caswell had been preparing to attack the British outpost at Lynches Creek. The combined forces now marched toward that objective unaware that the Crown forces had evacuated the post and moved back to Little Lynches Creek where reinforcements from Camden joined them. Lord Rawdon posted the Volunteers of Ireland, the 33rd Regiment, 23rd Regiment of Welch Fusiliers, and the 71st Regiment Highlanders at the creek to delay General Gates's approach while he waited for British dragoons to arrive from Charleston and light infantrymen from Ninety Six. General Gates's army outnumbered the Crown forces four to one, so Lord Rawdon did not want to attack nor did he want to retreat to defend Camden where Gates could defeat him and capture the British stores there.

General Gates feigned a flanking maneuver of the British defenses. When Colonel Charles Armand's [Charles-Armand Tuffin, Marquis de la Rouerie (d. 1793)] Legion drove in some British sentries, a skirmish ensued, but the creek banks were too steep, muddy and slippery and the swamp was too wide. Colonel Armand's cornet was captured. Gates refused to make a frontal attack and engaged the British sentries with long-range rifle fire which didn't hit any of them. Gates waited a day or two before going up the creek to cross.

Lord Rawdon withdrew to Camden to avoid a major fight and camped in Log Town. The thick woods blocked the view of both armies and neither wanted to attack, for fear of being detected and ambushed. Lord Rawdon discovered a pass through the swamp that came out 2 miles from the Continental camp, but he did not want to attack since he was outnumbered. Unable to cross the river, Gates moved his army to Rugeley's Mill on August 15th by way of Hanging Rock. This took him 35 miles from Camden—20 miles farther away than he had been at Lynches River. The Battle of Camden took place the next day, Tuesday, August 16, 1780.[59]

★ Brigadier General Thomas Sumter (1734–1832) retreated toward the Waxhaws with a force of 250 men to avoid the British at Camden after retreating from his aborted attempt to take Fort Watson. He traveled by way of the Lynches River and stopped by his plantation at Great Savannah to gather his paralytic wife and his young son. He then moved about 40 miles northeast, hoping that Brigadier General Francis Marion (1732–1795) would still join him. But Marion did not come. Sumter wrote to Marion on March 4, 1781:

> I made no doubt but your route to me would be by the way of King's Tree or the Ferry, and after receiving yours of the 28th ultimo, informing me what the number of your men were, I found you to be very weak and the enemy near at hand in force, this determined me to move on to meet you—to concert measures for our further operations, which is still absolutely necessary. I shall therefore remain at or near this place for that purpose, and beg that you may come this way with all possible speed; if not convenient with all your men to facilitate an interview, please come with a few. My horses are so worn out that I can scarce move at all, and officers and men are quite discouraged—finding no force in these parts, not even men enough to join to guide me through the country. But notwithstanding little may be done now, yet much good might be expected to result hereafter from a personal consultation, which I hope to have the favor of by to-morrow night.[60]

Sumter waited a day or two in vain for Marion. His men somewhat rested and refreshed, Sumter resumed his retreat from the High Hills of Santee to the Waxhaws by way of the Black River on Monday, March 6, 1780. He marched north along the road that follows the west side of Lynches River.

The Crown forces were trying to capture Marion, and he was certainly busy avoiding them. Nevertheless, even though Marion was less than a day's journey from Sumter, he does not seem to have responded to Sumter's appeal for a conference or even to have communicated to Sumter his own difficulties.

Lord Francis Rawdon (1754–1826) sent Major Thomas Fraser's (d. 1820) considerable body of South Carolina Royalists to intercept Sumter before he joined forces with Marion. They surprised him on the west side of Lynches Creek later that same day. A sharp conflict ensued. The first volley drove Sumter's militiamen back, but they dismounted and advanced again. Fraser's troops repelled the second attack and pursued the militiamen south for about 11 miles in a running battle. When they got to Ratcliffs Bridge, Sumter got his troops safely across, and burned the bridge to stop the British pursuit. Neither party gained a decided advantage. Fraser claimed a victory, but Sumter escaped, having lost about 10 men killed and 40 wounded. Fraser lost 20 killed and had to retreat. General Sumter returned to the Waxhaws without incident.

With General Sumter at the Waxhaws, Lord Rawdon now began a concerted move to crush Marion. He sent his own regiment under Colonel John Watson Tadwell Watson (1748–1826) along with Major John Harrison's (ca. 1751–) regiment of Loyalists in pursuit. The force of less than 500 men marched from Nelson's Ferry (Fort Watson) down the Santee toward Snow Island.

Lieutenant Colonel Welbore Ellis Doyle (1732–1802) (later General Sir John Doyle) left Camden a short while later with the Volunteers of Ireland. They crossed at McCallum's Ferry to the east of Lynches Creek and traveled down Jeffers's Creek to the Pee Dee where they were supposed to join Watson.

★ Brigadier General Francis Marion (1732–1795) sent a small detachment to watch the enemy's movements in Camden in late March or early April 1781, probably around Friday, April 13. They "took at the mouth of Kershaw's Creek, a boat laden with corn, killed 2, wounded 4, and took 6 British soldiers and 1 tory."[61]

Johnsonville, Florence County
Williamsburg, Richland County
Port's Ferry (Sept. 4, 1780)

> A state historical marker on route SC 41|SC 51 about 1.5 miles south of the junction with routes SC 51 and S-21-57 (River Road, Johnsonville, SC) calls attention to Port's Ferry on the nearby Great Pee Dee River. To get to the site itself, turn left on route SC 21-99 (East Trinity Road which becomes Ports Ferry Road) and drive east for 3.3 miles. There are supposed to be remains of fortifications on the east side of the ferry.
>
> Frances Port (1725–1812), the widow of Thomas Port, a member of the South Carolina Provincial Congress, operated a ferry in what is now Johnsonville during the American War for Independence. Lieutenant Colonel Francis Marion (1732–1795) used the ferry extensively during the autumn of 1780 in his operations against the Crown forces. He constructed a redoubt here and mounted two old cannons to defend his position from the Loyalists.
>
> The engagement between Lieutenant Colonel Marion and Major Micajah Ganey occurred about 17 miles north of the ferry along route SC 41, about 2.5 miles north of its junction with route U.S. 501 S|SC 576.

Lieutenant Colonel Francis Marion (1732–1795) had his men place white cockades on their hats to distinguish them from the Loyalists. They crossed the Pee Dee River at Port's Ferry to attack Major Micajah Ganey and a large body of Crown forces stationed on Britton's Neck between the Great and Little Pee Dee rivers on Monday, September 4, 1780. The dawn attack surprised the enemy who lost a captain and several privates. Marion had only two men wounded.

Major John James, Sr. (1732–1791) and a volunteer band of dragoons attacked the Loyalist cavalry. Major James singled out Major Ganey as his prey. Ganey fled with James in close pursuit, nearly within the reach of his sword. About half a mile away, they encountered a group of Loyalists in a thicket. Major James called out: "Come on, my boys! Here they are! Here they are!" The frightened Loyalists broke ranks and rushed into the swamp.

Another force of Loyalists farther up the river held their ground, making Marion hesitate to attack them. Marion feigned a retreat and led them into an ambuscade where they were defeated.[62]

Browns Creek, Union County (Aug. 12, 1780)
Hollingsworth Mill, Browns Creek, Union County (Oct. 5–8, 1780)
John Mayfield killed, Union County (ca. March 15, 1782)

> Browns Creek, now Big Browns Creek, joins the Broad River about 8 miles east of Union.
>
> John Mayfield was probably killed on Big Browns Creek about 0.9 miles north of route SC 49 (Lockhart Highway) on Big Browns Creek Road about 3.75 miles northeast of Union.
>
> Hollingsworth Mill may have been located about 5 miles due northeast of Union near where Vanderford Road crosses Little Browns Creek. While the actual location of Hollingsworth's Mill is unknown, there was an old corn grist mill at this site.

Lieutenant Alexander Chesney (1755–1843) and the Loyalist militia moved "down towards the Fish Dam Ford on Broad River" after the skirmish at Wofford's Iron Works. At Browns Creek, "there was a fight near the mouth of Brown's Creek with Neale's [Andrew Neal, Sr.] Militia where we [Loyalists], made many prisoners" on Saturday, August 12, 1780.[63]

★ A party of eight or ten Whigs hid in the thickets along Browns Creek near the Broad River in early October 1780 to observe what was happening in the area. Late Thursday afternoon, October 5th, they captured a Loyalist who told them that a party of about 250 intended to camp at a school house near Hollingsworth Mill on Browns Creek that night. The Whigs planned to attack the house on a high hill covered with thick woods that night.

They approached the camp in the dark and spread themselves in open order (see Photo SC-7) around the hill at some distance from each other. They agreed to advance until the sentries challenged them. They would then lie down until the sentries fired before rushing toward the camp to begin firing one at a time. When the firing began, the Loyalists fled into the woods.

The attackers entered the camp and saw wagons with horses hitched to them. The muskets were stacked against the trees. Cooking utensils were near the fires and clothing, hats and caps scattered around but there was nobody left in camp. The Whigs posted a guard, expecting the Loyalists to return.

The next day, they brought the animals, weapons, baggage and baggage wagons around the hill to a secluded spot some distance away. They remained there for several

SC-7. Reenactors deploying in open order

days before the sentry saw a party of 15 horsemen approaching rapidly. He notified the others who consulted for a moment and decided that the horsemen were the advance guard of an army coming to retake the spoils. They decided to hold their ground.

The Whigs fired at the horsemen who fled. A single horse stopped, unable to proceed, and his rider surrendered. His captors learned that the party of Loyalists had just come from Kings Mountain and were trying to escape as best they could. The Whigs gathered as many friends as they could to take their spoils away.[64]

★ Loyalist Lieutenant Colonel John Mayfield (ca. 1738–1782) had sent his family to Charleston for their safety early in 1782. He remained at his home, on a 300-acre tract on Brown's Creek, to protect his farm and store. Several Whigs disguised as British soldiers murdered him in his home between February and April 1782, probably around Friday, March 15, 1782.[65]

Camden and vicinity, Kershaw County

Camden (May 31, 1780; Aug. 16, 1780; April 21, 1781)
Wateree Ferry/Fort Carey/Carey's Fort (Aug. 9, 1780)
Ford of the Wateree (Aug. 15, 1780)
Battle of Wateree Ferry
Gum Swamp also known as Parker's Old Field, Saunder's (Saunders) Creek, Green Swamp and Sutton's Tavern (Aug. 16, 1780)
Antioch (Oct. 14, 1780)
Rugeley's Mill, also called Clermont or Rugeley's Fort (Dec. 4, 1780)
Hermitage Mill (April 15, 1781)
Major William Downes's house (April 15, 1781)
Logtown (April 19–20, 1781)
Near Camden (April 22, 1781)
Hobkirk Hill (April 1781; April 25, 1781)

> The Battle of Camden site (websites: www.historic-camden.net/ and www.battleofcamden.org/) is on Flat Rock Road (SC 58) north of Camden. From Camden take route U.S. 521 and U.S. 601 north 5.6 miles, bear left, and immediately afterward turn left on County Road 58 for 2 miles to a stone monument on the right.
>
> The Historic Camden Revolutionary War site (see Photo SC-8) on route U.S. 521 south of town is a restoration and reconstruction that recreates life in colonial Camden. It includes several of the earthen redoubts constructed by the British which General George Washington explored on a visit on May 25, 1791. It also includes the 1777 powder magazine with 48-inch walls built under the supervision of Joseph Kershaw (1728–1791). General Charles Cornwallis (1738–1805) used Kershaw's house as his headquarters. The house was burned during the Civil War and reconstructed.
>
> The terrain of the battlefield is partially developed with interpretive markers and trails. There is a stone memorial erected by the Daughters of the American

SC-8. 1909 DAR marker at the battle of Camden site

Revolution in 1909 on the spot where Major General Johann Baron de Kalb (1721–1780) was mortally wounded. A short stone obelisk in front of Bethesda Presbyterian Church between Lytleton and Broad Streets marks Baron DeKalb's grave. Robert Mills (1781–1855), a South Carolinian, designed the monument erected by the Town of Camden in 1825. Marie Jean Paul Joseph du Motier Marquis de Lafayette (1757–1834), who sailed to America with de Kalb in 1777, laid the cornerstone. The inscription on the monument states de Kalb's "love of liberty induced him to leave the old world to aid the new in their struggle of INDEPENDENCE."

Fort Carey, or Cary, also known as Wateree Ferry, protected the Wateree Ferry which is located just south of Camden where route I-20 crosses the Wateree River. Lieutenant Colonel James Cary, a leading Loyalist officer, had built a fort on the west bank of the Wateree River that guarded the main ferry crossing a mile from Camden. Some accounts date the August 9 event as happening on August 15, 1780. The exact site of the fort is unknown but it was probably located near Ward Road. To get to the site from Exit 92 off Interstate 20, take route U.S. 601 north for about 0.4 miles, then turn right onto Lachicotte Road. Drive 3 miles and turn right onto Ward Road. Drive about 1 mile to where a road goes to the left. This is the closest approach to the area where Fort Carey probably was located.

Wateree Ford was located on the Wateree River about 0.3 miles north of where route I-20 crosses the river.

Gum Swamp (see Photo SC-9) is also known as Parker's Old Field, Saunder's Creek, Green Swamp and Sutton's Tavern. It is 7.8 miles north-northeast of Camden and near the northeast end of Gum Swamp Creek.

Antioch is about 8.5 miles east of Camden. The site of this action was probably on the north (left) side of SC 34 (Bishopville Highway) just before Antioch Road bears to the left.

Rugeley's Mill was on route S-28-58 (Flat Rock Road) near the bridge over Grannies Quarter Creek. The site is about 10 miles north of Camden and 4 miles north of the Camden Battlefield site. Remains of Colonel Henry Rugeley's house, barn, mill, and pond have been found but are no longer evident, possibly buried in the construction of the new bridge. The August 16, 1780 skirmish took place about 600 yards south-southeast of the mill while the December 4, 1780 action occurred about 600 yards north of the mill.

Henry Rugeley's estate is known as Clermont, Rugeley's Fort, and, more commonly, Rugeley's Mill or Mills. Several historic events occurred here during the American War for Independence because, in addition to the house and mill, there was a large barn that could be adapted for many military uses.

Rugeley was commissioned a colonel when the British invaded the South. He is credited with saving Governor John Rutledge (1730–1800) from capture by Lieutenant Colonel Banastre Tarleton (1744–1833) in May 1780, just before the Battle of the Waxhaws. The governor had stopped at Rugeley's house when Tarleton was pursuing him. Rugeley warned Rutledge in time for him to get away safely. Colonel Abraham Buford (1749–1833) also camped here just before the Battle of the Waxhaws.

Major General Horatio Gates (1728–1806) camped here before marching on Camden in August. When General Charles Cornwallis (1738–1805) marched from Camden to attack Gates, Gates retreated to Rugeley's. Colonel Tarleton encountered some stiff resistance here from a few officers who tried to protect the baggage train from Whig looters.

Hermitage Mill was on Big Pine Tree Creek at the western end of Hermitage Mill Pond. To get there, go east from the junction of routes U.S. 1 and 521, in Camden, for about 1.4 miles, then turn right (south) onto route SC 34 (Bishopville Highway). The mill was about 0.3 miles east of where Bishopville Highway crosses Big Pine Tree Creek.

Major William Downes's house was about 2.5 miles further east, near the corner of routes SC 34 (Bishopville Highway) and SC 329 (Dr. Humphries Road). It was about 170 yards down Dr. Humphries Road (SC 329), about 180 feet north of the creek and about 80 yards from the road.

"Log Town" was a tract of 250 acres at the northern and most elevated portion of Camden. Joseph Kershaw (1728–1791) owned the property and named it for the log houses of Camden's first settlers.

SC-9. Gum Swamp

> After General Charles Cornwallis (1738–1805) captured Camden in 1780, he had four redoubts built at the four corners of the town and a large stockade, surrounded by high walls, in the center. He had a fifth redoubt built a little north of the town on the Salisbury Road to defend the jail. He commandeered the Kershaw house (on Highway 51) as his headquarters and had defensive works built around it. The 23rd and 33rd Regiments of Foot, the Volunteers of Ireland, a legion of cavalry, the Royal North Carolina Regiment, the Prince of Wales Volunteers and a detachment of artillery defended the town. The soldiers were housed in the stores and churches in the town.
>
> The "near Camden" action may have occurred near the intersection of York Street and route U.S. 521 (Broad Street) in Camden.
>
> Hobkirk Hill Battle Site is on route U.S. 521 about 1.1 miles north of the intersection of routes U.S. 521 and U.S. 601 (Broad Street) and U.S. 1 (SC 34|East Dekalb Street) in Camden. The location of the battle is along a ridge crossing north Broad Street near the intersection with Kirkwood Lane. A residential neighborhood covers the site of the battle at Hobkirk Hill. One can only see the ridge above the town where General Greene and his men camped.
>
> Lieutenant Samuel Bradley was hanged near the intersection of Kirkwood Lane and Lyttleton Street.
>
> General Nathanael Greene's headquarters was near the intersection of Kirkwood Lane and Broad Street. A historical marker is located on the right just past Kirkwood Lane.

Two boys, Kit Gales (d. 1780) and Samuel Dinkins (1762–), began sniping at the British column as it approached Camden on Wednesday, May 31, 1780. They fired several shots with no effect before the Crown forces captured them. The Crown forces hanged Kit Gales on a tree. Samuel Dinkins was brought to Camden in chains the next day.[66]

Camden, Kershaw County (May 31, 1780 or June 1, 1780)

★ Lieutenant Colonel Banastre Tarleton (1744–1833) dispatched a party of dragoons under quartermaster John Tuck to search for Whigs on Wednesday, May 31, 1780 or Thursday, June 1, 1780, two or three days after the battle at the Waxhaws. Tuck and his dragoons rode to Samuel Wyly's (Wiley, Wylie Wylley or Wyllie) (1756–1780) house in Camden, Kershaw County, mistaking him for his brother, John, the sheriff of the Camden district. (John Wyly (1750–1783) had supervised the execution of a Loyalist for treason.) Tuck accused Samuel, a young Quaker, of serving in the militia during the siege of Charleston. Wyly admitted that he had been there but stated he had been paroled. When Wyly showed Tuck his parole document, Tuck refused to recognize it and swore they would kill him and all others who had turned out to oppose the British forces. They then proceeded to cut him to pieces.

This story bears a striking resemblance to the descriptions of William Strong's (1760–1780) death (see **Fishing Creek Church** p. 14). William Dobein James's version says that the dragoons left two men posted behind two large gate posts at the entrance of the yard while the rest broke into Wyly's house and demanded his shoe buckles. When Wyly bent down to unbuckle them, the sergeant aimed a stroke of his sword at Wyly's head. Wyly saw the blade gleam as it descended and raised his hand to parry the blow. He lost some fingers and ran out the door toward the gate where the two guards beat him to death.

Family tradition believes that the Loyalists sentenced Wyly to be drawn and quartered and his body placed on pikes along the roadside as a warning to others. This incident provoked the Whigs in the region to join forces and soon the Crown forces needed larger and larger units to secure their outposts.[67]

★ Before the Battle of Camden on Wednesday, August 16, 1780, Brigadier General Thomas Sumter (1734–1832) requested Major General Horatio Gates (1728–1806) to send Colonel Thomas Taylor (1779–1783) and a small detachment of infantrymen and two small pieces of artillery to disrupt the enemy's line of communications to Charleston and to confuse reinforcements coming to Camden. Gates also sent Lieutenant Colonel Francis Marion (1732–1795) and his guerillas on a similar mission south of Camden.

Reinforced with 100 Maryland Continentals, 300 North Carolina militiamen, and two guns, all under the command of Lieutenant Colonel Thomas Woolford (1735–1794) of the 5th Maryland Regiment, Colonel Taylor proceeded to Carey's Fort to determine if it could be taken. They approached cautiously and silently and surprised the fort early Wednesday morning, August 9, 1780 and found its whole garrison of 37 Loyalists asleep. They killed seven Loyalists and captured Colonel Cary, 30 men, and 36 wagons loaded with provisions. This prevented any reinforcements from reaching Camden from the west.

Colonel Taylor learned that a supply train was coming to the fort from Ninety Six. Since all his men looked like Loyalist militiamen, he set a trap and captured the supply train of six baggage wagons and several hundred head of cattle and 70 more prisoners from the 71st Highlanders later the same day.

Sumter wrote, on the 11th, that he had taken possession of all the crossing points over the Wateree River and that all the British guards had been ordered into Camden. He reported that the British Regulars in Camden did not exceed 1,200 men and the militia was less than one thousand. These were "generally sickly and dispirited," and a reinforcement of 500 was expected to arrive from Charleston in two days. Sumter's information was accurate. He captured Elias Langham, a sergeant with the Royal artillery, and he reported that, on August 11th, the force at Camden was 2,365 men. Of these 1,770 were British Regulars.[68]

Camden (August 16, 1780)
★ After General Henry Clinton's (1730–1795) return to New York, General Charles Cornwallis (1738–1805) left a garrison in Charleston and divided the rest of his army into three columns for simultaneous expeditions into the interior in preparation to invade North Carolina. One column would march to Ninety Six; another would go up the Savanna and Saluda Rivers to Savannah and Augusta, Georgia, while the third would go to Camden by way of the Santee River.

The British occupied Camden on Friday, June 1, 1780, only 20 days after capturing Charleston. They began immediately to develop it as their main interior outpost in South Carolina. On June 22, two understrength Continental brigades from General George Washington's (1732–1799) army arrived at Hillsboro, North Carolina, to form the nucleus of a new Southern army around which militiamen could rally and which could serve as the nerve center of guerrilla resistance. Major General Baron Johann de Kalb (1721–1780), who commanded this army of about 1,400 men, was the highest ranking Continental officer in the South after Major General Benjamin Lincoln's (1733–1810) surrender at Charleston on May 12, 1780. In July, Congress, without consulting General Washington, provided a commander for this army in the person of Major General Horatio Gates (1728–1806), the hero of Saratoga.

Gates soon lost his northern laurels. Gathering a force of about 2,000 men, mostly militiamen, he set out to attack the British post at Camden. He arrived in North Carolina on July 25 and set out two days later. Acting against the advice of officers who knew the country, he took the more direct road, 50 miles shorter, through deserted areas where he could not find supplies. The men came down with dysentery from eating green corn and unripe peaches which was the only food they could find. They suffered from exhaustion and debilitation. Gates made rendezvous with 2,000 North Carolina and Virginia militiamen under Colonel Richard Caswell (1729–1789) on August 3, doubling the size of his army.

Cornwallis hurried north from Charleston to reinforce Lord Francis Rawdon (1754–1826) and meet General Gates outside Camden which would be the jumping-off point for his campaign. His army consisted of:

    1,500 Veteran Regular and Loyalist troops
      200 Veteran cavalry of Banastre Tarleton's Legion
      550 Militiamen and comparable units
    2,250 Total

The Continentals had about 3,500 men ready for duty:

      900 Veteran Maryland and Delaware Continentals
      100 Charles Armand's Veteran Legion
    2,500 Militiamen
    3,500 Total

The Crown forces marched quickly and traveled the 8 miles to Saunder's Creek in four hours. They became disorganized crossing the creek, but they were quickly put back in order and continued marching. Three prisoners told Cornwallis of Gates's plan to attack on the morning of the 16th, causing him to order his army to be ready to advance at 10 PM. Both armies unknowingly approached each other in the night, meeting on a slight rise near Saunder's Creek at a place called Parker's Old Field in Gum Swamp between 1 and 2:30 AM on Wednesday, August 16, 1780.

The British Legion hailed Colonel Charles Armand's [Charles-Armand Tuffin, Marquis de la Rouerie) (d. 1793)] Legion. Then, by the light of the full moon, they spotted Lieutenant Colonel Charles Porterfield's (1750–1780) light infantry on the flank. Colonel Armand's lead horseman fired his pistol and rode quickly back to the security of the light infantry, 300 yards to the rear. When Colonel Armand rode back to his troops in the road, Lieutenant Colonel Banastre Tarleton's (1744–1833) Legion had already charged "at the top of his speed, every officer and soldier with the yell of an Indian savage—at every leap their horses took, crying out, 'charge, charge, charge,' so that their own voices and the echoes resounded in every direction through the pine forest." Armand's men held their ground, fired at the charging dragoons, then drew their sabers and rode toward the enemy. Armand ordered his right flank to come up on line where Porterfield's light infantry would protect their flanks. Guilford Dudley (1756–1833) recorded the scene:

> Porterfield ordered, "Halt, face to the road and fire." This order was executed with the velocity of a flash of lightning, spreading from right to left, and again the piney forest resounded with the thunder of our musketry; whilst the astonished British dragoons, looking only straight before them along the road, counting no doubt with certainty upon extirpating Armand's handful of cavalry, and not dreaming that they were flanked on the right and on the left by our infantry, within point-blank shot, drew up, wheeled their horses, and retreating with the utmost precipitation, were out of our reach before we could possibly ram down another cartridge.

Tarleton's Legion was caught in a crossfire from the light infantry on both sides of the road and was forced to withdraw. Porterfield's inexperienced Virginia militiamen fled back to the main body on the road, accompanied by Armand's Legion, causing confusion for a few minutes.

General Gates and his staff rode to the front of the column, and "remained there until the firing grew slack and the troops were beginning to be formed."

The British 23rd and 33rd Regiments of Foot marched up the road in a column and deployed across the road to block a flanking light infantry attack. Major John Armstrong's North Carolina light infantry fell back to the main army, leaving Porterfield's militia to face the British army alone.

Porterfield lost a field gun. Disorganized fighting continued for 20 minutes around the broken artillery piece in a wagon before both sides retreated to regroup. Porterfield lost his hat and most of his troops in the withdrawal. Dudley noted:

> At this fire, Porterfield with horse's head reined directly to the enemy, received a horrid wound in his left leg, a little before the knee, which shattered it to pieces, when falling forward upon the pommel of his saddle, he directed Captain Thomas Haynes Drew (1760–1854), who was close by his side, to order a retreat, which was done in a very deliberate tone of voice by the Captain, and instantly our little band retreated obliquely from the road, which was wholly secluded from us by the enemy.

Dudley assisted Porterfield:

> Locking my left arm in the Colonel's right to support him in the saddle on that side, and having completely turned his horse, we received another hot fire from the enemy directed solely upon us at the distance of thirty yards or less. Upon this the Colonel's horse, very docile and standing fire with the same steady composure as his master, having no doubt been grazed by a ball which he sensibly felt, reared, plunged forward and dropt his rider on the spot, who had a severe fall in his maimed condition, and had liked to have dragged me off my horse with our arms locked, and the horse going off with his accoutrements at the top of his speed, followed the track of the retreating soldiers. At the very instant Porterfield's horse reared and plunged forward, Captain Drew fell prostrate on his face, and that to naturally, that I entertained no doubt but he was killed. The Captain, however, receiving no injury, and being an active, nimble little man, was presently on his feet, and wheeling around the stern of my horse, was in a moment out of sight. Thus left entirely alone with the Colonel, who was flat upon the ground with his head towards the enemy and his shattered leg doubled under him, entreating me not to leave him, I sprang from my horse and seizing him with an Indian hug around the waist, by a sudden effort jerked him up upon his well leg. Then again the Colonel, in the most pathetic manner, apparently dreading instant death, brave as he was, or captivity, entreated me, as he had done before, not to forsake him; the blood, in the meantime gushing out of his wound in a torrent as big as a large straw or goose-quill, which presently overflowed the top of his large, loose boot and dyed the ground all around him. Pale as a piece of bleached linen, and ready to faint with the loss of blood and the anguish of his wound, he made another appeal to my feelings.[69]

Dudley tried to put Porterfield back on his horse but Porterfield was 6 feet 2 inches tall and weighed 210 pounds.

> In this dilemma I ceased to make any further efforts to throw him upon my horse and resolved calmly to wait the result whatever it might be, nor did Porterfield attempt to give me any direction in this emergency, or express an opinion how I ought to act for his relief or my own preservation, but appeared to be entirely resigned to whatever fate might await him in his exhausted and fainting condition.

Dudley saw

> two men at the distance of about 150 yards in my rear, running back with great speed, half bent and with trailed arms, towards where they supposed the main body, under Gates, was by this time halted. Although I could not at the moment divine where these men came from, I yet, nevertheless, with joy as well as surprise recognized them for American troops by their garb, their manner and by their clumsy wooden canteens slung over their shoulders upon their blankets and knapsacks.

Dudley called out to them for assistance with Colonel Porterfield. The two men laid down their muskets and fixed bayonets according to Dudley's orders. They then took Porterfield by both arms and placed him on Dudley's saddle. They managed to rescue Colonel Porterfield while "balls whizzed along six feet above our heads, while others struck the ground before they reached us, and rebounding passed off without doing much injury that I could perceive."

They rested Porterfield under some persimmon trees while they bandaged his leg with a piece of cloth cut from the blanket of one of the soldiers. Dudley cut "a bundle of twigs 10 or 12 inches in length and hastily trim them to apply all around the Colonel's leg before the bandage was wrapped over them." Even though the bandage became drenched in blood after it was put on, the three men proceeded another mile and a half to an open field where Dudley laid the colonel down to await the dawn.

After an indecisive but sharp 15- to 20-minute skirmish, both armies retired and prepared for battle later in the day. The infantry and advance picket suffered very much in the very hot fire. General Gates discovered, on the road, that he had stumbled into General Charles Cornwallis's (1738–1805) army of 2,000. Gates retreated to a defensive position across the Charlotte road and waited until morning to attack.[70]

When the soldiers awoke that morning, they found themselves in a pine grove with swamps on both sides, giving them no room to maneuver and forcing a head-on collision if they decided to fight. Both armies faced each other across the Waxhaw Road (now Flatrock Road) which went to the Waxhaw River from Camden and Charlotte. The centers of both lines were located just about at the road.

Major General Horatio Gates (1728–1806) occupied a position 5.5 miles north of Camden, at the ford on Saunder's Creek, prior to the Battle of Camden. He prepared his defensive works at this strategic location, the only fordable point on the "great road" leading to Camden. He had an army of about 3,500 men but he thought he had 7,000.

Gates deployed the Virginia militia on his left and the North Carolina militia in the center with the Delaware Continentals under Major General Johann de Kalb on the right. Brigadier General Charles Armand's [Charles-Armand Tuffin, Marquis de la Rouerie) (d. 1793)] Legion (previously Pulaski's Legion) and the 1st Maryland Regiment formed the second line to their rear, with 300 Continentals in reserve. His strength was on his right or west flank, while the militiamen in the center and on the left were not experienced in battle. The militiamen were still forming in the hazy dawn when Cornwallis struck, and they fled in panic before the British onslaught, scarcely firing a shot.

Cornwallis, to the south on the same road, posted his best men on his right or east flank, creating an opposite effect to Gates's arrangement. The first line consisted of Loyalist troops on the left and Regulars on the right, aligning British veterans opposite the militia. Regulars formed the second line. The Highlanders and Lieutenant Colonel Banastre Tarleton's (1744–1833) cavalry were held in reserve.

The battle began with a cannonade shortly after sunrise. As the British advanced, Gates tried to attack the right before it could deploy, but his militiamen did not get there fast enough and found the Redcoats already in formation, advancing on them. General Edward Stevens (1743–1820), seeing the enemy rushing on, ordered his men to fix bayonets; but the British advanced, firing and huzzaing (cheering), with such impetuosity that the militiamen panicked, broke formation and ran, throwing down their loaded weapons. Fog, dust, and smoke reduced visibility and contributed to the militia's panic. Two-thirds of Gates's army fled without firing a shot. The remaining third consisted of the Continentals under de Kalb.

After recovering from the confusion caused by the militia's flight, the 1st Marylanders in the second line charged, moving to the left of the 2nd Maryland and Delaware Regiments in the now-ragged first line. The British soon forced it back, eventually sending it racing to the rear.

Cornwallis moved his troops against the 2nd Maryland and Delaware Regiments on his left flank and in front of de Kalb's 900 Continentals. The Continentals held firm for a while, putting up a valiant but hopeless fight against 2,250 men. When de Kalb called for the reserve, those 300 men ran into the fleeing militia which rallied and tried to advance.

Brigadier General William Smallwood (1732–1792) was swept away by the runaways, but his 1st Marylanders formed under General Otho Holland Williams (1749–1794). Williams tried to bring the 1st Marylanders to reinforce the exposed flank of the 2nd Maryland, but Cornwallis prevented them from doing so and soon drove them from the field.

Tarleton's cavalry attacked the Continentals in the rear and captured Baron de Kalb who had 11 wounds and died three days later. Tarleton's cavalry pursued the fleeing Congressional troops for 30 miles, killing or capturing those who lagged. They also caught up with Brigadier General Thomas Sumter (1734–1832), whom Gates had sent with a detachment to raid a British wagon train, and virtually destroyed his force in a surprise attack at Fishing Creek on August 18 (see **Fishing Creek** p. 14). Gates himself fled too fast for Tarleton, riding 60 miles to Charlotte, North Carolina, that day and reaching Hillsborough, 180 miles away, in three and a half days.

Gates's army was so badly beaten that there are no accurate reports of his losses. He lost all his stores and baggage, all his seven brass cannons, and his reputation. He began the battle with about 3,500 men but only 800 reached Hillsborough. Estimates put the casualties at approximately 800–900 killed and 1,000 captured. Cornwallis claimed 1,000 killed and wounded, and 800 captured. Gates reported 700 killed, wounded, and missing. The Continentals suffered 650 casualties, over two-thirds of the total. Hundreds of militiamen disappeared, probably fleeing to their homes. Tarleton's cavalry killed or captured several hundred more during the days that followed the battle. An official inquiry into Gates's conduct was ordered, but charges were never pressed. British casualties totaled 324: two officers and 66 men killed and 256 wounded, including 18 officers.

The British seemed to have a firm hand on South Carolina. They evacuated Camden, after burning most of it, on Tuesday, May 8, 1781, 15 days after the battle at Hobkirk Hill, because General Nathanael Greene's (1742–1786) campaign to drive the Crown forces out of South Carolina put it in danger. A Loyalist newspaper printed this notice on September 15 about the British victory:

> REWARD Strayed, Deserted, or Stolen, from . . . [General Horatio Gates], on the 16th of August last, near Camden, in the State of South Carolina, a whole ARMY. . . . Any person or persons, civil or military, who will give information [about it] . . . so that . . . [it] may be recovered and rallied again, shall be entitled to demand from the Treasurer of the United States the sum of THREE MILLION of PAPER DOLLARS. . . .[71]

Antioch (Oct. 14, 1780) see **McCallum's Ferry** (p. 37).

★ Lieutenant Colonel William Washington (1752–1810) ended Colonel Henry Rugeley's military career when Washington and his dragoons found Rugeley with more than 100 Loyalist troops at Camden on Monday, December 4, 1780. They did not have enough artillery to assault the log barn encircled by a ditch and abatis. Musket fire would not inflict any serious harm and Washington was not foolish enough to attempt an assault, so he made a fake cannon and positioned it in full view of the defenders. He told them that he would blow them to bits if they did not surrender. Washington took the colonel, a major and 107 privates as prisoners and took them back to Brigadier General Daniel Morgan's (1736–1802) camp at New Providence. General Gates also came with his main force and established his camp there.[71a]

Near Camden (April 15, 1781; April 20, 1781)

★ A company of British soldiers guarded the Hermitage mill, a grist mill, at Camden a few days before the battle of Hobkirk Hill to prevent it from being destroyed. A party of Congressional troops under Lieutenant Aeneas McDonald, on patrol to observe the British at Camden and to interrupt their supply lines, approached the mill Sunday night, April 15, 1781, intending to set it on fire. One of the men disobeyed orders and shot and killed the sentry. The guards came out of the house "swarming like bees; and alarmed the horse in Camden, whose feet roared like thunder, as they came to their relief." The raiders were forced to flee or be captured.

★ The raiders found Major William Downes (d. 1781) and a group of Loyalists partying in the yard beside his house outside of Camden that night and ordered them to surrender. Downes could not determine their number in the darkness so he surrendered. When he realized he surrendered to only a few men, he ordered his men to fire. After a volley, the Loyalists ran into Downes's house and bolted the doors.

The raiders rushed forward and one was shot down in the yard. Angered by the violation of the original surrender agreement, the Whigs killed every man in the yard. Major Downes and his men fired out the windows while his wife and children loaded the weapons. They killed several of the attackers but Downes decided to surrender to protect his family. As Downes came out of the house, he was hit by nine bullets and killed in front of his wife and daughter. His daughter was wounded and crippled for the rest of her life. The attackers escaped into the night when they heard some dragoons approaching from Camden.[72]

★ Major General Nathanael Greene (1742–1786) received a report from Brigadier General Thomas Sumter (1734–1832) on the state of the British posts in South Carolina. He then decided to march toward Camden, hoping to surprise General Charles Cornwallis (1738–1805). If Cornwallis followed Greene, North Carolina and Virginia would be relieved. If he did not follow Greene, the Continental Army could capture the British posts in South Carolina.

General Greene sent Major William Richardson Davie (1756–1820) and all the heavy baggage to Oliphant's Mill, located at the head of the Catawba River, in case he had to retreat. He ordered Brigadier General Andrew Pickens (1739–1817) to concentrate on the British at Augusta, Georgia and Ninety Six to keep any reinforcements from marching to Camden. He then ordered Colonel Henry "Light-Horse Harry" Lee (1756–1818) to join forces with Brigadier General Francis Marion (1732–1795) to conduct operations on the Pee Dee River against Colonel John Watson Tadwell Watson (1748–1826) and Lieutenant Colonel Welbore Ellis Doyle (1732–1802) while General Sumter was in North Carolina recruiting three regiments to join Greene at Camden. He sent the wounded, spare weapons and heavy baggage to Salisbury and ordered that "the women who have children and all those unable to march on foot must also be sent off, as none will be permitted to ride on wagons or horses, on any pretext whatever." This allowed his army to march fast and hard through Loyalist dominated Carolina. They marched 311 miles in 33 days and were starving. Advised that the militiamen would help them find more food, Greene moved his troops to the north side of Camden, near Hobkirk Hill.

Captain Robert H. Kirkwood (1746–1791) and his Delaware Continentals advanced toward Camden at 10 PM on Wednesday, April 18, 1781 under the cover of darkness. They had full possession of Log Town by midnight, but the firing continued all night long. A sizable skirmish ensued at sunrise the next day. Kirkwood beat in the pickets and could see the advance works of the British army in Camden from his position. General Greene arrived near Log Town the next day and set up his camp half a mile from the British works. [73]

★ After Captain Robert H. Kirkwood (1746–1791) captured Log Town, Major General Nathanael Greene (1742–1786) withdrew his army 1 mile north to Hobkirk Hill. Realizing it would be suicidal to assault the fortifications at Camden, Captain Kirkwood and Lieutenant Colonel William Washington (1752–1810) conducted a diversionary raid to Camden on Saturday, April 21, 1781. They burned one house in a redoubt and captured 40 horses and 50 head of cattle. (Sergeant Major William Seymour wrote that it was 350 head of horses and cattle.)

General Greene learned, during the raid, that Colonel John Watson Tadwell Watson (1748–1826) was returning to Camden; so he mobilized his army to cut off Watson and prevent him from reaching Lord Francis Rawdon (1754–1826). He also wanted to prevent Rawdon from sending any reinforcements to Fort Watson which Colonel Henry "Light-Horse Harry" Lee (1756–1818) and Brigadier General Francis Marion (1732–1795) were besieging.[74]

★ Sergeant Major William Seymour recorded, in his memoirs, this incident that occurred near Camden on Sunday, April 22, 1781:
> a skirmish between a detachment of Colonel Campell's Regiment and a picquet of the enemy's at a mill near Campden, in which the enemy were obliged to abandon their post. Of our men were slightly wounded one Lieutenant and one private. Of the enemy were four killed and five wounded.[75]

Hobkirk Hill (April 1781; April 25, 1781)

★ Lord Francis Rawdon (1754–1826) sent Lieutenant Samuel Bradley (d. 1781) on a reconnaissance mission just before the battle of Hobkirk Hill (Wednesday, April 25, 1781). A patrol of South Carolina militiamen captured Lieutenant Bradley and hanged him from a tree on Hobkirk Hill in revenge. One of the militiamen had a brother who held a commission in the Loyalist militia and had deserted to Major General Horatio Gates (1728–1806). He was captured and hanged, so Lieutenant Bradley was hanged to avenge his death.[76]

★ Major General Nathanael Greene's (1742–1786) army, in better condition in April 1781, than six months earlier, pushed quickly into South Carolina to reduce the British posts in the interior. General Greene wanted to demonstrate the transience of British control and to teach the British that it is easier to conquer than to occupy. He planned to use partisans to harass the enemy's supply lines; seize their smaller bases, if only temporarily; and interrupt their communications so they could not co-operate effectively.

Greene would move against the larger garrisons with his main army which he had to preserve intact. He fought battles against the major British forces but never to the point where he lost so many men that he could not return to fight again.

While he sent Lieutenant Colonel Henry "Light-Horse Harry" Lee (1756–1818) and his Legion to Brigadier General Francis Marion (1732–1795) to take Fort Watson, Greene marched his army of some 1,200 Continentals and 250 militiamen plus Lieutenant Colonel William Washington's (1752–1810) 80 cavalrymen toward Camden against Lord Francis Rawdon (1754–1826). Lord Rawdon commanded 8,000 men in South Carolina and Georgia, but they were mostly Loyalist units scattered throughout the two states in small garrisons. The largest garrison was at Camden, where Rawdon commanded 900 men.

Greene took up a position on Hobkirk Hill, about a mile and a half north of Camden on Friday, April 19, 1781. Although he had the larger army, he realized the futility of attacking the strong Crown position and waited for reinforcements. Rawdon received a description of Greene's position from a deserter and decided to attack the Continental camp on Wednesday morning, April 25, 1781.

Lord Rawdon, age 26, armed every man who could carry a weapon and attacked the Continental outposts about 10 AM. He took his men, mostly Loyalists, on a long march through the forest to attack Greene's left flank. He used other Loyalists as snipers to pick off as many of their fellow-countrymen as they could as the narrow column pressed the main attack.

Greene's pickets gave him enough time to muster his men and assess the situation. Greene planned to overlap both flanks of the narrow Crown column. When Rawdon arrived about 100 yards away, Greene's front line (4th Virginia, 5th Virginia, 1st Maryland, and 5th Maryland regiments) moved quickly to the right and left, exposing three 6-pounders which immediately opened fire with grape shot. Rawdon's infantry recoiled under the heavy fire. While Greene's cavalry attacked his rear, two battalions of infantry advanced against the Crown center and two more against their flanks.

The Continentals tried to outflank Rawdon, who let them advance and pushed his reserves to either side of his front line, outflanking the Continentals. He escaped their trap and caught them in his own. Ferocious fighting continued for several minutes. Colonel Washington's cavalrymen surrounded Rawdon, and one of them demanded his sword. Rawdon pretended to comply and seemed to have difficulty in disentangling it. This gave his own infantry time to advance toward him and drive off his prospective captors.

Loyalist sharpshooters brought down several officers of the 1st and 2nd Maryland regiments. As the 1st Maryland Regiment proceeded down the hill, it became momentarily disorganized. Its commander tried to reform the ranks, but the resulting confusion allowed the Crown forces to close in on them before they could reorganize. The 4th Virginia and 5th Maryland regiments also retreated, leaving only the 5th Virginia holding its position. The Crown forces almost captured the three 6-pounders in a heated battle that raged around the guns. Greene tugged at the drag ropes himself until Colonel Washington, who had been occupied in taking prisoners, including several surgeons, galloped up to help him get them away. They saved the guns but left 100 men on the field to be taken prisoners. Greene retreated 2 or 3 miles to the old Camden battlefield to reorganize his troops.

Greene's losses were about 19 killed, 115 wounded, and 136 missing; the Crown forces lost 28 killed and 228 wounded or missing. Rawdon won an expensive victory like General Charles Cornwallis's (1738–1805) at Guilford Courthouse. The Battle of

Hobkirk Hill marked the beginning of a general British withdrawal from the interior of South Carolina. Rawdon was so weak, despite reinforcements of 500 men of the 64th Regiment who arrived on May 7, he decided to abandon his exposed position at Camden. He was now cut off from his supply base to the east, forcing him to retire to Charleston, thus leaving Camden to the Continentals.

Rawdon began to withdraw to Moncks Corner, on the Cooper River, 30 miles above Charleston, on Thursday, May 10, 1781. He destroyed the fortifications and most of the town before leaving. Greene took over Camden the next day and had Brigadier General Thomas Sumter (1734–1832) destroy the remnants of the British redoubts. The Crown forces lost several forts (Fort Motte, Orangeburg, Fort Granby, Georgetown, and Augusta) in the following months, leaving them with only Charleston and Savannah after a year and a half of campaigning.[77]

Kingstree, Williamsburg County (Aug. 6 or 7, 1780; Aug. 27, 1780; Nov. 20, 1780)
Mouzon's house burned (Aug. 6 or 7, 1780
Lower Bridge, Williamsburg County (March 10, 1781)

The Williamsburg County Courthouse is just east of the intersection of routes U.S. 52 (Main Street), SC 261 (East Main Street), and SC 527 (South Longstreet Street) in the heart of Kingstree. A state historical marker in front of the courthouse notes that the local militia mustered on this lot in the 18th century. The courthouse grounds have a monument to the Whigs of Williamsburg County during the Revolutionary War. It honors virtually every able-bodied man in the county aged 15 to 60 who fought under Brigadier General Francis Marion (1732–1795) for some or all of his two year campaign to reclaim South Carolina from control of the Crown forces.

Just west of the intersection is an island in the middle of route U.S. 52|SC 261. The Daughters of the American Revolution marker there identifies the site of the "King's Tree" which gave the town its name. An early explorer marked the white pine with an arrow to reserve it for use as a mast for the Royal Navy.

The Williamsburg County Museum, at the corner of Main and Academy Streets, directly across Main Street from the courthouse, has exhibits and displays that chronicle the area's long history, including the period of the American Revolution. On this site, at the head of Academy Street, Major John James, one of Brigadier General Francis Marion's most trusted men from Williamsburg, intercepted Major James Wemyss and a column of Crown troops on Sunday night, August 27, 1780. Major John James had served as a militia captain for King George III, but when the American War for Independence began, he resigned his commission and served the Congressional forces with distinction for the duration of the war as a leader of four militia companies.

The Mouzon house was located on Sumter Highway (SC 527) about 7.7 miles west of its intersection with Main Street (SC 261) in Kingstree. A house has been built on the site of the original house with the same style as the original. There's also a historical marker at the site.

Robert Witherspoon's (1728–1788) son, who was about five years old at the time, gives the date of the burning of Mouzon's house as July 25 in his account written at age 73. Other accounts put it at August 6 or 7, 1780.

> The location and dates of the burning of the William and Edward Plowden houses are unknown, but the event happened the same day or the day after Mouzon's house was burned.
> Lower Bridge crosses the Black River 5.5 miles south of Kingstree in Williamsburg County. The battle occurred where route SC 377 (Martin Luther King, Jr. Avenue) now crosses the Black River. The Lower Bridge historical marker is about 325 yards further south, in the point of the triangle formed by the roads. Patrick O'Kelley (vol. 3 p.126) dates this event March 14–27.
> Witherspoon's plantation was about 2.6 miles due north of Lower Bridge, about 0.9 miles west of the intersection of routes SC 377 (Martin Luther King, Jr. Avenue) and S-45-394 (Shaw Corner Road).

Major John James, Sr. (1732–1791) commanded four companies of South Carolina Whig militiamen meeting at Kingstree in late July 1780. Lieutenant Colonel Banastre Tarleton (1744–1833) learned of this and crossed the Santee River at Lenud's Ferry and arrived at Captain Gavin Witherspoon's (1748–1834) plantation near the Lower Bridge on Black River, south of Kingstree, around July 25. Major James sent Henry Durant (1755–1805) to spy on Tarleton's force at Witherspoon's plantation. However, Durant unexpectedly ran into Tarleton's force just after they crossed the Lower Bridge. The Crown forces chased Durant for three quarters of a mile, forcing him to abandon his horse, jump a high fence, and run through the pea-vines of Robert Witherspoon's (1728–1788) cornfield to escape.

Tarleton rode to the steps of Robert Witherspoon's house and demanded to know the name of the spy, the object of his mission, Major James's location and the size of his force. He learned that James was only 5 miles away with about 350 to 400 or more well-mounted men. As Tarleton only had 250 men, he changed his plans to avoid doing battle with James. He passed through Kingstree on his way to the Salem Black River community.

★ Along the way, Tarleton burned the home of Whig Captain William Henry Mouzon (1741–1807) on Sunday or Monday, August 6 or 7, 1780, because he was one of James's officers and spoke French. He destroyed 14 buildings and their contents. He also destroyed the houses of William and Edward Plowden (1744–1819) a little further on his way, possibly in Williamsburg, Clarendon or Sumter counties.[78]

★ Major James Wemyss (1748–1833) had destroyed property in the area around Kingstree several months earlier and treated the Whigs harshly. The people of Williamsburg hated him and Major John James, Sr. (1732–1791) couldn't wait to get revenge. Major James hid in a thicket close to Major Wemyss's line of march and formed a good estimate of his force by the light of the bright moon on Sunday, August 27, 1780. As the rear guard passed, James jumped from his hiding place and took some prisoners.

After he gained an accurate count of the number of troops sent to raid the Williamsburg area, Major James and his militia of about 150 men began a hit-and-run strike. He sustained heavy losses. Some accounts say he lost 30 men killed. It is more likely he had 30 total casualties: about five killed, 15 wounded and 10 captured. Yet, they rallied and drove Wemyss's larger force back into Georgetown County. James then galloped off to notify General Francis Marion (1732–1795) that the Crown forces were in the area. A few months later, James's militia became part of the core of Marion's Brigade. James killed or captured 30 enemy soldiers.[79]

★ Major Robert McLeroth and the 64th Regiment arrived at Kingstree on Monday, November 20, 1780 and encamped on the village green that evening. Instead of mounting an attack on the British camp at daybreak, General Francis Marion (1732–1795) quickly retreated on the road to Britton's Ferry. He had covered 26 miles and pitched his tents on the bluff which forms the western bank of the Pee Dee River by morning.

Colonel James Cassells requested Lieutenant Colonel Nesbit Balfour (1743–1832) for permission to move up the Pee Dee, the Great Pee Dee, and Lynches rivers in search of Marion "whom they all look upon only as a plunderer." Balfour agreed but McLeroth abandoned Kingstree on November 22 with 300 British regulars, 300 mounted militiamen and two cannons. They marched toward Murray's ferry on the Santee River.

Lieutenant Colonel Balfour hoped that Major McLeroth would stay on the north side of the Santee River. If he moved to the south side or marched off to Camden, he would leave only militiamen to oppose General Marion who was "too formidable to trust so near the boats, and stores, without something better than militia." Balfour had to strengthen Georgetown. He decided to send Lieutenant John Wilson, an engineer, with a galley and two cannons to Georgetown on November 24. A week's work on the redoubts there would make them "absolutely impregnable."[80]

★ Samuel Tynes led another large raiding party toward Kingstree in March 1781. However, William McCottry or McCottrey (1748–) commanding McCottry's Rifles, a unit of Brigadier General Francis Marion's (1732–1795) brigade, blocked them at Lower Bridge. General Marion, with 40 men, and Captain William McCottry, with 30 riflemen, held the Lower Bridge over the Black River. They removed the planks and set the eastern end of the bridge on fire. Lieutenant Colonel John Watson Tadwell Watson (1748–1826) tried to dislodge them with cannon sometime between March 10 and 14, 1781. However, the cannon could not be depressed enough to fire effectively on the Whigs without exposing his artillerymen to the Whigs' rifle fire.

The Crown troops prepared to make a frontal assault on the ford, but McCottry's riflemen killed the captain leading the charge and the men trying to carry him to safety. They lost 12 men killed and wounded while the Whigs lost five killed and eight wounded.

Watson withdrew to Witherspoon's plantation. He tried unsuccessfully to get Marion to attack him. He made another attempt to take the bridge, but McCottry's riflemen repelled him. While Watson was at Witherspoon's, Whig Colonel Archibald McDonald climbed a tree and shot Loyalist Lieutenant George Torriano in the knee from 300 yards.[81]

See also **Tearcoat Swamp** p. 58.

Hemingway, Georgetown County
Pee Dee Swamp (Sept. 1780)

> No one knows where this action took place other than somewhere in or along the Pee Dee Swamp. The swamp was near Conch Creek, along the Old Pee Dee Road 13 miles southeast of Hemingway, about 0.3 miles north of the junction of Route S-22-127 (Carvers Bay Road).

Brigadier General Francis Marion (1732–1795) sent out reconnaissance patrols to observe the movements of the Crown forces in his area in September 1780. Captain Gavin Witherspoon (1748–1834) and four men, on one of these patrols, discovered a Loyalist camp in the Pee Dee Swamp. When his men refused to approach the camp, Captain Witherspoon went alone, creeping up to the camp where he found seven Loyalists asleep with their muskets leaning against a pine tree. He secured the muskets and woke the Loyalists and demanded their surrender. When the Loyalists saw Witherspoon's men coming to assist him, they surrendered.[82]

Tearcoat Swamp (Tarcote Swamp), Clarendon County (Sept. 4, 1780; Oct. 25, 1780)
Blue Savannah, Little Pee Dee River, Marion County (Sept. 4, 1780)
Black River, Williamsburg County
Black River, Georgetown and Williamsburg Counties (Dec. 7, 1780; March 10, 1781; April 2, 1781)
Lower Bridge, Williamsburg County (March 10, 1781)

> Originally called Turncoat Swamp, it became known as Tearcoat or Tarcote Swamp. It is on route S-14-50 (Brewington Road, about 6.2 miles northeast of Alcolu), about 0.5 miles east of route I-95 but there is no access from I-95. It is also about 1.5 miles northwest of the intersection of Brewington Road and route U.S. 301 about 34 miles southwest of Florence. A state historical marker is on Brewington Road near the site of the skirmish.
>
> A state historical marker for the Battle of Blue Savannah, supposedly located near the junction of routes U.S. 501 and SC 41, southeast of Florence and giving the incorrect date of August 13 was not evident at the time of our visit. The battle site was probably along route SC 41 in Marion, about 1.3 miles northeast of the intersection with route SC 41A.
>
> This battle at Blue Savannah should not be confused with the battle of Great Savannah or any skirmish along the Savannah River which separates South Carolina and Georgia.

The British had sent about 250 Loyalist militiamen to search for Francis Marion (1732–1795), recently appointed to the rank of brigadier general. A detachment of 52 of Marion's mounted soldiers stumbled upon a band of about 45 to 50 of Loyalist Major Micajah Ganey's cavalry early Monday morning, September 4, 1780. They charged the Loyalists and routed them. Major John James, Sr. (1732–1791), the leader of Marion's advance detachment, pursued them alone, calling out orders to nonexistent officers. The ruse worked. Most of the Loyalists scattered. Major James captured three men who reported that Captain Jesse Barfield's (1738–1780) larger force of 200 men was only 3 miles away.

Marion's force soon encountered Captain Barfield's infantry which quickly formed for battle. Marion pretended to retreat, moving deep into a swampy region until he reached an area of sandy ground and dense scrub pines. At this point, along the Little Pee Dee River known as Blue Savannah, Marion circled back and ambushed the unsuspecting Loyalists later in the day.

Outnumbered almost five to one, Marion ambushed the Loyalist infantry who fired a volley, wounding three of Marion's men and killing two horses. Unable to reload quickly enough, the Loyalists scattered in the Little Pee Dee swamp. Marion lost only four men wounded and two dead horses in this decisive victory that destroyed Loyalist support east of the Little Pee Dee River. It also encouraged 60 local men to join Marion's unit. Marion and his men celebrated their victory with roasted pigs and turkeys and a half-pint of brandy each.

The following day, they went in search of any survivors of the battle. As they marched through the swamp, they found a dead British soldier but they saw no bullet holes. Marion's men wondered how the soldier died until one of them saw a rattlesnake slither into the nearby undergrowth. Someone raised a musket to kill the snake, but someone else pleaded to spare the snake's life. The serpent supposedly was ordered court-martialed and the rattler was brought to camp in a horsehair noose.

One of Marion's men served as attorney for the snake and argued: "If this creature is a murderer, then so are we all. This snake has killed one British soldier; we have killed many. This is not murder, gentlemen. This is war!" The sympathetic jury cried out in unison, "Not guilty!" and the snake was released immediately.[83]

★ Brigadier General Francis Marion (1732–1795) was under direct orders from Major General Horatio Gates (1728–1806) to continue harassing the enemy. He and his force of 150 soldiers surprised Colonel Samuel Tynes (d. 1795) and 200 Salem Loyalist militiamen just after midnight on Wednesday, October 25, 1780 at Tearcoat or Tarcote Swamp. These men were supposed to cover the departure of Major James Wemyss's (1748–1833) British regulars from the area on their way to Camden after the battle at Kings Mountain.

General Marion had learned that Colonel Tynes was gathering a large body of Loyalists in the fork of the Black River for an uprising. So Marion left his camp at Port's Ferry on the Pee Dee River and marched more than 50 miles west to Tearcoat Swamp. He crossed the north branch of the Black River at Nelson's plantation, marched some 30 miles southwest to Kingstree and divided his men into three units as he had done at Black Mingo. Marion's scouts reported that Tynes and his men were camped in a field with the swamp behind them. Marion ordered his men to rest and they attacked shortly after midnight in the early morning hours of Thursday, October 26, advancing from three directions—both flanks and the front. With the swamp behind them, the Loyalists were routed and many, including Colonel Tynes, were forced to flee into Tearcoat Swamp on the far side of the field.

Without losing a single man, Marion inflicted severe casualties leaving six dead, 14 wounded and 23 captured. He also captured 80 weapons, 80 horses, the baggage, and the ammunition at the camp. He prevented the uprising and many of the Loyalists "turned coat" (tearcoat) and joined Marion's forces following the attack. The prisoners were brought to a camp in North Carolina. Supply convoys traveling between Charleston and Camden now had to make long diversions to avoid Marion's roving patrols. A short while later, Marion took a position on Snow Island where the Pee Dee and Lynches rivers meet. His camp here was inaccessible except by water.[84]

★ Brigadier General Francis Marion's (1732–1795) cavalry commander, Colonel Peter Horry (1747–1815), stuttered which increased when he was excited. He tried to order his men to fire during an ambush. All he could say was, "fi-fi-fi!" Angered because his men awaited the complete order, he shouted, "SHOOT, damn you Shoot! You know what I would say! Shoot, and be damned to you!"

Colonel Samuel Tynes (d. 1795) had been released from jail in North Carolina and returned to the Black River area. General Marion sent Colonel Horry to reconnoiter Colonel Tynes's militia at Fort Upton. Horry's troops rode all night and stopped at a tavern kept by a well-known Loyalist on Thursday, December 7, 1780. While Horry questioned the owner about Tynes, the tavern-keeper's wife showed the men a barrel of apple brandy in a storehouse. The men filled their canteens and drank as much as they wanted. Horry, unaware that his men had been drinking the brandy, began to suspect something was amiss when they drank continually from their canteens and some grinned in his face "like monkeys, others looked stupid as asses, while the greater part chattered like magpies."

Colonel Horry, the only sober man among his troops, decided to retreat before they got captured. His men were boisterous as they traveled down the road along the Black River. Even though Horry's mission was a failure, the Loyalists along the Black River were terrified and 20 of Tynes's militiamen deserted. With his force severely depleted, Tynes resigned his command.[85]

★ Brigadier General Francis Marion (1732–1795) had engaged Colonel John Watson Tadwell Watson (1748–1826) twice previously at Wiboo Swamp and Mount Hope Swamp on March 6 and 9, 1781. Soon afterward, Watson pretended to continue down the Santee River, but he took the road to the Lower Bridge. General Marion expected Colonel Watson to march toward Kingstree, the county seat of Williamsburg County, so he crossed to the north side of the Black River to block Watson's advance. He destroyed the bridge and detached Major John James, Sr. (1732–1791) with 70 men, including Captain William Robert McCottry (1748–1805) and his 30 riflemen, to cover the bridge site and the nearby ford.

James and his men quickly removed the planks from the middle of the bridge and set fire to the stringers on the eastern end. The riflemen posted at the abutment could shoot directly across the ruined bridge. The musketeers were positioned on the flanks to defend the ford and to support the riflemen. Marion arrived a short while later with the rest of his men who were placed in the rear to support Major James's detachment.

Watson surveyed the landscape. The east bank of the Black River was low and swampy. The west bank was a high bluff and the road descended through a ravine to the bridge. The river was only 50 yards wide and James's riflemen commanded the defile. Watson brought his field artillery forward to clear a path, but the terrain was unsuitable for efficient fire because the elevation on the southwestern side of the river only allowed the artillery to fire above the heads of Marion's men, cutting off the tops and limbs of the trees. Watson brought his guns to the brow of the hill to fire on the riflemen on the low ground on the opposite side. However, McCottry's riflemen managed to pick off the artillerists before they could get their guns ready. The riflemen also prevented Watson's infantry from advancing.

Watson then tried to take the ford in a direct attack but McCottry's sharpshooters repelled the Loyalists who fled in disorder. McCottry shot the light infantry captain waving his sword at the head of the column leading his men on. Four men returned to remove the captain's body but they met the same fate. Colonel Watson remarked, "I have never seen such shooting before in my life." He succeeded in removing his dead and wounded that evening. He took a position at John Witherspoon's plantation, a mile north of the bridge and General Marion took a position on a ridge below the ford of the river (later called General's Island).

McCottry, considered the best marksman in his company, raised his rifle to aim at a Loyalist across the Black River and then lowered it. He took aim three more times and each time refused to fire. When his men asked him why he did not fire, McCottry replied, "That Tory is one of my neighbors, Captain John Brockington [(1727–)], and I cannot kill him."

The next day, Marion sent his marksmen to harass and snipe at Watson's pickets and sentries, forcing Watson to abandon his plan to attack Kingstree. Watson established his camp at Blakeley's plantation where he stayed about 10 days. He camped on an open field and McCottry's riflemen kept Watson's troops in constant fear, verging on panic.

When Blakeley's and Witherspoon's provisions ran out, Watson had to send his men foraging which invited daily skirmishes. On one occasion, Sergeant Alexander McDonald (1750–1804), who had been taken prisoner and rescued by Marion a year earlier at Nelson's Ferry, climbed one of the large oaks along the road leading to Gavin Witherspoon's (1748–1834) house and shot Lieutenant George Torriano in the knee at a distance of 300 yards, inducing panic among the Loyalists. Watson was now literally besieged with his supplies cut off on all sides. He supposedly lost so many men killed that he sank them in the Black River to conceal their number. He probably suffered 15–20 casualties to Marion's five killed and eight wounded. Watson abandoned the field and retreated toward Georgetown, never able to reach his goal at Snow Island.

Watson and his men paused at Ox Swamp, 6 miles south of the Lower Bridge, where Marion's men had destroyed the three bridges through the swamp and felled trees across the causeway, forcing the Loyalists to march through the thick boggy swamp. They had a more difficult passage at Johnson's swamp, 10 miles further. They crossed through the pine woods to the Santee road 15 miles ahead. Marion pursued them and sent Colonel Peter Horry (1747–1815) ahead with the cavalry and riflemen. Together, they harassed the Loyalists all the way to Sampit bridge, 9 miles from Georgetown where the last skirmish took place.

Colonel Horry's men annoyed the Loyalists in their flank and front while General Marion attacked their rear. Watson reached Georgetown with two wagon loads of wounded men. One of Watson's intercepted letters, dated March 20th, revealed that he took this route to Georgetown, 50 miles out of his way, to obtain supplies which he needed badly.

Watson broke camp on March 28th and moved rapidly toward the coast. He fought a final skirmish at the Sampit Bridge where Marion attacked his rear while his column was fording the river. Marion had sent an advance party to dismantle the bridge to make the crossing more difficult. [86]

★ Captain John Saunders (1754–1834) sent Lieutenant John Wilson with 20 Queen's Rangers to guard the men loading flatboats with forage from a Black River plantation on Monday, April 2, 1781. The Rangers became aware of the Whigs in the area after about two hours of uninterrupted work. Lieutenant Colonel Lemuel Benton (1754–1818) led about 60 South Carolina militiamen of Brigadier General Francis Marion's (1732–1795) brigade in an attack on the work party as they were completing their task. They charged twice in an attempt to overtake the Rangers who drove them back both times. Lieutenant Wilson then led a counterattack and drove Benton's force from the field. He and five of his men were wounded, but they killed one of Benton's lieutenants and wounded several of his men.[87]

Black Mingo Creek (Sept. 14, 1780; Sept. 28, 1780) Shepherd's Ferry

Black Mingo Creek is about 20 miles north-northwest of Georgetown near Rhems, north of the junction of routes SC 41 and SC 51. The site of the battle is undeveloped. Visitors can view the battle area but the only marker is about 100 yards north of the bridge across Black Mingo Creek.

> Shepherd's Ferry was about where route SC 41|SC 51 crosses the Black Mingo, about 20 miles northwest of Georgetown. Dollard's Tavern which accommodated the ferry passengers was about a mile south, in the vicinity of Edgewater Drive off route SC 41|SC 51, about 0.6 miles north of their junction at Rhems.

Brigadier General Francis Marion (1732–1795), at one of his camps at Port's Ferry, about 15 miles north of Black Mingo Creek on the Pee Dee River, was informed around Thursday, September 14, 1780, that Colonel John Coming Ball (1758–1792) and a band of about 46 Loyalists were posted on the south side of Shepherd's Ferry.

Marion's men were unanimous in wanting to engage in battle, so he decided to attack. They had to cross the creek at Willtown, about a mile upstream from Shepherd's Ferry. As they crossed over a boggy causeway and a bridge of planks around midnight on Wednesday, September 27, 1780, a sentry heard them and fired an alarm gun, alerting Colonel Ball. Marion swung around the ferry at full gallop and, in a few minutes, reached the main road that led to the ferry about 300 yards ahead. Most of his men dismounted and a group attacked a house, where the Loyalists were supposed to be posted, from the south (along what is now route SC 41). At the same time, Colonel Hugh Horry (1744–1795) and two companies attacked on the right (west) and the cavalry on the left. Several officers under Captain Thomas Waites moved in the center against Dollard's Tavern, while Marion himself followed with the reserves.

Horry's party encountered the enemy first. Colonel Ball's men had left the house and formed up in the field that Horry was advancing through, opposite the house. They held their fire until Horry's men came within 30 yards. The volleys killed Captain George Logan (d. 1780) and severely wounded Captain William Henry Mouzon (1741–1807) and Lieutenant John Scott. When Colonel Horry's troops started to retreat in confusion, Captain John James, Sr. (1732–1791) held his troops in order, rallied Captain Mouzon's men and began to advance in an attempt to turn Colonel Ball's right flank. They caught the Loyalists in a crossfire and routed them. The engagement lasted only 15 minutes. The Loyalists fled into Black Mingo swamp behind them. There were only about 50 men engaged on each side of this brief but sharply contested action. Marion lost two dead and eight wounded. The Loyalists lost three dead and one wounded and 13 captured. Marion also captured a sorrel gelding which he named Ball, after its previous owner. He rode the horse for the rest of the war.[88]

Williamsburg Township, Williamsburg County
McGill's Plantation (Sept. 15–20, 1780; Nov. 7–8, 1780)

> Williamsburg Township is about 9 miles east of Kingstree. McGill's plantation was about 4.7 miles southwest of Hemingway, about 400 yards south of the Hemingway Highway (SC 261) on Mount Carmel Road (S-45-85) where the road turns southeast (left). The Indiantown Presbyterian Church was located about 2.4 miles west on Hemingway Highway (SC 261) just past the intersection of Old Georgetown Road. A historic marker is located near this site. Captain John James, Jr. is buried in the graveyard of the reconstructed church and his house was located on Indiantown Swamp Road (S-45-290) between Greer Road and Chair Road (S-45-194), about 2.5 miles north of the church.

General Charles Cornwallis (1738–1805) ordered Major James Wemyss (1748–1833) to disarm all the Rebels "in the most rigid manner." His force of 200 Regulars of the 63rd Regiment and 100 Provincials of the Royal North Carolina Regiment and the South Carolina Rangers destroyed a 15-mile wide path along the 70-mile route from Kingstree to Cheraw from September 15 to 20, 1780. They plundered houses, burned mills and 50 plantations, shot milk cows and bayoneted sheep. They destroyed looms and killed the sheep, intending to deprive the people of clothing. They also took the slaves and hanged several men who opposed them. Only the corn was saved as it had not yet been harvested.

When they came to McGill's plantation, Captain John James, Jr. (1757–1825) and his men fired at Major Wemyss's Loyalists. One of his men shot at a Loyalist officer but missed and killed the officer's servant. The man's wife and children begged Major Wemyss for mercy. Had his officers not intervened, Major Wemyss's horse would have trampled the kneeling woman. The man was hanged in front of his wife and children. Dr. James Wilson had his home burned for trying to stop the hanging. Dr. Wilson then went to North Carolina to join General Francis Marion (1732–1795) with many others from the area. (Major Wemyss became Marion's best recruiting officer.)

Major Wemyss then proceeded to the Indiantown Presbyterian Church which he burned, calling it a "sedition shop." He then went to Major John James, Sr.'s (1732–1791) house. He told Mrs. James that her husband would be pardoned if he laid down his arm. She replied that she had no influence over her husband so Major Wemyss locked her and her children in a room without food or water for two and a half days. Captain David Campbell secretly passed them food through a window to keep them alive. They were released just before the troops burned the house in retaliation for Major John James's supporting the cause of independence, attacking the Crown troops in Kingstree and for firing on Wemyss's men at McGill's plantation. When General Marion learned of Major Wemyss's actions, he returned to South Carolina to stop the Loyalists.[89]

★ Colonel Samuel Tynes (d. 1795) managed to escape when Brigadier General Francis Marion (1732–1795) raided his camp at Tearcoat Swamp on Wednesday, October 25, 1780. General Marion sent Captain William Clay Snipes (1742–1806) to the High Hills of Santee to capture him. Captain Snipes captured Colonel Tynes and several other Loyalist officers and Justices of the Peace. This outraged Lieutenant Colonel George Turnbull (1752–1807) who commanded the area. Colonel Turnbull sent Lieutenant Colonel Banastre Tarleton (1744–1833) to search for Captain Snipes's party.

When General Marion learned of Colonel Tarleton's mission, he tried to surprise him, but Tarleton had set up a trap of his own at Woodyard Swamp. Dorothy Sinkler (1737–1793), General Richard Richardson, Sr.'s (1704–1780) wife, warned Marion of the ambush and he rode away immediately. Enraged at losing his prey, Colonel Tarleton began burning 30 plantations and houses, from Jack's Creek to the High Hills. He plundered General Richardson's widow's house to punish her for informing the enemy. Colonel Tarleton forced her to feed him dinner and ordered his troops to drive away all the cattle, hogs, and poultry in the barn, and set the barn on fire.

Tarleton was aware of Marion's skills, and each night he brought his Legion together to form a defensive perimeter. Marion tried every trick he knew to lure Tarleton into an ambush, but the men were evenly matched, neither falling for the other's traps. The chase soon ended when Tarleton was ordered back to find Brigadier General Thomas Sumter's (1734–1832) partisans. It seems that from this point on, Tarleton's luck changed for the worse. Due to his actions, Tarleton, like Major James Wemyss (1748–1833), became the best recruiting officer for Marion's forces.[90]

Society Hill, Darlington County
Adam Cusack hanged (ca. Sept. 20, 1780)
Darlington
Pine Log Bridge (early 1782)

> The hanging of Adam Cusack took place near the intersection of route U.S. 15 (U.S. 401|North Main Street) and West Depot Street, about 0.6 miles northeast of the junction of routes U.S. 52 (Cheraw Highway) and U.S. 401|North Main Street in Society Hill. There's a historical marker on the left about 400 yards up the road at Bradshaw Street.
> Pine Log Bridge was located where route U.S. 52 (U.S. 401|North Governor Williams Highway) crosses Black Creek in Darlington, about 10 miles south of Society Hill.

The Loyalists convicted Adam Cusack (1742–1780) for breaking his parole by firing across Black Creek into John Brockington's (1727–) plantation. Cusack was taken to Long Bluff [Society Hill] to be hanged around Wednesday, September 20, 1780. His wife and children followed. Major James Wemyss (1748–1833) personally supervised the hanging. As the noose slipped over Cusack's head, his family threw themselves upon the ground in front of Wemyss's horse in anguish and terror to plead for mercy. The enraged major seized his reins and spurred his horse to trample them, but a young officer snatched the bridle and held him back.[91]

★ South Carolina militia Captain Alexander McIntosh (1732–1780) commanded the Whigs on Black Creek, at a point nearest Society Hill, in early 1782. He had a brother wounded in a skirmish at Pine Log Bridge. This "excited [McIntosh] to Exasperation" and he killed every Loyalist he caught. When a Loyalist named Hughes was wounded, McIntosh fired his pistol at him but did not kill him. He made no further attempt to kill him and the Loyalists then pursued him closely.[92]

See also **Colonel Kolb killed** p. 80.

Bigger's Ferry, York County (Sept. 26, 1780)

> Bigger's Ferry became Mason's Ferry in 1811. The site of Bigger's Ferry is now under Lake Wylie. There's a granite historical marker on Charlotte Highway (SC 49) in the northeast quadrant of the intersection with Lake Wylie Road (S-46-1099) 7.3 miles east of Clover. Proceeding along Lake Wylie Road, one comes to Mason's Ferry Road. At the east end of the road, one can see the old road to the ferry by walking just beyond the last house on the left. The old road went through the front yard of that house.

The Crown forces were moving toward Charlotte when General Charles Cornwallis (1738–1805) learned that General Thomas Sumter's (1734–1832) brigade of South Carolina Whig militia was camped on the east side of the Catawba River at Bigger's Ferry in September 1780. He detached Lieutenant Colonel Lord Francis Rawdon (1754–1826) and his Volunteers of Ireland, along with Major George Hanger (ca. 1751–1824) and the British Legion dragoons and infantry, to find Sumter and attack him by surprise.

All of Sumter's men, their horses and baggage wagons had crossed the Catawba River using Bigger's Ferry and a nearby ford by Monday evening, September 25, 1780. They posted a strong guard at both the ferry and the ford with orders to sound the alarm if any Crown soldiers attempted to cross the river.

The British Legion dragoons, each with a Legion infantryman mounted behind, arrived at the east side of the Catawba River at the ferry at dawn on Tuesday morning. Sumter's riflemen picked their targets and opened fire to prevent the Crown troops from crossing the river. The Crown troops took cover, returned fire and both sides traded shots across the river. The skirmish prevented the Crown forces from crossing the river.[93]

Dillon, Dillon County
Rouse's Ferry (Sept. or early Oct. 1780)
"Sweat Swamp" (1782 or 1783)

> Rouse's Ferry was located at the modern Harlee's Bridge over the Little Pee Dee River north of the Little Rock neighborhood in Dillon.
> Sweat Swamp most probably ran from Harlee's Bridge northwest of the Little Pee Dee River into Marlboro County. "Sweat Swamp" William Bethea (1725–1785) lived along Sweat Swamp. Two other less likely locations for Sweat Swamp are where route U.S. 301 N crosses the Little Pee Dee River south of the junction of Kentyre Road and about 300 yards south of that point.

South Carolina militia Colonel Murphey (possibly Major Maurice Murphy who was later made a colonel) succeeded in defeating the Loyalists in a skirmish at Rouse's Ferry on the Little Pee Dee River after the Battle of Camden on the Wateree River (on August 16, 1780). The Crown victory encouraged the Carolina backcountry Loyalists who had been suppressed by the Whigs since 1776. They forced the Whigs to move from one swamp to another constantly in September or early October 1780.[94]

★ "Sweat Swamp" William Bethea (1725–1785) lived close to the line dividing the Marion and Marlboro districts on Sweat Swamp. Several Loyalists heard that he had hidden a considerable amount of money in his house and set out to rob him. They found him at home and began to torture him to reveal his hiding place. They even poured melted pitch over his head, but William would not tell them what they wanted to know. The Loyalists then departed, convinced that William would take his secret to his grave. William's son, "Sweat Swamp" John Bethea (1752–1812), also lived on Sweat Swamp and vowed that he would kill any of the Loyalists involved if he ever saw them.

After the war ended, "Sweat Swamp" John encountered one of the Loyalists, named Snowden, in the woods in 1782 or 1783. He subdued Snowden and began to hang him with a spare bridle, but he could not lift Snowden high enough to get his feet off the ground. He solved the problem by breaking both of Snowden's legs.

On an earlier occasion, John met a Loyalist at night and tied him after winning a struggle. He put the Loyalist on his horse and brought him to South Carolina militia Colonel George Hicks (1716–1793) as a prisoner.[95]

York, York County
Kings Mountain (Oct. 7, 1780)

> Kings Mountain is a narrow hogback 60 feet above the surrounding valleys. The plateau is a treeless summit about 600 yards long, 70 feet wide at one end and 120

> feet wide at the other. It is surrounded by a hardwood forest and slopes covered with rocks (see Photo SC-10).
>
> Kings Mountain National Military Park (website: **www.nps.gov/kimo/index.htm**) is south of the town of Kings Mountain, North Carolina, off route I-85. It is one of the largest military parks in the United States, covering 3,950 acres. It is a spur of the Kings Mountain Range that spreads across York and Cherokee counties in South Carolina. A self-guiding trail winds around the Whig lines and up to the summit passing all the significant battlefield sites. The park has the United States Monument, Centennial Monument and other memorial markers. A monument marks the spot where Patrick Ferguson was mortally wounded. A traditional Scottish stone cairn covers his grave. The visitor center offers exhibits, a film, and a diorama of the battle.
>
> There is also a Kings Mountain State Park on route SC 161, 12 miles northwest of the town of York.

Late in 1780, with General Henry Clinton's (1730–1795) reluctant consent, General Charles Cornwallis (1738–1805) set out on the invasion of North Carolina. He sent Major Patrick Ferguson (1744–1780), who had successfully organized the Loyalists in the South Carolina upcountry, to move north simultaneously with his "American Volunteers," spread the Loyalist gospel in the North Carolina back country, and join the main army at Charlotte, North Carolina, with a maximum number of recruits. Ferguson operated independently in the mountains to the west and didn't expect to find any serious opposition, but his advance northward alarmed the "over-mountain men" in western North Carolina, southwest Virginia, and what is now east Tennessee.

After Ferguson warned the frontiersmen to cease attacking the British outposts and threatened to march over the mountains with his Loyalist troops to "lay waste their country with fire and sword," a picked force of mounted militia riflemen gathered at Sycamore Shoals on the Catawba River in western North Carolina and set out to find him on Tuesday, September 26, 1780, the same day Cornwallis arrived at Charlotte. Ferguson learned of their approach from a deserter and retreated east to Kings Mountain, near the border of the two Carolinas, to await the attack. The 900 frontiersmen were joined by an equal or greater number of backcountry frontier militiamen from the region east of the mountains, totaling about 1,000. They found Ferguson and his 1,100 men early Saturday morning, October 7.

Ferguson believed the summit of Kings Mountain was impregnable, so he built no fortifications. He set the camp at the northeast end, the widest point on the ridge. The Carolinians crept around the flanks of the mountain in groups of one or two hundred, using the trees and rocks as cover. They intended to surround Ferguson and his men.

The battle began about 3 PM on October 7 when Ferguson's pickets discovered the mountainmen advancing up the slopes. The opening shots were fired about where the Visitor's Center is located. As the frontiersmen worked their way up the slopes, fighting from tree to tree, the defenders were unable to get clear shots at their attackers, firing downhill and probably too high.

Ferguson led a bayonet charge to drive the attackers down the hill, but they rallied and moved back up. He led two more bayonet charges to chase the mountainmen down the hill, but each time they returned to kill more Loyalists. The mountainmen pushed the Loyalists back to the summit and into their camp. Ferguson tried in vain to rally them, riding his horse from one end of the ridge to the other, blowing a silver whistle,

SC-10. Kings Mountain showing the hilly and rugged terrain of the approach to the plateau

and waving his sword with his one good arm. (The other had been shattered at Brandywine, Pennsylvania and was practically useless.) Ironically, Ferguson, who had improved the design of the breech-loading rifle, had to resort to the bayonet to defend himself against men who fired from cover with rifles.

Ferguson, the only person on both sides who was not an American, tried to break through the enemy lines, but eight or nine marksmen took aim on him, shooting him off his horse (see Photo SC-11). He died a few minutes later.

Captain Abraham de Peyster (1753–ca. 1799), of New York, assumed command and tried to rally the survivors, but he was forced to surrender. When the Loyalists began to lose heart and tried to surrender, few escaped death or capture. Some got the same "quarter" Lieutenant Colonel Banastre Tarleton (1744–1833) had given Colonel Abraham Buford's (1749–1833) men at the Waxhaws. After an hour of fierce fighting, the frontiersmen suffered 90 casualties, including 28 dead and 64 wounded, while they killed 225, wounded 163, and captured 716 Loyalist prisoners, taking with them those who were well enough to walk.

The next morning, the mountain men marched the surviving prisoners away, without food, down the mud-covered road toward Bethabara. Some fell down exhausted and despairing and were abandoned or stepped on and beaten. About 100 others managed to escape. One was shot and wounded trying to escape and was later executed. When they reached Bethabara they endured more brutalities. A drunken militia captain kicked a Loyalist officer out of the bed he had found. Dr. Uzal Johnson (1757?–1827), a Loyalist surgeon, was beaten for tending the wounds of an injured prisoner. Lieutenant Anthony Allaire (1755–1838), a friend of this surgeon, escaped with a few friends and found his way to Ninety Six.

The prisoners were court-martialed a week later, near Gilbert Town. Thirty were condemned to death as traitors, but only nine were actually hanged. Most of the others eventually escaped, as the mountainmen went back home, leaving them unguarded.

Kings Mountain was as fatal to General Cornwallis's plans as Bennington, Vermont/New York, had been to those of Major General John Burgoyne (1722–1792). The North Carolina Loyalists, cowed by the fate of their compatriots, gave him little support. On October 14, 1780, when Lord Cornwallis learned of the defeat at Kings Mountain, he realized that he could not continue his campaign of invading North Carolina. He was unable to recruit militiamen, his supplies at Camden were dwindling, and sickness spread through his army. He decided to withdraw to Winnsboro, South Carolina in the rain with militiamen harassing his progress. Cornwallis became ill with the fever that also affected many of his men, so he delegated his authority to Lord Francis Rawdon (1754–1826).[96]

Lake View, Dillon County
Bear Swamp (Oct. 30, 1780)

> Bear Swamp is located where North Bear Swamp Road crosses Bear Swamp about 1.5 miles due east of Lake View. There's a historical marker at Bear Swamp Baptist Church about 0.25 miles north. The skirmish most likely took place at or near the site of the church.

The government of North Carolina decided to impress large quantities of cattle to feed the Continental Army in October 1780. This angered the Loyalists of the Little Pee Dee area who opposed North Carolina militia Colonel Thomas Brown (not to be confused

SC-11. Monument memorializing Colonel Patrick Ferguson at Kings Mountain

with the Loyalist officer of the same name in Georgia) when he led an expedition through present Marlboro and Dillon counties to round up cattle. His regiment camped at Bear Swamp on Monday night, October 30, 1780. Some Loyalist farmers attacked Colonel Brown's militiamen during the night. The sentry challenged the Loyalists several times but received no answer. Major Jesse Barfield (1738–1780) shot the sentry and the Loyalists got so close to the Whigs that they could see their enemies' faces lit by the flashes of gunfire. Brown's officers finally succeeded in bringing order to their camp and formed their troops. They then drove off the Loyalists after firing only four rounds. Colonel Brown reported that the Loyalists only slightly wounded two men. One of them was Captain Robert Anderson (1741–1812) who, when he was shot, cried out, "O, Lord, I'm a dead man. What shall I do?" One veteran recorded that adjutant Robert Raiford (1754—1793), who stuttered very badly, replied, "G-God damn it, l-l-l-lye [lie] close, lye close!" [97]

Manning, Clarendon County
Ox Swamp (Nov. 8, 1780)

> Ox Swamp is located at the first bridge over the creek about 0.6 miles east of Manning on route U.S. 521. Brigadier General Francis Marion's (1732–1795) camp was located near Jacks Creek, about 2.3 miles northwest of the intersection of routes U.S. 15 (Church Street) and U.S. 301 (Main Street) in Summerton.

When Lieutenant Colonel Banastre Tarleton (1744–1833) received intelligence of Brigadier General Francis Marion's (1732–1795) position (near General Richard Richardson's (1704–1780) plantation) and had a guide, he immediately set out in pursuit. However, Marion had already departed and Tarleton pursued him to the Woodyard Swamp but could not pass it at night.

Marion, who camped at Richbourgh's Mill about 5 miles beyond the swamp, decamped the next morning and traveled 35 miles through woods, swamps and bogs to Black River. That night, he camped at Benbow's Ferry (Lowry's Bridge), about 10 miles above Kingstree on the east side of Black River. This position was the best defensible ground around and Marion could now defend himself. He made his first defense at Black River itself and then at each of three difficult-to-cross swamps—all within 10 miles on the east side of the river—before he reached Kingstree. Marion determined to make a stand at a defile on the road to the west of the river. He felled trees across the road to impede the Crown forces.

The next day, Wednesday, November 8, 1780, Lieutenant Colonel Banastre Tarleton (1744–1833) found General Marion's trail across the Woodyard Swamp but went around. He pursued "for seven hours, through swamps and defiles" about 25 miles to Ox Swamp. The swamp was wide, miry and had no road to pass it. Tarleton abandoned the pursuit supposedly telling his men, "Come my boys! Let us go back, and we will soon find the game cock, [Brigadier General Thomas Sumter (1734–1832)] but as for this damned old fox, the devil himself could not catch him." This incident supposedly earned Marion his nickname, the Swamp Fox.[98]

★ Colonel John Watson Tadwell Watson (1748–1826) was stopped at Ox Swamp because Brigadier General Francis Marion's (1732–1795) men removed the bridge planks about Thursday, March 15, 1781. He then made a dash for Georgetown via the Old Santee River Road. This is part of the Bridges Campaign in Williamsburg County.

Carlisle, Union County
Fish Dam (Nov. 9, 1780)
Near Carlisle (Nov. 23 or 24, 1781)

> The Fish Dam Battleground Monument is on route SC 72|121, 3 miles east of Carlisle, just east of the Broad River bridge on the north side of SC 72|121. The battle site is undeveloped. Only a sign and stone marker on the east side of the Broad River identify the site. Artifacts were found in this area. The "fish dam," which is a zigzag chain of rocks built by the Cherokees to trap fish and to cross the river, is visible when the water is low during the summer.

Major James Wemyss (1748–1833) with 100 mounted troops of the 63rd Regiment of Foot and 40 dragoons of Tarleton's Legion planned to surprise the camp of Brigadier General Thomas Sumter (1734–1832) at a place called Moore's Mill about 30 miles northwest of Winnsboro. But Sumter had moved his men 5 miles south to the east end of Fish Dam Ford. Wemyss ran into Sumter's pickets about 1 AM on Thursday, November 9, 1780, and drove them back after a quick volley.

Wemyss fell from his saddle with a broken arm and a wounded knee. Tarleton's troopers charged ahead and were badly shot up. The infantrymen attacked but withdrew after suffering heavy losses. Sumter escaped and returned to his camp about noon the next day to find his men reassembling and a British sergeant left behind to tend to the wounded.[99]

★ After Captain William "Bloody Bill" Cunningham (d. 1787) killed Colonel Edward Hampton (1746–1781 in Spartanburg County during his killing campaign known as the "Bloody Scout," he proceeded to the vicinity of Carlisle on the west side of the Broad River. Cunningham and his Loyalists captured and executed James Knox (1749–1781) and seemed to be planning to cross the river to raid the New Acquisition. However, they rode to John Boyce's (1745–1806) house, known as Walnut Grove, on Evans Creek in the southern portion of Union County.[100]

Chester District (Nov. 1780)

Captain Robert Cooper (1747–1794) learned of a "squad of Tories who had collected for the purpose of organizing to commit depredations in the neighborhood." He gathered his militiamen and rode toward them.

Cooper and his men approached the Loyalists, who had fortified themselves in a new log cabin around Chester, one night in November 1780. The Loyalists heard them coming and fired a volley, severely wounding William Hale in the foot and giving Cooper a flesh wound in the side. William Hale "was rendered lame all of his life afterwards."

Cooper tried unsuccessfully to burn out the Loyalists who refused to surrender. Since the Loyalists had not fired any shots from the house after the first volley, Cooper thought that they were out of ammunition. He had his men construct a battering ram "by swinging a log with ropes & battered down the door." They captured all the Loyalists. The following day, Cooper found the body of a young girl who was shot and killed in the Loyalists' first volley while she walked down the lane on her way to a neighbor's house.[101]

Chester, Chester County
Jenkin's Cross Roads (Nov. 8, 1780)

> Jenkin's Cross Roads was located at the junction of West End Road (SC 72|121) and Sandy River Road (SC 42) about 8 miles southwest of Chester. Fishdam Road was 5 miles west of the Chester Courthouse.

Colonel Edward Lacey, Jr. (1742–1813) seized a barrel of whiskey from a Loyalist named Knight on the Fishdam Road, 5 miles west of Chester Courthouse. Promising the whiskey to any new recruits, he persuaded 150 "warm hearted whiskey loving Irish" to enlist in his regiment in a single day. They drank their fill and grabbed "milk pails, milk piggins, noggins, pitchers, cups and any vessel" and mounted their horses. "They kept swigging at it till they all soon became gloriously befuddled and courageously brave."

Lacey's Whigs rode 4 miles to Jenkin's Cross Roads where they spotted a Crown patrol. Lacey's men yelled and the Crown troops fled. Lacey regained control of his men and avoided the road leading to Fishdam Ford where he was supposed to rendezvous with Brigadier General Thomas Sumter (1734–1832). Lacey didn't want his drunken mob to attract any Crown troops to the site so he and his men rode forward for a mile until he was sure that they were not being followed. They then turned on a road leading to Fishdam Ford. They "made frequent ludicrous tumbles from their horses, over the horse's heads, when drinking at their piggins" as they rode into the camp.[102]

Chester district
Broad River
Hopkins Place (Dec. 1780)
McKown's Mill, Cherokee County (Dec. 11, 1780)
Love's Ford, Chester County (Jan. 18, 1781)

> McKown's Mill was on the London Creek Branch, about 1.6 miles due southwest of the Broad River about 2 miles south of Cherokee Falls. John Nuckolls is buried on Whig Hill.
> Major Samuel Otterson's (1754–1837) residence was on the Tyger River in the vicinity of Hamilton's Ford which was probably on the west side of the Broad River, opposite the mouth of Bullock's Creek. There is a marker for Otterson's Fort on Whitmire Highway (U.S. 176) north of Beatty's Bridge Road (route S-44-278) between Union and Whitmire. The fort was 1 mile east of the marker, near the intersection of Beatty's Bridge Road and Lula Green Road. There was another Hamilton's Ford 4.3 miles south-southeast of the marker, just east of where route SC 72 (SC 121|Carlisle Whitmire Highway) crosses the Tyger River.
> Captain David Hopkins's home was near the Broad River in western Chester County.

Major Samuel Otterson (1754–1837) and eight or ten men were sent to spy on the Loyalists in the western Chester district in December 1780. When they reached the home of Captain David Hopkins, they found it deserted. Major Otterson noticed a fire on the west side of a ridge, a quarter mile away. He approached the ridge alone and "discovered Tories, double his strength. They must be Tories or they would have been at

Hopkins." He returned to his men and ordered them to crawl to the Loyalist camp and to fire at his signal.

Captain Moore, the Loyalist commander "who was advanced in his years," went to build the fire as the Whigs were approaching the camp. "He was on his knees blowing up a blaze" when Otterson gave the signal to fire. The attackers killed several Loyalists in their beds and hit Captain Moore from behind. He fell into the fire. "A few escaped like wild turkeys."

One of the Loyalists grabbed his musket and clubbed one of Otterson's men. He would have smashed his skull, but another Whig "who had just knifed his antagonist, came to the relief of the overpowered man and dispatched the Tory with his knife."[103]

★ Captain John Nuckolls (1732–1780), a Whig who lived on Whig Hill near Thicketty Creek, returned home to visit in early December 1780. He took his young son John, to McKown's Mill to get some meal for his family on Monday, December 11th. Even though McKown was a Loyalist, Nuckoll's trusted him. McKown told Nuckolls that he would not be able to grind any meal for him until the next day and gave him a room at the mill for the night. Meanwhile, McKown sent for some other Loyalists who went to Nuckolls's room during the night and woke him.

Nuckolls asked them if he could wake his son to give him some messages for his family. The Loyalists told him that if the boy awoke, he would also be killed. They took Nuckolls a short distance from the mill. Nuckolls asked for five minutes to pray, but while he was praying, he was shot through the head. The Loyalists threw the body into a hole where a tree had blown over and covered it with brush. An old woman found his bones a few months later and his family buried them at his home.

A few months later, a Whig patrol captured several of the Loyalists who killed John Nuckolls and executed them in the same way they murdered Nuckolls. The Whigs went to Mrs. Nuckolls's house and asked for a pick and a shovel because "they were going to settle her some new neighbors." She "hoped they would be good neighbors" to which the men laughed and said that "they would guarantee them to be quiet ones." [104]

★ Captain Samuel Otterson (1754–1837) and 10 badly mounted Newberry militiamen were on their way to join Brigadier General Daniel Morgan (1736–1802) prior to the battle of Cowpens. Finding that the battle was already begun on Thursday, January 18, 1781, he halted his men near a crossroad which he knew the enemy would take on their return and waited either "to make prisoners in case of their defeat or to attempt the rescue of our men who might be prisoners in their hands."

Before long, they discovered a considerable body of British dragoons coming down the road at full speed. They appeared evidently to have been defeated. Captain Otterson proposed to his men to follow the enemy and attempt to make some prisoners, but only one man was willing to join him. The two men mounted the best horses in the company and armed themselves in the best possible manner before pursuing the fleeing enemy. Captain Otterson prudently kept at some distance in the rear until dark. He occasionally stopped at some of the houses along the road, ascertained the situation, number, and distance of the enemy, and found his suspicions were verified. The Crown forces had indeed been defeated and that these horsemen were a part of Lieutenant Colonel Banastre Tarleton's (1744–1833) cavalry.

Captain Otterson's men found Colonel Tarleton's heavy baggage at Love's Ford on the Broad River. They captured it along with eight foot soldiers, 27 African Americans, 60 horses, 14 swords and 14 braces of pistols which they brought to a blockhouse (see Photo SC-5) on the Pacolet River.

Toward dusk, Captain Otterson and his companion pushed their horses nearer the Crown troops, and, when it was dark, dashed in among them with a shout. They fired their weapons, killed one man and ordered the Crown troops to surrender. The darkness prevented the enemy from knowing how many men surprised them and they surrendered at once. They were required to dismount, come forward and surrender their arms, which they did. When they were secured, their commanding officer was greatly mortified to find that he had surrendered 14 Legion dragoons, to two men.

One of the dragoons escaped and erroneously reported to Lieutenant Colonel Banastre Tarleton (1744–1833) that Lieutenant Colonel William Washington (1752–1810) was coming with his dragoons. Captain Otterson and his men rode for 100 miles before they caught up with Brigadier General Daniel Morgan (1736–1802) and handed over their prisoners. [105]

★ Captain Samuel Otterson (1754–1837) and four men later patrolled around Brigadier General Daniel Morgan's (1736–1802) army to observe enemy movements. On one occasion, they captured 30 British soldiers and their officers when they stopped at a spring to drink. On another occasion, Otterson discovered a group of Loyalists near the Catawba River and pursued them. He was thrown from his horse during the chase and broke his arm in the same place where he had been shot at the battle of Hanging Rock. His men killed all but three of the Loyalists. [106]

Chester, Chester County
Lee's Creek (Jan. 1781)

> This event was described as "south of Chesterville, about 10 miles." It was probably somewhere between the site of the Rocky Mount Engagement and that of the Fish Dam Engagement. This would place the site near the junction of Little Creek and East Fork. Chesterville is now Chester. Although no date is given for this incident, it occurred when General Charles Cornwallis was marching toward North Carolina.

General Charles Cornwallis's (1738–1805) army pursued Brigadier General Daniel Morgan (1736–1802) and the prisoners he captured at Cowpens on Wednesday, January 17, 1781. Bands of Whigs rode near the Crown troops as they marched toward North Carolina and took advantage of any opportunity to harass them. They captured two officers as they were making their breakfast after they crossed Lee Creek. Daniel Stinson wrote that the two officers "loitered in the rear, suspecting no danger until they were pounced upon by Jimmy Johnson and Captain John Mills (1757–1795), and taken prisoner." The prisoners were later exchanged for 11 Chester militiamen. [107]

Brierly's Ferry or Ford, Newberry County (Nov. 18, 1780)

> Brierly's Ferry or Ford was a critical point along the line of communications between Ninety Six and Camden. Accounts of operations in the area in 1780–81 mention it frequently. The ferry crossed the Broad River west of the Monticello Reservoir 5 miles northeast of Pomaria. To get to the site from exit 74 off Interstate 26, go northeast on route SC 34 for about 10.6 miles, then turn right (south) onto Broad River Road (S-36-28) and go about 5.25 miles. Brierly's Ferry was on the left at the river about 0.65 miles from the road.

Lieutenant Colonel Banastre Tarleton (1744–1833) pursued Brigadier General Thomas Sumter (1734–1832) toward Blackstock's plantation on the south side of the Tyger River in November 1780. On November 18, 150 mounted militiamen fired on Tarleton and his men until Major Archibald McArthur arrived from Cheraw with the 71st Highlanders and 80 survivors of Major James Wemyss's (1748–1833) engagement at Fish Dam Ford. McArthur and his Highlanders then joined Tarleton in pursuit of Brigadier General Daniel Morgan (1736–1802) to Cowpens.[108]

Sandy River (Dec. 5, 1780; ca. April 22, 1781; date unknown)

> The Sandy River community was an affluent Loyalist community in the western part of Chester County, about 7 miles due southwest of Chester. To get there, take route SC 72 (SC 121|West End Road) southwest from Chester for about 6.5 miles. Turn west (right) on Carter Road and go to the end. Turn right on Sandy River Road (SC 42). The settlement was just before the bridge over the Sandy River.
>
> The December 5, 1780 engagement most likely occurred about 5 miles northeast of the settlement, near where route SC 9 (Pinckney Road) crosses the Sandy River about 2.5 miles west of Chester.

Soon after the Battle of Blackstock's (November 20, 1780), Colonel Thomas Brandon (1741–1802) wanted to disrupt communications between General Charles Cornwallis (1738–1805) in Winnsboro and the Loyalists west of the Broad River. Captain Joseph McJunkin (1755–1846) wrote:

> In early December [Wednesday, December 5, 1780] Brandon, McJunkin [Daniel McJunkin (1756–1825), the diarist's brother], and such as they could collect, took post at Love's Ford on Broad River to prevent intercourse between Cornwallis and the Loyalists west of the Broad River. . . . While there a Scout, under the command of Captain [John] McCool [d. 1815], was ordered to cross the Broad River and attack the Tories on Sandy River. McCool was defeated and Daniel McJunkin was taken captive and sent to Winnsboro.

Colonel Brandon "proceeded after them and fell in with a small party—we killed three and wounded three, most notorious villains." The remaining Loyalists escaped with their prisoners. "Colonel Brandon sent a flag to Cornwallis and proposed to exchange Colonel Fanning [probably Edward Fanning] for Daniel McJunkin. Cornwallis declined and sent Daniel to jail in Camden. He remained there till April 1781, when he and some others made their escape, but nearly perished for the want of food before they reached their friends."

Captain Robert Wilson (1758–1850) wrote that the skirmish at Sandy River occurred before the battle at Blackstock's. He also wrote that Captain Manning Gose commanded the Loyalists.[109]

★ Brigadier General Thomas Sumter (1734–1832) retaliated for Brevet-Major John Coffin's (1756–1838) raid at the Waxhaws about Monday, April 9, 1781 by sending some men about two weeks later (ca. April 22 or 23) to burn and kill in the Loyalist settlements of Sandy River (Chester County) and Mobley (Fairfield County) (see **Gibson's Meeting House** or **Mobley's Meeting House** p. 6). General Sumter wrote to Major General Nathanael Greene (1742–1786) on April 26: "As I found some delay unavoidable, marched into Mobley's and Sandy River settlements, with a view to harass the enemy, which has been effectually done, and will, I hope, in a great measure relieve our friends in that part of the country from the unnatural cruelties that were daily exercised over them. Some small skirmishes have happened, I have lost no men. Several of the enemy have fallen; and many others taken prisoners. Upon the whole, they have been pretty well scourged." [110]

★ Thomas Young (1764–1848) rode with Colonels Thomas Brandon (1741–1802), Levi Casey (ca.1752–1807), Isaac Hughes (1747–1782), and Major Jolly on a scouting mission when they learned of a band of Loyalists hiding in a dense thicket on the Sandy River. The scouting party rode to Sandy River early in the morning and attacked the Loyalist hideout where a "great deal of plunder" was supposedly hidden. Young wrote:

> In the fight I took a little fellow, by the name of Tom Moore, prisoner. I ran him for some distance, shot at him, and broke his arm.—when I took him back Tom Salter wanted to kill him, because Moore had once had him prisoner, and would in all probability have killed him, if he had not escaped. I cocked my gun and told them no! He was my man, and I would shoot the first one who harmed him. During this skirmish I witnessed rather an amusing scene between Colonel Hughes and a tory. Hughes had dismounted to get a chance to shoot at some fellow through the bushes, when a tory sprang upon his horse and dashed away—Hughes discovered it in time, fired, and put a ball through the hind tree of the saddle and the fellow's thigh. The tory fell and Hughes got his horse. In this excursion we got a great deal of plunder, which had been concealed by the tories.[111]

Clarendon County, near Rimini
Halfway Swamp (Dec. 12, 1780)
Singleton's Mill, Sumter County (Dec. 13, 1780)

Halfway Swamp extends on both sides of the Santee River. It gets its name because the swamp on the right (west) bank was supposedly halfway between Moncks Corner and The Congarees. It still bears the name. The swamp on the left (east) bank was supposedly halfway between Moncks Corner and Camden. The Halfway Swamp astride the Old Santee Road to Camden is now known as Spring Grove Creek and is where Brigadier General Francis Marion (1732–1795) had the skirmish in December 1780.

A state historical marker for the "Encounter at Halfway Swamp" is on route S-14-76 (Old River Road) at Rimini, about 1 mile south of the intersection with route S-14-26 (Gov. Richardson Road). General Richardson's grave can be seen in the big field on the west side of Old River Road.

Singleton's Mill was an important point along the line of communications for the Crown forces. Brigadier General Marion seized it in late October 1780, as the Crown forces proceeded to winter quarters. General Charles Cornwallis (1738–1805) was furious and sent Lieutenant Colonel Banastre Tarleton (1744–1833) and his Legion to eradicate Marion's band. However, Tarleton never found Marion, allegedly saying to his men that "as for this damned old fox, the devil himself could not catch him." This statement gave Marion his nickname, the Swamp Fox.

The site of Singleton's Mill is at the western end of Poinsett State Park (Manchester State Forest), about 10 miles downstream from where the Congaree and Wateree rivers join to form the Santee. To get there, take route SC 261 (North Kings Highway) south for about 10 miles, then turn right onto Poinsett Park Road and go about 1.25 miles. Turn left at the intersection and go about 1.5 miles to the

> Park Headquarters Building on the left. The mill and mill race are to the right of the building. Melrose House, the Singleton residence, was on top of the hill to the right of the road.

Brigadier General Francis Marion (1732–1795) learned that Major Robert McLeroth (pronounced Mackeroth) and a large force of British Regulars of the 64th Regiment and 200 recruits of the Royal Fusiliers were moving from Charleston toward Winnsboro, General Charles Cornwallis's (1738–1805) headquarters. General Marion gathered his men and set out to stop them.

They encountered McLeroth's rear guard near Halfway Swamp on Tuesday, December 12, 1780. Marion's men killed a few pickets in what they thought would be a general engagement. However McLeroth fled another mile and a half north to an open field enclosed by a rail fence and prepared his defense. He prepared his troops for battle, but Marion's troops outnumbered him with about 700 mounted men. Captain John Coffin (1756–1838) and 140 Loyalist dragoons were close enough to support McLeroth; but, instead of coming to rescue McLeroth, Coffin turned around and posted his troops behind Swift Creek.

When Marion arrived, McLeroth sent a messenger under a flag of truce in an attempt to buy some time. He accused Marion of violating the rules of warfare by shooting his pickets. He proposed to Marion that the two forces fight out in the open. Marion made a counterproposal that each army select 20 of its best men to do combat. McLeroth tentatively agreed, and the two groups marched out to meet each other. When they got within 100 yards of one another, the Redcoats turned around and marched back to their lines.

Marion waited until dawn to engage the enemy, but he learned, just after midnight, that McLeroth and his troops had abandoned their baggage and slipped away under the cover of darkness. McLeroth's troops made huge campfires, shouted and sang during the night as a diversion while most of the troops withdrew to Singleton's Mill, 10 miles to the north.

Marion sent a detachment of 100 men under Major John James, Sr. (1732–1791) ahead to beat them there. Major James and his men were waiting for the Crown forces on the high ground near Singleton's Mill. They fired a single volley and abandoned their position for no apparent reason. They learned the Singleton family was ill with smallpox, so they refused to occupy the buildings. McLeroth, reinforced by Coffin, continued on his way unmolested. He reached Winnsboro on December 16.

Both sides lost several wounded in the skirmishing between Halfway Swamp and Singleton's Mill. Marion suffered six wounded in the skirmish while his men killed six and wounded one. McLeroth had all the wounded on both sides gathered (nearly half were Marion's men) and left them at a tavern under a flag of truce as he retreated. He left his own surgeon to care for them and gave money to the tavern keeper to pay for their subsistence—a very unusual act.

When Marion and his men stopped at the tavern, the old woman who ran it supposedly said, "If I ain't down right sorry to see you, then I'll be hanged. You are chasing the British to kill them. Ain't it so now, Colonel? . . . But pray now, my dear Colonel Marion, let me beg of you, don't you do any harm to that dear good man, that Major Mucklewort, who went from here a little while ago. For, oh, he's the sweetest-spoken, mildest-looking, noblest-spirited Englishman I ever saw in all my born days."

Marion left the tavern and rode a long time in silence then turned around and returned to Singleton's Mill. Many of his troops said that the Major's generosity had so won their hearts that they had none left to fight him. McLeroth was removed from command of British forces in South Carolina; and Major John Campbell (d. 1806) assumed command of the 64th Regiment.[112]

Wallace, Marlboro County
Cheraw, Great Pee Dee River, Chesterfield County (Dec. 20, 1780–Jan. 28, 1781)

> Cheraw was of considerable strategic importance during the American War for Independence. Located on a navigable stream about 100 miles north of the major port of Georgetown, it controlled the northeastern approaches to the colony from North Carolina. Welsh from Pennsylvania settled here around 1752. They completed building St. David's Episcopal Church in 1773 which is the last church built in South Carolina under the authority of King George III (1738–1820) and the major architectural attraction in modern Cheraw.
>
> Both armies occupied the town at various times during the war, and the church was used to house the troops. The Crown forces used it as a hospital during a smallpox epidemic, and 50 patients are buried in a common, unmarked grave in the churchyard. British officers were buried in separate brick-covered graves and there are graves for many veterans of both armies. The church is located on the southeast side of Church Street between Second Street and Front Street in Cheraw.
>
> A state historical marker on the eastern side of route U.S. 1, just past the Wallace Baptist Church, notes the site where Major General Nathanael Greene (1742–1786) and his army camped from December 20, 1780, to January 28, 1781.

Major James Wemyss (1748–1833) led a punitive expedition of Crown forces up the Pee Dee River as far as Cheraw soon after the surrender of Charleston on May 12, 1780. After establishing a base at Camden, they created an outpost at Cheraw in June. Major Archibald McArthur commanded the 1st Battalion, 71st Highlanders which garrisoned the place until they were moved to Brierly's Ferry five months later.

After the defeat of Major General Horatio Gates (1728–1806) at Camden, Major General Nathanael Greene (1742–1786) took over as commander of the southern army. He split his forces into two widely separated wings. Brigadier General Daniel Morgan (1736–1802) took one wing between the Broad and the Pacolet rivers, while Greene took the larger force to the Cheraw region. The decision to divide an inferior force in the face of a superior enemy violated the classic rules of warfare, as it invited the enemy to destroy each part separately. However, by separating his army into two parts, Greene made it easier for both to subsist on the country. Moreover, if General Charles Cornwallis (1738–1805) should come back into South Carolina, he would find a fighting force on each of his flanks.

Colonel Engineer Thaddeus Kosciusko (1746–1817) selected the camp site 2 miles northeast of the settlement (present-day Wallace). Greene and his army of 1,100 troops (650 Continentals, 303 Virginia and 157 Maryland militiamen) camped here during the period December 20, 1780, to January 28, 1781, while General Cornwallis, in Winnsboro, tried to figure out Greene's strategy. Cornwallis debated whether he should engage Greene in battle in South Carolina or go around Cheraw. Lieutenant Colonel Henry "Light-Horse Harry" Lee (1756–1818) and his Legion patrolled the area to guard against the threat of Cornwallis skirting Cheraw. When the threat did not materialize Lee's Legion passed through Cheraw to join Brigadier General Francis Marion (1732–1795) along the Pee Dee.

Ferry near Owen's Plantation (Dec. 22, 1780; Feb. 2, 1781)
Brierly's Ferry

> There were six plantations belonging to members of the Owen family (Job; Jonathan; Samuel; Thomas; Thomas, Sr. and Thomas, Jr.) clustered together in the center of the area now covered by the Monticello Reservoir. There is also an Owens Cemetery in Fairfield County south of the reservoir near the intersection of Penner Road and Fire Tower Cir. (S-20-275).

Colonel Archibald McArthur ordered his Loyalist militiamen to keep a guard at Brierly's Ferry near Colonel Owen's plantation while his own troops guarded the mill. Half a dozen Whigs under a man named Green (a common surname in South Carolina) came within 3 miles of the ferry on Friday, December 22, 1780. They fired at one man who was severely wounded, took his gun and rode off.

Sherwood Fort claimed he was involved in an engagement at Colonel Owen's plantation on Friday, February 2, 1781.[113]

Lisles's Ford (Dec. 24, 1780)

> Lisles's (Lyles) Ford was on the Tyger River.

Some 30 or 40 shots were fired near Lisles's Ford on Friday, December 24, 1780. Colonel Archibald McArthur immediately sent two trusty men to know the cause. They returned the following morning with a letter from Captain Hill informing General Charles Cornwallis (1738–1805) that a party of Captain Gillam's (probably William Gillam, royal militia) "had got plenty of rum, which made them feel bold" and began to celebrate Christmas early by firing their muskets.[114]

Sharon, York County
James Kirkpatrick killed (Jan. 1, 1781)

> James Kirkpatrick's (d. 1781) home was about 0.4 miles down Canupp Road from its intersection with Lockhart Road (SC 49) about 3.75 miles northeast of its junction with Pinckney Road (SC 49) east of Lockhart. The murder site was on the McKelvey branch of Turkey Creek about 0.35 miles from the road. A marker at the Bullock Creek Presbyterian Church is about 1.75 miles farther north on Lockhart Road. The church and marker are on the right.

James Kirkpatrick (1730–1781) served in Colonel Thomas Brandon's (1741–1802) regiment of the South Carolina militia. According to family tradition, James slipped through the Loyalist lines to visit with his family on Monday, January 1, 1781. He had just entered his home and was sitting on his wife's lap, surrounded by his children, when the Loyalists burst in and shot him.[115]

Amis's Mill (Jan. 17, 1781)
Hulin's Mill (Hulon's also known as Bass's mill) (Catfish Swamp), Dillon County (April 26–28, 1781)
The "Bull Pen," Marlboro County (April 28, 1781)
Colonel Kolb killed, Marlboro County (April 28, 1781)
Mrs. Wilds robbed, Marlboro County (April 28, 1781)
Two Redcoats killed, Marlboro County (April 28, 1781)
Mulatto slave killed, Marlboro County (April 28, 1781)
Mr. Cotton killed, Marlboro County (April 28, 1781)
Courtney killed (after Sept. 3, 1783)

> Amis's Mill was on Drowning Creek (Lumber River) near the North Carolina/South Carolina state line about 2.5 miles southwest of Fair Bluff, North Carolina.
>   The Hulin's (Hulon's) Mill incident is also referred to as Catfish Swamp. It is south-southwest of Latta where route U.S. 301 crosses Catfish Creek.
>   The other incidents all occurred along route U.S. 15 & 401 north of its junction with route U.S. 52 in Society Hill. Colonel Abel Kolb's grave is on Kolb's Tomb Road about 0.64 miles west of route U.S. 15 & 401.
>   To get to the site of Courtney's death, continue south on route U.S. 301 from Hulin's Mill on Catfish Creek. Go about 1.4 miles to route SC 38 W. Turn right (west) onto route SC 8 W and proceed about 1.45 miles. The site is on the left behind the houses there.

Colonel Hector MacNeil (1756–1830) and 150 Loyalists harassed the Whigs in the region of Amis's Mill on Drowning Creek. Major General Nathanael Greene (1742–1786) dispatched Major Archibald Anderson of the Maryland Line with a detachment of 200 light troops from his camp on the Pee Dee River on Wednesday, January 17, 1781. Brigadier General Francis Marion (1732–1795), at Snow Island, needed to keep an eye on enemy movements in his area and could not attack MacNeil himself. He ordered Colonel Abel Kolb (1750–1781) to attack MacNeil, but Kolb never obeyed. Colonel James Kenan (1740–1810), of Duplin County, and a force of North Carolina militiamen arrived before Major Anderson and dispersed MacNeil's force.

★ Colonel Abel Kolb (1750–1781) lived and operated a ferry on the Pee Dee River in Marlboro County and was the commander of the local militia. He learned that some of Major Micajah Ganey's Loyalist militiamen had mustered on Drowning Creek to resume fighting against Brigadier General Francis Marion's (1732–1795) forces. He surprised them on Thursday, April 26, 1781, sending them fleeing into the countryside. The next day, he surprised two of Ganey's followers, John Deer (d. 1781) and Osburn Lean, at Hulin's Mill. He killed Deer as he ran to Catfish Swamp and broke Lean's arm. Lean escaped into the swamp and hid in a hollow log while Kolb's men hunted for him. Kolb's men even sat on the log that concealed Lean at one point, frightening him so much that he thought they would hear his heart beating.

Kolb's men found another Loyalist and hanged him before returning home. The killings at Catfish Swamp infuriated Captain Joseph Jones, of Ganey's militia, who called for volunteers to pursue Kolb. He mustered 50 Loyalists who rode fast for 34 miles to surprise Colonel Kolb. They attacked him and his two houseguests at Kolb's home. Kolb and his guests held off the attackers for some time and killed some of them. Captain Jones ordered the house to be burned. Kolb decided to surrender to save his wife and children; but, as he came out the door with his wife, Sarah, one of the Loyalists, Mike Goings, shot him from behind. The two houseguests tried to run away and were shot. The Loyalists then plundered the Kolb house, took everything of value, and then set it on fire.

Sarah Kolb (d. 1785) kept the bullet-riddled dress she wore that day for many years. Her husband's death drove more outraged volunteers to join General Marion.[116]

★ The Whigs constructed a blockhouse (see Photo SC-5) called the "Bull Pen" to keep their prisoners. It was a few hundred yards away, between the Kolb house and the ferry and confined a number of prisoners, including two British officers and several soldiers, on the night of the attack on Kolb's house (Thursday, April 26, 1781). The Loyalists surprised the small guard and released the prisoners at the same time the others attacked the Kolb house.[117]

★ Two of the soldiers released from the "Bull Pen" had heard old Mrs. Wilds kept a treasure on her person or in her house. When they were released, they went down the river to her house, opposite Long Bluff (modern Society Hill), in search of the treasure. They found her alone, made a quick search of the house, treated her rudely and took her gold.[118]

★ A short, old, feeble shoemaker called Willis lived in the marshes south of the Kolb house. He tried to remain neutral; but, when he heard the commotion at the Kolb house, he took his long-barreled fowling-piece which he affectionately called "Old Sweet Lips" and mounted his old shaggy pony and set out for the Kolb house. He soon met a young man by the name of Ayer who was on his way to Kolb's to inform him of a new birth in his family. Willis asked him what all that shooting was about and learned of the Kolb incident. He encountered the two British soldiers who were returning from plundering Mrs. Wilds and shot them both. He took their shoe-buckles and valuables.

Willis went to visit Mrs. Wilds a few days later. He learned she had been robbed by two of the soldiers who escaped from the "Bull Pen" and that they had taken 101 guineas. Willis took out a package of coins which she recognized as hers so he gave them to her. She counted the money and, finding that not a guinea was missing, offered Willis a reward for his honesty. He refused, saying that it was hers and he was sufficiently rewarded by being able to return it to her.[119]

★ After leaving Mr. Willis, young Mr. Ayer went off the main road into a narrow cow path which crossed a large marsh. The narrow path was the only way to cross the marsh safely. The Loyalists coming from Kolb's house saw Ayer head into the swamp and tried to go directly across the marsh, hoping to get ahead of Ayer. When Ayer reached the opposite ridge, he looked back and saw all the Loyalists floundering in the mud in confusion. Ayer proceeded through the woods for several miles until he came to the road leading from Pledger's Mill to the Welch Neck road. The roads joined near Mr. Cogdell's house which was then occupied by a man named Cotton. The Loyalists surprised and killed Cotton, thinking he was trying to alert Captain Malachi Murphy, Jr.'s militiamen that they were coming.[120]

★ Captain Joseph Jones's Loyalists headed back to Catfish Creek and Tart's Mill after killing and robbing Colonel Abel Kolb (1750–1781). They intended to surprise Captain Malachi Murphy, Jr.'s militiamen who were at Brown's Mill on Muddy Creek (now known as Rogers Creek), about a mile above the crossing at the old Rogers mill. However, only a few men remained at the mill. Most of them had departed a few days before.

Captain Jones's Loyalists killed a mulatto man, the slave of Captain Daniel Sparks (1740–1810), along the way. When they arrived at Brown's Mill, they surprised and killed Captain Joseph Dabbs (1734–1781) and the few men who remained there. Ned Threwitts was the only man to escape with a bullet in his shoulder.[121]

★ A man named Courtney (d. 1781) acted as commissary for the Loyalist militias in Dillon County and was particularly obnoxious to the Whigs who tried unsuccessfully to capture him several times. Courtney frequently visited another Loyalist by the name of Shoemake. One day in 1783 (after September 3), a party of Whigs saw Courtney at Shoemake's house as they passed by. They positioned themselves some distance away from Shoemake's house, which was in an open field, to make sure that Courtney did not escape. However, Courtney saw them and tried to escape on his swift horse. He first approached Jordan Gibson who fired but missed. Enos Tart took better aim, and broke Courtney's leg and knocked him off his horse. As the Whigs gathered around Courtney, Levi Odom called on the others to shoot the wounded man, but they refused. So Odom did so, killing him.

The Whigs left Shoemake's and went to the Loyalist neighborhood where they captured several and planned to execute them immediately. However, many Loyalists in the area responded to the alarm and came to rescue the prisoners. The incident alerted the Loyalists to what they could expect if they continued to oppose the Whig government. They agreed to submit to the state government and keep the peace. This ended any problems with the Loyalists in this area.[122]

Johnsonville, Florence County
Snow Island
De Peyster's (or De Peister's) capture (Jan. 19, 1781; March 29, 1781)
Hasty Point (John Postell's plantation), Georgetown County

Snow (or Snow's) Island (see Photo SC-12, SC-13), named for former owners James and William Snow, is situated at the conflux of the Pee Dee River and Lynches Creek east of Johnsonville. It is of a triangular form with the Pee Dee on the northeast and Lynches Creek on the north. Clark's Creek, a branch of Lynches Creek, was the boundary on the west and south. Tradition says that Brigadier General Francis Marion (1732–1795) used this location for his base camp from August 1780, after the battle at Halfway Swamp, to March 1781 as it gave him command of the rivers and made his camp inaccessible except by water.

Recent archaeological research is questioning whether General Marion actually had his headquarters on Snow Island. Researchers have found very few Revolutionary War artifacts there and no evidence of a camp. They have found a large site on Goddard's plantation across the river from Snow Island that may be the location of the camp. The site has yielded many artifacts and burned remains of an 18th century camp seem to agree with the description of the raid on Marion's camp.

To get there, take route SC 41|51 (Kingsburg Highway) north to route U.S. 41|378 (East Myrtle Beach Highway). Travel east on route U.S. 41|378 for 5.5 miles to the

Northeastern South Carolina 83

SC-12. Snow Island viewed from across the river

SC-13. Typical swamp area on and around Snow Island

> first dirt road (Dunham Bluff Road) on the right, just past route SC 908. Proceed down Dunham Bluff Road for 1.7 miles. Snow Island is across the river. The island is still accessible only by boat.
>
> You can also view the island from the south at Clark's Creek. Take route SC 41|51 to Hemingway and route SC 261 (Broad Street) east for 0.2 miles. Turn north (left) on route S-45-34 (Muddy Creek Road). After 5.7 miles, turn left onto route S-45-488 (Snows Lake Road) and proceed for 1.7 miles where the road ends.
>
> Captain James De Peyster was most likely captured at Hasty Point plantation which was on the Great Pee Dee River, at the end of Hasty Point Drive. To get there, take route U.S. 701 (North Fraser Street) north from Georgetown for about 13.75 miles. Turn right (east) onto Plantersville Road and follow it for about 2 miles to Hasty Point Drive.

After the capture of Georgetown, Brigadier General Francis Marion (1732–1795) had his men gather provisions and collect boats along all the rivers that flow into Georgetown Bay. These were all brought to Marion's camp at Snow Island. This island is of a triangular form with the Pee Dee River on the northeast and Lynches Creek on the north. Clark's Creek, a branch of Lynches Creek, was the boundary on the west and south. This location gave Marion command of the rivers and made his camp inaccessible except by water.

Captain John Postell (1717–1782) and 28 men were sent down the Black River to the mouth of the Pee Dee to take all the boats and canoes, to impress all the African Americans and horses, and to take all arms and ammunition for the use of the service. He was also ordered to prevent anyone from carrying grain, stock or any sort of provision to Georgetown or anywhere that the enemy might get them. He was also instructed to bring to Marion all persons who would not join him.

Captain James De Peyster (d. 1793) and 29 grenadiers (see Photo SC-14) of the British Army occupied the home of Captain Postell's father on Thursday, January 18, 1781. Around dawn the following morning, Captain Postell, who knew the ground well, got around the guards and entered the kitchen which was detached from the main house. He demanded De Peyster's

SC-14. Members of the Brigade of the American Revolution portraying British grenadiers. This photo depicts Scottish Highlanders wearing red regimental coats with black facings, bearskin helmets, and a blue and green tartan kilt. Grenadiers were members of an elite unit selected on the basis of exceptional height and ability.

surrender but was refused. Postell immediately set fire to his father's kitchen and demanded De Peyster's surrender a second time, saying that he would burn the house if De Peyster did not surrender. The Regulars laid down their arms and surrendered immediately.[123]

★ After defeating Brigadier General Thomas Sumter (1734–1832) at Lynches Creek, Lord Francis Rawdon (1754–1826) turned his attention to crushing Brigadier General Francis Marion (1732–1795). He sent his own regiment under Colonel John Watson Tadwell Watson (1748–1826) along with Major John Harrison's (ca. 1751–) regiment of Loyalists toward Marion's camp on Snow Island which measures roughly 4.5 by 1.5 miles.

The force of less than 500 men (probably about 300) marched from Nelson's Ferry (Fort Watson) down the Santee to attack the island from the northeast. Lieutenant Colonel Welbore Ellis Doyle (later General Sir John Doyle) (1732–1802) left Camden a short while later with the Volunteers of Ireland, a band of New York Loyalists. They crossed at McCallum's Ferry to the east of Lynches Creek and traveled down Jeffers's Creek to the Pee Dee where they were supposed to attack from the southeast and join Watson.

However, Marion learned of these plans and took most of his men to skirmish with Watson for the next few weeks. He left a small detachment at the camp under Colonel Hugh Ervin (1730–1785). Doyle attacked the camp at Snow Island about Monday, March 19, 1781. He killed seven and wounded 15 of Marion's men and burned all the structures on the island. To prevent the enemy from capturing his arms and ammunition, Ervin threw them into the river.

Colonel Watson wrote to Captain John Saunders (1754–1834), the commander at Georgetown, on March 20, 1781 informing him that he would be in Georgetown or very near it that day.

Marion and Colonel Hugh Horry (1744–1795) moved their troops to Indiantown. Horry's and Captain William Robert McCottry's (1748–1805) riflemen killed or wounded nine Loyalists and captured or wounded 16. Doyle recrossed Clark's Creek and camped on the north side of Witherspoon's Ferry to avoid being caught in a trap. Marion learned of this and pursued Doyle after McCottry's riflemen had a fire fight with Doyle's rear guard at Witherspoon's Ferry.[124]

See **Witherspoon's Ferry** p. 104.

The loss of the camp was a blow to Marion, but it did not help the Crown forces as Major General Nathanael Greene (1742–1786) would soon arrive in South Carolina to begin large-scale operations.

According to legend, a British officer came to Marion's headquarters under a flag of truce to discuss an exchange of prisoners. Marion entertained him at a dinner that consisted entirely of sweet potatoes baked in a campfire. The officer was astounded that men were willing to fight for a cause that provided such meager rations. When he returned to Charleston, the officer supposedly resigned his commission, saying that the British could never defeat an army that would endure such hardships. Whether true or not, the story is part of Marion's mystique and illustrates his influence and the respect he had from his men and fellow countrymen. John Blake White illustrated the story in a painting which later became a Currier and Ives engraving.[125]

Cayce, Lexington County
The Congarees
Muddy Spring, Lexington County (Feb. 17, 1781)
Fort Granby, Lexington County (Feb. 19–20, 1781; May 15, 1781)
Friday's or Fridig's Ferry, Lexington County (Feb. 19, 1781; May 1, 1781; May 15, 1781; July 3, 1781; before April 17, 1782; May 1, 1782)
Hampton's Store
Vaudant's Old Field (Weaver's Old Field), Lexington County
(June 1, 1781)
Ancrum's Plantation, Richland County
Eggleston's capture, Lexington County (July 3, 1781)
Dreher Plantation, Lexington County (July 1781)

> Granby, once known as The Congarees, was built in 1718 as a trading post for trade with the Native Americans. It had grown into an important river depot by 1754. The British fortified the Cayce House, a strong two-story frame house built in 1765. It was a square redoubt enclosing a store. It had a parapet with bastions (see Photo SC-15) and guns, a ditch, and the usual abatis which protected the perimeter from 1780 until May 15, 1781 when Lieutenant Colonel Henry "Light-Horse Harry" Lee's (1756–1818) Legion captured it. It was garrisoned by 352 men, including 60 German mercenaries under the command of Major Andrew Maxwell, a Maryland Loyalist.
>
> Fort Granby protected a landing at Friday's or Fridig's Ferry on the Congaree River south of Columbia in what is now Cayce, named for John Cayce. Wade Hampton (1752–1832) and his brother, Richard (1752–1792) owned Friday's Ferry. President George Washington (1732–1799) crossed the river here on May 22, 1791 on his way to Columbia. A state historical marker for the eastern landing of Friday's Ferry was located on Bluff Road (SC 48) just southeast of its intersection with Rosewood Drive in Columbia but it was missing in the summer of 2004. The ferry itself was located 1 mile to the west on the river. Hampton's Store was situated about 5 miles southeast of Fort Granby across the Congaree River.
>
> The fort was located about 450 yards south-southeast of the junction of Frink Street and State Street (SC 2). The site is now a quarry.
>
> The Cayce Museum, located at 1800 12th Street 1.3 miles south of route U.S. 1, includes a reconstruction of the Cayce House and a strong two-story trading post constructed in 1765 by James and Joseph Kershaw (1728–1791). The ferry was about 1.65 miles east of the museum.
>
> Many of Brigadier General Thomas Sumter's (1734–1832) men called the period of heavy marching and constant fighting, in February 1781, "Sumter's Rounds."
>
> The Muddy Spring engagement occurred a mile southwest of the modern community of Barr Crossing, which is about 4.5 miles southwest of Lexington, on route S-32-77 (Two Notch Road). Paul Quattlebaum wrote that "The spring took its name from the turbid appearance of the water as it exceeds from the foot of the hill, showing traces of iron rust, which the superstitious & ignorant of that day & time regarded as the effects of the blood spilled in the battle." He doesn't give a date, but it probably occurred on Saturday, February 17, 1781.

SC-15. Bastions. Northeast stone bastion of Fort Ticonderoga (above) and earthen bastion with mortar at Yorktown, Virginia.

> Vaudant's Old Field is also known as Weaver's Old Field. The only references to this skirmish are in General Sumter's dispatches and in Lyman C. Draper's *Sumter Papers*. Sumter says this event occurred west of the Congaree and Santee Rivers. The site was just south of the intersection of Old Field Road (S-32-31) and Cedar Grove Road (S-32-54) in Leesville. The graves are located about 0.25 miles further north on Cedar Grove Road on the right side between the trees at the north side of the field about 60 feet from the road.
>
> The site of Eggleston's capture is on route S-32-66 near Congaree Creek, about 0.6 miles northeast of exit 2 off route I-77 (Southeastern Beltway) in West Columbia. The date is given both as July 3rd and July 8th.
>
> Captain Godfrey Dreher's plantation was on Twelve Mile Creek where Carley Mill Road crosses it about 1.5 miles north-northwest of exit 61 off Interstate 20 in Lexington.
>
> Ancrum's plantation was across the Congaree River from Fort Granby.

Loyalist Major Andrew Maxwell was sent to command the garrison and 100 militiamen at Fort Granby in January 1781. Colonel Wade Hampton (1752–1832), who owned a store nearby, supplied the garrison for a time. Aware of the fort's diminishing supplies, he informed Brigadier General Thomas Sumter (1734–1832) of Maxwell's vulnerability. General Sumter decided to attack the heavily fortified place on February 19, 1781. Lacking the artillery to breach the defenses, Sumter had his men construct "Quaker cannons" out of tree trunks and tobacco hogsheads and threatened to reduce the fort to splinters. Whether the defenders recognized the fake artillery or were warned by spies, they did not fall for Sumter's Quaker cannon trick and refused to surrender. General Sumter made an unsuccessful attempt to assault the fort and was repulsed.

Sumter then surrounded Granby and laid siege to it. He surrounded the fort and began to harass the defenders with slow continuous rifle fire. Colonel Thomas Taylor's (1743–1833) riflemen rolled tobacco hogsheads ahead of them, so that they could build a screen of logs in front of the fort. They built a "rail pen," a sort of Maham Tower (see Photo SC-16) "of logs some 20 feet square at the base, slightly tapering to the summit in the top of the tower the riflemen were placed who, overlooking the works of the fort pierced everyone that was not sheltered."

During the siege, which lasted between Monday and Wednesday, February 19–20, 1781, one of the defenders "repeatedly slapped his buttock to the Whigs and Taylor's men would shoot and so far would miss. Finally the fellow was so insulting that Colonel Taylor said to one of his men, a good shot, 'Can't you punish that fellow for his impudence?' He drew up his gun, took a good aim, fired, and the fellow tumbled over."

When General Sumter learned that Lord Francis Rawdon (1754–1826) sent Lieutenant Colonel Welbore Ellis Doyle (1732–1802) and his Volunteers of Ireland provincial regiment of 600 infantrymen, 100 dragoons and two pieces of artillery from Camden to reinforce the fort, General Sumter took his main force and a cannon and headed to the British post at Orangeburg. He left Colonel Thomas Taylor (1743–1833 and a detachment of South Carolina militiamen to continue the siege.

Doyle seized the fords above Friday's Ferry, expecting Sumter to retreat up the Broad River. He crossed the river 8 miles above Fort Granby and began to march down the opposite side to intercept any escape by Sumter. Sumter saw Doyle's force on the other side of the Congaree and destroyed the supplies and munitions in the Crown camp outside the fort. He then withdrew under the cover of darkness. He marched 20 miles before learning that Major Robert McLeroth had left Camden with the 64th Regiment, the New York Volunteers and a field piece to intercept his force. In addition, a detachment of Regulars and militiamen were coming at him from Ninety Six. Sumter's men gathered boats along the Congaree and crossed over, taking the boats with them.[126]

★ The engagement at Muddy Spring occurred on the main road between the Crown post of Fort Granby and Augusta, Georgia. Captain Philemon Waters (1734–1796) of Brigadier General Thomas Sumter's (1734–1832) corps had a running battle with some Crown forces in which the Loyalists captured Private James Calk (1755–1825) who later made a daring escape.[127]

★ Captain Henry Hampton's (1755–1826) dragoons surprised a guard of the Prince of Wales American Volunteers at Friday's Ferry near Fort Granby on Tuesday, May 1, 1781. They killed 13 Loyalists. They then ambushed another party Captain Hampton spotted on the road heading toward Fort Granby, killing five more.[128]

★ Lieutenant Colonel Henry "Light-Horse Harry" Lee (1756–1818) left for Fort Granby on Sunday, May 13, 1781, the day after the capture of Fort Motte. Aware that

SC-16. Maham tower at the Ninety Six National Historic Site. The tower is made of logs tapering slightly to the summit. Riflemen in the top could fire into a stockade, redoubt or fort. The remains of the zigzag trenches are visible at the base of the tower in the foreground.

Major Maxwell lacked courage and military ability and was inclined to plunder, Lee was convinced he could take the fort. He placed a 6-pounder within 600 yards of the fort, at the location of the 1748 fort which no longer existed, during the night of Monday, May 14, 1781. When the fog cleared the following morning, Lee fired the cannon while his infantry advanced to fire on Maxwell's pickets.

When Lee demanded Maxwell's surrender, he agreed to do so on condition that he and his men be allowed to keep their plunder and be kept at Charleston as prisoners of war until exchanged. Lee expected Lord Francis Rawdon (1754–1826) to arrive to save the fort, so he agreed and added the condition that all horses fit for service be surrendered. Maxwell's mercenaries, who were mounted, objected; and negotiations were suspended. As Lee considered Maxwell's proposal, he received intelligence from his cavalry scouts that Rawdon had crossed the Santee River at Nelson's Ferry and was heading toward Fort Motte. Lee agreed to Maxwell's terms. Maxwell surrendered before noon on Tuesday, May 15 and departed with two wagons of plunder.

Neither side suffered any casualties. The Whigs captured an important post, 280 Loyalists, 60 British Regulars, a large supply of ammunition, the garrison's weapons, two cannons, a number of horses, and some salt and liquor.

Lee's men escorted Maxwell's convoy only a short distance before they encountered Lord Rawdon's rescue force. Rawdon, forced to abide by the terms of the surrender and satisfied that Fort Granby was not worth the effort to retake it, ordered his army to return to Charleston.

★ Brigadier General Thomas Sumter (1734–1832) sent Lieutenant Colonel Richard Hampton (1752–1792) and Colonel Charles Middleton (Mydelton) (1750–1780) south from Ancrum's plantation around Friday, June 1, 1781. Their mission was to block any enemy attempt to relieve the siege at Fort Ninety Six. Colonel Hampton defeated Colonel Colton and Ensign Henry B. Livingston (d. 1781) and about 50 South Carolina Royalists at Vaudant's Old field. They "killed several" including Livingston and "made some prisoners, took a number of negroes, and thirty odd fine horses."[129]

★ Major General Nathanael Greene's (1742–1786) army followed Lord Francis Rawdon (1754–1826) after he abandoned Fort Ninety Six soon after June 19, 1781. Lieutenant Colonel Henry "Light-Horse Harry" Lee (1756–1818) had been trying to determine their exact numbers. Captain Joseph Eggleston (1754–1811), of Lieutenant Colonel Lee's legion, initially had estimated that Rawdon only had 500 men, but on Monday, July 2nd, he increased his estimate to 1,270 men after he interrogated a deserter. General Greene sent a message to Brigadier General Thomas Sumter (1734–1832) telling him of his plans to attack Lord Rawdon immediately before Rawdon could join forces with Lieutenant Colonel Alexander Stewart (1740–1794) in Dorchester.

Emily Geiger (ca. 1760–) may have carried that message, as Lyman Copeland Draper (1815–1891) said that James Chappel (1740–1781) told him that, after the siege of Ninety Six, "Emily Geiger was sent by Greene to search out Sumter.... She was intercepted by Maxwell's Tories and was given over to some of their women to search ... she found the opportunity to chew up and swallow the written dispatches, consequently she was not shot as a spy. The next day she reached Sumter's camp" at Cedar Springs.

As Lord Rawdon would need to send out foraging parties, Lieutenant Colonel Lee sent Captain Eggleston to ambush the foragers south of Friday's Ferry. Captain Eggleston rendezvoused with Captain William Armstrong (1737–1783), who had been on a reconnaissance mission in the area, on Monday night, July 2, 1781. The South Carolina Royalists went out to forage the following morning, disobeying Lord Rawdon's orders to stay with the army. Captain Eggleston's scouts reported that the South Carolina Royalists were approaching, escorting a British wagon. When the Royalists saw Eggleston's scouts, they mistook them for Sumter's militiamen and pursued them into an ambush. Eggleston's men captured three officers and 45 men with their horses, arms and equipment and most of the wagons. Only one dragoon escaped.[130]

★ A detachment of "Regulars" had been sent from Fort Granby to Twelve Mile Creek, a short distance from the Saluda River, to arrest Captain Godfrey Dreher (1731–ca. 1793) at his home in Lexington County in July 1781. Dreher's mill supplied provisions (flour, corn, beef, pork, and other items) to the Whig forces. Captain Dreher and his family drove them off.[131]

★ *The Royal Gazette* of April 17, 1782 reported "As they [prisoners from Fort Granby], were marching down to the ferry a most bare-faced assassination was committed. An officer of the State troops, said to be Colonel Wade Hampton, who formerly kept a store there, had conceived a pique against an old gentleman named Dawkins, one of the prisoners, and hired one of his own soldiers to shoot him, as he passed in the ranks. The fellow, whose name was Burke, an Irishman, and who had resided many years in North Carolina, stood by the side of the road, watching for an opportunity to fire at Mr. Dawkins, but feeling it would be difficult to get him by himself, as they marched in files, determined to take the first opportunity to kill him at any rate; therefore, as soon as Mr. Dawkins came abreast of him, he fired and killed him and the man who marched by his side, the bullet passing through them both, and wounding a woman who stood at a little distance. The name of the other man who was killed was John McWhartry. Burke was immediately confined in the provost guard, where the other prisoners were, but was not pinioned. It was said that Gen. Greene threatened to hang him." *The Royal Gazette* of May 30, 1782 also reported that Major General Nathanael Greene (1742–1786) ordered Burke released without trial or punishment.

★ Around Wednesday, May 1, 1782, Colonel Wade Hampton (1752–1832) had returned from the Wateree and launched a surprise attack on two parties of Loyalists. They killed a total of 18 soldiers—13 of the enemy's guard—at Friday's Ferry and five of another party going to Fort Granby. They also captured a number of horses and several African Americans.[132]

Orangeburg, Orangeburg County
Orangeburg County
Manigault's Ferry, Calhoun County (Jan. 31–Feb. 1, 1781)
Near Manigault's Ferry, Belleville, Calhoun County (Feb. 22, 1781)
Belleville Plantation, Thomson's (Thompson) Plantation, Calhoun County (Feb. 22, 1781; Feb. 23, 1781)
Big Savannah, Calhoun County (Feb. 23, 1781)
Santee
Summerton, Clarendon County
Fort Watson (Wright's Bluff), Clarendon County (Feb. 27, 1781; Feb. 28, 1781; March 1, 1781; April 16–25, 1781)
Metts Crossroads, Calhoun County (March 1, 1782)
Moore's surprise (ca. Nov. 12, 1781)
Rowe's Plantation (Nov. 13, 1781)
Richard Hampton's surprise (ca. Nov. 14, 1781)
Saint Matthews, Calhoun County (May 1781)
Calk brothers, Calhoun County (May 1781)
Edisto River (May 11, 1781; Aug. 1, 1781; ca. Nov. 12, 1781)
Orangeburg, Orangeburg County (July 8–10, 1781; July 25, 1781)
Fork of Edisto (late July, 1781)
Near Orangeburgh, Orangeburg County (Aug. 1781; April 27, 1782)
McCord's Ferry, Richland County (Aug. 3, 1781)

Edisto River, Battle of the Tory Camps, Bull Swamp, Orangeburg County (July 1780; Oct. 1780; May 1781; or Dec. 20, 1781)
Four Mile Branch, Orangeburg County (Aug. 15, 1781)
Below Orangeburg, Orangeburg County (ca. May 8, 1782)
Amelia Township close to Manigault's Ferry, Sharp's skirmish, Calhoun County (June 1, 1782)

> Big Savannah was probably located on route SC 267 (McCords Ferry Road) about 1.7 miles south of route U.S. 601 (Colonel Thomson Highway) in Saint Matthews.
>
> Orangeburg was settled in the 1730s at the intersection of two ancient Native American paths. During the American War for Independence, it was very important because it was equidistant from Charleston, Ninety Six, and Augusta, Georgia. Governor John Rutledge (1730–1800) made his headquarters in the Donald Bruce (1742–1795) house (ca. 1735, originally on Bull Street but now on route U.S. 301, 11.1 miles west of the junction with route U.S. 176), in 1779 before the Crown forces entered South Carolina.
>
> The Battle of Orangeburg was fought at the old jail and courthouse that were located on top of the hill east of the intersection of Amelia and Windsor streets. The action involving Captain John Watts and Major John Doyle occurred on Amelia Street between Lowman and Treadwell streets. Lee's Raid was executed at the intersection of Russell Street and Dorchester Street. The Loyalist ambush that freed his prisoners occurred on Old Cameron Road Northeast between Shadowlawn and Kennedy Drives.
>
> Richard Hampton's Surprise probably occurred on what is now Amelia Street near the corner of Sunnyside Street in Orangeburg.
>
> The British moved into the city a year later and established a base. Three significant clashes occurred in the area over a 6-month period in 1781. Nothing remains of the Orangeburg fortifications today but Brigadier General Thomas Sumter (1734–1832) said they were very strong and could have been defended if the British garrison had chosen to do so.
>
> The Edisto River divides into the North Fork and the South Fork about 16 miles south of Orangeburg. Turkey Hill is located 4 miles north of Orangeburg.
>
> Bull Swamp was located on Bull Swamp Creek south of Forrestcreek Drive (S-38-189) and east of Slab Landing Road (S-38-73) which runs south from route U.S. 178 (North Road) about 2.3 miles east of North.
>
> Four Mile Branch (now Fourmile Creek) was between the North and South Edisto rivers, about 5.8 miles west of Orangeburg.
>
> The May 8, 1782 action took place along the road in the area that is 7 miles southeast of Orangeburg on route U.S. 178.
>
> There were two Manigault ferries. One was about 5 miles northwest of Nelson's Ferry on the west bank of the Santee River (Lake Marion) and 2.3 miles due north of the town of Vance in Orangeburg County. The other was about 22.5 miles northwest on the east bank of the Santee River, It was about 4 miles east-southeast of Fort Motte. It is the latter one we're concerned with here. The site is at the end of a farm dirt road that may be named Sawdust Road. This whole area is composed of very large farms and the sites are on private property.

Belleville plantation (also known as Thomson's plantation) was around the location of the intersection of routes S-9-80 (Adams Road) and S-9-151 (Lang Syne Road) about 0.4 miles west of route U.S. 601 (Colonel Thomson Highway) northeast of Saint Matthews and 2 mile southeast of site of the action at Fort Motte. Note that there is also a town of Fort Motte about 2.3 miles southwest of Belleville plantation.

Belleville changed hands several times during the war and apparently remained under Whig domination after their capture of nearby Fort Motte in May 1781. A notice in *Colonials and Patriots* (1964) reads: "Among the historic remains at and near the plantation are earthwork fortifications overlooking the Santee; the Thomson Cemetery, said to contain the remains of troops who died in the area; a camp and hospital site; McCord's Ferry, a strategic crossing of the Camden Road over the river; and Gillon's Retreat, plantation of Alexander Gillon (1741–1794), a commodore of the South Carolina Navy during the War for Independence."[133]

Big Savannah was also known as Big Glades. It was a few miles southeast of Belleville plantation (Thomson's plantation) on route SC 267 (McCords Ferry Road).

When the British took control of South Carolina, they established a series of outposts to support the line of communication between Charleston and Camden. When General Nathanael Greene (1742–1786) assumed command of the Continental Army in the south, he embarked on a campaign to destroy these interior posts. He made Fort Watson his first objective. The fort was constructed atop an ancient 30- to 50-foot Native American mound on Wright's Bluff overlooking the Santee River, about 6.75 miles due southwest of Summerton along Fort Watson Road, about a mile north-northwest of routes U.S. 301 and 15.

The mound probably dates from around 1200 to 1500 A.D. and probably served as either a burial or temple structure. Steps now lead to the top. No trace of the fortifications remains. Water now covers most of the ground to the west of Fort Watson, probably including the site of the well and the trench the defenders dug. Granite memorials mark the common grave of the Whig dead. One of the stones replaces the original marker which is no longer legible.

Saint Matthews is about 13 miles north of Orangeburgh on route U.S. 601 (South Harry C. Raysor Drive) where it intersects with route SC 6 (Old Number Six Highway).

Metts Crossroads was at the intersection of route U.S. 176 (Old State Road) and Belleville Road (S-9-45) in Saint Matthews. A granite marker in the northwest corner of the crossroads is hard to spot.

The site of the Calk Brothers action is unknown but the British were operating in the Fort Motte area northeast of Saint Matthews in May 1781. The Calks may have camped at Halfway Creek, a little east of route S-9-46 (F. R. Huff Drive North or Railroad Avenue) about 0.5 miles north of route SC 6 (Bridge Street) in the center of Saint Matthews. The site is on the right between the road and the railroad at the creek.

Colonel Michael Christopher Rowe's (1715–1788) plantation was 3 miles south of Orangeburg along route U.S. 21 (Rowesville Road) north of route S-38-1449 and south of Faulkner Road. It was about 200 yards east of Rowesville Road between Kirby Lane and Wildeway Lane. The skirmish there is also known as Moore's defeat.

> McCord's Ferry was on the Congaree River southeast of Columbia and northeast of Fort Motte.
> Amelia Township and Manigault's Ferry were on the west bank of the Santee River in what is now Calhoun County. The site of this action was at the end of Sawdust Landing Way which runs northeast from McCord's Ferry Road (SC 267) 0.8 miles southeast of its intersection with route U.S. 601 (Colonel Thomson Highway).
> Sharp's skirmish occurred about 0.5 miles east of the intersection of routes U.S. 601 (Colonel Thomson Highway) and SC 267 (McCords Ferry Road) in Saint Matthews.

★ Major James Postell (1739–1824) was returning to Brigadier General Francis Marion's (1732–1795) camp on Wednesday, January 31, 1781, when he heard of a "great quantity of rum, sugar, salt, flour, pork, soldiers clothing and baggage" at Manigault's Ferry. The guard there had gone after his brother John at Keithfield. A guard of only four men remained at the wooden redoubt which Major Postell's men took easily. They destroyed the redoubt and all the stores without losing a single man.[134]

See also **Wadboo, Keithfield** and **Manigault's Ferry** (Jan. 31–Feb. 1, 1781) p. 181.

★ The Crown forces occupied Belleville plantation, the home of Colonel William "Danger" Thomson (1727–1796), in 1780 and turned it into a fortified post and supply depot. They made a stockade around Colonel Thomson's house and incorporated the outhouses into the defenses. As Lord Francis Rawdon (1754–1826) marched west from Camden, he expected Brigadier General Thomas Sumter (1734–1832) to retreat up the west bank of the Congaree River, so he had seized all the passes in the north. Instead, Sumter marched quickly in the opposite direction and arrived at Belleville plantation on Thursday morning, February 22, 1781.

Sumter's men met heavy fire that prevented them from crossing the open field to the fort. After an unsuccessful attempt to take the stockade by assault, a small contingent of men managed to reach the defenses and burn some of the buildings; but the defenders, under Lieutenant Charles McPherson, of the 1st Battalion of De Lancey's Regiment, extinguished the flames and the garrison would not surrender. After 30 minutes of fighting, Sumter withdrew his troops but maintained a siege.

★ After the battle at Belleville, Brigadier General Thomas Sumter (1734–1832) left some men at Belleville to continue the siege while he moved the remainder of his force to Manigault's Ferry to rest. He ordered Captain Wade Hampton (1752–1832) to patrol the approaches to his camp and to observe any enemy movements that might threaten his troops. Lieutenant Hicks Chappell (1757–1836), who was with Hampton, later wrote that on Thursday, February 22, 1781 "the advance of the British met them and a skirmish ensued in which Hampton retreated after losing several men being made prisoner." Hampton hastened to return to Sumter's camp.[135]

★ Brigadier General Thomas Sumter (1734–1832) received word early Friday morning, February 23, 1781, that a large British supply column was approaching his camp at Manigault's Ferry from the south. The convoy of 20 wagons and an escort of about 50 to 80 men (depending on the sources) was headed from Charleston to the British post at Camden with clothing, provisions, munitions and some pay chests to establish what would become Fort Motte.

General Sumter, informed of the approach of the convoy, moved his troops to a hill, known as Big Savannah. He, Colonel Edward Lacey, Jr. (1742–1813) and Colonel William Bratton (1740–1815) attempted to ambush the wagon train near Big Savannah, a few miles down the road from Thomson's plantation. They barely finished setting up an ambush when the British column arrived in a glade near the ambush site. The British saw a small detachment of Sumter's men coming to attack the column. Sumter's men fired on the Regulars who quickly formed a compact line and advanced on open ground and drove Sumter's men back. The rest of Sumter's troops outflanked the Regulars and surrounded the wagons. Both sides expected victory; but, after a short but decisive conflict, Sumter's men outflanked and defeated the Redcoats.

Colonel William Bratton's (1740–1815) men ignored a white flag the British raised at one point in the fighting and killed seven men and wounded several others. David Sadler (1762–1848), one of Sumter's militiamen reported that "the British guard fought hard until nearly all were killed." The British lost seven killed, seven wounded and 66 taken prisoners and the 20 wagons loaded with arms, ammunition and clothing for three regiments of Lord Rawdon's army, plus several chests full of gold. Toward the end of the day, General Sumter ordered a retreat.[136]

★ The Santee had overflowed its banks preventing the wagons from crossing but Brigadier General Thomas Sumter (1734–1832) had collected all the boats at Fort Granby and at Belleville plantation. He had all the booty placed on board the boats and directed an officer to take them down the Santee River to a point near Wright's Bluff where Sumter would meet him with the troops. He rested his exhausted men at Manigault's Ferry the following day, Saturday, February 24, 1781.

Lord Francis Rawdon (1754–1826) had been pursuing Sumter, and his lead troops, the 64th Regiment under Major Robert McLeroth, caught up with him at 3 PM on the way to relieve the post at Belleville plantation. Sumter had formed his men for battle, expecting only to deal with the light infantry. McLeroth did not want to engage Sumter's force alone; so he withdrew his unit 4 miles to wait for Rawdon's main force. When Sumter saw Rawdon's entire army, he retreated. Rawdon did not pursue him.

Sumter proceeded to Wright's Bluff (Fort Watson), about 10 miles north of Nelson's Ferry, to meet the boats. Lieutenant William Cooper and the 63rd Regiment captured Sumter's boats at Wright's Bluff. The pilot, Robert Livingston, "through ignorance or intentional, carried the boats to the British post." The men guarding the boats escaped, but the Crown forces captured all the supplies and brought them inside the fort. Sumter needed those supplies and particularly the boats to cross the river and the swamps. He decided to attack Fort Watson but did not reconnoiter the fort; so he was unaware that Lieutenant Colonel John Watson Tadwell Watson (1748–1826) and 400 provincial light infantrymen had reinforced it.

★ Brigadier General Thomas Sumter (1734–1832) decided to attack Fort Watson to try to regain his supplies and boats. He made a direct attack on the fort at noon on Tuesday, February 27, 1781. (Some accounts say this event occurred on Wednesday, February 28; others say it was March 1.) The fort had been reinforced a few hours earlier when Colonel John Watson Tadwell Watson (1748–1826) returned with 400 provincial light infantrymen. The frontal attack was repulsed with heavy casualties. British accounts claim 18 killed and 38 prisoners and 40 horses captured. Lieutenant Colonel James Hawthorne (1750–1809) was wounded in the thigh.

Sumter retreated to a secure position about 5 or 6 miles from the fort to tend to his wounded. After three quick defeats in one month, Sumter's men suffered from poor morale that led to many desertions, so he withdrew from the area and retreated to Farr's plantation in the High Hills of the Santee to rest and recover from their two-week campaign. He later had to explain his conduct during the campaign in a long discourse to his disgruntled men.[137]

★ Brigadier General Thomas Sumter (1734–1832) attacked Ensign Richard Cooper (ca. 1756–) and 20 men of the provincial light infantry at noon on Thursday, March 1, 1781, as they straggled behind the rest of the battalion to cover the men repairing a broken wagon. About 200 of Sumter's men quickly surrounded them and ordered them to lay down their arms. Ensign Cooper ordered his men to form a loose square behind trees. Outnumbered 10 to one, they held off Sumter's men in an intense fight until Major John Harrison (ca. 1751–) and his South Carolina Rangers arrived and drove Sumter's men away.[138]

★ Major General Nathanael Greene (1742–1786) then sent Lieutenant Colonel Henry "Light-Horse Harry" Lee (1756–1818) and his Legion to Brigadier General Francis Marion (1732–1795), the "Swamp Fox," to take Fort Watson. They converged at the fort on Monday, April 16, 1781. Marion's men immediately took control of the nearby lake which lay outside the Native American mound and served as the fort's water supply. The 80 defenders had sufficient ammunition and food to withstand a siege until relieved; but, without water, they could not endure very long. When demanded to surrender, British lieutenant James McKay politely declined and ordered his men to dig a well at the base of the Native American mound. They struck water on April 18.

Lee realized the great difficulty of forcing the defenders to surrender after they had acquired a source of water. He knew that he could not successfully assault the fort without any cannon, so he asked General Greene for a field piece to destroy the walls of the fort. Greene sent a small cannon, but the soldiers bringing it got lost trying to find Fort Watson and turned back. About this time, smallpox broke out among Marion's men. This caused many militia members to return home.

The Congressional troops had no cannon and would not risk storming the fort. Lieutenant Colonel Hezekiah Maham (1739–1789) found a solution. He proposed building a tower of logs outside the walls, higher than the stockade. Marion's men constructed a 60-foot tower of notched logs (see Photo SC-16) over the next five days. It had an oblong base and a platform on top that was protected on the fort side by a palisade, allowing the riflemen to shoot everything that moved inside the fort. Two units assaulted the stockade at dawn on April 23 while the riflemen shot at the defenders. McKay soon surrendered. The tower eventually came to bear Maham's name.

The capture of Fort Watson is significant in that it was the first of the interior forts to fall to the Congressional forces after the return of General Greene to South Carolina in April 1781. The Continentals would capture several more outposts over the next month. The British would withdraw from Camden on May 10. The siege of Fort Watson was also the first use of the Maham tower, which would become a standard fixture of Continental sieges in South Carolina and Georgia.[139]

★ James Calk (1755–1825) and his brother William Calk (1740–1823) were probably heading home soon after the battle at Fort Motte when a patrol sent out by Lord Francis Rawdon (1754–1826), or one of his officers, to look for stragglers from Brigadier General Francis Marion's (1732–1795) force found them observing British troop movements at Saint Matthews in Calhoun County in May 1781. The Regulars attacked them, Dexy Ward, and two others and took them prisoners to Moncks Corner. Because James Calk and his horse had such a slovenly appearance, the British did not disarm him. When the captain in charge began making fun of him because of his slovenly appearance, James got angry, drew his sword and struck the captain in the head, just above the ear, knocking him off his horse and leaving him lying on the road bleeding. James then spurred his horse and galloped through the pines. His brother, William, and the rest of the prisoners managed to escape later that night and went to join Captain Philemon Waters's (1734–1796) company of General Sumter's forces.[140]

★ When Lord Francis Rawdon (1754–1826) started regrouping his forces in the spring of 1781 to prepare for Major General Nathanael Greene's (1742–1786) campaign to liberate the South, Captain Henry Giesendanner, the commander at Orangeburg, did not receive the order to abandon his position.

When the Continental Army arrived at the Congaree River, they crossed and gathered at Beaver Creek. Brigadier General Andrew Pickens (1739–1817) was detached to observe the movements of the Crown forces at Ninety Six. Meanwhile, Brigadier Generals Thomas Sumter (1734–1832) and Francis Marion (1732–1795) joined the army with about 1000 state troops and militiamen.

Throughout the night of Thursday, May 10, 1781, Brigadier General Sumter fired his 6-pound cannon to weaken the post. The Crown forces occupied so strong a position and were so advantageously posted, that the Congressional troops had little hope of success in attacking it. The Crown forces held a large brick jail (on the lower floor of the court house) which was as effective as a good redoubt. It commanded the only pass, giving them a safe retreat over the Edisto River. One side was secured by an impassable river and the other was covered by strong buildings. The Crown troops were posted in the jail and in several other buildings near it.

Major Thomas Young (1764–1848) wrote, "The tories were lodged in a brick house, and kept up a monstrous shouting and firing to very little purpose. As soon as the piece of artillery was brought to bear upon the house a breach was made through the gable end; then another, a little lower; then about the center, and they surrendered." The garrison raised a white flag at 7 the next morning. The Crown forces lost one man killed and six officers, 83 enlisted men and an undetermined number of Loyalists as well as an immense storehouse of provisions and military supplies captured. Sumter had no casualties. Captain Giesendanner was jailed "stripped to shirt and breeches" and his captors threatened to make his 10- and 12-year-old sons drummers in a Continental regiment.

Sumter was prepared to return from Orangeburg on the 11th when he intercepted one of Rawdon's expresses and learned of his lordship's retreat from Camden. Sumter then set out for Fort Motte to join Brigadier General Francis Marion (1732–1795) and Lieutenant Colonel Henry "Light-Horse Harry" Lee (1756–1818) in opposing Lord Rawdon. The posts of Camden, Orangeburg, Fort Motte, and Fort Balfour had all fallen within a few days.[141]

★ Lord Francis Rawdon (1754–1826) returned to Orangeburg in full force in July 1781 after forcing Major General Nathanael Greene (1742–1786) to abandon the siege of Ninety Six. Rawdon left Lieutenant Colonel Alexander Stewart (1740–1794) in charge of the garrison with his regiment, the famous 3rd Foot ("Buffs"), and the provincial light infantry while Rawdon opposed Major General Nathanael Greene (1742–1786) in the field. Colonel Stewart began to march toward Orangeburg to reinforce Lord Rawdon on Sunday, July 8, 1781.

Meanwhile, Brigadier General Francis Marion (1732–1795) and 400 horsemen rode at night to intercept him. Stewart took a less-traveled road so the two forces passed by each other in the early morning hours. When General Marion realized his mistake, he sent Colonel Peter Horry (1747–1815) to overtake Stewart's forces. Horry captured

Stewart's supply trains, but his troops arrived in Orangeburg to join Lord Rawdon and increase his force to 1,500 men. Colonel John Harris Cruger (1738–1807) brought 1,300 more men from Ninety Six.

Major General Nathanael Greene (1742–1786) and the forces of Brigadier General Thomas Sumter (1734–1832), Brigadier General Francis Marion (1732–1795), Lieutenant Colonel Henry "Light-Horse Harry" Lee (1756–1818) and Lieutenant Colonel William Washington (1752–1810) took a position on the north side of Turkey Hill, 4 miles above Orangeburg, on Tuesday, July 10, 1781. They prepared for battle and tried to entice Lord Rawdon out of his well-defended garrison for two days.

Rawdon declined to do battle. His men had little food. Lieutenant Alexander Chesney (1755–1843) wrote "we had nothing but one pound of wheat in the straw served out to each man every 24 hours. The parties going out daily to forage had constant skirmishes with the enemy." Lieutenant Colonel Banastre Tarleton (1744–1833) noted, "During the greater part of the time, they were totally destitute of bread, and the country afforded no vegetables for a substitute. Salt at length failed; and their only resources were water, and the wild cattle which they found in the woods."

The Continentals also lacked food. Captain Robert H. Kirkwood (1746–1791) recorded, "Rice furnished our substitute for bread. . . . Of meat we had literally none. . . . Frogs abounded . . . and on them chiefly did the light troops subsist. Even the alligator was used by a few."

General Greene and his generals reconnoitered the British lines on July 12th and realized it would be suicidal to try to take the town. They then retreated across the Santee and marched to the High Hills of Santee to regroup their forces after sending the militiamen to strike Crown posts. General Greene ordered his cavalry and mounted militia to get behind Rawdon and to strike at Charleston. General Marion established a new base in a cleared cane brake at the western end of a swamp known as Gaillard's Island in upper St. Stephen's Parish at Peyre's plantation, a quarter of a mile from the Santee River (2 miles north of present-day route SC 45 and 2 miles south of the dam on Lake Marion).[142]

★ Major General Nathanael Greene (1742–1786) received intelligence that Ninety Six had been evacuated and that Colonel John Harris Cruger (1738–1807) and his troops were on the march to Orangeburg, the only fordable location for 30 miles in either direction. General Greene decided to attack the lower posts at Moncks corner and Dorchester, hoping to entice the Crown forces to withdraw from Orangeburg to protect the posts in the lower country.

General Greene detached Brigadier General Thomas Sumter (1734–1832) and Brigadier General Francis Marion (1732–1795), with the legion cavalry, to draw away the enemy troops. They began their march from Orangeburg on Friday, July 13, 1781, while Greene headed to the High Hills of Santee to refresh his troops and to join Major General Jethro Sumner (1735–1785) and a body of militia, expected from the Salisbury district.

One of the Continental regiments mutinied a few days later at Dorchester. Nearly a hundred men were killed and wounded in quelling the mutiny which arose because the men were employed in service different from what they expected.[143]

★ Lieutenant Colonel William Washington (1752–1810) sent Captain John Watts and 20 or 30 dragoons to harass the Crown forces during the siege of Orangeburg. Major John Doyle (ca. 1750–1834), of the Volunteers of Ireland, mustered the mounted troops in Orangeburg and rode out on one of the daily foraging parties to find supplies. Captain Watts encountered Doyle and his men at sunrise on Wednesday, July 25, 1781.

The quick furious fight left two Loyalists dead and seven captured. Captain Watts had only one man wounded.[144]

★ A force of Loyalists led by Captain William Connaway assigned to patrol the Orangeburg area attacked a company of Whigs under Captain Jacob Rumph (d. 1785) at Four Mile Creek several miles west of Orangeburg on Wednesday, August 1, 1781. They killed 18 Whigs and dispersed the others.

★ Major General Nathanael Greene (1742–1786) ordered Lieutenant Colonel Henry "Light-Horse Harry" Lee (1756–1818) to strike at the enemy's lines of communication from Orangeburg to Charleston. Lee circled around the British camp at McCord's Ferry with 60 men and crossed the Congaree River on Friday, August 3, 1781. His dragoons dispersed 32 wagons escorted by 300 men within sight of the garrison at Orangeburg. The forward part of the escort fell back, but the main body refused to surrender. Lee was obliged to break off the attack. Nevertheless, Lee captured 20 prisoners. He sent Cornet George Carrington (1711–1785) and 12 dragoons to escort the prisoners to a secure location. A party of 60 Loyalists ambushed Carrington near Orangeburgh and freed 17 of the 20 prisoners.[145]

★ Colonel Hezekiah Williams ordered Captain William Connaway to eliminate the nuisance of Captain Stirling Turner, of Colonel William Harden's (1743–1785) militia, who had been harassing Loyalists between the North and South Edisto rivers, a few miles west of Orangeburg. Captain Connaway's Loyalists attacked the militia at the head of Four Mile Branch on Wednesday, August 15, 1781. The militiamen drove the Loyalists back. The Loyalists shot Captain Ryan through the shoulder during the pursuit. Captain Connaway's cavalry then counterattacked and dispersed Ryan's men as they drew lots for the captured horses. Captain Turner lost 18 men killed and 25 horses captured as well as all the pistols, swords and other equipment.[146]

★ Brigadier General Thomas Sumter (1734–1832) crossed the Congaree River on Monday, November 12, 1781 just before the Crown forces withdrew from Orangeburg to Charleston in December. Major Blewford crossed early the next morning with 70 mounted men. Sumter sent him to find Loyalist Captain Henry Giesendanner who had just arrived in the Orangeburg area with some wagons escorted by 60 men. The scouts only found two men at Giesendanner's. After firing on the scouts, the men escaped.

Major James Moore (1737–1777), of the South Carolina militia, was supposed to join Major Blewford at Giesendanner's but went on to Orangeburg instead and proceeded toward Colonel Michael Christopher Rowe's plantation 2 miles from Orangeburg. (Colonel Rowe was away fighting with the Congressional forces.) Along the way, Moore encountered a large party of Loyalists under Major William "Bloody Bill" Cunningham (d. 1787) near Orangeburg. [General Sumter's report to Major General Nathanael Greene (1742–1786) mistakenly identifies the Loyalist commander as Brigadier General Robert Cunningham (1741–1813).] Moore attacked the Loyalists and drove them out of their camp into a swamp. However, Cunningham's larger force returned a heavy fire from the swamp and pushed Moore's men back. They scattered and fled in disorder. Some of Moore's men reached Major Blewford and joined General Sumter about 8 miles north of Orangeburg.

Cunningham's troops numbered more than 500 men to Sumter's 418. They killed four, wounded eight, and routed the rest of Sumter's forces. Although Sumter abandoned his advance, he checked Cunningham's advance to the upper country. This action is also known as Moore's Defeat. It is also referred to as Hampton's Surprise, since a newspaper of the period incorrectly identified Moore as Major Richard Hampton (1752–1792). Dates also vary between the 12th, 13th and 14th.[147]

★ Major William "Bloody Bill" Cunningham (d. 1787) was wanted by every Whig militia in the Edisto River area. He had his men set up numerous small camps scattered along the river. Brigadier General Andrew Pickens (1739–1817) pursued Major Cunningham to the Edisto River near Orangeburg. Pickens joined forces with some other Whig leaders at Bull Swamp and led his troops across the Edisto River to attack the Loyalist camps at sunrise on Thursday, December 20, 1781.

Pickens's troops attacked the first camp and killed every Loyalist in it, leaving 20 dead. The gunfire at this camp alarmed the other camps and all the other Loyalists fled, ending "Bloody Bill's" activities. Cunningham got away by swimming his horse Ringtail across the Edisto River. He reached the safety of Charleston and his horse died of fatigue a short while later. Cunningham reportedly showed more grief for his horse than for all the widows and orphans he left in the Ninety Six District. He gave Ringtail a funeral with full military honors.[148]

★ Governor John Adam Treutlen (1726–1782), the first state governor of Georgia, fled the colony when the British occupied it. Treutlen was living with his German kinsmen at Metts Crossroads in South Carolina on Friday, March 1, 1782, when an independent company of General Robert Cunningham's (1741–1813) Loyalist brigade under Captain James Swinney attacked and killed him.[149]

★ Loyalists captured a convoy of six wagons carrying artillery supplies and small arms from Major General Nathanael Greene's (1742–1786) camp on the upper Ashley River near Bacon's Bridge to Charlotte, North Carolina around Wednesday, May 8, 1782. The wagons were captured and burned 7 miles below Orangeburgh. One of the teamsters was killed and another wounded.[150]

★ General Alexander Leslie agreed to exchange three officers of the Royal North Carolina militia for "persons, of that Country" of equivalent rank and "line of service." He expected that the Loyalist officers would be released from confinement immediately and be allowed to travel to Charleston. However, he learned "with pain" that Captain Christian House (d. 1782) of the Royal Militia was "chain'd to the ground" in the Orangeburg jail.

Leslie did not order immediate retaliation as he did not know Major General Nathanael Greene's (1742–1786) motives and assumed there must be "reasons most cogent to justify so extraordinary a procedure." As there were "many privates, prisoners to each side" who would benefit from an exchange, Leslie would "willingly" name a commissioner to meet with any officer General Greene might appoint to "negotiate this business."

Captain House, an officer of the Orangeburg Loyalist militia, submitted a petition on September 13 in which he stated that he had been captured and confined in the Orangeburg jail but had managed to escape and flee into Charleston. He did not mention the reason for his confinement. Colonel William Thomson reported that House and eight other prisoners escaped on May 31, adding: "all the prisoners could have got away if they had tried."[151]

★ Captain James Sharp's (ca. 1730–1795) Loyalist militia found a party of South Carolina militiamen who were en route from the Congarees (Old Saxe Gotha and present day Cayce) to join Major General Nathanael Greene's (1742–1786) army on Saturday, June 1, 1782. Captain Sharp's men charged and defeated them in Amelia Township, which was in Calhoun County close to Manigault's Ferry, killing four and dispersing the rest.[152]

Buckhead
Buckhead Creek, near Fort Motte
Fort Motte (Feb. 24, 1781; May 12, 1781)

> Fort Motte stood on a hilltop overlooking the Congaree River near its junction with the Wateree to form the Santee River. The Daughters of the American Revolution erected a granite monument in 1909 on the site of Rebecca Brewton Motte's (1738–1815) home which became the fort/supply depot, but it is about half a mile from the nearest road.
> Colonel William "Danger" Thomson is buried at his Belleville plantation on Buckhead Creek, Fort Motte.

Loyalists captured and fortified Whig Colonel William "Danger" Thomson's (1727–1796) house at Belleville. Brigadier General Thomas Sumter's (1734–1832) troops attacked it unsuccessfully on Thursday, February 22, 1781. The Loyalists shortly afterward abandoned the post for Fort Motte which was attacked May 8–12, 1781.[153]

★ When the British occupied South Carolina, they selected the mansion of widow Rebecca Brewton Motte (1738–1815) as their principal supply depot between Charleston and Camden. The mansion, fortified with a stockade, ditch, and abatis, was garrisoned by 150 infantrymen and a few dragoons on Tuesday, May 8, 1781 when Brigadier General Francis Marion (1732–1795) and Lieutenant Colonel Henry "Light-Horse Harry" Lee (1756–1818) arrived after their victory at Fort Watson.

They intended to lay a formal siege to the fortress and had already begun digging trenches when they learned that Lord Francis Rawdon (1754–1826) was abandoning Camden and might rescue Fort Motte on his way to Charleston. Lee devised a plan to capture the fort by using fire arrows to ignite the shingle roof of the house which was dry after a period of sunny weather. Mrs. Motte, who was living in a nearby farmhouse which Lee and Marion made their headquarters, not only granted her permission but also produced a fine East Indian bow and a bundle of arrows.

When one of the siege trenches got within range of the house, about noon, one of Marion's men shot two arrows onto the roof. His artillery prevented anybody from knocking the burning shingles to the ground, forcing the defenders to surrender about 1 PM. After the fire was extinguished, Mrs. Motte served a sumptuous dinner to the officers on both sides. The only casualties of the action were two of Marion's men. The prisoners were paroled.[154]

Wiboo (Wyboo) Swamp (March 6, 1781)

> Wiboo Swamp is now a branch of Lake Marion. It is south of Manning and west of the intersection of routes SC 260 and S-14-410 (Old River Road East). Old River Road East follows the trace of the Old Santee Road which Brigadier General Francis Marion (1732–1795) blocked to check Colonel John Watson Tadwell Watson's (1748–1826) advance before retreating to Mount Hope Swamp. In the 18th century, seven bridges crossed seven branches of what was then Wiboo Creek. The river road crossed those bridges and continued on the other side. A historical marker is on Old River Road East just east of the junction of Wyboo Road (S-14-480).

Lord Francis Rawdon (1754–1826) sent Colonel John Watson Tadwell Watson (1748–1826) of the 3rd Foot Guards (Scots Guards) and a force of 500 Loyalists, mostly

Major John Harrison's (ca. 1751–) regiment of South Carolina militiamen, "for the purpose of dispersing the plunderers that infested the eastern frontier" in March 1781. Brigadier General Francis Marion (1732–1795) and his partisans had been cutting the line of communication between Camden and Charleston. Watson left Fort Watson on Monday, March 5th and headed down the Santee River toward Snow Island in search of Marion who was at Murray's Ferry. Marion's scouts informed him of Watson's movements, so he took the offensive. The two forces engaged each other four times over the next three weeks, but the action that occurred on Tuesday, March 6, at Wiboo Swamp, which is exactly midway between the two ferries, is the only one for which an exact date is known.

Marion's men were outnumbered and low on ammunition. They had only about 20 rounds per man. So Marion resorted to strategy to draw his enemy into an ambuscade. He placed Colonel Peter Horry (1747–1815) in the front line on a causeway. Marion and the rest of the brigade–about 400 men–remained in reserve, hidden to counter an anticipated charge on the flank. Watson's two field pieces dislodged Horry's men from the swamp and Major Harrison's Loyalist dragoons pursued them as had been anticipated. Marion placed Captain Daniel Conyers (1748–1809) and his dragoons in a concealed position to meet Major Harrison's dragoons. Conyers and his men charged into the Loyalists, killing their officer and dispersing the rest. Watson rested a day or two at Cantey's plantation (Clarendon County) before continuing his march down the Santee. Marion destroyed the bridges ahead of him and harassed Watson all the way.

The next three engagements were at Mount Hope Swamp (see below), Lower Bridge (see p. 55), and Sampit Bridge (see p. 103) on the Black River. At the end of this campaign, Colonel Watson admitted failure and complained that Marion "would not fight like a gentleman or a Christian." Watson took refuge at Georgetown.[155]

See **Kingstree, Lower Bridge** p. 55 and **Sampit Bridge** p. 103.

Near Greeleyville, Williamsburg County
Mount Hope Swamp (March 9, 1781)
Near Cantey's Plantation

Mount Hope Swamp is 3 miles south of Greeleyville. To get there, take route SC 375 south from its intersection with route U.S. 521. Proceed for 2.5 miles and turn right onto route S-45-148 (Lesesne Road). At the end of Lesesne Road, turn right onto River Road. Travel 0.6 miles just past St. John's Baptist Church to a small bridge over Mount Hope Swamp. Patrick O'Kelley (vol. 3 p. 126) gives March 13 as the date of this event. Others date it between March 10 and 28, 1781.

John Cantey's house was about halfway between Nelson's Ferry and Murray's Ferry. Joseph Cantey (in or before 1704–1763), John's father, purchased the Mount Hope plantation about 1739. It was located near the present Cantey Cemetery. From the intersection of routes SC 260 and S-14-323 (Santee River Road|Francis Marion Road), about 12 miles south of Manning, go east on Santee River Road for about 2.6 miles. A large brick and metal gate on the right (south) side of the road marks John Cantey's plantation.

The Battle of Mount Hope Swamp is the second encounter between Colonel John Watson Tadwell Watson's (1748–1826) Loyalists and Brigadier General Francis Marion's (1732–1795) militiamen. Colonel Watson encamped at John Cantey's plantation on

Friday, March 9, 1781. He then attempted to join Lieutenant Colonel Welbore Ellis Doyle (1732–1802) (later General Sir John Doyle) who was moving down the River Road from Camden but Marion's men were destroying the bridges behind themselves. When they got to Mount Hope Swamp, Marion had his men remove the bridge planks. He left Colonel Peter Horry (1747–1815) and a detachment of riflemen on the rising ground on the other side of the bridge to block Colonel Watson's advance. They were successful for several hours until Watson brought up a howitzer and cleared the road with a charge of grape shot (see Photo SC-17). Watson proceeded to Murray's Ferry where he passed the Kingstree road and headed to the Black River road, about 12 miles away, which crosses at the Lower Bridge, the site of his next encounter with Marion.[156]

See **Kingstree, Lower Bridge** p. 55.

Sampit
Sampit Bridge, Georgetown County (March 20, 1781)

> The Battle of Sampit Bridge occurred about 0.5 miles south of the intersection of routes U.S. 17A and 521 northeast of the present village of Sampit, 10 miles west of Georgetown where route U.S. 17A (Saints Delight Road) crosses the Sampit River just north of its junction with Pennyroyal Road (S-22-42). The bridge is about half way between Chovin's plantation and Georgetown. The site of the 18th-century bridge corresponds to the modern bridge. There's a historical marker on the south side of Saints Delight Road about 0.5 miles southwest of the bridge.

See also **Sampit Road** and **Snow Island** p. 82.

SC-17. Grape shot. Nine balls such as these were placed between two iron plates and tied together to resemble a cluster of grapes. When fired simultaneously from a cannon, the balls separate into multiple projectiles.

Colonel John Watson Tadwell Watson's (1748–1826) campaign, which was supposed to be a "search and destroy" operation to annihilate Brigadier General Francis Marion (1732–1795), began at Wiboo Swamp and ended at Sampit Bridge. Watson broke camp at Blakeley's plantation near Kingstree and marched his troops across more than 25 miles of forest and swamps toward Georgetown. Marion's men followed them closely, firing on them at every opportunity. Marion sent Colonel Peter Horry's (1747–1815) dragoons ahead to the Sampit River Bridge to destroy it. Horry posted Lieutenant John Scott and his riflemen at the river with orders to shoot any Crown troops that came within range.

Watson arrived at the crossing late in the afternoon or early Tuesday evening, March 20, 1781 on his way back to Georgetown from an unsuccessful campaign. His men formed a column and began to cross quickly. Marion's men attacked their rear while they forded the river. Watson tried to rally his men, but a rifleman killed his horse. He mounted another and ordered the cannon to fire grape shot into Horry's dragoons, driving them back.

Within a few minutes, Watson lost 20 men killed and about twice as many wounded. He later recalled, "I have never seen such shooting before in my life." Marion supposedly lost only one man. Marion learned that night that Lieutenant Colonel Welbore Ellis Doyle (1732–1802) threatened his camp at Snow Island so he abandoned the pursuit and returned to Snow Island. Watson and his men retreated to Georgetown, ending the encounters between these two officers. Watson was so low on supplies that he had to take a route that took him more than 50 miles out of his way to obtain more. He reached Georgetown with two wagonloads of wounded men.[157]

Fairfield County
Dutchman's Creek (ca. March 21, 1781)

> Dutchman's Creek is about 11 miles east of Winnsboro. From the intersection of routes U.S. 21 and S-20-55 (Wateree Road), about 5.25 miles south of Great Falls, take route S-20-55 (Wateree Road) east for about 4.7 miles, then bear to the left onto S-20-101 (River Road). Proceed for about 2.35 miles, and then turn right onto route S-20-317 (Wateree Estates Road). Go about 1 mile and turn right on Runic Circle to Heart Lane. The site is on the far shore of the lake. The encounter is also known as "Dunlap's Defeat."

Lord Francis Rawdon (1754–1826) sent a party of the New York Volunteers from Camden under the command of Captain Grey to disperse a body of militiamen who were gathering on Dutchman's Creek in March 1781. They killed two captains and 16 privates and took 18 prisoners without losing a single man.[158]

Florence County
Lynches River
Lynches River massacre, Florence County (ca. April 10, 1780)
Witherspoon's Ferry (March 1781; April 3, 1781)

> The site of the Lynches River Massacre occurred in Florence County about 300 yards south of Witherspoon's Ferry. It was west of route SC 41 (SC 51|Kingsburg Highway) where it crosses the railroad tracks.

> Witherspoon's Ferry (see Photo SC-18) was near where route SC 41 (SC 51|Kingsburg Highway) crosses the Lynches River in the town of Johnsonville, Florence County, about 6 miles west-northwest of Snow Island. A historical marker is about 0.28 miles south of the site. Patrick O'Kelley (vol. 3 p.176) gives the date of this skirmish as April 3.

Lieutenant Colonel Francis Marion (1732–1795) sent Lieutenant Roger Gordon (1750–1781) and a small patrol to reconnoiter Lynches Creek in early April 1780. When they stopped at a tavern to rest around Tuesday, April 10th, Captain Jeffery Butler's large Loyalist patrol surrounded the tavern and set it on fire when Gordon's men wouldn't come out. Outnumbered, Gordon surrendered. He and his men were all shot down and murdered when they grounded their arms.[159]

After the Battle of Sampit Bridge, Brigadier General Francis Marion (1732–1795) marched back to Snow Island. Along the way, he received intelligence that Lieutenant Colonel Welbore Ellis Doyle (1732–1802) had destroyed his camp on Snow Island about Tuesday, March 20, 1781 and had taken a position on the north side of Witherspoon's Ferry on Lynches River. Marion decided to retaliate for the destruction of his camp and proceeded to attack Doyle and his Volunteers of Ireland. General Marion went in search of Colonel Doyle to retaliate. His scouts reported to him at daybreak on Tuesday, April 3, 1781, that Doyle had sent foragers to the Whig plantations, south of the Lynches River.

Marion ordered Colonel Hugh Horry (1744–1795) and his mounted infantrymen to disperse them. Horry's men rode into a plantation and shot nine Loyalists ransacking a house and captured 16 more. When Captain William Robert McCottry (1748–1805) and his riflemen arrived, they found the Loyalist rear guard scuttling a ferry boat on the opposite side at Witherspoon's Ferry. The riflemen sharpshooters fired at the Loyalists, wounding an officer and a sergeant. The Volunteers of Ireland quickly

SC-18. Witherspoon's Ferry site

formed along the river bank and fired a terrific volley that cut twigs and leaves loose but did not harm any of Marion's men.

Doyle's Loyalists struck their tents, mounted their horses and headed toward the Pee Dee but Marion's men had to go 5 miles upriver where they swam across the river because Lynches Creek was too swollen, wide, and deep to cross at Witherspoon's Ferry and because the ferry boat had been scuttled. Marion pursued Watson for two days and halted when he learned that Doyle had destroyed all his baggage and was rushing toward Camden.[160]

Conway, Horry County
Bear Bluff (April 1, 1781)

> Bear Bluff is on the Waccamaw River about 9.5 miles due east of Conway. From Conway, take route SC 90 east for about 8.75 miles, turn left onto Bear Bluff Road, cross Old Reaves Ferry Road and continue on Bear Bluff Road for about 1 mile. The site is on Bear Bluff Drive between the road and the river just before Bear Bluff Road begins to bend to the right. Bear Bluff should not be confused with Bear Swamp in Dillon County.

Joshua Long and a large body of Loyalists surprised Captain Daniel Morrall's (Murrell) (1722–1835) company at Bear Bluff on Sunday, April 1, 1781. The Whigs defended themselves to the last extremity in severe fighting but were forced to surrender. However, instead of being captured by the Loyalists, Josias Sessions (1764–1837) and eight other soldiers escaped by swimming across the Waccamaw River. Local tradition says a stray bullet from this battle killed an elderly slave woman who was working at her loom in a nearby farmhouse. People then believed she haunted the house and they stayed away from the site for decades.[161]

Heath Springs, Lancaster County
Twitty's Mill, Lancaster County
Beaver Creek (April 1781)

> The location of the skirmish at Beaver Creek is unknown, but the Loyalists often met at local mills. Twitty's Mill might have been located on Beaver Creek 20.7 miles due north-northwest from Camden. There is a low area there that could have been Twitty's millpond. To get there, take route SC 522 (Stoneboro Road) from Heath Springs to Stoneboro. Turn left (east) onto Twitty Mill Road and proceed about 1.5 miles to the bridge over Beaver Creek.
>
> Another possible site is near where Beaver Creek Cemetery Road crosses the creek in Heath Springs about 4 miles due south of Stoneboro.

John Robinson emigrated from Ireland and settled on a plantation in the Waxhaws in South Carolina in 1771. He became a Loyalist when the war began. In August 1779, he joined with the Loyalists in the neighborhood of the Lynches River who pretended to stage and attend a horse race. Instead, they planned to seize the arms in a magazine close to Camden. They proceeded with their plan under Colonel Ponder in September or November 1779. The Whigs discovered their plan, took Robinson and four others prisoners and dispersed the rest of the party, about 70 men. The prisoners were paroled in November and remained peaceful until late in February 1780.

Robinson was promoted to the rank of major in the South Carolina Loyalist militia after the Battle of Camden and was taken prisoner when Colonel Henry Rugeley's fort surrendered on Friday, December 1, 1780. He was apparently paroled again and raised 30 men in March 1781. He was wounded in the thigh in a skirmish on Beaver Creek, probably at Twitty's Mill in April 1781.[162]

Lynchburg, Lee County
Willow Grove (April 6, 1781)

> Lynchburg was called Willow Grove until about 1850 because of a thick grove of willow trees growing there. The site is on the right (northeast) about 90 yards north of the intersection of routes U.S. 76 (Florence Highway|Willow Grove Road) and SC 41(Lynchburg Highway|Church Street). The Whig position was approximately where the first white house is on the right and the Crown position was in the tree line on the far side of the field where Big Branch goes through the trees.

Lieutenant Colonel Welbore Ellis Doyle (1732–1802) had discarded his heavy baggage in his haste to reach Camden. His route was well marked with abandoned canteens and knapsacks as Brigadier General Francis Marion (1732–1795) pursued him. Doyle stopped at Willow Grove and made a stand on Friday afternoon, April 6, 1781 at a log building, previously used as a rum shop and now as a Whig fort, on a knoll covered by a thick growth of willow trees and partially surrounded by a thickly wooded stream known as Big Branch. The Loyalists crossed the branch on the north side, while General Marion's troops stayed on the south side, taking shelter in the grove and in and behind the log fort. The Loyalists greatly outnumbered the Whigs who had the advantage of a strong position and the best marksmen. Both sides exchanged fire until nightfall. At dawn, General Marion discovered that Doyle had withdrawn during the night and proceeded toward Camden. Marion abandoned the pursuit.[163]

Cashua or Cashway Ferry, Marlboro County (April 17, 1781)
Brownsville Church

> Cashua or Cashway Ferry was a rendezvous on the Great Pee Dee River for Whig forces in the area. Cashua Ferry was located about where route SC 34 crosses the Pee Dee River today. Only the cemetery of the old Brownsville Church remains and is now called the Rogers Cemetery. It is located in the southwest corner of Screwpin Road (SC 18) and River Road in Latta, about 2 miles west of the junction of Screwpin Road and route SC 38. The closest approach to Brown's Mill is reached by continuing on Screwpin Road to the bridge over Rogers Creek. The site is about 15° right of due north about 0.34 miles.

The militiamen used the Brownsville Baptist Church on the Marlboro County side of the river, a short distance from the ferry landing, as their headquarters on weekdays. The Whigs and the Loyalists engaged in a furious skirmish here on Tuesday, April 17, 1781. It ended with the Loyalists being chased into the swamp. The doors and shutters of the ferry house were riddled with bullet holes from the skirmish.[164]

Prosperity, Newberry County
Camping Creek (ca. April 1781)

> Camping Creek flows south from Prosperity. The easiest way to get there is to take South Main Street (S-36-26) southeast from Prosperity for about 2.85 miles. The route changes name to Macedonia Church Road along the way. Turn left (east) on Long Road and take the first right onto Pugh Road and travel about 0.75 miles to the bridge over Camping Creek. There's another bridge over the creek about 1 mile south on Wheeland School Road (S-36-72).

A skirmish occurred on Camping Creek, about 8 miles from the Saluda River, sometime between March 1 and May 7, 1781, probably around April. The only information available regarding this skirmish is that Captain John Lindsay [Lindsey] commanded the Whigs.[165]

Sawney's Creek, Kershaw County (May 8, 1781)

> Wateree Dam Road (S-28-37) crosses Sawney's Creek about a mile south of Lake Wateree and about a mile west of the Wateree River.

Major General Nathanael Greene (1742–1786) knew that Lord Francis Rawdon (1754–1826) would attack him as Colonel John Watson Tadwell Watson (1748–1826) reached Camden. He learned that Colonel Watson's 600 men and four pieces of artillery arrived at Camden on Monday, May 7, 1781. He withdrew to strong ground at Sawney's Creek, protected by a rough area of pine and oak. Lord Rawdon marched to the Wateree Ferry on Tuesday morning, May 8th, to find that General Greene had moved his camp. Rawdon followed Greene to the lower side of Sawney's Creek where his advance troops met Lieutenant Colonel William Washington's (1752–1810) dragoons on picket duty. They engaged in a brief but deadly skirmish.

Rawdon observed Greene's troops on the heights in full view. The North Carolina militiamen were posted in the deserted houses near the ford of Sawney's Creek. When the militiamen discovered a second ford that the British could use to flank them, they notified General Greene of its location. Greene left the cavalry, light infantry and pickets in place and withdrew 4 miles to Colonel's Creek, as he did not have enough men to cover both fords.

Rawdon returned to Camden with his men about the same time and prepared to abandon the town, not wanting to risk his men in an attack on the heights at Sawney's Creek. Both commanders had averted a major battle. When Rawdon abandoned Camden on May 9th, he released the prisoners, set the jail on fire, burned the mills and many private dwellings and destroyed most of the town leaving it "a little better than a heap of ruins." He left 31 wounded Congressional soldiers from the battle at Hobkirk Hill and 58 of his own men, including three officers, all of whom were too badly wounded to be evacuated. General Greene moved into Camden the next day and had Brigadier General Thomas Sumter (1734–1832) destroy the remnants of the British redoubts.[166]

Bass's Mill, Marion County (Aug. 1781)

> Bass's Mill was on Marsh Creek, a few yards inside the Marion County line, the dividing line between Dillon and Marion Counties at this point. To get there, take

> route U.S. 76|U.S. 301 east from Florence. After crossing the Great Pee Dee River, the roads separate. Follow U.S. 301 north for about 1.25 miles to Blue Brick Road which soon becomes Hassie Road. Follow Hassie Road 2.75 miles to the mill site. However, locked gates on all the roads leading to the site deny access. This action should not be confused with the Hulin's Mill action in Dillon County, which is sometimes referred to as Bass's Mill.

Moses Bass operated a well-known tavern on an island in Naked Creek, now called Marsh Creek, near his mill about 12 miles south of Cashua Ferry. When the Loyalists learned that South Carolina militia Lieutenant Colonel Murphy made dinner reservations at the tavern in August 1781, they prepared to ambush him. A gunfight ensued as Murphy's party sat down to their meal and others relaxed on the front porch. The Loyalists had the advantage of surprise, but the Whigs could take shelter in and around the tavern. As Major Jesse Barfield and South Carolina Loyalist militiamen were retreating toward the entrance causeway, they heard one of the Whig soldiers exclaim in a loud voice, "Good heavens! What shall we do? The powder is out!"

Barfield's men quickly resumed their attack. Murphy's men escaped down the steep embankment behind the tavern into the thick woods across the creek. Captain Malachi Murphy, Jr. (d. 1781), one other Whig and an unspecified number of Loyalists were killed. The Whigs also lost their horses.[167]

Leesville, Lexington County
Hartley's Creek (Oct. 1781)
Mount Willing, Saluda County (Nov. 1781)
Lexington
Tarrar Spring, Lexington County (Nov. 16, 1781)
Clouds Creek (Carter's House, Carter's Old Field, Turner House Massacre, Big Lick, Lick Creek), Lexington County (Nov. 17, 1781)
Lorick's Ferry, Newberry County (ca. Sept. 1782)

> Hartley's Creek, now known as Hellhole Creek, is on the north shore of Brodie Millpond in Leesville. It is about 3.8 miles west of Interstate 20 and 1.25 miles east of route U.S. 178 (Fairview Road) and about 1 mile south of South Carolina route S-32-34 (Pond Branch Road).
>
> The action at Tarrar Spring occurred about 2 miles east of the Lexington County Courthouse in Lexington.
>
> The Battle of Clouds Creek, also known as the Clouds Creek Massacre, occurred just north of Batesburg and Leesville. Routes U.S. 178|SC 391 separate at Pine Street in Batesburg. Follow route SC 391 for 2.4 miles to route SC 245 (North Lee Street). Turn south onto route SC 245 for 0.2 miles to route S-32-59 (Devil's Backbone Road). The site is 0.4 miles from this intersection.
>
> The actual site of the Lorick's Ferry action is not known. It could have happened in Saluda or Newberry counties. Lorick's Ferry was on the Saluda River that divides the two counties. A probable site is about a mile northwest of where route SC 395 crosses the Saluda River.

> Captain William Butler is buried in the family plot in the cemetery of the Butler Church. To get there, return along route S-41-138 (McNeary Ferry Crossing) to the intersection of routes U.S. 378 and SC 391. Follow route U.S. 378 west for 9.4 miles. At route S-41-39 (Cherry Hill Road), proceed northwest for 2.6 miles where the road is numbered S-41-122. Proceed 0.1 miles to route SC 194 (Denny Highway). A state historical marker near this intersection calls attention to William Butler's nearby grave site. Proceed down route SC 194 a short distance and turn onto route S-41-51 (Butler Road). Proceed west for 0.7 miles and turn right on route S-41-161. The grave is 0.1 miles north.
>
> Bloody Scout is the name given to Major William "Bloody Bill" Cunningham's (d. 1787) killing rampage through South Carolina in December 1781. Various groups went to Rowe's plantation (Orangeburg County), Tarrar Spring and Clouds Creek (Lexington County). One group continued on to Mount Willing (Saluda County), where Cunningham rejoined them before proceeding to Captain Caldwell's house, then to Hayes Station and O'Neal's Mill (Laurens County), Swancey's ferry and Anderson's mill, Walnut Grove, the houses of James Woods, Colonel John Woods, Mr. Lawson, Hilliard Thomas, and Wofford Iron Works (all in Spartanburg County). They also killed John Snoddy (1762–1781) and Colonel Edward Hampton in Spartanburg County, John Boyce (Union County), captured and hanged a few of his stragglers in Laurens County, and attacked the Pinewood House (Edgefield County) and McCord's Creek (Abbeville County). They proceeded to Bull Creek Swamp in Orangeburg County and then to Slaughter Field in Barnwell County.

Cunningham and his men killed 79 Whigs and burned more than eight plantations during this expedition and in other actions. This earned him the nickname "Bloody Bill." He only lost 25 men.

Major William "Bloody Bill" Cunningham (d. 1787) massacred 28 Whigs at Hartley Creek and dismembered and mutilated the bodies sometime in 1781, possibly around October. The creek later became known as Hellhole Creek. This action is sometimes referred to as John W. Lee's Tavern or Lee's Tavern as it is close to Hellhole Creek.[168]

★ Another Loyalist raid occurred in the neighborhood of Mount Willing in present Saluda County in November 1781. They plundered the area and captured considerable booty.

★ Whig Captain Stirling Turner and Captain James Butler (1737–1781), recently released from captivity in Charleston, pursued Colonel Hezekiah Williams. They chased the Loyalists to Tarrar Spring in Lexington County on Saturday, November 16, 1781. Both sides exchanged shots at the spring, but both sides soon decided to negotiate. They agreed that Turner's militiamen would not harm the Loyalists if they returned the stolen cattle and left the area.[169]

★ Captain Stirling Turner and his band of 23 camped at Clouds Creek, a branch of the Little Saluda River, in mid-November 1781 on their return home from Tarrar Spring. Turner, ignoring Captain James Butler's (1737–1781) warnings that Major William "Bloody Bill" Cunningham (d. 1787) and his Loyalists were in the area, selected an open location and failed to use basic precautions. Cunningham's 250–300 Loyalists attacked the camp at dawn on Saturday, November 17, 1781. The surprised campers took refuge in an unfinished log house without doors or windows.

The Loyalists set fire to the shed and the Whigs surrendered. They were promised good treatment and were to march out with clubbed arms (see Photo SC-19) and to

SC-19. Clubbed muskets. Reenactors in the center are carrying their muskets in clubbed position to show that they have surrendered. Clubbed muskets can also be used as a weapon when one has run out of ammunition.

ground them in front of the house. Captains Turner and James Butler, Jr. (1737–1781) came out of the house first. As soon as they passed the door of the house, Cunningham recognized Butler as the man who had killed Captain Radcliffe (d. 1781). He drew his sword and swung it at Butler but missed him. Butler struck one of the Loyalists to the ground with his clubbed rifle.

Cunningham refused any terms which would free young Butler. Butler's father offered his life instead. Knowing that Cunningham would not spare his life, the young man fired his rifle, killing a Loyalist and ending the parley. Return fire left James Butler, Jr., mortally wounded as he prepared for a second shot. Captain Butler grabbed a pitchfork to defend himself until a sabre stroke severed his right hand. James Butler, Jr.'s death produced panic in the little party which was greatly outnumbered. Cunningham got an unconditional surrender and slaughtered all but Hendley Webb (1753–1828) and Bartley Bledsoe (1760–1811), who were spared through the intercession of friends in Cunningham's band, and Benjamin Hughes (1759–1849) who escaped. This struggle, which lasted an hour, is best known as the Clouds Creek Massacre, but it is also referred to as Carter's House (Mr. Carter owned the unfinished log house on the premises), Carter's Old Field or Big Lick, a creek nearby the location.

Cunningham left a detachment to meet any burying party that might come to bury the victims. He hoped to capture William Butler (1759–1821), another of Captain James Butler's sons. However William, a captain of rangers, was too far away to arrive in time. The bodies were buried in a large pit, except for Captain Butler and his son. Captain Butler's body was so badly cut up that his wife could only identify him from the bible in his pocket. She put the parts of his body into a basket and then buried her husband and son in separate graves.

Cunningham's men then went to Oliver Towles's (1734–1781) blacksmith shop to get their horses shod. Cunningham's men killed Towles, after he finished the job, along with his son and an African American boy. They then set fire to all the buildings as they left.[170]

★ After defeating Major Moore at Rowe's plantation Major William "Bloody Bill" Cunningham (d. 1787) crossed the fork of the Edisto River and rendezvoused with the other detachments of his "Bloody Scout." Two of the detachments under Colonel Hezekiah Williams and Captain Radcliffe (d. 1781) moved to Mount Willing and began plundering the settlers.

A disorganized band of Captain Stirling Turner's Whig militia assembled and pursued Colonel Williams. This band of Whigs did not have a leader and acted more as a mob than a military force. They pursued Williams across the Saluda River into what is now Newberry County, and surprised the Loyalists, killing Captain Radcliffe. The rest of the Loyalists dispersed into the surrounding countryside.[171]

★ Colonel William "Bloody Bill" Cunningham (d. 1787) probably timed his raids in the Saluda River area to take advantage of Brigadier General Andrew Pickens's (1739–1817) absence while he was conducting his expedition against the Cherokees between September 10 and October 22, 1782. Pickens foresaw the possibility of such a raid and left some troops behind to counter Cunningham who would usually split his large force into smaller groups to invade enemy territory. The groups would then rendezvous and conduct their raids.

Captain William Butler (1759–1821), the son of James Butler (1737–1781) whom Major Cunningham had killed at Clouds Creek, learned that Cunningham was operating in the Saluda River area in September 1782. He set out on a raid to avenge his father's death. His party consisted of men who had lost brothers, fathers and neighbors in previous raids by Cunningham. He wanted to avenge the deaths of his father and brother, so he sent his brother, Captain Thomas Butler (1754–1805), to the home of Joseph Cunningham, one of Bloody Bill's relatives, under cover of darkness to find out exactly where Cunningham was.

Thomas was a talented voice imitator, so he pretended to be a member of Cunningham's band and requested directions to the Loyalist camp. Unable to recognize Thomas in the dark, Joseph Cunningham's wife gave him the information that led to her husband's capture. Butler then emerged from the darkness, seized Joseph Cunningham, put a pistol to his head and forced him to lead Butler and his men to Bloody Bill's camp.

Butler's 30 men surrounded the camp at sunrise and attempted to take Cunningham alive. However, as Butler's men approached the camp, the 20 Loyalists were drying their blankets around the fire. They mistook Butler for Bloody Bill because they resembled each other and continued with their business. When Butler got close enough, his men charged the Loyalist camp at Lorick's Ferry. The Loyalists fled in all directions. Bloody Bill, immediately realizing his predicament, jumped on his horse, Silver Heels, and raced for the Saluda River. Butler pursued Cunningham closely on his horse Ranter. Cunningham tried to fire his pistols repeatedly, but they misfired every time because the powder was damp from the previous night's rain. One pistol eventually fired when Cunningham pointed it over his shoulder.

When Cunningham drew his sword, the bushes tore it out of his hands. Butler was only armed with a sword and he couldn't get close enough to strike Cunningham whose horse plunged into the Saluda and swam to safety. As he returned to join his men, Butler found Cunningham's sword and kept it. When he got to the camp, he found that his men had murdered one of the captured Loyalists who had whipped the mother of one of Butler's men.

The Whigs pursued the Loyalists, overtaking some of Cunningham's men at the Saluda River. They fired on the Loyalists in the water. One man's pistol misfired. He reprimed it and fired at another Loyalist named Davis, killing him on the river bank. Butler ordered his men to cease firing. Cunningham escaped to Charleston and then to the Spanish territory of Florida but never managed to raise another band. Butler represented South Carolina in the United States House of Representatives after the war.[172]

Near Salley, Aiken County
Dean Swamp (May 24, 1782; May 25, 1782; Oct. 1782)
Battle of John Town

> The southern banks of Dean Swamp, a branch of the South Edisto River, are on route SC 394 (Salley Road) 1.2 miles west of its junction with route SC 39 (Railroad Avenue) in Salley once known as John Town. The John Town Memorial on the right where route SC 52 (Voyager Road) meets route SC 394 (Salley Road), just before the bridge over the creek, marks the site of the Battle of John Town which was fought here on May 24, 1782.

A band of Loyalists, part of Major William "Bloody Bill" Cunningham's (d. 1787) force, had been detached to liberate British and Loyalist prisoners held in two bull pens near John Town. Brigadier General Andrew Pickens (1739–1817) sent Captain Michael Watson (1726–1782) and Captain William Butler (1759–1821) with a contingent of militiamen to intercept them. Watson's men were mounted militiamen armed with rifles and muskets. Butler's troops consisted of cavalry armed with pistols and sabers. The party set out from Edgefield at sunset Thursday, May 23, 1782 with Captain Watson in command. They advanced quickly, intending to surprise the Loyalists.

They captured a prisoner along the way, but the man escaped as the militiamen approached the Loyalist camp. He alerted the Loyalists of Watson's approach, and the Loyalists prepared an ambush on the edge of Dean Swamp. After the prisoner escaped, Watson wanted to cancel the expedition but Butler convinced him to continue. As they approached the edge of the swamp on Friday, May 24, 1782, the Whigs saw two men trying to hide themselves. Watson and some of his men rode forward rapidly to capture them. Watson soon realized that these men were only a decoy and warned the others but it was too late. The entire body of Loyalists rose up and fired on the attackers, mortally wounding Watson and Sergeant Vardell (d. 1782) and wounding several other men.

Butler assumed command and removed the wounded men under heavy fire. Outnumbered two to one and low on ammunition, Butler led a desperate charge to counter the enemy advance. This unexpected move threw the Loyalists into confusion. His men mingled in the enemy's disordered ranks, preventing them from rallying. This turned the tide of battle and sent the Loyalists fleeing to the safety of the nearby swamp. Sergeant

Vardell was buried in the field; Watson died the next day and was buried in Orangeburg. In addition to these two casualties, the Whigs had eight men wounded.[173]

★ Captains Tenison Cheshire (1726–1794), Joseph Jones and Oldfield led an active community of Loyalist settlers along the Salkehatchie River. The Whigs and the Loyalists observed a truce in the area since late spring 1782; but Captain William Goodwyn and 18 Congaree militiamen broke this truce on Saturday, May 25, 1782, when they tried, unsuccessfully, to kidnap Captain Cheshire at Dean Swamp and bring him to Major General Nathanael Greene's (1742–1786) camp.

★ Captain John Carter (1761–1820) of Hammond's militia rode with his Volunteer Scout of Horse Company to break up an assembly of Loyalists at Dean Swamp in October 1782. Captain Tenison Cheshire (1726–1794) and 25 Loyalists ambushed them on the way to the swamp, inflicting several casualties. Yet, Captain William Goodwyn's men managed to drive the Loyalists into the swamp.[174]

Bowling Green, Marion County (June 3, 1782)
Burch's (Birch's) Mill, Florence County (June 8, 1782)
Black Lake, Horry County (June 8, 1782)

> As these sites are often grouped together, one might infer that they are quite close to each other, but that is not the case. Burch's Mill is 33.4 miles from Black Lake and 15 miles from Bowling Green. This sequence of events would have taken two or more days.
>
> The savannah known as Bowling Green is located about 4 miles north of Marion, in the fork of routes U.S. 501 and S-34-23 (Temperance Hill Road). The site is between St. Phillips A.M.E. Church and Forks Chapel. A state historical marker for the Battle of Bowling Green is on route U.S. 501 about 5.5 miles north of Marion.
>
> Burch's mill is thought to have been located on Mill Branch in Florence County, east of route S-21-57 (North Old River Road) and about a mile south of the confluence of Jefferies Creek and the Great Pee Dee River.
>
> Black Lake is now an inlet on the east side of the Great Pee Dee River a short distance below Britton's Neck. It is located in present Horry County about 2 miles north of Yauhannah Bridge, the modern bridge on route U.S. 701 (North Fraser Street) across the Great Pee Dee River about 22 miles northeast of Georgetown. The lake was larger in the past than it is now.[175]

Major Micajah Ganey's Loyalists had caused trouble to the people of North Carolina and had not observed the treaty of neutrality with Brigadier General Francis Marion (1732–1795) which was made on Sunday, June 17, 1781. South Carolina Governor John Matthews (Matthewes) (1744–1802) and North Carolina Governor Alexander Martin (1740–1807) agreed to form a joint expedition to subdue the Loyalists. They appointed General Marion in command.

General Marion had already drawn up plans for this operation and sent three columns to proceed from different directions. The Loyalists offered no significant resistance to Marion's men during this expedition. The only incident reported to have occurred involved Colonel John Baxter's company, which had been assigned to patrol Britton's Neck, the narrow strip of land between the Great and Little Pee Dee rivers just above their junction in modern Horry County. Colonel Baxter learned that the Loyalists had seized a boatload of rice near the mouth of Black Lake. When he and his men arrived on the scene, the Loyalists fled. However, as Baxter's company was proceeding up the lake in canoes to recover the boat, the Loyalists fired on them, wounding Robert James, a personal friend of General Marion.

★ Brigadier General Francis Marion (1732–1795), commanding the North Carolina and South Carolina militiamen, defeated Major Micajah Ganey and a force of 500 Loyalists at Bowling Green, approximately 0.5 miles northeast of the marker, on Monday, June 3, 1782. Marion had only one man wounded. The Loyalists began to sue for terms. As the treaty was to expire on June 17, 1782, Ganey signed another treaty at Burch's mill on the west side of the Pee Dee River on Saturday, June 8, 1782 in which the Loyalists agreed to

- lay down their arms and to become peaceable citizens,
- deliver up all stolen property,
- apprehend all who did not accede to the treaty now made,
- deliver all deserters from the Congressional army,
- return to their allegiance and abjure that of his Britannic Majesty.

In a letter dated June 3, 1782, Marion wrote to Ganey: "Colonel Richardson acquaints me that there was some men who did not, or would not, submit to the terms sent you. All such men will be allowed to go to Charlestown, and be considered as prisoners of war, to be exchanged for the American prisoners. Their wives and children, and such property as is theirs, they will be allowed to take with them, except stock and arms, and shall be safely conducted to town on Saturday, or sooner, if possible. I shall be glad to see you at Mr. Burches'."[176]

Major Ganey asked permission to go to Charleston saying, "Honor, sir, requires that I should yield my commission to Colonel Balfour, from whom I received it. But this done, I shall immediately return to the country and seek your protection." True to his word, Ganey returned to Marion's headquarters, enlisted with many of his followers to obtain full pardon, and served loyally until the end of the war.

General Marion remained at the camp at Burch's mill until June 16. He then marched north and crossed the river in the vicinity of Mars Bluff within a few days and proceeded to the Bowling Green, between the Great and Little Pee Dee rivers, in Marion County, where at least 500 Loyalists laid down their arms.[177]

Bryan's Station, South Carolina (now Kentucky) (Aug. 15–17, 1782)

This event occurred in what is now Kentucky and will be treated in the Kentucky chapter of the next volume: *The Guide to the American Revolutionary War in the Deep South and the Frontier.*

2
CHARLESTON AND VICINITY

See the map of Charleston and vicinity.

Fort Johnson, James Island (Sept. 14, 1775; Nov. 10, 1775; May 12, 1779; Feb. 26, 27, 28, 1780; March 2, 1780; March 10, 1780; March 21, 1780; April 20, 1780; Nov. 14, 1782)

Oohey River, Wallace's Road, James Island (Feb. 26, 1780)

James Island (Oct. 10, 1782)

Horses captured (Oct. 10, 1782) (some accounts date this event as Nov. 4, 1782)

Dill's Bluff (Nov. 14, 1782)

Fort Johnson is on James Island, west of Charleston on the Stono River, at the entrance to Charleston Harbor opposite Fort Sumter and Fort Sullivan. The fort, built between 1704 and 1708, was the first fortification in Charleston and was the city's principal defense guarding the port from attack by sea in colonial times. It had 20 guns, 18- and 24-pounders. There was also a battery of 12 heavy guns on the same island, nearer the town. When South Carolinians received news of the battles at Lexington and Concord, Massachusetts, the Council of Safety ordered local militiamen to seize the fort on Friday, September 15, 1775. The council even discussed capturing Lord William Campbell (d. 1778), the royal governor himself. The governor took refuge on the HM sloop of war *Tamar* and never again set foot on Carolina soil. Colonel Francis Marion (1732–1795) served as commander of the fort after his illustrious military career.

Fort Johnson was a major part of the Charleston Harbor defenses for the Whigs from 1775 to 1779. The fort was reinforced with earthworks and palmetto logs. A line of earthworks with batteries was added about 500 yards west of the fort to protect the peninsula from attack by land. Colonel Christopher Gadsden (1724–1805) and 380 men of the 1st South Carolina Regiment held Fort Johnson along with a small detachment of artillerists. Captain Thomas Pinckney (1750–1828) and a company from Gadsden's regiment occupied the other battery on James Island.

The Redcoats recaptured the fort in 1780 when they attacked it from the land. General Henry Clinton's (1730–1795) men took the fort's garrison by surprise early in 1780 and eliminated one of the two positions dominating the entrance to the harbor, allowing Royal Navy ships to enter Charleston harbor unhindered, except for a few shots from Fort Moultrie across the water.

To get to Fort Johnson from the junction of routes U.S. 17 (Savannah Highway) and SC 171 (Wesley Drive) across the Ashley River south of Charleston, follow route SC 171 (Wesley Drive) south for 4.5 miles to Fort Johnson Road. Turn left (east) and proceed 4.4 miles to the brick powder magazine and the ruins of Fort Johnson, located on the grounds of the Marine Laboratory of the College of Charleston.

The site of the plantation of Eliza Lucas Pinckney (1723–1793), the mother of Colonel Charles Cotesworth Pinckney (1746–1825) and Captain Thomas Pinckney

Charleston and Vicinity **117**

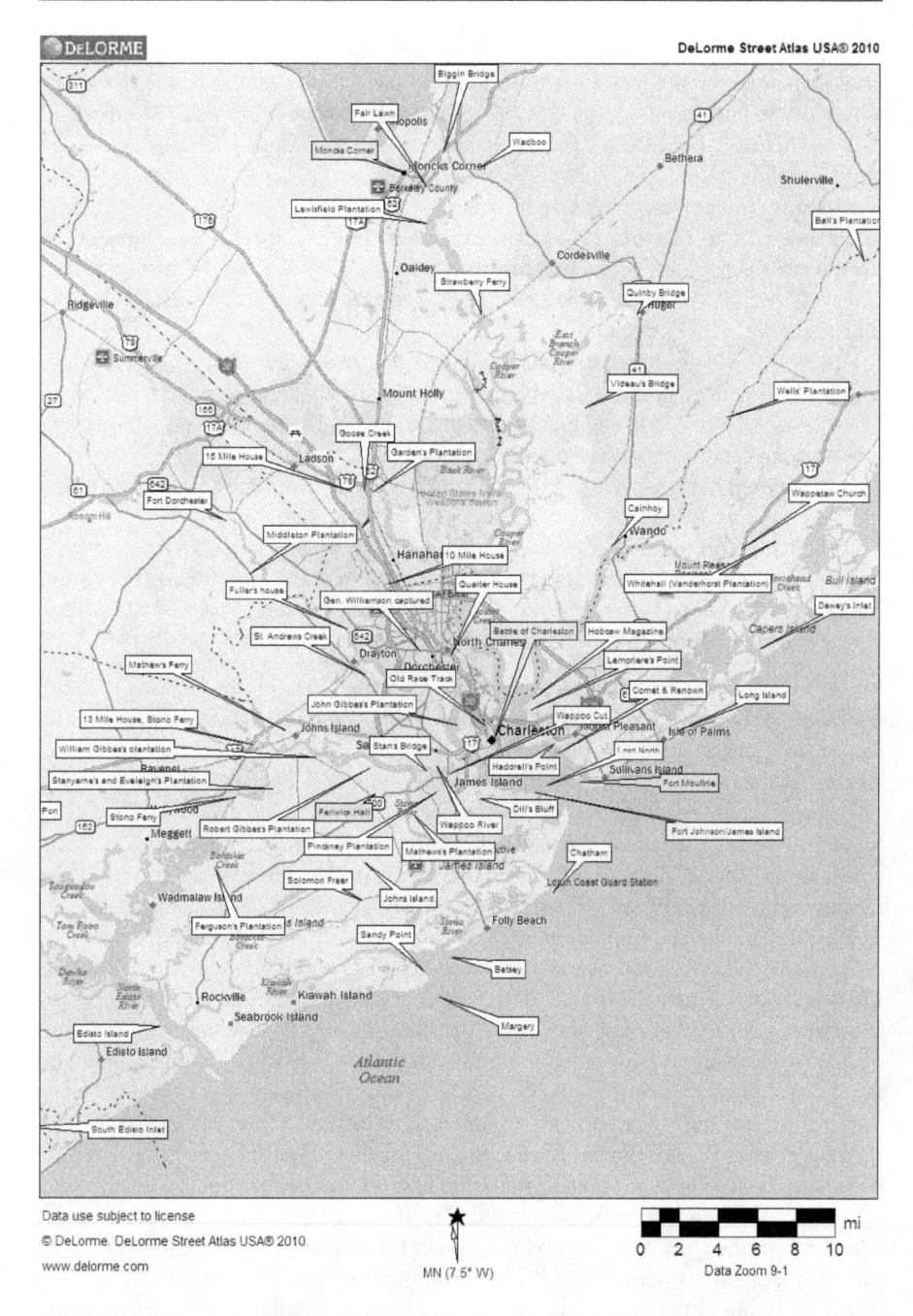

Charleston and vicinity: Map for The Guide to the American Revolutionary War in South Carolina
© 2012 DeLorme (www.delorme.com) Street Atlas USA®

> (1750–1828) is also in the area. As a teenager, Eliza established the indigo industry that subsequently produced great wealth for Low Country planters. About 1 mile south of the junction of routes U.S. 17 (Savannah Highway) and SC 171 (Wesley Drive), route SC 171 (Wesley Drive) meets route SC 700 (Maybank Highway). Turn right (west) onto route SC 700 (Maybank Highway) and proceed 0.8 miles to Wappoo Creek. The plantation was near here.
> Colonel William Moultrie (1730–1805) commanded 413 men of the 2nd South Carolina Regiment and 22 men of the 4th Artillery at Fort Sullivan. He raised a flag with a blue field and three white crescents. The state flag of South Carolina incorporates the design of that flag.
> The Rebels also erected a redoubt with 16 guns at the town's southern extremity, at what is now called the Battery, and a line of six small "forts" along the Ashley River. Each of these forts had four to nine guns. On the Cooper River side, they built seven more redoubts, each with three to seven guns.
> The captured horses site is at Fort Johnson Road and Deepwood Drive, less than a mile from Fort Johnson.
> Dill's Bluff is on the Stono River on the west end of James Island. After crossing the river on Harbor View Road, take the first right onto North Shore Drive and proceed to the second intersection (Waites Drive) and the site of Dill's Bluff. (A little further down the road, North Shore Drive becomes Dills Bluff Road.)

The HM sloop of war *Tamar* was posted in Charleston Harbor in August 1775 and was awaiting the arrival of the HM Sloop *Scorpion* and the transport ship *Palliser* to help remove the guns and military stores from Fort Johnson. The citizens became alarmed because the fort was the city's main naval defense and stored a large number of cannonballs for the fort's heavy cannons. The HMS *Cherokee* arrived in the harbor on Thursday, September 7, 1775, alarming the Council of Safety even further. They appointed Lieutenant Colonel Isaac Motte (1738–1795) to command 150 men from Captain Thomas Pinckney's (1750–1828) and Captain Barnard Elliott's (1740–1778) 4th South Carolina Artillery companies and Captain Francis Marion's (1732–1795) light infantrymen.

They marched from the barracks in silence at 11 PM on Thursday, September 14, 1775. They proceeded to Gadsden Wharf where they embarked on board the *Carolina* and *Georgia Packet*. After setting sail, Colonel Isaac Motte (1738–1795) convened the officers in the cabin and informed them that they were ordered to capture Fort Johnson. Even though there were only a few men in the garrison there, he expected reinforcements from the HM sloop of war *Tamar*, so he ordered Lieutenant Henry Mowat (1734–1798) and a detachment from Captain Pinckney's grenadiers and the cadets to serve as the forlorn hope to scale the walls on the south bastion (see photo SC-15) while he and Captain Pinckney's grenadiers and Captain Marion's light infantrymen would enter or force the gates over the ravelin. Captain Elliott and his grenadiers would enter into the lower battery over the left flank. All this was to be done in silence.

About an hour after sailing, the expedition crossed the harbor and anchored about half a mile from the opposite shore near Captain Stones landing. They disembarked with great difficulty as they only had two small boats which could only ferry 15 men at a time. The men had to drag the boats part way over a long muddy flat and then wade through waist-deep water. Captain Pinckney's grenadiers landed first and occupied the sea beach to cover the others. Captain Elliott's grenadiers boarded the small boats as soon as his company was landed. Captain Elliott boarded one boat and Colonel Motte the other.

Colonel Motte convened Captains Pinckney and Elliott about dawn to determine whether they should try taking the fort before day with the troops that were landed or to wait for the rest of the grenadiers and the light infantrymen. They decided on an immediate assault. Captain Marion's light infantry company and Lieutenant Richard Shubrick's (1751–1777) grenadiers would march to their assistance as soon as possible after landing. Lieutenant Mowat's detachment of grenadiers from the 1st Regiment and the cadets set out to scale the wall of the south face of the southwest bastion which had a ladder already fixed to it, making it easy to perform their task. Colonel Motte followed the first detachment with Captain Pinckney and the rest of the grenadiers while Captain Elliott brought up the rear.

Anticipating the militia's action, the crew of the *Tamar* dismounted and spiked the fort's guns, completing the task two hours before the militiamen arrived at the fort. The militiamen captured "Gunner" George Walker, the fort's caretaker, and five of the *Tamar*'s crew. They found the guns were dismounted but not spiked. They captured Fort Johnson and its 20 guns.[178]

Lord William Campbell (d. 1778), the Royal Governor, dissolved the South Carolina Commons House of Assembly and sought his personal safety on board the *Tamar*, anchored in Rebellion Road, on Friday morning, September 15, 1775. The *Tamar* unmoored at 9 PM and went to Sullivan's Island where she remained in company with other ships all night after the capture of Fort Johnson.

Lieutenant Thomas Heyward, Jr. (1746–1809) and a detachment of the Charles Town Artillery company arrived at Fort Johnson with a gin (see Photo SC-20) and other implements to remount the cannon. It was pretty late in the day before they were ready

SC-20. Cannon gin. A cannon gin (or engine) is used to mount and dismount a cannon barrel from its carriage.

for work and they only mounted three cannons. As the Charles Town Artillery company was under orders to return to the city that night, Captain Elliott and his grenadiers remounted the other cannons and manned them while residents fled the city, fearing an attack by the British fleet.

★ During that night, Saturday, September 16th, the *Tamar* and the *Cherokee* weighed anchor with a sloop of war and the packet *Swallow*. By dawn, they came within point blank range of the fort. Colonel Motte ordered his troops to withdraw under the cover of the fort when the ships began to fire, as their three cannons were no match for the ships' guns. They were to proceed between the fort and enemy fire. If the ships landed any men, they were instructed to attack them, expecting that the British cannon would not fire at their own men. However, due to an ill wind or another reason, the ships veered about and anchored at their old station. Once the guns were remounted on the east side of the battery and pointed to the *Tamar*, she weighed anchor, followed by the *Cherokee* and *Swallow,* and headed with the ebb tide to the lowest point of Sullivan's Island where they anchored out of gun range.[179]

★ The citizens of Charleston resolved to obstruct the passage through the channel to Hog Island Creek, one of the approaches from Rebellion Road, in November 1775. About 2 PM Saturday afternoon, November 9th, Captain Simon Tufts (1722/1723–1799), commander of the South Carolina schooner *Defiance*, mounted with two 9-pounders, six 6-pounders, and four 4-pounders, and with 70 seamen and marines on board, towed four hulks into the channel to sink them on the bar of Hog Island Creek, within gun shot distance of the sloops of war *Tamar* (16 6-pounders) and *Cherokee* with six or eight guns.

The *Tamar* fired six shots at Captain Tufts as he approached his destination. Captain Tufts, who had just anchored, responded with two shots. The *Tamar* continued the cannonade, but Captain Tufts returned only one other shot and proceeded to sink the hulks of three large schooners in the Marsh Island Channel. The fourth hulk did not arrive before the ebb tide, so Captain Tufts remained at his station through the night to sink her when the tide was more favorable.

The *Tamar* and *Cherokee* warped closer to Captain Tufts during the night and fired about 130 shots at the *Defiance* about 4:15 AM on Sunday morning. The cannonade continued until about 7 AM but the vessels were too close for accuracy. Most of the shots passed between the rigging and struck the mainland. The citizens of Charleston watched the latter part of the cannonade and drums called the militiamen to arms. Fort Johnson fired three 26-pound shots. One fell within a few yards of the *Tamar* and two passed through the enemy's riggings.

Captain Tufts brought the hulk to her proper station, scuttled her in various places, and left her sinking. He then withdrew. The hulk was loaded with sand and took a considerable time to sink. When Captain Tufts retreated a long distance, the *Tamar* sent an armed boat which burned the hulk and towed her into shallow water, where she sank a short while later. Captain Tufts fired a shot at the armed boat but to no effect; so he prudently refrained from wasting ammunition. Captain Tufts received one shot under his counter, one in his broadside, and another cut his fore starboard shroud. Nobody was wounded. He reported to the Provincial Congress the next day that six shots were fired at him before he could anchor and he returned fire with two shots from a pair of 9-pounders, his heaviest weaponry.

★ Two schooner hulks were sunk in the Marsh Island Channel on Tuesday, November 21st. This blocked the channel, forcing all large vessels to pass within musket shot of Fort Johnson. The fort was also strengthened with some additional works.[180]

★ Some enemy movements in early May 1779 gave reason to believe that they intended to attack Fort Johnson. As most of the forces near Charleston were required to defend the city, Fort Johnson was blown up on Wednesday, May 12, 1779, after the ammunition was removed. British Major Valentine Gardiner and a superior number of men attacked Captain Matthew's company of 30 Charleston militiamen who were sent down to cover a party engaged in removing some more of the iron work on Saturday. They lost seven wounded and one taken prisoner. [181]

★ Seven vessels arrived in Charleston from Savannah laden with military stores and provisions for the British army. The crews of the Congressional cruizers captured two and destroyed one.

★ Lieutenant General Sir Henry Clinton, the Commander in Chief of the British Army in North America, set out from New York with some 8,700 soldiers aboard a fleet of ships in December 1779. Vice Admiral Marriot Arbuthnot commanded the fleet. Clinton launched his new offensive against Charleston with a landing on Simmons (now Seabrook) Island on February 11, 1780 and gradually deployed his forces about the city.[182]

★ Major Chevalier Pierre-Jean François Vernier (1736–1780) and the remnants of Brigadier General Casimir Pulaski's (1747–1779) Legion were on James Island along the Stono River on Saturday, February 26, 1780. Residents informed him that the Crown forces sent a large number of men to rustle cattle and forage in the area every day. This day, the foraging party consisted of detachments from the British 7th and 23rd Regiments with 50 men. Vernier followed them as they marched back to camp. His men had only four rounds each, so he set an ambush in a narrow passage between two ponds. When the troops entered the narrow area of the ambush, Vernier's cavalry attacked them from all sides. The British had little room to maneuver and fired at their attackers too soon. Vernier's dragoons killed three soldiers and wounded many others before they could reload their muskets. The British camp, alerted by the gunfire, rushed to assist their comrades. An intense firefight ensued in which 10 British were killed and nine wounded. Vernier captured several horses before retreating.[183]

★ Fort Johnson, on James Island, was dismantled, disarmed and evacuated when British Major General Augustine Prevost (1723–1786) advanced from Savannah in 1779. It was subsequently occupied by the Continentals who demolished it on Sunday, February 20, 1780 as General Henry Clinton (1730–1795) advanced for the second invasion of Charleston. The Hessians took the destroyed fort from the rear or landward side on Saturday, February 26, 1780. They garrisoned it but found that it no longer provided any protection. The Continental Navy vessels *Ranger* and *Providence* fired into the fort with little or no effect.

★ The next day, the Continental Navy vessels *Boston* and *Ranger* and the South Carolina frigate *Bricole* came from Sullivan's Island to fire on Fort Johnson. The cannonade killed three men and the Crown forces installed a 24-pounder, a 12-pounder and an 8-inch howitzer to fire at the Continental Navy.

★ The *Providence, Boston* and *Ranger,* stationed in the channel at Sullivan's Island, came up the river Monday afternoon, February 28th and anchored off the left bank, an unprotected side, below Fort Johnson and cannonaded a work party repairing a redoubt in the fort. A Hessian captain brought up some grenadiers, from the Grenadier Battalion von Graff, and two artillery pieces to return fire. A shot from the *Boston* killed a gunner and two grenadiers and forced them to move their camp farther back. The pickets of the Hessian grenadiers extended from the mouth of Newtown New Cut to Lighthouse Island. The 42nd Highlanders placed a field piece in the road leading to Fort Johnson and fired upon the *Boston*. In the afternoon, four more schooners with large pieces went up the river to the Wappoo.[184]

★ The *Providence, Boston, Ranger, Bricole, Notre Dame* and several galleys fired into Fort Johnson again at 3 PM on Thursday, March 2, 1780 with no effect. They ceased firing when the first British schooners came over the bar.[185]

★ Congressional vessels fired grape shot at the Hessians constructing gun batteries at Fort Johnson with no effect on Friday, March 10, 1780. The attack caused the Crown forces to strengthen the fort that spring by adding cannon on the unprotected sides and building a fortification at Wappoo Cut on James Island with a redoubt between it and Fort Johnson to defend against a land attack.[186]

★ Captain Thomas Simpson's (ca. 1728–1784) *Ranger* exchanged fire with Fort Johnson, now occupied by the Crown forces, as he sailed to Charleston on Tuesday, March 21, 1780.

★ The batteries at Fort Johnson fired on four British ships as they approached the fort on Thursday, April 20, 1780. Another battery on Mount Pleasant exchanged fire with the HMS *Sandwich* on the 23rd.[187]

★ Colonel Engineer Thaddeus Kosciusko (1746–1817) and about 20 dragoons went to Fort Johnson on James Island on Thursday, October 10, 1782. As they approached the British picket, he ran away. The fort fired two alarm guns but the Continental raiders captured 48 horses and sent them to the Quartermaster General. They also wanted to capture the cattle in the pasture with the horses but they were too strongly guarded.[188]

★ Captain William Wilmot (d. 1782), of the Maryland Line, reconnoitered James Island on Wednesday, October 23, 1782, and discovered that 50 to 100 British sailors arrived at Dill's Bluff every morning at the same time to cut wood. He reported his finding to Colonel Engineer Thaddeus Kosciusko (1746–1817) who led Captain Wilmot and his 50 to 60 Marylanders onto James Island that night. They waited until late the next morning to ambush the sailors; but the sailors never arrived because the British had learned of the attempted ambush and changed the woodcutters' schedule. They also increased the woodcutters' escort from 20 men to a force of infantry and cavalry from the command of Major William Dansey, of the 33rd Regiment, at Fort Johnson.

★ Colonel Engineer Thaddeus Kosciusko (1746–1817) made a second attempt on the woodcutters three weeks later with Captain William Wilmot's (d. 1782) Marylanders and Lieutenant John Markland's (1755–1837) Pennsylvanians. They engaged the woodcutting party's escort on Thursday morning, November 14, 1782. The British were better prepared than Kosciusko had anticipated. They quickly brought reinforcements and Kosciuszko soon faced at least 300 men and a field piece. The intense fight left Captain Wilmot dead and Lieutenant Markland wounded. A number of casualties were left on the field, including a mulatto slave named William Smith who was wounded and taken prisoner as the Congressional forces withdrew. British Regulars killed five and captured about five. Four musket balls pierced Kosciusko's coat and another musket ball shattered a spontoon (see Photo SC-21) in his hand but he was not harmed. A British dragoon came close to cutting him down but William Fuller, a young volunteer, killed the dragoon.[189]

SC-21. Spontoon. The spontoon is a sergeant's symbol of authority. It can be used as a weapon; but it is more commonly used to line up and manage the troops. The sergeant leading the column is carrying a spontoon.

Sullivan's Island, Charleston County

Fort Sullivan/Fort Moultrie (Sept. 18, 1775; Dec. 19, 20, 1775; Jan. 5, 1776; June 21, 1776; June 25, 1776; June 28, 1776; Nov. 1777; April 8, 1780; April 12, 1780; April 20, 1780; April 25, 1780; Sept. 1, 1780)

Ash's Plantation, Haddrell's Point (Dec. 5, 1775; Dec. 13, 1775)

Haddrell's Point (Pest House) (Dec. 19–20, 1775) (see also **Charleston Harbor** p. 150)

> Sullivan's Island was named for Captain Florence O'Sullivan, one of the earliest settlers of South Carolina. It is southeast of downtown Charleston and is the site of Fort Sullivan, called Fort Moultrie (website: **www.nps.gov/fomo/index.htm**) after the battle in 1776. It was neglected after the American War for Independence and little of it remained by 1791. It was replaced by a new fort in 1794, but the sea destroyed it within 10 years. The present fort (see Photo SC-22) was built between 1807 and 1811 a little to the rear of the first one. The fort saw no action during the Civil War and remained active until World War II when it was deactivated in 1947. The National Park Service assumed administration of the site as part of Fort Sumter National Monument in January 1961. It is at 1213 West Middle Street, Charleston. It can be reached via routes U.S. 17B and SC 703.
>
> Thomson Park is a small public park on Sullivan's Island at 3241 Middle Street near the Thompson Memorial Bridge. It marks the site of the battle at Breach Inlet.

SC-22. Fort Moultrie was constructed of palmetto logs. The reconstructed fort in the background is made of stone. A palmetto tree grows in the foreground.

> Dedicated on June 28, 2011, the 235th anniversary of the battle of Breach Inlet, it has several interpretive markers.
>
> Haddrell's Point goes from Shem Creek to the Inland waterway between Mount Pleasant and Sullivan's Island.
>
> There were several Pest Houses at different times and locations on Sullivan's Island. They were used to quarantine all slaves coming into Charleston. The Pest House of interest here was about 400 yards northwest of Fort Moultrie.

Captain Edward Thornbrough (1754–1834) sent some men from the HM Sloop *Tamar* ashore on Sullivan's Island on Monday morning, September 18, 1775, to cut down the wood to prevent the Rebels from raising a battery on the island. The *Tamar* fired one 6-pounder with round shot and seven swivels with round and grape shot to cover the landing party.[190]

★ Captain Jacob Milligan (1747–1796) observed huts being built with slave labor on Sullivan's Island when the HM Sloop *Scorpion* captured his vessel, the *Hetty*. These huts were part of an encampment being built to house the crews of the British warships in Rebellion Road during the winter months. Milligan reported his observations to the Council of Safety which also learned that "Lord William Campbell had gone to great lengths in harboring & protecting Negroes on Sullivant's Island from whence these villains made nightly sallies and committed robberies & depredations on the Sea Coast of Christ Church Parish." The island had been public property and the British warships were using the only structure standing, an old quarantine station or pest house, as a watering station.

William Henry Drayton (1742–1779) and Doctor David Oliphant (1720–1805) were appointed commissioners on Saturday, December 2, 1775, to determine a location for a battery at Haddrell's Point to counter the activity of the Royal Navy ships. The work at all the other fortifications across from Charlestown Neck ceased on December 6th and the workers and their equipment were transported over the Cooper River to Mount Pleasant.

Colonel William Moultrie (1730–1805) cleared Sullivan's Island of all English sailors "and Negroes, who are said to have deserted to the enemy" before construction of the battery on Haddrell's Point. He was also ordered to drive the British off the island by burning the "pest house" that they were using as living quarters.

Moultrie sent Major Charles Cotesworth Pinckney (1746–1825) and 150 men to Haddrell's Point on Saturday, December 9, to "surprise, seize and apprehend a number of negroes who are said to have gone over to the enemy together with every person on the island." Pinckney headed to a fording place that had recently been discovered between Haddrell's Point and Sullivan's Island but he was unable to find the ford or any boats to cross; so he returned to Charleston. Since none of the Carolinians wanted to be bombarded by three armed vessels, the delay may have been intentional.

Captain John Tollemache took the HM Sloop *Scorpion*, the *Palliser*, "two Bermudian Sloops, and a Schooner, along with thirty to forty slaves and an excellent black pilot" and returned to the Cape Fear River (North Carolina) because there was no longer any opportunity of getting food from the town of Charleston. This left only the HM Sloop *Cherokee* and the HM Sloop *Tamar* at Charleston.

★ The British "fleet" in Charleston harbor numbered six vessels in December 1775. The Provincial Congress and Council of Safety realized that they needed professional soldiers to man the harbor defenses. Colonel Job Rothmaler and the Prince George County Militia Regiment assumed those duties from Major Francis Marion's (1732–1795) company of the 2nd South Carolina Regiment.

★ The British ships began to execute small raids on the undefended northern side of Charleston harbor. Captain Joseph Maybank's (1735–1783) militiamen had patrolled Haddrell's Point in early October. Captain John Allston's (1740–1787) Raccoon Company, consisting of Native Americans, was ordered to patrol the same area at the end of November. Yet, the British continued to raid the northern part of Charleston harbor to obtain food and supplies to maintain their position in Rebellion Road.[191]

★ The British reconnoitered Hog Island Creek with small boats on Tuesday, December 5, 1775. Men under "Governor Campbell's command" "robbed" John Ashe's (1720–1781) plantation near Haddrell's Point that night.

★ "Men from the Men of War" raided Ashe's plantation again Wednesday night, December 13, 1775 and took some livestock.[192]

★ Captain John Allston's (1740–1787) Raccoon Company of riflemen had been waiting in vain to ambush British troops and did not wait for Major Charles Cotesworth Pinckney's (1746–1825) forces. They crossed over to Sullivan's Island, Tuesday night, December 19, 1775. Lieutenant William Withers (1726–1804 or 1731–1806) and a party of 54 Native American rangers surprised the King's troops and burned the Pest

House on Sullivan's Island at 7 AM the following day. They also destroyed some water casks, and burned "Gunner" George Walker's house. There were no white casualties, but four African Americans "who would not be taken" were killed. The Native Americans captured four white men, four women, and three children. Three of the men were crewmen from the Sloop of War *Cherokee* and one of the prisoners was a boy belonging to Captain Edward Thornbrough's (1754–1834) sloop *Tamar*. He was returned to the ship in the morning.[193]

★ Several British sailors from the HM Sloop *Cherokee* hid from the Native Americans throughout the night. The following morning, when they were taken off the island in boats with about 20 slaves, the Native Americans "were permitted to fire (being all rifle men) and must have killed every sailor what appear'd in the boats." The Whigs had no casualties but a Whig source reported that the British sailors were "much frightened by the whooping & appearance of a party from our Indian Company." Lieutenant John Withers (1755–1800) captured 16 prisoners, both fugitive slaves and Loyalists. He also destroyed a number of water casks belonging to the ships and left the island unsafe for future British landing parties. The Native Americans were ordered to stand guard on the island until regular troops could relieve them.

The Carolinians could now build the battery on Haddrell's Point that would consist of four 18-pounders. The 200 Continentals constructed 228 fascines to build the 58-foot long battery on December 22. They worked all through the night and the next day before the British ships observed them. The battery had walls that were 24 feet thick and two guns ready for action that were larger than those on the ships. The British ships weighed anchor and moved to a position near the Bar before the Whigs constructed another battery on Cummings Point that would trap them in the harbor.[194]

★ Captain John Ferguson's HM Sloop *Cherokee* exchanged shots with a Rebel battery on Sullivan's Island at 9 AM on Friday, January 5, 1776. She fired round shot from four 4-pounders and six 3-pounders at a large pettiauger (see Photo SC-23) full of armed men who were trying to carry off the fishing boat which the *Cherokee* had detained. Fort Johnson, on the north shore, fired eight guns at the *Cherokee* which weighed her best bower (see Photo SC-24) at 10 and anchored farther east.[195]

★ After the evacuation of Boston on Sunday, March 17, 1776, General William Howe (1732–1786) stayed at Halifax, Nova Scotia, from March until June, awaiting the arrival of supplies and reinforcements. While he tarried, the British government ordered another diversion in the South, aimed at encouraging the numerous Loyalists who, according to the deposed royal governors watching from their refuges on board British warships, were waiting for the appearance of a British force to rise and overthrow Rebel rule. The British believed large numbers of Loyalists in the South would rise and support the military.

Without an exact plan, they wanted to see which colony offered the best conditions for military operations. General Howe saw this as an opportunity to rid himself of his subordinate, General Henry Clinton (1730–1795), as the two had quarreled over strategy since Howe assumed command from General Thomas Gage (1719–1787) in April 1776.

Clinton wanted to accede to the wishes of the deposed royal governor of Virginia, Lord John Murray, 4th Earl of Dunmore (1732–1809), and conduct operations in Virginia. But Admiral Sir Peter Parker's (1721–1811) recent reconnaissance mission to Charleston showed that the Rebel fortifications guarding the harbor were not completed, so General Clinton agreed to seize the port of Charleston.

Charleston and Vicinity   127

SC-23. Pettiauger Mercury (replica). Courtesy of Gene Tozzi, Sailing Master, Pettiauger Mercury.

SC-24. HMS Victory, a British frigate, man-of-war or ship of the line. The best bower is the large anchor at the starboard front of the ship.

Unfortunately, Admiral Parker's naval squadron, sent from England, was delayed and did not arrive in the Charleston area until June 1, 1776. By that time, all hopes of effective cooperation with the Loyalists had been dashed. Loyalist contingents had been completely defeated and dispersed in Virginia, North Carolina, and South Carolina. Parker remained undeterred and determined to attack Charleston, the largest city in the South.

The Second Continental Congress sent Major General Charles Lee (1731–1782) to command 6,500 Continental soldiers and the Southern defenses. Lee and Governor John Rutledge (1730–1800) clashed over the utility of Fort Sullivan. Rutledge wanted to use it against the approaching British fleet. Lee, fearing that the garrison would be easily overwhelmed and defeated, wanted to abandon it.

Fort Sullivan, a fortification located on the western end of Sullivan's Island, was still under construction to guard the entrance to Charleston Harbor. It was made of three walls of palmetto logs (see Photo SC-22). Each one had a forward section of palmetto logs and another section 16 feet behind the first. Sand filled the space between the sections. The combination of the spongy wood of the palmetto logs and the sand acted as a shock-absorber under fire. Moreover, palmetto does not splinter like other woods or shatter like stone. Only the two walls and two bastions facing the sea were completed when the British attacked. An existing but old fort, Fort Johnson, guarded the other side of the harbor entrance.

Colonel William Moultrie (1730–1805) commanded a garrison of approximately 750 men at Fort Sullivan, renamed Fort Moultrie after the battle. The defenders consisted of the South Carolina militia and Continentals from North Carolina and Virginia as well as newly raised troops. They manned 25 guns ranging from 9- to 25-pounders.

★ An advance party of Colonel William "Danger" Thomson's (1727–1796) South Carolina militiamen, at the northeast of Sullivan's Island, fired several shots at the British armed schooner *Lady William*, another armed sloop, and a pilot boat on Friday, June 21, 1776. Several shots hulled the vessels anchored in Breach Inlet between Long Island and the mainland. The British retaliated by firing shells (see Photo SC-25) for several mornings and evenings at the vessels and firing field pieces at the advanced post with little effect.[196]

★ The battery on the northeast point of Sullivan's Island began firing at the schooners and armed vessels in the creek at daybreak on Tuesday, June 25, 1776. Some shots struck the vessels, forcing them to retire farther into the creek. A party of Highlanders then took a position at Oyster Bank opposite the Rebels' works on the northeast point of Sullivan's Island and kept up a brisk fire.[197]

★ Admiral Sir Peter Parker (1721–1811) decided to attack Fort Sullivan at 11 AM on June 28, 1776. The naval attack was an unwise decision, somewhat comparable to that at Bunker Hill. Fortunately for the defenders, the British had to mount an uncoordinated attack in haste. General Henry Clinton (1730–1795) landed his troops on Long Island, now known as the Isle of Palms. After landing 2,500 men on the island, he learned that Breach Inlet, the narrow channel between Long Island and Sullivan's Island, contained very swift currents and deep holes—even at low tide—preventing his troops from wading across. The Rebels had also constructed breastworks across Breach Inlet to challenge any attempt to cross from Long Island and Colonel William "Danger" Thomson's (1727–1796) riflemen prevented any British attempt to cross over to Sullivan's Island from the mainland.

Two 50- and two 28-gun ships moved to within 400 feet of Fort Sullivan. Two 28-gun ships and another with 20-guns positioned themselves behind them. Another 28-gun

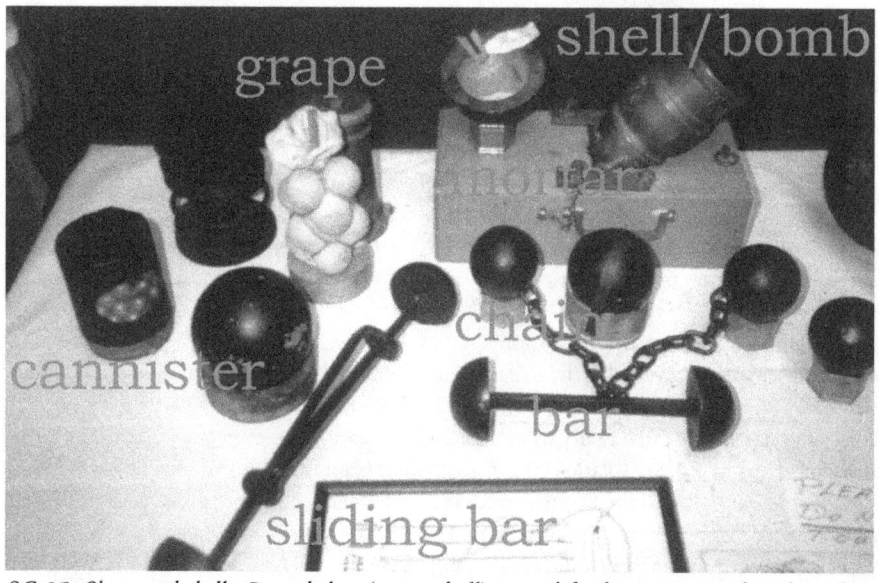

SC-25. Shots and shells. Round shot (cannonball) is used for battering an obstacle such as a fort wall or ship's hull. The ball can be heated (hot shot) to embed in a ship's hull and set it on fire. Grape and canister shots are fired against troops. Chain, bar, sliding bar and star shots are used against vessels to destroy the rigging and immobilize a vessel. A shell, also called a bomb, is a hollow metal ball filled with gunpowder. It has a large touch-hole for a slow-burning fuse which is held in place by pieces of wood and fastened with a cement made of quicklime, ashes, brick dust, and steel filings worked together with glutinous water.

SC-26. Mortar used for firing shells (also known as bombs) in a high arc over fortifications, particularly to get behind walls and other high obstacles that cannons cannot reach. The shell often detonates in the air, raining metal fragments with high velocity on the fort's occupants.

ship and the HM Bomb Brig *Thunder* with a 10-inch mortar (see Photo SC-26) were stationed about a mile and a half southeast of the fort.

The *Thunder*'s mortar exploded when its crew used a larger charge of powder in an attempt to increase its range. About 12:30 PM, the 20-gun *Sphynx*, 28-gun *Actaeon* (or *Acteon*), and 28-gun *Syren* tried to slip to the western end of the fort and ran aground on the Middle Ground of the Charleston Bar where Fort Sumter was later built. Some historians speculate that slave pilots who favored the Whigs may have been responsible for grounding the three vessels and for keeping the others at a considerable distance from the fort. The crews managed to extricate the *Sphynx* and *Syren* but could not dislodge the *Actaeon*.

The *Actaeon* had one lieutenant killed and Captain Christopher Atkins (1728–1791) set her on fire to prevent her from falling into enemy hands. Captain Jacob Milligan (1747–1796) of the Carolina warship *Prosper* boarded the *Actaeon* and took her bell, colors and as many sails as his three boats could carry. He even managed to fire the *Actaeon*'s guns at Admiral Parker's flagship *Bristol*. Captain Milligan escaped before the *Actaeon* blew up. She burned to the waterline and at least 16 of her guns were recovered and later used to arm Congressional shore batteries.[198]

The defenders in the fort were low on gunpowder, so they conserved their cannon fire and concentrated on the two 50-gun vessels. Their limited firing was very effective. The *Bristol*, sustained over 70 cannon hits. Her sister ship, the 50-gun *Experiment*, received almost as many hits. Moreover, Sir Peter Parker suffered the ultimate indignity of losing his pants. Some accounts say they were set afire from cannon fire. Others say they were destroyed by splinters from a cannon shot.

Meanwhile, the British cannonballs bounced off Fort Sullivan's walls. The vessels could not get close enough to the fort to allow the marines to snipe at the Rebels from the rigging. The British took severe casualties, and many of the ships sustained heavy damage in the engagement. The battle raged until 9:30 PM when the British ships ceased firing. Parker ordered his fleet to withdraw from the harbor entrance about 11 PM that night. The crew of the *Actaeon* burned her and sailed with the fleet, but the Rebels later salvaged equipment from the ship.

Casualties in this battle vary in different sources. Estimates put the Whigs' losses at 12 men killed and 20 wounded and British casualties at approximately 225, including 64 dead. The *Bristol* alone suffered an estimated 40 battle deaths and 71 wounded. The Continental Congress declared the independence of the 13 American colonies six days later.

General Clinton's forces remained on Long Island for another three weeks and then withdrew from the area by sea. Parker's battered fleet, already behind schedule, sailed northward to join Admiral Richard Howe (1726–1799) in New York on Monday, July 31, 1776. The Continentals used the *Actaeon*'s own guns to fire on the retreating navy. The British left the south unmolested and the many Loyalists there without support for three years following the fiasco at Charleston. They returned in 1779 to capture Savannah and then Charleston in 1780. South Carolina added a palmetto tree to its state flag to commemorate the victory at Sullivan's Island. One grateful Charlestonian sent a hogshead of old Antigua rum to the fort's garrison.[199]

★ Captain John Ferguson's 32-gun British frigate *Brune* sank Captain Eliphalet Smith's (d. 1777) South Carolina privateer schooner *Volunteer* about 75 miles east-southeast of Sullivan's Island in November 1777. The December 2, 1777 issue of the *Gazette of the State of South Carolina* reported the *Brune* "inhumanely" fired a full broadside into the small schooner killing the captain.[200]

★ When the British returned to Charleston in early 1780, Fort Moultrie commanded the approach to the harbor and threatened any advance on the city. Admiral Marriot Arbuthnot (1711–1794), aboard Sir Andrew Snape Hamond's HMS *Roebuck*, led eight frigates and three transports out of Five-Fathom Hole at 4 PM on Saturday, April 8, 1780. The squadron sailed in the following order: 50-gun *Roebuck*, 32-gun *Richmond*, 44-gun *Romulus*, 31-gun *Blonde*, 32-gun *Virginia*, 31-gun *Raleigh*, armed ship *Sandwich*, and 50-gun *Renown*. They had "a splendid wind and a strong tide, and aided by fog" when they passed Fort Moultrie at 4:30. The fort's 43 cannon, mostly 24-pounders, belched fire until the *Roebuck* came by. She "replied with a broadside and then sailed by without loss and without delay." The *Richmond* followed without engaging Fort Moultrie. She attacked another fort just beyond and lost her fore-topmast in the ensuing cannonade. Several cannonballs went through the ships without doing any damage. The *Romulus* relieved the *Richmond*, attacking in the same manner. The rest of the ships followed and gave a broadside as they passed the fort.

After two hours, and extensive damage to the *Richmond*, the *Aeolus (Eolus)*, one of the three transports, loaded with guns, ammunition, and supplies, ran aground on a sandbank off Haddrell's Point and endured a terrific cannonade from the fort. The incoming tide re-floated her, but she was so shot to pieces that her crew set her on fire and abandoned her after removing her equipment.

When the rear guard passed the fort, the *Renown* took in her sails and covered the rear of the squadron. She gave such an unrelenting fire that the whole ship seemed to flare up. The squadron anchored at Fort Johnson on the opposite shore by 6:30 PM. They lost seven killed and one midshipman and 13 men wounded, most of them from the *Renown*.

The occupants of the fort considered this place impassable and were so dumbfounded when the squadron passed that they suddenly ceased firing. The Hessians finished constructing the sailors' battery (Number 2) during the night. The guns of Fort Moultrie cannonaded them the next day but without effect.[201]

★ A British frigate and two schooners passed the works on Sullivan's Island on their way up the Ashley River to join the fleet which had arrived from New York. The vessels passed about 5 PM on Wednesday, April 12, 1780, under very heavy gunfire and joined the other vessels without firing a shot. The Crown forces did not want to lose any time in cutting off all communications with Charleston. The 23rd, the 33rd Regiments and the British Legion marched to the rear to cross the Cooper River and take post at Cainhoy (see **Cainhoy** p. 177) in the afternoon. [202]

★ Continental batteries fired on four British ships heading to Fort Johnson on the 20th.

See **Charleston** (p. 132) for the account of the siege of the city.

★ Lieutenant Colonel Banastre Tarleton (1744–1833), surprised and captured nine Congressional sloops with goods, stores, etc., and twenty cannons on Thursday, April 20, 1780. They were probably captured in the Cainhoy area or further up the Wando River where the river is only about 0.25 miles wide.[203]

★ The HMS *Germain* exchanged fire with Fort Moultrie as she passed Sullivan's Island on Tuesday, April 25, 1780.[204]

★ The Whig privateer *Rhodes*, with a crew or 130 men and armed with 20 6-pounders, captured the British ship *Lyon*, 12 leagues (36 statute or nautical miles) from Charleston around Friday, September 1, 1780.[205]

Charleston (April 21, 1775; April 29, 1775; April 21, 1777; May 20, 1779; March 20, 1780; March 21 1780; March 30, 1780; Feb. 11 to May 12, 1780: April 1, 3, 4, 8, 10, 11, 12, 13, 14, 16, 17, 18, 19, 20, 21, 22, 23, 24, 25, 26, 27, 28, 30, 1780; May 1, 2, 5, 6, 12, 1780; April 14, 1782)

Hobcaw Magazine (April 21, 1775)

Near Charleston (Sept. 4, 1777; Aug. 13, 1781)

Old Race Track (May 11, 1779)

Snider House (April 14, 1782)

> The Old Exchange and Provost Dungeon (see Photo SC-27) (122 East Bay Street at Broad Street website: **www.oldexchange.com/**) was built in 1771 as the Customs House and Exchange for the prosperous city of Charles Town. The British imprisoned prominent Whigs in the cellars during the American War for Independence. The excavated half-moon battery portion of the wall that surrounded Charles Town in the late 1600s is visible in the dungeon.
>
> The *London* landed at Charleston with 257 chests of tea and an assortment of other goods destined for New York on December 2, 1774. Protesters persuaded merchants not to import the tea. When the twenty-day period for payment of the duty expired, customs officers confiscated the tea and put it in storage in the

SC-27. The Old Exchange and Provost Dungeon was the Customs House and Exchange for the prosperous city of Charles Town. The British imprisoned prominent Whigs in the cellars during the American War for Independence.

Exchange. One report said that the tea was rotting from dampness. Another account says that it was subsequently sold at auction in July 1776, to pay for war expenses. George Washington (1732–1799) was entertained several times in the Great Hall which also served for the election of delegates to the First Continental Congress, the reading of the Declaration of Independence and the ratification of the U.S. Constitution.

Charleston has many historic buildings and 18th-century sites of interest, but urban development has obliterated any traces of both lines and the parallels the Crown forces dug as they moved closer to the Continentals. All that remains of the battle is a small section of the defensive hornwork (see Photo SC-28) on the west side (King Street side) of Marion Square.[206]

Hobcaw Magazine was in the Mount Pleasant section of Charleston near the mouth of Molasses Creek. On the east side of the Arthur Ravenal, Jr. Bridge, follow Johnnie Dodds Boulevard (route U.S. 17 (U.S. 701 Bypass) to Mathis Ferry Road (S-10-56). Proceed about 0.75 miles on Mathis Ferry Road to Muirhead Road (S-10-503) and turn left, then left again at Hobcaw Drive. Proceed to the end and turn left onto Wandolea Drive and go to the end of the road. The site is near the end of the road.

Cochran's Magazine was a bit beyond the end of Shipyard Creek Road in North Charleston. The original colonial era Powder Magazine is at 79 Cumberland Street in Charleston between Church Street and Meeting Street. The State House Armory was in the northwest corner of Broad and Meeting Streets at 77 Meeting Street. General Henry Clinton (1730–1795) and General Charles Cornwallis (1738–1805)

SC-28. Remains of hornwork, Charleston. This tabby block on the west side (King Street side) of Marion Square is all that remains of the hornwork which stood at the center of Charleston's inner defenses during the siege of 1780.

> made their headquarters at Rebecca Brewton Motte's (1738–1815) house at 27 King Street, between South Battery Street and Lamboll Street, during the occupation of Charleston in 1780.
>
> There were several powder magazines located on Magazine Street at various times. The one that exploded on May 15, 1780, might have been near the intersection of Magazine Street and Logan Street.
>
> The Quarter House Tavern was on Meeting Street between Tant Street on the west and just south of Success Street on the east side of Meeting Street. The "Near Quarter House Tavern" site is about a mile southeast of the tavern in the vicinity of Meeting Street and Arbutus Avenue in North Charleston.
>
> General Williamson was captured along Dorchester Road between Dewey Street and Ranger Drive.
>
> Reports of the May 1779 engagement vary between May 8, 9, 14 and 20, 1780.
>
> The site of the action near the Old Race Track was probably near the corner of route U.S. 78 (King Street) and Race Street, about 220 yards west of exit 221A off Interstate 26 in Charleston.

The powder in the old colonial era powder magazine was located in the middle of Charleston near many houses. It was moved to Cochran's Magazine, on Charleston Neck; the Hobcaw Magazine, at Mount Pleasant; and to Forts Sullivan and Johnson, out of the city, prior to April 21, 1775 to prevent destruction of a large part of the city in the event it blew up. The powder remaining in the warehouse and the colonial era magazine was used in the defense of Charleston during the British naval attack on Fort Sullivan in 1776 and the Siege of Charleston in 1780. Some of the powder was shipped to the Cherokees for tribute payments.

★ Charleston Whigs broke into the powder magazines at Cochran's, Hobcaw and the State House Armory on Friday, April 21, 1775, two days after the Battle of Lexington in Massachusetts. They removed all the weapons and ammunition at all three locations in less than three hours. They took the cutlasses, cartridge boxes, matches, flints, and 800 muskets from the State House Armory (stored in the attic of the State House) and 1600 pounds of gunpowder from Cochran's and Hobcaw magazines. When Royal Lieutenant Governor William Bull, Jr. (1710–1791) learned of the theft, he offered a reward for the capture of the perpetrators. However, since the perpetrators were prominent citizens, including Governor Bull's nephews, and many were in the South Carolina legislature, nobody would inform on them.[207]

★ The Royal Navy frigate *Galatea* was cruising off the coast of Charleston on Monday, April 21, 1777, when she spotted two vessels on the horizon. She gave chase and fired three shots at one of them, the privateer *François* bound from St. Eustatius to North Carolina with a load of salt. The *François* slowed and was captured.[208]

★ Captain Nicholas Biddle (1750–1778), commander of the 32 gun Continental Navy frigate *Randolph*, captured Thomas Venture's *True Britain*, after a little resistance, 30 leagues southeast of the Charleston Bar on Thursday, September 4, 1777. The *True Britain* had a crew of 74 men and a complement of 20 6-pounders. Captain Biddle also captured Captain Lyon's brig *Charming Peggy*. Both vessels were headed from Jamaica to New York, laden with rum for the British Army and Royal Navy.

A Congressional cruiser, headed from Jamaica to London, captured Captain James Henderson's ship *Severn* (eight 4-pounders) which the *True Britain* recaptured. Captain Biddle also took a French brig laden with salt going from the West Indies to Charleston which the *True Britain* had also captured. A small sloop accompanying those vessels escaped in the stormy weather while Captain Biddle was manning his prizes.[209]

★ As Major General Augustine Prevost (1723–1786) approached Charleston, he sent five armed galleys through the Callibogie Sound, down Skull Creek and into the Broad River, to capture Fort Lyttleton in Port Royal. As the British vessels approached, the South Carolinians burned the fort and abandoned it on Tuesday, May 11, 1779. They also burned another fort on St. Helena. The British salvaged the guns from both of the forts.

The South Carolinians slowed the advancing army by felling trees across the road and burning bridges along the route of march. General Prevost's troops crossed the Ashley River and proceeded south down the Charleston Neck. Brigadier General William Moultrie (1730–1805) ordered the Charles Town Militia to occupy the left of the line at Charleston Neck to reinforce Colonel Francis Marion (1732–1795) and the 2nd South Carolina Regiment holding the redoubt there. The Upcountry Militia was on the right of the line where Lieutenant Colonel Alexander McIntosh (1732–1780) and the 5th South Carolina Regiment occupied the redoubt. Lieutenant Colonel Harris occupied the advance redoubt in front of the line with the Camden Militia. The remainder of the 2nd South Carolina Regiment and Brigadier General Casimir Pulaski's (1747–1779) infantry occupied the half-moon redoubt in the center of the line as a reserve force.

When Pulaski discovered General Prevost's advance on Tuesday, May 11, 1779, he immediately ordered his infantrymen to prepare an ambush at the Old Race Track within sight of the city's defenses. He left Colonel Michael de Kowatch or Kovats (1724–1779) to position the infantry while he went forward to lead the British cavalry into the ambush. Continental Major James Moncrieff (1744–1793), commander of the engineers, was in charge of the vanguard.

When Captain Thomas Tawse (Taws or Tawes) spotted Pulaski, he ordered his Georgia Loyalist Dragoons to charge Pulaski's Legion. Pulaski and his legionnaires turned about and galloped back to the ambush but Kowatch did not have his men in place. Tawse attacked Pulaski's infantrymen and drove them into the woods, killing Kowatch and 15 of his men and capturing 4. Tawse only had three of his men killed and three others wounded. Pulaski retreated into Charleston with the British in pursuit. The British then besieged the city.

Two Continental armies arrived at Charleston just prior to the siege to aid in its defense; but Southern Department commander Major General Benjamin Lincoln's (1733–1810) army did not arrive from the Augusta area in time. General Moultrie and Governor John Rutledge (1730–1800) negotiated with General Prevost, stalling for time and hoping that General Lincoln's army would arrive soon. When General Prevost received intelligence that General Lincoln was approaching from the west, he evacuated his army under the cover of night.[210]

★ Major General Augustine Prevost's (1723–1786) army of about 3500 men and six 9-pounders plus field pieces and mortars (see Photo SC-26) attacked Charleston (near the Old Race Track) on Sunday, May 14, 1779. Brigadier General William Moultrie (1730–1805) and 1500 men repulsed them with great slaughter. General Andrew Williamson (ca. 1730–1786) was in Moultrie's rear, and within a day's march, with 2000 men. The Crown forces attempted a second, more vigorous, attack when a column of Major General Benjamin Lincoln's (1733–1810) 3000 man army appeared. The Crown forces had to retire from the attack to oppose General Lincoln's corps. The action became general and the Crown forces were routed, leaving 1400 killed and wounded on the field.

The Crown forces crossed the Ashley River and advanced toward Charleston the next day. They attacked the town about 5 PM and kept up their fire until 9:30 when they were repulsed, leaving about 650 men on the field. The Continentals lost about 120. The Crown forces retreated about 5 miles that night and were hemmed in between the Ashley and Cooper rivers.[211]

★ General Henry Clinton (1730–1795), urged on by the British government, had determined to push the southern campaign in earnest in 1780. Unable to win a decisive victory in the North, he withdrew the British garrison from Newport, Rhode Island in October 1779, pulled in his troops from outposts around New York, and prepared to move south against Charleston with a large part of his force. With Admiral Comte Jean-Baptiste-Charles-Henri-Hector d'Estaing's (1729–1794) withdrawal, the British regained control of the sea along the east coast, giving Clinton a mobility that General George Washington (1732–1799) could not match.

Applying the lessons of his experience in 1776 (see **Sullivan's Island** p. 123), General Clinton carefully planned a coordinated army-navy attack for this attempt to take Charleston. Leaving Lieutenant General Wilhelm von Knyphausen (1716–1800) in command in New York with more than 15,000 men, Clinton set sail on Sunday, December 26, 1779, with 11 warships and some 8,500 men aboard 90 transports.

Winter storms off the Outer Banks of North Carolina scattered the ships. Two frigates foundered. The transport *George* sank. One transport with Hessian troops even washed ashore on the coast of Cornwall in England. The winds ripped the sails to shreds and blew masts down on the decks. The storm killed many horses, and the troops tossed their carcasses overboard, along with horses they sacrificed to lighten cargoes.

Clinton landed his force on Johns Island, about 30 miles south of Charleston, on Friday, February 11, 1780, then moved up to the Ashley River, investing Charleston from the land side 47 days later. He called for more men from Savannah and from New York. They arrived in March and April. This brought his force to about 14,000, including sailors from the fleet. Washington was able to send only piecemeal reinforcements to Major General Benjamin Lincoln (1733–1810) over difficult land routes. General Clinton laid siege to the city.

★ A band of militia cavalry under Captain William Sanders (1760–1847) surprised a party of Loyalists at Charleston on Monday, March 20, 1780. They killed two and captured one.

★ The Continentals withdrew all their frigates and armed ships into the Cooper River and sank seven schooners when they were confronted by the ships of the Royal Navy on Tuesday, March 21, 1780. They sank the frigate *Queen of France* and an old two-decker between "Shutes Folly" and the city to prevent the British ships from cutting off their retreat by way of the Cooper River if they managed to pass Fort Moultrie.[212]

★ The Crown forces marched down King Street, the main route to Charleston, at 9 AM on Thursday, March 30, 1780, with two 12-pound cannons and two 6-pounders. Major General Benjamin Lincoln (1733–1810) did not have enough men to oppose them. He placed the light infantry companies of the North Carolina brigade and the 2nd and 3rd South Carolina regiments under Colonel John Laurens (1754–1782) and ordered them "to watch the motions of the Enemy and prevent too sudden an approach."

Colonel Laurens posted his troops in a forward redoubt on King Street, about a mile from the city (in the vicinity of Ann and Mary streets), and a detachment of riflemen 1.5 miles ahead of them, about a mile east of John Gibbes's plantation (Lowndes Grove) and about 400 yards west of the Old Race Track. The riflemen set up an ambush in a wooded area along the road which a jaeger officer described as "three hundred Rebels, consisting of Light Infantry and Negroes who had lain in ambush along both sides of the road, in the woods, and had a small defensive position behind them to cover their retreat."

General Henry Clinton (1730–1795), General Charles Cornwallis (1738–1805) and Brigadier General Alexander Leslie (1740–1794) led the Crown troops into the ambush area around noon when they came under fire from the riflemen. John Barriedale, the eleventh Earl of Caithness (d. 1780), was shot through the stomach as he stood beside General Clinton.

As the jaegers returned fire, the light infantrymen flanked the riflemen who, outnumbered, began to withdraw. They "fell back but kept up a considerable fire from behind the Trees," keeping up a running battle until they reached the protection of the redoubt. Colonel Laurens took Major Edmund Hyrne (1748–1783), deputy adjutant general of the Southern Department and commander of the 3rd South Carolina light infantry, to reconnoiter the advancing enemy force. They came too close to the jaegers moving through the trees. A jaeger bullet wounded Major Hyrne in the cheek and knocked him from his saddle. Colonel Laurens "had barely time to cover his Retreat and drive off his horse" to prevent its capture. He then helped Major Hyrne to safety.

When Colonel Laurens returned to the redoubt, he waited for the jaegers to make the first move. Captain Johann von Ewald (1744–1813) ordered the jaegers to bring up an amusette (see Photo SC-29) while the light infantrymen flanked the redoubt. Unaware of the number of cannon in the redoubt, the Hessian light infantrymen advanced slowly, as they only had two amusettes. The light infantrymen fired the amusettes at the redoubt until General Clinton ordered them to stop.

SC-29. Amusette or wall gun. The bottom weapon is a wall gun. It is an oversize musket or rifle (compare with the rifles above it). It is usually mounted on fort walls or fortifications. Because of its weight, it is usually supported in a device such as the one at the bottom of the photo to facilitate aiming.

General Lincoln sent some reinforcements and some artillery with Jean-Baptiste Ternant (1750–1816), a French officer serving with the Continental Army, to support Laurens. Ternant told Colonel Laurens, who was outnumbered, to fall back one platoon at a time because General Lincoln did not want to engage in a battle at this time. General Lincoln also sent countermanding orders which did not arrive before Laurens left the fleches. A small detachment of jaegers occupied the redoubt after Laurens's light infantrymen withdrew.

Colonel Laurens had requested two cannons when the fighting began. Six field pieces arrived by late afternoon. Laurens was puzzled, wondering why they had been sent if General Lincoln wanted to avoid a major encounter. He decided to attack the redoubt he had previously held. He ordered a swift bayonet counterattack. The Continental light infantrymen advanced against the jaegers with bayonets fixed and yelling. They attacked "with considerable violence" and drove off the small jaeger force that left one man dead, one slightly wounded and another missing. The dead jaeger was found two days later with three bullets in his body, clutching Major Hyrne's hat which he had grabbed earlier as a souvenir.

The Crown light infantry counterattacked, forcing the Carolinians to retreat back to their main lines. Suspecting a trick to lure his men into a larger ambush, General Clinton ordered his men to retreat to the redoubt. Major Lowe reinforced the Crown forces in the evening with 90 men and two field pieces. Both sides exchanged artillery fire until nightfall.

This skirmish took place in view of both armies. Many Charleston ladies came out to the works to watch the cannonading. They continued to do so even after the firing from the town had begun. Captain John Bowman (d. 1780) was killed by a British cannon ball. Major Edmund Hyrne (1748–1783) and seven privates were wounded. Major Hyrne's minor facial wound kept him out of action for the rest of the siege. The Crown forces had John Barriedale, the eleventh Earl of Caithness (d. 1780), aide-de-camp to the Commander in Chief, one of the jaegers and several men wounded. The Continental light infantry re-occupied the redoubt.

General Clinton rode to the left of the battlefield after the skirmish and observed a hill which dominated Charleston. It was Hempstead Hill near the Cooper River, 800 yards from the city. He placed his artillery park, powder magazine and laboratories here on Gibbes Farm during the siege of Charleston. Colonel Laurens retired into the city at dusk. He wrote, "Upon the whole it was a frolicking skirmish for our young soldiers." Most of the Crown army camped at John Gibbes's plantation, 2 miles from Charleston. General McIntosh pronounced the whole affair a mere point of honor without advantage! [213]

★ General Clinton landed south of the city, crossed the Stono and the Ashley rivers without opposition, captured Fort Johnson by surprise, and cut the city from the outside world on three sides by Saturday, April 1, 1780. Rather than try to assault the hornworks, he decided to besiege the city. His troops began digging entrenchments that night.

About 3,000 soldiers and laborers marched from John Gibbes's plantation at sunset on Saturday, April 1, 1780. They headed to the place that Major James Moncrieff (1744–1793), General Henry Clinton's (1730–1795) chief engineer, had chosen to begin the siege of Charleston. They were less than 800 yards from the Whig defenses at Hempstead Hill, near the Cooper River. Half of the force began digging the trenches while the light infantrymen and the grenadiers guarded against any attack.

All the wooden buildings in the area were torn down and the wood was used to construct a wall of mantelets 6 feet high and 16 feet long for the troops to work behind. They dug the trenches quickly because the soil was sandy. They built redoubts number 3, 4, and 5 and a communication trench to each of them in a single night without being fired upon. The communication trench used a trench that the Whigs did not fill in so it was the easiest to make.

★ The South Carolinians were surprised to find three redoubts facing them the following morning. They fired a single 24-pounder at the Crown forces who watched boats going up the Cooper River all day on April 2nd, moving civilians and their property out of the city. They strengthened their three redoubts that night and began building Redoubt Number 1 on the Ashley River.

★ A party of Hessian troops worked on two crescent-shaped redoubts about 200 feet from their camp outside Charleston on Monday, April 3, 1780. One redoubt was on the right near the bank of the Ashley River. The other was on the left close to the Cooper River. The Congressional troops brought up some artillery to fire at the work parties. British Captain Russell wrote "The Rebels fired near 300 shot and 30 small Shells but did no manner of Injury." However, one 6-inch bomb killed four British grenadiers and wounded two Hessian grenadiers. The Congressional troops stopped firing at sunset and the Crown troops resumed work on the trenches, focusing on building a battery on Hempstead Hill, about 350 yards away from the Congressional lines. The battery became Redoubt Number 6 but it was only partially completed during the night. It had only one wall toward the enemy batteries and another toward the Cooper River. It was designed for nine cannons with masked embrasures.

Since the Hessians expected a sortie against the two redoubts, Major Ludwig Johann Adolph von Wurmb (d. 1813) and 100 jaegers reinforced the guard of the redoubt on the bank of the Ashley River while Captain Johann von Ewald (1744–1813) took 100 jaegers to the one along the Cooper River. The Continentals fired several shots and a few shells (see Photo SC-25) during the night and, at daybreak, "they directed their entire fire on the two advanced works, killing three soldiers of the 33d Regiment and severely wounding 3 together with two Hessian grenadiers." The Congressional forces directed their fire toward the new battery. They brought three more guns to reinforce the two already in place. They fired more than 600 shots from 12-, 18- and 24-pounders.

★ The 32-gun Continental frigates *Boston* and *Providence,* both anchored in the Cooper River Monday night, April 3, 1780. They set sail about 10 AM and got in position to fire on the flank and rear of the Cooper River redoubt. The *Providence* and two galleys sailed closer to the battery and fired broadsides, but most of the shots went over the battery which was low to the ground. The *Providence* moved away and fired shells into the redoubt. The jaegers were protected by a trench and no one was wounded.

Heavy cannon fire lasted more than an hour before the Hessians brought up two 12-pounders and a howitzer and placed them on a promontory along the Cooper River. The first shots damaged the *Boston*. The frigates fired several more sharp salvos and withdrew. Toward evening, Captain Thomas Simpson's (ca. 1728–1784) brigantine *Ranger* ran up Town Creek and fired. Her deck was crowded with people of both genders. She fired 23 shots at the working party on the unprotected side of the fort and sailed away. Captain Johann von Ewald (1744–1813) wrote that for "over an hour we had to endure heavy cannon fire." One British soldier was killed and another was wounded as they tried to get to the redoubt. Lieutenant MacLeod, of the Royal Artillery, ordered 80 sailors to move a 24-pound cannon and a howitzer close to Town Creek and fired two shots at the *Providence*, forcing her to withdraw. One shot hit the *Ranger* in the bow and lodged in her hull. Captain Simpson then ordered the *Ranger* to return down river. The jaegers withdrew at nightfall.[214]

★ The *Ranger* proceeded up Town Creek and fired on the Crown forces' camp outside the city again on Tuesday, April 4, 1780. She was forced back by enemy gunfire.

★ The Crown forces closed the back of Redoubt Number 6 during the bombardment and began constructing Redoubt Number 2 about 200 paces in front of the parallel after sunset. The Congressional forces fired at the workmen all night. One of the bombs fell into Redoubt Number 6, between two powder kegs that were just in front of the position occupied by General Henry Clinton (1730–1795) and General Charles Cornwallis (1738–1805). Neither man was hurt.

The firing continued for 24 hours, supported by the *Boston* and the *Providence*. It continued on the morning of the 5th. A total of 573 shells were directed at the two redoubts. Three soldiers of the 33rd Regiment were killed and three others wounded as well as two Hessian grenadiers. Major James Moncrieff (1744–1793) placed two 12-pounders and a howitzer on a promontory on the Cooper River and drove off the frigates.

A Congressional brigantine, whose deck was "crowded with men and women," sailed toward the British works in the early evening and fired 23 shots. She then sailed back and the army resumed firing during the evening. A cannonball struck Alexander Grant of the 42nd Highlanders but he survived. A grenadier of the 23rd Fusiliers lost an arm, and a fusilier of the 7th Regiment deserted. A British battery fired randomly onto the Cooper River to prevent any frigates from approaching the flanks of the redoubts.

General Clinton ordered the Fenwick batteries across the Ashley River to fire upon the city, and not the enemy defenses, at 9 PM. Two British row galleys also fired hot shot into the town. They fired more than 200 24 and 32-pound balls. One killed a carpenter called Morrow as he was leaving his house. A soldier of the 3rd South Carolina Regiment was wounded at the battery on Cumming's Point. Two balls tore through General Lachlan McIntosh's (1727–1806) quarters and killed two of his horses. Five others hit a house and the outbuildings.

The Congressional batteries replenished their ammunition and supplies throughout the following day, April 6th. Each battery was ordered to have 100 rounds per gun and an equivalent amount of powder. Meanwhile, the British placed a battery of nine 24-pounders in the first parallel. Sailors and slaves had to carry the guns and the ammunition across the swamps from the landing place at Gibbes's plantation. The battery was manned by 200 sailors. The Crown forces also dug straight, instead of zigzag, approach trenches from the first parallel toward the Congressional works. They had completed a parallel of 2 miles in three days.[215]

★ A squadron of 11 British warships successfully forced the passage past Fort Moultrie (formerly Fort Sullivan) and exchanged fire with the fort as they proceeded up the Ashley River on Saturday, April 8, 1780. The attackers lost 27 seamen killed or wounded and succeeded in investing Charleston from the sea. The siege then proceeded in traditional 18th-century fashion for almost a month.

At 1 PM that same afternoon, 11 Congressional schooners and sloops sailed down the Cooper River bringing reinforcements of 750 Virginia Continentals under Colonel William Woodford (1734–1780) and 120 North Carolina militiamen under Lieutenant Colonel Henry William Harrington (1747–1809). They landed at Gadsden's Wharf and marched to the lines where they were greeted with cheers and a 13-gun feu-de-joie. They were positioned to the left and right of the hornwork.

★ General Clinton already had cannon in place within 800 yards of the Continental Army's defenses by April 8. On April 10, he began cutting their line of supplies from the north which Brigadier General Isaac Huger (1743–1797) and three regiments of cavalry kept open 30 miles upriver at Moncks Corner. Clinton sent the Queen's Rangers and Lieutenant Colonel Banastre Tarleton's (1744–1833) British Legion to destroy the Continental camp in a surprise attack by night.

Major General Benjamin Lincoln's (1733–1810) 5,150 Continentals and militiamen were greatly outnumbered, even with the reinforcements General George Washington (1732–1799) sent from Morristown, New Jersey. But they had to try to defend the city for political reasons, even though Lincoln knew that it was more important to preserve his fighting force than to defend the city. He concentrated his forces in a citadel on the neck of land between the Ashley and Cooper rivers, leaving Fort Moultrie in the harbor lightly manned. Forts Moultrie and Johnson had fallen into disrepair after the attempted invasion in 1776.

Governor John Rutledge (1730–1800) pressed some 600 slaves into building new fortifications across the neck between the two rivers. The enemy would encounter a water-filled ditch, then two rows of abatis, followed by a trench filled with logs and branches. Large holes in the ground would impede a charge before the enemy reached the redoubts and breastworks. The center of the earthworks consisted of a hornwork (see Photo SC-28) made of tabby, a mixture of lime and oyster shells. This hornwork comprised two bastions (see Photo SC-15) connected by a curtain or wall and a wall running back from each bastion.

The defenders stood behind these fortifications which the British described "as a kind of citadel." What appeared as a good defense was just an illusion, as the Continentals had no escape route if Clinton and the British fleet chose to attack. They also had no hope of getting adequate reinforcements anywhere. Instead of taking advantage of the two rivers as lines of defense, General Lincoln left them virtually unguarded.

★ The Hessians dug several hundred feet of trenches between their redoubt on the right, near the bank of the Ashley River, and the sailors' battery during the night of Tuesday, April 11, 1780. The engineer laid out a demiparallel from the advanced battery up to an inundated area on the right front of the Continental outer works. Meanwhile the besieged did their best to disturb this work.

The Congressional forces fired artillery at the Hessians all night. They continued bombarding the trenches the following morning, firing 300 cannon shots and 41 shells. They killed one jaeger and five Hessian grenadiers. One cannonball took off the head of one of the Hessians. One of the shells burst close to General Henry Clinton (1730–1795).

The Crown troops dug a trench from the first parallel to the advanced Hessian battery that night. The Congressional forces brought up two heavy mortars and four howitzers to the right of the parallel. Each time they fired, the British battery at Fenwick's Point silenced them. One of the mortars exploded when it was overcharged.[216]

★ Brigadier General Alexander Leslie (1740–1794) ordered Captain Johann Hinrichs (d. 1834) to send an officer and 20 men to him at 4 AM on Wednesday, April 12, 1780. Since day was breaking, Captain Hinrichs lost no time. He took 20 men and occupied a half-finished trench which was still out of range to use rifles effectively against the parapet. All the batteries had been ordered to be ready at a moment's notice. Battery Number 2, on the right wing, had one 12-pounder, eleven 24-pounders, and one 9-inch howitzer. Battery Number 6, on the left wing had hot shot. However, at 11 o'clock, the batteries were ordered not to open fire during the day. Captain Hinrichs's party fired "a few shells and twenty to thirty grape shot and cannon balls, without losing a man."

The Hessians posted a Captain and 60 men in Batteries Numbers 3, 4 and 5 in place of the two regiments. They spent the day and night carrying ammunition to the magazines for the 21 24-pounders, two 12-pounders, two howitzers, and one mortar (see Photo SC-26) mounted in the batteries. The Continentals fired several gunshots at the workmen every half hour, killing one Hessian grenadier.[217]

★ The British had mounted 17 24-pounders, two 12-pounders, three 8-inch howitzers, and nine mortars in three of the seven batteries by Thursday, April 13, 1780. They then began to dig a second parallel about 750 feet from the canal.

General Henry Clinton (1730–1795) demanded the city's surrender. When Major General Benjamin Lincoln (1733–1810) refused, Clinton's batteries began to bombard the city at 9:30 AM. Redoubt Number 2, manned by navy gunners who were unfamiliar with ricochet fire, silenced, with the first 20 shots, a front redoubt on the Ashley River which had three embrasures and two 18-pounders. Redoubt Number 6 fired several hot shots at the defenders' works; "but they accidentally fell into the city and set fire to a few buildings [seven or eight houses]." Both sides fired fiercely throughout the day, killing two British sailors and one artilleryman and wounding one light infantryman and two sailors. A Hessian grenadier (see Photo SC-30) had his head shot off.

Three British soldiers became casualties when their artillery piece exploded during loading. John Peebles (1739–1832) wrote, "an artillery man lost an arm & an assistant kill'd by one of our own Guns hanging fire & going off when they put in the spunge, a man of the 37th Light Infantry had his backside shot away looking for Balls."[218]

The Crown forces maintained very brisk gunfire through the night; but the Continental gunfire was moderate. Both sides had to make repairs and procure fresh ammunition. The Crown troops

SC-30. Re-enactors portraying Hessian grenadiers wearing blue regimental coats with buff facings, buff waistcoats and breeches, full gaiters with 21 buttons, and miter helmets with brass face plates

opened a second parallel about 130 paces from the right wing of the first parallel, on the left of Battery Number 2 without much interference. Captain Johann von Ewald (1744–1813) occupied the approach on the left with 60 jaegers before daybreak and exchanged rifle fire with the enemy all day long. The three Crown batteries opened a little after daybreak and fired three shots every hour. Their mortars and howitzers fired over 40 shells (see Photo SC-25) but only got a few shells and less severe gunfire in response.[219]

★ Clinton's troops moved to the upper side of the Cooper River to seal off one evacuation route on the 14th. Both sides began a heavy cannonade that would go on for the next three days. Lieutenant Colonel John Faucheraud Grimke (1752–1819) moved some mortars to the right of the Continental line so that they could fire on the Crown work parties all night. Brigadier General William Moultrie (1730–1805) ordered the advanced battery on the left to fire solid shot, "en ricochet," down the Crown trenches. He also ordered a 12-pounder and three 4-pounders in the Cooper River redoubt to keep up a continuous fire of grape shot at the ground between the two parallels. Captain Johann Hinrichs (d. 1834) wrote that 19 18-pound balls and 13 mortar shells had fallen into the second parallel. A British grenadier was killed by a cannonball. A British light infantryman of the 16th Regiment was shot through the eye and four Regulars were killed. Captain Jackson of the row galley *Comet* had his leg shot off and another sailor was wounded during the intense bombardment. The firepower was so effective that the Crown work parties had to "retire for a while."

One North Carolina sergeant was killed by a cannon ball. One of the Charleston artillerymen was killed and another was wounded. Two matrosses of the 4th South Carolina Regiment were also killed.[220]

★ On Saturday, April 15, 1780, the Continentals wounded two British Regulars working on the new parallel.

★ The Hessians continued constructing the approaches, despite very severe fire on Sunday, the 16th. They occupied the advanced work and exchanged fire with Continental riflemen the whole day. The riflemen were protected by a counterapproach which they had constructed from their right up against the advanced trench. Since the Hessians had advanced within rifle range, the besieged fired mostly grape shot (see Photo SC-17) which was answered by 12 coehorns. A light infantryman was shot through the eye as he looked over the wall of the trench and four infantrymen were killed. The so-called Admiral's Battery of six 24-pounders was opened in the afternoon. Admiral Marriot Arbuthnot (1711–1794) had the battery erected close to the mouth of the Wappoo Canal on James Island opposite Charleston.

★ The Crown forces extended the approaches considerably on the 17th and constructed a demiparallel on each side during the night. The Continentals fired at them continuously with grape shot and musketry, killing five Hessian grenadiers and three British and wounding 14. They also enfiladed some of the trenches, firing scrap iron and broken glass which caused the Hessians to lose their composure and seek shelter, even though there was no place to hide. Nine men were wounded in the legs.

The Continentals kept up constant grape shot and small-arms fire through the night as the Hessians tried to finish the trenches. The Continentals killed one light infantryman and either killed or wounded 10 artillerymen and infantrymen and wounded two. British and jaeger snipers and artillery fire wounded 30 Congressional troops.

★ The Crown troops completed the communication trench of the second parallel within 250 yards of the Continental lines during the night of Tuesday, April 18th. They built trestles over the swamp to connect them and placed baskets filled with sand on the trestles for protection. They lost two Hessians and two British grenadiers wounded in this work and they mounted several more coehorns in the second parallel. Reinforcements of almost 3,000 men from New York arrived by ship to reinforce General Henry Clinton (1730–1795). They disembarked at Hamilton's landing place on James Island.

That same day, a cannonball took off part of Philip Neyle's (d. 1780) head. He was Brigadier General William Moultrie's (1730–1805) aide. The Congressional troops built another rifle breastwork to the left of the hornwork to harass the approach of the Crown troops. They killed one British light infantryman and wounded two others along with 10 British artillerymen killed or wounded. Jaeger rifle fire killed five Congressional troops and a shell wounded three others. A 12-pounder from the HMS *Acteon* which was brought into the hornwork burst and wounded two men, including a sentinel who had his arm blown off.

★ The British brought up more coehorns to the second parallel on April 19th and placed them 450 yards from the hornwork. They fired bombs and grenades into the hornwork. Most of the shells fell in the North Carolina camp and killed one man and wounded two others. One highlander of the 71st Regiment was killed in the bombardment and two Hessian and two British grenadiers were wounded.

The Crown forces discovered that a swamp prevented them from connecting the second parallel to the first. They had to dig a third parallel within 800 feet of the main enemy lines with no connection in the middle. The batteries on James Island continued to fire into the Congressional lines throughout the night.[220a]

★ One Anspach jaeger was killed by a cannonball as he rested behind the sandbags (about two feet long and one foot thick and placed 3 or 4 inches apart) on Thursday, April 20, 1780. A party of jaegers occupied the new trench and fired several well-placed rifle shots into the embrasures (see Photo SC-31) which flanked them on the right every time they opened, keeping the guns silent for the rest of the day. The Crown batteries fired so effectively all day that two powder magazines were demolished.

The Crown troops constructed a mortar battery that night and erected a battery for three 6-pounders in the second parallel, right on the highway in the middle of the main road. The Congressional troops fired briskly upon the working party with both cannon and musketry. The Hessians responded with many shells. The Congressional troops shelled their lines, killing three and wounding five. Grape shot killed two British light infantrymen and wounded seven. General Henry Clinton (1730–1795), who was inspecting a partially built redoubt within 70 yards of the enemy lines, wrote in his journal "I run too much risk for my station."[220a]

★ Continental batteries fired on four British ships heading to Fort Johnson on Thursday, April 20, 1780.

★ Captain Adam Sanders (1732–1820) ordered William Hargis (1760–1836) and about 50 men to go up the Wando River in boats to collect all the vessels they could find and bring them to Charleston. Only about 30 of these troops reached Charleston with the boats they had found. Hargis and the rest of his party only reached what was called the old Brickyard on the Wando River on their return on Thursday, April 20, 1780. They had to leave their boats behind to avoid being captured. They escaped into the woods on the east side of the Wando River and went to the Santee River. They crossed the Santee at Duprees and Lippees ferry, since Captain Sanders knew one of the ferry operators.[221]

The situation in the city was beginning to look hopeless. Major General Benjamin Lincoln (1733–1810) could not expect any more reinforcements from Virginia and only

SC-31. Embrasures are openings in a wall for guns. These embrasures are in an earthen wall and are part of the Grand French Battery at Yorktown, Virginia.

received 300 militiamen from North Carolina instead of the 2,500 troops he requested. His commissaries informed him that there were only provisions for 8 to 10 more days and his engineers expected the Crown forces would penetrate their defenses in about a week.

General Lincoln called a Council of War to consider his two options: evacuate Charleston or surrender. The Council adjourned and reconvened twice more before deciding to request a parley on Friday afternoon, April 21. The Council of War drafted proposed terms of surrender which were so generous that General Henry Clinton (1730–1795) and Admiral Marriot Arbuthnot (1711–1794) rejected them as being preposterous. They gave Lincoln until 10 o'clock to surrender. Negotiations were broken off about 9 PM and General Clinton continued bombarding the city. Severe gunfire resumed about 10:30 PM and lasted over two hours.

★ A battery of four 6-pounders was erected during the night to demolish the gate and barrier of the forward ditch on the highway. Both sides engaged in violent firing. The besieged loaded their mortars with anything which could injure the enemy. Continental riflemen used all their power to silence the fire of the jaegers on the 22nd and killed one of them. A grenadier was killed in the trenches by cannon fire and three Whigs were wounded. A servant of a British officer was "blown all to pieces with a shell."[222]

★ Brigadier General William Moultrie (1730–1805) told the Continental batteries to "keep up the fire on the Enemy's Works as usual this night," Sunday, April 23, 1780, as a diversion. They ceased firing at 3:30 AM and were ordered to load all the cannons with grape shot. Meanwhile, Lieutenant Colonel William Henderson (1748–1787) assembled a group of 200 men in the advanced work on the left of the line. He ordered his men to fix bayonets as they would attack Captain Johann Hinrichs (d. 1834) and 30 jaegers and 50 light infantrymen entrenched on Charleston Neck with unloaded muskets. They charged across a temporary bridge into the Crown third parallel before daylight on Monday, April 24. The work parties had finished their work for the night and noticed the attackers coming over the side. The jaegers defended themselves with their hunting swords as the work party fled to the second parallel in panic.

Captain Hinrichs "heard a loud yelling" in the other sections and realized that the Congressional troops had gotten behind the trenches. When the men in the second parallel began firing volleys at the third parallel, Colonel Henderson ordered the men to retreat back to their lines, covered by the artillery firing canister made up of "old burst shells, broken shovels, pickaxes, hatchets, flatirons, pistol barrels and broken locks." General Moultrie wrote in his memoirs "they brought in twelve prisoners, and bayoneted fifteen or twenty more." Seven of the prisoners were wounded.

Two jaegers were bayoneted and killed and four severely wounded. Two Hessians, a British corporal and eight privates were captured without firing a shot. Two grenadiers of the 38th Regiment deserted in the confusion. Henderson lost one man killed [Captain Thomas Moultrie (ca. 1740–1780) of the 2nd South Carolina Regiment, who was General Moultrie's brother] and three wounded. His men left 16 muskets behind which probably belonged to the dead or wounded who were carried back.

General Charles Cornwallis (1738–1805), the Volunteers of Ireland and the North and South Carolinians crossed the Cooper River at the governor's house that night in armed boats and some commandeered craft. They captured a 6-gun privateer which ran aground on the left bank of the Cooper River. The vessel was loaded with rum and rice and waiting for the tide when she was captured. [223]

★ Captain Johann Hinrichs (d. 1834) continued firing the next day and had to move his mortars constantly because of heavy enemy fire. His men would wait until the Congressional troops would open a firing port. They would then fire 100-bullet canisters into them.

Colonel Richard Parker (1751–1780), of the 1st Virginia Detachment, was killed at 8 AM when a sniper's ball hit him in the forehead while he was looking over a parapet. Two privates were also killed and seven wounded.

Major General Benjamin Lincoln (1733–1810) expected the Crown forces to attack, so he recalled most of Colonel Charles Cotesworth Pinckney's (1746–1825) 1st South Carolina Regiment from Fort Moultrie and John Laurens's (1754–1782) light infantry from Lempriere's Point. This added 200 men to the lines.

★ Congressional troops attacked Crown working parties on Monday night, the 24th and killed one officer and wounded two of the 71st Regiment which had some 20 noncommissioned officers and soldiers killed and wounded. The Hessian grenadiers had two killed and 11 slightly wounded. A lieutenant of the engineers was severely bayoneted by his own men through some misunderstanding.

The Congressional troops suddenly appeared behind their abatis on the other side of the ditches around midnight. They opened up severe small-arms fire on the workers causing a terrible panic among the workers who rushed back into the rear trenches and threw the guard there into disorder. The guard began firing indiscriminately, without considering what they fired at. The Hessians reassembled about 3 AM and a severe cannonade continued all night long.[224]

★ Both sides anticipated an attack Tuesday night, April 25, 1780. Some nervous Congressional sentries heard noises at 1 AM and thought the Crown troops were attacking in force. They fired their muskets. The main force in the trenches thought that this was a signal that the Crown troops were assaulting the works. Muskets, rifles and artillery fired across the line at the Crown trenches, causing panic. The Crown forces fired muskets into the night for more than an hour before fleeing to the rear. The men in the first and second parallels saw the men from the third parallel running toward them. Mistaking them for Congressional troops, they fired at their fleeing comrades, killing and wounding many.

★ On Wednesday, April 26, 1780, the Crown forces erected a battery of six pieces to fire on the hornwork. However snipers fired on them as they completed the work, killing two jaegers, two light infantrymen and two grenadiers. Lieutenant Arthur Beaver, of the 33rd Regiment, and eight grenadiers were wounded. A soldier from the 42nd Regiment was killed by a double-barreled blunderbuss when he got too close to a house.

★ Three British row galleys and two schooners fired on the battery at Mount Pleasant on Wednesday, April 26, 1780. Both sides maintained a severe cannonade on the 26th and 27th. The British lost one killed and four wounded during the night of April 27th when a 12-pounder took a direct hit and was disabled. Redoubt Number 7 was "shot to pieces." The Whigs lost one private killed and five wounded. Five militiamen from the James Island Company deserted from the city in a boat.

★ The Crown forces brought four 9-inch mortars and 12 coehorn mortars to the first parallel on Friday, April 28, 1780 so they could fire on the Congressional works. The artillery pieces in the second and third parallels could no longer fire on enemy lines without hitting their own forward defenses. The bombardment killed two privates and wounded Captain James Campbell (1750–1813) (also referred to as Campaign or Campen) and two privates of the North Carolina Line.

Artillery and small arms fire continued against the Crown work parties the entire night, killing six British grenadiers and wounding 14 British and Hessian grenadiers. A Hessian grenadier, who deserted that night, revealed several passwords and informed the Congressional forces of the precise time of relieving the work parties and pickets. This resulted in three British soldiers killed and two others and one Hessian wounded.[225]

★ On Sunday, April 30, 1780 and Monday, May 1st, an Englishman was killed and several men severely wounded, including a jaeger whose arm was shot off. Another Englishman and a jaeger were killed and two Englishmen and one jaeger wounded on Tuesday the 2nd.[226]

★ Cannon and small arms fire continued on May 1. Over 300 rounds were fired that night, killing four British and three Hessian grenadiers, and wounding an equal number. A jaeger and a light infantryman were killed after sunrise and another jaeger had his right arm shot off. Captain Joseph Montford (1728–1798) of the 3rd North Carolina Light Infantry was wounded.[227]

By Friday, May 5, 1780, a third parallel opened only 40 yards away from the Continental earthworks. People could not buy meat, rice, sugar, or coffee. When General Henry Clinton (1730–1795) learned that a new fleet had set sail from France, he wanted to return to New York as soon as possible. He granted Major General Benjamin Lincoln (1733–1810) a truce to discuss terms which were subsequently refused because he thought the Continentals were "not yet sufficiently humbled to accept" British terms. He offered to pardon all Continentals who took an oath of loyalty to the royal government and required those who did not actively support the British to be treated as though they were rebels. Instead of clearly differentiating between friends and enemies, these proclamations forced those who had decided to remain neutral to take sides. Loyalists complained that rebels could gain the privilege of British subjects by taking an oath they would break at the first opportunity.

★ A landing force of sailors and marines took Fort Moultrie on Saturday, May 6, 1780. After the truce expired at 8 PM on May 9th, both sides resumed the cannonade which lasted through the night. Brigadier General William Moultrie (1730–1805) describes the Continentals' final desperate act:
> It was a glorious sight, to see them [the shells] like meteors crossing each other, and bursting in the air; it appeared as if the stars were tumbling down. The fire was incessant almost the whole night; cannon-balls whizzing and shells hissing continually amongst us; ammunition chests and temporary magazines blowing up; great guns bursting, and wounded men groaning along the lines: it was a dreadful night! it was our last great effort, but it availed us nothing.[228]

★ Three days later, at 11 AM on Friday, May 12, 1780, with the enemy within 90 feet of the hornwork, the town surrendered after almost ceaseless bombardment. Major General Benjamin Lincoln (1733–1810) accepted the terms that General Henry Clinton (1730–1795) had offered on April 10. The Union Jack was raised over Charleston at 2 PM, causing one Loyalist to gloat that "the thirteen stripes [were leveled] with the dust."

General Lincoln surrendered all four of South Carolina's remaining Continental regiments, two North Carolina regiments and six Virginia Continental regiments, as well as a large number of North and South Carolina militiamen. The Continentals would remain prisoners of war until exchanged, but the militiamen "were to be permitted to return to their respective homes, as prisoners on parole; and while they adhered to their parole, were not to be molested by the British troops in person or property."[229]

The capture of Charleston, the fourth largest city in the colonies, was one of Britain's greatest victories of the war. Although General Lincoln had very few casualties—only 240 killed and wounded, he surrendered his entire force of 5,466 men, the greatest disaster to befall the Continentals during the war. It ranks as the third largest surrender of Americans in history, after Bataan in World War II and Harpers Ferry in the Civil War. Surprisingly, General Clinton's siege took three months to accomplish what he might have done in half the time.

Clinton also captured 391 guns, 5,916 muskets, 15 regimental flags, and large quantities of supplies. The Crown forces lost 265 men killed and wounded. They lost several more on Monday, May 15, 1780, when they British collected all the Congressional weapons in Mount Pleasant and Charleston. They were warned that some of the weapons were still loaded and should be handled carefully as the Crown troops loaded the wagons. The wagons were then driven to a warehouse on the far west side of Charleston, a sparsely populated area bordered by a creek and marsh. The warehouse there contained 4,000 pounds of ammunition. A Whig powder magazine, only 200 paces away, contained 10,000 pounds of black powder. As the troops began tossing the weapons into the warehouse, there was an explosion.

The exact cause of the explosion is not known, but it most likely was caused by the discharge of a loaded musket. Some accounts say one of the prisoners threw his loaded musket into the magazine. The magazine exploded with such force that debris and body parts were blown about 0.3 miles to the intersection of Meeting and Cumberland streets. It also set fire to several nearby buildings but not the Whig magazine which had a high brick wall around it. Between 200 and 300 people died in the explosion and fire, almost as many as were killed during the Siege of Charleston.

Hessian Captain Johann von Ewald (1744–1813) was going to a Charleston coffeehouse when the explosion occurred. He recalled:
> I had hardly entered the house, when such an extraordinary blast occurred that the house shook. I ran out of the house, saw a thick cloud of vapor a short distance

away, and rushed there. The most dreadful cries arose from all sides of the city. I saw that the magazine into which I intended to go some eight or ten minutes earlier, had blown up with all the people who worked in and around it, along with several adjacent houses. The view was horrible. Never in my life as long as I have been a soldier, have I witnessed a more deplorable sight. We found some sixty people who were burnt beyond recognition, half dead and writhing like worms, lying scattered around the holocaust at a distance of twenty, thirty, to forty paces, and in the confusion one could not help them. We saw a number of mutilated bodies hanging on the farthest houses and lying in the streets. Nearby and at a distance, we found the limbs of burnt people. Many of those who hurried to the scene were killed or wounded by gunshots which came from the loaded muskets in the cellars.

The explosion scattered and mutilated bodies so that it was impossible to "make out a single human figure."

The Continental Army was further humiliated by having to march without music and with flags furled when it surrendered. The British, however, let the officers keep their swords until repeated shouts of "Long Live Congress!" provoked their captors into confiscating them. The British occupied Charleston until Wednesday, December 14, 1782. [230]

★ Part of Brigadier General Francis Marion's (1732–1795) brigade, under Colonel John Irwin (1754–1810), fell in with a party escorting a wagon loaded with flour on Monday, August 13, 1781. The wagon was headed from Charleston to the British at Congaree. The militiamen captured three officers (Captain Niel Campbell and Lieutenants Robison and McGregor) and one private with 200 guineas. Captain John Leacraft or Leacroft (1766–1838), of Colonel William Harden's (1743–1785) regiment, went to Port-Royal where he captured Lieutenant Colonel William Kelsall and several other officers. He also liberated a number of Whig prisoners. [230a]

★ Lieutenant Colonel James Jackson (1757–1806) stopped at a Mr. Snider's house with five of his Georgia Legionnaires to let them rest. Major Philip Dill (d. 1782) and 30 Loyalists landed near Knox and attacked Snider's house before daylight on Sunday, April 14, 1782. Seventeen balls were fired through the house during the fight. Snider and the dragoons returned fire and killed Major Dill and wounded two other Loyalists. The dragoons then chased Dill's men back to their boats, where they managed to escape. [231]

★ Brigadier General Alexander Leslie (1740–1794) evacuated Charleston 19 months after the city's surrender. He agreed not to destroy the city if the Whigs allowed his troops to depart in safety. They moved out of their forward defenses after the firing of the morning cannon on Saturday, December 14, 1782. General "Mad Anthony" Wayne (1745–1796) then moved in with his Continentals. Major General William Moultrie (1730–1805) wrote in his memoirs, "This fourteenth day of December, 1782 ought never be forgotten by the Carolinians; it ought to be a day of festivity with them, as it was the real day of their deliverance and independence."

The British promised freedom to the slaves who came in of their own free will. They honored their commitment. An estimated 25,000 slaves left South Carolina during the British occupation. More than 5,000 slaves and former slaves sailed away with the fleet. Many settled in the Caribbean or in Canada.

The day after the British evacuation, the Maryland Line considered their enlistments ended and prepared to return home. Major General Nathanael Greene (1742–1786) rode to the camp to remind the troops that the war was not yet over. The Treaty of Paris which ended the war would not be signed until September 3, 1783. [232]

Charleston Harbor

Haddrell's Point (Dec. 5, 1775; Dec. 13, 1775; April 28, 1780; April 30, 1780; March or April 1780; May 2, 1780)

Charleston Bar (Nov. 1775, May 21, 1776, May 29–June 3, 1777, July 25, 1777; Jan. 23, 1780; Jan. 27, 1780)

Rebellion Road (Oct. 18, 1775; Nov. 9, 1775; Dec. 5, 1775; June 29, 1781)

Bull's Inlet (March 7, 1778; March 10, 1778; March 17, 1778)

Lemprière's Point (April 26, 1780)

> Haddrell's Point is at the end of Hibben Street at the harbor in the old village of Mount Pleasant. There was a Whig battery there. The fort on the causeway from Haddrell's Point to Sullivan's Island and Fort Sullivan was about 150 yards from the mainland. At high tide, it became an island on the causeway. The area between Shem Creek and The Cove (modern Intercoastal Waterway is considered Haddrell's Point.
>
> Lemprière's Point is southwest of Hobcaw Magazine at the end of 5th Avenue.
>
> The Charleston Bar was a shallow sand bar—only 4 feet deep at points—where the rivers emptied into the ocean southeast of Charleston. To navigate around the Bar, ships would have to go through narrow channels in the Bar and then sail up another channel, while being under the guns of Fort Moultrie. The Bar was Charleston's first line of defense for any naval attack.
>
> Rebellion Road was a shipping channel in Charleston Harbor that was east of Shutes Folly Island.
>
> Bull's Inlet is the entrance to Bull's Bay southwest of Cape Romain.
>
> The April 30, 1780 action occurred in Charleston Harbor less than a mile south-southeast of Haddrell's Point.
>
> The June 29, 1781 action occurred in Charleston Harbor, north of Fort Johnson on James Island.

The HM Sloop *Tamar*, in Rebellion Road, Charleston Harbor, fired 6-pound shots at a boat from Fort Johnson Wednesday afternoon, October 18, 1775, forcing the boat back to the fort.[233]

★ Charleston Bar (Nov. 1775) see **Fort Johnson, James Island** (Nov. 10, 1775) p. 120.

★ Two Provincial armed pilot boats chased the HM Sloop *Tamar*'s pilot boat into Rebellion Road, Charleston Harbor, at 1 PM on Thursday afternoon, November 9, 1775.[234]

★ The Royal Navy was anchored in Charleston Harbor in early December 1775. Fort Johnson blocked one side of the harbor and the Whigs had shut off the Hog Island channel on the other side. The South Carolinians outfitted the frigate *Prosper* to counter the British ships, and the 1st and 2nd South Carolina Regiments manned two pilot boats to prevent any boats from delivering supplies to the British ships. Moreover, South Carolina purchased five more pilot boats to cruise between James Island and Shutes Folly Island and in Hog Island Creek.

Captain Edward Thornbrough (1754–1834) of the *Tamar* outfitted the captured merchant vessel *Polly* with swivel guns in an attempt to capture the two pilot boats in the harbor. Meanwhile, the British ships continued to capture any craft that came into the harbor. The royal sloop of war *Scorpion* arrived in Charleston at the end of November with North Carolina Royal Governor Josiah Martin (1737–1786) on board. Governor Martin and South Carolina Royal Governor William Campbell (d. 1778) disagreed on whether the British squadron in Charleston should attack Charleston or go to Cape Fear (North Carolina).

A large "quantity of fire arms and military stores" arrived in Charleston from the Dutch island of St. Eustatia in the West Indies to arm the Whigs. This induced Captain Tollemache to enforce the blockade of Charleston and stop all traffic from entering the harbor.

The *Scorpion*'s small boats captured the *Hetty* and the *Thomas and Stafford*, their crews and two Charleston pilots at the mouth of Charleston harbor on Tuesday, December 5, 1775. Captain John Tollemache thought that the *Hetty* was such a fine vessel that he commissioned it as a British warship and renamed it the *General Clinton*, bringing the British "fleet" in the harbor to six vessels.

Mr. Fenwick Bull protested the seizure of the ships and that "several Negroes" were on the *General Clinton*. Captain Tollemache "did not deny his having some of our negroes on board, but said they came as free men and demanded protection; that he could have had five-hundred who had offered; that we were all in actual rebellion; and that he had orders to distress America by every means in his power; that had his advice been taken, Fort Johnson should have been attacked on the day of his arrival, if the attack had cost fifty men, and that this town should soon be laid in ashes; but that it would soon be destroyed: that upon his honor he expected soon, two frigates and a bomb to arrive here," Captain Tollemache also carried off an African American harbor pilot when Colonel William Moultrie (1730–1805) refused to return some British seamen who had deserted the *Scorpion* and joined the 2nd South Carolina Regiment.[235]

★ Captain Anthony Hunt, of the HMS *Sphynx*, spotted the privateer brig *St. James* heading for the Charleston Bar with a prize at 5 AM on Tuesday, May 21, 1776. The *Sphynx* fired two guns for the boats to return at 7 AM. The prize ran aground at 11 AM when Captain Hunt ordered lieutenants Bowen and Popple to man all the boats and the schooner with seamen and marines. They boarded the prize in the afternoon, set her on fire and captured two Rebels and three of the brig's crew.

The following morning, the schooner tender *Comet* chased a sailing boat ashore. She came alongside the *Sphynx* with her prize, an open boat, at 6 PM. The boat had 11 casks of turpentine aboard. Captain Hunt turned her adrift and set her on fire.[236]

★ The HMS *Daphne* was headed to St. Augustine, searching for merchantmen along the way. She encountered Captain Elkanah Hathaway's (ca. 1747–1796) sloop *Polly* bound from Charleston to Dartmouth between Thursday, May 29, 1777 and Tuesday, June 3. The *Daphne* captured the *Polly*. Captain St. John Chinnery (1727–1787) sent a midshipman and four sailors to board her as a prize crew to take her to a safe port.

The *Daphne* tried to capture the schooner *Angelina*, bound from Charleston to Curacao the same day. However the British crew could not board her due to the high wind. The *Angelina* escaped in the night.

The *Daphne* continued cruising toward St. Augustine, attacking any merchantmen she encountered. The *Daphne* and her prize ship *Polly* disguised themselves as French ships by flying French colors on Sunday, June 1. The two vessels surrounded six canoes at the Charleston Bar. They captured the canoes which had 25 "very valuable negroes, chiefly tradesmen" on board, 22 of whom were sold at St. Augustine for £13,741. The other three were returned to their Loyalist owners. The *Daphne* also captured Captain Ridley's schooner a few days after leaving the Charleston Bar. The schooner was burned and the *Daphne* continued on her way. These actions may have happened off the Outer Banks of North Carolina.[237]

Captain Francis Morgan's privateer *Experiment* fell in with a 16-gun British brig and a 10-gun sloop off the Charleston Bar Thursday morning, July 25, 1777. He managed to escape "with the loss of a Negro boy killed." However, he saw the sloop capture a Bermudian sloop.[238]

★ The *Daphne* and the *Unicorn* harassed any vessels coming out of Charleston harbor in early March 1778. They drove Captain Joseph Chapman's Boston-based schooner *Live Oak* on the reef of South Santee River on Saturday, March 9th. They drove in a brig within sight of the town on Wednesday, the 10th.[239]

★ Two other British ships, a 10-gun schooner and an 8-gun sloop, saw Captain Howland coming out of Bull's Inlet with a cargo of 25 hogsheads of tobacco on Tuesday, March 17, 1778, and chased his ship back into the inlet. They sent two boats with a total of 16 men to seize Howland's vessel. Howland had a crew of 13 men and four swivel guns (see Photo SC-32) and four muskets but no cutlasses or pikes to repel any boarders. As the boats approached, Howland's crew managed to fire only one volley before the British clambered over his side. A brief but fierce fight ensued until Howland and another man were severely wounded and one of his crewmen was killed. The wounded man was hit in the neck by a shot from a swivel gun. The attackers lost a lieutenant, a boatswain and a carpenter killed and four men wounded. The British stripped their prisoners of all their clothes and shoes and put them ashore in a boat.[240]

★ Commodore Abraham Whipple (1733–1819) and four Continental ships were ordered south from Massachusetts to assist in the defense of Charleston. The ships were the frigates *Queen of France* and *Boston*, and the sloops *Providence* and *Ranger*. They took

SC-32. Swivel gun. The gun mounted on the tree stump is a swivel gun. The mount allows it to rotate in any direction.

27 days to arrive in Charleston, delayed by a heavy gale northeast of Bermuda which damaged the *Queen of France* so much that a "jury of carpenters" condemned her. The fleet arrived on Thursday, December 23, 1779.

Major General Benjamin Lincoln (1733–1810) dispatched the *Ranger* and the *Providence* on Monday, January 17, 1780 to patrol between Cape Romain and St. Augustine, Florida, to give an early warning when any British troop ships might approach Charleston. However, they were becalmed outside the harbor for three days. On January 23rd, they spotted a brig in the fog outside the bar to Charleston harbor. The Captain of the brig mistook the Tybee River for the Savannah River and followed the Continental ships into the harbor and was captured with 17 reinforcements for the New York Volunteers on board. The captured brig was renamed the *General Lincoln* and given to Captain Hoysted Hacker (1745–1814).

★ Commodore Abraham Whipple (1733–1819) and Captain Thomas Simpson (ca. 1728–1784) put out to sea at sunrise on Monday, January 24, 1780. They headed south in search of British vessels. They spotted two Royal Navy sloops and a brig which they quickly overtook and captured off the Tybee Lighthouse in Georgia. The vessels were carrying a few infantrymen, 40 light dragoons of the British Legion and the Bucks County Light Dragoons, seven or eight officers, and an equal number of passengers. A gale off of Cape Hatteras had blown the vessels off course. They had two horses on board, along with the gear for 40 more horses, which was all thrown overboard.

As soon as Commodore Whipple saw the approaching British fleet, he returned to Charleston to alert Major General Benjamin Lincoln (1733–1810). Lincoln wanted Whipple to defend the Bar, but Whipple responded that it was too shallow to allow room to maneuver and couldn't be defended. Three days later, during another reconnaissance, a British ship captured the *Eagle*, the *Ranger*'s tender, outside the harbor and chased both the *Ranger* and the *Providence* back into Charleston harbor.[241]

★ When the British fleet sailed into Charleston Harbor, the fortifications at Haddrell's and Léprière's points prevented it from going up the Cooper River. Colonel Bernard François Lellorquis Marquis de Malmedy (1766–1832) held Léprière's Point with 100 South Carolina Continentals and 200 North Carolina militiamen. The Crown forces marched from Wappetaw Meeting House to the Haddrell's Point Battery on Wednesday, April 26, 1780. Colonel Malmedy learned of their movements and thought that they were planning to attack his position. He panicked, abandoned the fortification and withdrew to Fort Moultrie. The withdrawal was disorganized. The men who tried to escape by boat went to Hog Island by mistake and were captured.[242]

★ The Crown forces captured a small work on Haddrell's Point on the mainland across the Cooper River opposite Charleston on Friday, April 28, 1780. The Continentals fired several shells (see Photo SC-25) into the Crown earthworks but did little damage. A deserter from the Continental artillery showed the Crown bomb batteries the location of their powder magazine.

The American Volunteers and the New York Volunteers marched to Léprière's Point on Mount Pleasant to verify that the post had been abandoned. Meanwhile Admiral Marriot Arbuthnot (1711–1794) organized a brigade of 500 sailors to capture Léprière's Point. They landed at daybreak on Saturday, April 29, 1780, and marched to join the American Volunteers and the New York Volunteers before proceeding to Léprière's Point. The Crown forces captured four 18-pounders, two 4-pounders and five swivel guns (see Photo SC-32). Captain Charles Hudson of the Royal Navy raised the British flag over the fort. The flag was clearly visible to the residents of Charleston who now knew that the

British had control of the east side of the Charleston harbor and Cooper River. Malmedy was not popular with the people of Charleston after that. He was advised to leave the city and was soon surprised and taken prisoner along with about nine others.[243]

★ British Captain Jackson's galley *Comet* and the frigate *Renown* intended to attack the bridge battery on Haddrell's Point on Sunday, April 30, 1780. Both vessels ran aground. The *Renown* got off but the *Comet* was stuck. The Whigs still occupied Fort Sullivan [Fort Moultrie] and temporarily moved some of the cannons from the fort to Mount Pleasant to destroy the *Comet*.[244]

★ A British store-ship had its rudder disabled in the Charleston harbor in March or April 1780. Without navigational control, it went aground on the eastern end of Shutes Folly Island in a gale, within range of the guns at the Half-Moon Battery, located at the eastern end of Broad Street in Charleston. Her crew set her on fire to prevent her from being taken by the Whigs. After burning a while, the ship blew up.[245]

★ Major Patrick Ferguson (1744–1780) and 60 American Volunteers marched to Haddrell's Point on Tuesday, May 2, 1780 to attack the small fort on a causeway leading to Fort Moultrie. Taking the fort would sever communications between Fort Moultrie and the mainland. Major Ferguson divided his force into two groups of 30. He led one group to attack from the right while Captain Abraham De Peyster's (1753–1799) group attacked the center. Major Ferguson advanced at low tide, so his men marched on dry land while Captain De Peyster's men marched in knee-deep water.

The 200-man garrison surrendered without resistance but the four cannons in Fort Moultrie fired at the British continually until dark but didn't inflict any casualties.[246]

★ During a thunderstorm on Thursday, June 29, 1781, lightning struck the British privateer sloop *Lord North* at anchor in Rebellion Road. The sloop sank quickly but all on board were saved.[247]

Sandy Point (March 14, 1776)

> Sandy Point was on the south side of Stono Inlet.

Two South Carolina tenders traveling up the Cooper River encountered a small Loyalist vessel coming down the river with a cargo of flour on Thursday, March 14, 1776. The Loyalists ran aground at Sandy Point and abandoned ship. The two tenders captured the vessel and tried to refloat her. Some Loyalists regrouped along the shore and fired "pieces of iron, and a variety of shot" at them and the tenders, mortally wounding one of the crew. The tender returned fire, possibly killing three Loyalists. The incoming tide refloated the vessel which was then taken to Charleston as a prize of war.[248]

Dewey's Inlet (July 21, 1776)

> Dewey's (Dewee's) Inlet, also known as Spencer's Inlet, is on Horseshoe Creek, northeast of the Isle of Palms, between it and Dewee's Island. The Isle of Palms was called Long Island in the 18th century.

When General Henry Clinton (1730–1795) evacuated his forces from Long Island after his first attempt to take Charleston, he had most of the transports taken over the Bar to Dewey's Inlet. His troops at the lighthouse boarded the transports on Friday, July 19, 1776; but some of them were left behind, including almost an entire company of Royal Highland Emigrants who may have missed the order recalling them off Long Island or may have been in a fight with the militiamen because of an unconfirmed report that Lieutenant Stratton was dead and that Captain Alexander Campbell (d. 1779) and Ensign Duncan McDougall were wounded.

Some of the Royal Highland Emigrants managed to get off Long Island on the transport brig *Glasgow Packet,* the last ship off the Bar, since it had some small guns on board that could be used to cover the withdrawal. However, the Highlanders lost 38 men and seven officers who were left on the beach and taken prisoner.

All the ships, except the *Glasgow Packet,* crossed the Bar and got under way on Saturday, July 20th. The *Glasgow Packet* became calmed as she arrived at the Bar and dropped her anchor to wait for assistance. Admiral Sir Peter Parker (1721–1811) replied that he was sending the *St. Lawrence* to help the *Glasgow Packet* but the *St. Lawrence* never arrived.

The wind picked up on Sunday morning and the *Glasgow Packet* crossed the Bar only to get stuck on a shoal. Captain Porterfield, her captain, fired signal guns to get the attention of anyone in the fleet and tried to row his ship off the shoal. His men rowed out, dropped the anchor, and then pulled on the anchor to tug the ship. Captain Porterfield also sent Captain Alexander Campbell (of the Royal Highland Emigrants aboard a rowboat to alert the British fleet that they were stuck.

Captain Campbell rowed 12 miles before reaching Admiral Sir Peter Parker's (1721–1811) flagship *Bristol.* Admiral Parker sent the schooner *St. Lawrence* to accompany a flat-bottomed boat with a kedge anchor to help pull the *Glasgow Packet* off the shoal. Because of the lack of wind, the *St. Lawrence* trailed behind the rowboats. All of the vessels arrived too late, however.

The *Glasgow Packet*'s signal guns alerted Lieutenant Francis Pickering's 2nd South Carolina Regiment. The Carolinians rowed toward the British brig and used some smaller boats to tow her. A row battery sent to annoy the fleet fired round ball and grape shot at the *Glasgow Packet* which could not return fire because of the angle she was stuck on the shoal.

Captain McNicoll, of the Royal Highland Emigrants, ordered his men to throw their muskets overboard to prevent their capture by the Carolinians who boarded the transport and captured her at 4 PM along with 43 Royal Highland Emigrants, "6 sailors, and 2 Negro Boatswains." The flatboat with nine sailors sent to help the *Glasgow Packet* was captured later that day.

Captain Campbell pleaded with Lieutenant John Graves, the captain of the *St. Lawrence*, to go to rescue the *Glasgow Packet.* Graves responded that he did not have any orders to cross over the Bar to rescue the Royal Highland Emigrants. Admiral Parker ordered the *St. Lawrence* over the Bar to rescue the *Glasgow Packet* the next morning but it was too late. The Carolinians set the transport on fire just as the *St. Lawrence* reached the Bar. [249]

Off Cummings Point (Sept. 28, 1775)
Tamar vs. 3 Canoes

> Cummings Point was probably what is now known as Mount Pleasant. This incident probably occurred off James Island, east of the Fort Sumter National Monument and north of the tip of Morris Island.

Captain Edward Thornbrough's (1754–1834) HM Sloop *Tamar* weighed anchor Thursday afternoon, September 28, 1775 and set sail after firing a gun as a signal to the HM Armed Vessel *Cherokee*. She anchored off Cummings Point at 4 PM on Thursday, September 28, 1775, to intercept about 30 armed men in three canoes from Fort Johnson. After running aground and getting free again, the *Tamar* fired two 6-pound shots at the same men after 5 PM. The men retreated to the fort. There were no casualties.[250]

Near Stono River (1777; July 25, 1777; July 26, 1777; Aug. 21, 1777; Aug. 22, 1777; June 1779; Feb. or March 1781)

Mathews's Plantation (Massacre of the Beaufort Company) (May 20, 1779)

Stono Inlet (June 16, 1776; June 14, 1777)

13 Mile House, Stono Ferry (May 31, 1779)

Stono River, mouth (June 26, 1779; Feb.18, 1780; Feb. 22, 1780)

Stono Ferry (May 23, 1779; June 20, 1779; June 21 1779; Feb. 18–22, 1780; March 26, 1780)

Mathew's Ferry (March 5, 1780 March 26, 1780)

Stanyarne's and Eveleigh's Plantation (June 22–23, 1779)

Rantowles (Rentowle) Bridge (March 26, 1780)

New Cut, Johns Island

Robert Gibbes's Plantation, Charleston County (March 29–30, 1780)

William Gibbes's Plantation, Charleston County (Jan. 12–15, 1782)

Fenwick Hall, Charleston County (Jan. 15, 1782)

Folly Island (ca. Jan. 18, 1782)

Chatham

> The mouth of the Stono River is between Kiawah Island and James Island. New Cut is the name of a branch of the Stono River that connects the river to Bohicket Creek near its mouth. It is simply named New Cut with no creek or river attached to the name. It had that name at the time of the Revolutionary War and still retains it.
>
> Stanyarne's and Eveleigh's plantation were on the Stono River, Johns Island, west of Stono Ferry.
>
> Fenwick Hall (**www.fenwickhall.com/fenwickhallhomepage.html**) is on Johns Island about 0.3 miles northwest of the intersection of route SC 700 (Maybank Highway) and Fenwick Hall Allee and about 0.3 miles east of the intersection of route S-10-91 (River Road) and Santa Elena Way. It is a privately owned residence.
>
> William Gibbes's (1722–1789) plantation was north of route S-10-91 (River Road) about 1.5 miles east of its junction with route S-10-20 (Main Road) on the south side of the Stono River.
>
> Mathews's plantation is about 2.5 miles southeast of Fenwick Hall near the end of Exchange Landing Road east of route S-10-91 (River Road). The road to the west of the intersection is Plow Ground Road and the street sign may indicate either road.
>
> Robert Reeve Gibbes's (1732–1794) plantation, also known as Peaceful Retreat Plantation, The Muck, or Gibbes Farm, was on Johns Island 8 miles west of Charleston on the Stono River. It was about 1.5 miles due north of Fenwick Hall, located in the area of Rushland Landing Road on the south side of the Stono River. Elizabeth Ellet (1818–1877) described it: "a few hundred yards from a fine landing on Stono

> River, upon John's Island, about two hours' sail from Charleston, stands a large, square, ancient-looking mansion strongly built of brick, with a portico fronting the river. On the side towards the road, the wide piazza overlooks a lawn; and a venerable live oak, with aspen, sycamore, and other trees, shade it from the sun. On either side of the house, about twenty yards distant, stands a smaller two story building, connected with the main building by a neat open fence. In one of these is the kitchen and out-offices; the other was formerly the school-house and tutor's dwelling; Beyond are the barns, the overseer's house and the negro huts appertaining to a plantation. The garden in old times was very large and well-cultivated, being laid out in wide walks, and extending from the mansion to the river. The 'river walk,' on the verge of a bluff 8 or 10 feet in height, followed the bending of the water, and was bordered with orange-trees. Tall hedges of the ever-green wild orange-tree divided the flower from the vegetable garden, and screened from view the family burial ground. The beautifully laid out grounds, and shaded walks, gave this place a most inviting aspect, rendering it such an abode as its name of 'Peaceful Retreat' indicated."[251]
>
> Stono Ferry was located on the Stono River at the end of Trexler Drive off route SC 162, south-southeast of Rantowles.
>
> Rantowles refers to the Kennedy Tavern. It was located where route U.S. 17 crosses Wallace Creek, in Ravenel, west of Rantowles Creek. Mathew's Ferry was in the same area.
>
> The *South Carolina and American General Gazette* (August 28, 1777) dates the engagements of July 25 and 26, 1777 as occurring on August 21, 22, 1777. However, a letter from Mr. John Raven Bedon, dated New Providence, August 2, 1777 published in *The Pennsylvania Ledger: or the Weekly Advertiser* on October 10, 1777 indicates that they occurred on July 25 and 26, 1777.

Captain Francis Morgan's privateer sloop *Polly* tried to run past some British ships and get into Charleston harbor on Sunday, June 16, 1776. The *Polly* almost made it into the harbor with her cargo of 300 barrels of gunpowder, 20 chests of cartridges, several hundred stands of arms and 90 barrels of rum, sugar and gin from St. Eustatia. She ran aground on the bar at the mouth of the Stono River and her crew scuttled her and abandoned ship that night.

The Royal Navy man of war *Bristol* (see Photo SC-24) sent Lieutenant Molloy and eight boats to investigate the *Polly*. The sailors boarded her but were unable to float her since she had 5 feet of water in her hold. They set her on fire and she "blew up with a great Explosion. . . . It would have been much greater but she had 5 feet of water in her hold, which had damaged a great deal of Powder."[252]

★ The British chased a ship ashore near the Stono River sometime in 1777. The ship was bound from Boston to Charleston.[253]

★ The Royal Navy 20-gun frigates *Galatea* and *Perseus* and a tender patrolled the mouth of Charleston harbor for several weeks in June 1777. Captain Alexander Bell's brigantine *Union*, which had been captured by Captain William Sutton Jr.'s (1727–1778) Philadelphia privateer *Lively* on June 5, 1777, approached the harbor and was chased by the *Galatea* and *Perseus*. The *Union*, coming from the Mississippi River bound for Jamaica with a cargo of barrel staves, ran aground between Stono Inlet and the Charleston Lighthouse on Saturday, June 14, 1777 and was abandoned. The tender sent her boats to board the abandoned brig and then to set her on fire to prevent her from falling back into enemy hands.[254]

★ Captain Charles Morgan's Letter of Marque [privateer] brig *Fair American* fell in with a British convoy of 80 vessels from Jamaica on Thursday night, July 25, 1777. The convoy was led by Captain Sir Charles Thompson's (ca. 1740–1799) 28-gun *Boreas* and the 14-gun *Hornet*. He captured Captain John McNeil's schooner *Margery* which was headed from Jamaica to New York with a cargo of 52 hogsheads, 13 tierces (each 42 gallons) and 25 barrels of sugar, 30 casks of coffee, six pipes of Madeira wine and 50 Barcelona handkerchiefs.

The next day, he captured Captain Samuel Boyd's (1734–1801) schooner *Betsey* also bound for New York with a cargo of sugar, wine, rum, coffee and limes. The *Margery* ran aground on Saturday trying to enter one of the inlets. The vessel was lost but most of her cargo was saved.

The *Betsey* was sent to Charleston as a prize of war but ran aground on the Stono Breakers and was destroyed but more than 100 puncheons of her cargo were saved. (A puncheon is a cask of 84 gallons.)[255]

★ After the raid on Charleston in May 1779, Major General Augustine Prevost (1723–1786) returned to Savannah on Wednesday, May 12, leaving a force of 1,500 men under his brother Lieutenant Colonel James Mark Prevost (1736–1781). The Crown forces withdrew across the Ashley River to James Island before crossing the Stono River to Johns Island. They established a bridgehead on the northern side of what is now called New Cut Church Flats to cover Stono Ferry. They built three redoubts surrounded by an abatis. The British Army set up their camp on one side of the Stono River and the Hessian regiments set up their camp on the other side. Lieutenant Colonel John Maitland (1732–1779) commanded about 900 Highlanders and the von Trumbach Regiment of Hessians (later known as Regiment Von Bose (1779)) and some Loyalist militiamen here where they could forage on the mainland and protect their escape route down the river and to the Atlantic Ocean.

When he learned that Major General Benjamin Lincoln (1733–1810) was advancing on his army at Stono Ferry, Colonel Prevost collected all the boats in the area to build a floating bridge across the Stono inlet to Johns Island. He never built the bridge.

★ Crown troops, guided by Loyalist Thomas Fenwick, surprised two companies of South Carolina militiamen at Captain John Mathews's (1744–1802) plantation on Johns Island on Thursday May 20, 1779. They gave no quarter and cut two companies to pieces: Captain (later governor) John Mathews's Colleton County company and Captain Robert Barnwell's (1761–1814) Beaufort Company (St. Helena Volunteer Militia Company).

Barnwell's unit was not far from the home of Thomas Fenwick whom they thought was a friend. Fenwick dined with some Whig officers one evening and learned the strength of the companies. He notified the British commander who sent a detachment that quickly surrounded Captain Mathews's Colleton County company at his plantation. They surrendered.

The Loyalists demanded Captain Barnwell's surrender as well. Captain Barnwell demanded to know what quarter his men would receive. The response was "No quarter to rebels." Barnwell ordered his men to charge and defend themselves. The Loyalists immediately fell back. A British sergeant soon promised Barnwell's men honorable quarter if they surrendered. He assured them that his word was as good as any officer's. Barnwell and his men surrendered, and the soldiers immediately began to attack them with their bayonets, killing and wounding most of the Beaufort company. The Loyalists burned the Solomon house and raided other nearby residences on Johns Island.

Elizabeth Ellet (1818–1877) wrote, "When the conflict was over, Mrs. Gibbes sent her servants to search among the slain left upon the battleground, for Robert Barnwell, her nephew, who had not returned. They discovered him by part of his dress, which one of the blacks remembered having seen his mother making. His face was so covered with wounds, dust and blood, that he could not be recognised. Yet life was not extinct; and under the unremitting care of his aunt and her young daughter, he recovered."

Sarah Reeve Gibbes (1747–1825), wife of Robert Reeve Gibbes (1732–1794) and Colonel Barnwell's aunt, nursed him back to health at her husband's plantation, Peaceful Retreat. He had been left for dead, with 17 bayonet wounds. Yet he survived to command his unit at the siege of Charleston the following year. Robert Gibbes later took protection from the British and moved to his plantation on Kiawah Island.[256]

★ As Charleston prepared for a major assault, a party of South Carolinians went to Fort Johnson to re-spike the guns with steel spikes instead of the nails used when the fort was abandoned and burned. Lieutenant Colonel Francis Marion (1732–1795) returned to Fort Moultrie from Charleston Neck with the 2nd South Carolina Regiment and patrols scouted British activities day and night.

A galley provided cover for the Hessians on the north side of the Stono River, opposite the British camp, but it was not much help because it was unable to maneuver in the narrow river. The galley did fire her cannons to keep the Whigs at a distance. When they tried to get in a deep ravine behind the Hessian camp on Sunday, May 23, 1779, the row galley's cannon killed or wounded 40 of them. The militiamen then directed their fire at the row galley instead of at the Hessians, forcing the vessel to withdraw from the fight.

The Whigs on the high ground overshot their targets and the bullets flew over the Hessians' heads into the water behind them. The British gathered all the boats they could find and crossed the river to reinforce the Hessians. They charged but the South Carolina Navy schooner *Rattlesnake* began firing on the rear of the Crown forces. The Regiment de Wissenbach fired at the *Rattlesnake* with two field pieces. The *Rattlesnake* repulsed an assault by the Royal Americans and the Hessian grenadiers with heavy losses.

The 60th Regiment lost their commander during the assault and the Hessians had six men killed and 38 wounded, including their commander. Captain Paul Frisbie decided that he could not escape with his ship so he set the *Rattlesnake* on fire and then led his crew through the British lines to Charleston.[257]

★ Brigadier General Casimir Pulaski's (1747–1779) dragoons were sent to reconnoiter near 13 Mile House on Monday, May 31, 1779 and to drive away the Crown defenders if possible. Colonel Isaac Huger (1743–1797) and 1,000 infantrymen joined him. The light infantry and the South Carolina militia were on the right of the line, Brigadier General John Butler (1728–1796) and the North Carolina militia formed the left of the line, and the 1st and 6th South Carolina Regiments were in the center with four field pieces. The remainder of Major General Benjamin Lincoln's (1733–1810) army was in reserve, a mile to the rear.

The defenders fired at Pulaski's dragoons, wounding two officers. Pulaski had his horse killed under him with 14 musket balls, but he himself was not hurt. Pulaski withdrew into the woods and was ready to order a general assault when he learned that the Crown forces had received reinforcements. Estimating their force at 1,500 men and knowing their defenses were too strong for an attack, Pulaski ordered a retreat.[258]

★ Lieutenant Colonel James Mark Prevost (1736–1781) left for Savannah, Georgia on Wednesday, June 16, 1779 with all the boats and most of his troops. He left Lieutenant

Colonel John Maitland (1732–1779) in charge of only 500 men at Johns Island. Almost a week before the battle, Maitland had decided to abandon the base and head to Beaufort, but he was delayed by lack of water transportation. The next three days after Colonel Prevost's departure were spent transporting the sick and wounded across Stono Inlet, along with the African Americans and Native Americans, and the baggage and horses belonging to the garrison. The Crown forces also destroyed all unnecessary huts and buildings.

Major General Benjamin Lincoln (1733–1810) decided the camp was now weak enough to attack. He would lead the main attack while Brigadier General William Moultrie (1730–1805) would command a secondary attack against Johns Island, to the east. With few boats to ferry his troops across the Ashley River, Moultrie only had half his force on James Island when the battle began on Sunday, June 20th. By the time he got his 700-man army in position, the battle was over.

General Lincoln's 1,400 troops left camp about midnight Saturday, June 19, 1779 and marched 8 miles from the Ashley Ferry (modern Drayton where the railroad bridge crosses the Ashley River). They became bogged down in the marsh and dense woods as they advanced in two wings to attack at dawn. Major General Jethro Sumner (1735–1785) commanded the Carolina militia on the right with two guns. Brigadier General Isaac Huger (1743–1797) (pronounced Eugee) commanded the Continental troops with four guns on the left wing. They faced the 71st Highlanders, a seasoned unit. The light infantry, under Lieutenant Colonel John Henderson (1756–post 1833), protected the left flank. Virginia militiamen and two field pieces under General Mason, Brigadier General Casimir Pulaski's (1747–1779) cavalry and a small body of North Carolina horsemen, under the command of Major William Richardson Davie (1756–1820) were in the rear in reserve.

Colonel Maitland had about 40 Highlanders in a circular redoubt on his right, with the remainder of the 71st Regiment of Highlanders between the circular and central redoubts. North and South Carolina Loyalists under Lieutenant Colonel John Hamilton (d. 1817) manned the central redoubt and a Hessian regiment held the left flank.

The Continental light infantry first engaged two companies of Highlanders Colonel Maitland sent as a scouting party about 7:30 AM on Sunday, June 20th. The Continentals attacked the enemy lines, defended by abatis and pickets, about 40 yards away and continued until almost 9 o'clock. They mauled the Highlanders who refused to surrender or retreat until all their officers were killed or wounded. Only 11 Highlanders returned and joined with the 2nd Battalion of the 71st Regiment of Highlanders, one battalion of Hessians and a contingent of Loyalist troops.

The initial attack of heavy firing of small arms and cannon lasted for an hour. When General Lincoln's militia pressed forward and broke a Hessian battalion, Colonel Maitland shifted a number of Highlanders from the redoubts to reinforce them. The Hessians rallied and reserves were brought across the bridge.

Lincoln ordered the Continentals to stop firing and to prepare for a bayonet charge. The men refused to charge and the firing continued. When he saw reinforcements running for the ferry, Lincoln realized that he could not capture the redoubts and ordered a retreat which became disorganized. Maitland took advantage of the confusion and ordered a counterattack.

Lincoln brought his reserve of cavalry forward to check Maitland's counterattack and to give his troops time to withdraw. Maitland formed his men in two parallel lines and closed ranks. As the first rank knelt on one knee with the butts of their muskets on the ground, presenting a row of bayonets to the cavalry, the second line, still standing, fired a volley. The front rank rose and fired another volley while the second line reloaded. The bayonets and bullets stopped the cavalry charge.

Then, the reserve of Virginians came up and managed to hold off the Crown forces until Lincoln's troops could leave the field. Lincoln lost about 34 men killed and 113 wounded, including General Huger, and an equal number of "missing," most of them deserters. The Crown forces claimed no prisoners. They lost three officers and 23 men killed and 10 officers and 93 men wounded and only one missing.

Although the Crown forces technically won the battle, they failed to capture Charleston and abandoned their fortifications here. Maitland started moving to Beaufort on June 21 and completed his withdrawal from Johns Island on the night of June 24.[259]

★ Brigadier General William Moultrie (1730–1805) ordered Captain James Pyne (or Payne) to "proceed . . . to Stono-ferry, there you are to endeavor to destroy a bridge of boats the enemy have thrown over the river. In your passage up, and on your return, you are to sink, burn, and destroy any of the enemy's boats or vessels that you may meet with." He took three galleys up the Stono River to harass the British on Tuesday, June 22, 1779, two days after the Battle of Stono Ferry. The Captains of the other galleys were Captains Paul Frisbie and Boutard.

Brigadier General Casimir Pulaski (1747–1779) and his Legion were ready to support the landing of Colonel Marquis de Britigney and his Corps of Frenchmen who were with the galleys and were to try to make a landing, if possible. The galleys sailed through the Wappoo Cut during that night but did not find any bridge of boats. The British were unable to get enough boats to build the proposed bridge, so the galleys passed by Gibbes's plantation undetected. However, they were fired upon "with field-pieces and small arms" for 45 minutes when they passed Stanyarne's plantation.

Captain Pyne captured a British schooner during the fight and silenced the batteries at the plantation. He then continued up the river to the next bluff, where "a battery consisting of three field-pieces and a great deal of musketry" fired upon him again. The galleys managed to silence that battery also. The vessels then anchored at Eveleigh's plantation as the sun was rising and the tide was going out.

When the sun came up, the sailors realized that there were 1,200 Crown troops at Eveleigh's plantation and cannons were entrenched on the causeway leading to it. Although the galleys were safe where they were, moving in any direction would place them "within pistol shot of their intrenchment" so Captain Pyne decided to wait until dark.

Aware that the galleys were nearby, the Crown forces sank a schooner in the river to block the enemy's escape. The Carolina gunners fired cannonballs into the Crown camp throughout the day. The vessels rushed down the river after nightfall, running the gauntlet of men and cannons (the largest were 9-pounders) firing along the riverbank. The galleys returned fire only when necessary as they were low on ammunition. Captain Boutard's galley, in the rear, received the heaviest fire which killed six men and wounded several others. All three galleys returned with the British schooner as their prize.[260]

★ The slaves and plunder the Crown forces had taken from around Charleston slowed their withdrawal. As Lieutenant Colonel James Mark Prevost (1736–1781) did not have enough ships to take them all back to Savannah, Georgia, he decided to shuttle his forces from island to island, back toward Savannah.

When they reached Edisto Island, the Crown troops fortified their positions and waited for more ships to help them evacuate South Carolina; but General William Moultrie (1730–1805) ordered Captain Hezekiah Anthony to do everything possible to impede their evacuation because Major General Benjamin Lincoln (1733–1810) was trying to bring in artillery.

A Whig fleet, composed of Captain William Hall's (1757–1814) South Carolina brig *Notre Dame*, Captain Tryon's brig *Beaufort*, Captain Hezekiah Anthony's brig *Bellona* and four armed South Carolina State Navy vessels, attacked seven British ships bringing supplies to Gibbes's plantation on Saturday, June 26, 1779. They captured two British ships at the mouth of the Stono River and took them safely into Charleston. The men blew up one of the British ships. Two other vessels were captured and four escaped.[261]

★ Major John Jameson (1758–1842) and the 1st Continental light dragoons captured three British soldiers of the 23rd Regiment when they wandered too far from their lines on Friday, February 18, 1780. The following night, a British row galley blew up in the Stono River. Two drunken sailors who had a "nymph" with them were blamed. Captain George Keith Elphinstone, viscount Keith (1746–1823) came from the fleet with two schooners carrying a 24-pound cannon and a flatboat armed with a 12-pounder to cover the movement of the transports to the mouth of the Stono River for protection. Meanwhile, the British light infantry marched down the river to Mathew's Ferry to reduce the distance that the ships would have to move.

Captain Elphinstone got the transports to Mathew's Ferry on Sunday, February 20, 1780 and they began unloading supplies for the army. On Tuesday, Major Hezekiah Maham (1739–1789, of Colonel Daniel Huger Horry's (1737–1785) (pronounced Orry) South Carolina dragoons, and Captain William Sanders (1760–1847), of the Round O Company, reconnoitered the British lines near Stono Ferry.[262]

★ Major Hezekiah Maham (1739–1789) and 20 militia dragoons seized Lieutenant Aeneas McDonald and eight sentries with their muskets and side arms, without firing a shot on Tuesday afternoon, February 22, 1780. Lieutenant McDonald's party was sent half a mile beyond the posts occupied by the fusilier pickets at Stono Ferry to fetch a grindstone from William Ashley's house.

Brigadier General Alexander Leslie (1740–1794), Lieutenant Colonel James Webster (ca. 1743–1781), Lieutenant Colonel Alured Clarke (1745–1832), the fusilier picket and 20 jaegers advanced half an hour later to see which way the dragoons had gone. The next day, 20 jaegers and 30 British Regulars lay in ambush near William Ashley's house but nobody came. The Regulars finished the fortifications at Stono Ferry on February 24th. General Charles Cornwallis (1738–1805) brought his men onto James Island the following day.[263]

★ Some of Brigadier General Casimir Pulaski's (1747–1779) legionnaires scouted the Crown redoubt at Mathew's Ferry late Saturday afternoon, March 4, 1780. They returned at 11 o'clock the next day to test the defenses and were fired upon, losing several men and horses. Captain Johann von Ewald (1744–1813), commander of the position, expected the attackers to return, so he placed six Highlanders and six jaegers in two ambuscades along the main road. He placed two other jaegers in a sentry position in the open, in front of the works, as a decoy.

Pulaski's dragoons circled the sentries to cut them off from the works about 7 PM that night. When the dragoons entered the ambuscade, the sentries fired, giving the signal for the hidden soldiers to fire also. The Crown troops shot or bayoneted almost all the dragoons but a few managed to escape.

Captain Ewald abandoned the earthworks at Mathew's Ferry the next day. He demolished them and set the abatis on fire before crossing the Stono River. He then destroyed the boats he had used to cross. General Henry Clinton's (1730–1795) entire army was now on James Island, except for a small detachment.[264]

★ Lieutenant Colonel William Washington (1752–1810) and his dragoons rode toward the British lines on Monday, March 26, 1780. His men created an ambuscade near an old rice field, along a main road, 12 miles from the British lines. A few South Carolina militiamen "wearing bright clothes" made a vain attempt to draw out the Crown troops. Colonel Washington then moved his men a half mile to the east and then took an advance party to Governor William Bull, Jr.'s (1710–1791) house. They captured eight prisoners along the way.

As he returned to Bacon's Bridge, Colonel Washington received word that Lieutenant Colonel Banastre Tarleton's (1744–1833) British Legion was approaching from the rear. When Tarleton's Legion arrived, Washington's Legion turned in their direction and charged. One of Tarleton's officers charged down a narrow causeway that was only wide enough for one rider. The troops ran into Washington's dragoons waiting at the end of the causeway with superior numbers and better horses.

Colonel Tarleton ordered his men to retreat across the causeway and back to his lines, leaving many wounded behind and eight dragoons captured. Colonel Washington had one man wounded through the knee and a sergeant major killed.[265]

★ Gout contracted and crippled Robert Reeve Gibbes's (1732–1794) hands and feet early in life and confined him to a wheelchair. Yet, his mansion, named Peaceful Retreat, was well known as a place of hospitality and elegant taste during the American War for Independence. It commanded the attention of the Crown forces when Major General Augustine Prevost (1723–1786) invaded the city in 1779. A battalion of British and Hessians, intending to quarter themselves at the plantation, arrived at the landing about 10 or 12 PM on Wednesday, March 29, 1780, and marched in silence to surround the house, unaware that the residents were informed of their presence. They heard Mr. Gibbes's wheelchair rolling toward the front door about dawn. Thinking the sound was caused by a cannon being rolled to the door, the soldiers advanced and stood prepared to rush for an assault when the signal was given. As the door opened, the soldiers saw Mr. Gibbes in his wheelchair surrounded by women and children. The occupation was accomplished without firing a shot.

When the city officials in Charleston learned that the Crown forces had occupied Gibbes's plantation, they sent two galleys to dislodge the troops. These galleys arrived opposite the plantation at night and opened a heavy fire upon the encampment near the house. They had orders not to fire on the house itself to avoid injuring any of the family. Mr. Gibbes, unaware of the orders, sent his wife and children to seek shelter away from the house. The cannon shots cut the bushes and struck the trees around them as they fled. They continued running, as fast as possible, for about a mile until they were out of range of the guns.[266]

★ In February or March 1781, the South Carolina Navy schooner *Rattlesnake*, loaded with ammunition and stores for the Continental Army, came up the Stono River and grounded at Stono ferry. The British on the Island tried to board her. Brigadier General Francis Marion (1732–1795) ordered a redoubt to be raised to prevent the boarding. The *Rattlesnake*'s crew found it impossible to defend the vessel and put a slow match to the magazine. They escaped to the opposite shore shortly before some of the enemy boarded her and were blown up with her.

Major Thomas Ladson (1749–1785) commanded the Whigs in an engagement that continued across the river before the explosion which caused the Crown forces to retreat to the island.[267]

★ The British had troops in only three Southern port towns after General Charles Cornwallis (1738–1805) surrendered at Yorktown, Virginia, on October 19, 1781. Lieutenant Colonel James Henry Craig (1742–1812) and his 82nd Regiment evacuated

Wilmington and went to Johns Island near Charleston to tend to the British cattle. He made his headquarters at William Gibbes's (1722–1789) plantation on the eastern end of Johns Island. His troops were stationed at Fenwick Hall and some British dragoons were stationed 4 miles away.

Meanwhile, the Continentals were moved from Yorktown into the Carolinas to reinforce Major General Nathanael Greene's (1742–1786) army. Major General Arthur St. Clair (1737–1818) marched into South Carolina with a force of 2,000 Pennsylvania, Maryland and Delaware Continentals, driving 400 beef cattle through knee-deep mud. They arrived at Round O on Friday, Jan. 4, 1782.

Lieutenant Colonel Henry "Light-Horse Harry" Lee (1756–1818) and Lieutenant Colonel John Laurens (1754–1782) devised a plan to steal the British cattle on Johns Island and presented the idea to General Greene.

Lieutenant Colonel James Henry Craig's 400 to 500 troops were camped at William Gibbes's plantation on the eastern end of Johns Island. They posed a great threat to the South Carolina government in Jacksonboro, where the legislature moved after the surrender of Charleston and would reconvene on January 8. Greene knew that the only threat to the legislature was the British on Johns Island. He decided to eliminate this threat with a surprise raid on the island.

Since the Continentals didn't have any boats, they could only approach the island by a narrow canal to the Stono River called New Cut. The canal could only be crossed two times each month, shortly after midnight when "the depth of water was not more than waist high." The British knew about the strategic value of New Cut and they placed a galley and two gunboats 400 yards apart to guard it. The vessels had to remain apart so they could still stay afloat at low tide. The gap between them allowed the Continentals to pass through but the tide gave them only a small window of opportunity.

Lieutenant Colonels John Laurens and Henry Lee, supported by the main army under General Greene, forded New Cut at low tide, under cover of darkness, on a cold and rainy Saturday night, January 12, 1782, in an attempt to surprise and capture the entire British force. Laurens divided his force into two columns. Lee commanded one; Major James Hamilton (ca. 1710–1783), of the Pennsylvania Line, commanded the other. The crossing began at 1 AM. Lee sent Captain Michael Rudolph (1758–1793) across first with the Legion infantry. They crossed onto Johns Island easily.

Major Hamilton's guide had deserted him, so his column missed the turnoff to the ford and got lost. Laurens searched for an hour before he found Major Hamilton. This gave the British time to evacuate and eliminated any possibility of Laurens surprising them.

Laurens did find a schooner in the Stono River, probably near William Gibbes's plantation where a wide creek connects to the Stono River. The British had loaded all their baggage, supplies and military stores onto her. Laurens ordered his men to attack the schooner. His men fired a volley that "threw the Crew into great confusion" almost making the schooner run aground. The crew stacked the baggage and used it as protection against the musket balls. They returned fire as the schooner moved away slowly. Laurens remarked, "If I had a three pounder...perhaps She might still be taken."

When the tide came in, Laurens had to call off the operation and recall Lee's troops from Johns Island to James Island. Lee's men found themselves waist deep in "mud, weeds and water" on the march back. Several soldiers became stuck in the mud and "were obliged to be pulled out."

British Brigadier General Alexander Leslie (1740–1794) learned of Greene's plan the following day and ordered all Crown troops off Johns Island. They evacuated the island on January 13 and 14 and Lieutenant Colonel Craig went to James Island, where the British engineers had constructed a pair of redoubts.

Greene had his men search the riverbank, on January 14th, for a boat to ferry Laurens's troops back across the inlet to try again. He brought up his cannon to fire on the galleys to cover the crossing. The artillery fired on the British vessels throughout the day, but the boats refused to withdraw until Craig evacuated the island that night.

Laurens and a small force of cavalry and infantry crossed the Cut in a boat on Tuesday, the 15th. They found the remains of the abandoned camp and captured a few stragglers at Fenwick Hall.

Greene remarked, "We have got the territory but we missed the great objective of the enterprise." He withdrew to Skirving's plantation, 6 miles from Jacksonboro on the road to Charleston. The expedition was a failure, but it eliminated the threat to Jacksonboro.[268]

★ Captain Charles Douglas's (1727–1789) HMS *Chatham* captured a brig from the West Indies with a cargo of coffee, etc. around Friday, January 18, 1782. The prize was sent to Charleston, but it went aground on Folly Island (Coffin Land) south of the Charleston Bar and was lost. The crew was saved, but the brig was burned.[269]

Parker's Ferry, Colleton County (May 7, 1779; Aug. 31, 1781)
Charleston Road (Aug. 31, 1781)

> Parker's Ferry was located on the primary colonial highway. The site is now on route S-15-705 (Parkers Ferry Road) about 5.2 miles northeast of the intersection with route S-15-40 (Jacksonboro Road). About 0.3 miles along Parkers Ferry Road are the ruins of the Pon Pon Chapel, an old brick chapel which was constructed in 1754 at a site where John Wesley (1703–1791) preached in 1735. (The Edisto River is called Pon Pon in this region.) The church survived the American War for Independence and the fighting at nearby Parkers Ferry but it was destroyed by fire in 1801. It has since been known as the "Burnt Church." A state historical marker for the chapel is at the intersection of routes SC 64 (Charleston Highway) and S-15-40 (Jacksonboro Road), 0.9 miles south of this road's intersection with route S-15-705 (Parkers Ferry Road).
>
> Charleston Road was probably the road from Charleston to Dorchester which corresponds to today's Dorchester Road (SC 642) in Charleston County.

Major Butler and a party of horsemen fell in with a Crown foraging party in the vicinity of Green Pond, about 13 miles southwest of Parkers Ferry and about 8 miles west of Jacksonboro, about Friday, May 7, 1779. Three of the horsemen belonging to the 71st light infantry were taken prisoners and a few horsemen were killed and wounded.[270]

Charleston Road (Aug. 31, 1781) see **Ashley River Church** p. 168.

Santee River (March 7, 1779; June 21, 1779; Jan. 1781; Aug. 16, 1781)
Charleston Road (Aug. 16, 1781)

> The Santee River runs from Lake Marion to the Atlantic Ocean. It forms the northern boundary of Francis Marion National Forest.
>
> The Charleston Road corresponds to route SC 6 (SC 45|Old Number Six Highway) which runs along the Santee River. The incident that occurred here probably took place about 6.8 miles southeast of Nelson's Ferry and 4.8 miles from Eutaw Springs.

★ Several British privateers drove a New England schooner ashore on the reef off the mouth of the Santee River in South Carolina on Sunday, March 7, 1779.[271]

★ After the battle of Stono Ferry, two small privateers from St. Augustine, Florida came into the Santee River to plunder on Monday, June 21, 1779. The militiamen stationed there captured one of the vessels and killed the captain. They also captured the lieutenants of both ships, the crew of 10 men and "16 Negroes who had been captured from the plantations." The prize was brought to Charleston; the other privateer escaped.[272]

★ Captain Daniel Conyers (1748–1809) and a party of 16 of Brigadier General Francis Marion's (1732–1795) militiamen surprised and captured 46 British Regulars and a considerable number of horses and wagons and a large quantity of salt and other stores on the west side of the Santee in January 1781. They destroyed what they could not take with them and took their prisoners safely across the Pee Dee River.[273]

★ Crown troops captured Colonel Isaac Hayne (1745–1781) in July 1781 and brought him to Charleston. He was tried, found guilty of violating his parole and hanged for treason on Saturday, August 4th. Hayne became a martyr for the cause of independence. Major General Nathanael Greene (1742–1786) wrote to the British "that retaliation shall immediately take place, not on the tory militia officers, but it shall fall on the heads of regular British officers." See p. 169.

★ Major General Nathanael Greene (1742–1786) ordered Brigadier General Francis Marion (1732–1795) to strike at the enemy's lines of communication to Charleston. General Marion dispatched Colonel John Ervin (1754–1810) to the Santee River on that mission. Colonel Ervin captured a convoy on the Charleston Road south of the Santee on Wednesday, August 16, 1781 and took Captain John Campbell (d. 1806), two other officers and a private prisoner. The officers were kept for possible reprisal for the death of Colonel Hayne.[274]

Washington's Raid, Berkeley County (July 9–18, 1781)

Lieutenant Colonel William Washington (1752–1810) was sent on a raid to disrupt British communications between the Santee River and Charleston. His dragoons patrolled the roads between McCord's Ferry and Charleston between July 9 and 18, 1781 when they defeated two parties of cavalrymen and captured 50 prisoners.[275]

Saint Andrews, Charleston County

Hammond's Plantation, Savage's Plantation or St. Andrews Church (March 12–15, 1780)

Saint Andrews Creek (Armstrong's skirmish) (March 22, 1780; Dec. 30, 1781)

Drayton's Plantation (March 23, 1780)

John Gibbes Plantation (Lowndes Grove Plantation), Charleston County (March 30, 1780)

Saint Andrews is on the west bank of the Ashley River where the Ashley River Road (SC 61) crosses Church Creek about 2 miles northwest of exit 11A of Interstate 526 (Mark Clark Expressway). The Old Saint Andrews Episcopal Church is about 300 yards further down Ashley River Road on the right.

> Hammond's plantation is also known as Savage's plantation or St. Andrews Church.
>
> Armstrong's Skirmish probably occurred on the road to Ashley Ferry (Ashley River Road|SC 61) about a mile northwest of where it crosses Saint Andrews Creek, now called Church Creek and Long Branch Creek.
>
> John Gibbes's plantation, also known as Lowndes Grove, was on the Ashley River between 5th and 6th Avenue and Saint Margaret Street and Grove Street in Charleston.

Lieutenant Colonel Robert Abercromby's or Abercrombie's (1740–1827) light infantry marched to Hammond's plantation at dawn on Sunday, March 12, 1780 in search of forage for the artillery horses. They brought two huge wall guns, called amusettes (see Photo SC-29), which were giant muskets resembling cannons. They fired a 1-inch ball capable of hitting a target at 800 yards. Lieutenant Colonel James Webster's (ca. 1743–1781) 33rd Regiment and a detachment of jaegers marched along the left bank of the Stono River to cover Abercromby's flank. Webster's regiment encountered a patrol of 50 dragoons and about 100 infantrymen at Savage's plantation and skirmished with them for more than two hours. He had two jaegers wounded. The Congressional force withdrew and attacked Abercromby's light infantry. When Webster heard the amusettes firing, he sent the jaegers to reinforce the light infantry. They set up an ambuscade which the Continentals detected and avoided.

★ Lieutenant Colonel Thomas Dundas (1750–1794) and his 2nd Battalion of light infantry (500 men) were sent to the right side of Saint Andrews Creek at daybreak on Wednesday, March 15, 1780 to forage at the plantations located there. Meanwhile, Colonel Webster's force went to John Gibbes's plantation (Lowndes Grove) to forage there and divide the Congressional forces. The jaegers skirmished with a number of riflemen near a bridge that had been demolished at Saint Andrews Church until the foraging was done. Neither side suffered any casualties.[276]

★ Brigadier General Alexander Leslie (1740–1794) led the jaegers, the 33rd Foot and the light infantry toward Drayton Hall and the Middleton plantation on Wednesday, March 22, 1780. Continental artillery fire greeted them at the bridge crossing St. Andrews Creek. General Leslie halted and asked Captain Johann von Ewald (1744–1813) if the creek could be forded farther upstream to drive the artillery from the bridge. Otherwise, Leslie would have to bring up artillery to drive the enemy away from the bridge as Ewald's force only had four amusettes.

Captain Ewald and 50 jaegers, supported by Captain St. Lawrence Boyd (d. 1780) and three companies of light infantry, crossed the creek at 7 PM on Thursday, March 23, 1780 and found a swamp that was so deep that many of the jaegers sank up to their chests. When they emerged from the swamp half an hour later, they found that the enemy had abandoned their position. They had a brief skirmish with retreating militiamen and had two or three men wounded. Captain Ewald posted his men in the churchyard and began repairing the bridge, allowing General Leslie and his large force to proceed to Drayton's plantation on the Ashley River.

Ewald and Boyd received orders at 8 AM the next morning to try to get to Drayton's plantation, the home of Vice Governor William Henry Drayton (1742–1779). A detachment of South Carolina cavalrymen discovered Captain Ewald and his light infantrymen about 8:30. Captain Ewald immediately attacked with his riflemen, keeping his cavalry at a distance. The South Carolina cavalry continued to observe without attacking.

The jaegers and light infantrymen reached Drayton's plantation at noon. Captain Ewald posted his men in the zoological gardens and asked Mrs. Drayton for some food. She gave him some bread and wine for the troops. General Leslie arrived in the afternoon and took up quarters at Drayton's plantation.[277]

★ Captain James Armstrong (1728–1800) and a mounted scouting party of 40 of Lieutenant Colonel Henry "Light-Horse Harry" Lee's (1756–1818) dragoons clashed with British dragoons under Major John Coffin (1756–1838) (or Captain Ludwig Kienen or Lewis Kenan) on the road to Ashley Ferry, about a mile north of the St. Andrews Church, about 11 AM or noon on Sunday, December 30, 1781. Most of the dragoons were killed or captured and Captain Armstrong captured Captain Kienen and seven other prisoners. Captain Armstrong was himself taken prisoner the next day at Garden's plantation near Goose Creek along with a man named Ellis who resided 5 miles from the town. Mr. Ellis had a commission to command and arms to accouter 30 dragoons. He and his men joined the Congressional forces and Ellis was acting as Armstrong's guide when he was captured.[278]

Dorchester and vicinity
Dorchester Road (March 25, 1780)
Fuller's Plantation (The Muck) (March 29, 1780; ca. March 24, 1782)
Horse Savannah (July 5, 1781)
Cypress Swamp, Dorchester
Ashley River Church (Ashley River Baptist Church) (Aug. 31, 1781)

> Dorchester Road is now route SC 642.
> Fuller's plantation was on the Ashley River, about 370 yards northwest of the end of Covington Drive off route SC 642 (Dorchester Road) in North Charleston. It was opposite Drayton's house on the other side of the river.
> The Ashley River Baptist Church was a little farther up Dorchester Road on the right before the intersection with Great Oak Drive, less than 3 miles from the Dorchester County line.
> Horse Savannah was a plantation on the Dorchester Road, 7 miles from Charleston, probably in the area between Dewey Street and Ranger Drive.
> Cypress Swamp was 21.5 miles southwest of Moncks Corner.

Brigadier General Alexander Leslie (1740–1794) received information that 600 of Lieutenant Colonel William Washington's (1752–1810) dragoons and Pierre-Jean François Vernier's (1736–1780) Legion had occupied the pass to Bacon's Bridge in March 1780.

A party of South Carolina cavalry approached Captain Johann Hinrichs's (d. 1834) jaeger post on the Dorchester Road at daybreak on Saturday, March 25, 1780. Several jaegers went into the woods on their right to be able to fire on the flanks of the dragoons. However, they only hit a sergeant of the 3rd Regiment of Continental Light Dragoons who rode far in front of the others and was mortally wounded in the stomach.[279]

★ British grenadiers and light infantrymen, Hessian grenadiers, jaegers and 200 infantrymen from the 7th Regiment of Foot, 33rd Regiment of Foot and two battalions of the 71st Regiment departed at 3 AM on a foggy Wednesday morning, March 29, 1780. They headed for a landing site on the east side of the Ashley River, opposite Drayton Hall, where there was high ground with a narrow marsh. When the fog cleared, all the troops landed with the field artillery and all the horses and went to Benjamin Fuller's house, about 12 miles from Charleston. They arrived by 3 PM and began the Siege of Charleston.[280]

★ Colonel Isaac Hayne (1745–1781), commander of the Colleton County Regiment, had resigned his commission because of some intrigue and served as a private. After the surrender of Charleston (May 12, 1781) and Ninety Six (June 19, 1781), he returned to his plantation on the Edisto River. The Articles of Capitulation provided that "the militia now in garrison shall be permitted to return to their respective homes as prisoners of war on parole." Some people interpreted the provision to apply to the outposts as well as to the garrison. However, General Sir Henry Clinton (1730–1795) issued a proclamation revoking paroles of everyone who was not actually in the garrison at the time of surrender. When informed that he was ordered to take the oath of loyalty to the King or report to the commandant at Charleston, Hayne claimed the benefit of the terms of capitulation under which he had surrendered. Rather than leave his family—all his children were sick with smallpox, one had already died, and his wife was close to death and died a short while later—Hayne wrote that he engaged "to demean himself as a British subject so long as the country should be covered by the British army."

Hayne had to go to Charleston on behalf of his wife. He reported to the commandant and requested permission to return home. The permission was refused and Hayne was told he would have to become a British subject or be imprisoned. Forced to take the oath of allegiance, Hayne declared "that when the regular forces could not defend the country without the aid of its inhabitants, it would be high time for the Royal army to quit it." He received permission to return to his family, but the British authorities violated Hayne's reservation and repeatedly called upon him to take arms against his countrymen. They threatened to imprison him if he continued to refuse.

Hayne visited Charleston but Brigadier General James Pattison (1724–1805) refused to let him return home unless he signed a declaration of allegiance to the King, even though Hayne showed him the paper he had already signed. Hayne signed the declaration, but considered it null and void after the Congressional forces reoccupied his district.

Hayne accepted a commission as colonel from Governor John Rutledge (1730–1800), raised a regiment, and joined Colonel William Harden (1743–1785). He and 100 horsemen rode to the Charleston area on Thursday, July 5, 1781, and captured Brigadier General Andrew Williamson (ca. 1730–1786), who was known as the "Benedict Arnold of the South." Williamson, who led the militia in the Ninety Six district, took British protection after the surrender of Charleston and was living on a plantation at Horse Savannah. Hayne and his men surrounded the house and got Williamson out of bed without giving him the time to dress properly. The British could not allow the militia to discredit their protection so easily, so it became a political necessity for them to rescue General Williamson.

Hayne was captured on July 8, 1781 and was imprisoned in the provost (the basement of the Exchange in Charleston (see Photo SC-27)). Despite a petition from a number of ladies on his behalf, Hayne was tried on Friday and Saturday, July 27–28. However, Lord Francis Rawdon (1754–1826) took the record of the court proceedings with him when he sailed for Europe a short while later. When he was captured at sea, he threw the records overboard. Nevertheless, Hayne received the following judgment dated the day after the trial:

> To Mr. Hayne in the Provost Prison
> Memorandum
> Sunday 29 July 1781
>
> The Adjutant of the town will be so good as to go to Colonel Hayne in Provost Prison and inform him that in consequence of the court of enquiry held yesterday and the preceding evening Lord Rawdon and the commandant Lieutenant Colonel Nisbet Balfour have resolved upon his execution on Tuesday the thirty-first instant at six o'clock, for having been found under arms raising a regiment to oppose the British government, though he had become a subject and had accepted the protection of that government after the reduction of Charlestown.

Hayne appealed his sentence and received the following answer at 1 PM on Monday, the 30th:

> I have to inform you that your execution is not ordered in consequence of any sentence from a court of enquiry, but by virtue of the authority with which the Commander-in-chief in South Carolina and the commanding officer in Charlestown are invested. And their resolves on the subject are unchangeable.

After a few days' reprieve, Hayne was hanged in the forenoon of Saturday, August 4th somewhere near the junction of Saint Phillip and Calhoun streets in Charleston.

Controversy over Isaac Hayne's execution grew in late August 1781. Brigadier General Francis Marion (1732–1795) vowed to retaliate. Some 450 Loyalists took up arms in the region and the British dispatched Major Thomas Fraser (d. 1820) and 200 dragoons from Fort Dorchester and Stono to help them. Colonel William Harden sent a desperate plea for assistance to Major General Nathanael Greene (1742–1786) at his headquarters in the High Hills of Santee. Greene sent Marion and 100 men. They traveled 100 miles at night to intercept Fraser's column at Parker's Ferry.

Marion's scouts rode headlong into the British force about 1 mile west of Parker's Ferry on Thursday, August 30, 1781. Fraser ordered his dragoons to pursue them as Marion had expected. His riflemen, hidden in a thick wood, within a mile of the ferry, about 40 yards from the road, waited for the dragoons. When they appeared, the marksmen opened fire, inflicting heavy casualties. Major Charles Harden commanded a division of about 80 men on the right. Marion ordered him to retire 100 yards from the line and to march up when the firing began on the left. He then sent Major Samuel Cooper (1757–1840) with 60 horsemen and the swordsmen to attack the enemy's rear as a diversion and to follow them whenever they moved and to charge when the firing became general.

Marion's men waited in this position until sunset when part of the Loyalists from the ferry were allowed to pass. When they discovered one of the militiamen, they challenged him. They began firing when they received no answer. The militiamen returned fire, driving the Loyalists back. Marion sent a few horsemen after them, forcing them across the river. The Loyalists heard the fire and immediately sent their cavalry to their support. The dragoons rode at full speed and received the fire of the entire line.

Fraser ordered Lieutenant Stephen Jarvis (1756–1840) and his South Carolina dragoons to charge forward while he deployed three other divisions on the road and along both sides. Some of Marion's dragoons charged at Jarvis's troops who returned to the main body in the road. Fraser ordered his cavalry to advance at full gallop toward Marion's troops in the road. They flanked Marion's right, throwing his men into confusion. The Loyalists took advantage of the time it took Marion to rally and form his men to capture their field pieces and wounded.

Jarvis pursued a mounted officer who had shot at him. When the cavalry reached the ambush site Marion gave the signal. His men fired buckshot at the dragoons at a distance of 40 yards. Jarvis wrote "we received the most galling fire ever Troops experienced." Fraser rallied his men and tried to charge but his men were struck by several volleys, unable to retreat and unable to attack in the swamp. He was forced to retreat down the causeway, the entire length of the ambush. Jarvis wrote, "We only saw the flash of the pieces, the enemy was so complete hid from our view, and we only had to push forward, men and horses falling before and behind."

They retreated "on a trot, leaving 20 men and 23 horses dead on the spot." Jarvis's commander, Captain Archibald Campbell (1739–1791), had been wounded twice. Fraser's horse was killed and the rest of the cavalry rode over him as he lay in the road, badly bruising him.

Marion immediately marched up and took possession of the ground and remained there for three more hours. He then retired 2 miles to refresh his men who were low on ammunition and had not eaten for 24 hours. He sent a party to bury the dead early the next morning; but they withdrew when a superior force of British arrived with their field pieces. The British crossed the river and headed toward Charleston. "A party sent after them found a number of horses dead and wounded on the road, amounting to upwards of 40 in the whole. The enemy had upwards of eighty men and several officers wounded." Jarvis wrote, "We lost one hundred twenty-five killed and a great many wounded." Marion lost one man killed and three wounded. [281]

See **Snipes's Plantation** p. 240.

★ Loyalists were using the Ashley River Baptist Church, a brick building that was no longer used for worship, as a military station in 1781. Brigadier General Francis Marion (1732–1795) sent Captain George Cooper and a detachment of mounted militiamen to create a diversion near Charleston when he set out to attack the British at Parker's Ferry. Captain Cooper raided down the east side of the Ashley River and routed a party of Loyalists at Cypress Swamp on Friday, August 31, 1781. He then proceeded toward Charleston. He drove off the cattle from in front of the British post at Fort Dorchester and attacked a group of Loyalists at the Ashley River Church. He charged and drove the Loyalists in front of him. He took a number of prisoners but had no casualties in these engagements. He then retreated by way of Goose Creek.[282]

★ A British vessel anchored off Fuller's plantation to land a foraging party between Wednesday, March 20th and Thursday, March 28, 1782. Lieutenant George Foster (1756–1810), of Lieutenant Colonel Henry "Light-Horse Harry" Lee's (1756–1818) Legion, was patrolling the area when he saw the landing party heading for shore. His legionnaires took the foragers prisoners without firing a shot when they landed. Lieutenant Colonel John Laurens (1754–1782) paroled the prisoners and sent them back to Charleston under a flag of truce.[283]

Near Summerville, Dorchester County
Fort Dorchester (ca. July 14, 1781); Dec. 1, 1781; Jan. 14, 1782; April 21, 1782 [Howard Peckham dates this event as occurring on April 24, 1782])
Dorchester (Fair Spring) (May 28, 1782)

Congregationalists from Dorchester, Massachusetts, established a town of the same name at the headwaters of the Ashley River in 1697. The market town grew into a trade center with about 40 houses by 1781. Although most of the Congregationalists abandoned the town in the 1750s, it remained prosperous and was the third-largest town in the colony but it was abandoned by 1788.

Fort Dorchester (see Photo SC-33) was in what is now Old Dorchester State Park off route SC 642 (Dorchester Road) south of Summerville and about 25 miles northwest of Charleston. To get there, take route U.S. 17A (Boonehill Road) south of Summerville. Travel about 6 miles to route SC 642 (Dorchester Road). Follow route SC 642 east for 4.9 miles to route S-18-373 (Old Dorchester State Park Road). A state historical marker at this junction chronicles the history of Fort Dorchester. Follow route S-18-373 (Old Dorchester State Park Road) for 0.5 miles to the entrance to Old Dorchester State Park to see the remains of the fortifications.

Just past the park entrance, on the right, are the brick remains of the bell tower of the St. George parish Church, constructed in 1737. The British burned the church, then partially restored it before it fell into disuse. These ruins and the adjacent cemetery are the few tangible reminders of Old Dorchester. The remains of the fort walls, just beyond the parking area at the end of the road, are made of tabby, a building material made with oyster shells as a binder. A substantial portion of the tabby walls of the old fort survive. The fort's remains consist of a squarish, empty enclosure that resembles a pinwheel. The design is unique in North America. There are bastions to the right and left and the remains of the powder magazine in the interior. The old sally port, or rear exit, is directly opposite the main entrance.

The fort, constructed on a bluff above the Ashley River during the Seven Years' War (French and Indian War) (1756–1763), changed hands several times during the American War for Independence. The Council of Safety of South Carolina

SC-33. Remains of the fort walls and the powder magazine of Fort Dorchester

> ordered the establishment of a depot here in 1775 to store public records and ammunition. A detachment of local militiamen garrisoned the fort in the early days of the war. Continental soldiers from the 2nd South Carolina Regiment under Captain Francis Marion (1732–1795) replaced them. The British took control of the fort after they captured Charleston. They held the fort until late November 1781 when Major General Nathanael Greene (1742–1786) tricked them into abandoning it.
>
> Fair Spring was located on the east side of the Ashley River about a mile west-northwest of Bacon's Bridge at the intersection of route SC 165 (Bacons Bridge Road) and Tom Pike Lane on the east side of the Ashley River. The site is about 0.8 miles down Tom Pike Lane.

Lieutenant Colonel Henry "Light-Horse Harry" Lee (1756–1818) was ordered to capture Fort Dorchester and proceed to Charleston about Saturday, July 14, 1781. He met no resistance at the fort because Lieutenant Colonel Alexander Stewart (1740–1794) had greatly reduced the garrison by draft and a mutiny resulted in many dead and wounded. Lieutenant Colonel Wade Hampton's (1752–1832) sudden appearance at Goose Creek Bridge alarmed the demoralized garrison who abandoned the fort. Colonel Lee arrived in time to seize about 200 horses, three empty wagons, and a fourth one filled with much-needed ammunition.[284]

★ General Charles Cornwallis (1738–1805) had surrendered at Yorktown in October 1781. Major General Nathanael Greene (1742–1786), in command of the Continental Army in the South, came to the Dorchester area to quell a Loyalist uprising and decided to take Dorchester which was garrisoned by 850 Redcoats.

General Greene and Colonel Wade Hampton (1752–1832) [Lieutenant Colonel William Washington (1752–1810) was a prisoner and Lieutenant Colonel Henry "Light-Horse Harry" Lee (1756–1818) was an invalid at this time] approached with about 200 Maryland and Virginia Continental infantrymen and 200 of Lee's, Washington's, and Brigadier General Thomas Sumter's (1734–1832) cavalrymen. The Redcoats assumed Greene had his full army with him. They were unaware that General Otho Holland Williams (1749–1794) and most of the army was camped at Round O more than 20 miles to the west.

The British commander at Dorchester prepared his fort for an attack, but, when the attack did not occur by dawn on Saturday, December 1, 1781, he sent 50 dragoons of the South Carolina Royalists to reconnoiter. They encountered Colonel Wade Hampton and his 300 light dragoons, Greene's vanguard, who drove them back across the bridge, killing 8 or 10, wounding 15 or 20 more, and taking several prisoners. The survivors returned to the fort and told their commander that Greene's entire army was approaching.

The commander at Dorchester ordered the South Carolina Royalists out again to intercept the approaching Continentals. Colonel Hampton mistook the cavalrymen for militiamen, but soon realized they were well-armed dragoons. Hampton's infantrymen chased the Royalists off the field after a tough fight.

The British commander recognized General Greene riding with the troops and thought the entire Continental Army was coming. He ordered the stores destroyed and the artillery thrown into the Ashley River. The Redcoats then burned all their military stores and threw the cannons into the Ashley River before abandoning their base during the night. They withdrew to the Quarterhouse on Charleston Neck where they rendezvoused with the main army under Lieutenant Colonel Alexander Stewart (1740–1794).

General Greene captured the fort without firing a single shot and captured two iron artillery pieces there.

General Greene withdrew his army of 800 men on Friday, December 7th and returned to his camp at Round O. His troops only had four rounds of ammunition per man as the month's supply of ammunition had all gone to Brigadier General Francis Marion's (1732–1795) troops. The Crown forces only held Charleston and its immediate vicinity in South Carolina. The garrison consisted of 3,300 men and a considerable body of Loyalists. Rumors exaggerating General Greene's strength caused "wild alarm" throughout the town.

★ Major John Coffin (1756–1838) and 45 New York Volunteers surprised Lieutenant John Kelty's (1751–1812) 3rd Regiment of Continental Light Dragoons near Dorchester on Monday, Jan. 14, 1782. They captured Kelty and seven of his men.[285]

★ The situation in the Continental camp outside Charleston was pretty grim in the spring of 1782. Major General William Moultrie (1730–1805) wrote in his memoirs:

> While the American army lay on the south side of the Ashley-river, the greater part of the men were so completely ragged, that their clothes would scarcely cover their nakedness: every little piece of cloth was taken up to tie about their waists; and that was not the worst of their grievances; the want of provisions was severely felt by them. Sometimes they had meat without bread or rice, sometimes bread and rice without meat, and sometimes were without either. In this situation did they continue for several months, and only sixteen miles from Charleston, where the British army was in garrison, with a greatly superior force; fortunately, Ashley-river was between them. By their being encamped so long in one place at this season of the year...they began to be sickly, discontented and mutinous.

Major General Nathanael Greene (1742–1786) wrote to General George Washington (1732–1799) that the troops were "so naked as to be unfit for duty.... Not a rag of clothing arrived to us this winter. It is true we get meat and rice, but no rum or spirits." He also wrote, "For upwards of 2 months, more than one third of our men were entirely naked, with nothing but a breech-cloth about them, and never came out of their tents; and the rest were as ragged as wolves."

It was during this time that Sergeant George Gornell (d. 1782) began to foment a conspiracy in the Pennsylvania Line. The Pennsylvania Continentals had mutinied earlier, in January 1781, because they claimed that soldiers who had enlisted for three years were being detained on the pretext that they had enlisted for the duration of the war, violating their enlistment contracts. This time, the Pennsylvanians complained that they were not used to the fighting conditions in the South. Major General Arthur St. Clair (1737–1818) wrote, "Can soldiers be expected to do their duty, clothed in rags and fed on rice."

Captain Philip Pendleton (1741–1811) went to Charleston, under a flag of truce, to negotiate with the British about the treatment of his brother, Henry Pendleton (1750–1788) who was the Chief Judge of South Carolina. Pendleton's servant stole his horse as Captain Pendleton returned from Charleston. The servant then rode to claim protection from the British. Pendleton sent Sergeant Peters [William? (ca. 1746–1801)] to retrieve the horse. Sergeant Peters belonged to the Maryland Line and was Major General Nathanael Greene's (1742–1786) cook He sided with Sergeant Gornell who had deserted the British Army and joined the Pennsylvania line.

When Sergeant Peters arrived in Charleston the British offered him a large bribe to get the disgruntled Pennsylvanians to seize General Greene and deliver him to the British on the Dorchester causeway. Sergeants Peters and Gornell were instructed to secure all the officers at a certain hour and fire a gun as a signal whereupon 150 British dragoons, waiting within 1 mile of the camp, would rush in and take possession of Greene and his staff.

Sergeant Peters's wife learned of the plan and warned Greene who had Gornell, Peters and four other Pennsylvanians arrested. A dozen other Pennsylvanians deserted to the British shortly after the arrests. While the court-martial was in session, Greene sent out his dragoons to search for the British counterparts to the conspiracy. Captain Ferdinand O'Neal or O'Neale (ca. 1758–ca. 1817) and some of Lieutenant Colonel Henry "Light-Horse Harry" Lee's (1756–1818) Legion crossed Bacon's Bridge to patrol the east side of the Ashley River Sunday morning, April 21 or Wednesday, April 24, 1782. O'Neal spotted three soldiers of the Independent Troop of Black Dragoons led by Captain March, a Black officer near Dorchester.

Captain Michael Rudolph (1758–1793) was in the lead of Lee's Legion with two other troopers. They attacked the Loyalists and killed one of the Black Dragoons and captured a second. The third one escaped. One of the prisoners informed Captain Rudolph that Captain George Dawkins (ca. 1754–1805) took a troop by the way of the Goose Creek bridge and would return by the way of Dorchester; so O'Neal set out in pursuit. He discovered Dawkins as he passed through the village of Dorchester. Both sides charged simultaneously and a desperate fight began. At the sound of a bugle, dismounted Crown cavalry rose from their hiding places where they were awaiting the Pennsylvanians to deliver General Greene. They fired a volley into O'Neal's flanks.

O'Neal ordered his men to retreat down Gaillard Road, his only option to escape. He lost three or four men killed, nine men and 15 horses captured. Sergeant Major William Seymour, of the Delaware Regiment, wrote in his journal, "One of our men engaged and killed 2 of the enemy's negro horse, and a third, which happened to be a Major, thought to make his escape by running into a swamp where he came up with him, and with one blow of his sword severed his head from his body."

When the Pennsylvanians learned of this incident, 12 more deserted to the British lines. However, two British officers and 20 of their men deserted to the Continental lines with their weapons that night. Gornell was sentenced to be executed on the 23rd.[286]

★ Ralph Izard (1741–1804), an aide to General Isaac Huger (1743–1797), was visiting his plantation, known as Fair Spring on Tuesday, May 28, 1782. When Captain George Dawkins (ca. 1754–1805) was informed that Izard was at home, he surrounded the plantation house with 30 of his South Carolina Royalists. Mrs. Izard let the Loyalists come into her home to search after she concealed her husband in a clothespress. After the Loyalists left, Izard crossed Bacon's Bridge to notify Lieutenant Colonel John Laurens (1754–1782) that the Loyalists were nearby. Laurens and his dragoons went in search of the Royalists, overtook them and defeated them in a brief skirmish. They captured one Royalist lieutenant, seven dragoons and their 10 horses. Laurens had three men wounded and two horses killed.[287]

Ferguson's Plantation, Charleston County (March 6–7, 1780)

Ferguson's plantation, called Spring Grove, was 14 miles from the Wappoo River, possibly along the Wadmalaw River or Bohicket Creek.

Two British light infantry battalions tried to surprise some of Major Hezekiah Maham's (1739–1789) South Carolina dragoons near Ferguson's plantation on Monday night, March 6, 1780. They crossed the Wappoo River and marched through the night, but an officer's servant had deserted and warned the dragoons who fled before the British arrived. The 14-mile march fatigued the infantrymen and eight were left behind, too tired to return.

Major Maham sent word to the Continental light dragoons that the British were on the mainland. The light dragoons, who had spent the night partying at Ferguson's plantation, headed toward the retreating British and captured seven of the eight stragglers. The other man had rejoined his unit.[288]

Mouth of Wappoo Creek, Charleston County (March 11, 1780)
Wappoo Cut, Charleston County (March 21, 1780)
Near Stan's Bridge (April 23–24, 1782)

> Wappoo Creek and Wappoo Cut are about 2.25 miles east of where route SC 700 (Maybank Highway) crosses the Stono River and a little east of where route SC 171 (Folly Road) crosses it.
> Stan's Bridge crossed the Stono River near the present location of Plymouth Avenue on James Island.

The Crown forces raised a 6-gun battery on the right, at the mouth of Wappoo Creek at Mr. Fenwick's store. They had one 32-pound brass cannon mounted. The brigantine *Notre Dame* and two galleys went up to fire upon them at dawn on Saturday, March 11, 1780. The *Notre Dame* received a shot by her mainchains that beat in two of her knees.[289]

★ Two British grenadier (see Photo SC-14) battalions left Fort Johnson to join the forces at Hudson's house on James Island on Saturday, March 18, 1780. Major Thomas Mecan, of the 23rd Regiment, and 120 men of the Hessian Regiment von Benning occupied the fort constructed there to protect the fleet and transport vessels coming to Charleston. They surrounded Hudson's house with a breastwork 12 feet thick by Sunday and constructed two redoubts 300 feet away from the fort. The left redoubt was on the Stono River and the right one was on the Wappoo Canal. Each had an abatis of sharpened apple and peach tree limbs.

Captain Johann von Ewald (1744–1813) reconnoitered the Congressional lines on the 21st. He discovered the quarters of the main guard and the individual guard posts. He placed a corporal and five men on the path to one of the guard posts. He gave them each "a guinea, a bottle of water, and some bread" and ordered them to stay there until they could ambush one of the guards.

A party of dragoons rode up to the redoubt on the Wappoo Canal about midnight and fired their pistols. When the dragoons returned to their lines, the jaegers ambushed them, wounded a sergeant major and his horse and captured them.[290]

★ Two hundred Loyalists on James Island crossed the Wappoo Cut at Stan's Bridge to plunder houses along the Ashley River on Tuesday, April 23, 1782. The Whigs captured one of them, Thomas Farr, and discovered that he was a deserter from the North Carolina Line.

The Loyalists crossed over again the next night and took John Linning (d. 1782) prisoner. They released him after a few hours, but Linning was shot dead as he was returning home. The crew of a British galley found Linning's body on the ground, wrapped it up in a blanket and threw it in a creek.[291]

Charleston and Vicinity

Wando River (April 13, 1780; Feb. 1781; Jan. 3, 1782)
Cainhoy (Nov. 2, 1781; Dec. 30, 1781)
Colonel Maham's tour

> Cainhoy is on the Wando River about 1 mile southwest of Wando. The Cainhoy Tavern was at the end of Fogarty Lane which runs south from Clements Ferry Road (S-8-33) in Francis Marion National Forest. The fence at the eastern edge of the boatyard property is as close as you can get. The Cainhoy Tavern was about 75 feet inside the fenced area, near the water. This was an ideal location for a fortification as it was at a bend in the river, allowing cannon to be fired easily in either direction up or down the river.
>
> Both sides used the two-story Cainhoy Tavern as a fort. The building stood until the late 1970s or early 1980s when the boatyard that now occupies the site acquired the property, leveled the building and covered the area with at least 3 feet of sand.

Colonel Bernard François Lellorquis Marquis de Malmedy (1766–1832) was ordered to Cainhoy, on the north side of the Wando River, 9 miles from Charleston, to fortify that post with 200 men on Thursday, April 13, 1780. Colonel Richard Richardson, Jr. (1741–1817), of the South Carolina militia, commanded the post which also served as a supply depot.

★ Colonel Hezekiah Maham (1739–1789) patrolled the Cainhoy area about Tuesday, November 2, 1781 when he captured a British dragoon and burned a sloop and schooner that were collecting provisions for the Crown forces.[292]

★ A party of British from Haddrell's Point went to Cainhoy about Sunday, December 30, 1781, to surprise Colonel Benjamin Screven. The outcome of the brief skirmish is unknown.[293]

★ Brigadier General Francis Marion (1732–1795) and a party of mounted militiamen proceeded from Pee Dee down the country in early February 1781. They destroyed enemy stores and damaged their quarters in different parts, particularly at Wando Landing, within 15 miles of Charleston, where they destroyed all the Crown stores and took 30 prisoners, including several officers, before proceeding to Dorchester.[294]

★ A British force landed in the area of Cainhoy from a ship in the Wando River on Thursday, January 3, 1782. Details of the skirmish are unknown.[295]

Moncks Corner and vicinity, Berkeley County
Moncks Corner (April 14, 1780; Oct. 16, 1781)
Fair Lawn
Moncks Corner Road (Sept. 9, 1781)
Biggin Bridge (April 14, 1780)
Biggin Church (July 17, 1781)

> Moncks Corner is about 30 miles north of Charleston.
> Moncks Corner Road probably corresponds pretty much with Old Moncks Corner Road which runs northeast of route U.S. 176 (Saint James Avenue) about 1.1 miles

north of its junction with route U.S. 52 (North Goose Creek Boulevard) in Goose Creek.

Biggin Bridge crossed the West Cooper River about 2.5 miles northeast of Moncks Corner and about 1 mile south of the junction of routes SC 402 and U.S. 17A|U.S. 52).

St. John's Berkeley Church, known as the Biggin Church (see Photo SC-34) from the creek in front, is located about 0.5 miles south of routes U.S. 17A|U.S. 52 on SC 402. It was constructed between these two roads in 1755 to replace an earlier building destroyed by a forest fire. Located at the intersection of three roads in the 18th century, the church was a strategic point for both armies. Henry (1754–1782) and William Moultrie (1730–1805) worshipped here. The Crown forces garrisoned the church and used it as a supply post for part of the war until Lieutenant Colonel John Coates burned it when he had to abandon it. The church was restored after the war, but a forest fire in 1890 damaged it beyond repair. The ruins of the Biggin Church, which was 60 feet long by 40 feet wide with three-feet thick brick walls at the base, are still visible.

To get to the Biggin Church site from the intersection of routes U.S. 17A and SC 6 in Moncks Corner, go 1.4 miles east on route SC 6 to route U.S. 17A. Bear left onto route U.S. 52 and go north 1.6 miles, then turn right on route SC 402 for 0.6 miles. The Biggin Church ruins and cemetery are on the right on route SC 402 just before the intersection with Biggins Road. A historical marker explains the site.[296]

The adjacent cemetery contains many 18th-century graves. The low-arched vault supposedly was used to imprison Turpentine John Palmer and his brother because

SC-34. Biggin Church was a strategic point for both armies. The Crown forces garrisoned the church and used it as a supply post for part of the war. Lieutenant Colonel John Coates burned it when he had to abandon it. The church was restored after the war, but a forest fire in 1890 damaged it beyond repair.

Charleston and Vicinity **179**

> John's son was one of Francis Marion's soldiers. The two men were buried alive in the vault for two days before they were released. The bricks have indentations identifying the men's efforts to cut their way out. They were so weak when they were released that it took them two days to walk the 10 miles to their homes.
>
> Among the parishioners at Biggin Church during the Revolutionary War era were Brigadier General Isaac Huger (1743–1797) and Lieutenant Colonel William Washington (1752–1810), General George Washington's (1732–1799) cousin, who kept a supply line and a possible escape route open at Biggin Bridge.

General Henry Clinton (1730–1795) landed his force on Johns Island, about 30 miles south of Charleston, on Friday, February 11, 1780. He then moved up to the Ashley River investing Charleston from the land side. He called for more men from Savannah, Georgia, and from New York who arrived in March and April. This brought his army to about 14,000, including sailors from the fleet.

On Saturday, April 8, British warships successfully forced the passage past Fort Moultrie, investing Charleston from the sea. On April 10, Clinton began cutting the defenders' line of supplies with the north which three regiments of cavalry under Brigadier General Isaac Huger (1742–1797) kept open 30 miles upriver at Moncks Corner. General Clinton sent Colonel John Graves Simcoe's (1752–1806) Queen's Rangers and Lieutenant Colonel Banastre Tarleton's (1744–1833) British Legion to destroy the Continental camp in a surprise attack by night. They left from the Quarter House, a well-known tavern and British stronghold on the outskirts of Charleston.

Lieutenant Colonel James Webster (ca. 1743–1781) was detached with a corps from the third contingent, the 33rd Regiment, and the cavalry under Lieutenant Colonel Tarleton, to the bridge near the head of the Cooper River [Biggin Bridge]. They arrived at 3 AM and struck at 3:30 on Friday, April 14, 1780. Colonel Webster came upon the Congressional cavalry and militia so unexpectedly and quickly that General Huger's guards could not even fire a cannon. The guards immediately fell back toward their camp, with the raiders in pursuit. General Huger, Lieutenant Colonel William Washington (1752–1810), and other officers fled on foot into the swamps. The British killed those who tried to defend themselves.

Colonel Webster took possession of the bridge and some forty wagons, boats, and sloops, all loaded with provisions and munitions. Tarleton reported: "Four hundred horses belonging to the officers and dragoons with their arms and appointments fell into the hands of the victors. About one hundred, officers, dragoons and hussars, together with fifty wagons loaded with arms, clothing and ammunition, shared the same fate." The British captured 73 dragoons and militiamen and about 100 horses. The prisoners included General Huger and Colonel Washington, who later escaped on his swift horse, which they had neglected to take away from him. The casualties totaled a major and 12 privates dead, 19 wounded and 64 captured. The militia also lost 50 wagonloads of supplies and ammunition and 400 horses while the British reported only three casualties. The successful brutal attack closed the Continental supply route to Charleston which would surrender on May 12.[297]

★ The British controlled the Moncks Corner area for over a year until Brigadier General Thomas Sumter (1734–1832) moved against the forces here in July 1781. He sent a detachment to attack the picket guarding the bridge on Monday, July 16. The pickets drove off the attackers without much difficulty. Lieutenant Colonel Henry "Light-Horse Harry" Lee (1756–1818) and his dragoons rode in from the west, expecting to find Sumter's troops in control of the Biggin Bridge. To their chagrin, they found it still in the possession of Lieutenant Colonel John Coates's 19th Regiment and mounted infantry of the Loyalist South Carolina Rangers. Colonel Coates withdrew his troops from Moncks Corner when he learned that Brigadier General Sumter was approaching. He crossed to the east side of the Cooper River to St. Johns about a mile and a half away on Biggin Creek. He stored his weapons and supplies in the church.

★ When Lieutenant Colonel John Coates left the Moncks Corner area to move closer to Charleston, about 29 miles to the south, on Monday evening, July 16, 1781, he ordered his men to burn the Biggin Church, which was being used as a supply depot, and all the supplies he could not take with him. The fire broke through the church's roof about 3 AM, long after Coates had departed. The fire burned itself out after destroying the church. Only the church's 3-foot brick walls remained. It was reconstructed after the war, destroyed again by a forest fire, and never rebuilt. All that remains are parts of the west and south walls.[298] (See **Quinby Bridge** p. 189.)

★ After the battle of Eutaw Springs on Saturday, September 8, 1781 (see p. 243), Colonel Alexander Stewart (or Stuart) (1740–1794) retreated toward Moncks Corner with his force of nearly 2,000 men. He halted a few miles away and encamped at Wantoot, Mr. Daniel Ravenel's (1762–1807) plantation, 20 miles from Eutaw. Major General Nathanael Greene (1742–1786) intended to renew the action the next day but Colonel Stewart called up Major Archibald McArthur and 400 men from Fair Lawn. He left 70 of his wounded to the enemy and many of his dead unburied. He broke the stocks of 1,000 stand of arms and threw them into the spring and destroyed his stores before joining Colonel Stewart on Sunday morning, September 9, 1781 "about two miles above Fergusons Swamp. They Immediatly turn'd down the road & Crossed that Swamp, & is now there halted."

Greene turned back from Burdell's plantation and followed McArthur for some distance; but as Stewart continued his retreat, Greene halted and sent Brigadier General Francis Marion (1732–1795) and Lieutenant Colonel Henry "Light-Horse Harry" Lee (1756–1818) to try to keep reinforcements from reaching Stewart. They took a circuitous route intending to take a position between the two British forces. The plan failed, however, because Stewart retreated so quickly for 15 miles that his first division came within a few miles of McArthur before Marion and Lee reached their destination at Ferguson's Swamp.

Colonels Lee and Hezekiah Maham (1739–1789) got within 4 miles of Moncks Corner and fell in with a party of 300 infantrymen and 15 cavalrymen going down to meet some reinforcements. Maham led the Continental detachment past the post at Wantoot in an attempt to decoy the British cavalry into the field. The maneuver did not succeed, but it did bring out a strong detachment which pursued him closely. Lee and Marion had two horses killed and two men wounded. Marion reported: "We have taken 24 British & 4 toreys prisoners," 14 of them dragoons captured by "six men of Lee and Maham."

The two known accounts of this engagement differ considerably. Major General Henry "Light-Horse Harry" Lee (1756–1818) wrote in his memoirs that his detachment had been in pursuit of the enemy's "rear guard, with a portion of their wagons conveying the wounded." They overtook the rear guard and Lee detached Captain Joseph Eggleston (1754–1811) to fall upon the enemy's flank while he moved to "force the enemy in front." Eggleston's troops had to ride through woods "thickly set with black jack" to attack. This gave the Crown forces time to form and fire a volley before fleeing. Lee recorded that "Eggleston and his troop were roughly handled; his horse being killed,— himself happily escaping although five balls pierced his clothes and equipments." Lee's party encountered "none of the impediments" and was little injured. When he examined his captured wagons, Lee discovered that he had captured wagons filled with "miserable wounded," who "supplicated so fervently to be permitted to proceed" that Lee assented, not wishing "to add to their misery and to his trouble."

Samuel Hammond (1757–1842) noted in his memoir that Lee, Maham, and he had obtained reliable information that the detachment they were pursuing consisted of 50 or 60 British infantrymen, escorting "several wagons" and all of the Congressional prisoners taken at Eutaw Springs, including Lieutenant Colonel William Washington (1752–1810). The Whigs, who remained undiscovered until they were within a mile of the convoy, found that part of the infantry escort was in the rear, the wagons and prisoners were in the center, and the remainder of the escort was in front. As the Congressional cavalrymen came into view, the escort "formed in the road with the wagons in the rear." Hammond continued: "We were halted. Colonel Lee gave orders to Captain Eggleston to charge with his troops and take the escort." The rest of the dragoons were held in reserve. "Eggleston charged the enemy breasted by their bayonets and covered by their wagons; he lost several brave men, with a Sergeant of great merit, and was compelled to retreat in disorder. We saw this with great concern, but expected the attack would be immediately renewed successfully; but, to our astonishment, a retreat was ordered. Chagrin and ill humor pervaded the detachment; Colonel Maham and myself requested Colonel Lee's permission to make an attempt with our own commands, and pledge ourselves the responsibility of the attack. We were peremptorily refused."[299]

★ Another engagement occurred at Moncks Corner on October 16, 1781 when a Whig raiding party attacked a British encampment and captured 80 men.

Berkeley County
Wadboo, Keithfield and Manigault's Ferry (Jan. 31–Feb. 1, 1781)
Keithfield Plantation (also known as Kitfield Plantation)

Keithfield was about 2.4 miles north-northeast of Moncks Corner, about 1 mile due south-southwest of where the Cooper River exits from Lake Moultrie. Keithfield plantation was located inside the circle or loop encompassed by Belleview Circle at the end of Keithfield/Kitfield Road which branches right (east) of Broughton Road about 0.75 miles north of route SC 6 (East Main Street).
This engagement happened the day after the raid on Wadboo Bridge. One source asserts that it occurred on January 24th.

See **Huger** p. 189.

Brigadier General Francis Marion (1732–1795) sent Major James Postell (1745–1824) and his brother, Captain John Postell (1717–1782), and 70 men to destroy British supply bases on January 29, 1781. This was after the raid on Georgetown and was intended to support Major General Nathanael Greene's (1742–1786) planned offensive against Fort Ninety Six or Camden. Captain John Postell, of the Kingstree Regiment, and a party of 39 unassigned officers made a forced march to Wadboo to "burn all British stores of every kind." They destroyed 15 hogsheads of rum, a quantity of pork, flour, rice, salt and turpentine on Wednesday, January 31, 1781.[300]

See also **Manigault's Ferry, Calhoun County** (Jan. 31–Feb. 1, 1781) p. 91.

★ They then proceeded to the Keithfield supply depot, near Moncks Corner, on their way back. They surprised the depot the same day and killed two guards, wounded two, and captured two surgeons, one quartermaster, one wagon master, one steward, and 25 non-commissioned officers and privates. They burned 14 wagons loaded with soldiers' clothing and baggage and 20 hogsheads of rum. They also captured seven other wagons and retired with their prisoners without losing a single man.

Captain Tarleton Brown (1757–1845), who rode with Postell, recorded:

> Just about the break of day we charged upon the enemy, and our appearance was so sudden and unexpected that they had not time even to fire a single gun. We took thirty-three prisoners, found twenty odd hogsheads of old spirits, and a large supply of provisions. The former we destroyed, but returned with the latter and our prisoners to the army on the Santee.[301]

★ Major James Postell (1739–1824) and 40 men went to Colonel Benjamin Thompson's (1753–1814) plantation on the Congaree, but found no supplies there, as they had all been removed a few days earlier. Lieutenant Colonel Brown wrote that Major Postell had found the camp too heavily guarded to attack.[302]

Lewisfield Plantation (also known as Little Landing) (ca. July 15, 1781)

> Lewisfield plantation is at the end of Lewisfield Plantation Road on the West Branch of the Cooper River about 3 miles from the center of Moncks Corner. To get there, go south on route U.S. 52 from Moncks Corner until it turns right at a traffic light. Continue straight for about 1.5 miles to Lewisfield Plantation Road and turn left. There's a historical marker on the right immediately after the turn. The plantation is at the end of Lewisfield Plantation Road. It is a private residence and not open to the public.

Colonel Wade Hampton (1752–1832) made a surprise attack at Lewisfield plantation in mid-July 1781. He destroyed two boats with supplies and took 78 Crown prisoners in a skirmish that took place in the area 100 to 150 feet between the plantation house and the Cooper River.[303]

Fair Lawn (also known as Fair Lawn Barony or Colleton House) (Aug. 29, 1781; Nov. 17 or 27, 1781)

> The Fair Lawn plantation was the property of Sir Peter Colleton (1673–1674), one of the original eight lords proprietors. After Sir Peter's death, the estate passed to his eldest son Sir John Colleton (d. 1750). By the last quarter of the 18th century, the estate was so large that it was more like a small village. It had a landing on the Cooper River which was protected by a redoubt. The Crown forces used the large brick mansion as a hospital. The British usually maintained a large garrison here but with the army much farther north, it was now considered unnecessary and its garrison was weakened.
>
> Fair Lawn, the old Colleton house, was on what is now Pascal Drive (S-8-756) about 1.25 miles east of Moncks Corner in Berkeley County. To get there, from the fork of routes U.S. 52 and U.S. 52 Bypass (Rembert C. Dennis Blvd.), take the route U.S. 52 Bypass for about 0.3 miles to route S-8-757 (Edward Drive), the entrance to the Old Santee Canal and Berkeley County Museum. Turn right for one block

Charleston and Vicinity **183**

> and turn right again onto Pascal Drive (S-8-756). About halfway down this street, a path on the right leads into the woods where the old Colleton house was. The path returns to Pascal Drive just below Old Fort Road. Bricks from the house can still be found along the path.

August 29, 1781 see **Wadboo (Watboo)** p. 189.

★ After General Charles Cornwallis (1738–1805) surrendered at Yorktown, Virginia, a large number of Continental soldiers were dispatched to South Carolina to escort the last of the British forces back to Charleston for their departure to England. Brigadier General Francis Marion's (1732–1795) brigade was reinforced with nearly 600 over-mountain men who had fought at Kings Mountain. Major General Nathanael Greene (1742–1786) decided to concentrate his forces against Fair Lawn which was guarded by Captain Murdock MacLaine and 50 men from the 84th Regiment of Foot. He soon received reinforcements who had seen the Continentals on their way to Fair Lawn.

When General Marion arrived on Saturday morning, November 17, 1781, he dispatched Major Hezekiah Maham (1739–1789) with 180 men and Colonel Isaac Shelby (1750–1826) with 200 over-mountain men to storm the Colleton house. The British were using the house as a hospital. It was protected by a redoubt about half a mile away which also guarded the nearby Cooper River landing. Marion expected that MacLaine would leave the redoubt and fight in the open. But MacLaine, strongly outnumbered, refused to take Marion's bait. Marion ordered a party of riflemen to dismount and to move as infantrymen. Meanwhile, the rest of his men advanced into the field behind the cavalry. They demanded surrender and received no resistance.

Marion's forces captured about 150 Crown soldiers and doctors, 300 stand of arms, many stores of value, some sick, and 80 convalescents. They took the convalescents on horseback behind Maham's men. The doctors and those who were too ill to be moved were paroled.

Within half an hour of the arrival of the Continentals, the Colleton house was in flames, according to Dr. Dowse, the senior surgeon on duty. Colonels Maham and Shelby claimed that they were the last men to leave and that there was no sign of smoke or fire when they left. The question of who actually burned the house has never been resolved, but the Colleton family held the British responsible for burning the house to the ground.[304]

Sir John Doyle (1732–1802), Deputy Adjutant General to Lieutenant Colonel Alexander Stewart (1740–1794), conveyed the general's complaint to General Marion on November 20, 1781:

> The burning an Hospital and dragging away a number of dying people to expire in swamps is a species of barbarity hitherto unknown in civilized nations—especially when that hospital has been left without a guard for its defence—that could justify an attack upon the defenceless inhabitants. For the sake of humanity, sir, the General is unwilling to believe that such unmanly proceedings could meet your countenance, and he therefore expects that those unhappy sufferers may be sent immediately as prisoners on parole, to prevent their perishing for want of necessaries and medicines. The sick and helpless seem not proper objects for military prowess, and attacks on Hospitals are among your own Continental army hitherto unprecedented.[305]

When General Greene learned of General Stuart's complaint, he wrote to General Marion on November 24, 1781:

The enemy complains of Colonel Maham in attacking and dragging off a number of their distressed sick from their Hospital. I shall be obliged to Colonel Maham to give me a particular report of the condition of the prisoners he made as well as the manner of making them, also the special reasons which induced him to burn the Hospital. I have not the least doubt that the burning the Hospital was to destroy the stores, which could not be effected in any other way; but I wish to have materials to contradict their charges with.[306]

No record of the requested report exists; but, as the Continentals captured 80 prisoners, all able to bear arms, the complaint was considered baseless. An enemy has no right to protect a depot of stores and arms with a hospital flag.[307]

15 Mile House and 10 Mile House (July 11–14, 1781)
Goose Creek (Dec. 19, 1781)
Garden's Plantation (Dec. 20, 1781)
Head of Goose Creek (Dec. 10, 1782; Dec. 12, 1782)

> The 10 Mile House was probably located west of exit 211-B of Interstate 26, about 100 yards southeast of the intersection of route S-10-1342 (Aviation Avenue) and Core Avenue. It might also have been on the left of Remount Road (S-10-13), about 400 yards east of Interstate 26 after Exit 212A and just before route U.S. 52 south (Rivers Ave).
>
> The 15 Mile House, so named because it was 15 miles north of Charleston, was probably located about 100 yards east of the end of Wheaton Street which runs east, off route S-10-544 (Deerwood Drive). To get there take exit 205-B off Interstate 26. Travel east on route U.S. 78 (University Boulevard) for about 0.7 miles to route S-10-1427 (Dantzler Drive) which becomes Deerwood Drive.
>
> Dr. Alexander Garden's (1728–1791) plantation was called Otranto and was probably located about 0.3 miles east of the intersection of routes U.S. 78 (University Boulevard) and U.S. 52 (Rivers Avenue) and east of the Otranto Plaza Shopping Center and North Basilica Avenue. There's a historical marker on Otranto Boulevard about 100 yards west of Andrea Court and Andrea Lane.
>
> John Parker's (1736–1802) house at Goose Creek was on Antler Drive about halfway between Fawn Street and Melvin Court about 2 miles east of exit 205 off Interstate 26, 15 miles north of Charleston. The head of Goose Creek is about 1.25 miles due north-northwest, at the end of Tuscany Drive. To get there from exit 205 off Interstate 26, go east on route U.S. 78 (University Boulevard) for about 0.7 miles. Turn north (left) on Elms Plantation Boulevard to Delancey Circle East. Tuscany Drive branches off Delancey Circle East.
>
> Goose Creek Bridge was located where route S-8-43 (Goose Creek Road) crosses Goose Creek about 0.5 miles east of route U.S. 52 (Rivers Avenue).

Brigadier General Thomas Sumter (1734–1832) ordered Colonel Wade Hampton (1752–1832) to ride toward Goose Creek Bridge and harass any Crown troops in the area. He attacked 15 Mile House on Wednesday, July 11, 1781. William Brotherton wrote in his pension application, "they had a skirmish at the 15 Mile House and took prisoners but no person was killed." Hampton then attacked the next post, the 10 Mile House on Saturday, the 14th. Brotherton noted "no person was killed." Hampton then proceeded to the Goose Creek Bridge which he captured without opposition on Sunday, July 15th.[308]

★ Captain James Armstrong (1728–1800), of Lieutenant Colonel Henry "Light-Horse Harry" Lee's (1756–1818) Legion, defeated Captain Ludwig Kienen's (or Lewis Kenan) South Carolina Royalist dragoons at Goose Creek on Wednesday, December 19, 1781. Captain Armstrong captured Captain Kienen and seven other prisoners.[309]

See also **Saint Andrews Creek (Armstrong's Skirmish)** p. 182.

★ Captain James Armstrong (1728–1800) was supposed to meet with a spy from Charleston at Dr. Alexander Garden's (1728–1791) plantation on Thursday, December 20, 1781. While he waited for the spy, Captain Armstrong spotted Major John Coffin (1756–1838) and his New York Volunteers and a company of South Carolina Royalists who were searching for Captain Ludwig Kienen's (or Lewis Kenan) captors. Captain Armstrong's dragoons chased the New York Volunteers who led them into an ambush. Captain Armstrong made a bold charge and got out of the trap, but most of his men were killed or captured. Armstrong's horse stumbled on a rock in the road and he was captured.

Loyalist Lieutenant Stephen Jarvis (1756–1840) said to him, "Give me your hand Captain Armstrong, I'll protect you" and he took him to the rear where "Some of our men made a blow at him, and one came near taking off his scalp. I drew my pistol and said. If you touch the prisoner I'll blow your brains out." Armstrong was exchanged for Captain Kienen a short while later.[310]

★ Captain James Robins (d. 1782) and a detachment of Charleston Loyalists went to John Parker's (1736–1802) house in Goose Creek to kill him. When they arrived at Parker's house on Tuesday, December 10, 1782, Parker defended his house and killed Captain Robins, their leader. The Loyalists then gave up the fight.

★ Another detachment of Loyalists went out to avenge Captain James Robins's (d. 1782) death two days later, on Friday, December 12, 1782. Meanwhile, anticipating the British evacuation of Charleston, Lieutenant Colonel Henry "Light-Horse Harry" Lee' (1756–1818) sent out a detachment of his Legion. They entered the Parker property by the front gate while the Loyalists were entering by the back gate. The Loyalists soon fled to avoid engaging the well-armed and trained dragoons.[311]

Charleston County
Ashley River
Ashley Ferry
Quarter House (July 15, 1781; March 18, 1782; Nov. 4, 1782)
Near Quarter House Tavern (Sept. or Oct. 1782)
Dewee's Tavern (March 1782)

> The Quarter House Tavern was north of the city of Charleston, on Meeting Street (S 10-39), about midway between Tant Street and Success Street. The near Quarter House Tavern action probably occurred on Meeting Street (U.S. 52) at the intersection of Arbutus Avenue in North Charleston.
>
> Howard Peckham dates the capture of the *Alligator* as March 19, 1782. It occurred in the Ashley River just west of I-526 (Mark Clark Expressway) slightly to the right at the end of Ashley View Lane. Dewee's Tavern must have been in this vicinity also as it was frequented by Crown forces. The Whigs who captured the *Alligator* rowed there afterward.

Lieutenant Colonel John Coates commanded the Crown forces' garrison at Moncks Corner in July 1781. His troops consisted of the raw Irish recruits of the 19th Regiment, who had arrived in Charleston on June 1, and some mounted Loyalists of the South Carolina Rangers. Coates, realizing that Brigadier General Thomas Sumter (1734–1832) was trying to isolate him, retreated a mile and a half to Biggin Creek on Saturday, July 14, thinking his position at Moncks Corner was weak. He occupied St. John's Berkeley church, commonly called Biggin Church after the creek that flowed in front of it. The church was considered impregnable because its brick walls were three feet thick and it was on an elevation that controlled the approaches to the church. He constructed defensive works and set up a double abatis around the church. When he received reports of Sumter's movements, Coates thought he was going to be attacked by Major General Nathanael Greene's (1742–1786) entire army. He realized his position could leave him exposed and cut off from all possible aid, so he prepared to abandon it and retreat toward Charleston.

Sumter's troops patrolled the various approaches to Charleston to disrupt communications, to destroy outposts, and to harass the enemy at every opportunity. Colonel Henry Hampton (1755–1826), one of Sumter's officers, captured the bridge across Four Holes Creek and was supposed to assist Lieutenant Colonel Henry "Light-Horse Harry" Lee (1756–1818) in an attack on Fort Dorchester. Henry's brother, Colonel Wade Hampton (1752–1832), captured Goose Creek Bridge with no opposition. He was supposed to meet Lee here; but, when Lee did not show up, Hampton proceeded to St. James Church (on Vestry Lane east of route S-8-208 (Snake River Road)) at Goose Creek on Sunday, July 15, 1781. He surrounded the church during Sunday services, captured the congregation and their horses and then released them all on parole. He then proceeded to Charleston.

As he approached the Quarter House, a large garrison of Crown forces 5 miles north of Charleston, some South Carolina dragoons (a Loyalist unit) were saddling their horses preparing to go in search of Hampton's cavalry. Captain John Reid (1745–1818), at the head of Hampton's dragoons, charged and dispersed the Loyalists. Lieutenant David Waugh (d. 1781), of Hampton's dragoons killed Captain John Wright (d. 1781) and two others before being captured. British reports state that, when Waugh tried to surrender his sword, he was killed in retaliation for killing Captain Wright.

The garrison surrendered after a brief fight. Hampton captured a total of 50 prisoners, including several officer and 19 loyal South Carolina dragoons. William Trusler (1736–1781), a butcher, was shot trying to escape. Hampton lost one man killed. He and his men burned four vessels loaded with military supplies and rested for a couple of hours before going up the Ashley River for the night.[312]

★ The British had stationed the galley *Alligator* in the Ashley River to prevent any communication with Charleston. Major General Nathanael Greene (1742–1786) requested that Lieutenant Colonel John Laurens (1754–1782) remove the vessel. Laurens had command of the light troops and Lieutenant Colonel Henry "Light-Horse Harry" Lee's (1756–1818) Legion. Colonel Henry Lee had returned to Virginia and Captain Michael Rudolph (1758–1793) now commanded the Legion. Rudolph was placed in charge of planning and conducting the clandestine raid on the British galley.

Captain Rudolph and 13 dragoons, who were covering the left flank of the Crown army encamped at the Quarter House Tavern and guarding the passage to Charleston, concealed themselves under straw in an armed sloop mounting two 12-pounders, eight 6-pounders, two 3-pounders, and a number of swivels (see Photo SC-32) about 10 PM on

Sunday, March 18, 1782. The sloop, disguised as a boat carrying provisions to market in Charleston, had nine soldiers concealed under vegetables, four disguised as slaves and Captain Rudolph dressed as a farmer. They rowed down the Ashley River, intending to pass the British galley *Alligator*. When the Captain got within 60 yards of the *Alligator* at about 10 PM, the sentry challenged him. He answered in Gullah (a dialect spoken by local slaves), "that some poor negroes were going to town to sell some live stock: Massa, we got some fat goose, will you buy?" "Yes, yes," replied the sailor, "heave too and let us look at them."

As soon as the boat came alongside the *Alligator*, Captain Rudolph and his men "jumped, mounted the deck, knocked the sentries' brains out, and shut down the hatches." They killed two or three of her crew. They took possession of the *Alligator* and took the captain, three commissioned and two warrant officers, and 23 seamen prisoners. Some of the crew jumped overboard and swam for shore. Rudolph released the others, took what supplies he wanted and blew up the *Alligator* because the wind and tide were unfavorable for sailing her away. The Crown forces lost four killed and 28 captured.[313]

★ Shortly after the capture of the *Alligator*, Lieutenant Ballard Smith (d. 1794) took 12 men and Sergeant Du Coin and rowed to the other side of the Ashley River to Dewee's tavern which British officers frequented. Lieutenant Smith took a "Negro as a guide" but the guide became scared and did not take them to the exact spot. Sergeant Du Coin's boat landed in a marsh. He went overboard to reconnoiter the tavern but the mud was deep and had much difficulty getting to shore. As he approached the tavern, Sergeant Du Coin heard music and revelry and saw a large number of British and Hessian officers dancing. Alone and unarmed, Du Coin decided not to risk a fight and he returned to camp.

Sergeant Du Coin led a boat to the exact location of the tavern the following night. His men surrounded the house and kicked in the doors. However, instead of finding 20 or 30 British and Hessian officers, they only found one Hessian major and a lieutenant from the Volunteers of Ireland. Lieutenant Smith paroled these two men then returned to the other side of the river.

The capture of the *Alligator* and the raid on Dewee's Tavern lowered the morale of the Crown troops in Charleston. It also increased the number of false alarms each night.[314]

★ Lieutenant John Markland (1755–1837), of the Pennsylvania line, fought an action near the Quarter House Tavern, 4 miles from Charleston, in September or October 1782 when he ambushed a party of British dragoons. He killed 8 or 10 dragoons and captured two others, along with a number of horses, without any casualties of his own.[315]

★ After Colonel John Laurens (1754–1782) was killed, Colonel Engineer Thaddeus Kosciusko (1746–1817) assumed his duties as commander of the advance position near the enemy lines. Kosciusko and a small party captured 60 Crown horses on James Island on November 4, 1782.[316]

See **James Island** (Oct. 10, 1782) p. 122.

Wappetaw Meeting House (fall 1781; Nov. 17, 1781)

> Wappetaw Meeting House was located about 13 miles north of the modern community of Mount Pleasant, in a church building that the British had converted into a fortified stronghold. The site is on route S-10-584 (15 Mile Landing Road) in Awendaw, in Charleston County, just west of route U.S. 17. Wappetaw Bridge crosses the Wando River on Guerins Bridge Road (S-10-98) a little over 1 mile west of its intersection with route U.S. 17.

★ Colonel Hezekiah Maham (1739–1789) and a corps of state troops and militiamen attacked the British post at Wappetaw Meeting House in St. Thomas Parish sometime during the fall of 1781, probably on Saturday, November 17, 1781. They killed or captured a number of the King's troops. The British burned the meeting house and the church records when they abandoned the post at the close of the war.[317]

Johns Island (Dec. 29, 1781)
Murder of Solomon Freer (1780)

> The site of Solomon Freer's murder was very close to the intersection of River Road (S-10-91) and Edenvale Road (S-10-633) at Huskum Corner Cross Roads on Johns Island.

Solomon Freer (1722–1780) was a Whig but his uncle, John Freer (1715–1787), was a staunch Loyalist. John told his nephew that if Solomon's son [also named Solomon (1764–)], went to join Brigadier General Francis Marion (1732–1795), he would kill the young Solomon. Solomon saddled a horse for his son late one night and sent him to join Marion's partisans. John killed his nephew about 5.5 miles northeast of his home three days later.[318]

★ The British force in Wilmington, North Carolina withdrew to Johns Island, south of Charleston on Sunday, November 18, 1781. Lieutenant Colonel Henry "Light-Horse Harry" Lee (1756–1818) tried to attack this force on Saturday, December 29, 1781. However, his men became disoriented and he aborted the attack.

Middleton Plantation, Ashley River (March 15, 1782)

> Middleton plantation, now known as Middleton Place (4300 Ashley River Road, Charleston; phone: 800-782-3608) is a 65-acre historic plantation with gardens. It is 10 miles southeast of Summerville on route S-61 or 12.5 miles northwest of Charleston on route S-61. The plantation was established in 1741 by Henry Middleton (1717–1784), President of the First Continental Congress. It was the home for generations of the family, including Henry's son, Arthur Middleton (1743–1787), a signer of the Declaration of Independence.
>
> Middleton Place imported water buffalo from Constantinople in the late 1700s. These water buffalo were the first in the United States. Union troops burned and looted the plantation in 1865, near the end of the Civil War in retaliation for the owner's signing of the Ordinance of Secession. The soldiers killed and ate five of the water buffalo and stole 6.
>
> The south building, built in 1755, was the only portion of the plantation that survived. It is now the Middleton Place House Museum which contains a collection of Middleton family furniture, paintings, books, and documents dating from the 1740s through the 1880s. The formal gardens consist of symmetric landscaped terraces, allées, ponds, and garden rooms.
>
> Arthur Middleton was born at the house, and is buried there.

Brigadier General Francis Marion (1732–1795) raided in the vicinity of the Middleton plantation on the Ashley River on Friday, March 15, 1782. He and his militiamen killed three Loyalists and captured one.[319]

Huger, Berkeley County
Wadboo (Watboo) (July 15, 1781; Aug. 29, 1782)
Biggin Church (July 16, 1781)
Strawberry Ferry (July 17, 1781)
Quinby Bridge and Shubrick's Plantation (July 17, 1781)
Bull Head
Wells's Plantation (Aug. 24, 1781)

> Wadboo Bridge and plantation and Strawberry Ferry are near the junction of Wadboo Swamp with the Cooper River near Moncks Corner and Biggin Bridge and Church. Wadboo Bridge crosses a prong of the western branch of the Cooper River, known as the Fair Forest Swamp (some maps show this as Wadboo Swamp), about 25 miles north of Charleston.
>
> The ruins of the Biggin Church (see Photo SC-34) are 3 miles northeast of Moncks Corner. The skirmish at Biggin Church is often incorrectly called Wadboo Bridge. Wadboo Bridge was where the modern bridge on route SC 402 crosses the creek in Wadboo Swamp. The British post consisted of a redoubt and Biggin Church, a fortified brick church. Lieutenant Colonel John Coates commanded eight companies of the 19th Regiment stationed here.
>
> Strawberry Ferry was on the western branch of the Cooper River about 8 miles due west of Huger. To get there from Moncks Corner, take route U.S. 52 south to Cypress Gardens Road (S-8-9). Proceed about 2.5 miles to the fork in Tarry Town. Bear left onto Pimlico Boulevard (S-8-260) and go to the end. The ferry was about 500 yards ahead, where the railroad now crosses the river. Strawberry Chapel and a historical marker are across the river at the junction of Comingtee Road and Strawberry Chapel Road.
>
> Bull Head is the source of a southern tributary of Quinby Creek that is today known as Northampton Creek. The site is in present-day Berkeley County about 5 miles southeast of Huger and less than 2 miles from the Charleston County line.
>
> Quinby Bridge crossed Quinby Creek about 0.25 miles southwest of Huger. Coming up route SC 41, turn left onto Clements Ferry|Cainhoy Road before the junction of routes SC 41 and SC 402 in Huger and follow the road 0.25 miles to Quinby Bridge. A state historical marker on the right immediately before the bridge (west of it) marks the battle site. A modern house sits on the site of the Quinby plantation. The site is not marked.
>
> Shubrick's plantation was about 0.4 miles northwest of Quinby Bridge.
>
> The site of Wells's plantation is in the Huger area in the Francis Marion National Forest. To get there, go north from Wando on route SC 41 and turn right onto Halfway Creek Road (S-10-98). Go about 7.9 miles on Halfway Creek Road to South Hampton Road on the left. The site is about 350 yards up South Hampton Road and about 150 yards on the right.

When Colonel Wade Hampton (1752–1832) stopped at a house near Wadboo Bridge and Strawberry Ferry on Sunday, July 15, 1781, a woman told him "that 2 sloops had landed a small distance up the river, with British soldiers and they were in the cornfield getting roasting corn and beans." Colonel Hampton immediately rode to the river bank and ordered half of his men to dismount and "run into the vessels." They found only one soldier on the sloops. The soldier aimed his musket at them but it misfired. He tried to fire several times with the same result. Hampton's men killed him and then searched the neighboring fields where they found 30 others. They took the soldiers prisoners but paroled them and burned the two sloops loaded with indigo.[320]

★ The Crown forces controlled the Moncks Corner area for over a year until Brigadier General Thomas Sumter (1734–1832) moved against the forces here in July 1781. Lieutenant Colonel Henry "Light-Horse Harry" Lee (1756–1818) arrived outside Charleston to find that the Crown forces had been warned of his arrival and fortified themselves. He returned to rejoin General Sumter on Monday, July 16th after being forced to return by the long way because the enemy held Biggin Bridge.

Colonel Hezekiah Maham's (1739–1789) troops destroyed the Wadboo Bridge on July 16th along with two schooners moored alongside. They took the crews prisoner and then withdrew to camp about 1.5 miles from the Biggin Church. Colonel Peter Horry (1747–1815) and Captain Edward Lacey, Jr. (1742–1813) had reinforced Maham and set up their camp near the Wadboo Bridge. A slave came into the British camp about 2 PM and reported that Horry and his men were at Wadboo Bridge and that their horses were running loose in a field.

As Maham's men were resting and cooking or eating their evening meal, about 4 or 5 PM, Major Thomas Fraser's (d. 1820) South Carolina dragoons charged suddenly in what Peter Horry described as "a most confused cowardly attempt." Most of Colonel Horry's men fled. Captain Lacey's riflemen broke the charge. Horry rallied his men who killed several of the attackers and took 10 prisoners. They discovered one of the prisoners was a deserter and executed him for treason. Major Fraser withdrew to Biggin Church. Lieutenant Colonel Coates sent out the infantry (the 19th Regiment of Foot) to meet Horry's horsemen who pursued Major Fraser back to camp. Horry's men wheeled about and returned to their camp to finish their supper.

Captain Lacey's regiment behaved particularly well, and Brigadier General Thomas Sumter (1734–1832) proudly wrote to Major General Nathanael Greene (1742–1786), who had little respect for the militia, "Noble militia! What think you now of their charging British Dragoons with Rifles & pursuing them to their lines." He also wrote that Horry's men had "killed some and took away two subs and eight dragoons of Colonel Innis [Colonel James Inness (Innis)] Corps." He discovered one of the prisoners had deserted from the Continental Army and executed him the next morning. The Congressional forces lost two officers and 10 men killed. This skirmish is sometimes referred to as Wadboo Bridge, but the action took place from Wadboo Bridge to about 1 mile or more north of the Biggin Church. It was also a delaying action to allow Lieutenant Colonel John Coates time to put all of his stores into Biggin Church which he then burned in the middle of the night before retreating toward Charleston.[321]

★ Lieutenant Colonel John Coates burned his stores and the Biggin Church, which was being used as a supply depot, about 3 AM on Tuesday, July 17, 1781. He ordered Major Thomas Fraser's (d. 1820) dragoons to cover his evacuation. He then retreated 18 miles down the Cooper River toward Charleston, stopping at Quinby Bridge that afternoon. Coates posted his men in strong defensive positions behind the creek. Major Hezekiah Maham's (1739–1789) men loosened the planks on the bridge over the wide and deep creek, leaving enough of the bridge to allow the rear guard and the baggage to cross.

Lieutenant Colonel Henry "Light-Horse Harry" Lee (1756–1818) and his Legion, arrived at Quinby Bridge about noon, ahead of Brigadier General Thomas Sumter's (1734–1832) infantry. They were in pursuit of Lieutenant Colonel John Coates. Some of the Legionnaires spotted the enemy across the creek. They captured Coates's rear guard, and two sections of cavalry galloped over the bridge, catching the enemy by surprise. Crossing the bridge, they knocked many planks into the water, making it impossible for the main force to repair the bridge in time to join the action on the other side. All but a few Loyalists fled, leaving Coates alone with only a few men. They rallied, and the dragoons escaped to cross a ford further upstream where they were met by Lee with his main body and Brigadier General Francis Marion's (1732–1795) men.

Brigadier General Sumter could see the glow of the burning church from his camp. He marched his troops to Moncks Corner at double time in an attempt to get to the bridge over the Cooper River before the Loyalists. When he discovered that Lieutenant Colonel Coates had retreated along the east bank of the Cooper, he set out in pursuit. Colonel Lee's cavalry preceded the slower units, but he and Colonel Henry Hampton (1755–1826) were delayed at Wadboo because the Loyalists had completely destroyed the bridge. They lost time searching for a ford farther upstream. They discovered a fork in the road at the Wadboo River. The infantry marched to Quinby Bridge by the left fork. Colonel Hampton took the right fork in pursuit of the South Carolina Royalists headed toward Strawberry Ferry. However, the Royalists had already reached the ferry, crossed the river and secured the boats on the other side.

Meanwhile, Lee's legion and Hampton's militia cut off Coates's rear guard of 100 men of the 19th Regiment near Shubrick's plantation about a mile north of Quinby Bridge. Lee sent Captain Joseph Eggleston's (1754–1811) troop into the woods to come around their left flank while the rest of the cavalry formed in close order on the road facing the British. When Lee's bugler sounded the charge, the dragoons galloped forward with drawn sabers. Lee's men clearly heard the order to fire, but the recruits of the 19th Regiment threw down their arms without firing a shot. The Continentals captured almost all the baggage and the men.

Lee then rode toward the bridge half a mile away. As Coates was still expecting his rear guard, he was completely taken by surprise when Captain William Armstrong (1737–1783), leading the first section of the Lee's Legion cavalry, and Lieutenant George Carrington (1711–1785), the second, charged across the bridge. The horses kicked up the loose planking from the stringers creating gaps in the flooring. The first two sections managed to cross but the gap increased, preventing Captain Ferdinand O'Neal or O'Neale (ca. 1758–ca. 1817) and the third section from crossing.

Captain Armstrong's section rode through a fatigue party that remained on the bridge removing the planks. They were in the line of fire of a howitzer at the end of the bridge. They drove off the gunners and took cover in the woods because of heavy musket fire. Captain Armstrong lost two men and four horses killed. Major Maham, who was with the advance, had his horse killed under him. Some of the fatigue party fired a single volley, then fled, frightened by the sudden charge.

Coates and a few of his men were left standing in front of a wagon. They defended themselves as best they could with their swords. Some of Coates's men returned to the fight and tried to display into a line of battle; but Colonel Taylor "had a superior rifleman with a long range gun who would pick off the British at the bridge." The British rolled the howitzer back to protect the bridge. Several of Lee's men were wounded by the artillery fire. Captain Armstrong and Lieutenant Carrington were driven off and rode to find a ford to rejoin the legion. Captain O'Neal remained helpless on the opposite bank which was too marshy for the men and horses to get a good footing. Some men who went into the stream to repair the bridge found the bottom too deep in silt to gain a firm footing.

Coates moved his regiment to the protection of some buildings attached to the Quinby plantation owned by Captain Thomas Shubrick (1756–1810). They used the rail fences and outbuildings of the plantation to form a square. Coates placed his remaining howitzer in the center to cover his front. Lee and Marion decided not to attack because they did not have many bayonets and Sumter had left all of his artillery behind. They decided that the position was too strong to attack without artillery.

They waited until 3 PM for General Sumter to arrive with his artillery. This delay gave Coates more time to prepare his defenses. When Sumter did arrive with the rest of the infantry about 5 PM, he did not bring his artillery. He overruled Lee's and Marion's decision and ordered an attack without waiting for a 6-pounder to arrive. He divided his forces to attack the plantation from three different angles. Sumter's brigade took the center where the plantation's slave buildings offered them some protection. Marion's brigade attacked the right, across open fields, with no cover except for a fence 50 yards in front of the plantation. The dragoons were kept in reserve. The attack began about 5 PM and lasted until near 8.

Colonel Thomas Taylor's (1779–1783) infantry began the attack by charging across an open field and forming a line along a fence. Coates counterattacked and retook the position. Marion's infantry re-captured the fence line but were driven back with heavy losses while Sumter's men fired from behind the buildings.

Colonel Taylor's riflemen, down to seven cartridges each, "reached the negro cabins, fired around the corners and the British were driven to the refuge of the house." Taylor rushed to a fence on the left of the house with 45 men, "Each man screening himself behind a stout fence post, and as the British appeared to fire out a window Taylor's men would fire at them and sometimes a ball would hit a fellow who would bound up in his death agony and then be out the window. The posts were pretty well battered by the enemy's bullets."

The riflemen continued firing until they ran out of ammunition and were repulsed in a bayonet charge. Marion's men rushed to cover Taylor's retreat across the repaired bridge. They suffered heavy casualties because Sumter failed to bring the artillery. One lieutenant was hit by five balls and killed. Colonel Taylor was the last to retreat. He "had a swing pistol at his side which in running and dodging struck him on the knee, producing much pain, that it retarded his progress and he was the last of his men to get beyond the reach of danger." He found Sumter "sitting cooly under the shade of a tree." He said 'Sir, I don't know why you sent me forward on a forlorn hope, promising to sustain me and failed to do so, unless you designed to sacrifice me. I will never serve a single hour under you' and then retired from Sumter's command."

General Greene reported to Congress:
> The firing was close and warm. By the enemy being advantageously posted in the range of house where our cavalry could not act, and our artillery left behind, they maintained their ground though every effort was made to dislodge them. The troops kept up a fire until the whole of their ammunition was consumed, when they were ordered to retire, our loss was about 10 or 12 killed and between 20 and 30 wounded. As the firing was not more than from 40 to 50 yards distance, and most of our people good marksmen, it is thought the enemy must have suffered considerably.

The gallantry of the militia, and state troops upon the occasion, would have done honor to veteran soldiers.

Lord Rawdon, with part of the troops at Orangeburg, being on the move downwards, and judging the position of our people ineligible, Gen. Sumpter ordered them to retire towards Nelson's ferry. There were taken in the expedition, in the different attacks, near 140 prisoners, 8 or 10 of whom were officers, between us and one and two hundred horses, several wagons, one loaded with ammunition, and all the baggage of the 19th regiment, in which was found 720 guineas. The General had ordered the whole to be divided among the troops as a reward for their bravery.

Sumter retreated 3 miles and waited for the artillery piece. All but 100 of Marion's militiamen deserted that night and Marion and Lee, also angry over the loss of their men, left Sumter's command the next morning, determined never to fight under Sumter again. With reinforcements coming to join Coates, Sumter withdrew his remaining men. He retired from the army shortly afterward. Crown casualties were six killed, 38 wounded and captured, together with several wagons, a load of ammunition and the baggage of the 19th Regiment.[322]

★ South Carolina militiamen and Continental cavalry raided down as far as Daniel Island across the Cooper River from Charleston on Friday, August 24, 1781. Captain McNeil, the commander of the British post at Wappetaw Meeting House, near the head of the Wando River, sent out a party of regular troops from the Prince of Wales American Regiment and the South Carolina Militia (Loyalist). They picked up the trail of the Congressional forces as they retreated northward and overtook a party of Brigadier General Francis Marion's (1732–1795) militiamen commanded by Captain William Bennett (1717–1815) after sundown at Wells's plantation on Bull Head. They surrounded the plantation house but a barking dog alerted the South Carolinians. Captain McNeil lost the element of surprise. His men killed one Whig and wounded several others in the skirmish. They took 16 horses with all their equipment but failed to capture most of the Congressional force The Wells family owned the firm that published Charleston's Loyalist newspaper, which may account for the excellent press coverage that this small affair received.[323]

★ Shortly after Brigadier General Francis Marion (1732–1795) marched from the Santee, around the middle of July 1781, Major General Nathanael Greene (1742–1786) asked him to take a post at Wadboo. Marion kept his men constantly on the move, changing his camp continually as he patrolled east of the Cooper River. He camped at Fair Lawn (see p. 182) whenever possible, because Sir John Colleton's (d. 1750) plantation had a large house with wings of slave quarters on each side. The house served as his headquarters and the cabins quartered his men. The buildings were strong enough to withstand rifle and musket fire and the long cedar-lined lane could offer a perfect ambush against attackers.

Major Thomas Fraser (d. 1820) and 100 Loyalist dragoons and some African American dragoons crossed the Cooper River on Friday morning, August 29, 1782, to surprise the guards at Biggin Bridge and Strawberry Ferry. General Marion learned of the raid and posted his marksmen among the cedars. He sent Captain Gavin Witherspoon (1748–1834) out on a reconnaissance mission. Fraser met Witherspoon in the woods and charged.

Witherspoon's men withdrew toward Fair Lawn. As they galloped toward the plantation, Witherspoon bore to the left and then fell back as if to cover the retreat. One of Fraser's dragoons rushed forward to cut him down. As the attacker rose in his stirrups to strike Witherspoon, Captain Witherspoon fired his carbine and killed him.

Witherspoon's concealed men, on the left, gave a roaring shout and fired from the cover of three small houses when the Crown troops came within 30 yards of them. Surprised, the Crown troops broke their ranks, wheeled about, and retreated toward the cedars in confusion. Witherspoon's marksmen fired, killing four men and five horses and wounding about 14. They captured one prisoner, three horses and a mule.

The horses drawing General Marion's ammunition wagon bolted when the driver got frightened and drove off at the sound of the volley. Five mounted militiamen ran out and recovered the wagon, but they fled when Fraser's dragoons chased them. Major Fraser's dragoons made several attempts to flank Marion's men who changed positions and stayed in the pines where the dragoons dared not go. Without powder, Marion ordered his men to retreat again to the Santee.

Marion bade farewell to his troops at Wadboo plantation, about half a mile east of Wadboo Bridge. Some sources say this occurred at Fair Lawn plantation, the estate of Sir John Colleton (d. 1750) also about half a mile east of the bridge. The Crown forces burned that estate.[324]

Berkeley County
Between Huger and Cainhoy
Videau's Bridge (Jan. 2, 1782)

> Videau's Bridge was on route S-8-98 (Cainhoy Road) where it crosses French Quarter Creek. To get there, take Clements Ferry|Cainhoy Road south from Huger and proceed 6.25 miles to the bridge over French Quarter Creek. A state historical marker for Brabrant plantation is another 1.2 miles further. A short distance further south is a marker for Silk Hope plantation which was General Charles Cornwallis's (1738–1805) headquarters. It is now a private residence.

The Battle of Videau's Bridge was fought on the Brabrant plantation on the Cooper River just south of French Quarter Creek on January 2, 1782. The Crown forces in Charleston were in desperate need of food for their horses. British General Alexander Leslie (1740–1794) sent out a foraging party of 350 infantrymen and cavalrymen under Major John Coffin (1756–1838). Colonel Richard Richardson, Jr. (1741–1817), who was monitoring enemy movements, immediately requested reinforcements to pursue Coffin's party which had already reached Brabrant plantation.

Coffin sent a scouting party across Videau's Bridge while the remainder of his force rested. Richardson managed to get ahead of them and approached the bridge from the north. His troops clashed with Coffin's scouts and initially repulsed them. However, Richardson's band contained many untrained recruits who quickly became disorganized. The Redcoats soon routed them with heavy casualties—some say as many as 77—and pursued them for 6 miles. The British were able to forage as far as Quinby Bridge before returning to Charleston.

Richardson lost 57 killed and 20 captured while the British lost one man killed and one wounded. Lieutenant Colonel Archibald Campbell (1739–1791), known as "Mad Archy" and considered one of the most colorful officers in the British Army, was taken captive in the battle. He was later shot when he attempted to flee.[325]

Whitehall (Vanderhorst Plantation), Charleston County
(Aug. 29, 1782)

> Whitehall, the Vanderhorst family plantation, was located in Christ Church Parish about 10 miles northeast of Mount Pleasant on the Georgetown road (route U.S.17). It was probably about 1.8 miles east of the Wappetaw Church and about 0.5 miles east of the intersection of route S-10-584 (Seewee Road) and Pointing Brittany Lane in Awendaw.

Brigadier General Francis Marion (1732–1795) sent Captain George Sinclair Capers (1755–1809) and 12 of Colonel Peter Horry's (1747–1815) dragoons into southeastern Berkeley County to observe Crown activities in August 1782. Captain Capers found Captain March and Lieutenant Mingo and 26 Black Dragoons, also known as the Black Pioneer Troop at the Vanderhorst plantation on Friday, August 29, 1782. Captain Capers charged the Black Dragoons and routed them, freeing three of his neighbors bound in handcuffs. He had two men wounded and may have wounded Captain March in the knee.[326]

3
SOUTHEASTERN SOUTH CAROLINA

See the map of southeastern South Carolina.

Daufuskie Island
Bloody Point (July 7, 1775; July 9, 1775)
Ash's Point, Port Royal River (Aug. 30, 1779)
Captain Martinangel killed (Dec. 25, 1781)

> Bloody Point is on the southern tip of Daufuskie Island, about 4 miles south-southwest of Hilton Head Island. It gets its name from a place in Beaufort County where a Native American massacre occurred in the early 1700s. The actual site of the naval action is in the Atlantic Ocean off Cockspur Island on the South Carolina side of the border with Georgia.
> Ash's Point is another name for Bloody Point.
> The site of Captain Martinangel's killing is on the southern end of Daufuskie Island on the high ground to the right, near the end of Martinangele Road.

Rebel vessels with many armed men from South Carolina guarded the inlet to the Savannah River near Bloody Point in early July 1775. They awaited the arrival of a ship from London, intending to seize her cargo of gunpowder. The Georgia schooner *Liberty* with 8 or 10 carriage guns and many swivel guns along with two barges departed from Bloody Point, Daufuskie Island, to meet the convoy escorted by Captain Richard Maitland's armed schooner *Phillipa*. They met about 4 leagues from the Bar on Friday, July 9th. As the pilot was guiding the shipment and the *Phillippa* to the Tybee Bar, the *Liberty* closed on the British vessels and fired two musket shots at the *Phillippa*. That night, the *Liberty* anchored beside the *Phillippa*.

The next day, the British vessels were ordered to anchor off Cockspur Island. The South Carolina militiamen on the island rowed out to the British vessels, surrounded them and inspected their papers. The militiamen then took 15,000 pounds of powder and "seven hundredweight of leaden bullets" and all the bar-lead, sheet-lead, and arms destined to be traded with the Native Americans. They sent 5,012 pounds of powder to Charleston and the Georgians kept the rest. Later, South Carolina urged Georgia to send 5,025 pounds of this gunpowder to the Congress in Philadelphia for the Continental Army.[327]

★ Lieutenant John Hamilton (1720–1790) and nine men crossed the Port Royal River to Ash's Point Monday night, August 30, 1779. They surprised a Crown picket, bayoneted and later shot one of the guards. The gun fire alerted the rest of the camp and forced Lieutenant Hamilton to withdraw before he could attack the Captain's Guard at Ash's House, about 350 yards away. Two other sentries escaped but the attackers captured a corporal and three men.[328]

★ Captain John Leacraft or Leacroft (1766–1838) led a party of Whigs known as the "Bloody Legion" to Daufuskie Island to kill Captain Phillip Martinangel (d. 1781) (Filippo de Martinangelo) (also spelled Martinangele) to avenge the killing of Charles Davant (1750–1781). Captain Martinangel was at home sick in bed on Tuesday, December

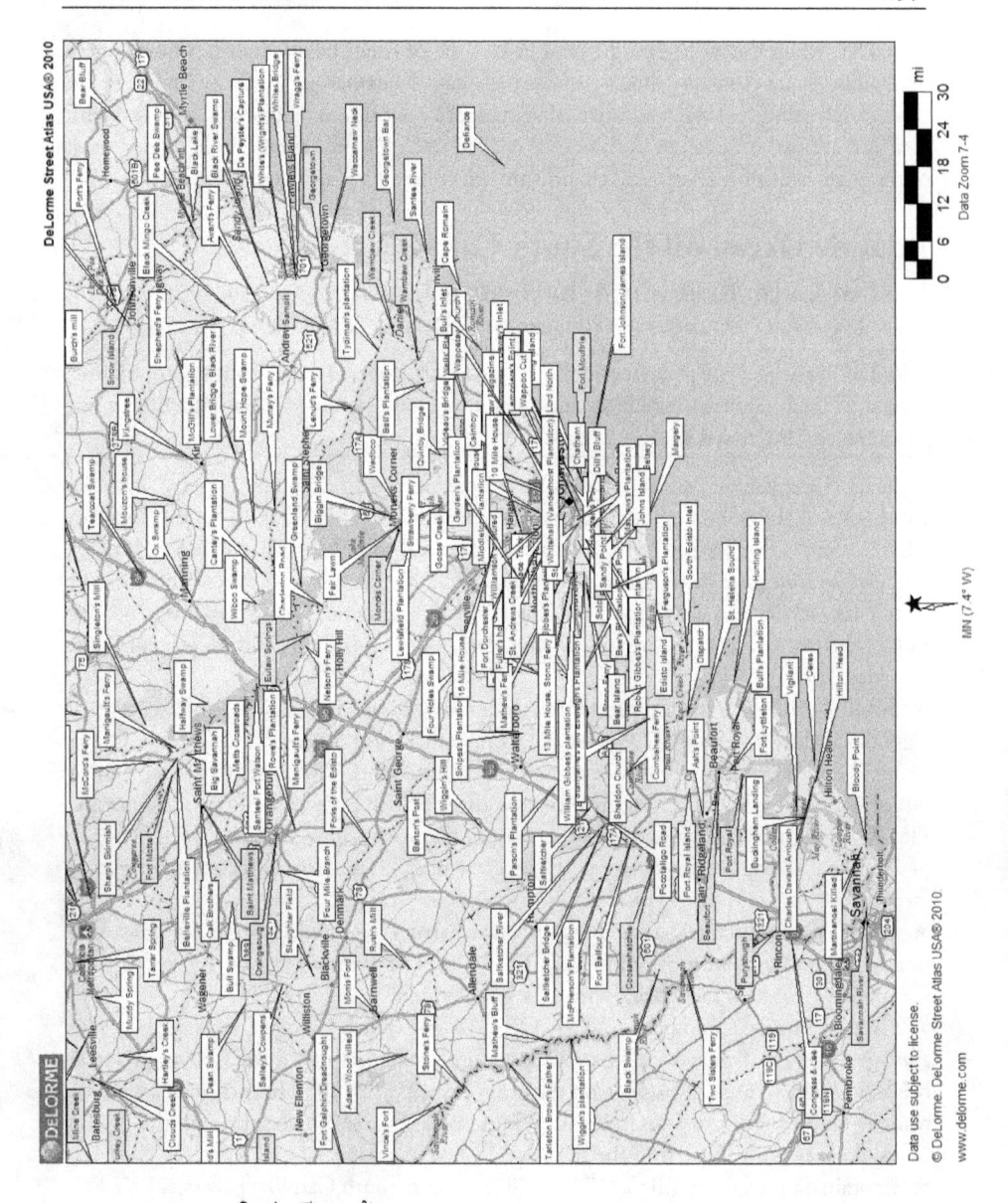

Southeastern South Carolina: Map for The Guide to the American Revolutionary War in South Carolina © 2012 DeLorme (www.delorme.com) Street Atlas USA®

25, 1781, when the Whigs paid him a visit. Two of them held Captain Martinangel's wife while Israel Andrews shot and killed Captain Martinangel in his bed and cut his throat. According to local tradition, Martinangel's 3-week-old daughter was in bed with him and almost drowned in his blood. She lived to be 94 and, at one time, owned most of the plantations on Daufuskie Island through inheritance and marriages.[329]

Atlantic Ocean off the South Carolina coast
East of Cape Romain, Charleston County (April 24, 1776; June 19, 1778; May 17, 1779; April 1, 1780; Sept. 6, 1781; Oct. 7, 1781; Oct. 14, 1781)

> Most of these actions occurred in the open ocean, several miles from shore, off the coast of Cape Romain which is about 22 miles due south of Georgetown. Some occurred off the coast of Charleston.

Israel Thompson's British transport *Golden Rule*, with Captain Dauzey and two companies of the 33rd Regiment on board, fell in with Whig Captain John Chace's or Chase's sloop *Defiance* off Cape Romain at daybreak on Wednesday, April, 24 1776. The *Golden Rule* gave chase for half an hour, fired a few shots and captured the *Defiance* which was taken into the Cape Fear River, North Carolina. The *Defiance* was headed to Charleston with a cargo of coffee, chocolate, cider, whale oil candles, oil, rum, etc. valued at £500.[330]

★ South Carolina Navy Commodore Alexander Gillon (1741–1794) took charge of Captain Samuel Smedley's (1753–1812) Connecticut brig *Defiance* and Captain Oliver Daniel's South Carolina sloop *Volant* on Friday, June 19, 1778. As the two vessels sailed out of Charleston Harbor, they encountered three British privateers from St. Augustine, Florida by nightfall. They captured the 12-gun *Governor Tonyn's Revenge* with her crew of 75 men and the 8-gun *Ranger* with her crew of 35. The third privateer managed to escape.[331]

★ The Congressional frigates *Boston* and *Confederacy* captured Captain Thomas Ashburn's sloop *William* on Sunday, May 17, 1779. The *William* was en route from the Caribbean Islands to New York with a cargo of rum.[332]

★ Captain Samuel Champlin's (1739–1782) 14-gun South Carolina privateer brig *Fair American* and the Pennsylvania privateer sloop/brig *Argo* captured the Crown privateer brigs *Elphinstone* and *Arbuthnot* on Saturday, April 1, 1780. The privateers were en route from New York to St. Kitts. The Whigs sailed their two prizes through the British blockade fleet into Charleston the next day.[333]

★ Captain Samuel Champlin's (1739–1782) 14-gun South Carolina privateer brig *Fair American* and Captain Roger Kean's (1756–1801) 16-gun privateer brig *Holker* captured the brig *Rodney* from Liverpool, England, bound for Charleston on Sunday, October 7, 1781. The following day, the *Fair American* and the *Holker* captured another brig from England bound for Charleston. They also attacked and captured the British armed transport *Richmond* (or *Richard*) after a brief action on Sunday, October 14, 1781. The prizes were all sailed to Delaware. The British had no casualties, except for the loss of their armed transport, two merchant vessels and their crews. The Whigs had one man killed and another wounded on the *Holker*.[334]

★ Captain Charles Stirling's (1760–1833) British vessel *Savage* was sailing south from the Potomac River when he spotted the Pennsylvania privateer *Congress* about 10 leagues (30 statute or nautical miles) east of Charleston about 11 AM on Thursday, September

6, 1781. The *Congress* fired a shot across the *Savage*'s bow. Captain Stirling mistakenly believed the *Congress* was a common privateer and poorly armed. He soon discovered she was a frigate with 20 12-pound cannons.

The crew of the *Savage* responded to the *Congress*'s first shot with muskets. Both vessels then fired cannons at each other. The *Savage*'s main and mizzenmasts were shot away. When the crews could no longer fire the cannons, they resorted to muskets and pistols. By this time, the *Savage* was a wreck. Her masts, rigging and sails were all shot to pieces. Only five of her 16 cannons remained in operating condition and most of her crew was killed or wounded. Yet, the *Savage* continued to fight for another hour.

At times, the ships were so close that the cannon fire from one scorched the crew of the opposing ship and the crews threw various items at the enemy. After an engagement of three hours, the *Savage* was on fire and had only 40 men left in fighting condition. As the Whigs were coming aboard the *Savage* in three places, Captain Stirling lowered his colors and surrendered.

The British frigate *Solebay* pursued the *Congress* after the battle and re-took the *Savage* which could not sail fast enough to escape the *Solebay*. Captain Stirling and his crew remained prisoners. The British lost 8 killed, 26 wounded and 40 taken prisoners. The Whig crew of 215 men lost 11 killed and 30 wounded.[335]

South Edisto Inlet, Charleston County (Dec. 16, 17, 1778)
Edisto Island, Charleston County (Sept. 1782)
Lacey vs. Landing Party, Charleston County

Edisto Island is on the west bank of the North Edisto River opposite Wadmalaw Island and Johns Island. The South Edisto inlet is at the mouth of the South Edisto River between Edisto Island and Pine Island. Colonel Edward Lacey's encounter with the landing party occurred about 0.3 miles from the river and about 100 yards south of the creek which runs parallel with Clark Road.

Captain Joseph Fickling (1752–1781) and the Edisto Island Volunteer Company manned a position with a 4- or 6-pound cannon as a signal gun at the Edisto Island lookout when a privateer came into the South Edisto inlet on Wednesday, December 16, 1778. The privateer had ambushed the sloop *Sally* and was coming to Beaufort for provisions. She dropped anchor at the South Edisto inlet and sent a boat ashore. The Edisto Island militiamen spotted the privateer, assembled, and moved their signal gun within range of the privateer. They then fired on her, forcing her to leave the inlet, leaving behind the five sailors who had gone ashore for provisions. The militiamen captured them and placed them on board a schooner bound for Beaufort. The prisoners tried to overpower the crew of the schooner, but the Edisto Island militiamen stopped them and brought them to the jail in Beaufort.[336]

★ A British privateer from St. Augustine captured a schooner carrying indigo and rice near the Edisto inlet on Thursday, December 17, 1778. The cargo belonged to the estate of George Austin, William Moultrie's (1730–1805) father-in-law. The schooner was set adrift on Edisto inlet bar and lost on December 20th.[337]

★ South Carolina militiamen refused to turn out to defend the coast against British foraging parties coming from Charleston by the middle of 1782. Many were offended because Colonel William Harden (1743–1785) had not been promoted to brigadier general and they did not want to serve under General John Barnwell (1748–1800). So

Major General Nathanael Greene (1742–1786) and South Carolina militia Lieutenant Colonel William Henderson (1748–1787) had to use backcountry militia units to defend the coast. South Carolina militia Colonel Edward Lacey, Jr. (1742–1813) and his men were ordered to protect the neighborhood of Edisto Island.

A British foraging party landed on Edisto Island in September 1782. Colonel Lacey set out with a party of 15 or 20 men and captured two boats loaded with provisions. He burned and sank both of them. The foraging party pursued Lacey as he withdrew toward the west. They overtook him after a short distance, but Lacey had stationed his riflemen in a very advantageous position. They fired two effective volleys and routed the British.[338]

Beaufort and vicinity
Port Royal Harbor (Dec. 16, 1778)
Bull's Plantation (Feb. 1–2, 1779)
Port Royal Ferry (Feb. 3, 1779; Sept. 1, 1782)
Port Royal Island (Feb. 3, 1779; July 1779; July 23, 1779)
Battle of Halfway House
Fort Lyttleton (May 1, 1779)
Hunting Island (ca. July 22, 1779)
Beaufort (March 4–25, 1782; March 4, 1782; March 13, 1782)
Capers Creek (ca. March 15, 1782)

> Port Royal is in Beaufort County between Charleston and Savannah on route U.S. 21. There are historical markers on route U.S. 21 at Grays Hill. The battle site was about 0.5 miles north of the marker at U.S. 21 and Bruce K Smalls Drive. The low, swampy ground in the area may correspond to the swamp area General William Moultrie mentions in his account of the battle. He wrote that he tried to reach that area before the British, probably to get his men under cover, but the enemy beat him.
>
> The arsenal (see Photo SC-35) on Craven Street between Scott and Carteret Streets, Beaufort, is now the site of the Beaufort Museum, which is permanently closed.
>
> The Port Royal Ferry was where route U.S. 21 (Sea Island Parkway) crosses the Coosaw River to Port Royal Island.
>
> Port Royal Island extends from Beaufort in the south to Seabrook in the north and from the Broad River in the west to the Coosaw River in the northeast. The Port Royal Island engagement of February 3, 1779 is also known as the Battle of Halfway House. British Lieutenant William Calderwood (d. 1779) and Ensign John Finlay (d. 1779), of Lieutenant Colonel James Mark Prevost's (1736–1781) troops, were killed in this engagement near Gray's Hill. They were buried in the cemetery at St. Helena Church in Beaufort on February 5, 1779. A marker is in the post office area on Church Street near King Street southbound.
>
> The two galleys were anchored off the town in the vicinity of Waterfront Park. The schooner was recaptured in the Beaufort River northwest of Ladys Island.

SC-35. Beaufort arsenal is now the site of the Beaufort Museum

> Bull's plantation was located in the area now occupied by the Laurel Bay Naval Housing Unit on the Broad River.
> Hunting Island is about 14 miles east of Beaufort and is accessible by route U.S. 21 (Sea Island Parkway). The site of this action is about 1200 yards offshore of Harbor Drive.
> Capers Creek, now known as Chowan Creek, was at the end of Hunters Grove Road on Saint Helena Island. To get there from Beaufort, take route U.S. 21 (Sea Island Parkway) for about 6.5 miles and turn right onto Martin Luther King Drive. Go about 1.35 miles to the fork in the road and bear right (Lands End Road). Go about 0.4 miles and turn right onto Sam Doyle Drive. Turn right on Hunters Grove Road and follow it to its end.
> Fort Lyttleton was on Spanish Point Drive on Port Royal Island in Beaufort.

The merchants of Charleston outfitted the sloop *Sally* with eight guns to patrol the coast and to prevent the privateers from attacking the merchant ships. Captain Benjamin Stone spotted a large transport ship at the mouth of Port Royal harbor on Wednesday, December 16, 1778, and sailed to investigate. The wind died as he came alongside the ship. The crew, previously hidden, now appeared on deck and fired their muskets at the *Sally*, killing six men and wounding 12. Captain Stone had his crew row the *Sally* away from the privateers and managed to escape.[339]

★ British General Augustine Prevost (1723–1786) sent Major Valentine Gardiner and a landing party of 200 men north to occupy Port Royal Island within one month of seizing Savannah, Georgia on Monday, December 29, 1778. He hoped to attract Major General Benjamin Lincoln's (1733–1810) army, about 30 miles away, into an engagement and thus, draw off any Continental troops that could stop Lieutenant Colonel Archibald Campbell (1739–1791) from capturing Augusta, Georgia.

Captain Dougherty's militiamen fired at the British troops as they landed on Hilton Head Island on Monday, February 1, 1779. Lieutenant Breitenbach's landing party of the 60th Regiment chased the militiamen and burned the two houses they had occupied. Meanwhile, the vessels accompanying the landing party headed up the Broad River and anchored opposite Governor William Bull, Jr.'s (1710–1791) plantation on Port Royal Island. The landing party planned to burn the plantations of the owners who had fled. They began with the house of Captain Thomas Heyward, Jr. (1746–1809), one of the signers of the Declaration of Independence, after they removed all the furniture and took a tierce of indigo. They spared the overseer's house for use by the women of the plantation. A light infantry sergeant found and captured two of Captain Heyward's slaves, who had armed themselves and waited in ambush under a bank of the creek.

Some militiamen posted in Bull's house fired rifles and muskets at the raiding party that evening as they returned to their vessels. They continued sniping throughout the night.

The armed brig *Lord George Germain* bombarded (see Photo SC-25) the house the next morning to chase the militiamen out into the open. Lieutenant Breitenbach's landing party drove them into the woods. They finished removing the furniture from Bull's house except a billiard table. The 120 dozen bottles of liquor were distributed to the men. The soldiers got the ale while the wine was sent on board the ships for the officers. They then burned the plantation.

When the British crossed the Savannah River, Captain John Francis de Treville (1742–1790), who guarded Fort Lyttleton with 20 Continentals, ordered the guns spiked and the fort blown up. The Crown troops then proceeded to capture Port Royal after three prisoners from the Port Royal artillery told them that the smoke on the horizon was from the evacuation of Treville's artillery.[340]

★ Congress sent Major General Benjamin Lincoln (1733–1810) to replace Major General Robert Howe (1732–1786) as commander of the Southern Department in September of 1778. Lincoln assumed command of the 1,500 Continental troops remaining in Charleston on December 7. He called out the militia and increased his force to 3,500 men. He then marched to Purysburg on the Savannah River where he met the remnants of the Georgia and South Carolina troops who had escaped from Savannah, Georgia.

General Lincoln and Major General Augustine Prevost (1723–1786) faced each other across the Savannah when General Prevost took advantage of his naval supremacy and moved against Port Royal Island, about 30 miles in Lincoln's rear and 60 miles south of Charleston.

Major Valentine Gardiner, of the 60th (Royal American) Regiment, captured Port Royal because it was one of the few harbors south of the Chesapeake that could receive British warships. An African American came alongside the transport *Margaret and Martha* around midnight Tuesday, February 2, 1779 and reported that Brigadier General John Ashe (1720–1781) had left 300 sick at Pocotaligo Bridge.

The following morning, at daybreak, three British companies landed in 13 minutes, at Laurel Bay on Port Royal Island, about 30 miles up the South Carolina coast. Two artillerymen with a howitzer and six sailors accompanied them. The column landed behind the Continental Army, in an attempt to outflank General Lincoln. They marched 2 miles before the advanced troops encountered some dragoons and exchanged shots with them. As the cavalry retreated, the British fired the howitzer at them, but to no effect. Major Gardiner organized his troops into nine platoons and headed toward Roupelles Ferry, unaware that Brigadier General William Moultrie (1730–1805), General Stephen

Bull (1734–1779) and 300 South Carolina militiamen, 20 Continentals and three guns had arrived in Beaufort the day before.

General Moultrie was reconnoitering the fort there when he learned that Major Gardiner was about 5 miles from Beaufort. He gathered his men at the arsenal on Wednesday, February 3, 1779, and marched north (on what is now route U.S. 21) to block Major Gardiner's advance from the Broad River.

The two armies met about 4 PM. When Moultrie tried to deploy his forces in a wooded swamp, he discovered that the British had already occupied the area. He lined up his South Carolina militiamen across the road, 200 yards from Gardiner's troops. They were in the open near the Halfway House with two 6-pounders in the middle of the road and a 2-pounder on the right in some woods. Captain Thomas Heyward, Jr. (1746–1809) and Colonel Edward Rutledge (1749–1800), both signers of the Declaration of Independence, commanded the artillery in the road but they only had 40 rounds. Captain John Francis de Treville (1742–1790) commanded nine men, the only Continental troops in the engagement, manning the brass 2-pounder. They only had 15 rounds for their cannon.

When Major Gardiner demanded surrender, he was told that he was outnumbered and that he should surrender instead. Neither side would surrender, so the British howitzer fired on Heyward's artillery and killed Lieutenant Benjamin Wilkins (1745–1779). Heyward's artillery returned fire at the howitzer and disabled it on the second shot, killing Lieutenant Calderwood (d. 1779) and Ensign John Finlay (d. 1779) and wounding Major Gardiner's horse. The sailor manning the howitzer ran away with the slow match (see Photo SC-36).

SC-36. Cannon and linstock with slow match. A 3-pound cannon (also called a butterfly) with a linstock (foreground). The linstock holds a slow match to ignite the powder charge. The device resting on the cannon's left wheel is a worm which is used to remove debris from the barrel.

Meanwhile, the militiamen advanced toward the British in the woods and were ordered into the trees on the side of the road when they started taking casualties. Both sides made futile attempts to flank each other. The British left wing charged the riflemen in the trees who fled, as they had no bayonets. Very heavy firing continued on both sides for about 45 minutes until both sides ran low on ammunition. The British pressed both of General Moultrie's flanks.

The British had only 93 cartridges left. Even after searching the dead of both sides, they could only come up with 300 more cartridges. They stopped their advance and the militiamen retreated. General Moultrie ordered his artillery back when there was a lull in the fighting. That gave his artillerymen a chance to withdraw the cannons with their horses, while the infantrymen covered the flanks of the artillery.

The British withdrew from the town about sunset, leaving behind a wounded officer, a sergeant and three privates in a house near the battlefield. Every officer fighting for the British was wounded. Major Colin Graham was wounded in the thigh by two buckshot. Captain George Bruere (1744–1786) was wounded "through the ribs" by grape shot. Captain Patrick Murray was wounded in the shoulder by a rifleman when he tried to charge General Moultrie's artillery.

When Moultrie realized his opponents were retreating toward the ocean, he ordered his men to pursue. His few mounted troops captured 15 men, including the wounded Captain Bruere, and 12 "fuzees" (fusils, musket carbines). The British light infantrymen regrouped, rushed the cavalry, and rescued Captain Bruere and seven prisoners. The British marched back to their landing place in the darkness. General Moultrie sent his aide de camp to the British ships to ask for bark and other medicines for his wounded.

Major Gardiner left Port Royal on Thursday, February 5, 1779, after a final raid of the plantations in which he took 400 slaves which he gave to the Commissary's Department in Savannah. A week later, seven deserters from the armed brig *Lord George Germain* told General Bull that the Crown forces lost 40 killed and wounded in this engagement.

The engagement at Port Royal Island was successful in blocking the British attempt to outflank General Lincoln. It cost the Whigs eight men killed and 22 wounded. We don't know the number of British casualties, but they are assumed to have been very heavy, including every British officer involved in the action wounded.[341]

★ Fort Lyttleton was a triangular fort built of tabby to guard Beaufort against a Spanish attack from the sea. South Carolina militiamen seized the fort in 1775 but abandoned it on Friday, May 1, 1779, when the British landed a raiding party of 200 men on the opposite side of the island, even though the British made no attempt to assault it. The fort's commander, unable to defend the position with only 20 Continentals remaining, spiked the guns and abandoned the fort.[342]

See also **Old Race Track** (May 11,1779) p. 132.

★ Major General Augustine Prevost (1723–1786) had only evacuated a small portion of his force to Beaufort by Thursday, July 1, 1779 and he did not have enough men to occupy the town. He assigned 200 troops to construct a defensive position on Edisto Island to protect his retreating forces. Colonel Daniel Huger Horry (1737–1785) monitored the British forces on Port Royal Island but he did not have enough men to attack them.

The remainder of General Prevost's army arrived at their camp at Beaufort by July 6th but the troops remained on board the ships to avoid any snipers after dark. Only a few men went on shore to get water and wood.

Colonel Charles Cotesworth Pinckney (1746–1825) and the 1st South Carolina Regiment were ordered to Port Royal ferry to reinforce Colonel Horry on July 7th. The British vessels had begun shuttling the troops to St. Helena Island but Major General Benjamin Lincoln (1733–1810) anticipated an attempt to take Beaufort.

The Hessians were posted on a narrow neck of land at Mile-end (present day Parris Island). Horry's dragoons under Lieutenant Lewis (Louis) Ogier (1726–1780) met a party of Loyalists driving 300 head of cattle to General Prevost's army in mid-July. They attacked, drove the Loyalists into the river and captured most of the cattle. Only the 71st Highlanders remained near Beaufort by July 17th.[343]

★ A short while later, about Thursday, July 22, 1779, a British 10-gun sloop carrying 216 stolen slaves from Charleston ran aground on a large shoal off the tip of Hunting Island, near Port Royal, as she turned south toward St. Augustine, Florida. The crew took most of the supplies and guns ashore before a local militia unit attacked. The commander ordered the slaves to scatter and then set the sloop on fire. The militiamen recovered a few of the slaves but the fate of the others is unknown. The British managed to remove the guns and stores.[344]

★ Major Andrew Deveaux (also spelled DeVeaux) (1758–1812) and the Granville County Loyalist militia set out from the Stono River with the galleys *Scourge* and *Adder* and a private sloop and headed to Beaufort in late February 1782 to recover Loyalist property. General John Barnwell (1748–1800) could not offer any serious opposition with his small force of 50 men of the St. Helena Volunteer Militia Company. Nor could he execute his orders to destroy the rice the British stockpiled on Hutchinson's Island in the Savannah River.

Deveaux anchored in Beaufort on Monday, March 4, 1782, where he remained for three weeks while his men searched for Loyalist property confiscated by the Whigs and for Whig boats and ships hidden in the rivers and creeks surrounding Beaufort. A Whig vessel brought a British schooner to the port of Beaufort on Wednesday, March 13, 1782. The Whigs probably escaped when they saw the British galleys in port and Deveaux's men recaptured the schooner.

They found the sunken British vessel *Vigilant* at the mouth of Moss Island Creek and another captured British vessel in the vicinity of Capers Creek on Friday, March 15, 1782. Deveaux sent 14 men in rowboats to recover the vessel. General Barnwell's 50 militiamen followed the boats and ambushed them near the vessel as they attempted to free it. The engagement lasted about 15 minutes, leaving three militiamen wounded. The Crown forces had no casualties.[345]

★ Brigadier General Mordecai Gist (1743–1792) pursued the Crown forces to the Port Royal Ferry with his Maryland Continentals and a company of the Delaware Regiment after the battle at Combahee Ferry. Two of the British galleys, the *Balfour* and the *Shark*, had been at the action at Combahee Ferry and were now guarding the Port Royal Ferry. General Gist's infantry opened fire on the two galleys with a 6-pound field gun on Sunday, September 1, 1782.

Both galleys slipped their anchors, but the *Balfour* ran aground. Her crew quickly spiked the guns and abandoned her. The Whigs captured the *Balfour* and one prisoner, repaired the galley and re-armed her with two 9-pound cannons.

This was the last engagement of the Delaware Regiment in the Carolinas. The Continentals marched to rejoin the main army after this action. William Seymour wrote "this expedition among the rice-fields in the month of August and September had nearly ruined the light infantry."[346]

St. Helena Sound (Dec. 31, 1778; Aug. 16, 1781)
Coosaw Island
Brigantine *Dispatch*

> St. Helena Sound separates St. Helena Island and Hunting Island from Edisto Island and Hutchinson Island to the north. There are no roads close to the Brigantine *Dispatch* site. The closest is Carissa Lane, 4 miles from it, on Coosaw Island. To get there, take route U.S. 21 (Sea Island Parkway) from Beaufort to Ladys (or Ladies) Island. Turn left on route SC 802 (Sams Point Road). Proceed about 5.6 miles, then turn right onto Coosaw River Drive after you cross the bridge to Coosaw Island. Go about 1 mile and turn left onto Piney Lane, and then take the right fork, Carissa Lane. Then, take the left fork to its end.

When the British fleet headed south after the battle of Savannah, the bad weather blew several ships off course. One of these vessels, the transport *Sally*, entered St. Helena Sound, 40 miles northeast of the Savannah River, to get her bearings on Thursday, December 31, 1778. Congressional forces captured her and 19 horses on board. Two other transports with horses on board were believed lost; but they arrived at St. Augustine on January 16, 1779.[347]

★ A 14-gun privateer schooner drove the British brigantine *Dispatch* ashore in St. Helena Sound on Thursday, August 16, 1781. The crew escaped in their boat and headed to Combahee.[348]

Beaufort County
Near Sheldon
Sheldon Church (May 1779)
Savannah River (Feb. 24, 1782)

> The Prince William Parish Church, known as Sheldon Church (see Photo SC-37) is located about 2 miles off route U.S. 17 between the towns of Yemassee and Beaufort on the Old Sheldon Church Road. The Savannah River, just north of Savannah, Georgia, constitutes South Carolina's southern boundary.
>
> Construction of the red-brick Anglican church began in 1745 and finished around 1755. William Bull, Sr. (1683-1755), who donated the land, was buried here in 1755. (The graveyard is in back of the church but the remains of the Bull family were removed and buried elsewhere when vandals began to desecrate the above-ground vaults.) The porch, supported by four free-standing Doric columns, covered an equestrian statue of Prince William for whom the parish was named. Burned by Crown forces in 1779, the church was partially restored around 1825 and was burned again on January 14, 1865 by General Oliver Otis Howard (1830–1909), commanding General William Tecumseh Sherman's (1820–1891) right wing coming out of Beaufort. The church was never rebuilt. The ruins are now owned by St. Helena Episcopal Church.
>
> Thousands of pounds of gunpowder confiscated from the British ship *Little Carpenter* were stored in the Prince William Parish Church in June 1775. The church was then used frequently to store gunpowder and weapons.

SC-37. Ruins of Sheldon Church. An equestrian statue of Prince William, for whom the parish was named, graced the porch of the church which was supported by four free-standing Doric columns. Thousands of pounds of gunpowder confiscated from the British ship Little Carpenter *were stored in the church in June 1775. The church was then used frequently to store gunpowder and weapons.*

Major Andrew De Veaux, Jr. (also spelled DeVeaux or De Veaux) (1758–1812), a leading Loyalist of the Beaufort region, left the Stono River, just south of Charleston, bound for Beaufort with the galleys *Scourge* and *Adder* and a private sloop about Friday, February 22, 1782. He arrived at Beaufort two days later where he was met by a party of gentlemen that evening. The men represented themselves as an advanced guard of a large Congressional force and foiled De Veaux's attempt to land his men. De Veaux did, however, succeed in destroying two galleys that General John Barnwell (1748–1800) was planning to use for General "Mad Anthony" Wayne's (1745–1796) expedition.

★ Colonel Robert Barnwell (1761–1814) and his St. Helena Volunteer Militia Company attempted to cross the Savannah River at Beaufort on Sunday, February 24, 1782. They intended to burn the British stores in Georgia but Lieutenant Colonel Andrew De Veaux, Jr. (b. 1757) (also spelled DeVeaux) and the Beaufort Loyalist militia attacked them and drove them back across the river. Barnwell lost six men killed and five captured.[349]

★ Major Andrew De Veaux, Jr. (also spelled DeVeaux) (1758–1812) burned the Sheldon Church in May 1779 and destroyed Sheldon plantation, the Bull family estate. [350]

Sheldon, Beaufort County
Battle of Chehaw Point (Aug. 27, 1781)
Combahee Ferry (Aug. 27, 1782)

Combahee Ferry was where route U.S. 17 crosses the Combahee River about 7.75 miles northeast of Sheldon. From the bridge across the Combahee River, follow route U.S. 17 northeast for 2.2 miles. At the junction with route S-15-162 (Wiggins

> Road), turn right (east) and proceed 6.5 miles to route S-15-161 (Wiggins Road) and go to the end of the road at the river.
>
> Middleton Place (4300 Ashley River Road, Charleston; phone: 800-782-3608) is a 65-acre historic plantation with gardens. It is 10 miles southeast of Summerville on route SC 61 or 12.5 miles northwest of Charleston on route SC 61. The plantation was established in 1741 by Henry Middleton (1717–1784), President of the First Continental Congress. It was the home for generations of the family, including Henry's son, Arthur Middleton (1743–1787), a signer of the Declaration of Independence.

On Sunday, August 26, 1781, Brigadier General Francis Marion (1732–1795) detached Colonel Hugh Horry (1744–1795) and a guard of 30 men to Chehaw where three schooners were taking in rice. The boatmen heard of Horry's approach and went down the river before the party arrived there.

General Marion sent out reconnoitering parties, which determined that the Crown forces consisted of 180 Hessians, 150 British, 130 Loyalists, and 80 Queen's Rangers equipped as dragoons. They were too strong to make any attempt at attacking them seem feasible; so General Marion placed a guard at the causeway at Godfrey Savannah, 2 miles away from his main body of troops. He ordered them to defend that pass until he arrived.

About midnight the following day, General Marion's patrols encountered the Crown forces, 2 miles from the causeway, heading toward Marion's main force. The guards abandoned the causeway without firing a shot before General Marion could get his troops in motion. The Crown troops passed the causeway and proceeded to Mr. Hyrne's plantation near the Fish Ponds, 5 miles above Ashepoo.

General Marion marched after them on Tuesday morning but found they were posted in too strong a position to attack. He arranged his men in order of battle in a wood, in sight of the Crown forces. Marion's reconnoitering parties exchanged a few shots with the enemy picquets and wounded two men.[351]

★ General Charles Cornwallis (1738–1805) surrendered at Yorktown, Virginia on Friday, October 19, 1781; but it would take two more years to complete negotiations of the peace treaty which would result in the withdrawal of all British armies from the new United States of America. The British still held New York City in the North and Charleston in the South.

Major General Alexander Leslie (1740–1794), in command at Charleston was running low on supplies to feed his 3,300 troops and a considerable number of Loyalists, as the city was surrounded on the land side. He requested to cross Continental lines to purchase food and other provisions in the countryside and to allow his men to forage. Major General Nathanael Greene (1742–1786) refused, so General Leslie gave notice that he would proceed into the surrounding country to take provisions by force. He assembled a sizable foraging party under the command of Major William Brereton of the 64th Regiment. It consisted of about 300 Regulars, 200 Loyalists, and 18 sailing vessels consisting of two row-galleys (the *Balfour* and the *Shark*), some topsail schooners and other small craft.

General Greene then prepared to counter the British operations. He organized a light brigade under the command of Brigadier General Mordecai Gist (1743–1792). It included the infantrymen of Lieutenant Colonel Henry "Light-Horse Harry" Lee's (1756–1818) Legion, the Delaware troops, 100 infantrymen from the other Continental regiments, and the dismounted dragoons of Colonel George Baylor's (1752–1784) 3rd and 4th Virginia regiments, all under the command of Lieutenant Colonel John Laurens (1754–1782) who was ill with a fever.

Twelve miles below the Combahee Ferry, on the north side of the Combahee River, the extreme end of Chehaw Neck approaches the river bed which is generally bordered by extensive swamps and rice fields between these points. General Greene ordered Gist to protect the rice plantations along the Combahee River on Friday, August 23, 1782 because provisions and other supplies there provided a tempting target for the British. General Gist ordered a defense work to be constructed here to impede an enemy retreat. Colonel Laurens requested command of this task. He received a detachment of 50 infantrymen, some matrosses and a howitzer. He moved down the river on Monday evening, the 26th, and halted at the Stock plantation close enough to Chehaw to occupy it by daylight the following morning.

The Continentals used their howitzer so effectively that the Crown troops found their retreat cut off. Major Brereton sent a party ashore to silence the battery. He then landed a large force of 140 to 300 infantrymen, consisting of parts of the 17th and 64th Regiments and a detachment of provincial regulars at Middleton's plantation on the south side of the river. He posted troops on the north side of the river that evening and ordered the cavalry to go around by the Salkehatchie bridge to join the militiamen foraging in that area.

Gist tried unsuccessfully to block the movements of the Crown forces at Combahee Ferry early Tuesday morning, August 27, 1782. He then ordered Colonel Laurens, stationed just south of Combahee Bluff, to march to Chehaw Point with the Delaware battalion, consisting of several hundred light infantrymen, to reinforce the few artillerymen there and to confront the enemy on their return trip down the river; but the Crown troops beat him into position and set up an ambush, catching him in a double envelopment.

Laurens, who had served as a personal aide to General George Washington (1732–1799) and as a European diplomat, rode at the head of his column without the aid of scouts. Three hundred Redcoats hid in the fennel and tall grass waiting for him. When he recognized the ambush, he decided not to retreat or surrender, leaving him the only alternative of a charge. He dashed forward but the first volley knocked him out of his saddle, killing him. His force sustained approximately 50% casualties, including one corporal killed, 19 men wounded and three reported missing. The Crown forces captured the howitzer and re-formed in a wood near the river's edge. The Continentals retreated a quarter of a mile before they met General Gist who reorganized his forces.

A second engagement began when General Gist arrived sometime later. He tried unsuccessfully to dislodge the Crown troops who were covered by logs and brush, making them inaccessible to the cavalry. Moreover, the Crown infantry greatly outnumbered Gist's.

Realizing that his cavalry had insufficient room to maneuver and the Crown troops were going to make effective use of the captured howitzer, he called off the attack.

Brereton's troops traveled to Fields Point, a short distance downstream, where they boarded their vessels and departed. They had one man killed and seven wounded while Gist's losses were very serious for such a small force. In addition to the deaths of Colonel Laurens, Captain Smith (d. 1782) of the artillery and a corporal of the Legion cavalry, two captains, one lieutenant, two sergeants, one corporal, and 13 privates were wounded. Three others were missing and assumed captured. Colonel Laurens was buried on the grounds of the Stock plantation near where he fell. When General Washington learned of his cousin's death, he remarked, "He had no fault that I could discover—unless it was an intrepidity bordering on rashness."

The British continued foraging around the Broad River country, bringing their provisions and cattle to Beaufort. Gist got more men and a 6-pounder, crossed the Combahee, and proceeded to Port Royal Ferry to oppose them. The two forces engaged in a brisk encounter. Gist captured one of the two armed galleys there and drove off the other. He then rejoined the main army. The foragers eventually withdrew and returned to Charleston with about 300 barrels of rice and a number of cattle.

Although the Continental forces held the field at the end of the fighting, they lost a promising young leader for the new nation and the British had achieved their goal of obtaining food. This action is also sometimes known by the names Combahee Ferry or Chehaw Neck.[352]

Georgetown Bar (snow lost) (May 1778)
Georgetown, Georgetown County (Feb. 21, 1779; March 6, 1779; July 1, 1780; Dec. 25, 1780; Dec. 27, 1780; Jan. 6, 1781; Jan. 24–25, 1781; Feb. 14, 1781; May 28, 1781; June 6, 1781; July 25, 1781; Aug. 2, 1781)
Winyah Bay (brig *Peace & Harmony*) (March 28, 1779; July 20, 1780)
White's Bridge (Nov. 15, 1780; Jan. 24, 1781)
White's (Wright's) Plantation (Dec. 28, 1780)
Alston's Plantation (Jan. 14, 1781)
Waccamaw Neck (Jan. 14, 1781)
Waccamaw River (mid-Feb. 1781)
Avant's Ferry (1781)
Wragg's Ferry (April 2, 1781)
Black River Road (ca. July 1781)
Hanging of Loyalist Bradley
Black River Swamp (late 1781)

> The Pee Dee and three other rivers empty into the bay at Georgetown to form one of the state's three major harbors.
>
> A Daughters of the American Revolution plaque at Front Street and Broad Street, across the street from Francis Marion Park, marks the site of the British headquarters (see Photo SC-38) during the war. There are also two state historical markers nearby. One of them summarizes the early history of Georgetown. The second honors Brigadier General Francis Marion (1732–1795), the liberator of Georgetown. Francis Marion Park, nearby, overlooks Harborwalk. A monument in the park erected by the Daughters of the American Revolution is dedicated "to the honor and glory of Francis Marion and his men who under extreme hardships did such valued service for the independence of their country in the war of the American Revolution."
>
> Another Daughters of the American Revolution tablet affixed to the exterior of the Rice Museum (at the intersection of Front and Screven streets) commemorates the

SC-38. British headquarters, Georgetown. This building occupies the site of the British headquarters in Georgetown. A Daughters of the American Revolution plaque between the two canopies on the right marks the site.

150th anniversary of Major General Marie Jean Paul Joseph du Motier Marquis de Lafayette's (1757–1834) landing. The inscription reads: "He came to draw his sword for the young republic in the hour of her greatest need." Lafayette Park, adjacent to the Rice Museum, displays a bust of the young French soldier. Georgetown also has more than 40 18th-century houses and buildings worth visiting. They are identified in Georgetown's Historic Trail of Old Homes and Buildings.

A marker in a traffic island on route U.S. 17 (Ocean Highway) across the Pee Dee River about 2.25 miles east of Georgetown commemorates the battle.

There is much confusion about the location of the site of White's Bridge because the texts say White's plantation. White's plantation was close to White's Bridge west of Georgetown on the Sampit Road where it crosses Whites Creek in the vicinity of where route U.S. 17A|521 (Highmarket Street) crosses it today at the western perimeter of Georgetown. The garrison was nearby. The event on January 24, 1781 may have occurred at White's plantation which accounts for the name given to the bridge and the road leading to the plantation. The December 28, 1780 action, also called White's plantation, may have occurred near the bridge over 6 Mile Creek about 3.5 miles northwest of the junction of routes SC 51 (Browns Ferry Road) and U.S. 701 (North Fraser Street) north of Georgetown.

A state historical marker at route U.S. 17 (Highmarket Street) and Broad Street marks the site of the Prince George Parish Church, Winyah, near the Episcopal church. The brick Jacobean-style church was completed in 1753 and has remained in continuous use since that time, except for brief periods of restoration to repair damage suffered in the American War for Independence and American War of Rebellion (Civil War). A plaque near the front entrance notes that the British Army used the church to quarter soldiers during the war and also stabled their horses here.

The army burned most of the interior before leaving town. The church's cemetery contains the graves of local men who fought for independence.

A state historical marker (see Photo SC-39) at the junction of routes U.S. 17 (Highmarket Street) and White's Bridge Drive west of the town commemorates the murder of Lieutenant Gabriel Marion (1761–1780), the Swamp Fox's nephew, by Loyalists about a quarter mile north of here.

Winyah Bay is south of Georgetown and the Georgetown Bar is at the mouth of Winyah Bay.

Colonel William Alston's (1747–1795) plantation was also known as The Pens. It was likely located northeast of Georgetown about 250 yards east of the intersection of Landgrave Street and Huger Drive, a short distance southeast of the intersection of route U.S. 701 (North Fraser Street) and Black River Road. Colonel Alston had another plantation called Brookgreen, from nearby Brookgreen Creek. It was probably near where Brookgreen Gardens is now located within the William Alston Loop at the end of Kings River Road opposite Huntington Beach State Park.

SC-39. Marker commemorating Gabriel Marion, Georgetown

> A state historical marker on route U.S. 701 just north of Georgetown marks the spot where Sergeant McDonald bayoneted Major Micajah Ganey in January 1781.
> Belle Isle plantation, Francis Marion's boyhood home, was south of the town [route S-22-23 (Whitehall Avenue) off route S-22-18 (South Island Road) 3.3 miles south of its intersection with route U.S. 17]. Perry Horry, one of Marion's greatest subordinates, acquired Belle Isle in 1801. Nothing remains of the plantation and the site became a Civil War fortification (Battery White). The Belle Isle Gardens, a 20th-century housing development, incorporated the old breastworks into the landscape. The remains of the fortifications can still be seen among the azaleas and oaks.
> Waccamaw Neck, the narrow strip of land extending from the Atlantic Ocean to the Waccamaw River, produced large quantities of badly needed salt during the American War for Independence. A state historical marker on route U.S. 17 at a turnout between the two bridges crossing the Great Pee Dee and Waccamaw rivers east of Georgetown commemorates the Revolutionary War battles at Georgetown. The site also offers a panoramic view of Georgetown, the third oldest town in South Carolina.
> Avant's Ferry was on the Black River about 13 miles north-northwest of Georgetown about 100 yards east of Browns Ferry Road (SC 51) where it intersects with Indian Hut Road. A historical marker is about 200 yards further on Browns Ferry Road near the original Prince George Winyah Church and the Winea plantation.
> Black River Road runs northwest to southeast on the eastern end of Georgetown. The hanging of Loyalist Bradley most likely occurred near the southern end of Huger Drive about 200 yards east of Black River Road north of Bonds Street|Willow Bank Road. Black River Swamp is along the Black River north of White Bridge and west of Jackson.

A snow, loaded with provisions, was sailing from Cork, Ireland, to Barbados, in May 1778. The South Carolina brig *Notre Dame* captured her on the Georgetown Bar.[353]

★ A British privateer drove a New England vessel ashore near the Lower Fort in Georgetown on Sunday morning, February 21, 1779. Captain Paul Trapier (1749–1778) and his Georgetown Artillery Company, stationed at the Lower Fort, captured a lieutenant and five privateers when they came ashore to claim the vessel.

★ Captain Paul Trapier's (1749–1778) militiamen struck again almost two weeks later when a St. Augustine privateer entered Georgetown harbor on Sunday, March 6 and cut loose some of the vessels moored there. The Georgetown militiamen captured a lieutenant and seven sailors.[354]

★ British Captain Dean's British privateer snow *Vengeance* drove Captain Rogers's brig *Peace & Harmony* ashore near Winyah Bay on Sunday, March 28, 1779. The British then burned the brig.[355]

★ The Crown forces wasted no time in establishing a base in Georgetown after the surrender of Charleston. They captured all the vessels then in port and raided and plundered nearby plantations. These actions outraged the residents who would soon become the nucleus of Lieutenant Colonel Francis Marion's (1732–1795) brigade. That army attacked Georgetown on several occasions over the next eleven months in an attempt to liberate it.

Captain John Plummer Ardesoif (d. 1790), of the Royal Navy, arrived at Georgetown about the end of June 1780 to invite the people to swear allegiance to King George III (1738–1820). Many of the inhabitants took the oath. According to local tradition, a public meeting was called to deliberate upon the situation. Major John James (1732–1791) was selected to meet with Captain Ardesoif on Saturday, July 1, to inquire if his proclamation required them to take up arms against their countrymen. Major James headed to Georgetown, dressed as a country planter, and was introduced to the captain who lodged a considerable distance from his ship.

Major James explained the nature of his mission. The captain seemed surprised and demanded unconditional submission, explaining that the King offered the people a free pardon which they did not deserve for rebelling against His Majesty for which they ought all to be hanged. If they take the oath of allegiance, they must also take up arms in support of his cause. As the angry captain wore a sword and Major James had none, Major James supposedly seized the chair on which he sat, brandished it in the captain's face, and left through the back door of the house, mounted his horse, and escaped into the country.

When news arrived that Major General Horatio Gates (1728–1806) was approaching with his army, the people called a public meeting and decided to take up arms in defense of their country and Major James was appointed to command them. They formed four companies consisting of about 200 men. They were soon joined by two more companies. They took prisoner most of the officers appointed over them by the British and positioned themselves at the pass of Lynches creek, at Witherspoon's ferry.

Lieutenant Colonel Banastre Tarleton (1744–1833) and 70 mounted militiamen and cavalrymen crossed at Lenud's ferry and advanced to surprise Major James who was notified of his movement and requested reinforcements. His company of about 50 mounted militiamen then headed to battle Colonel Tarleton at Kingstree. They approached around midnight, but Tarleton had left a few hours earlier. Colonel Tarleton was informed of the militia's approach and rode 30 miles from Kingstree to Salem where he took a prisoner the next day. [356]

★ Captain Peter Mansen's (1733–1793) Charleston, South Carolina, privateer schooner *Peggy* chased a sloop ashore near Winyah Bar around Thursday, July 20, 1780. The sloop was hulled and her cargo lost, except for a small quantity of indigo and a few other articles that were saved.[357]

★ After the battles of Black Mingo and Tearcoat Swamp, Brigadier General Francis Marion (1732–1795) received an influx of militiamen. With these reinforcements, he decided to attack the garrison at Georgetown, about 60 miles northeast of Charleston. He thought that the garrison consisted of 50 invalid British Regulars when he attacked on Thursday, November 15, 1780. He was unaware that the Redcoats expected a move on Georgetown and had reinforced the town with 200 Loyalist militiamen the day before the attack.

Marion sent Colonel Peter Horry (1747–1815) and his horsemen across White's Bridge to reconnoiter in the Black River area. He sent Captain John Melton to the Sampit road and concealed the rest of his men in the swamp north of the town near Alston's plantation which became known as The Camp. (This is probably Gapway Swamp, about 2.25 miles north northwest of White's Bridge.) Here, Marion could conduct raids in the north, along the Black River Road or the west, along the Sampit River road.

Captain James Lewis's (d. 1780) Loyalists, who were slaughtering cattle at White's plantation, fled when Colonel Horry's men approached. Horry's men heard the sound of shooting and ran out of the village, leaving Horry alone with a boy. A party of 10 men galloped toward Horry and the boy. The boy fired his musket, knocking Captain Lewis from the saddle with buckshot. Lewis fired as he fell, killing Horry's horse. Horry's men returned and chased the Loyalists away.

Captain Melton's patrol, moving down the Sampit Road, learned of a Loyalist party camping at The Pens, Colonel William Alston's (1747–1795) plantation. His scouting party included Lieutenant Gabriel Marion (1761–1780), the general's nephew. As Melton's horsemen were passing through a dense swamp, they encountered a strong force of Loyalists under Captain Jesse Barfield (1738–1780). Both sides fired at the same time. Barfield was shot in the head and body with a load of buckshot, but got away. Lieutenant Marion had his horse shot from under him. As the two armies disengaged, the Loyalists captured "Gabe" Marion and began clubbing him until he lost consciousness. Gabe recognized one of them from seeing him at his uncle's house and pleaded for mercy, taking hold of the man. When he was recognized as General Marion's nephew, a mulatto named Sweat (d. 1780) put a musket against Gabriel's chest and fired a load of buckshot into his heart, killing him instantly and setting his linen shirt on fire. General Marion's men captured Sweat the next day. An officer shot him in the head with his pistol that night as they were crossing the swamps. General Marion supposedly reprimanded the officer later, as he did not condone such actions.

General Marion lost two dead and three wounded, one of whom died later. He killed two enemy soldiers, captured 12 and wounded an undetermined number before withdrawing. The Crown forces had withdrawn into a well-defended redoubt (80 Regulars plus militiamen with swivels and coehorns on the parapet) and Marion's men were running low on ammunition (6 rounds per man) so Marion withdrew his forces from the area. A short while after the skirmish, the Redcoats evacuated Kingstree and Marion's men began requesting permission to return to their homes. With dwindling forces, Marion retreated to his camp on Snow Island. Some accounts date this event as occurring in January 1781.[358]

★ Major General Nathanael Greene (1742–1786), from his camp on the Pee Dee River in December 1780 rued the fact that "the great Bodies of Militia that have been in Service this year employed against the Enemy & quelling the Tories have almost laid Waste the Country & so corrupted the Principles of the People that they think of nothing but plundering one another."[359]

Lieutenant Colonel George Campbell (1732–1799) led a patrol of the Queen's Rangers in the vicinity of Georgetown on Monday, December 25, 1780. When they encountered 50 mounted militiamen, Lieutenant John Wilson charged with his 13 dragoons and dispersed them. He was wounded in the skirmish. His men captured an officer but the rest of the militiamen escaped into the woods. Their horses outran those of the Rangers and they escaped.[360]

★ Brigadier General Francis Marion (1732–1795) sent Peter Horry (1747–1815), Captain John Baxter, and 30 men to reconnoiter the strength of the Crown forces in Georgetown on Wednesday, December 27, 1780. They set up an ambush and waited. Cornet Thomas Merritt (1759–1842) and some Queen's Rangers were sent to provide cover for some slaves sent to neighboring plantations to recover cattle that had wandered away from the garrison.

Cornet Merritt, another officer and a party of the Queen's Rangers were escorting two young women past Horry's ambush about midmorning. Horry decided not to ambush them since they had women with them. Horry and his men had not eaten in 36 hours so they rode to White's plantation to seek a late breakfast. They found Mrs. White, her daughter, and the two ladies escorted by the Rangers inside the house. When Peter Horry asked Mrs. White for food and drink for his men, she begged him to leave. He was confused because he knew the family supported General Marion. He followed

Mrs. White to the kitchen and asked her to explain. She told him that the two visiting women were Loyalists and that he should pretend to take what he wanted by force.

When Horry returned to the room with the Loyalist women, the sentries fired a warning shot and ran to the house to report that the Queen's Rangers were coming down the road. Horry's men mounted their horses and charged the Rangers who saw they were outnumbered and fled back toward Georgetown.

Cornet Merritt remained in the rear to fight off Horry's men as they caught up with him. Captain Baxter fired his pistols at Merritt but missed. Captain James Postell (1745–1824) or John Postell (1717–1782) and another man attacked Merritt with swords, but they were driven back. Merritt had two horses killed under him. The fall from the second one so stunned him that he was left for dead. Horry's men took his boots, helmet and weapons. When Merritt regained consciousness, he escaped and hid in the swamp.[361]

★ Brigadier General Francis Marion's (1732–1795) camp on Snow Island was near Major Micajah Ganey's or Gainey Loyalists. By crossing the river and marching two or three hours, Marion could forage in enemy country. With his force growing daily, Marion kept a close watch on the enemy. Colonel Peter Horry (1747–1815) led 32 cavalrymen against some Queen's Rangers who retreated into Georgetown on Thursday, December 28, 1780. Major Ganey's mounted Loyalists rode out to meet Horry, but they were routed and Ganey wounded.[362]

★ Brigadier General Francis Marion (1732–1795) sent Colonel Peter Horry (1747–1815), Captain John Baxter, Sergeant McDonald and a reconnaissance force of 30 men (British accounts say 50) to patrol the Black River Ferry Road. They left from Indiantown on Thursday morning, December 28, 1780, to determine the strength of the Crown forces in Georgetown. The Whigs entered a house to request some food, later that morning. Lieutenant John Wilson (Bass says Cornet Thomas Merritt) and a small group of Queen's Rangers charged down the road toward the house. The militiamen quickly mounted their horses and headed toward the Queen's Rangers. Realizing he was outnumbered, Lieutenant John Wilson quickly headed back to Georgetown.

Major Micajah Ganey and a mounted force of Loyalists came out to counterattack Horry's party as the Queen's Rangers retreated to Georgetown, They engaged in a bloody clash at "The Camp," just north of Georgetown, probably Gapway Swamp about 2.25 miles northwest of White's Bridge. Major Ganey fled toward Georgetown with Sergeant McDonald in hot pursuit. As McDonald caught up with Ganey, he plunged his bayonet into his adversary's back but the bayonet detached from McDonald's musket and Ganey rode into town with the weapon in his back and blood gushing from his wounds. The wound prevented Ganey from returning to the field to fight until April 1781. Lieutenant John Wilson, of the Queen's Rangers, was also wounded in the encounter, but not seriously. Horry's casualties are unknown but he captured 16 men.[363]

★ Brigadier General Francis Marion (1732–1795) sent Colonel Peter Horry's (1747–1815) troops to Waccamaw Neck in early January 1781 to collect boats and drive off cattle to prevent the Crown forces from getting them. Lieutenant Colonel George Campbell (1732–1799), the British commander at Georgetown, decided to lead a British patrol in the countryside around Georgetown on Saturday, January 6, 1781. They intended to find some of Marion's men who had been raiding the countryside and continuously attacking the Crown forces.

The two forces met near Alston's plantation, named Brookgreen, some distance south of Socastee Swamp which flows into the Waccamaw River about 12 miles south of Conway in Horry County. Lieutenant John Wilson had recovered from the wounds he received on Christmas day and took part in the action. Colonel Campbell saw a dozen mounted men in the middle of the road and ordered Lieutenant Wilson to charge. The men were a decoy for an ambush hidden on the side of the road. When the Queen's Rangers reached the ambush site, they received a volley and lost a corporal killed, three others wounded and three horses killed and two sergeants taken prisoner. The Rangers turned and charged into the ambush site putting Marion's men to flight. Horry was thrown from his horse and almost trampled by one of the Queen's Rangers. Fortunately for him, the dragoon mistook him for a British lieutenant colonel at the last moment. Marion reported this skirmish, which is also known as Waccamaw Neck, to Major General Nathanael Greene (1742–1786) on January 14, 1781.[364]

★ Lieutenant Colonel Henry "Light-Horse Harry" Lee (1756–1818) joined Brigadier General Francis Marion (1732–1795) at Snow Island on Tuesday, January 23, 1781. Marion planned to attack and seize Georgetown with his reinforcements the next day. The defenses in Georgetown were weakened as Captain John Saunders (1754–1834) was given permission to withdraw his Queen's Rangers from the town. He rode to Charleston on January 19th to board a ship and leave South Carolina. (The sailing orders were revoked after the defeat at Cowpens (January 17) and Captain Saunders was ordered to assume command of the garrison at Georgetown.)

Captain Michael Rudolph (1758–1793), Captain Patrick Carnes and Lee's infantry companies moved down the Pee Dee in boats after midnight and traveled across the rice fields to Georgetown where they hid until nightfall. Meanwhile, Marion and Lee approached the town by land and waited for the first shots. Rather than attack the main brick redoubt in Georgetown, the infantry concentrated on smaller objectives.

Later, Captain Carnes rushed into the British headquarters and, without firing a shot, captured Lieutenant Colonel George Campbell (1732–1799) who commanded 200 soldiers defending the town. Lieutenant James Cryer's men surrounded a tavern housing Adjutant John Crookshanks (1754–1822) and Major Irvine (d. 1781). When Major Irvine heard the soldiers surrounding the tavern, at the intersection of Screven and Front streets, he ran into the street, fired his pistol, saw that he was outnumbered and tried to surrender. Lieutenant Cryer killed him with a bayonet in revenge because Irvine had once sentenced Cryer to receive 500 lashes. When Cryer turned to bayonet Major Crookshanks, the tavern-keeper's daughter threw her arms around the major's neck and begged for his life. Cryer accepted the major's surrender. Major Irvine and about 104 officers and privates were killed in the night attack which only used the bayonet.

When Marion and Lee arrived with their cavalry, they had not seen a single British soldier. The Crown troops remained in their brick redoubt which could not be taken without artillery to breach the walls, battering rams or scaling ladders. Not wanting to make a direct assault which would be tantamount to suicide, Marion paroled Colonel Campbell and withdrew. Marion sustained no losses; Lee lost one private killed, two wounded, and two horses disabled; and the losses of the Crown forces are not known. Lee reported to Major General Nathanael Greene (1742–1786) that "many were killed, few taken."

Although Marion failed to capture the garrison as he had hoped, the attempt prevented reinforcements from being sent to General Charles Cornwallis (1738–1805) and even required reinforcements to be sent to Georgetown.[365]

★ Brigadier General Francis Marion (1732–1795) sent Captain John Postell (1717–1782) to collect rice on the Pee Dee River and to bring 50 slaves to Major General Nathanael Greene's (1742–1786) army to impede the flow of supplies into the British post at Georgetown. The rice was to be moved by boats to be stored at Alston's plantation on Bull's Creek. When Captain Postell learned that Captain James De Peyster (d. 1793) and 29 men of the King's American Regiment had occupied his father's home north of Georgetown, between the Black and Pee Dee Rivers, he planned to drive De Peyster out of the house. Postell and 14 men crept near the kitchen of the house on Tuesday night, February 13, 1781 and waited until morning to attack.

Captain Postell formed his men in four ranks, at sunrise, to make their numbers seem larger than they were. They rushed the house and demanded De Peyster's surrender. De Peyster asked for some time to consider the demand. Captain Postell refused and began to set the house on fire. He demanded De Peyster's surrender again whereupon De Peyster and his men marched out, stacked arms and surrendered. When De Peyster surrendered his sword, he asked Captain Postell where his men were. Postell told him that he only had 14 men. Captain De Peyster became enraged that he had surrendered to a force less than half his size. Postell's men removed the prisoners before reinforcements arrived, but some of them escaped later and returned to Georgetown with some cattle and a few captured militiamen.[366]

★ Captain John Saunders (1754–1834), of the Queen's Rangers, sent Lieutenant John Wilson and 35 to 40 Queen's Rangers up the Waccamaw River to capture Captain John Clarke, one of Colonel Peter Horry's (1747–1815) officers, in mid-February 1781. The Rangers traveled to Clarke's house by boat but the heavy rain prevented them from traveling more than 20 miles—half the distance to Clarke's house. Lieutenant Wilson sent the boats back to Georgetown and concealed his men in a house until nightfall.

The Rangers marched to Clarke's house after dark and, to ensure a surprise, took prisoner anybody they encountered along the way. They surrounded Clarke's house at daylight and captured Clarke, the only one of his company there. Lieutenant Wilson freed the civilian prisoners he captured during the night and marched back to Georgetown.[367]

See also **Georgetown** (Jan. 24, 1781) p. 217.

★ If Brigadier General Francis Marion (1732–1795) could capture Georgetown, the line of British posts spreading out from Charleston would collapse. He decided to attack the town again and called for his militiamen to assemble at Cantey's plantation. They set out for Georgetown on Sunday, May 27, 1781. Marion was unaware that Lieutenant Colonel Nesbit Balfour (1743–1832) told Captain Robert Gray to evacuate his post if he should become "so press'd by the enemy as to make a retreat necessary." Marion's men began to dig trenches to lay siege to the post, but the Crown forces spiked their three 9-pounders and a carronade and knocked them off their trunnions (see Photo SC-40) before boarding their vessels that night.

Marion's men entered the town and destroyed the earthworks as the British ships waited outside the bar to Winyah Harbor. Marion left Lieutenant Colonel Peter Horry (1747–1815) in command of a small force in the town and took the captured baggage on the backs of mules to go help Major General Nathanael Greene (1742–1786) with the siege at Fort Ninety Six.[368]

★ Brigadier General Francis Marion (1732–1795) made a third attempt to take Georgetown on Wednesday, June 6, 1781. This time, he brought a large force and the necessary tools for a proper siege. The Crown forces abandoned the fort and sailed to Charleston, leaving behind their stores. Marion and his men captured the goods and destroyed the enemy fortifications. Some of Brigadier General Thomas Sumter's (1734–1832) men plundered the homes and plantations of area Loyalists in late July 1781. British gunboats entered the Sampit River just south of the town and opened fire in retribution on

SC-40. *Trunnions. Trunnions are two pieces of metal sticking out of the sides of an artillery piece. They serve to hold the artillery piece on the carriage and allow it to be raised or lowered. The trunnions are generally as long as the diameter of the cannonball and have the same diameter.*

August 2. The barrage of shells (see Photo SC-25) destroyed more than 40 houses and buildings, virtually destroying the town.

In his diary, General George Washington (1732–1799) recorded his reflections on the town: "George Town seems to be in the shade of Charleston—It suffered during War by the British, having had many of its Houses burnt. . . . The Inhabitants of this place (either unwilling or unable) could give no account of the number of Souls in it, but I should compute them at more than 5 or 600.—Its chief export, Rice."[369]

★ Brigadier General Thomas Sumter (1734–1832) ordered Captain William Ransom Davis (1755–1799) to go to Georgetown to "secure all articles of property belonging to the enemy & all persons abetting or in any wise acting inimical to the interests of the United States of America" on Wednesday, July 25, 1781. Sumter instructed Davis to seize slaves, horses, indigo, salt, hospital stores, "& all other articles suitable & wanted for the army . . . except so much as may be necessary for family use." The goods included much linen cloth and other supplies left there by Loyalists and which were for sale. After General Sumter's men had plundered the Loyalists' property, the British retaliated by burning 42 houses in the town in August.[370]

★ Lieutenant Colonel Nesbit Balfour (1743–1832) ordered Captain Manson, commander of the Loyalist privateer schooner *Peggy*, to destroy Georgetown. Captain Manson sailed the schooner over the Winyah Harbor Bar and demanded permission to land his men on Thursday, August 2, 1781. When Captain Davis denied the request, Manson brought up a galley and bombarded Georgetown. The shelling (see Photo SC-25) evacuated the streets and sent everyone to seek shelter. Manson sent his sailors ashore to set fire to the stores, warehouses and 42 houses. He continued to shell the streets to prevent anyone from extinguishing the flames. Georgetown did not recover from this attack until 1830, almost 50 years later.[371]

★ After John Futhey (d. 1781) was promoted to captain, he was killed in a skirmish with some Loyalists at Avant's Ferry on the Black River in 1781.[372]

★ Wragg's Ferry was a strategic ferry on the Black River north of Georgetown. Captain John Saunders (1754–1834) sent Lieutenant John Wilson and a detachment of 20 Queen's Rangers to cover a foraging party loading flatboats with forage from a plantation on the Black River on Monday, April 2, 1781. After a few hours, toward the end of their detail, Lieutenant Colonel Lemuel Benton (1754–1818) and about 60 of Brigadier General Francis Marion's (1732–1795) men charged the plantation twice in an attempt to capture the Rangers. The Rangers drove them off both times. After the second attack, Lieutenant Wilson counterattacked, and drove Lieutenant Colonel Benton away. Wilson and five of his men were wounded. Benton lost one lieutenant killed, and "several others wounded." Lieutenant Wilson received a commendation.[373]

★ Lieutenant Colonel John Baxter pursued some Loyalists who had captured a loaded ship. They exchanged fire at Black River Swamp in late 1781. Colonel Baxter had one man wounded.[374]

Purysburg, Jasper County
Savannah River south of Purysburg (March 29, 1779; ca. April 16, 1781)
Black Swamp (April 22, 1779)
Yamasee (Yemassee) Bluff (April 22, 1779; Aug. 13, 1779)
Congress and Lee (March 21 or 29, 1779)
Harden's men search for boats
Near Purysburg (before July 19, 1779)
Hardeeville, Jasper County

> Black Swamp is about 20 miles north of Purysburgh.
>
> The engagement of the *Congress* and *Lee* with a British galley probably occurred in the Savannah River about 2.9 miles due south-southwest of Purysburg. There is no close road access to the site.
>
> Purysburg is at the end of route S-27-31 (Church Road) where it intersects with route S-27-34 (Purysburg Road), about 2 miles west of route U.S. 321 in Hardeeville. Some accounts date the event here as occurring in April 1781.
>
> Nobody knows where the Black Swamp camp was located. James Owenby's (Ownby or Ownbey) (1761–1850) pension application gives us the best idea. He stated "That he marched from there to South Carolina and joined the Army under the command of Genl Lincoln [Benjamin Lincoln] at Purysburg. From there he was marched up the [Savannah] River to a place called the Two Sisters Ferry where he remained for some time and then marched 8 miles further up the River to a place called the Black Swamp where he remained until discharged on the 10th of April 1779. . . ."[375]
>
> It might have been near the intersection of routes U.S. 321 and SC 462 southeast of Garnett about 6.5 miles from the Two Sisters Ferry. There is high ground here

> that allowed control of the access to two main roads of the time. Another possible location is about 0.5 miles east of the Two Sisters Ferry. However, neither location is across from Abercorn, Georgia, which is across the Savannah River from Purysburg.

Major General Benjamin Lincoln (1733–1810) was camped at Purysburg in mid-March 1779. Small parties of his troops frequently skirmished with the Crown forces across the Savannah River. Colonel John White had taken command of the remnants of the Georgia Navy before the Crown forces captured Savannah and managed to get several vessels up the Savannah River away from the Crown forces. The British moved two galleys, Lieutenant Stone's *Comet* and Lieutenant McKenzie's *Hornet,* and the HM Sloop *Greenwich* upriver to Yemassee Bluff to prevent the Continental vessels from approaching Savannah.

General Lincoln ordered Captain Robert Campbell's (1753–1779) galley *Congress* and Captain Jacob Milligan's (1747–1796) galley *Lee* and Captain Marshal Boitard's French sloop to try to capture the *Comet* and the *Hornet*. They sailed at midnight. The river was treacherous enough in daylight with a river pilot. At night, without lights, it was almost impossible to sail through the shoals of the twisting channel.

Meanwhile, a detachment of 40 militiamen was ordered to march down along the river bank to take possession of a house opposite the British vessels to support the galleys. The attack was planned to begin at dawn on Sunday, March 21 or Monday, March 29, 1779. The militiamen completed their task, but the *Congress* ran aground within range of the British guns. The vessels were delayed in reaching their positions until 9 AM, losing the element of surprise. The galleys and the militiamen opened fire on the British. Lieutenant Terrill moved the British galley *Thunderer* to assist the *Comet* and the *Hornet*. Her guns forced the militiamen to withdraw. The *Lee* put up a valiant fight for about an hour but could not conquer the British galleys without the assistance of the *Congress*.

The British then manned their boats to board the Continental galleys. The Whigs "took to their boats, and as many as could be accommodated, escaped." The British lost one man killed and one wounded. The Whigs lost Captain Robert Campbell (1753–1779) and three men killed, six wounded and 10 taken prisoner. They also lost their last two Continental galleys which the British renamed *Scourge* and *Vindictive*.[376]

★ Lieutenant Colonel William Henderson (1748–1787) and a company of 40 men of the 6th South Carolina Regiment guarded Yemassee Bluff, near Black Swamp, on Thursday night, April 22, 1779, when 30 Loyalists, disguised as Native Americans, attacked a small guard post of six men there. Brigadier General Thomas Sumter (1734–1832) was certain that no Native Americans were involved because all the raiders knew how to use the bayonet. The Loyalists surprised the entire company without a shot being fired.

Colonel Henderson sent for the rest of the regiment "but could not come up with them." The Loyalist attack was a complete surprise because neither the guard post nor any of the 6th Regiment ever fired a shot. The raiders burned Captain Joachim Hartstone's house where the rest of the guards were sleeping. Hartstone was a rice planter who lived at Great Swamp on the road from Purysburg to the Coosawhatchie Bridge. The raiders murdered and scalped an old negro woman but Hartstone and his family escaped. The Carolinians abandoned their position but returned after the raiders had gone.

Some Hessian deserters informed the Whigs that there were about 50 Native American warriors stationed in the swamps opposite Purysburg to prevent desertions from the

British Army. A party of Native Americans crossed the river a little below Purysburg a short time later, but one of the Continental picket guards drove them back.

Lieutenant Colonel Alexander McIntosh (1732–1780) and 100 men of the 5th South Carolina Regiment reinforced the post at Black Swamp. Brigadier General William Moultrie (1730–1805) requested that the governor send an additional 20 Catawbas to Black Swamp to counter the Loyalist raids. Colonel McIntosh abandoned the post on April 28 when Major General Augustine Prevost (1723–1786) landed 300 men at Purysburgh.[377]

★ A party of Crown forces attacked Captain Smith's militia company near Purysburg before July 19, 1779. They captured two militiamen.[378]

★ A party of Loyalists and Native Americans crossed the Savannah River near Black Swamp on Friday, August 13, 1779, and attacked Captain William Stafford's (1750–1819) guard post but most of the guards were out on patrol. The Loyalists killed one guard and wounded two.[379]

★ Colonel William Harden (1743–1785) dispatched some of his South Carolina militiamen to destroy seven supply boats that were coming up the Savannah River around Monday, April 16, 1781, presumably to supply the British at Purysburg. It is not known if Harden's men succeeded in destroying the boats.[380]

Savannah River (April 19, 1779; July 23, 1779)
Two Sisters Ferry (March 12, 1780)
Mathew's Bluff, Allendale County (Aug. 1780 or April 1781; Jan. 22, 1781)
Wiggin's Hill, Allendale County (Jan. 23–24, 1781)
Wiggin's (Wiggan's) Plantation, Allendale County (Jan. 23–24, 1781)

> The Savannah River constitutes South Carolina's southern boundary. The Two Sisters Ferry crossed the river between Garnett, South Carolina and Clyo, Georgia, about 30 miles upriver from Savannah.
>
> Mathew's Bluff was near Brier Creek on the Savannah River at the end of route S-3-41. It is accessible by road only from the South Carolina side. To get there, take route U.S. 301 west of Allendale to route SC 3. Follow route SC 3 for a little less than 9 miles to route S-3-41. Go right (southwest) for 1.4 miles to the boat ramp. Georgia authorities place Mathew's Bluff about 3 miles farther north on the Savannah River, around the place now called Red Bluff Point. Thomas Brown (1744–1814) says that this event occurred in August 1780. Another account says it happened in April 1781.
>
> Wiggins (or Wiggan's) Hill and Wiggin's plantation were located within the borders of modern Allendale County. They were not far south of Brier Creek near where it empties into the Savannah River.

See also **Georgia** in the volume *The Guide to the American Revolutionary War in the Deep South and on the Frontier.*

Sergeant William Jasper (ca. 1750–1779) and Sergeant John Newton (1757–1787), pretending to be deserters, crossed the Savannah River on Monday, April 19, 1779 and captured captains Scott and Young and brought them to Major General Benjamin Lincoln (1733–1810) in Charleston.[381]

★ Sergeant William Jasper (ca. 1750–1779) and a detachment of four Georgia Continentals went up the Savannah River on Friday, July 23, 1779, hoping to surprise a picket post. They captured seven Georgia Loyalists on a patrol, recovered 12 stolen slaves and sent the prisoners to Charleston.[382]

★ Brigadier General James Pattison (1724–1805) and a column of 1,500 Crown troops from Savannah, marching to the siege of Charleston. They crossed the Savannah River into South Carolina at the Two Sisters Ferry on Saturday, March 11, 1780, and camped a quarter of a mile from the river. Captain John Campbell's (d. 1806) foraging party dispersed a party of Continental light horsemen the next day. Campbell was slightly wounded in the skirmish.[383]

★ About 150 British Regulars and militiamen gathered on a bluff along the Savannah River at the Two Sisters Ferry on Sunday, June 4, 1780. Several of this group crossed the river and killed two men in South Carolina.[384]

★ Whig Captain James McKay plundered boats bound for Augusta, Georgia, along the swamps of the Savannah River in January 1781 in retaliation for Colonel Daniel McGirth's (d. ca. 1789) raid on the Brier Creek settlements in Georgia. Lieutenant Colonel Thomas Brown (1750–1825), who commanded the Crown garrison at Augusta, Georgia, wanted to stop the frequent capture of boats laden with provisions and supplies. He ordered Captain Alexander Wylly, of the King's Rangers, to proceed down the South Carolina side of the river to eliminate any threat to the shipping. He sent Lieutenant Kemp (d. 1781) and 25 King's Rangers and 20 Loyalist militiamen ahead of his force. Their hired guide did not like the Loyalists and alerted Captain McKay who set up an ambush on Mathew's Bluff and waited to attack the Crown forces, although greatly outnumbered.

When Kemp's troops rode into the ambush site, his militiamen all fled at the first volley, without firing a shot. Lieutenant Kemp and his Rangers surrendered. McKay invited Kemp to join him, but he refused. McKay's men shot Kemp dead, along with 15 of his men in retaliation for the Brier Creek massacre. The lone survivor pretended to join McKay. He escaped at his first opportunity and reported what had happened to Colonel Brown.[385]

★ After Captain James McKay's men killed Lieutenant Kemp (d. 1781) at Mathew's Bluff, Lieutenant Colonel Thomas Brown (1750–1825) learned that Colonel William Harden (1743–1785) was near Augusta, Georgia; so he ordered Captain Alexander Wylly and 40 King's Rangers and 30 Native Americans to search for McKay and his men. Captain McKay had joined Lieutenant Colonel William Harden's force of about 100 South Carolinians near Augusta. Captain Wylly informed Colonel Brown of McKay's location as soon as he discovered it. Colonel Brown marched his men (about 100 soldiers and 70 Creeks) 60 miles from Augusta in two days to avenge Lieutenant Kemp's death. He was joined by 100 Loyalist militiamen along the way.

Colonel Brown and his men camped in an open field at Wiggin's plantation, about 30 miles from Black Swamp on Tuesday, January 23, 1781. Lieutenant Colonel Harden, unaware of Brown's approach, advanced less than a mile from Brown's camp. Both parties were within striking distance of the other and both were ignorant of the other's position. Harden was the first to learn of the enemy's position and decided to attack immediately, hoping to catch Brown by surprise. Brown had retired to a house a short distance from the camp and had gone to sleep. Some of his officers informed him of Harden's approach. The Crown forces were forming for battle shortly after midnight when Harden's men rode into the camp and terrified the Loyalist militia. The Rangers formed their ranks and repulsed the attack. Outnumbered by more disciplined troops, Harden was forced to retreat.

★ Colonel William Harden's (1743–1785) men struck again at 8 AM, dismounted. Lieutenant Colonel Thomas Brown (1750–1825) was forewarned and counterattacked. His 170 troops, including Rangers and Creeks, outnumbered Harden's men and scattered them in the swamp in an engagement that lasted half an hour. Harden lost seven killed and eleven wounded. The Loyalists lost at least as many and possibly more. Colonel Brown reported that his entire militia deserted during the battle and joined Harden. The Creeks caught the guide who betrayed them at Mathew's Bluff and "ripped him open with their knives in Browne's presence and tortured him to death." Brown claimed that the chief killed the guide with a tomahawk.

Brown hanged one of McKay's men who confessed to killing Kemp's troopers. He also burned the plantations of several people who had helped McKay's men. He wanted to hang the 13-year-old son of Captain Rannal McKay (or Ranald McCoy) who was taken prisoner. Brown was told that the boy was last seen at the garrison, spying for Harden. The boy's mother came to the fort at Augusta to plead for her son's life. Captain Ranald MacKinnon (1737–1805), of the 84th Regiment, told Colonel Brown that he thought that hanging a 13-year-old boy was murder. Brown ignored him and hanged the boy anyway.

★ Lieutenant Colonel Harden attacked again the following morning, but was repulsed again. He returned to his headquarters on an island in Coosawhatchie Swamp.[386]

Coosawhatchie, Jasper County
Coosawhatchie River (May 3, 1779; May 11, 1779)
Black Swamp

> The Coosawhatchie River flows east of the town of Coosawhatchie. The bridge over the Coosawhatchie River is on route SC 462 (right off Exit 28 of I-95), about 1 mile past where it turns right. A historical marker is a short distance before reaching the bridge on the right. The engagement took place just north of the river on May 3, 1779.

Colonel John Laurens (1754–1782) and 350 North Carolina light infantrymen comprised the rear guard of Brigadier General William Moultrie's (1730–1805) army when they tried to hold back Major General Augustine Prevost's (1723–1786) 2,400 man expeditionary force marching from Georgia to capture Charleston in early May 1779. Laurens, on the western bank of the Coosawhatchie River, was outnumbered and was no match for Prevost's heavy guns, but he managed to gain General Moultrie some valuable time.

Major Thomas Fraser (d. 1820) and a party of about 300 Regulars of the 71st Regiment landed 9 miles below Purysburgh on Thursday, April 28, 1779. Lieutenant Colonel John Maitland (1732–1779) landed 4 miles higher up the Savannah River the next morning with the light infantry of the line and 2nd battalion of the 71st Regiment. They took possession of the town that afternoon.

The Crown forces intended to attack General Moultrie, who was posted at Black Swamp with about 800 men, before Colonel Lachlan McIntosh (1727–1806) could join him. Major General Benjamin Lincoln (1733–1810) was 80 miles farther up the country with the main body of the army at this time.

Moultrie, outnumbered three to one, was forced to retire on the 30th. That night he met Colonel McIntosh at Black Swamp, coming to join him. They halted at Coosawhatchie that night and proceeded to Tulifiny before dawn the next morning. They left a field officer's guard at the bridge and took their post there.

Moultrie received intelligence early Saturday morning, May 2, 1779, that the enemy was in motion. He placed about 100 men on a slight ridge along the Tulifiny River, about 2 miles east of the Coosawhatchie River. He placed guards at all possible crossing points and 100 men at the main crossing point with orders to guard the crossings and warn Moultrie when the Redcoats arrived. Moultrie also requested Governor John Rutledge (1730–1800) to send 100 dragoons but they never arrived. Moultrie sent Laurens's light infantry and 150 select riflemen to bring the rear guard back to the main force before it was cut off. Colonel Laurens was supposed to lead them back to Tulifiny Hill, and Moultrie sent 250 men to help cover Laurens's flanks. An advanced party of Crown light infantrymen attacked the bridge at 2 PM on Sunday afternoon. The guard had been reinforced by 1500 riflemen but they were still outnumbered and couldn't stop the Crown advance.

Colonel Laurens disobeyed his orders, crossed the river and formed his 400 men and Captain Thomas Shubrick's (1756–1810) company of the 5th South Carolina Regiment for battle on the west bank of the Coosawhatchie River. He did not occupy the high ground and the Crown forces, equipped with artillery, occupied the houses on the west bank. Heavy enemy fire, from cover, inflicted many casualties, even wounding Laurens in the right arm and killing his horse. Laurens ordered Captain Shubrick to hold this position while he went for medical care; but, once Laurens left, Shubrick ordered a retreat to the main force at the Tulifiny. Had he not retreated, the entire force, one third of Moultrie's army, would have been captured. They lost three killed and eight wounded.

Although Laurens lost the skirmish here, he delayed General Prevost enough for the Congressional forces to regroup and force General Prevost to abandon his siege.

Moultrie retreated toward Charleston, in successive stages, by the Saltketcher road. The retreat was marked by rear-guard skirmishes, burning the Tulifiny and Pocotaligo bridges behind him. He notified Governor John Rutledge and Major General Benjamin Lincoln of the threat to the city. The army halted for a few hours at the meeting house and then marched on to Ashepoo. They passed the bridge in the morning of May 4th and occupied the high grounds near Mr. Pickney's houses for the rest of the day.

That night, General Moultrie received intelligence that the enemy's advanced party had reached Godfrey's Savannah and that their main body had crossed the Saltketcher River, even though the bridge had been destroyed. As Moultrie's outnumbered troops could not make a stand without being surrounded, they were forced to leave Ashepoo between 3 and 4 AM on the 3rd. They halted at Mr. Ferguson's plantation, called Spring Grove, that night after destroying the Jacksonboro Bridge. They reached Bacon Bridge the next night.[387]

★ Brigadier General William Moultrie (1730–1805) received intelligence Monday evening, May 10, 1779, that the British Army was encamped on the south side of Ashley Ferry. They appeared so suddenly that the ferry boats could not be destroyed. They began to cross Ashley Ferry at 1 AM on Tuesday. Their advanced party of light infantrymen and cavalry took their post half a mile from the ferry.

Brigadier General Casimir Pulaski (1747–1779) reconnoitered the Crown forces and left a detachment to watch their movements, as he went to town to confer with the council. Meanwhile, the Crown forces completed their passage over the river and were advancing toward the town in three columns with 200 horsemen, 400 highlanders and some Native Americans in the lead. The cavalry comprised the rear guard.

Some of General Pulaski's men, 5 miles from town, were ordered to fire to announce the enemy's approach. The Crown troops halted frequently to explore the ground over which they were to pass.

General Pulaski had ordered his infantry to form an ambuscade and directed a detachment of volunteer horsemen to support his infantry while he prepared to entice the enemy cavalry to attack. A close fire began and both Pulaski's cavalry and infantry charged. However, the volunteer horsemen misunderstood their orders and hindered the infantry's movements. Despite these difficulties and being outnumbered, General Pulaski's men put up a good fight but were eventually forced to retreat. The Crown forces did not pursue and escaped artillery fire. They lost 45 soldiers and officers, while the Continentals had 30 casualties.

★ General Pulaski attacked a detachment of Crown forces on Tuesday, May 11, 1779. He took several prisoners and forced the rest to flee. One of the sentries sounded an alarm about 10 PM. A general fire of cannon and musketry ensued from the lines and the armed vessels stationed on the flanks. Major Benjamin Huger (d. 1779) and a party were sent to burn a gap in the abatis. The major and three privates were unfortunately killed and the Crown forces had several men killed, primarily on the ships.

General Pulaski went out with a small party of horsemen to reconnoiter early Thursday morning, the 13th, and found the Crown forces had decamped and recrossed Ashley ferry. His men brought eleven deserters and about as many prisoners into town during the course of the day.[388]

General Barnwell repulsed, Jasper County (ca. March 1, 1782)

This action occurred in South Carolina on the approach to Rochester's Ferry across from the southeastern tip of Hutchinson Island. The Island was considerably smaller in 1782 and has grown toward the ocean since then.

There was a considerable quantity of unthreshed rice on Hutchinson Island, opposite Savannah, Georgia, and a large amount of stacked rice on Royal Governor Sir James Wright's (1714–1785) plantation, about half a mile southeast of the town about Friday, March 1, 1782. Brigadier General John Barnwell (1748–1800) was ordered to burn the rice on Hutchinson's Island and Brigadier General "Mad Anthony" Wayne (1745–1796) was to destroy the rice at Governor Wright's plantation.

Loyalist militia Lieutenant Colonel Andrew De Veaux, Jr. (1758–1812) (also spelled DeVeaux) arrived at Beaufort and destroyed all the boats General Barnwell had collected for this mission. Despite the loss of his boats, General Barnwell ordered his brother, Lieutenant Colonel Edward Barnwell (1757–1808), to take 50 men in boats to cross the river to burn the rice on the island.

Lieutenant Colonel De Veaux learned of the plan and sailed to the Back River, between Hutchinson Island and South Carolina, to prevent Barnwell's troops from reaching the rice stores. His men fired on Lieutenant Colonel Barnwell's men as they approached Rochester's Ferry. Barnwell lost five or six men killed and an equal number taken prisoner. He was forced to retreat, most likely by land, hoping to find vessels along the river or to use Rochester's Ferry, while Deveaux travelled by boat.[389]

Yamassee, Hampton/Beaufort/Colleton Counties
Near Yemassee
McPherson's Plantation, Hampton County (March 18, 1780)
Jacksonboro, Colleton County (March 14, 1780; March 17, 1780; April 1781)
Six Miles from McPherson's (Saltketcher Bridge) (March 17, 18, 1780)
Saltketcher (Salkehatchie or Salkahatchie) River (March 18, 20, 1780; May 25, 1782)
Saltketcher Swamp (Oct. 1782)

> McPherson's plantation was probably about 2 miles west of where Interstate 95 crosses Pocotaligo Road about 1.5 miles south of exit 38. It was near the intersection of routes S-25-17 (Pocotaligo Road) and S-25-286 (McPhersonville Church Road) 2.8 miles west of Yemassee. The area is known as McPhersonville. A historical marker is also near this intersection. No information has yet been found that identifies the exact location of either of these two skirmishes but they most likely occurred near the present town of McPhersonville probably where route U.S. 17A crosses the Salkehatchie River (also called the Saltketcher River in some accounts) near Yemassee.
>
> The event named "6 Miles from McPherson's" most likely occurred at the Saltketcher Bridge which was where route U.S. 17A (U.S. 21) crosses the Salkehatchie River about 5.5 miles due east of McPherson's plantation and about 1.85 miles east of Yemassee.
>
> A state historical marker on route U.S. 17A, 6 miles south of route S-15-41, marks the site of the Salkehatchie Presbyterian Church and Cemetery. The church was constructed around 1766 and destroyed during the Civil War but the 18th century cemetery survives. Some of the most prominent Scotch-Irish settlers of the Low Country are buried here.
>
> About 1.7 miles further on route U.S. 17A, a bridge crosses over the Salkehatchie/Combahee River. Warring armies destroyed the bridge here during the American War for Independence. President George Washington (1732–1799) crossed the river here on Wednesday morning, May 11, 1791 over a bridge built by Thomas Patterson.
>
> Saltketcher Swamp was south of Islandton and west of Ricepatch Creek.
>
> Jacksonboro is located on the Pon Pon or Edisto River about 30 miles west of Charleston. It consisted of about 60 houses—all owned by Whigs.

Brigadier General James Pattison (1724–1805) and British reinforcements marched from Savannah, Georgia to assist General Henry Clinton (1730–1795) who was beginning the siege of Charleston. His troops fought several skirmishes with South Carolina militiamen before they arrived at Charleston.

General Pattison sent an order to Lieutenant Colonel Banastre Tarleton (1744–1833), from his headquarters at Port-Royal Island, instructing Tarleton:
> to join him with the cavalry, then lying at Beaufort, if he had assembled a sufficient number of horses to remount the dragoons; the number was complete, but the quality was inferior to those embarked at new York by the detachment of the 17th

light dragoons, and by the legion. The corps felt not discouraged by this circumstance, but instantly joining General Patterson, sought for occasion to acquire better horses by exertion and enterprise. The inhabitants of Carolina having heard of the loss of the cavalry horses at sea, had flattered themselves that they could not be speedily recruited. In order to confine the British troops as much as possible to the line of march, and to prevent their collecting horses in the country, some of them accoutred themselves as cavaliers, and a few days after the junction of the dragoons from Beaufort, ventured to insult the front of General Patterson's corps, which composed of his cavalry, who made a charge, unexpected by the Americans, and without any loss took some prisoners, and obtained a number of horses.[390]

Meanwhile, Colonel James Ladson (1753–1812) and a detachment of 80 Colleton County militiamen had been busy felling trees across the roads leading to the Saltketcher Ferry in early March 1780. Colonel Ladson had his men destroy all the boats along the river so the Crown troops couldn't use them to cross. Captain Abraham De Peyster (1753–1799) pursued the militiamen and captured three of them and several horses.

General Pattison ordered Major Patrick Ferguson's (1744–1780) American Volunteers and Major Charles Cochrane's (1749–1781) detachment of Tarleton's Legion to secure the river crossing. When Majors Ferguson and Cochrane received intelligence that two parties of Whig militiamen were in the area, they set out in pursuit. Major Ferguson took a part of his American Volunteers and 20 men of the British Legion to Isaac McPherson's plantation at 4 PM on Monday, March 13, 1780. They planned a surprise attack at night, but, when they arrived about 9 PM, they learned that 50 Continental dragoons had just left. Major Ferguson sent a party to pursue the dragoons but they were unsuccessful. The troops rested at McPherson's plantation for the night.

★ Major Charles Cochrane's (1749–1781) Legion infantry pursued another party of militiamen, but his guide led them the wrong way. Major Cochrane arrived in front of Major Patrick Ferguson's (1744–1780) pickets at daybreak and mistook them for the militiamen he had pursued all night. The pickets discovered the infantrymen moving into position to attack and fired upon them. Major Cochrane ordered his men to fix bayonets. They rushed the pickets to drive them from a nearby house where a detachment of the American Volunteers (Loyalists) were located.

The American Volunteers fired on the British Legion, thinking they were being attacked by Congressional troops. Major Ferguson was wounded in the arm by a bayonet and had to hold his horse's reins in his teeth. A lieutenant was also wounded in the arm and hand. When majors Cochrane and Ferguson recognized each other's voices, they stopped fighting. They lost three men killed and several badly wounded. Captain Abraham De Peyster then secured the Coosawhatchie Bridge with 60 American Volunteers and 20 British Legionnaires. The troops camped at McPherson's plantation from Saturday March 17 to Tuesday, March 20, 1780.[391]

★ Lieutenant Colonel Banastre Tarleton (1744–1833) and his Legion met a body of mounted South Carolina militiamen as he passed through Jacksonboro on Friday, March 17, 1780, after stealing horses from Port Royal. They killed three, wounded one and captured one and took several good horses.

★ Captain Abraham De Peyster (1753–1798) was ordered to pursue a party of Whigs headed toward Charleston on Friday, March 17, 1780. The Whigs got intelligence of his pursuit and escaped. He captured three prisoners, who were probably stragglers, and several horses that night.

The next day, De Peyster set out at 8 AM and marched to the Salkehatchie River crossing where Colonel James Ladson (1753–1812) and 80 militiamen held a position on the north side of the river to oppose the British crossing. Colonel Ladson's men had destroyed the bridge and occupied a tavern on the north side of the river to oppose any crossing by Brigadier General James Pattison's (1724–1805) army. A company of legionnaires exchanged fire with them while the light infantrymen and the remainder of the legionnaires crossed the river downstream and attacked Colonel Ladson's rear by surprise. They bayoneted Captain Mills (d. 1780) and 16 privates to death, badly wounded four others and captured one man who was unharmed. Captain De Peyster had Major Colin Graham and two privates of the light infantry and Major Wright of the Georgia Loyalists slightly wounded.

The Crown troops spent a cold, rainy night at Ogilvie's plantation and, the following day, swam the horses and crossed the Salkehatchie River in boats that they brought with them. The bridge had already been destroyed and the causeway on both sides of the river overflowed with water 2 to 3 feet deep from the ferry house to about a quarter of a mile from the river. As a detachment of New York Volunteers was placing the boats back onto the carriages, some snipers from Captain William Sanders's (1760–1847) Round O Company fired upon them from the far shore and killed three on Monday, March 20, 1780.[392]

Saltketcher (Salkehatchie or Salkahatchie) River (May 25, 1782) see **Dean Swamp** p. 114.

Saltketcher Swamp (Oct. 1782) see **Dean Swamp** p. 114.

Pon Pon, Charleston County
Bee's Plantation, Charleston County (March 23, 1780)

> Some authorities give this skirmish the name "Pon Pon," which is what the Cherokees called the Edisto River. There are no remains of Lieutenant Governor Thomas Bee's (1725–1812) 1,500 acre plantation which was on the east bank of the Edisto River, opposite Jacksonboro. The town, founded in 1735, served as the provisional capital of South Carolina after the surrender of Charleston.
>
> A state historical marker for Pon Pon Chapel is a little to the northwest of the junction of routes SC 64 (Charleston Highway) and S-15-40 (Jacksonboro Road) about 2 miles west of the intersection of routes SC 64 and U.S. 17. The site of the chapel is 0.9 miles north to route S-15-705 (Parker's Ferry Road) and 0.3 miles to the east (right). The chapel was constructed in 1754 on a spot where John Wesley (1703–1791) preached in 1735. The building was a well-known landmark during the American War for Independence. It survived the war, including the fighting at nearby Parker's Ferry, but a fire destroyed it in 1801 and it has since been known as the "Burnt Church."

Several months before the surrender of Charleston, Lieutenant Colonel Banastre Tarleton (1744–1833) led a successful attack against a party of mounted Catawbas and Whig militiamen at Bee's plantation just east of Jacksonboro and the Edisto River on Thursday, March 23, 1780. He killed 10 militiamen and captured four in a heated skirmish. He also captured some badly needed horses.[393]

Jamestown, Berkeley County
Ball's Plantation, Berkeley County (May 5, 1780)
Lenud's (Lanneau's) Ferry, Jamestown, Berkeley County (May 6, 1780)
Near McClellanville, Charleston County
Wambaw Creek, Berkeley County (Feb. 24, 1782)
Tydiman's Plantation, Berkeley County (Feb. 25, 1782)

> Ball's plantation was in what is now the Francis Marion State Forest near where Wambaw Creek meets Victor Lincoln Road north of the Awendaw Bridge. Lenud's Ferry is on route U.S. 17A|SC 41 at the northern edge of the Francis Marion National Forest 1.7 miles north of the junction of routes U.S. 17A, SC 41 and SC 45 (French Santee Road) at Jamestown. A state historical marker about 0.8 miles southeast of the bridge calls attention to the Battle of Lenud's Ferry which was fought here on the Santee River. The battle actually took place between the marker and the concrete bridge, a half mile further north, which replaced the ferry that once crossed the Santee River here. The old ferry landing is near the old railroad bridge, accessible from a boat landing near the bridge over the Santee River.
>
> The place name comes from the Acadian Lanneau family who came here with other refugees after being evicted from Nova Scotia in 1755. They settled about 5 miles west of the present-day Jamestown bridge on route U.S. 17A. Yellow fever took its toll on the family and many of the Acadians had left before the American War for Independence. The site has many variations of the Lanneau name but they are all mispronounced "Lenoo." The more generally used name now is "Lenud."
>
> Tydiman's plantation was on the Berkeley County side of Wambaw Creek, which is northwest of McClellanville. From the intersection of routes U.S. 17 N (U.S. 701|N U.S. 17|N Highway 17) and SC 45, go north on route U.S. 17 for 6.5 miles then turn left (northwest) onto Rutledge Road (S-10-857). Go 4.3 miles, cross Wambaw Creek and proceed 2.6 miles on Echaw Road. Turn right onto Forest Road 204B and go 1.7 miles.
>
> Some sources place the site of the battle about 6 miles north where a bridge on Echaw Road crosses Wambaw Creek. The action took place about 125 yards west of the bridge. It started at the bridge and ended about 100 yards past the bridge into Berkeley County. Route S-10-857 (Rutledge Road) crosses route U.S. 17 about 1 mile south of the Santee River. At Wambaw Corner, when the road forks to the right and left, bear right for 0.7 miles where the road turns into Echaw Road. The bridge is less than 0.25 miles ahead. Jack Parker places the site about 285 yards due northeast of this site or about 0.25 miles east, as the creek flows.
>
> Two roads met at Wambaw Creek in the 18th century. One went northwest to Lenud's Ferry; the other went to a plantation belonging to Elias Horry, one of Colonel Peter Horry's (1747–1815) relatives. Horry's own plantation was on the north side of the Santee River.

Colonel Anthony Walters White (1750–1803) took command of all the Whig cavalry in South Carolina after Lieutenant Colonel Banastre Tarleton's (1744–1833) attack at Moncks Corner. He and Lieutenant Colonel William Washington (1752–1810) began to assemble their troops on the north of the Santee River at Lenud's Ferry toward the end of April 1780 under the protection of two Virginia infantry regiments and the Carolina militia. Colonel White and 300 New Jersey Continentals crossed the Santee River Friday morning, May 5, 1780. They attacked a British foraging party at 9 AM the next morning at Elias Ball's (1709–1786) plantation, 19 miles from Strawberry Ferry. They caught the British by surprise with only one pistol being fired. They surrounded and captured a British officer and a detachment of 17 of Tarleton's dragoons in what is known as the Battle of Wambaw. They then marched up to Lenud's Ferry with their prisoners to recross the Santee, unaware that a Loyalist informant reported their movements to Tarleton. Tarleton rushed to the ferry, arriving at 3 PM. He records:

> On the road, the British were overtaken by a loyal American, who had been a witness to the success which had attended Colonel White in the morning, but had luckily escaped his power. The description of the troops, the assurance of their intention to pass the river at Lenew's, and the hope of retaking the prisoners, stimulated Tarleton to push forward his patrole with the greatest expedition: At the same time, the distance of Lord Cornwallis's camp (at Huger's bridge 26 miles away), the fatigue of the march, the heat of the weather, and the sight of their infantry on the opposite bank, threw the Americans quite off their guard.[394]

★ When the Continentals arrived at the ferry to join Colonel Abraham Buford (1749–1833) and the 3rd Virginia, who had been trying to get to Charleston to assist in its defense, Lieutenant Colonel Banastre Tarleton's (1744–1833) 50 dragoons struck them by surprise as they were crossing about 3 PM and routed them. Although the Continentals outnumbered Tarleton's Legion, they were no match for the cavalry. Colonel Anthony Walton White (1750–1803), Lieutenant Colonel William Washington (1752–1810), Major David Jamieson (1715–1799), and several officers and men, escaped by swimming the river. Tarleton reported killing and wounding five officers and 36 men and capturing seven officers and 60 dragoons while he lost only two men and rescued all his light infantrymen. The Continentals actually lost about 11 killed, including those who drowned trying to swim the river to escape, 30 wounded and 67 captured as well as their prisoners. The dragoons lost only two men killed and four horses. They lost more than 20 horses from fatigue on the way back to Lord Charles Cornwallis's (1738–1805) camp.

Tarleton annihilated the corps of Congressional cavalry and infantry in the open field and caused fear and terror to spread through the country from the Saltketcher to the Santee, a distance of 120 miles. It took about six months before the dragoons could take the field again because of a lack of horses and equipment.[395]

★ Brigadier General Francis Marion (1732–1795) had been elected a member of the general assembly and was attending a meeting at Jacksonboro (Charleston was still occupied by the British) in January 1782. Even though General Charles Cornwallis (1738–1805) had surrendered at Yorktown, Virginia, almost three months earlier, there were still many British troops in the South and fighting continued. Marion placed his two principal officers, Colonel Hezekiah Maham (1739–1789) and Colonel Peter Horry (1747–1815), in charge during his absence, but they found various pretexts to delegate their command duties to subordinates.

When Colonel Benjamin Thompson (Count Rumford) (1753–1814), in Charleston, learned that Horry and Maham were feuding, he took advantage of the opportunity. He crossed the Cooper River with 200 mounted troops, 500 infantrymen, and two cannons. He headed to Wambaw Creek where Marion's men were encamped from Wambaw Creek to Echaw Creek on the northwest side.

Horry decided to visit his home on the north side of the Santee River on Sunday, February 24, 1782. He delegated command to Colonel Adam McDonald (ca. 1740–1778).

Maham, also a legislator, was in Jacksonboro with Marion. Maham's brigade was camped at Mepkin plantation on the Cooper River. Colonel Thompson mounted the infantrymen behind the cavalrymen for part of the way and, by forced marches, approached the camp from the west.

Not believing reports of the enemy's proximity, most of the Whig officers were sitting down to dinner when the firing started. Horry's dragoons advanced over the bridge and formed about 100 yards down the road facing Thompson's mounted militiamen. The rest of Thompson's force came up and charged suddenly. Most of Horry's men were recruits. They broke ranks during the charge and fell back across the bridge. The Crown forces pursued them, shooting; but the bridge broke under the weight of the men and horses, ending the chase. Horry lost 40 men dead and seven prisoners.

When news of the battle reached Jacksonboro, about 40 miles away, Marion and Maham hurried back to Wambaw Creek, not stopping until they reached the Tydiman plantation north of Wambaw Creek and about 1.5 miles from the Crown forces.

Thompson had captured a herd of cattle and discovered two pickets near the Tydiman home as he was driving the cattle to Charleston. He knew immediately Marion's men were nearby so he formed his line quickly and advanced. Marion's men rushed to take up their positions. The infantrymen deployed along a rail fence while the dragoons formed in a column. The dragoons charged but had to incline to the left to avoid a pond. As they broke ranks, Thompson charged and routed them. The fleeing dragoons headed toward the Santee River, about a half mile from Tydiman's plantation, and escaped by swimming the river.

A band of Horry's men managed to get to the Wambaw bridge as the rest of Thompson's men advanced. They were repairing the bridge, and even though they had had enough warning to form, the Whigs lost about 20 killed and 12 taken prisoners.[396]

Brier Creek, Allendale County
Tarleton Brown's father and 17 others (May 1780)

> Tarleton Brown's father lived on Brier Creek south of route U.S. 301 and about 0.75 miles east of the Savannah River.

Georgia Loyalists often crossed the Savannah River near the home of Captain Tarleton Brown's (1757–1845) father to plunder the South Carolina Whigs. One of these raids occurred in May 1780 while Tarleton Brown, of the South Carolina militia, was visiting his father. A band of Loyalists arrived about midnight intending to kill Captain Brown and his brothers, but barking dogs woke Captain Brown, who was sleeping in the hallway.

Someone knocked loudly at the door and requested shelter claiming they were friends and part of Major General Benjamin Lincoln's (1733–1810) army on their way home. Captain Brown looked through a crack in the door and realized they were Loyalists. When they asked for water, he told them to get it from the well in the yard. The men became angry and swore vengeance upon Brown and the entire household.

The Loyalists tried unsuccessfully to break down the door and then fired several shots at it. (The light at the end of the hallway revealed the cracks in the door.) The shots missed Captain Brown but killed his little brother who was awakened by the noise. The family and friends had armed themselves by this time, but their shots were ineffective because the Loyalists had moved some distance away from the house.[397]

★ Captain Tarleton Brown (1757–1845) went to Virginia while his father, mother and sisters stayed at home to look after their property in May 1780. Colonel Daniel McGirth (d. ca. 1789) (McGirtt) and his Loyalist militia crossed the Savannah River from Georgia at Stone's Ferry and marched along the Savannah River through South Carolina, killing everyone who had not sworn loyalty to the King. This included Brown's father and 16 others in that area, including Henry Best (d. 1780) and a Mr. Moore (d. 1780). John Cave was left for dead but later recovered. Brown's mother and sisters escaped into the woods as McGirth burned their house to the ground and destroyed all their property. They remained in the woods until the Loyalists left.[398]

Silver Bluff, near Jackson, Aiken County
Fort Galphin (May 21, 1781)
Fort Dreadnought

> Silver Bluff was near route SC 315 (Bluff Landing Road) about 100 yards north of Fort Galphin/Dreadnought.
> Fort Galphin, also known as Fort Dreadnought (the British name for the fort), was on the north side of the Savannah River about 12 miles south of Augusta, Georgia, on Silver Bluff. To get there, from the junction of routes SC 5 (Main Street) and SC 62 (South Silverton Street) in Jackson, drive northwest on route SC 5 for 2.2 miles to the junction with an unimproved road (Bluff Landing Road). Turn left and follow that road west for 3 miles to the Savannah River at Silver Bluff.

The home of George Galphin (1709–1780), Deputy Superintendent of Indian affairs, was turned into a small stockaded place which the Whigs called Fort Galphin and the Crown forces, who occupied it for most of the war, called Fort Dreadnought, suggesting it was invincible. Two Loyalist companies garrisoned it in May 1781 during the final days of the siege of Augusta, Georgia.

Colonel Elijah Clarke's (1733–1799) forces strengthened with each passing day. One of these new arrivals was Brigadier General Andrew Pickens (1739–1817) with about 400 men from Colonel Robert Anderson's (1741–1812) regiment. Pickens immediately invested two forts across the river near Augusta to cut off assistance to Fort Galphin at Silver Bluff. He also requested Major General Nathanael Greene (1742–1786) for aid.

Greene sent Lieutenant Colonel Henry "Light-Horse Harry" Lee (1756–1818) and his Legion, consisting of three companies of cavalry under captains Joseph Eggleston (1754–1811), Ferdinand O'Neal or O'Neale (ca. 1758–ca. 1817), and James Armstrong (1728–1800) and three companies of infantry commanded by captains Patrick Carnes, Michael Rudolph (1758–1793), and Levin Handy (1754–1799). He also had some of Brigadier General Thomas Sumter's (1734–1832) men and part of a battalion of North Carolina militiamen.

Lee was moving rapidly toward Augusta because General Greene feared that Colonel John Harris Cruger (1738–1807) might withdraw his garrison from Ninety Six and join Colonel Thomas Alexander Browne (1744–1814) at Augusta when he learned of Lord Francis Rawdon's (1754–1826) retreat after the battle of Camden. One of Rawdon's messages intercepted from Camden expressed his desire for Cruger to do just that.

Lee had his dragoons and infantrymen share the horses. They covered the 75 miles from Fort Granby in less than three days. Along the way, Lee learned that Cruger was preparing for a siege and strengthening his fortifications. Some of Clarke's militiamen had attacked several boats bringing the king's annual gifts to the Cherokees and Creeks and forced them into port at Fort Galphin (Dreadnought) where the fort's heavy guns, overlooking the river, kept them at bay. As he approached Augusta, Captain Neal informed Lee that the annual king's present had recently arrived at Fort Galphin for temporary storage. This was a considerable quantity of material, including weapons. Lee wanted to capture these supplies or prevent them from going to the Native Americans.

Lee sent some of his Legion reinforced by Captain Michael Rudolph (1758–1793) and parts of two regiments of Georgia and South Carolina militiamen to help Clarke capture Fort Galphin. They hastened to the fort, mounting the infantry behind the dragoons, with the artillery to follow later. They arrived at Fort Galphin the next morning, May 21st, and found the stockaded farmhouse garrisoned by two companies of Colonel Thomas Brown's (1750–1825) Loyalist militia. They hid in a pine grove along an open field surrounding the fort and prepared for the assault. Rudolph and Clarke, knowing that the Crown forces in the garrison held the local militiamen in contempt, sent a small force in front of the fort, as a decoy, to feign an attack and make a hasty retreat while most of the Continentals hid.

When the fort's defenders rushed out to pursue Rudolph's bait, Clarke's militiamen and Lee's regulars rushed through the open gates, surprising the enemy soldiers inside and capturing them. Captain Rudolph chased the first group back, quickly surrounding and subduing them with little opposition. Clarke and Rudolph killed three or four defenders, wounded a few others, and captured 126 prisoners, including 70 British Regulars who would be sorely missed in the defense of Augusta. A few escaped into the woods. The attackers lost only one man who died of sun stroke. They also captured a large store of blankets, clothing, small arms, ammunition, rum, salt, medicines, and other articles.

Lee then reassembled his troops, crossed the river, and headed to Augusta that evening to join Pickens for an attack on Fort Cornwallis and Fort Grierson two days later. With the Continentals in control of the fort, British reinforcements in Augusta could not reach Ninety Six, Major General Nathanael Greene's (1742–1786) next objective. Lee was now free to march on Savannah.[399]

Eutawville, Orangeburg County
Great Savannah, Clarendon County (Aug. 20, 25, 1780)
Nelson's Ferry (Dec. 14, 1780)

> Nelson's Ferry was a major crossing of the upper Santee River in the 18th-century. It was about 9 miles downstream from Fort Watson on the county line due north of Eutawville. It is now under the waters of Lake Marion.
> General Thomas Sumter's plantation, Great Savannah, is also under the waters of Lake Marion. Some sources say it was 6 miles above Nelson's Ferry. Others say it was just north of the ferry. Many accounts use the two names (Nelson's Ferry and Great Savannah) interchangeably. This engagement should not be confused with the Battle of Blue Savannah or any of the skirmishes along the Savannah River.

Lieutenant Colonel Banastre Tarleton (1744–1833) raided and burned General Thomas Sumter's (1734–1832) plantation, Great Savannah, in the summer of 1780. Shortly afterward, on Sunday, August 20, British Captain Jonathan Roberts

(1735–1825) was escorting to Charleston about 150 Maryland Continental prisoners captured four days earlier at Camden. A Loyalist deserter informed Francis Marion (1732–1795), recently promoted to brigadier general of the state militia, of the movement on August 24. Marion, along with Colonel Hugh Horry (1744–1795) and his troops, surprised and ambushed the Redcoats at the plantation site. Horry's men stumbled across a sentry who fired a shot. Horry attacked the front of the house immediately while Marion's men attacked the back. Horry captured the Crown muskets stacked outside the front door. This put the Crown troops at a disadvantage. The attackers quickly killed or captured 22 British Regulars and two Loyalist guides. They also rescued 147 Maryland and Delaware Continentals who were captured at Camden but 85 of the prisoners refused to return to service and insisted on imprisonment in Charleston. Of those who joined Marion, three deserted on the way to Snow Island.[400]

★ Lieutenant Colonel Nesbit Balfour (1743–1832) changed the shorter supply route from Charleston to Camden via Nelson's Ferry and the Santee Road to the much longer one going from Moncks Corner to Friday's Ferry on the Congaree River in mid-December 1780. He also ordered that boats on the Santee River stay below Murray's Ferry. Brigadier General Francis Marion's (1732–1795) men captured and burned one boat which did not receive the directive in time at Nelson's Ferry on Thursday, December 14, 1780. The 64th Regiment was posted at Nelson's Ferry but they did not have enough men to pursue Marion's mounted men.[401]

Hilton Head (Sept. 24, 1779; Sept. 2, 1780)
Hilton Head Island (1780; Oct. 20, 1781)
British privateer *Vigilant* (between Feb. and May 12, 1780)
Ceres
Charles Davant ambushed (Oct. 22, 1781)
Two Oaks Plantation (also known as Big Gate, Bear Island, Buckingham Landing)

> Hilton Head is northeast of Savannah, Georgia. The closest land approach to the site of the action involving the *Ceres* is at the end of any of the streets, to the right, off Folly Field Road, east of William Hilton Parkway (U.S. 278) on Hilton Head.
>
> The site of the Privateer *Vigilant* action is in Mackays Creek at the mouth of Moss Creek west of Buzzard's Island. There is no convenient road access to the site.
>
> Charles Davant (1750–1781) was ambushed near the intersection of Mathews Drive and Marshland Road on Hilton Head Island. There's a marker in the median on Mathews Drive.

The HMS *Experiment* was on her way from New York to Savannah with Major General George Garth (d. 1819) and 20 British officers and £30,000 in silver to pay the Crown troops in Georgia when she lost her masts and bowsprit in a gale. General Garth was supposed to replace Major General Augustine Prevost (1723–1786) as commander in Savannah.

★ The frigate *Lively* was cruising in the same area and captured two vessels loaded with provisions. When the *Lively*'s captain learned that the vessels became separated from the *Experiment* in the storm, three ships were dispatched to find the *Experiment* off Port Royal.

The *Experiment* rendezvoused with a British store ship and a navy victualer from New Providence near Hilton Head on Thursday, September 24, 1779. The captain of the store ship, which had 65 prisoners aboard, warned Sir James Wallace (1731–1803), the captain of the *Experiment,* that he had seen 20 large ships south of Hilton Head.

The *Experiment* spotted three large ships in the distance at 3:45 PM and tried to outrun them. About 45 minutes later, Captain Wallace saw two more ships heading toward him from the west. The unknown ships hoisted the French colors at 8 PM and closed with the *Experiment*. The French man-of-war (see Photo SC-24) *Sagittair* gave the *Experiment* two broadsides but only a few shots reached the *Experiment* due to the distance between them. Captain Wallace hoisted more sail to get farther away from the *Sagittair*. He hoisted his colors at 8:30 and prepared to fight. All the French ships, two ships of the line and two frigates soon came within the *Experiment*'s range. They dismasted the *Experiment* and Captain Wallace struck his colors.[402]

★ Captain Thomas Goldesbrough's 20-gun British vessel, *Vigilant*, was formerly the *Empress of Russia* which the British purchased in 1777. (This is not the same vessel as the 64-gun third-rate HMS *Vigilant* launched on October 6, 1774.) The *Vigilant* was in such bad condition by 1779 that she could not be used for ocean service. Her masts, rigging and ballast had been removed and she was used as a troop carrier and gun platform in inland waterways. She had to be towed by rowing vessels through the narrow creeks and waterways. A British flotilla of longboats towed the *Vigilant* through Skull Creek behind Hilton Head Island when a Congressional armed vessel spotted her between February and May 12, 1780. The boats towed her into Mackays Creek where she ran aground on a mud flat at the mouth of Moss Creek. The boats did not have enough power to pull the *Vigilant* free, so the crews burned her at the mouth of Moss Creek, west of Buzzard Island at Hilton Head, because of her poor condition and to prevent the Whigs from using her or her parts. Another company of British soldiers discovered the *Vigilant*'s hulk about March 15, 1782 when they patrolled the rivers and creeks around Beaufort in search of hidden Congressional vessels.[403]

See also **Beaufort and vicinity, Capers Creek** (ca. March 15, 1782) p. 205.

★ The HMS *Ceres* ran aground on a sand bar "in going round from" Tybee, Georgia, to Beaufort, South Carolina about Saturday, September 2, 1780. A party of militiamen captured her.[404]

★ A hurricane caught Captain George McCumber's (1756–1841) galley *Tuger* off Hilton Head on Friday, October 19, 1781. The *Tuger* capsized and two crewmen drowned. Captain John Howell (1756–1830), a Georgia privateer, rescued 30 other crewmen and the combined crews captured two schooners loaded with rice the next day. They also captured 30 slaves bound for the West Indies; but a British galley appeared with two boats before they could take the captured schooners away. Captain Howell set the vessels on fire and escaped with the slaves. The British captain arrived in time to save the schooners.[405]

★ Hilton Head Island was dominated by the Whigs while neighboring Daufuskie Island was a British stronghold known as "Little Bermuda." The Crown forces on Daufuskie Island decided to raid Hilton Head Island. Loyalist Colonel Thomas Brown (1750–1825) assembled a force of regulars and militiamen under the immediate command of Major Arthur Maxwell and Loyalist Captain Phillip Martinangel (d. 1781) (also spelled Martinangle or Martinangele) of the Royal Militia. The force burned many houses on Hilton Head Island and laid an ambush that resulted in the killing of Charles Davant (1750–1781), a local Whig soldier and planter on Monday, October 22, 1781. They also took John Andrews prisoner. Charles Davant was a prominent resident and an influential citizen of Hilton Head. His plantation, known as Two Oaks plantation, Big Gate, and Gardiner's or Gardner, was 1,424 acres in size.[406]

Bear Island (Dec. 20, 1780)

> Bear Island is between the South Edisto River and the Ashepoo River south of Jacksonboro.

Captain James Doharty (d. 1780), of the South Carolina militia, took command of Fort Lyttleton, near Beaufort, with 50 men in March 1779. He pursued the Loyalists to the point that many wanted to kill him. Richard Pendarvis (1744–1780/1781) was a staunch Loyalist who lived about 12 miles from Captain Doharty's home on Bear Island. Even though they had been friends and neighbors before the war, they now hated each other.

Doharty was home on Wednesday, December 20, 1780, when he learned that Pendarvis and a party of Loyalists would attack him that night. His three nephews, Lieutenant John Leacraft or Leacroft (1766–1838) of Hilton Head and his 14-year-old brother William (1766–) and Captain Thomas Talbird (1755–1804) were with him. They decided to ambush Pendarvis and his Loyalists; but they waited too long to set the trap. The Loyalists hailed Doharty as he stepped onto the porch of his home and asked if he was Captain Doharty. Doharty turned to his nephews to inform them that the Loyalists were already outside and that they should flee, then admitted that he was Doharty. The Loyalists then shot Captain Doharty on his porch but did not kill him.

Captain Doharty held his gun in his hand and asked to shake hands with his attackers, hoping for some sort of retaliation but the Loyalists refused. From the light of a fire in the yard, the Loyalists saw where Captain Doharty lay and fired a second volley that killed him. They then entered the house and hanged William Leacroft (1766–) until he was half-dead in a futile attempt to get information on the hiding places of the others. The Loyalists admired the young man's courage and did not complete the hanging. Captain Doharty's friends buried his body at Whale Branch on Port Royal Island.[407]

★ In one of Captain James Doharty's (d. 1780) excursions, he attacked a British galley anchored in the Savannah River. His well-directed fire killed several and cleared the decks, but he had no boats or any means of cutting the cable, and warping the galley on shore. As his party retreated, the British fired their cannon with grape shot into the woods, but without injury. When the men had retired far enough, they were halted and seated on a tree to rest. A random shot from the galley now struck a sapling close to them, cut it off and struck one of the men on his body. However, as the charge was spent, the shot fell harmless at his feet.

Buckingham Landing (ca. Dec. 24, 1780 or April 13, 1781)
Richard Pendarvis killed

> Buckingham Landing is at the end of Fording Island Road, sometimes called Buckingham Landing Road, which is off route U.S. 278 (William Hilton Parkway) at the end of Fording Island Road Ext. about 0.6 miles west of Calibogue Sound.

A few days after Richard Pendarvis (1744–1780/1781) and his Loyalists killed Captain James Doharty (d. 1780,) Pendarvis prepared to move to St. Augustine, Florida, where he expected to find a safe haven. Lieutenant John Leacraft or Leacroft (1766–1838), one of Captain Doharty's nephews, and five others killed Pendarvis and his friend, Patterson, at Buckingham Landing, on the May River, shortly before embarking about Sunday, December 24, 1780 or Friday, April 13, 1781. Leacraft retired to his plantation on Hilton Head after the signing of the peace treaty. He lived a long life but left no family.[408]

Colleton County
Saltketcher Bridge (Patterson's Bridge) (April 5, 1781; April 8, 1781)
Four Holes Swamp, Dorchester County (April 7, 1781; June 16, 1781)
Barton's Post, Colleton City (April 8, 1781)
Pocotaligo Road (April 8, 1781)
Fort Balfour, Beaufort County (April 8 and 13, 1781)

> The event at Patterson's Bridge is also known as Saltketcher Bridge, Fort Saltketcher or Pocotaligo Road. It occurred just east of the Combahee (Salkehatchie) River on route U.S. 17-A (Hendersonville Highway).
> Colleton County is about 30 miles south of Orangeburg.
> Four Holes Creek or Swamp is a branch of the Edisto River west of Summerville and south of Dorchester. Route U.S. 78 north out of Summerville meets route SC 173 (School Street) east of Ridgeville. Follow route SC 173 (School Street) into Ridgeville to route SC 27 (Church Street). Take Church Street south for 0.16 miles. Turn right (west) on South Railroad Avenue and proceed one block to Main Street. Turn left onto Main. About 0.3 miles down the road, you will come to route S-18-19 (Ridge Road). Turn left onto Ridge Road and proceed for 5.6 miles to where it crosses Four Holes Swamp.
> Barton's Post at Red Hill was approximately 2 miles from the Saltketcher Bridge. Some references indicate Barton's Post at Red Hill was at Four Holes Swamp. It was in Colleton County about 2 miles east of the Saltketcher Bridge.[409]
> Fort Balfour overlooked the Pocotaligo River Bridge, two thirds of the way between Charleston and Savannah. It was near the intersection of routes U.S. 17 (Castle Hall Road) and U.S. 17A|U.S. 21 (Trask Parkway) about 1.8 miles northeast of route I-95 exit 33. There's a historical marker in the far right corner of the church parking lot around the right side of the church. Named for Lieutenant Colonel Nesbit Balfour (1743–1832), the British commander at Charleston, Fort Balfour was garrisoned by Colonel Edward Fenwick (d. ca. 1785?) and 100 officers and men in April 1781.

Brigadier General Francis Marion (1732–1795) sent Colonel William Harden's (1743–1785) company of 100 men to conduct operations into the low country between Savannah and Charleston in the middle of March 1781. Harden planned to recruit local people to increase his force but was unsuccessful. Nevertheless, he continued on his mission to disrupt enemy communications. Captain Tarleton Brown (1757–1845), who was with Harden, later wrote in his memoirs: "Crossing the Edisto at Givham's Ferry, we fell in with a man who assisted Brown in hanging the 5 brave fellows at 'Wiggin's Hill'. We gave him his due, and left his body at the disposal of the birds and wild beasts."

The party proceeded down the Pocotaligo Road on Wednesday, April 4, 1781, and prepared to ambush Loyalist Captain Edward Fenwick (d. ca. 1785?) and 35 South Carolina dragoons near the Saltketcher Bridge. Fenwick learned of Harden's approach and tried to surprise him instead. When Harden's advance party met the Loyalists and hailed them, Harden ordered his men to turn out in the woods, but they went too far from the road. Harden fired a few shots when they retreated and rushed out. The Loyalists charged. Although Harden's company outnumbered the dragoons, his men became disoriented in the dark and were dispersed. Paul Hamilton (1762–1816), one of Harden's men, wrote, "At midnight encountered a body of British cavalry near Saltketcher Bridge. The onset was in our favor, but, Harden being an indifferent commander, we were defeated and in the rout I suffered a hard pursuit.... Our whole party was dispersed, and about 15 severely wounded with the sabre."

Harden was defeated and a force of Loyalist dragoons pursued him for a long distance to Patterson's bridge by way of the Four Holes Swamp. Harden captured a Loyalist captain and 25 privates at a muster field at Four Holes Swamp and paroled them. He reported he had one man captured and two wounded and said he killed one of Fenwick's men and wounded seven.[410]

★ On Saturday, April 7, 1781, Colonel William Harden (1743–1785) with 70–100 mounted men, surprised and captured a captain and 25 Loyalists as they were drilling at a muster field at the Four Holes. (*The Royal Gazette* of April 11, 1781 reports the date as the 7th while Harden's letters written on the 18th seems to indicate the date as the 14th.) Harden learned that a body of Loyalists was gathering at Barton's Post at Red Hill, a small post garrisoned by Captain John Barton (d. 1781) and six men. When he arrived within 6 miles of Barton's post Sunday night, the 8th, Harden detached Major John Cooper (1751–1819) and 15 men to surround the house and demand a surrender. When Barton refused to surrender, Cooper's party opened fire in what became a brisk engagement that lasted an hour. Cooper and another man were wounded and one other man killed. Barton lost three men killed and two wounded and was forced to surrender. He was also mortally wounded and taken prisoner.[411]

★ Three days after Colonel Edward Fenwick's (d. ca. 1785?) encounter with Colonel William Harden (1743–1785) at the Saltketcher Bridge (which Captain Tarleton Brown (1757–1845) called Patterson's Bridge), Harden was riding down the Pocotaligo Road toward the Saltketcher Bridge after defeating the Loyalists at Red Hill. He learned that Colonel Edward Fenwick and his 35 South Carolina Loyalist mounted dragoons were at Fort Balfour on the Pocotaligo River. The fort controlled the Pocotaligo River Bridge, Kings Highway (the road to Charleston), and U.S. Highway17A to Walterboro.

Colonel Harden advanced on Fort Balfour on Sunday, April 8, 1781, to surprise Colonel Fenwick, but Fenwick heard of Harden's approach and advanced to meet him. Captain Tarleton Brown wrote, "Soon after we left Red Hill we entered upon a long, high causeway; a man came meeting us and told us Colonel Fenwick, with the British horse, were marching on just behind. We paid no attention to him not knowing who he was, but went ahead; however, we did not go many rods before the advance parties met and hailed each other."

Harden saw Fenwick's advanced party searching for him around midnight and attempted an ambuscade around Patterson's Bridge. As the vanguards met, Harden ordered his men to turn into the woods but most of them went too far to be recalled. Harden ordered his men out of the woods to charge Colonel Fenwick's dragoons.

However Colonel Fenwick's dragoons charged the small group in the road, scattered and routed them, wounding two and capturing one. Rather than pursue Harden's troops, Fenwick retreated. Harden claimed to have killed one of the South Carolina dragoons and wounded seven more and captured two. He lost one man killed, seven wounded and two taken prisoners the following morning. *The Royal Gazette* of April 11 reported Harden's losses as 14 killed and wounded and some horses. This skirmish is called the Battle of Pocotaligo Road.[412]

★ Colonel William Harden (1743–1785) withdrew about 10 miles with his two prisoners the next day and rested two days before crossing the Salkehatchie River and marching on Fort Balfour again. He arrived in sight of the fort about noon on Friday, the 13th and posted his men. He and the rest of his men hid in the wilderness around the fort. Harden sent Captain Tarleton Brown (1757–1845) and 13 of his best dragoons to lure the Crown forces out of the garrison.

At this time, Colonels Edward Fenwick (d. ca. 1785?) and Nicholas Lechmere (1733–1805) were returning from visiting troops wounded in the Battle of Pocotaligo Road who were recuperating at Vanbiber's tavern nearby. The two officers, caught by surprise, began running for the safety of the fort and were captured along with seven dragoons. With the two commanding officers held prisoner, Colonel Harden demanded the surrender of the fort, but the senior officer, Colonel William Kelsall or Kelsell refused. Harden sent another messenger to tell Kelsall that if Harden had to storm the fort, he would give no quarter. Kelsall requested half an hour to consider his alternatives. Harden gave him 20 minutes after which Kelsall agreed to surrender.

In two hours, Colonel Harden took the fort without firing a shot or losing a single man. The garrison marched out and piled their arms outside the abatis. One militia colonel, Major Andrew Deveaux (also spelled DeVeaux) (1758–1812), three captains, three lieutenants, and 60 privates and one lieutenant and 25 dragoons were taken prisoners and paroled. Colonel Harden's men worked all night and the next day paroling the prisoners and arranging transportation for them. They threw the 6-pounder into a nearby creek.

Captain Brown, describing the surrender, stated that the Loyalists had a force of 110 men while Harden only had 80. He also thought that 1,000 men could not have dislodged the Loyalists if they were determined to resist, as the fort was well fortified and all three approaches were well protected by deep creeks and cannons.

When he learned that Loyalist Colonel Robert Ballingall was on his way from Charleston with 100 men of the 71st Regiment, 30 Highlanders, and about 40 militiamen to relieve the garrison, Harden destroyed the fort.[413]

★ Major Hezekiah Maham (1739–1789) dispersed a band of Loyalists at Four Holes, in Dorchester County, on Saturday, June 16, 1781.[414]

Walterboro, Colleton County
Snipes's Plantation (May 6, 1781 or June 3, 1781)
Ford's Plantation (July 7, 1781)
Ford's Horseshoe Plantation
Horseshoe, Colleton County (July 7, 1781)
Parson's Plantation (Aug. 7, 1781)

> Snipes's plantation, also known as the Snipes's Horseshoe plantation, (there was also a Ford's Horseshoe plantation) was located about 6 miles east of Walterboro on Fuller Swamp Creek. It was west of Featherbed Road (S-15-199) and south of

> Barracada Street west of Round O. The land is now owned by a lumber company. A historical marker is located about 2 miles further north on Cottageville Highway (U.S. 17A) about 75 yards west of Round O Road (S-15-45). According to Lyman Copeland Draper (1815–1891), this event occurred on May 6, 1781. The "Horseshoe" is a depressed horseshoe-shaped geographical feature of the land in this area.
> Ford's Horseshoe plantation was also called the Horse Neck. It was south of Snipes's Horseshoe off Charleston Highway (SC 64) east of Featherbed Road (S-15-199).
> Parson's plantation was located on Black Creek near the end of Iron Bar Road about 1.25 miles due west-southwest of Low Country Highway (U.S. 21) 5.75 miles north of Yemassee.

Captain William Clay Snipes (1742–1806) formed an independent militia company and refused to serve under Brigadier General Francis Marion (1732–1795) because he resented being passed over for promotion when Marion was made a brigadier general. He operated under Brigadier General Thomas Sumter (1734–1832), but Sumter denied that he interfered with any militia operations east of the Santee River when Marion protested to him.

Snipes decided to stop and spend the night at his home when he was nearby in early June 1781. He was unaware that Captain John Saunders (1753–1834) and a party of the Queen's Rangers, a troop of the South Carolina Royalists and Colonel Robert Ballingall's Colleton County Regiment had followed him. The Crown forces swam their horses across the Edisto River and approached the plantation on Saturday night, June 2, 1781 after Snipes had retired for the night. Lieutenant Alexander Chesney (1755–1843) described the crossing:

> We crossed Pond Pond River at parker's Ferry, and the boats having been removed to impede our march I swam my horse over, accompanied by some others, and procured feather beds to transport those who could not swim across the river; we then proceeded rapidly and reached Snipe's Plantation by daylight.

The Loyalists came within 50 yards of the house. Captain Saunders saw a large gate that would slow their progress and give away their surprise raid. He ordered Cornet Thomas Merritt (1759–1842), Corporal Theobald Franks, and four men to widen the opening for the detachment. Someone in the house spotted Merritt and fired at him. He managed to create a hole in the gate and fence strengthened by an ox chain. Captain Saunders and his Rangers rushed through the opening. As Lieutenant Chesney jumped his horse over the fence, a man hidden there wounded him in the leg with a spear. Lieutenant Stephen Jarvis (1756–1840) of the South Carolina Royalists described the attack:

> We received the fire of the Enemy which wounded some of our men. We charged them. They quit the house and retreated towards the woods. There was an open field between the house and the wood where we came up with them and cut them to pieces. They were much scattered and every one singled out his man. I saw one who had nearly gained the wood before I should overtake him and as I was the only person who was in pursuit he deliberately turned and faced me, recovered his rifle and waited until I came very close. I was aware of his intentions. I could not retreat. My only chance was to charge him, I laid my head down by the side of my horse and put him at full speed. He levelled his piece and fired. He missed both myself and horse and before he could recover his rifle I gave him a blow across the face and he fell to rise no more. He died without a groan.

When the cries of his African American driver awakened him, Snipes headed to his barn for shelter; but the driver indicated that the barn was already ablaze. Snipes barely escaped the house in his nightshirt and hid in a briar patch 50 yards from the house. The briars ripped the shirt off his back.

The Loyalists grabbed the slave and demanded to know where his master was. The driver refused to answer; so they tied a rope around his neck and ran him up a tree. When he was on the verge of choking to death, they let him down and demanded him to reveal Snipes's location. They repeated this process three times; but the driver never revealed his master's hiding place. The militiamen were still firing from the mill house; so the Loyalists were wary of going into it. They set it on fire which spread to Snipes's plantation house. The heat blistered Snipes's skin while he lay hiding in the briar patch.

Captain Saunders captured 18 of Snipes's men. Snipes and three of his men were the only ones to escape. The 18 prisoners were killed after they surrendered and the fire may have killed others. Lieutenant Jarvis noted:

> Only one man was taken prisoner and he was ordered to be killed, by Captain Saunders. The most disgraceful thing I ever heard of a British officer. The poor fellow was severly hacked, but whether he died of his wounds or not I do not know. I once pulled out my pistol to put the poor fellow out of his misery but I had not the power to discharge, and said to myself "This blood shall not be charged to me." I do not know but have reason to believe that as many as twenty were killed.[415]

Snipes and his driver immediately went to join General Marion's forces after the raiders left.

★ After Colonel Isaac Hayne (1745–1781) and his men captured Brigadier General Andrew Williamson (ca. 1730–1786) at Horse Savannah on Thursday, July 5, 1781, they withdrew to Snipes's Horseshoe where Captain William Clay Snipes's (1742–1806) men had been captured. When Major Thomas Fraser (d. 1820) learned of this, he sent 90 of his dragoons to search for the perpetrators the next day. After a circuitous march of more than 70 miles through the woods, they surprised Colonel Hayne and his men in their camp at Ford's plantation, or Ford's Horseshoe, on Saturday morning, July 7th. They "killed 14 on the spot, wounded several, took Colonel Isaac Hayne, their Commander, prisoner, and released General Williamson from his confinement at a house in the neighbourhood." The dragoons cut Lieutenant Colonel Thomas McLaughlin (d. 1781) to pieces for attempting to kill Major Fraser with a pistol. Colonel Hayne was taken to town on Sunday and imprisoned in the provost jail. He was later hanged as a spy. The British account says that Colonel Hayne was captured at the plantation of Mrs. Mary Ford, wife of Tobias Ford (Horseshoe) which was located on the east side of Horseshoe Road, now Featherbed Road.[416]

★ Major Thomas Fraser's (d. 1820) South Carolina Royalists attacked Major John Cooper (1751–1819) and 86 men of Colonel William Harden's (1743–1785) Regiment in a swamp at Parson's plantation on Tuesday, August 7, 1781. The swamp was so deep that the horses were mired up to their bellies. Fraser reported killing 15 and capturing 4, while only losing two men killed and one wounded. Major Cooper tried to exchange Crown prisoners for his four men.

When Captain John Melton and Simon Fraser (1726–1782) went to Major Fraser with a flag of truce, Major Fraser noticed Simon Fraser's name on the flag and asked if he was the same Simon Fraser who had killed a man named Ingles (d. 1781) at the house of Major James Clitherall (d. 1782), surgeon of the South Carolina Royalists, earlier in the year. Simon Fraser responded that he was that man. (Colonel Harden had sent his men out to round up Loyalist officers. Simon Fraser and some other men surrounded the house of Major Clitherall and ordered him to open the door. A man named Ingles opened the door and quickly tried to slam it shut when he saw the armed men. Fraser fired through the door and struck Ingles in the chest, killing him. He then took Major Clitherall prisoner.) When Simon Fraser confirmed his identity, Major Fraser had him arrested and put in irons.[417]

Loyalists hanged by Captain Joseph Vince, Orangeburg County (ca. Aug. 5, 1781)
Captain Vince wounded, Orangeburg County (ca. Aug. 6, 1781)

> Captain Joseph Vince probably hanged the Loyalists near a mill at the "Forks of the Edisto." To get to the site from the junction of routes U.S. 21 and 178 north of Orangeburg, go northwest on route U.S. 178 for about 4.6 miles, then turn left onto Shillings Bridge Road and to the site at the bridge over the North Fork of the Edisto River.
>
> Captain Vince was probably wounded along the Caw Caw Swamp about 1.5 miles north of Wannamaker Catfish Ponds. From the junction of routes U.S. 21 and 178 north of Orangeburg, go north about 2 miles on route U.S. 21, then turn left onto Benjamin Boulevard and go to its end. The old mill is slightly to the left about 0.35 miles at Caw Caw Creek.

Colonels Baley (Baily) Chaney (ca. 1740–) and Hezekiah Williams led a force of Loyalists that captured Captain James Roberts (1734–1802) north of Orangeburg around Sunday, August 5, 1781. They butchered several of Roberts's men, but left him alive.

Captain James McKay's cavalry was returning from an attack on a small force of Loyalists on the Ogeechee River in Georgia when they learned of the attack. McKay and 36 of his men volunteered to go with Captain Joseph Vince (1745–1811) in search of the Loyalists, even though only 17 of them had weapons. They set out from the area of Vince's fort on the Savannah River. They rode through the woods at night and ran into a band of Loyalists before they had time to deploy. Both sides fired simultaneously without harming anyone. The Loyalists disappeared, leaving McKay and his men frustrated and angry. The Whigs captured six of the Loyalists, held a quick trial and hanged them at the "Forks of the Edisto."

Captain Vince then rode to Salley's Cowpens close to Turkey Hill north of Orangeburg to make camp. After his men set up the camp on Monday, August 6, 1781, Vince rode alone to a nearby mill, unaware that he had been observed by some Loyalists who ambushed him when he got close enough. They shot Vince in the leg seriously wounding him, "in consequence of which he was disabled from doing duty for some time." It took him almost two months to recover enough to be able to ride again. His next engagement was against Colonel Daniel McGirth (d. ca. 1789) at Stone's Ferry in Allendale County about September 29, 1781.[418]

Eutawville, Orangeburg County
Eutaw Springs, Orangeburg County (Sept. 8, 1781)
White Meeting House

> The site of the battlefield (sciway3.net/outdoors/park-eutawsprings.html) is just west of the intersection of routes SC 6 (SC 45|Old Number Six Highway) and Fredcon Road (S-38-137) in Eutawville. A small park with interpretive signs is located on

> route SC 6 (SC 45|Old Number Six Highway) near Fredcon Road (S-38-137). There are two informational markers, between the fence and the creek, that describe the engagement and a stone erected by the Daughters of the American Revolution to commemorate it. The British redoubt and Nelson's Ferry are also under Lake Marion. The closest land access to these sites is the end of Dogwood Drive.
> Major John Marjoribanks (d. 1781) was originally buried at a spot now submerged beneath the lake. Daniel Barefoot, in *Touring South Carolina's Revolutionary War Sites*, says the major's grave was moved to its present location in 1941. This probably refers to the tombstone, rather than to the actual remains.
> The Old White Meeting House was on the Dorchester Road (SC 642) about 3 miles east of its junction with route U.S. 17A and 2 miles northwest of Fort Dorchester.

After the siege of Ninety Six (see p. 252), General Nathanael Greene (1742–1786) rested his army for six weeks on the banks of the Wateree River, south of Camden. The long summer campaign ruined Lord Francis Rawdon's (1754–1826) health and spirit. After chasing General Greene in vain after the siege of Ninety Six, Rawdon turned his command over to Lieutenant Colonel Alexander Stewart (1740–1794) and sailed for England, only to have his ship captured by Admiral François Joseph Paul Comte de Grasse's (1722–1788) fleet.

On Wednesday, August 22, 1781, Greene moved his army of 2,300, about half of them Continentals, north to Camden and turned south toward Lieutenant Colonel Alexander Stewart's (1740–1794) camp at Eutaw Springs, about 50 miles northwest of Charleston.

Stewart left the initiative to the Continentals on Saturday morning, September 8, 1781. His army numbered about 2,000, including Colonel John Harris Cruger's (1738–1807) men evacuated from Ninety Six. Stewart learned of Greene's approach about 8 AM when some of his men, sent to harvest yams for the army's rations, encountered the advancing front line. They fled to tell Stewart who deployed his men in a line crossing the road that led to Charleston, about 100 yards to the west of his camp.

Stewart reinforced his exposed left flank with some infantrymen and his cavalry. Major John Marjoribanks (d. 1781) took his position with 300 men by the waters of Eutaw Springs. He placed the guards and grenadiers (see Photo SC-14) on his right flank, near a tangle of blackjack oak. The cavalry was on the left and his three guns on the road in the middle of the front line.

Greene had the advantage of knowing the enemy's location. Declining Loyalist support for the British allowed his army to get 4 miles from Stewart's camp without Loyalist citizens informing Stewart. Greene arranged his troops into battle order about a mile from the enemy. He put the South and North Carolina militia in the first line, the Continentals in the second, and the light infantry and cavalry in the third.

Brigadier General Andrew Pickens (1739–1817) and Brigadier General Francis Marion (1732–1795) led the South and North Carolina militiamen against Marjoribanks shortly after 9 AM. They encountered very heavy cannon and musket fire as artillery on both sides fired grape shot at each other. One of Stewart's guns and two of Greene's were put out of action. The militiamen did not falter, astounding the Regulars on both sides. They fired about 17 rounds before the 64th Regiment and some Loyalist troops charged with their bayonets and drove them back.

The British right and center held for a while, but Greene sent three brigades of North Carolina Continentals under Major General Jethro Sumner (1735–1785) to reestablish the line. He followed with a charge by the relatively fresh Maryland and Virginia Continentals, as the troops on the right poured heavy fire into the British left, collapsing that flank and then Stewart's front. The Crown forces soon retreated with heavy losses. Only Marjoribanks's troops continued to fight on the right.

Greene sent Lieutenant Colonel William Washington's (1752–1810) cavalry forward, but Marjoribanks routed them as they attempted to reach his rear. Colonel Washington's horse was hit by a musket ball and he was captured.

When the Congressional infantry pushed the British into their camp, the Whigs ran into the tents and plundered the camp. They opened casks and bottles and drank so heavily that they were soon uncontrollable. This gave Major Marjoribanks time to organize his troops, rush forward to capture the Congressional guns, and drive off the looters, shooting many of them as they drank. Sharpshooters also killed several officers. Although mortally wounded, Marjoribanks ordered an attack that forced the Continentals back. Greene's units were completely disorganized, so he stopped fighting and withdrew instead of risking the destruction of his army.

Greene's cavalry covered the retreat, while Stewart's cavalry tried to stop them. After collecting his exhausted men, Greene left Stewart in possession of the battlefield. The Continentals suffered about 25% casualties: 139 killed, 375 wounded, and eight missing. The number of missing is undoubtedly higher because a large part of the army was involved in plundering British tents and drinking. Stewart reported British casualties as 85 killed, 351 wounded, and 257 missing—35% of his army, the highest percentage of losses sustained by any force during the war. Stewart returned to Charleston, and the British did not leave their strongholds in Charleston and Savannah for the rest of the war.

The four-hour Battle of Eutaw Springs was one of the most violent of the war. It essentially ended the campaign in the south. It forced the Crown forces back to Charleston where they remained cooped up until they evacuated the city in December 1782. It also left Greene master in South Carolina. Greene had lost battles but won a campaign. In so doing, he paved the way for the greater victory to follow at Yorktown. The Whigs regained control of South Carolina and Georgia.[419]

★ After the battle of Eutaw Springs, the British troops, who were heading to Yorktown, Virginia to reinforce General Charles Cornwallis (1738–1805), were exhausted after the 4-hour battle. They retired to the Old White Meeting House on the Dorchester Road to rest and recover. While they were there, they burned the interior of the brick church and may have also burned the colonial records which had been removed from Charleston to Dorchester. They never went to Yorktown.[419a]

Girard, Georgia
Stone's Ferry (modern Stoney Landing) (ca. Sept. 29, 1781)
Colonel McGirth repulsed

Stone's Ferry (modern Stony Bluff Landing) is on the Georgia side of the Savannah River at the end of Stoney Bluff Landing Road 9 miles east of Girard. The South Carolina side has a high bluff of 10 to 20 feet that would have given Captain Joseph Vince's men the high ground and good cover, leaving Colonel Daniel McGirth's men exposed on the lower Georgia side of the river and while crossing the river.

A band of Loyalists ambushed Captain Joseph Vince (1745–1811) north of Orangeburg about Monday, August 6, 1781 and wounded him seriously. When he recovered enough to ride a horse, he and 17 of his men were returning to the area of Vince's fort on Steel Creek in Barnwell County about Saturday, September 29, 1781. Local residents informed Vince and his men that Colonel Daniel McGirth (McGirtt) (d. ca. 1789) was crossing the Savannah River. Captain Vince didn't have time to muster more men. They attacked Colonel McGirth and his 370 men as they were crossing the Savannah River from Georgia. The attack was so ferocious that Colonel McGirth and his men fled back to Georgia. Several of them panicked and drowned in the river. The Whigs captured McGirth's baggage and many horses that had already made the river crossing.[420]

Barnwell County
Vince's Fort (Oct. 23, 1781; Oct. 28, 1781)

> Vince's Fort was an outpost on Steel Creek in present-day Barnwell County. The site is a branch of the Savannah River within the boundaries of the Savannah River Nuclear Plant near the Georgia border.

Captain Joseph Vince (1745–1811) and 80 militiamen garrisoned Vince's Fort on Steel Creek when a larger group of Loyalists attacked it around Tuesday, October 23, 1781. Captain Vince lost one man killed but drove the Loyalists away.[421]

★ Captain Tarleton Brown (1757–1845) recognized Colonel Hezekiah Williams on one of his raids along the Savannah River below Augusta, Georgia and counted 150 Loyalists riding with him. Brown hurried across the Savannah to warn Captain Joseph Vince (1745–1811) who was sick in bed. When Colonel Williams and Colonel Baley [Baily] Chaney (ca. 1740–) prepared to attack Vince's fort on Sunday, October 28, 1781, they found the fort empty. Tarleton Brown had miscounted Williams's men who numbered only 25 instead of 150. The Loyalists captured a few stragglers and burned the fort before returning to Orangeburg.[422]

Barnwell County
Adam Wood killed (Oct. 27, 1781)
Mr. Collins killed (Oct. 29, 1781)

> Adam Wood was killed near Hayes Mill Pond, north of Poplar Road where it crosses a brook about 300 yards southeast of Woodland Road. Mr. Collins's home was close to Lower Three Runs Creek, about a mile and a half northwest of where Adam Wood was killed. Access to the property is restricted as it's part of the Atomic Energy Commission's Savannah River Plant. A marker at the Three Runs Baptist Church in the area of 5117–5334 route S-6-20 (Patterson Mill Road) commemorates the event.

Adam Wood (d. 1781) lived near Colonel Joseph Hayes's (d. 1781) residence, called the "Big House." Captain Tarleton Brown's (1757–1845) family lived there also. A band of Loyalists stopped at Wood's house Saturday night, October 27, 1781, and killed him. Captain Brown heard the sound of gunfire coming from the direction of Wood's house and went there with three other men. They hid by the roadside near the house. When the Loyalists rode by, Brown estimated the force at 150 men led by Colonel Baley [Baily] Chaney (ca. 1740–) and Colonel Hezekiah Williams, who were on their way to Vince's Fort.[423] (See previous account.)

★ After Colonel Baley (Baily) Chaney (ca. 1740–) and Colonel Hezekiah Williams burned Vince's Fort (see above) on Sunday, October 28, 1781, they headed toward their headquarters on the Edisto River. They stopped at the home of Mr. Collins (ca. 1696–1781), along the old Augusta Highway, the next day and killed him. Mr. Collins was an old man who remained neutral in the War for Independence.[424]

Blackville
Slaughter Field (Dec. 22, 1781)

> Slaughter Field, also known as Windy Hill, was about 3.4 miles due northeast of the town limits of Blackville. To get to the site from Blackville, go north on route SC 3 (Solomon Blatt Avenue) for about 2.75 miles. A historical marker is on the right just before the intersection with Healing Springs Road. Turn right (east) on route S-6-32 (Healing Springs Road) and proceed about a mile to route S-6-87 (Jones Bridge Road) and turn left (north). Travel about another mile to Kammer Road and turn right (east). Go about a mile further to a point just before the road turns sharply to the left (north). Slaughter field is about 0.5 miles south of this point and about 300 yards west of Windy Hill Creek. The site is on private property.

A group of Loyalists attacked Captain Benjamin Odom (d. 1781) and a detachment of Colonel William Harden's (1743–1785) regiment, stationed at Windy Hill Creek, at sunrise on Saturday, December 22, 1781. They killed Captain Odom and 16 men whose bodies were left in the open field. The bodies were not recovered until three days later.

According to a family legend, Patrick Cain's (1741–1781) widow retrieved his body; but, as she did not have any digging tools, she put him in a hole left by a giant tree uprooted by a storm. Some accounts report that all of Captain Odom's men were killed and that Benjamin Odom and his wounded brother Daniel Odom (1757–1840) both survived. This action fits with the timeline of Major William "Bloody Bill" Cunningham's (d. 1787) Bloody Scout and some authorities think he was the leader of the Loyalist band.[425]

Olar, Bamberg County
Rush's Mill, Barnwell County (1782)
Georges Creek

> Rush's Mill was on Georges Creek where Mulberry Road crosses the creek about 100 yards west of where Mulberry Road becomes Crazy Horse Road at the intersection with route S-5-90. The earthen dam is still visible just inside the tree line. A granite marker, placed by the relatives of George Hartzog, is located on route S-5-90 at the intersection with Sears Road. It is flat on the ground and hard to see from the road. Some of the information on this marker is not correct, as the family has found new information since its placement.

Many Loyalists wanted to kill George Hartzog (1736 or 1738–1782) because he supplied the Continental forces with beef and other foods during the war. His brother, Tobias, had over 750 acres of land on or near the Edisto River and also supplied the Continental Army with corn, forage, and at least 1,200 pounds of beef. A Loyalist named Blitchington stabbed George to death at Rush's Mill in 1782. There is no record of Blitchington's fate after he killed George Hartzog.[426]

Greenland Swamp, Berkeley County (Nov. 27, 1782)

> Greenland Swamp was about 1.75 miles north-northwest of Eadytown. It is now under Lake Marion.

★ Charleston Loyalist Mr. Gaillard's slave Harry had been assigned to the Quarter Master General's Department and was frequently employed to spy on the Whigs and militia groups around Charleston. Harry was sent to Moncks Corner to gather intelligence on Brigadier General Francis Marion's (1732–1795) troops on Wednesday, November 27, 1782 when a party of Whig militiamen captured him at Greenland Swamp. They cut off his head and placed it on a stake on the side of the swamp as a warning to others.[427]

4
Western South Carolina

See the map of western South Carolina.

Mount Carmel, McCormick County
Fort Charlotte (July 12, 1775)

> The site of Fort Charlotte no longer exits. It was on the Savannah River, the state boundary of South Carolina and Georgia, about 50 miles northwest of Augusta, Georgia in McCormick County. A state historical marker at the junction of routes SC 81 and S-33-91 (Fort Charlotte Road) in Mount Carmel commemorates the fort, the scene of some of the earliest fighting of the American War for Independence.
>
> The site of Fort Charlotte was on the Savannah River along route S-33-91, 5.3 miles southwest of this intersection. Before the Lake Strom Thurmond dam was constructed, the stone fort was dismantled and the stones were removed and placed along the shore. Some of them have been used to construct a monument. Others remain in a pile nearby. A campground now occupies the site.
>
> The location of the fort is of historical importance because later accounts of military operations in the Savannah River region mention it frequently. It is opposite the mouth of Georgia's Broad River, covering Cowens Ford. The site is now under the waters of Clark Hill Reservoir also known as J. Strom Thurmond Lake. Route S-33-91 ends at the Clark Hill Reservoir in the general vicinity of the site.
>
> The British built the stone fortification about 1765 to protect local settlers from Native American attacks. They named it after Queen Charlotte Sophia of Mecklenburg-Strelitz (1744–1818), the wife of King George III (1738–1820). It became the site of the first overt act of rebellion in the state on July 12, 1775 when the Council of Safety ordered Major James Mayson (1739–1799), the commander of Fort Ninety Six, to capture Fort Charlotte on the Savannah River west of Ninety Six.
>
> Loyalist leader Thomas Brown (1750–1825) described this fort as second only to the stone castle at St. Augustine, Florida, in being the most formidable fortification in the south. He wrote that it had a garrison of 60 men.[428]

Major James Mayson's (1739–1799) small force at Ninety Six captured Fort Charlotte without opposition on Wednesday, July 12, 1775. They seized 1,055 pounds of gunpowder, 18 cannon, 15 muskets, 83 casks of cartridges, 2,521 musket balls and 343 cannonballs. Mayson returned to Ninety Six with the captured supplies, but a group of Loyalists re-captured the booty.

Cherokee Campaign of 1776 (July 1, 1776–May 20, 1777) see the Tennessee chapter of the next volume, *The Guide to the American Revolutionary War in the Deep South and on the Frontier*.

New Richmond, Edgefield County (Aug. 2, 1775)

> New Richmond was on the South Carolina side of the Savannah River, across and north from Augusta, Georgia, about 500 yards north of route I-20. To get the closest by road take route SC 230 (Martintown Road) northwest. Go just past Interstate 20 and turn left onto Bergen Road.

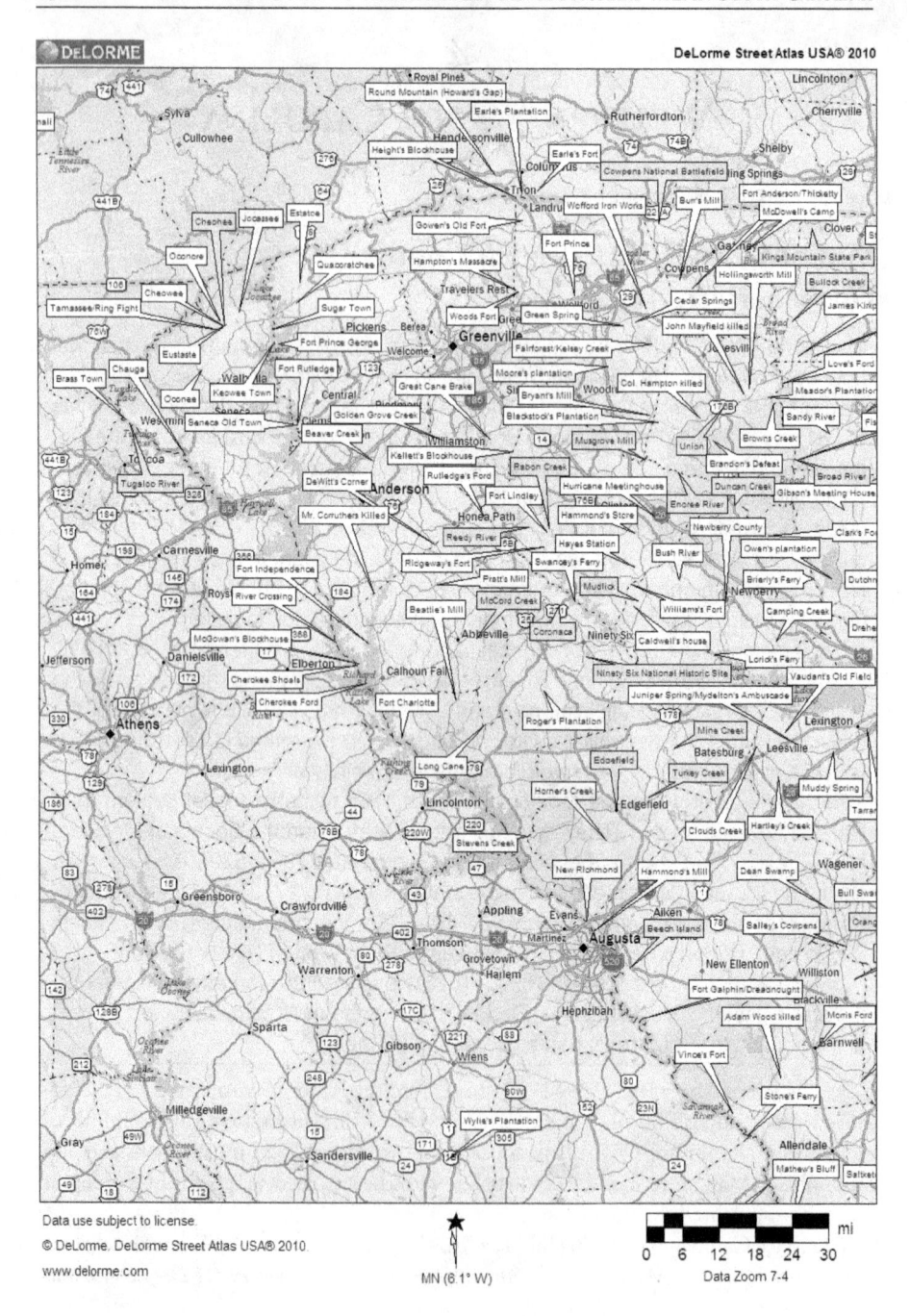

Western South Carolina: Map for The Guide to the American Revolutionary War in South Carolina
© 2012 *DeLorme (www.delorme.com) Street Atlas USA®*

Captain Robert Hamilton and a mob of men calling themselves the "Liberty Boys" attacked Loyalist Thomas Brown (1750–1825) at New Richmond on Wednesday, August 2, 1775. They demanded that Brown sign the Articles of Association, an agreement that stopped trade with Britain, banned horse racing and pledged allegiance to Congress.

Brown refused, stating that he did not want to take up arms against his country and did not want to fight against the people who were his neighbors. Captain Hamilton told Brown that he could not remain neutral and threatened to destroy his property if he did not sign the Association. Brown went inside his house and got two pistols. When he returned, Brown told the mob that they should respect private liberty as well as public liberty. Fifty "Liberty Boys" left, but the rest rushed at Brown who fired at them. He shot Chesley Bostick (1740–1808), their leader, through the foot and drew his sword. One of the "Liberty Boys" struck him in the head from behind with a rifle butt before he could strike a single blow. The "Liberty Boys" cut Brown's hair off with knives, applied burning pine knots to the soles of his feet and tarred him so badly that he lost two toes from the hot tar. Brown survived and allegedly asked Colonel Thomas Fletchall (1725–1789), the next morning, to use his command of more than 700 men at Ninety Six "to make reprisals" against those who had mistreated him. Brown later became the leader of the King's Rangers and wreaked his vengeance on Georgia, South Carolina, and Florida. After this action, Thomas Brown was known as Colonel Thomas "Burn Foot" Brown.[429]

Congaree River (Oct. 31, 1775)
Mine Creek, Saluda County (Oct. 31, 1775)
Near Ninety Six, Greenwood County (Nov. 3, 1775)

> Howard Peckham dates this event as occurring on Friday, November 3, 1775 near Ninety Six. It probably occurred near where the Old Charleston Road crosses Mine Creek about 30 miles southeast of Ninety Six. To get to the site from the junction of routes U.S. 378 and SC 121 (South Main Street) in south Saluda, go south on route SC 121 for about 3.6 miles, then turn left (east) onto Old Charleston Road and go about 1.9 miles to the bridge over Mine Creek and the site.[430]

The South Carolina Provincial Congress received intelligence, in late October 1775, that the pro-British Cherokees might go to war again "unless the Indians were furnished with some small supplies of ammunition, to enable them to procure deer skins for their support and maintenance." In order to head off trouble, Henry Laurens (1724–1792), President of the South Carolina Council of Safety, sent 1,000 pounds of gunpowder and lead to the frontier for use in hunting to appease the Cherokees and avert an outbreak of Cherokee raids. Lieutenant Thomas Charleton (1745–1795) and a detachment of 20 Rangers escorted Moses Cotter (1742–) who drove the powder wagon. Loyalist Captain Patrick Cunningham (d. 1794) decided to intercept the shipment to prevent the Cherokees from becoming allies with the Whigs and to avenge the arrest of his brother Robert. He delayed the first wagon at Mine Creek on Tuesday, October 31, 1775.

Cunningham asked Cotter what he had in the wagon. Cotter responded that it was rum. Sixty men then rose out of the roadside and Cunningham said, "I order you to stop your waggon in his majesty's Name as I understand you have ammunition for the Indians to kill us, and I am come on purpose to take it in his majesty's name." The Loyalists removed the kegs of powder and emptied them into bags they had prepared earlier. They also cut the lead bars into small pieces with their tomahawks.

When Lieutenant Charleton and his rangers appeared in the distance, the Loyalists quickly hid in the trees and soon surrounded them. Outnumbered and facing rifles at close range, Charleton surrendered when one of the Loyalists fired into the air. The Loyalists marched off with the ammunition and their prisoners, who were soon released. Moses Cotter immediately went to Ninety Six and reported the incident to Major James Mayson (1739–1799).

When they learned of the incident, president Laurens and the council immediately dispatched letters to obviate a panic, assuring the people that the powder had been sent only after "long and mature deliberation." They based their decision on the premise that it would require a smaller amount of powder to keep peace with the Cherokees than it would to fight them.

Major Andrew Williamson (ca. 1730–1786) in the Long Cane militia district learned on Saturday, November 4th, that the powder had been taken. He mustered his militia regiment and marched to Ninety Six to retake "that ammunition and bring those people to justice." As Colonel Richard Richardson, Jr. (1741–1817) had been capturing Loyalists before this incident, in violation of the Ninety Six Treaty, Major Williamson's motive was a pretext to round up even more Loyalists.[431]

Gilbert
Lexington County
Ninety Six, Greenwood County (July 17, 1775; Aug. 30, 1775; Nov. 18–21, 1775; June 15, 1776; June 13, 1780; Dec. 25, 1780; May 22 to June 19, 1781; June 19, 1781; March 23, 1781)
Near Ninety Six (May 20, 1781; May 22, 1781)
Road to Ninety Six (June 18, 1781)
Middleton's (Mydelton's) Ambuscade (also known as Juniper Spring, West's Old Field or Middleton's Defeat) (June 18, 1781)
Old Man Palmer killed (ca. June 18, 1781)
Laurens County
Cunningham's Raid, Laurens County (Aug. 1, 1781)
Saluda River (Aug. 1, 1781)
Rawdon's/Cruger's baggage train captured

Ninety Six supposedly received its name because the fort was 96 miles from Fort Prince George and the Cherokee village of Keowee in the Blue Ridge foothills on the Keowee River. In addition to the fort, it was a trading post with the Cherokees in the 1730s. It became a convenient campground along the Cherokee Path, a major trade route connecting the Cherokee towns of the backcountry with Charleston, the capitol of South Carolina in the 18th century. This trading post was the farthest one from the coast and soon became a settlement. In 1769, it became the center of the court for the Ninety Six district which covered an area equivalent to 12 of the state's modern counties.

Ninety Six National Historic Site (website: **www.nps.gov/nisi/index.htm**) is 2 miles south of Ninety Six on route SC 248. Visitors can explore the earthworks, old road beds, traces of the village, a reconstructed stockade fort, and an early log cabin along a mile-long trail. An observation tower provides an excellent view of the star redoubt and the zigzag trenches (see Photo SC-16) used to attack it. Inside the earthworks are the remains of a 25-foot well, dug through the hard-packed clay in a futile attempt to get water for the besieged fort. The Loyalists were forced to rely on slaves slipping past Major General Nathanael Greene's (1742–1786) pickets at night to bring water into the redoubt. The visitor center houses a museum and an auditorium.

The June 18, 1781 event is also known as Juniper Spring, West's Old Field or Middleton's Defeat.

Juniper Spring is northwest of the town of Gilbert. It ran from route U.S. 1 (Augusta Highway) south along route S-32-24 (Peach Festival Road) for about 2 miles to Twelve Mile Creek, about 200 yards north of Spring Hill Road. A state historical marker for the skirmish is about a mile further south near the intersection of Main Street and Church Street. It is 38.5 miles from Ninety Six.

Old man Palmer was killed 5 miles from the Juniper Springs battlefield, near where Cedar Grove Road (S-32-54) crosses Hollow Creek in Leesville.

Cunningham's Raid probably occurred near the intersection of route U.S. 76 Bus (East Main Street) and East Public Square in Laurens.

The Saluda River is about 6 miles east of Fort Ninety Six.

Most baggage was captured at creek or river crossings during the American War for Independence. There are eight likely sites between Ninety Six and Orangeburg where Lieutenant Colonel John Harris Cruger's baggage might have been captured. Arranged in order from Ninety Six to Orangeburg, they are:

1. Halfway Creek Swamp where Pheasant Road (S-41-98) crosses Halfway Swamp Creek about 7 miles due southeast of the Ninety Six National Historic Site.
2. Red Bank Creek near where Old Charleston Road (S-41-66) crosses it about 5 miles west-northwest of Saluda.
3. Mine Creek where Old Charleston Road (S-41-66) crosses it in Johnston about 1.9 miles southeast of route SC 121.
4. Indian Creek where Old Charleston Road (S-41-177) crosses it in Ward.
5. Peters Creek where Ridge Spring Highway (SC 39) crosses it about 2 miles northwest of Ridge Spring.
6. Dean's Swamp Creek, Aiken County, where route SC 39 (Old 96 Indian Trail) crosses it about 6.25 miles northwest of Wagener.
7. Great Branch (Orangeburg County) where route SC 4 (Neeses Highway) crosses it about 6.5 miles due east-southeast of Orangeburg.
8. The North Fork of the Edisto River (Orangeburg County) where route U.S. 301 (U.S. 601|SC 4|John C. Calhoun Drive) crosses it.

Captain Moses Kirkland (1730–1787) decided to switch sides after being passed over for promotion. His company also changed allegiance with him and became Loyalists. Captain Kirkland commanded the fort at Ninety Six. He invited Colonel Thomas Fletchall (1725–1789) and his Loyalist militiamen to raid the fort on Monday, July 17, 1775. Colonel Fletchall sent a detachment of 200 militiamen from his main force to capture the fort. When they arrived at the fort, Captain Kirkland persuaded all his men to desert and the Loyalist militia took it over and threw Major James Mayson (1739–1799) in the fort's jail. They released him on bail a few hours later to answer charges of robbing the King's fort at Fort Charlotte five days earlier.[432]

★ As tensions increased between Whigs and Loyalists, the South Carolina Council of Safety sent William Henry Drayton (1742–1779), a member of the Provincial Congress, and the Rev. William Tennent (1740–1777) inland to organize Whig forces during the month of August 1775. Colonel Drayton, commander of a regiment of Charleston militiamen believed that Captain Moses Kirkland (1730–1787) was raising men to attack Augusta, Georgia. He sent Major Andrew Williamson (ca. 1730–1786) to a river crossing 30 miles above Augusta to prevent such an attack. At the same time, Colonel Drayton sent Colonel William "Danger" Thomson (1727–1796) to the ridge 40 miles to the east, and Colonel Richard Richardson, Sr. (1704–1780) to the Enoree River to intercept any support Loyalist Colonel Thomas Fletchall (1725–1789) might send to Ninety Six.

Meanwhile, Colonel Fletchall, Captain Kirkland, Robert and Patrick Cunningham (d. 1794) and Colonel Thomas Brown (1750–1825) turned out near Ninety Six with their armed supporters on Wednesday, August 30, 1775 to attack Augusta and Fort Charlotte.

Drayton's men dragged four cannons from Snow Hill to Ninety Six. Along the way, they were joined by 84 Georgians and 141 South Carolinians under Captain LeRoy Hammond (1728–1789). They arrived at Loyalist Robert Cunningham's (1741–1813) house on Wednesday, August 30, 1775, hoping to surprise him; but Cunningham had already fled, leaving all of his papers and letters which Drayton's men seized.

As Drayton's army approached Ninety Six, Captain Kirkland's men deserted. Kirkland himself was on board the HM sloop *Tamar* in Charleston Harbor conferring with the royal governor. When Drayton learned, on the 31st, that another group of Loyalists was gathering near Saluda, he sent 100 horsemen to disperse them. Drayton also learned that Cunningham had joined Colonel Fletchall at Bullock's Creek and that the combined force was going to attack Drayton's force at 2 AM. Instead of retreating toward Colonel Thomson's Rangers holding a ridge 40 miles to the west, Drayton seized Ninety Six and prepared to defend it against any Loyalist attack. He placed his men in the prison building on Friday, September 1st, and placed a swivel gun in each room of the building. He also placed a small guard with each gun.

Drayton also sent Major James Mayson (1739–1799) with 100 mounted men to a ford on the Saluda to ambush anyone coming to attack the jail. While both armies were eager to fight, they did not. An uneasy peace lasted a few weeks. On Saturday, September 16, 1775, Drayton invited Fletchall to Ninety Six and offered him plenty to drink. When Fletchall was drunk, Drayton persuaded him to sign a treaty that stated neither side would give aid and comfort to any British troops, nor would they dispute the authority of Congress. This treaty became known as the Treaty of Ninety Six.

After Fletchall signed the treaty, his men were furious and wanted to do battle; but Colonel Thomas Brown (1750–1825) sent them home with instructions to prepare to muster at the appropriate time. Robert Cunningham (1741–1813) returned home and was taken "by the Liberty people in Charleston" and imprisoned there. He was released and ran as a Tory for election to the South Carolina Senate in 1778, defeating James Williams (1740–1780).[433]

★ On Tuesday, November 7, 1775, the Provincial Congress ordered Colonel Richard Richardson, Jr. (1741–1817) to assemble militiamen from his own regiment and the regiments of Colonels William Thomson, John Savage (1750–1812), Thomas Neal, Sr.

(1730–1799) and John Thomas, Sr. (1720–1811) along with six companies of Rangers from the Third South Carolina Regiment and Captain William Polk's (1758–1834) company of volunteers who had previously withdrawn from Thomson's Rangers. These men received orders to march toward Fort Ninety Six to recover the stolen munitions (see **Congaree River and Mine Creek** p. 251) and arrest Patrick Cunningham (d. 1794) and his party.

A force of 532 Whigs under Major Andrew Williamson (ca. 1730–1786) and Major James Mayson (1739–1799) built a crude fort of fence rails, cowhides, and straw bales on John Savage's plantation. They came under attack by Colonel Joseph Robinson (1748–1807), Patrick Cunningham and 1,890 Loyalists on Saturday, November 18, 1775. Both sides sustained a number of casualties and the defenders ran low on powder after three days of fighting. The aggressors could not capture the fort and its swivel gun (see Photo SC-32) and feared impending reinforcements, so both sides agreed to withdraw and the defenders demolished the fort.[434]

★ William Cunningham (d. 1787) was in the Whig militia at the beginning of the war, but became disillusioned after the Snow Campaign and fled to Savannah, Georgia. When Captain William Ritchie (d. 1776) learned of his desertion, he rode to Cunningham's house and beat William's lame brother, John and later returned to beat William's father and mother.

Cunningham returned to Laurens County to avenge the beatings of his family. He pursued Ritchie to his house at Ninety Six on Saturday, June 15, 1776. He fired and wounded Ritchie. A second shot killed him. Cunningham then rode away to join the Loyalist militia. He became one of the most vicious Loyalist partisans and became known as "Bloody Bill."[435]

★ Lieutenant General Charles Cornwallis (1738–1805) believed Ninety Six would be crucial to controlling the backcountry when the British Army moved northward out of South Carolina so the Crown forces secured the area in Greenwood County in June 1780. The troops built a stockade around the town, the earthwork star fort and several blockhouses. They fortified the farmhouse of Loyalist James Holmes (also known as the Stockade Fort) with a palisade in 1781 to protect the spring that was the fort's sole water supply.

Lord Cornwallis left Lieutenant Colonel John Harris Cruger (1738–1807), a New York Loyalist, in charge with instructions to be "vigorous" in punishing rebels and maintaining order in the area. Lieutenant Colonel Cruger used the fortified town of Ninety Six as his base of operations for many raids and skirmishes against the local Whigs.[436]

★ Lieutenant Colonel John Harris Cruger's (1738–1807) 1st Battalion of DeLancey's brigade garrisoned the fort at Ninety Six in Greenwood County. They were joined by Lieutenant Colonel Isaac Allen's (d. 1806) 3rd battalion of the New Jersey Volunteers when South Carolina Whigs conducted some minor raids on the fort. Ensign John Massey Camp (d. 1780) was captured outside the walls of the fort in a raid on Christmas day 1780. He was murdered and his body left outside the walls.[437]

★ Later, when the British took control of the South, they made their dominant strongholds at Augusta, Georgia and Ninety Six. They built a stockade flanked by two forts. A covered way connected to both the stockade on the west and to the strong, star-shaped redoubt on the east side of the fort.

Colonel George Rogers Clark (1752–1818) engaged Major James Dunlap (d. 1781) at Beattie's Mill, McCormick County, near Ninety Six on Friday, March 23, 1781. He killed 34, including the major, and took 42 prisoners.[438]

★ After the battle of Hobkirk Hill (April 25, 1781 see p. 53), Lord Francis Rawdon (1754–1826) retired to Charleston. Over the next five weeks, other posts fell rapidly:
- ♦ Brigadier General Francis Marion (1732–1795) and Lieutenant Colonel Henry "Light-Horse Harry" Lee (1756–1818) took Fort Motte,
- ♦ Brigadier General Thomas Sumter (1734–1832) took Orangeburg,
- ♦ Lieutenant Colonel Henry "Light-Horse Harry" Lee (1756–1818) took Fort Granby (later the site of Columbia),
- ♦ Brigadier General Francis Marion took Georgetown and
- ♦ Brigadier General Andrew Pickens (1739–1817) and Lieutenant Colonel Lee captured Augusta, Georgia on June 5, 1781.

★ As the Continental Army marched toward Ninety Six, the last important British outpost on the South Carolina frontier, in May 1781, Major General Nathanael Greene (1742–1786) sent out scouting parties to find any information about the fortifications there. He also ordered Lieutenant Colonel William Washington's (1752–1810) cavalry and the Delaware light infantry to eliminate any Loyalist militia on their route. When Colonel Washington learned that Major William Young, Sr. (1730/35–1787) and a party of Loyalists were nearby, he prepared to attack their camp. They marched 23 miles and crossed the Saluda River.

Some accounts say that when Washington's cavalry arrived, they found the camp abandoned and pursued the Loyalists through the surrounding forests and swamps. After the cavalry rode off, some of the Loyalists came out of their hiding place in the swamp near the camp on Monday, May 20, 1781. They mistook Captain Robert H. Kirkwood's (1746–1791) Delaware Continentals, who marched at their own pace, for Loyalists, as they wore hunting frocks and had not fired upon them. When they eventually realized their mistake, they took one of the men prisoner and fired on the rest. The Continentals returned fire, killing one Loyalist and taking his horse. The others rode away. When Washington's dragoons heard the musket fire, they returned to pursue the mounted Loyalists. They killed four and captured six more before returning to Kirkwood's force.[439]

★ Other accounts say that Lieutenant Colonel William Washington's (1752–1810) cavalry and the Delaware light infantry surprised a party of Loyalist militiamen near Ninety Six on Tuesday, May 22, 1781. They attacked the Loyalists and killed four within sight of the fort's garrison. They then reconnoitered the fort in preparation for General Nathanael Greene's (1742–1786) siege, which began that night. Despite desertions and the inability to get siege artillery, Greene raised a 3-gun battery 130 yards from the Loyalist fort and exchanged fire with the garrison's defenders throughout the night.[440]

★ When General Nathanael Greene (1742–1786) arrived at Ninety Six on Tuesday, May 22, 1781, he examined the position and concluded that, "the fortifications are so strong and the garrison so large and so well furnished that our success is very doubtful." His army of 1,000 Continentals had no heavy artillery, so he decided to lay siege to the garrison defended by Colonel John Harris Cruger (1738–1807) and 550 battle-toughened Loyalists. Greene put Polish engineer Thaddeus Kosciusko (1746–1817) in charge of the siege operation. Kosciusko had the men dig parallel trenches up to the star redoubt and protect them with a zigzag approach pattern. When the third trench line reached 40 yards from the fort, the men built a 30-foot rifle tower (see Photo SC-16).

The longest Continental siege of the war was heading into its 28th day in mid-June. Lord Francis Rawdon (1754–1826) brought up a powerful relief column of 2,000 men from Charleston that included three fresh regiments from England. Greene had to attack. Lieutenant Colonel Henry "Light-Horse Harry" Lee successfully fought through the defenses at the western redoubt on Monday, June 18, but Greene's initial assessment of the position, made a month earlier, proved correct. The Continentals could not break into the star redoubt. The 45-minute assault left 40 Continentals dead. Greene ordered a retreat to Charlotte.

★ Colonel Charles Middleton (Mydelton) (1750–1780) commanded about 300 cavalrymen and mounted militiamen from Brigadier General Thomas Sumter's (1734–1832) troops in the area west of Lexington in June 1781. Their mission was to harass the rear guard of Lord Francis Rawdon's (1754–1826) forces of more than 1700 infantrymen and 150 horsemen marching from Charleston to the relief of Ninety Six and to obstruct foraging parties from collecting cattle. Lieutenant Colonel Welbore Ellis Doyle's (1732–1802) troops marched from Moncks Corner and joined him along the way.

Major John Coffin (1756–1838), at the head of the royal cavalry, surprised and routed Middleton and his men at Juniper Spring in Lexington County on Monday morning, June 18, 1781. Their cavalry surrounded Middleton's flanks and rear. Middleton's men had no swords and were not prepared for close combat, so they were decimated, losing four officers and 20 or 30 men killed or taken prisoner. Lieutenant Colonel Richard Hampton (1752–1792) saw that they were surrounded and ordered his men to retreat. Some stragglers rejoined Middleton, but many were killed and many more were too demoralized to return to the service. Middleton could only muster 45 of his party.[441]

★ After the action at Juniper Spring, some of Lord Francis Rawdon's (1754–1826) troops encountered an old man named Palmer and killed him without mercy about Tuesday, June 19, 1781.[442]

★ That same day, Tuesday, June 19, 1781, after a 4-week siege of the fort at Ninety Six, Major General Nathanael Greene (1742–1786) and about 1000 Continentals tried to storm the garrison of 550 Loyalists under Colonel John Harris Cruger (1738–1807) before Lord Francis Rawdon's (1754–1826) reinforcements arrived. The Loyalists repulsed the attack but lost 27 killed and 58 wounded. The Continentals lost 59 killed, 72 wounded, one captured, and 20 missing. General Greene raised the siege on Wednesday, the 20th and withdrew his army behind the Saluda River, to a strong position about 16 miles from Ninety Six. Lord Rawdon arrived at Ninety Six on the 21st.[443]

★ Lord Francis Rawdon (1754–1826) regained the fort at Ninety Six and ordered its evacuation. He also ordered Lieutenant Colonel Alexander Stewart (1740–1794) to proceed with his regiment from Charleston to Friday's Ferry. Rawdon then divided his force, leaving a part of it with Colonel John Harris Cruger (1738–1807) at Ninety Six to protect the Loyalists and the retreat of the garrison while he marched with 800 infantrymen and 60 cavalrymen to meet Stewart. The hot sun and the heavy humidity caused 50 of his men to die of sun stroke or exhaustion on the march. Lieutenant Colonel Banastre Tarleton (1744–1833) describes their hardships:

> During a renewed succession of forced marches under the rage of a burning sun, and in a climate, at this season peculiarly inimical to man, they were frequently, when sinking under the most excessive fatigue, not only destitute of every comfort, but almost of every necessary which seems essential to his existence. During the greater part of the time, they were totally destitute of bread, and the country afforded no vegetables for a substitute. Salt, at length, failed; and their only resources were water and the wild cattle which they found in the woods.[444]

The British crossed the Saluda on Saturday afternoon, June 23, 1781. General Greene received intelligence that they were advancing rapidly to attack him; so he immediately put the army in motion and retired toward Charlotte, North Carolina. He had previously ordered provisions and forage to be provided along the route. Lord Rawdon's troops pursued General Greene's army for two days. They marched as light as possible, leaving even their knapsacks and blankets behind them. However, General Greene had sent his sick, wounded and stores ahead earlier, so the British advance had little effect. The British advanced as far as the Enoree River. The Continentals dismantled the mills as they retired, making it difficult for the Crown forces to subsist, so they returned toward Ninety Six on Tuesday morning, the 26th with Lieutenant Colonel Henry "Light-Horse Harry" Lee's (1756–1818) legion close behind them.

Lord Rawdon remained at Ninety Six only two days before marching for the Congaree with a little more than half his force, leaving Colonel Cruger at Ninety Six with the remainder. He intended to establish a post on the Congaree at Friday's Ferry. General Greene left his baggage, stores, and invalids behind at Winnsborough and proceeded to Camden. He marched the army for the Congaree as quickly as possible, but Lord Rawdon arrived there two days ahead of him. Stewart was on his way to Friday's Ferry as ordered but was recalled to Charleston. Rawdon was disappointed by Stewart's recall and decided to move south to Orangeburg when Greene approached. Captain Joseph Eggleston (1754–1811) attacked Lord Rawdon's dragoons in Lexington County, increasing his fears.[445]

★ As Colonel John Harris Cruger (1738–1807) was withdrawing from Ninety Six, through the Fork of Edisto, about Sunday, July 1, 1781, Captain James Ryan, of Edgefield County on Horse Creek, planned to attack his rear-guard and capture the baggage with his small company of about 50 militiamen. Ryan ordered his men to attack, except three or four who sounded bugles and beat a drum or two to indicate that a much larger force was advancing to do battle.

A severe skirmish ensued and Captain Ryan's men captured the wagons loaded with supplies of arms, ammunition and clothing. Every man in the company was allowed to take something home to his family as a prize. The baggage wagons were set on fire before any other force could arrive. The militiamen then dispersed. They "went from home almost destitute, returned to their families well-armed, well mounted, well clothed and much elated. They were much more punctual than usual at the next rendezvous, in hopes of equally good luck."[446]

★ William "Bloody Bill" Cunningham (d. 1787) left Charleston with a party of 150 men to punish the Whigs at Ninety Six who allegedly had committed injuries against the wives and children of some of his men. He began his operations in the area that is now Laurens County, between the Enoree and Saluda Rivers, on Wednesday, August 1, 1781. He killed eight "noted Rebels" in his first raid and attracted to his forces 60 Loyalists "who availed themselves of the opportunity to get rid of the blessings of independence, which have lately been forced upon them by their new masters." The recruits were escorted back to Cunningham's base at Cane Creek to join his dragoons. Cunningham continued to raid western South Carolina's frontier areas into September and October and became known as "Bloody Bill" or "Murdering Bill" because of his brutal attacks.[447]

See **Clouds Creek** p. 109.

The Crown forces soon evacuated Ninety Six. After a year and a half of campaigning, the British only held Charleston and Savannah in August 1781, leaving them at the same point they had started. The long summer campaign ruined Lord Francis Rawdon's (1754–1826) health and spirit. After chasing Major General Nathanael Greene (1742–1786) in vain after the siege of Ninety Six, Rawdon turned his command over to Lieutenant Colonel Alexander Stewart (1740–1794) and sailed for England, only to have his ship captured by Admiral François Joseph Paul Comte de Grasse's (1722–1788) fleet.[448]

Pelzer, Greenville County
Golden Grove Creek (ca. Nov. 30, 1775)

> Route SC 8 (Lebby Street|Pelzer Highway) crosses Golden Grove Creek (now Grove Creek) about 1.8 miles east of Pelzer. The Golden Grove Creek Mill was about half a mile south-southwest of the bridge over the creek.

Captain Thomas Sumter (1734–1832) and a force of Whigs fought a band of Loyalists at Golden Grove Creek Mill around Thursday, November 30, 1775. They captured about 95 Loyalist prisoners.[449]

Near Simpsonville, Greenville County
Great Cane Brake
Cane Brake (Dec. 22, 1775)
Snow Campaign

> The Battle of Great Cane Brake is sometimes referred to as the Snow Campaign because of an unusually heavy snowfall that dropped 15 inches of snow as the troops were camped at Hollingsworth's mills on December 25, 1775, during the return march. The battle diluted Loyalist strength in South Carolina until the fall of Charleston four and a half years later.
>
> The actual battle site is unknown, as it was a "running battle" but it is close to the Reedy River which is now on private property. It most likely extended from the area near where route SC 418 crosses the Reedy River to near the end of Derrick Lane in Simpsonville, a distance of a little more than a mile. Canebrakes still grow at the battle site.
>
> There is a highway marker on route S-23-146 (Fork Shoals Road), in Pelzer, just south of Old Hundred Road and about 0.75 miles north of route SC 418.

Whigs and Loyalists were sharply divided in South Carolina long before the British Army arrived in any significant numbers. The Provincial Congress, composed mostly of Whigs, first met in Charleston in January 1775. They ordered Colonel Richard Richardson, Jr. (1741–1817) to "silence the discontents of the backcountry" and "deliver up the bodies of all principal offenders" i.e. the Loyalists. Richardson had mustered a formidable force of over 3,000 men and pursued Patrick Cunningham (d. 1794), the leader of the Loyalists in November 1775. The two forces clashed in the First Battle of Ninety Six on November 17. The Loyalists besieging a Whig militia unit were persuaded to sign a cease-fire and depart when Richardson's force arrived.

See **Ninety Six** p. 252.

Richardson continued marching northward and was joined by 700 North Carolina militiamen and 220 Continentals. As they advanced, local Loyalist militia units chose to disperse and Richardson arrested many prominent Loyalists. A party was sent to the Loyalist camp on the Reedy River on Friday morning, November 24. The Loyalists and Native Americans ran off without making much resistance. One major was wounded and the campaign broke up when the party returned.[450]

When Richardson learned that Cunningham was camped along the Reedy River near the Cherokee lands with 200 men, he sent Colonel William "Danger" Thomson (1727–1796) and 1,300 men in pursuit. They marched all night, covering 25 miles, and attacked the sleeping Loyalists completely by surprise at the Great Cane Brake at dawn on Friday, December 22, 1775. Cunningham jumped out of bed, mounted his horse bareback, and shouted to his men to "shift" for themselves. Cunningham was one of the few to escape, narrowly escaping to the Cherokee lands. Colonel Richard Richardson Jr.'s (1741–1817) cool-headedness and restraint prevented the deaths of many Loyalists who lost only six killed and 130 taken prisoners. Richardson had one man wounded. He also captured much-needed supplies, arms, and ammunition, including the powder and lead which helped set up the First Battle of Ninety Six. A snowstorm that lasted for thirty hours dumped 15 inches of snow so many of the men suffered frostbite on the return trip. The expedition has since been known as the Snow Campaign.[451]

Landrum, Spartanburg County
Earle's Fort, Polk County, North Carolina (May 1776)
Earlesville
Fair Forest Spring
Earle's Plantation
Near Wellford, Spartanburg County
Hampton Massacre (June 30, 1776)
Height's Blockhouse, Greenville County (July 1776)
Near Gowensville, Spartanburg County
Gowen's Fort, Spartanburg County (July 14, 1780; Nov. 1, 1781; ca. Nov. 3, 1781)
Fort Prince/McDowell's Camp/Shiloh Church, Spartanburg County (July 15 and 16, 1780)
Earle's Ford, Spartanburg County (July 15, 1780)

> Earle's plantation was located east of Landrum near exit 1 off route I-26. It was north of route SC 14 (Landrum Road) between route I-26 and Earles Fort Road. A Daughters of the American Revolution granite historical marker is on the left of route SC 14 (Landrum Road) about 300 yards east of Earles Fort Road. It is on the left of the driveway into Four Columns Mansion, almost hidden in juniper hedges.
>
> Earle's Ford is about 0.4 miles further on the right, about 435 yards from the road, just before reaching the bridge over the river. Earle's Fort was about 1.6 miles due north of the plantation site on Hunting Country Road 4.9 miles east of what is now Tryon, North Carolina. Other names of this location are Earlesville, Fair Forest Spring, and Earle's plantation.
>
> The Hampton massacre site is in the vicinity of the junction of routes S-42-9764 (Carriage Drive) and S-42-9761 (Lantern Drive) in Greer. To get there, take route S-42-908 (Gap Creek Road) northwest from route SC 357 (Arlington Street). Travel 0.8 miles to route S-42-9767 (Colonial Drive). Turn right (north-northeast) on Colonial Drive. Go 0.2 miles and turn left (west) on route S-42-9765 (Rollingreen Road) to Carriage Drive.
>
> Colonel Height's Blockhouse was about 2 miles northwest of Landrum on the North Carolina border. To get there, take North Trade Avenue north from Landrum.

> After about 1.6 miles, it becomes Blockhouse Road. Continue on Blockhouse Road for about 0.6 miles to the site of Colonel Height's Blockhouse. There's a marker on the original site of the blockhouse in the field on the right.
>
> Several years ago, the blockhouse was moved to the new location and incorporated into a modern house about 500 feet north. The driveway to that house is just past the marker.
>
> Fort Prince was built in 1756 and served as a refuge in times of Cherokee uprisings. Whigs occupied it early in the American War for Independence but the Crown forces used it as an outpost later in the war. It was located about 250 yards southeast of the intersection of route S-42-123 (Mount Zion Road) and Fort Prince Road in Spartanburg. It was in what is now a small grove of trees about 135 yards to the left near 350 Fort Prince Road. The Daughters of the American Revolution placed a granite marker for the colonial fort at the site but it erroneously says the Patriots captured the position. The incident that occurred here is listed as having happened on both July 15 and 16, 1780.
>
> Gowen's Fort and Wood's Fort were also located within a few miles of this location. Nothing remains at the site of either fort. Gowen's Old Fort was on route S-42-183 (South Blackstock Road) about 1.12 miles southeast of its intersection with route SC 14 in Landrum.
>
> Wood's Fort was located about 11.5 miles south of Gowen's Fort and 9.2 miles west of Fort Prince. It was in the area north of route S-42-908 (Gap Creek Road) between route S-42-9767 (Colonial Drive) and Ashlan Woods Court, about 2.75 miles north-northeast of Greer.
>
> The location of the "McDowell's Camp" action is controversial. Some authorities say it occurred just north of the state line. Others say the action of July 16 took place at Earle's Ford on the Pacolet River just south of the state line.

The Hannon family moved south, as did many other families from Pennsylvania and Virginia. They unknowingly settled in Cherokee territory along the North Pacolet River, about a mile upstream from Earle's Fort. The British instigated the Cherokees to keep the settlers from encroaching on their territory.

Mr. Hannon and his wife were planting corn in their field in May 1776 when a band of Cherokees attacked and killed both of them in view of their two sons, 10-year old Edwin (1766–1825) and his younger brother John (1773–). Edwin heard the Cherokees coming toward him. He had to drop his brother to escape across the river. He hid himself in the canebrake and heard the Cherokees kill his brother.

Seven-year-old Winnie Hannon (1769–) grabbed her infant brother and ran into another canebrake nearby. When the Cherokees returned to the hills, the three children made their way downstream to Earle's Fort, the home of Baylis Earle (1734–1825). As the Cherokees proceeded upstream on their return trip, they killed David Anderson's (1741–1827) father near Fort Prince (in Spartanburg County) and burned his house. Colonel John Earle (1737–1815) adopted the Hannon children. The boys became his sons-in-law when they grew up.[452]

★ The "Block House" was a trading post for traders from Charleston to exchange guns, ammunition and other articles with the Cherokees for skins and furs. When the war began, the Cherokees allied with the British against the Whigs. Major Francis Ross (1743–1779) and a battalion, mostly of York men, were ordered out against the Cherokees. As they headed to the "Block House" in Greenville County, in July 1776, the York battalion learned that the Cherokees had killed Colonel Height (d. 1776), a Whig

Indian trader, and taken his wife and two daughters. Mrs. Height's young son tried to follow and rescue them, but he was murdered. The fate of Mrs. Height and her daughters is unknown.[453]

★ A band of Loyalists left their stronghold at Ninety Six and headed north into Spartanburg County in July 1780. They were defeated at Cedar Spring on Wednesday, July 12. The following day, Colonel Alexander Innes (ca. 1737–post 1791) sent Major James Dunlap (d. 1781) and a raiding party from Fort Prince. They encountered Whig Colonel John Thomas, Jr. (1751–1819) and his men on their way to join Colonel Charles McDowell (1743–1815).

Loyalist Colonel Zacharias Gibbs (1741–) learned that a Whig force was in the area. He sent Lieutenant Alexander Chesney (1755–1843) to infiltrate the camp to "learn their numbers, their commanders names, what carriages they had, how many horse and foot, and whenever they made any movement towards Colonel Ferguson [James Ferguson (1740–1780)], to return and let him know, and that there would be a handsome reward."

Chesney "set out immediately and at Pacolet got a man to go with me, who was acquainted with the North Carolina people; we went down to McDole's [Charles McDowell's (1743–1815)] camp at night without being noticed, counted all their tents and wagons, found out who were their leaders, and that 500 horsemen were gone down to attack Nicholas's Fort. With this news I returned, and on my way found a loyalist in whom I could confide and sent him off with the particulars by one route to Colonel Ferguson whilst I went by another."

★ The group of Loyalists pursuing Whig Colonel John Thomas, Jr. (1751–1819) camped at Gowen's Old Fort Thursday night, July 13, 1780. Gowen's Fort was a rendezvous and a place of safety for the Whig families of both North and South Carolina in that area. Colonel Thomas was on his way to join Colonel Charles McDowell (1743–1815), who was gathering an army near the North Carolina border. Colonel John Jones (1728–1793) and 35 Georgia militiamen were also going to join McDowell when they encountered 40 Loyalists here at 11 PM. They passed themselves off as Loyalists and were admitted into the fort. They surprised the garrison, killed one, wounded three and took 32 prisoners along with some horses and guns and damaged those guns he could not take with him. They were then guided to McDowell's camp at Earle's Ford on the high ground on the eastern side of the North Pacolet River, just across the North Carolina line. They delivered their prisoners and joined Colonel McDowell's force of 300. Both forces were tired. McDowell's men had just finished a "tedious march" and Jones's men had been on the move for three days and nights.

The Crown forces under Colonel Alexander Innes (ca. 1737–post 1791) occupied Prince's Fort about 20 miles away. It was located on high ground at the head of one of the branches of the North Fork of the Tyger River 7 miles northwest of Spartanburg. Colonel Innes had intelligence of Jones's unit but was unaware of McDowell's force of more than 300 men. He sent Major James Dunlap (d. 1781) with 14 mounted infantrymen from the American Volunteers and Colonel Ambrose Mills (1722–1786) with about 60 Loyalist militiamen to find and attack Jones.

Dunlap crossed Earle's Ford during the night of July 14 and attacked Jones's militia camped just across the river on the east side of the ford, near Colonel McDowell's main camp. A sentry spotted them and ran back to warn the others. Dunlap's men rushed into Jones's camp with sabers drawn, surprised the sleeping men, killed two and wounded six before most of the men were awake. Anthony Hampton's (1715–1776) son, Noah

(d. 1780), was one of the dead. When the Loyalists awakened him and asked his name, they bayoneted him. Colonel Jones received eight saber cuts on his head. The rest of his men rallied and joined Major John Singleton behind a rail fence about 100 yards away. Colonels McDowell and Hampton "formed the main body on Singleton's right," and ordered a counterattack which forced the Loyalists to retreat across the river. Dunlap had only one man wounded while McDowell had eight killed and 30 wounded. When a prisoner informed Dunlap that the militia had over 300 men, he retreated quickly toward his base at Fort Prince.

Major Joseph McJunkin (1755–1846) records:
> While this army was in South Carolina and lying near the home of Colonel Hampton it was surprised by the British, but held its ground and drove the British from the field. Captain Thompson was not in the main action. His captain, Joseph McDowell, had been ordered to reconnoiter, but failed to find the British. While engaged in searching for them they came and attacked the main army. He returned just as the British were retiring from the conflict, and finding that they had taken a number of prisoners, he rallied his men and as many others as would follow him, pursued the British, retook his friends and made a large number of prisoners. Living witnesses have stated to the writer that Colonel Hampton's residence was on the Enoree River not far from Ford's Bridge. After this engagement General McDowell retired toward North Carolina and took post near Cherokee Ford on Broad River.

Colonel Andrew Hampton (1716–1805) blamed McDowell for the Whig losses because Hampton had urged McDowell to place sentries on the west side of the ford to guard against such an attack. McDowell had sent his brother, Major Joseph "Quaker Meadows" McDowell, Jr. (1756–1801), on a scouting expedition earlier in the day and thought it was safe to not post guards when he received no report of enemy activity.[454]

★ When the Whigs learned of the murder of Anthony Hampton's (1715–1776) son, they wanted revenge. Colonel Charles McDowell (1743–1815) sent Captain Edward Hampton (1746–1781) and 52 men, mounted on the best horses in camp, in pursuit of Major James Dunlap (d. 1781). They set out before dawn on Saturday, July 15, 1780, and, after a two-hour chase, found Dunlap and his dragoons about 15 miles away, on the Blackstock Road, 5 miles from Fort Prince (near the Shiloh Church which is on Blackstock Road (S-42-40) about 4.25 miles northwest of exit 17 off Interstate 26) and attacked.

Unaware that he was being pursued, Dunlap lost eight men killed in the first volley. The Loyalists fled to Fort Prince, garrisoned by Regulars under Colonel Alexander Innes (ca. 1737–post 1791). Hotly pursued by Hampton's men, they reached the fort but lost 13 men killed and one captured. Hampton halted his men 300 yards from the fort, unsure of what awaited him inside the fort and not knowing that the only troops inside were the men he had been pursuing. (Some accounts say 300 British and Loyalist troops were inside the fort.) Hampton returned to camp at 2 PM with 35 horses, the Loyalists' arms and equipment and some of the enemy's baggage. He only lost one man captured who reported, under questioning, that McDowell's strength was around 400 men.

Dunlap reported the attack to Captain Abraham De Peyster (1753–1799) and abandoned Fort Prince, fearing an all-out attack by McDowell. De Peyster and 100 American Volunteers and Loyalist militiamen marched to support Dunlap. The two parties met at McIlwain's Creek.[455]

★ Another incident occurred at Gowen's Fort, in November 1781, that was very similar to what happened at Fort Lyndley in 1776. Cherokees and white men disguised as Cherokees, attacked this station around Thursday, November 1st or Saturday, November 3,

1781 and made several unsuccessful attempts to capture it. *The Royal Gazette* of November 24, 1781, reported that, about three weeks earlier, a party of loyal militiamen and Cherokees under the command of Mr. Tuft attacked and captured a rebel fort on the Pacolet River, Gowen's Ferry. The Mr. Tuft mentioned in the *Gazette* is unknown.

The party was most probably led by Captain William "Bloody" Bates (d. 1781) and Dragging Canoe (ca. 1730–1792) who commanded a large band of Chicamaugas and Loyalists painted like Cherokees in western South Carolina. They came down the Saluda Mountain frequently at night to kill and plunder the Pacolet, Enoree, and Fair Forest country. The settlers in the area fled to Earle's Fort and Gowen's Fort.

The raiding party attacked the fort where the local Whig settlers had taken refuge. Lacking ammunition, the fort's occupants surrendered on the condition that they would be protected from the Chickamaugas. Bates agreed but, as soon as the gates were opened, he ordered his men to kill everyone. They slaughtered all the men, women, and children, except for a few who escaped, some of them horribly mangled. When the raiders left, the bodies of 10 settlers lay in the dirt. Abner Thompson's wife survived being scalped and lived another 50 years. The sole surviving son of the Motley family later avenged the murder of his father, mother, brothers, and sisters. The raiders took the commander, Major John Gowen (1740–1810), and some of the defenders back to the mountains to burn them at the stake, but a relief expedition, led by Captain Major Parsons, overtook Bates at a place beyond the headwaters of the Tyger River, defeated him and freed Gowen. Bates escaped and his force dispersed.

Many years after the war, Bates returned to the state from the Cherokee Nation where he had taken refuge. He stole some horses and was pursued, arrested and imprisoned in the Greenville jail. When Mr. Motley heard of Bates's arrest, he procured a pair of pistols, went to the prison where Bates was incarcerated, and demanded the keys. After opening the cell door, Motley grabbed Bates by the collar and ordered him to say his prayers. He then fired a pistol at Bates's head and buried his body a few yards from the jail. Nobody interfered or prosecuted Motley. [456]

See also **Mill's Station** in the North Carolina chapter of *The Guide to the American Revolutionary War in Pennsylvania, Delaware, Maryland, Virginia and North Carolina* p. 276.

Earle's Fort (ca. Nov. 22, 1781) see **Union County and vicinity.**

Middle Tyger River, Spartanburg County (Hampton Massacre)
(June 30, 1776)

Woods Fort, Spartanburg County
Mountain Rest
Round Mountain (Howard's Gap), Polk County (June 30, 1776)

> Woods Fort was also called Thompson's Fort because it was built (or rebuilt) in the latter part of 1777 by an expedition from Fort Prince under the command of Captain William Wood (1737–1804) and Lieutenant Elisha Thompson. It was located between the South and Middle forks of the Tyger River near Beaverdam Creek. It also seems to have been near a small tributary of the South Tyger that is called Hampton Branch. It was located about 150 yards northeast of route S-42-908 (Gap Creek Road) between route S-42-9765 (Rollingreen Road) and Ashlan Woods Court near Beaverdam Creek, 2 miles north of Greer.[457]

Western South Carolina **265**

> The exact location of Captain Preston Hampton's (1752–1832) house is unknown. It was probably at the end of Fairway Estates Road north of route S-42-908 (Gap Creek Road) about 2900 feet northwest of Wood's Fort.
>
> Some historians think that the Hampton massacre occurred at Round Mountain, also known as Howard Gap, just over the state line in Saluda, North Carolina. This site is about 0.28 miles south of route I-26 (U.S. 74). Route SC 1188 (Indian Mount Road) becomes route SC 1122 (Howard Gap Road then Old Howard Gap Road, then Warrior Mountain Road). It is 59.25 miles as the crow flies between the Hampton house and Round Mountain. It is more likely that the Hampton Massacre happened in Spartanburg County and the revenge killing of the Cherokees occurred at Round Mountain.

Captain Edward Hampton (1746-1781) and his brother, Captain Preston Hampton (d. 1776), were sent to the Cherokee nation on a peace-seeking mission in June 1776. Cherokees and Loyalists visited their father, flax broker Anthony Hampton's (1715–1776) house, near Wood's Fort, on Sunday, June 30, 1776. (Some accounts say the Hampton house was near Earle's Ford.) Anthony Hampton settled here with his wife, his daughter, and his many sons in 1774. Elizabeth (Hampton) Harrison (1758–1799) was visiting her parents while her husband, James Harrison (1748–1815), was away recruiting militiamen. Only her brother Preston was home. He was returning from a conference with the Cherokee chiefs concerning a peace treaty and had stopped to talk with his father.

When the Cherokees and Loyalists arrived in the yard, Preston recognized a chief and went outside to greet him. His father Anthony followed and gave the chief a cordial welcome and a handshake. As he was shaking hands with Chief Big Warrior (Tustanagee Thlucco) (d. 1826), another Cherokee fired and mortally wounded his son, Preston. The chief released the old man's hand and embedded a tomahawk in Mr. Hampton's skull. When Mrs. Hampton arrived, they killed her the same way. The Cherokees and Loyalists entered the house, drank all the brandy and pillaged the family possessions. The Cherokees burned the Hampton estate before leaving. The event became known as the Hampton Massacre.

Elizabeth Harrison and Mrs. Sadler heard the war whoops and rode as close as possible. They then crept through the canebrake to investigate. When they approached the house, they saw the mutilated bodies of Mr. and Mrs. Hampton and Preston in the yard. The terrified women watched as a Cherokee warrior carried Elizabeth's and Preston's infant son into the yard, holding him by the feet. The warrior then bashed the baby's head against a tree, killing him. Mrs. Sadler clasped her hand over Elizabeth's mouth to stifle her scream and pulled her back through the canebrake to their horses. They mounted their bareback horses and galloped to Wood's Fort for help.

The men of the settlement then met at the blockhouse on the Pacolet River and chose 16-year-old Thomas Howard (1760–1838) to lead them in an attack to exact revenge. A Native American, named Skyuka (d. 1776), said he knew that the raiders were on top of Round Mountain and guided them. Skyuka suggested they pitch camp at the base of Round Mountain. They lit several bonfires when it got dark and left three men in the camp with instructions to shout and yell as if they were having a big celebration and to pass in front of the fire constantly, hoping to deceive the Cherokees into believing many men were preparing to attack them the next day. Meanwhile, Captain Howard and his men took a circular route to approach the Cherokees from behind. They surprised the

Cherokees and killed almost all of them. The Loyalists later captured Skyuka and hanged him from a sycamore tree at the base of Round Mountain in Polk County.[458]

See **Round Mountain (Howard's Gap)** (June 30, 1776) p. 264.

When the search party arrived at the Hampton house, they found it burned. The attackers took Preston's wagons, horses, guns and a case of pistols as well as the Hamptons' 9-year-old grandson, John Bynum (1767–), and held him for many years. They returned over the mountains into Cherokee country (Greenville County).

According to local tradition, the raiding party stopped at Preston Hampton's house on the way to Anthony Hampton's house. Preston's wife fled through the swamp and was found several days later wandering through the woods. She was so frightened that she went crazy and never fully recovered her mind.[459]

Laurens, Laurens County
Fort Lindley (Lyndley) (Rayborn, Raeburns, Rabun's, Rabon or Creek) (July 15, 1776)

> The battle of Fort Lyndley, also known as Rayborn, Raeburns, Rabun's, or Rabon Creek, occurred near Laurens in Laurens County. The fort was about 0.75 miles east of Rabon Creek. A highway marker is on route S-30-398 (Fort Lindley Road) 2 miles south of route SC 252. (SC 252 is approximately 5 miles west of Laurens off route U.S. 76 (West Main Street). The site of the battle is on private property but it can be seen from the road.

See also **Cherokee Campaign of 1776** in the Tennessee chapter of the next volume, *The Guide to the American Revolutionary War in the Deep South and on the Frontier.*

The strategy of the Crown forces in South Carolina relied on the recruitment of Loyalist Americans. They also tried to win the allegiance of the Native Americans. Major Andrew Williamson (ca. 1730–1786) and a group of about 580 Whigs gradually moved throughout the back-country recruiting men to oppose the Loyalists and the Cherokees. They stopped at Fort Lyndley, an old log stockade, on Monday night, July 15, 1776, to reinforce a small group of settlers who had taken refuge there. Captain Jonathan Downs (1738–1818) and 150 backwoods militiamen on their way to join Major Williamson had stopped there for the night.

At 1 AM, 88 Cherokees and 102 white Loyalists, some disguised as Cherokees, attacked the fort, unaware that Downs had reinforced the site the night before. The fighting continued for three hours when the attackers learned that Major Williamson and his army were approaching. As they departed, leaving several dead, Downs's men rushed from the fort and captured 13 Loyalists who were sent to jail at Ninety Six.

Colonel James Williams (1740–1780) and Lieutenant Colonel John Lisle arrived the next day with 430 men to reinforce Captain Downs. They were joined by two companies of Colonel Richard Richardson, Jr.'s (1741–1817) regiment. Major Williamson and his men arrived on July 17.[460]

Colonel Andrew Williamson's Indian Campaign (Aug. 1, 1776–Oct. 1776)
Cherokee Campaign (Aug. 1, 1776–May 20, 1777)
Seneca Old Town, Pickens County

Seneca (Esseneca), Oconee and Pickens Counties (Aug. 1, 1775; July 1, 1776)
Cherokee Town (June 26, 1776)
Cherokee Indian Town (Seneca/Esseneca) (Aug. 1, 1776)
Keowee (ca. Aug. 4, 1776)
Sugar Town (ca. Aug. 6, 1776)
Jocassee (Aug. 8, 1776)
Oconee (Aug. 8, 1776)
Oconore (Aug. 8, 1776; Aug. 12, 1776)
Estatoe (Aug. 8, 1776)
Tugaloo River (Aug. 10, 1776; July 1781)
Brass Town (Aug. 11, 1776)
Tamassee (Tomassy, Ring Fight) (Aug. 11, 1776)
Cheowee (Cheowie, Chehohee, Cheohee, Chehokee) (Aug. 12, 1776)
Eustaste (Eustustie, Oustestee) (Aug. 12, 1776)
Chauga (1776)
Quacoratchee (also known as Warachy, Tockorachee, Takwashua) (1776)
Oconee County
Indian Villages, Lower Settlements
Cherokee Villages (early March 1782)
Oconee Creek or River (early March 1782)
Keowee Town
Cherokee Campaign of 1782 (Sept. 16–Oct. 17, 1782)
See the Tennessee chapter of the next volume, *The Guide to the American Revolutionary War in the Deep South and on the Frontier.*

Ustanali (Oct. 8, 1782)

> The Native American towns moved from place to place but kept the same name. Therefore, it is hard to give accurate locations for all the towns and actions. The Cherokee Villages, Lower Settlements consisted of Brass Town, Cheowee (Cheowie, Chehohee, Cheohee, Chehokee), Esseneca (Seneca), Estatoe (Estatoie, Estatoee), Eustaste (Eustustie, Oustestee) (Frog Town), Jocassee (Jocasse, Jocassie, Jocassy), Keowee, Ostatoy, Soconee, Sugar Town, Tamasee (Tomasee, Tomassee), and Tugaloo. The names in parentheses are variant spellings.
> Esseneca was a town on both sides of the Seneca River which was dammed downstream to create Lake Hartwell in the 1960s. The site of Seneca Old Town is

on the campus of Clemson University. Tillman Hall, the administration building, occupies the site of Fort Rutledge. A monument to the fort is on the shore of modern Lake Hartwell. To get to the site, take route U.S. 76 (Anderson Highway) south from Clemson. Turn right onto Old Stone Church Road which becomes Cherry Road. Turn left onto Old Stadium Road and left toward the conference center and inn complex. Turn right onto the service access road that leads toward the pumping station. Cross over the dike and go just past the third building on the right (the one closest to the road). The monument, a fanciful design of a miniature fort of dressed stone, is straight ahead about 50 yards into the woods (see Photo SC-41).

SC-41. Fort Rutledge monument. This fanciful design of a miniature fort of dressed stone commemorates Fort Rutledge.

A diorama in the B'nai B'rith Klutznick Exhibit Hall, 1640 Rhode Island Ave., Washington, D.C. shows Captain Francis (Daniel Jezurun Rodriguez) Salvador (1747–1776) being shot from his horse and about to be scalped.

Keowee, an important Cherokee village, is located on the western shore of Lake Keowee, at the end of Keowee Landing Road in Salem. To get there, take route SC 130 north from Seneca to the fork with route S-37-128 (Nimmons Bridge Road). Bear right on the fork and go north for 1.6 miles to route S-37-98 (Keowee Town Landing Road). A state historical marker, noting that Keowee Town was approximately 1 mile east, supposed to be at this junction was not evident. Turn right on route S-37-98 (Keowee Town Landing Road) and travel 0.9 miles east to the banks of Lake Keowee to see the site. There's a Daughters of the American Revolution marker near the end of the road.

Fort Prince George (see Photo SC-42) was almost directly across the lake. The fort, constructed by the British in 1753 to protect frontier settlers from the Native Americans and their French allies, was a square log stockade surrounded by a ditch. It had four cannons and a garrison of 100 men. Both Keowee and Fort Prince George are now under Lake Keowee.

Western South Carolina 269

SC-42. Fort Prince George site

> Oconee was on the east bank of Cane Creek about a mile south-southeast of the Walhalla Reservoir in Walhalla.
> Oconee Station State Historic Site (see Photo SC-43) (500 Oconee Station Road, Walhalla, SC 29691 (864) 638-0079; **southcarolinaparks.com**) is 3 miles southwest of Tamassee. Follow route SC 11 (Cherokee Foothills Scenic Highway) south from Tamassee or north from West Union. Turn onto route S-37-95 (Oconee Station Road) and proceed 4.1 miles northwest to Oconee Station.

SC-43. Oconee Station served as a military base during the American War for Independence and was garrisoned until 1799. Frontier families probably sought refuge here during the Cherokee wars. The reconstructed buildings are part of the Oconee Station State Historic Site.

Oconee Station, constructed before 1760 as one of three fortified outposts on the South Carolina frontier, was a fieldstone structure and the oldest building in Oconee County. It served as a military base during the American War for Independence and was garrisoned until 1799. Frontier families probably sought refuge here during the Cherokee wars.

About 1.2 miles further north on route S-37-95 (Oconee Station Road) is a monument to Brigadier General Andrew Pickens (1739–1817) who made his home here after the war. Impressed by the beauty of the wilderness along Tamassee Creek when he did battle with the Cherokees, Pickens returned to live here toward the end of his life.

Oconee Creek runs east-west in Walhalla, about 2.2 miles south of Tamassee and 4.5 miles due west-southwest of Keowee Town.

The closest road access to Sugar Town is at the end of Hunter's Road off Nimmons Bridge Road about 2.25 miles north of the Keowee historical marker.

Jocassee was south of SC 130 (Whitewater Falls Road) and north of Talley Road on the west bank of Burgess Creek in Salem.

Estatoe was located about 0.5 miles south of where Estatoee Community Road crosses Laurel Creek in Sunset. To get there from the intersection of routes U.S. 178 and SC 11, go northwest on route U.S. 178 for about 3.25 miles. Turn left onto Cleo Chapman Highway (S-39-100) and go about 1.9 miles, then turn right (north) onto Estatoee Community Road. The site is on the left.

The Tugaloo River, which flows into Harwell Lake, constitutes South Carolina's western boundary with Georgia. The only notation of a date for the July 1781 event is that it happened "soon after the siege of Ninety Six."

Brass Town was on the Tugaloo River near Brasstown Creek. To get there from the junction of routes U.S. 76 and S-37-88 (Welcome Church Road), about 5.25 miles northwest of Westminster, go southwest on route S-37-88 (Welcome Church Road) for about 5.25 miles to route S-37-160 (Cleveland Pike Road) and turn right. Go about 2.25 miles, then turn right (northwest) onto Barton Creek Road (S-37-217) and go about 0.85 miles. Turn left (northwest) onto Cooper Road and go about 0.75 miles to the Tugaloo River site on the left. Proceed for about 1.2 miles to the Brass Town site about 185 yards on the left.

Chauga was at the mouth of the Chauga River where it emptied into the Tugaloo River. It was about 0.8 miles south of where route U.S. 123 (Toccoa Highway) crosses the Chauga River. The site is now submerged under Hartwell Lake.

Quacoratchee was about 400 feet south of where route S-39-49 (Little Eastatoee Road) crosses Little Eastatoe Creek in Sunset.

The site of Tamassee and the Ring Fight is about 5 miles west of Tamassee in Oconee County. Brigadier General Andrew Pickens (1739–1817) was so impressed by the natural beauty of the area that he later settled here and built his "Red House" on Tamassee Creek. To get to the site, take route S-37-172 (Dynamite Road) from Tamassee and go about 1.2 miles to route S-37-375 (Cheohee Valley Road). Turn right (west) and go about 1 mile to route S-37-95 (Tamassee Knob Road). A stone marking the site of the battle is located about 300 yards north of the junction of Cheohee Valley Road and Tamassee Knob Road. Go about 0.5 miles on Tamassee Knob Road to Jumping Branch Road. A small stone, called the "General Pickens Monument," on Tamassee Knob Road about 100 yards south of the intersection

> marks the house site on the creek. Proceed about 0.7 miles on Jumping Branch Road to the site of the Ring Fight.
> Oconore was probably in Tamassee on the eastern shore of Lake Isaquenna. Oconoree Creek may be what is now known as Oconee Creek in Walhalla.
> To get to Cheowee, return to Cheohee Valley Road and go about 1.4 miles north.
> To reach the Eustaste site, take Cheohee Valley Road south for about 0.7 miles and turn left (east) onto The Bear Boulevard. The site is along Mud Creek, about 200 yards northeast from the northeast most point on The Bear Boulevard.
> Ustanali was located about 2.25 miles north of Topton in what is now the Nantahala Gorge Recreation Site and the Nantahala National Forest in North Carolina.

The Peace Treaty of 1763, ending the Seven Years War (1756–1763) (French and Indian War), forbade any English subjects from settling west of the Appalachian Mountains. As this provision of the treaty was often ignored, the Cherokees sided with the British, hoping that their allies could stop encroaching settlers. The Cherokees cut off the wagon trains west through the Cumberland Gap which prevented movement into Kentucky for a while.

A detachment of 3rd South Carolina Rangers had been patrolling near Seneca Town on the South Carolina frontier on Tuesday, Aug. 1, 1775. They stopped for the night and set up camp, but they failed to post sentries. A party of Cherokees surprised them as they slept. A brief firefight ensued which left four rangers dead and six wounded.[461]

★ A delegation of Shawnee, Delaware and Mohawks arrived in the Cherokee country from the north, in May 1776, advocating war. They came to plan for a coordinated attack along the frontier with the Shawnee, Cherokee, Chicamauga, Creek, and Iroquois which would coincide with the British attack on Charleston. Two days before Admiral Sir Peter Parker (1721–1811) and General Henry Clinton (1730–1795) attacked Fort Moultrie, the Cherokees attacked Captain James McCall's (1741–1781) party of 33 militiamen and rangers which had entered their territory in search of Alexander Cameron (ca. 1720–1781), a Scot who was deputy Crown Superintendent for Indian Affairs in the South. Cameron moved into the Cherokee lands when the war broke out in 1775 and was thought to be encamped on Oconore Creek with a force of Native Americans and Loyalists. The scouting party wanted to capture Cameron before he could instigate the Cherokees to cause trouble along the South Carolina frontier.

McCall's mission was to penetrate the Lower Cherokees (the branch of the nation living in the foothills east of the mountains) and find Cameron who was Colonel John Stuart's (ca. 1710–1779), Superintendent of the Southern Indian Department, chief means of exercising influence over the Cherokees. The Cherokees permitted McCall's party to proceed through two of their towns, located in present-day Pickens County, without incident. After visiting a third village (probably near modern Clemson) without incident, McCall's men camped some distance away.

A strong body of about 200 Cherokees, outraged that an armed party entered their lands, perceived this action as a provocative act. They attacked the camp Wednesday night, June 26, 1776, killed four rangers, wounded Captain James Baskin (1739–1790) and captured Captain McCall and his interpreter. They lost about six warriors in the attack. On Monday, July 1st, three days after Parker's and Clinton's unsuccessful attempt to take Fort Moultrie at the mouth of Charleston harbor, the Cherokees joined in a general offensive against South Carolina. McCall, who witnessed the torture and death of at least one white captive, eventually managed to escape. He rode 300 miles on horseback, without a saddle, until he arrived in Virginia, joined a body of Virginia troops and returned to South Carolina.[462] See **Cherokee Campaign of 1776** in the Tennessee chapter of the next volume, *the Guide to the American Revolutionary War in the Deep South and on the Frontier.*

Another version of the story says that the Cherokees at Seneca encouraged Colonel Andrew Williamson (ca. 1730–1786) to send Captain James McCall and 20 men to bring back their prisoners because they trusted Captain McCall. When the soldiers approached Seneca, the Cherokees came out to meet them and invited McCall, his lieutenant, and one other soldier to eat dinner with the chief. Instead of eating dinner, the Cherokees attacked the Carolina camp that night. The soldiers let their guard down and many fled into the night. McCall and six others were captured.[463]

★ Cherokee raiding parties began attacking settlements in South Carolina in the summer of 1776. When they attacked Lyndley's (Lindley's) Fort on Monday, July 15, 1776, Major General Charles Lee (1731–1782), commander of the Continental forces in the south, urged Congress to send a major punitive expedition against the Cherokees before the British could invade the south and draw Continental troops away from the frontier. Within two weeks of the Cherokee invasion, the Continental Congress authorized the expedition.

Governor William Henry Drayton (1742–1779) ordered Colonel Andrew Williamson (ca. 1730–1786) to invade the Cherokee territory and burn every town and cornfield he encountered. Williamson had difficulty raising militiamen, as the men were afraid to leave their families. However, after a few quick victories, he raised a force of several thousand. Many Loyalists even offered their assistance. Colonel Williamson led a campaign of terror through the Lower Cherokee towns, following Drayton's orders explicitly. He stopped just short of Choate, Georgia when the Cherokees sued for peace as winter approached.[464]

Colonel Andrew Williamson (ca. 1730–1786) mustered between 1,150 and 1,800 militiamen by the end of July 1776. He began his campaign by attacking and destroying the Cherokee "capitol" of Seneca (Essenecca). Captain Francis (Daniel Jezurun Rodriguez) Salvador (1747–1776), who lived on Corn-acre Creek, now known as Coronaca, mounted a horse and galloped 28 miles to warn Colonel Andrew Williamson (ca. 1730–1786) that the Cherokees were on the warpath and to help assemble the militia. When he arrived, he found that one of Captain Aaron Smith's (1720–1776) sons who had managed to escape the massacre on Little River had already brought a warning. Williamson set out on Wednesday night, July 31, 1776, to subdue and punish Alexander Cameron's (ca. 1720–1781) Loyalists and Cherokees who attacked Fort Lyndley.

Colonel Williamson and Captain Salvador were riding at the head of the advance guard when the Cherokees ambushed them about 2 AM on Thursday, August 1, as they crossed the Keowee River near the village of Seneca Old Town or Essenecca, as the Cherokees called it. This was the only place they could cross the Seneca River to attack Cameron.

The Cherokees and Loyalists hid behind a fence parallel to the road. They fired into the flank of Williamson's column throwing the militiamen into confusion until Captain LeRoy Hammond (1728–1789) rallied a group of about 20 men and charged the fence where the heaviest fire was coming from. This startled the Cherokees so much that they dropped their weapons and fled into the woods. Williamson had his horse shot out from under him and Captain Francis Salvador,[465] his young Jewish aide, was shot three times and scalped alive before his friends found him in the dark. It appeared, after the action, that Captain Smith saw the Cherokees taking off the scalp in the dark. Thinking it was

Mr. Salvador's servant assisting his master, he did not interfere to save his friend. (Captain Smith was the son of Captain Aaron Smith who had been murdered with his wife, five children, and an African American on Little River.)

When morning came, the militiamen counted five killed and 13 wounded. The Cherokees lost only one man killed and three wounded. Colonel Williamson ordered his men to level the town on the eastern side of the Keowee River and to destroy the corn, estimated at 6,000 bushels, and all other food stores in retribution for the deaths of Salvador and other settlers. Colonel Hammond later crossed the river and burned the part of Esseneca town on the western side as well on Friday, August 2nd. They then fell back and established a base camp at 23 Mile Creek for future incursions against the Cherokees.[466]

When Williamson returned to the ruins of Esseneca, he found many of his men had gone home for want of clothes and other necessaries. Of those who remained, many were equally distressed. They built Fort Rutledge on the site of Esseneca. It was named for John Rutledge (1730–1800), South Carolina's wartime governor. It was also called Fort Salvador to honor Captain Francis Salvador.[467]

★ Colonel Andrew Williamson (ca. 1730–1786) camped at Twelve Mile River and sent Captain Benjamin Tutt's (1737/38–1790) regiment to burn the villages of Keowee about Sunday, August 4, 1776, Soconee (Sugar Town) about Tuesday, August 6, 1776; Jocassee and Estatoe on Thursday, August 8, 1776. The soldiers also destroyed Oconee, and Estatoy during this same four day period.[468]

★ Henry Hampton (1755–1826) was one of Colonel Andrew Williamson's (ca. 1730–1786) captains. Henry found a Cherokee brave wearing the coat of one of his slain brothers and killed him. Five of Henry's brothers served as officers in the Congressional forces, including Edward (1740–1781) who pursued Major James Dunlap (d. 1781) after the clash at Gowen's Old Fort. Edward was later killed by Major William "Bloody Bill" Cunningham (d. 1787).

★ Major Andrew Pickens (1739–1817) and a column of troops proceeded up the east side of the Tugaloo River on Saturday, August 10, 1776, when they spotted a party of Cherokees following them on the west side. When they reached a ford across the river, Pickens ordered his men to charge the Cherokees. The Cherokees fled under heavy fire; but none of Pickens's men were wounded.[469]

★ Colonel Robert Anderson (d. 1813) and three companies marched against the Cherokees on the Tugaloo River in July 1781. They took "one white man prisoner" but were not strong enough to attack the town. They destroyed what they could and then returned. William Morrow (1765–1835), who was with the expedition, wrote that they "accomplished very little." He also wrote that the force consisted of "three companies under Colonel Robert Anderson (1741–1812), or Major Taylor." He could not remember which.[470]

★ Colonel Andrew Williamson's (ca. 1730–1786) scouting party of 25 men encountered a large war party of about 185 to 300 Cherokees who surrounded and ambushed them at Tamassee (Tomassy) on Sunday, August 11, 1776. The ambuscade had been prepared for General Griffith Rutherford's (ca. 1731–1800) North Carolina army.

Williamson's scouting party was crossing a cornfield about 2 miles from camp when the Cherokees, posted on the crest and sides of a mountain in the form of a horseshoe, ambushed them. As Williamson and his men defiled through the gorge, or the heel of the horseshoe, they were allowed to proceed to the part which may be called the toe. All of a sudden, the war whoop sounded all around them. The soldiers fired and the

Cherokees had an equally deadly aim, forcing the soldiers into a circle. The main army advanced to the rescue as soon as they heard the firing begin.[471]

The skirmish continued for several hours until Major Andrew Pickens (1739–1817) arrived with the main body. Pickens ordered his men to form two circles, one inside the other, and to fire in relays. Two men would fire, then crouch in the tall grass to reload, while the next two would fire. Some Cherokees rushed at the ring but were killed. When Major Pickens's brother, Captain Joseph William Pickens (1737–1781), arrived with a rescue party, Captain Edward Hampton (1746–1781) spotted some Cherokees hidden behind trees and fired. All the hidden Cherokee and Catawba warriors immediately began a heavy fire. The militiamen rushed against the Cherokees causing them to flee into the mountains, leaving 16 or 83 dead, depending on the source.

Pickens later claimed setting fire to a nearby canebrake to save his men. The moist reeds filled with steam and exploded with a loud popping noise that sounded like gunfire. The Cherokees, mistaking these sounds for gunfire from reinforcements, fled in confusion.

John Drayton (1766–1822) claims this event occurred on Wednesday, September 18 and recorded in his memoirs:

> These heights were occupied by twelve hundred Indian Warriors; nor, were they discovered, until the advance guard of one hundred men began to mount the height, which terminated the valley. The army, having thus completely fallen into the ambuscade of the enemy, they poured in a heavy fire upon its front and flanks; compelling it to recoil, and fall into confusion. Great was the perturbation which then prevailed, the cry being, "We shall be cut off;" and while Colonel Williamson's attention was imperiously called to rally his men, and charge the enemy, he was at the same time obliged to reinforce the baggage guard, on which the subsistence of the army depended for provisions, in this mountainous wilderness. In this extremity, Lieutenant-Colonel Hammond caused detachments to file off for the purpose of gaining the eminences above the Indians, and turning their flanks; while, Lieutenant Hampton with twenty men, advanced upon the enemy, passing the main advance guard of one hundred men; who, being panic struck, were rapidly retreating. Hampton, however, clambered up the ascent, with a manly presence of mind; which much encouraged all his followers: calling out, "Loaded guns advance—empty guns, fall down and load;" and being joined by thirty men, he charged desperately on the foe. The Indians, now gave way; and a panic passing among them from right to left, the troops rallied and pressed them with such energy, as induced a general flight: and the army was thereby rescued from a total defeat and massacre. Besides this good fortune, they became possessed of so many packs of deerskins and baggage; that they sold among the individuals of the army, for £1,200 currency; and which sum, was equally distributed among the troops. In this engagement, the killed of Williamson's army, were thirteen men, and one Catawba Indian; and the wounded were, thirty-two men, and two Catawbas. Of the enemy, only four were found dead; and their loss would have been more considerable, if many of them had not been mistaken for the friendly Catawbas, who were in front.[472]

The soldiers proceeded along a narrow path through laurel swamps and thickets when they spied a lone squaw and fired, wounding her in the leg and shoulder. They questioned her and learned that the Cherokees were 4 miles ahead preparing to give battle again. As the woman could not travel, the "men favored her so far, that they killed her to put her out of pain."[473]

Colonel Thomas Sumter (1734–1832) and his regiment were ordered to a mountain about a mile away to prevent the Cherokees from capturing the baggage. When the battle was over, the ground was littered with moccasins, guns, deer skins, coats, and blankets but only four dead Cherokees were found. Pickens lost 14 killed and 34 wounded. The army camped to bury the dead and care for the wounded as best they could. On September 20, Pickens detached 100 men to bring the sick and wounded to General Griffith Rutherford's (ca. 1731–1800) camp.[474]

★ Colonel Andrew Williamson (ca. 1730–1786) destroyed Brass Town on Sunday, August 11, 1776 and headed to Cheowee (Cheowie, Chehohee, Cheohee, Chehokee) and Eustaste (Eustustie, Oustestee) on Monday, August 12.

He observed a recent trail used by the Cherokees at Eustaste and pursued the Cherokees. He encountered a large band of about 300 warriors whom he attacked and defeated, killing 16. Williamson had nobody killed and 17 wounded. He destroyed the towns of Tamassee (Tomassy), Chehohee, and Eustash and all the corn in the lower settlements, forcing the Cherokees to survive on roots, berries, and wild fruit. Many died of starvation during the winter.[475]

★ Colonel Andrew Williamson (ca. 1730–1786) sent a detachment to burn Chauga in 1776. The detachment consisted of Colonel Samuel Jack (ca. 1742–1807) and his 240 Georgia militiamen, Major Andrew Pickens (1739–1817) and 230 South Carolina militiamen and Captain Samuel Boykin (1749–1791) with 20 Catawbas. Colonel William Thomas joined this force with 33 of his rangers (3rd South Carolina Regiment).[476]

★ The regiments of Colonel Thomas Neel (1739–1779) and Colonel William Thomas (3rd South Carolina Regiment) burned Quacoratchee also known as Warachy, Tockorachee, or Takwashua.[477]

★ Colonel Andrew Williamson (ca. 1730–1786) then marched to attack British Indian agent Alexander Cameron (ca. 1720–1781), who was with a large body of Essenecas and Loyalists, camped at Oconore in September. He defeated them and destroyed their town and about 6,000 bushels of corn, in addition to peas and beans. He also destroyed the two towns, Ostatoy and Tugaloo. He destroyed a total of 32 towns in three months.[478]

Within a few weeks, the Cherokees began returning to their villages where some of the few standing houses had been plundered. They could erect shelters rather quickly, but, as their food supplies had been ruined, their survival in the approaching winter was a major problem.

In May 1777, delegates from the Lower, Middle, and Valley towns traveled to DeWitt's Corner (about 200 yards west of where SC 20 (Due West Road) crosses Corner Creek in Due West, South Carolina) to negotiate with the representatives of South Carolina and Georgia. North Carolina could not commission representatives in time for the meeting, so the other two states represented her interests. The terms of the agreement included peace, an exchange of prisoners, and a land cession of all the remaining land in South Carolina except for a narrow strip along the Chatooga in present Oconee County, along the western border.

The Treaty of Long Island of Holston, signed on Sunday, July 20, 1777, officially ended the Cherokee Campaign of 1776. The Overhill Cherokees ceded, to the state of South Carolina, all their lands east of the Unicoi (Blue Ridge) Mountains and north of the Nolichucky River (the present-day counties of Anderson, Pickens, Oconee, and Greenville). The treaty expelled the Cherokees from Virginia and cut their possessions in Tennessee and North Carolina in half.[479]

★ Loyalist Colonel Thomas Waters (ca. 1738–after 1810) settled among the Cherokees on Hightower River at the mouth of Long Swamp Creek in Georgia. The Cherokees collected there whatever plunder they took from the Whig settlers and slaves. The Cherokee raids prompted Brigadier General Andrew Pickens (1739–1817) and Brigadier General Elijah Clarke (1733–1799) to plan an attack on the Cherokees remaining in Georgia.

Generals Pickens and Clarke (1733–1799) and 300 militiamen were ordered to patrol the Cherokee territory in Oconee County in November 1781, after many of Major William "Bloody Bill" Cunningham's (d. 1787) Loyalists took refuge there. Pickens wrote "Some of the worst tories went to the Cherokees + were almost continually harassing + murdering the frontier inhabitants + made no distinction of the sexes."

Pickens wrote that there was a "scarcity of ammunition, which prevailed, often being reduced to a few rounds per man to endeavor to put a stop to those murderers of women + children." He gave "orders that no Indian woman, child or old man, or any unfit to bear arms, should be put to death on pain of death on the perpetrator. . . . My order was readily obeyed + the Indian soon followed the example."

Since he was low on ammunition he had to rely on surprise. Pickens wrote:

> The Indians had notice of our coming by a tory who left us when we began to collect, but not knowing the rout I intended to take, the Indians expected us the same way we had formerly gone + had their spies out on that way. I met Clarke at the place appointed. We proceeded with almost 500, all mounted + nearly one third with swords. I had not more than five or six rounds of ammunition for each man. It may be thought rash to have gone, with so little ammunition against a powerful tally of Indians, aided by a banditti of desperadoes. We went the whole way through the woods unexplored by any of us before. We entirely avoided their spies + completely surprised one of their town + made prisoners of more than 50 women + children with a few men. We had marched the whole night before guided by two Indians whom we accidentally met with the day before + made prisoners of. They faithfully performed the task allotted them. After surprising the town + waking the prisoners in the evening I sent out three of the most active Indian men that we had taken + told them to go + tell their people that I was there, that I did not blame the Indians so much as the white men that were amongst them who encouraged or assisted them in the war against us.

Pickens told the Cherokees that, if they released their prisoners, he would release his prisoners, including any slaves, and he would advance no further. He gave the Cherokees two days to comply, otherwise he "would destroy as many of their towns + as much of their provisions as possible + if they wished to fight, they knew where to find me."

Chief Terrapin (1736–post 1796) headed a delegation that met with Pickens and told him that they would surrender Thomas Waters and his men if Pickens would leave their settlements alone. The Cherokees surrendered six of Waters's men; but Waters escaped when he learned that he was going to be turned over to Pickens.

Some Georgia militiamen joined Pickens, bringing his force to 4500 men. They then marched against the Cherokee towns in March 1782 to prevent the Cherokees from raiding the settlements. Pickens also took revenge for his brother's death. His men burned 13 villages, killed 40 Cherokees and took 40 prisoners in the 19-day expedition.[480]

★ Colonel Elijah Clarke (1733–1799) captured 24 slaves at Ustanali on Tuesday, October 8, 1782. Pickens recorded "We remained in this nation till we had collected all the white prisoners that could be got, with a number of negroes." Twelve chiefs and 200 warriors met with Pickens and Clarke at Selacoa on October 17th and agreed to "temporary terms of peace" to be ratified by the tribe. The Native American delegation surrendered all of their land between the Chattahoochee and Savannah Rivers to the state of Georgia. The permanent treaty was signed in Augusta, Georgia in May 1783 but this did not end the hostilities.[481]

Reedy River (Aug. 1777)
Ridgeway's Fort, Laurens County (Aug. 1, 1781; Sept. 3, 1781)

> Ridgeway's Fort consisted of two blockhouses (see Photo SC-5) erected on the Reedy River to protect the frontier settlers from Native American, and later Loyalist, attacks. They were about 1.5 miles apart and were garrisoned by the Little River Regiment under the command of Captain John Ridgeway. The north blockhouse was about 0.3 miles northeast of the intersection of routes S-30-36 (Ekom Beach Road) and S-30-64 (Poplar Springs Road), east of Ware Shoals. The south blockhouse was on the north bank of the Reedy River, about 400 yards northeast of where route S-30-6 (Indian Mound Road) crosses the river.
>
> Captain Richard Pearis (d. 1804) raised about 400 men to go to Mobile [West Florida, now Alabama] to fight for the British in 1777. When the local militiamen learned of this, they raided Pearis's camp on the Reedy River in August 1777. They captured many Loyalists, including Pearis, but most scattered. Pearis managed to escape to the Cherokee settlements and then to Florida where he was made Captain of the West Florida militia. The other prisoners were taken to Ninety Six to await trial for "high Treason for Rising in arms against the United States of America" but they were acquitted.[482]

★ Major William "Bloody Bill" Cunningham (d. 1787) made two attacks on Ridgeway's Fort in 1781. One account says the first one occurred on Wednesday, August 1. Nothing is known about this action other than that the attack was successful.

★ Major William "Bloody Bill" Cunningham (d. 1787) made an unsuccessful attempt to capture the other blockhouse the following month. He crossed the Saluda River on Tuesday, September 3, 1781 (Some accounts date this event as September 5th.) and attacked Captain John Ridgeway, Jr. (d. 1781) who garrisoned the blockhouse with 30 men of the Little River Regiment. Cunningham killed Captain Ridgeway, another officer and eight privates and captured the fort without losing a single man. Thomas Arnold's pension application states that Captain Ridgeway was killed at Dirty Creek. This would be at the bridge over the creek on Fort Lindley Road about 1.25 miles south of Fort Lindley.[483]

Edgefield County
Edgefield (Feb. 1779 or Sept. 5, 1781)
Roger's (or Rogiard's) Plantation (June 1781)
Turkey Creek (Sept. 6, 1781)
Stevens Creek (Sept. 5, 1781; Oct. 5, 1781)

> Edgefield is east of Sumter National Forest on route U.S. 25 about 19 miles north of its intersection with route I-20 near North Augusta, Georgia.
>
> Roger's plantation was near the intersection of route SC 23 (Main Street) and Courthouse Square in Edgefield.
>
> Hezekiah Williams was an Edgefield Loyalist who lived on Log Creek, a branch of Turkey Creek. As Log Creek is long, nobody knows exactly where his house was located, except that it was on Log Creek. One possibility is near where route U.S. 430 (Meeting Street Road) crosses Log Creek about 2.7 miles north of Edgefield.

> Another likely location would be near where route U.S. 25 crosses Log Creek about 6 miles northwest of Edgefield.
> Turkey Creek begins about 5.5 miles east of Edgefield and flows in an arc around the city until it flows into Stevens Creek about 12 miles west of Edgefield. There are several possible sites for the Turkey Creek action. One is where route U.S. 430 (Meeting Street Road) crosses Turkey Creek about 3 miles north of the first possible site of Hezekiah Williams's house.
> A second option is where route U.S. 25 crosses Turkey Creek about 5.25 miles northwest of the split of routes U.S. 25 and SC 430 (Crest Road) at the bridge over Log Creek.[484]
> Another option is about 0.5 miles northwest of where route SC 23 (Columbia Road) crosses Turkey Creek. A state historical marker on Main Street west of Twigg Street South (SC 10) in Troy and another on route SC 28, 2 miles north of route S-33-38, in McCormick recount the Battle of Long Cane.
> The section of Stevens Creek that interests us is near where route SC 23 crosses the creek about 1.5 miles east of its junction with routes U.S. 221|SC 28 in Modoc.[484a]
> About 2 miles north of the intersection of routes SC 230 (Martintown Road) and S-19-432 (Delaughter Drive) is Big Stevens Creek Baptist Church, the first Baptist church in the county, which was established in 1762. The cemetery adjacent to the church contains Revolutionary War era graves. There's a state historical marker for the church nearby. At least one account says this event happened on Thursday, September 6, 1781, right after the skirmish at Turkey Creek.

Howard Peckham notes that Colonel LeRoy Hammond (1728–1789) and his militiamen defeated a party of Loyalists at Edgefield in February 1779. However, *The Royal Gazette* (Vol. 1: #65.) places this action at Stevens Creek on Wednesday, September 5, 1781.[485]

★ Colonel Samuel Hammond (1757–1842) sent Captain Thomas Harvey (d. 1781) and 24 dragoons to protect the countryside when Lord Francis Rawdon (1754–1826) was marching to the relief of Ninety Six. Captain Harvey's dragoons attacked Colonel James Cotton's Regiment of more than 70 men at Roger's plantation in June 1781. They routed the Loyalists and captured almost all their arms. Captain Harvey "met his death in the arms of victory" and was the only casualty.[486]

★ Colonel Hezekiah Williams attacked a body of militiamen patrolling the Turkey Creek area in Edgefield County on Thursday, September 6, 1781. He killed or wounded 10 militiamen and scattered the rest without losing a single man.[487]

★ Colonel Hezekiah Williams and his 30 Loyalists marched from the forks of Edisto in the wake of William "Bloody Bill" Cunningham's (d. 1787) raiding and harassing the Whigs at Ninety Six. Major Hugh Middleton (1740–1803) and a band of 70 men of Colonel LeRoy Hammond's (1728–1789) regiment attacked them on Stevens Creek on Friday, October 5, 1781. (Some accounts date this action as occurring on Wednesday, September 5, 1781.)

Outnumbered more than two to one, the Loyalists defeated Middleton's men in a heated skirmish. Middleton lost eight men killed, 17 severely and others slightly wounded. The Loyalists only had a few minor casualties. As Colonel LeRoy Hammond was advancing with considerable reinforcements, Williams retired and went on to attack Vince's Fort, a small post on the Three Runs, a branch of the Savannah River. However, the occupants of the garrison evacuated the fort before Williams arrived on the 28th. He only captured a few stragglers.[488]

See also **Vince's Fort** p. 246.

McGowan's Blockhouse, Abbeville County (Feb. 10, 1779)

> McGowan's blockhouse was on the South Carolina side of the Savannah River, approximately 70 miles northwest of Augusta, Georgia. The nine-man garrison covered the Cherokee Ford crossing which is now under the Richard B. Russell Reservoir. Cherokee Ford was an important crossing of the Savannah River between Georgia and South Carolina. It played a significant role in the American War for Independence, as many military units used it. McGowan's blockhouse defended the area as early as 1778. It was north of the Rocky River and was well fortified and well stocked with military supplies. There was another nine-man garrison in this area, Carr's Fort in Wilkes County, Georgia.[489]
>
> Fort Independence was located about 3.6 miles due northeast of McGowan's blockhouse, on the western shore of Richard B. Russell Lake.

Colonel Andrew Pickens (1739–1817) called for Captain Robert (1741–1812) to bring reinforcements before he left Carr's Fort in Georgia for South Carolina. Captain Anderson's men were ordered to patrol the Savannah River to prevent the Loyalist forces from crossing it.

Colonel John Boyd (d. 1779) and 600 to 800 Loyalist militiamen from North Carolina were marching south toward Georgia. They arrived at Cherokee Ford on Wednesday, February 10, 1779. McGowan's (McGowin's) blockhouse, located on a hill overlooking the ford, commanded the crossing. ("A high ridge that reaches the river here allowed travelers to avoid the low swampy river bottoms while the thousands of huge rocks in this shallow area formed a natural and partially manmade bridge across the river.")

Lieutenant Thomas Shanklin (1725–1829) [also identified as Ramsey (1741–1813) or Calhoun (1722–1786)] and eight South Carolina militiamen garrisoned the blockhouse. They had two swivel guns (see Photo SC-32).

When the Loyalists arrived at Cherokee Ford, Colonel Boyd demanded that Lieutenant Shanklin surrender the fort and allow the Loyalists to cross into Georgia. Even though he had received reinforcements of 40 Wilkes County (Georgia) militiamen under Captain James Little (1737–1807), Shanklin's force was still outnumbered by almost a hundred to one. Yet, he refused both requests. One account says that a man in the blockhouse by the name of Alexander McCopin had a blunderbuss (see Photo SC-44) and that the men prepared a round from their own shot bags and powder horns. McCopin loaded it and fired it at the enemy. Meanwhile, Captain Little sent a dispatch to Captain Anderson to apprise him of the situation at Cherokee Ford and to request assistance.

Colonel Boyd did not want to take any unnecessary casualties, so he decided not to attack the blockhouse and marched northward to search for an easier, undefended crossing of the Savannah River. He proceeded approximately 5 miles north to the South Carolina side of the mouth of Georgia's Vanns Creek. He divided his men into small groups. They transported their baggage on rafts and swam across with their horses.

Captains Robert Anderson (1741–1812), William Baskin (1737–1794), John Miller (1756–1804), and Joseph William Pickens (1737–1781) arrived at Cherokee Ford with some 80 South Carolina militiamen. The reinforcements and the 50 already stationed there marched north, hoping to prevent Boyd's forces from crossing Vanns Creek. They

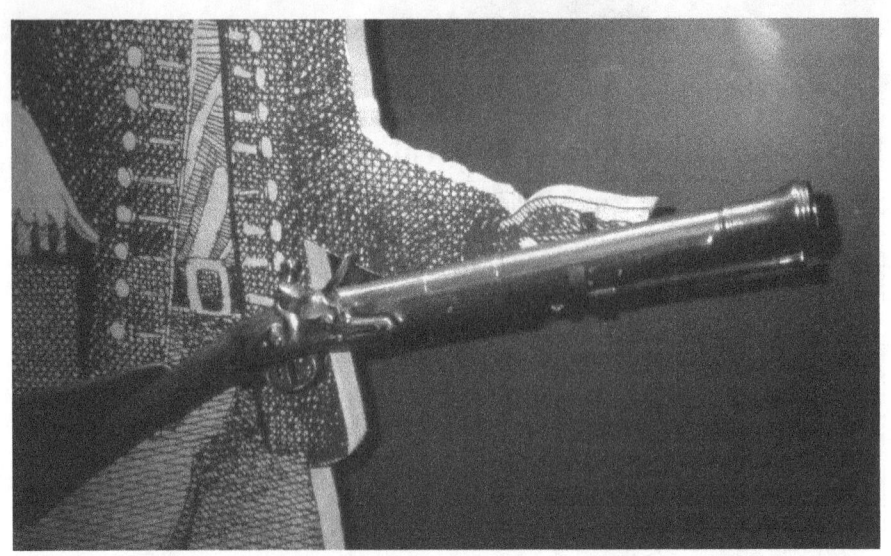

SC-44. A blunderbuss or musquetoon is used to fire shot with a scattering effect at close range. It is very effective for clearing a narrow passage, door of a house or staircase, or in boarding a ship.

arrived as the Loyalists were still crossing the river on Friday, February 12th. Most of the Loyalists were on the Georgia side when Anderson began his attack. The low ground and the cane brakes along the riverbank shielded many of Boyd's men, some of whom crossed the river and attacked Anderson from behind. Caught between two overwhelming forces, Anderson retreated to Cherokee Ford. He lost one man killed, 15 wounded, and 18 captured. Boyd probably lost about 100 men, most of them deserters.

Anderson rejoined Colonel Andrew Pickens's (1739–1817) main force which had crossed from South Carolina into Georgia at Cedar Shoals. Reinforced by Anderson's retreating men, Pickens had about 400 men to confront Boyd and the Loyalists as they proceeded toward Augusta. Pickens caught up with Boyd and defeated him at Kettle Creek on Saturday, February 14th.[490]

See also **Cherokee Ford** (Feb. 10, 1779) and **Vanns Creek** (Feb. 12, 1779) in the Georgia chapter of the next volume, *The Guide to the American Revolutionary War in the Deep South and on the Frontier.*

Fountain Inn
Kellett's Blockhouse, Laurens County (June 1, 1779; Sept. 3, 1781)

> Joseph Kellett (1728–1785) and some neighbors built a blockhouse and palisade fort in Laurens County, about 1778, as a refuge and defense in the event of Cherokee attacks. To get to the blockhouse site, take exit 19 off route I-385 in Gray Court. Go south about 2.5 miles to route SC 101 west. Travel about 4.6 miles on SC 101 and turn right (northwest) on Greenpond Road (S-30-76). Go about 2.9 miles, then turn left (west) onto Knickerbocker Road (S-30-308). The blockhouse was on the left side of Knickerbocker Road, opposite the cemetery, before getting to the bridge over South Rabon Creek.

Captain Benjamin Kilgore's (ca. 1740–1810) company and another company were stationed at Kellett's blockhouse about 12 miles from Ellison's Fort around Tuesday, June

1, 1779. Some Cherokees killed a man about 2 miles from the blockhouse, scalped him and "left a war tomahawk sticking in his back and a war club laying at his head."[491]

★ A British officer and many Cherokees were killed at Kellett's blockhouse in an overnight skirmish on Monday, September 3, 1781.[492]

Iva
Wilson's Creek, Abbeville County (ca. 1779)
Mr. Corruthers killed and Adam Files captured

> The site of this incident is located on the Abbeville/Anderson County line 2.8 miles southeast of Iva in Anderson County. Wilson's Creek follows the Old Indian Line (new county line) for about 100 yards at the site.

Adam Files, Sr.'s (d. 1779) sons were out hunting horses sometime in 1779 when they encountered a band of Loyalists and Native Americans. One of the boys ran home to alert his father and the others in his house of the danger. Captain William Baskins (1737–1794) and his brother Hugh Baskins (1743–1797), who were also in the house, ran and escaped. An African-American woman, named Rose, ran away with William's infant child. She hid the child in a hollow log until the danger passed. Adam and his other sons, along with Mr. Corruthers (d. 1779), hid in Wilson's Creek, a tributary of Rocky River. The raiders shot Mr. Corruthers as he was ascending the bank of the creek. They also shot Adam Files, Sr. at his hiding place in the creek and took him prisoner. They took him across the Savannah River, tortured and killed him. Adam Files, Jr. and his brother managed to escape.[493]

Cedar Springs
Lawson's Fork, Spartanburg County (July 1780; ca. Nov. 21, 1781)
First Battle of Cedar Springs, Spartanburg County (July 13, 1780)
Second Battle of Cedar Springs (the Peach Orchard Fight, The Old Iron Works Engagement or Wofford's Iron Works), Spartanburg County (Aug. 8, 1780)
Clark's Ford, Newberry County (spring 1781)
James Woods killed, Spartanburg County (ca. Nov. 21, 1781)
Colonel John Woods killed, Spartanburg County (ca. Nov. 21, 1781)
Hilliard Thomas killed, Spartanburg County (ca. Nov. 21, 1781)
Duncan's Creek, Newberry County and Lawson's Fork, Spartanburg County (ca. Nov. 22, 1781)
John Boyce's house, Union County (ca. Nov. 24, 1781)

> The battle of Cedar Springs was fought in the area west of Kelsey Creek and Kelsey Creek Road where Carolina Country Club Road crosses Kelsey Creek. The site is 1.1 miles south of the junction of routes SC 56 (Cedar Springs Road) and SC 295 (Southport Road) on the southeast edge of Spartanburg. At the foot of the hill

occupied by the South Carolina Deaf and Blind School is a pipe on Carolina Country Club Road spewing the waters of an ancient spring known as Cedar Spring. The site, which is only about 1 mile from Wofford's Iron Works, gave its name to two little battles of the American War for Independence.

The site of Wofford's Iron Works and the historical marker are near the intersection of routes S-42-47 (Country Club Road) and S-42-30 (Whitestone-Glendale Road) near Lawson's Fork Creek in Spartanburg. It is about 1.25 miles north of the junction of routes S-42-30 (Whitestone-Glendale Road) and U.S. 176 (SC 9|South Pine Street). A state historical marker at the intersection of routes S-42-30 (Whitestone Glendale Road) and SC 295 (Southport Road) calls attention to Wofford's Iron Works (often called simply the Old Iron Works), the first of its kind in South Carolina. The Iron Works was erected in 1773 on Lawson's Fork Creek about 0.25 miles west of the intersection of routes S-42-47 (Country Club Road) and S-42-30 (Whitestone Glendale Road). It was an undershot mill that stood here until it was burned late in the American War for Independence. The mill race is a cut through a large flat rock that can still be seen.[494]

The running battle began at Green Spring, near where Old Canaan Road crosses Fairforest Creek, about 1.75 miles west-southwest of the intersection of routes SC 56 (Cedar Springs Road) and SC 295 (Southport Road). It ended near the Pacolet River, about 7 miles northeast, near Mitchell Street about 300 yards beyond South Main Street. The peach orchard was located along the north side of SC 295 (Southport Road) about 0.3 miles east of its intersection with route SC 34.

James Wood was killed at his home on Hanging Rock Road 1.9 miles south of Boiling Springs. To get there, take exit 75 off Interstate-85 and go north on route SC 9 (Boiling Springs Road) for about 0.3 miles. Turn left (west) onto 4th Street and go to the end. Turn left (south) on Valley Falls Road (SC 79) and go about 85 yards, then turn right (west-northwest) onto Hanging Rock Road and go about 0.6 miles to the site on the left side of the road.

To get to the site of Colonel John Wood's house, return to Valley Falls Road and turn right (south). Proceed about 0.5 miles on Valley Falls Road. Make a hard left turn (northeast) onto Ranch Road (S-42-8390) and go to its end. This is the closest land access to the site, which is about 450 yards ahead, on the opposite side of Lawson's Fork Creek.

Clark's Ford crosses the Enoree River in the Sumter National Forest about 8.75 miles southeast of the town of Whitmire.

Duncan's Creek is on the Enoree River in Sumter National Forest about 1.4 miles south of Whitmire. The action occurred between where route U.S. 176 (Whitmire Highway)|SC 121 crosses Duncan Creek to where route SC 66 crosses it about 1.6 miles due west.

Mr. Lawson was killed near the western end of Lake Saranac about 4.25 miles due northeast of Spartanburg. From the intersection of route U.S. 29 and Plainview Drive and Zion Hill Road, go northwest on Plainview Drive about 0.6 miles, then turn right onto Saranac Drive and go about 0.6 miles. The site is on the left about 50 yards from the road.

Major William "Bloody Bill" Cunningham's men were hanged south of Whitmire, Newberry County, near the intersection of routes U.S. 176 (Whitmire Highway)|SC 121 and S-36-578, 190 yards south of South Church Street.

> Hilliard Thomas may have been killed on Lewis Chapel Road about 30 yards northeast of its intersection with Whitestone Glendale Highway (S-42-30).
> John Snoddy (1762–1781) may have been killed about 200 yards northwest of the intersection of Old Wofford Iron Works Road and Glen Forest Boulevard.
> John Boyce's house may have been about 3 miles east of Whitmire. From the intersection of routes U.S. 176 (Whitmire Highway) and SC 72 and 121, proceed east on SC 72 and 121 (Carlisle Whitmire Highway) for about 1.6 miles, then turn right (south) onto Maybinton Road (S-44-45) and go about 1.35 miles. The site is on the left about 0.9 miles from the road.[495]

Major Joseph Dickson (1745–1825) and Captain William Johnston (d. 1850) searched for any escaped Loyalists after the battle of Ramsour's Mill (North Carolina, June 20, 1780). They overtook Captain Patrick Moore's troops at Lawson's Fork in July 1780. (Patrick Moore was the brother of Colonel John Moore (1758–1836) who commanded the Loyalists at Ramsour's Mill.) A brief skirmish ensued. Captains Moore and Johnston personally fought each other. Johnston received several wounds on his head and the thumb of his right hand, but he captured Moore and escorted him to friendly forces nearby. When they encountered a mounted British patrol, Johnston tried to fire his musket but the blood from his wounded thumb wet the priming charge and his musket would not fire. Captain Moore escaped and Captain Johnston jumped into a nearby thicket to elude the dragoons.[496]

First Battle
★ Captain John Thomas, Sr. (1720–1811) owned Cedar Springs. He was in prison at Ninety Six with two of his sons for violating their parole in July 1780. Colonel John Thomas, Jr. (1751–1819) and his regiment of 168 men used Cedar Springs as a campsite as they prepared to join Brigadier General Thomas Sumter's (1734–1832) army.

While visiting her husband in prison at Ninety Six on Wednesday, July 12, 1780, Mrs. Jane Black Thomas (1720–1811) overheard two of the Loyalist soldiers' wives discussing the plans to attack the younger Thomas's encampment at Cedar Springs. She left Ninety Six before dawn and rode 60 miles nonstop, arriving at Cedar Springs on the night of July 13, to warn her son.

Colonel Thomas waited for the attack. He left his campfires burning the following evening and moved his 60 soldiers to the rear. The enemy force of 150 volunteer mounted riflemen and 60 well-equipped dragoons spotted the fires and charged into the empty camp. Immediately, they came under heavy fire from Colonel Thomas's regiment. The Loyalists lost 28 killed and several wounded before retreating. Thomas had four killed and 23 wounded, all with the broadsword.

Second Battle
★ The second battle was fought nearby three weeks later, on Tuesday, August 8, 1780. It has a variety of names: the Second Battle of Cedar Springs, the Peach Orchard Fight, and the Old Iron Works Engagement or Wofford's Iron Works. It was a running battle with most of the action taking place about half-way between the spring and the iron works.

Lieutenant Colonel William Washington (1752–1810) had his horses shod at Wofford's Iron Works as Colonel Daniel Morgan (1736–1802) retreated from Lieutenant Colonel Banastre Tarleton (1744–1833) before the Battle of Cowpens. Colonel Elijah Clarke (1733–1799) was on his way from Georgia to North Carolina with his militia regiment to join the Continental Army in late July 1780. Major Patrick Ferguson (1744–1780), upon hearing this news, dispatched Major James Dunlap (d. 1781) and 14 mounted American Volunteers and 130 militiamen to intercept Clarke.

Colonel Isaac Shelby (1750–1826), Colonel Elijah Clarke (1733–1799), and William Graham (1742–1835), in command of an army of 1,000 men, were alerted at dawn on Tuesday, August 8, 1780, that Major James Dunlap and a sizable detachment of Major Patrick Ferguson's (1744–1780) dragoons and mounted riflemen were on the move. The Whigs hurried from their camp near Cedar Springs to Wofford's Iron Works, on Lawson's Fork Creek, where they prepared to defend themselves.

Along the way Dunlap saw three of Clarke's horsemen, chased them, captured two of them, and pursued the last man into the center of Clarke's camp at the Iron Works. One of Major Dunlap's soldiers fired a musket that alerted the enemy to the danger. The man pretended that his musket went off accidentally and was not suspected of treason.

Patrols from both armies met in a peach orchard as Major Dunlap's party was gathering peaches. The Whigs fired on them and chased them away. As the Whigs entered the orchard, they came under fire. Hearing the gunfire, Shelby sent a strong detachment. The captain of the patrol, seeing Shelby's men approaching, withdrew his men to the cover of a fence along the ridge at the edge of the field in front of the woodland. The Whigs were greatly outnumbered in the furious conflict until Shelby's reinforcements arrived to change the tide. Clarke's and Shelby's forces now confronted the entire Crown force of 600 to 700 men. Clarke's men fought with such great energy and skill that Shelby often said that he stopped in the midst of the engagement to watch Clarke fight. Clarke received two saber wounds, one on the back of his neck and one on his head. The buckle of his neck stock saved his life. He was captured by two of Dunlap's men but he knocked them down a few minutes later and escaped. Dunlap was slightly wounded.

Dunlap charged the Iron Works twice and realized his men could not overcome the well-entrenched Whigs, so they began a retreat. The Crown forces lost 50 prisoners, most of them British, including some officers. Ferguson wanted to retake the prisoners so he pursued for 5 miles and maintained a running battle. The Carolinians slowed him down so much that the prisoners were soon out of reach. Dunlap retreated until he re-joined with Ferguson and the main army. They headed back to the Iron Works for another attack; but Clarke and Shelby had already withdrawn and resumed their march toward North Carolina. The half-hour battle was indecisive but it led to gradually increasing Whig supremacy in the region. One of the dead men supposedly had some peaches in his pocket when he was buried in a mass grave. A peach tree later grew there and bore fruit for years afterward. The tree has long since disappeared and the grave can no longer be located.[497]

★ The Whigs and Loyalists fought a fierce skirmish at Clark's Ford on the Enoree River in the Spring of 1781. Captain Thomas Jones (1740–1781), the Whig commander, and John Clark, the owner of the land at the ford, were wounded and captured by the Loyalists as Jones tried to summon reinforcements.[498]

★ Major William "Bloody Bill" Cunningham (d. 1787) rode to John Boyce's (1745–1806) house, known as Walnut Grove, on Evans Creek in the southern portion of Union County in November 1781. Boyce had just returned home to his family after fighting at Kings Mountain, Cowpens and Eutaw Springs. He heard horses approaching as he sat down to dinner one evening. He rushed to the door, saw "Bloody Bill" and his gang, and knew that he would die if he did not escape. He ran directly toward the Loyalists' horses and threw his hat in their faces and continued running into the woods.

"Bloody Bill" Cunningham caught up with him and struck Boyce with his sword. Boyce defended himself with his hand and the blow almost severed three fingers. Cunningham's horse couldn't follow Boyce in the thick woods.

When Boyce saw Cunningham and his men ride away, he mounted his horse and rode to Captain Christopher Casey's, his militia commander's, house. Casey mustered 15 men and pursued the Loyalists, capturing four stragglers at Duncan's Creek on the Enoree River. Captain Casey took his prisoners to the intersection of Charlestown Road and Ninety Six Road (Newberry County) and hanged them from a hickory tree. He then buried them at the foot of the tree.

★ After raiding Walnut Grove, Major William "Bloody Bill" Cunningham (d. 1787) rode to James Wood's (d. 1781) house on Lawson's Fork around Wednesday, November 21, 1781 Wood was a prominent Whig and the Commissioner of Sequestered Property. Cunningham dragged him out of his house and shot him. Wood's wife begged for her husband's life, as he lay wounded, but Cunningham hanged him from a dogwood tree.

★ The Loyalists hated and feared Colonel John Wood, a prominent Whig and brother of James Wood (d. 1781). Both brothers lived on Lawson's Fork. Colonel Wood's house was about 5 miles north of what is now Spartanburg. Colonel Wood was home recuperating from an illness. He had nearly recovered and was preparing to return to his command when Major William "Bloody Bill" Cunningham (d. 1787) raided the house. Had Cunningham arrived a day or two later, he would not have found Colonel Wood at home. The Loyalists surrounded the house. Colonel Wood went out to confront his enemies, followed by his wife and young son. Realizing that resistance was futile and that there was no possible way to escape, Colonel Wood offered to surrender. Cunningham ordered him to be shot, despite the pleas of his wife and son. His wife caught his lifeless corpse in her arms as he fell and gently laid his body on the ground. The raiders then pillaged the house, taking any valuables they could carry.[499]

★ Major William "Bloody Bill" Cunningham (d. 1787) then visited the house of a Mr. John Lawson (d. 1781) who lived near the Zion Hill Church. Lawson and another man were standing in the doorway when Cunningham arrived just before sunset. Cunningham shot and killed Lawson. The other man escaped through the back door. The gang then went to Hilliard Thomas's (d. 1781) house. When they rode up to the door at sunset, Mr. Thomas came out to greet them, Cunningham shot and killed him. Another man in the house escaped out the back.[500]

★ Major William "Bloody Bill" Cunningham (d. 1787) and his Loyalist militiamen camped at Wofford's Iron Works on Wednesday, November 21, 1781. Either before arriving at, or after leaving, Wofford Iron Works, Cunningham went to John Snoddy's (1762–1781) house and killed him. Before leaving the next morning, he set fire to the buildings. An account by an eyewitness says Major William Young, Sr. (1730/35–1787) led this raid. Young owned a plantation adjacent to Benjamin Wofford's property on James' Creek, now Jimmies Creek, which is a branch of the South Tyger River before he became a Loyalist in 1779.[501]

Green Spring (Aug. 8, 1780) see **Union County and vicinity** p. 15
Wofford's Iron Works (Old Iron Works) (2nd Cedar Springs)
(Aug. 8, 1780)
This engagement is also known as the Second Battle of Cedar Springs and is sometimes dated Aug. 1, 1780. See **Second Battle of Cedar Springs, the Peach Orchard Fight, the Old Iron Works Engagement or Wofford's Iron Works** p. 283.

Cross Anchor, Spartanburg County
Musgrove Mill, Spartanburg County (Aug. 19, 1780)
Cross Anchor vicinity
Blackstock's Plantation, Union County (Nov. 20, 1780)
Tyger (Tiger) River, Spartanburg County

> The Musgrove Mill State Historic Site (see Photo SC-45) [398 State Park Road, Clinton, SC 29325 (website: **www.discoversouthcarolina.com/stateparks/parkdetail.asp?PID=3888**)] is on route SC 56, 3 miles south of Cross Anchor. The site and its interpretive center are a hub for the Cradle of Democracy project which seeks to further the understanding of South Carolina's pivotal role in the creation of the nation. A memorial stone on the ridge just north of the Enoree River and alongside route SC 56 marks Captain Shadrack Inman's (d. 1780) grave. The Continental camp was probably along Cedar Creek about 3 miles from where Captain Inman is buried. Vandals burned the Musgrove [Edward Gordon Musgrove (ca. 1716–1792)] house in 1971. Fighting occurred all along the route from the ambush to the river. The most intense fighting occurred about 1.4 miles due north of the Musgrove Mill State Historic Site along Avinger Road and across SC 56.
>
> Blackstock's plantation, also known as Blackstock, is on the south side of the Tyger (Tiger) River, about 3.7 miles due northeast of Cross Anchor. To get to Blackstock's plantation from the intersection of routes SC 49 and SC 56 in Cross Anchor, take route SC 49 east 2.3 miles to Blackstock Road (S-44-51). There's a historical marker and a sign for Blackstock Battlefield at this intersection. Turn left on

SC-45. Musgrove Mill. Vandals burned the Musgrove house in 1971. The Musgrove Mill State Historic Site preserves what remains of the house and site.

> Blackstock Road and go 1.2 miles to a fork in the road. Battlefield Road bears to the right and Monument Road to the left. Follow Monument Road to the end where there's a sign and a stone monument (see Photo SC-46) on a prominent hill to mark the site of this engagement. None of the plantation buildings remain.

After the British returned to South Carolina and occupied Charleston in May 1780, Loyalist support began to increase, causing fear throughout the region. Two days after the defeat of Major General Horatio Gates (1728–1806) at the Battle of Camden, Colonels James Williams (1740–1780), Elijah Clarke (1733–1799), and Isaac Shelby (1750–1826) led about 200 militiamen to attack a Loyalist force consisting of the First Battalion of DeLancey's Brigade and the Third Battalion of the New Jersey Volunteers, both under the command of Colonel Alexander Innes (ca. 1737–post 1791), and a detachment of the South Carolina Royalists militia regiment, under Major James Fraser, near Edward Musgrove's plantation on the Enoree River on Friday, August 18, 1780.

The attackers learned that the Crown forces had been reinforced during the night and now numbered about 500, so they decided to ambush the Loyalists instead of attacking them. The Congressional forces hastily assembled a semicircular breastwork of fallen trees and brush 2 miles upriver from the Loyalist camp. A volunteer unit of 25 horsemen, led by Captain Shadrack Inman (d. 1780), attacked and fired into the Loyalist camp and raced back toward the ambush position. The lure worked well. The Loyalists ran right into the concealed riflemen who held their fire "till they could distinguish the buttons on their clothes." The Whigs waited for the Loyalists to get within 70 yards before the first shot was fired, followed by a volley. The Loyalists rallied and began gaining on the Whigs' right flank when their leader was wounded. The Whig right charged,

SC-46. Blackstock's battlefield marker

forcing the Loyalists back. The Loyalists retreated, then fled. The Whigs, outnumbered more than two to one, killed 63 Loyalists, wounded 90, and captured 70 while only losing four dead and eight wounded, including Inman who was fatally shot in the forehead by a retreating Loyalist.

The Whig forces left the area before enemy reinforcements arrived. During the retreat, the men ate green peaches and raw corn which, coupled with lack of sleep and exposure to the sun, blackened their faces and led to swelling of the eyes. After recuperating, the units separated. Clarke returned to Georgia. Shelby went to the Watauga in North Carolina to recruit additional militiamen. Williams took the prisoners to Hillsborough, North Carolina, where he later claimed credit for the victory.

The Battle of Musgrove Mill showed that militiamen could perform just as effectively as professional soldiers in some cases. It also demonstrated that Whig militiamen could still maneuver and defeat Loyalist units despite a devastating defeat only days earlier.

Major Joseph McJunkin (1755–1846) records:

> It was soon ascertained that the enemy were formed near the ford of the river with the intention of giving battle. A corresponding preparation took place among the Whigs. The command of Williams was placed in the centre. That of Shelby on the right and that of Clark on the left. At his own request Captain Inman was sent forward with a party to skirmish with the enemy at the moment they began to peep forward and gave them a hot reception. The word of command passed along the American line, "Reserve your fire until you can see the whites of their eyes!" Meanwhile, Inman's command gradually fell back from place to place until the enemy made a general charge under the impression that they were driving the main body of the British and Tories were rushing forward in the utmost confusion within seventy yards of their foes. A stream of fire revealed the hidden battalions of liberty. The British sank down in great numbers, the survivors recoiled, rallied and again pressed forward, but the fire from the American line continued with little abatement for one hour to thin their ranks, while their own produced little effect.
>
> Cuthbertson's party, under cover of trees, was pouring in a deadly fire upon the flank and rear. Innis and other leaders were shot down and the whole of the royal forces fell back in consternation. Captain Inman immediately rallied a party and pursued the fugitives to the river, but this onset proved fatal to the gallant Inman. In this engagement the royal force exceeded that of the Americans by at least 300. The British lost sixty-three killed and 160 wounded and prisoners. The American loss was four killed and nine wounded.

The Whigs were greatly exhilarated by the result of this conflict. They mounted their horses with the determination of being at Ninety Six that night. At this moment, an express arrived with a letter from Brigadier General Charles McDowell (1743–1815) for Colonel Shelby and one from Governor Richard Caswell (1729–1789) dated on the battleground where Gates's defeat occurred, giving an account of that disastrous engagement. McDowell advised Shelby and his companions to provide for their own safety. This intelligence led to a change of operations. It was necessary to avoid Major Patrick Ferguson's (1744–1780) army, which lay between them and McDowell. And there was a strong probability that Ferguson would lose no time in pursuing.[502]

★ Captain William Blackstock's (1710/1720–1798) plantation was situated on high hills on the Tyger River's west bank. It was an advantageous position for Brigadier General Thomas Sumter (1734–1832) when he stopped there about 4 PM on Monday, November 20, 1780, to strike at Lieutenant Colonel Banastre Tarleton (1744–1833) who was pursuing him. The river protected the plantation's rear and part of its right side. The front of the plantation dropped down to a creek which was bordered by a fence and brushwood. Sumter placed some of his men in the barn and some in small outbuildings on the farm. He put the rest of his 1,000 men near the tops of the hills running roughly northwest of the farm and sent some men forward.

Tarleton, expecting Sumter to cross the Tyger, approached with an advanced corps of about 250 men to try to block him a little after 5 PM. However, Tarleton relented and decided to wait for the rest of his force before attacking. Sumter decided to strike before Tarleton's main force arrived. He placed his center on high ground around five log houses and along a rail fence. Colonel Elijah Clarke (1733–1799) led 100 Georgians around Tarleton's right flank to encircle it and to block the advance of his reinforcements. Sumter led the main attack with 400 militiamen against 80 dismounted Regulars of the 63rd Regiment.

The attack surprised Tarleton but he rallied quickly. He sent his infantry forward, forcing Sumter to retreat back up the hill. The men positioned on the ridge line blasted Tarleton's troops. Tarleton led a charge but was forced back by the forces on Sumter's right and left. Tarleton attempted a charge on Sumter's left where the hill was less steep. He gained the hilltop after pushing through a stubborn group of Georgia militiamen, but the militiamen in the barn stopped Tarleton's advance and forced him to retreat.

The battle left three militiamen dead and five wounded, including Sumter who was hit in the chest and right shoulder with buckshot. His wounds incapacitated him for several months. Tarleton's casualties totaled about 50 killed and wounded.[503]

Saluda River
Rutledge's Ford, Abbeville County (Nov. 1780)
Hoil's Old Place, Greenville County

> Rutledge's Ford was on the Saluda River about where Erwin (Ervin) Mill Road crosses it. The Saluda River forms the northeastern boundary of Saluda County and flows into Lake Murray. This rocky ford was located about three quarters of a mile south of the Indian Boundary line which now divides Anderson and Greenville counties from Abbeville and Laurens counties. The ford has been replaced by a bridge on a secondary road.
>
> Hoil's Old Place was in the vicinity of where SC 86 (Main Street) crosses the Saluda River in Piedmont, Greenville County. It was about 19 miles due north-northwest of Rutledge's Ford or about 26 miles by river. An early settler in Ninety Six District was named Hoyle and the site was probably named after him. The Loyalists erected a fort at this location.

Brigadier General Thomas Sumter's (1734–1832) forces headed north after the battle of Blackstock's. The Georgians under Colonel Elijah Clarke (1733–1799), Colonel John Twiggs (1750–1816), and Colonel Benjamin Few (1744–) or (1763–1815) headed west when they passed Lawson's Fork Creek. The South Carolina militia under Samuel Hammond (1757–1842), Lieutenant Colonel James McCall (1741–1781) and Captain Moses Liddell (1755–1802) joined them. They headed to a Loyalist fort known as Hoil's Old Place on the Saluda River. The Loyalists learned of the approaching army and abandoned the fort. They crossed the Saluda River at Rutledge's Ford, about 19 miles downstream, where they exchanged rifle fire with the Whigs at long range across Rutledge Shoals. Both sides lost several men killed. Clarke's army then headed to Long Cane, a pro-Whig settlement, on their way to the fort at Ninety Six.[504]

Near Troy, McCormick County
Long Cane, McCormick County (Dec. 4, 1780; Dec. 11, 1780; Jan. 1781)
Near Ninety Six, McCormick County (Dec. 15, 1780)

The skirmish at Long Cane was fought on the same creek where 150 settlers were murdered in a Cherokee attack on February 1, 1760. One authority places the battlefield at Long Cane Creek (see Photo SC-47) near route SC 28 about 5.5 miles southwest of Troy. Another places it about 0.25 miles west of Troy off route S-24-24 (Church Street West). To get to Church Street West, take Main Street West off route SC 10 (Twigg Street). Follow the signs to Indian Massacre Grave (on Greenwood Street) just before it turns onto Church Street West. Proceeding a little further, route S-24-24 (Church Street West) leads to Hall Street which comes to a fork. Take the right branch (Charleston Road) for 2.4 miles to the site of the massacre. The left branch (Murrell Street) will lead to the battle site, 0.7 miles down the road.

The Long Cane action probably began around Mount Sinai Road about 3 miles north of Troy. It was a running battle covering about 4.5 to 6 miles in a big arc from its beginning near the Crown camp, through Georgia militia Colonel Elijah Clarke's camp, to its end at Georgia militia Colonel Benjamin Few's camp. The Crown camp may have been on the east end of Mount Sinai Road (also known as Puckett Town Road) where it meets route SC 10 (McCormick Highway). Clarke's camp may have been at the fork in the Reedy Branch, about 3.6 miles west of the Crown camp. Few's camp was probably near route S-33-117, about 2 miles southwest of Clarke's camp. The graves of the victims of the Long Cane Massacre are about 0.4 miles

SC-47. Long Cane Creek. The skirmish at Long Cane was fought along Long Cane Creek near where 150 settlers were murdered in a Cherokee attack on February 1, 1760.

Western South Carolina 291

> away near route S-33-141 on the right. There are state historical markers on Main Street west of Twigg Street South (SC 10) in Troy and another on route SC 28, 2 miles north of route S-33-38 (Old Charleston Road) that recount the Battle of Long Cane.

Captain Richard Creech, Captain Joshua Inman and Captain Patrick ("Paddy") Carr or Samuel Kerr (1741–1781) commanded companies in Colonel James McCoy's regiment. They engaged in a skirmish with the Crown forces at Long Cane on Monday, December 4, 1780. Captain Kerr, of the Rangers was mortally wounded.[505]

★ Colonel Elijah Clarke (1733–1799) led an advance column of 100 men and headed to Long Cane (about 30 miles southwest of Ninety Six). He hoped to gain the support of the populace, get some new recruits and eventually raise enough men to attack the fort at Ninety Six. Colonel Benjamin Few (1744–) or (1763–1815) and some Georgia Loyalists joined them, and Few took command. Lieutenant Colonel John Harris Cruger (1738–1807), commander of the fort at Ninety Six, learned of Clarke's plans and sent Lieutenant Colonel Isaac Allen (1741–1806) to stop them. Colonel Allen left Ninety Six on Sunday December 10, 1780 with 200 British Regulars, 200 Loyalists and 50 dragoons, hoping to take Clarke and Few by surprise. They marched about 20 miles and halted on Monday afternoon, camping about 3 miles from Few's camp.

Some of Colonel Allen's foragers bumped into one of Colonel Clarke's patrols and a brief skirmish ensued. The Whigs drove the foragers back and discovered the Crown camp. Few ordered Clarke, Colonel James McCall (1741–1781), and Major John Lindsay (1750–1780) to begin the action and to sustain it until he could bring up the main body. Clarke, McCall, and Lindsay advanced about a mile and a half, dismounted, and tied their horses about 100 yards in front of the Loyalist militiamen and engaged them, chasing them into their camp. They were unaware that Colonel Allen and the Provincials were on the other side of a hill, unseen. Clarke discovered the trap when his men came within 40 yards of the Provincials.

Although badly outnumbered, Clarke's men held their own for a while and even forced the Loyalists to retreat after about 10 minutes. Some of them fled; others formed behind the Regulars. Clarke sent another messenger to Colonel Few, urging him to hurry. However, Colonel Few failed to bring up the main body and ordered a full retreat instead, leaving six wagons and 30 head of cattle to be captured. Colonel Allen's men fired a volley and the British Regulars charged Clarke's men with the bayonet. The Loyalists came up on Clarke's flank and forced them to flee.

Clarke was wounded in the shoulder and was carried from the field. McCall was also wounded when his horse was killed and fell on him. McCall barely escaped with his life. With all their leaders fallen, the Whig forces retreated east toward Troy and crossed the Saluda River on Wednesday morning. The Loyalists chased them for 2 miles or more but stopped as nightfall approached. Captain Lang of the dragoons sabered Major Lindsay on the head and arms and cut off one of his hands as he lay on the ground. Fourteen Whigs were killed, seven wounded and nine captured. Several others, who were wounded and unable to resist, were also slain. Seven wounded men escaped. The Crown forces claim to have killed and wounded about 60 and admitted losing two militiamen killed, six wounded, and three Regulars wounded. Captain John Lindsay [Lindsey] (1750–1808) recovered from his wound and was "compensated for the loss of his right hand by covering it with an ornamental silver bandage. From this, Lindsay became known as 'Old Silver Fist.'"[506]

★ Colonel Benjamin Few's Georgia militiamen clashed with some Crown forces near Ninety Six on Friday, December 15, 1780. They had about 10 men wounded.[507]

★ General Charles Cornwallis (1738–1805) ordered Colonel John Harris Cruger (1738–1807), commander of the fort at Ninety Six, to seize "Negroes, cattle and other property" that might be useful to the Whigs in January 1781. Cruger delegated the task to Major James Dunlap (d. 1781) who took his dragoons to the Long Canes to plunder the home of Lieutenant Colonel James McCall (1741–1781). They abused McCall's wife and daughter and burned Colonel Andrew Pickens's (1739–1817) farm, driving his family into the woods where one of his children died of smallpox. This led General Pickens to notify Colonel Cruger that he considered his parole violated. (Pickens turned himself in and had been paroled after Charleston had surrendered.) General Pickens resumed his military activities and became a major enemy of the Crown forces in the Carolina backwoods.[508]

Clinton, Laurens County
Hammond's Store, Laurens County (Dec. 28 or 30, 1780)
Williams's Fort, Laurens County (Dec. 31, 1780)

> Hammond's Storehouse most likely was 3 miles south of Clinton. Take route SC 56 (Jacobs Highway) south for about 0.9 miles, then bear right (southwest) onto route SC 72 (Broad Street). Go about 2.4 miles, then turn left onto Greenplain Road (S-30-50) and go about 1.3 miles. The site was where the house is located on the left.
>
> Williams's plantation, also known as Mudlick and Mount Pleasant, was probably 5.5 miles due east of Cross Hill, near Mud Lick Creek. From Cross Hill, take route SC 560 east for about 5.25 miles, then turn right onto Mountville Road (S-30-38) and go about 1 mile to the locked gate. This is the closest public access to the site.

On Christmas Day 1780, Brigadier General Daniel Morgan (1736–1802) established a camp at Grindal Shoals on the Pacolet River (Union County) where Colonel Andrew Pickens (1739–1817) and Lieutenant Colonel James McCall (1741–1781) joined him with about 100 men. Colonel Elijah Clarke (1733–1799) was absent, still recovering from his wounds at Long Cane. Major John Cunningham (1750–1829) led Clarke's men.

General Morgan received intelligence that Colonel Thomas Waters (ca. 1738–after 1810) had gotten about 250 Georgia Loyalist militiamen together at Fair Forest and that they were destroying the settlements of Whig families between Ninety Six and Winnsboro. Morgan sent Lieutenant Colonel William Washington (1752–1810) and his band of 80 3rd Continental Light Dragoons and 200 of Lieutenant Colonel James McCall's mounted militiamen on a 40-mile ride to stop the Loyalist plundering on Thursday, December 28, 1780.

The Loyalists heard of the force sent to destroy them and moved about 20 miles away to Hammond's Store on the Bush River, in Laurens County. Here, on Saturday, December 30, 1780, Washington's dragoons attacked a force of 250 Loyalist raiders sent from Savannah to upstate South Carolina. The Loyalists could not offer effective resistance so they tried to flee. Washington's dragoons, in hot pursuit, hacked them to pieces, killing or wounding 150 and taking 40 prisoners without any loss of his own men.

Thomas Young (1764–1848), a militiaman riding with Washington that day, wrote in his memoirs:

When we came in sight, we perceived that the Tories had formed in line on the brow of the hill opposite to us. We had a long hill to descend and another to rise. Colonel Washington and his dragoons gave a shout, drew swords, and charged down the hill like madmen. The Tories fled In every direction without firing a gun. We took a great many prisoners and killed a few.

He also wrote of an incident during the massacre:

In Washington's corps there was a boy of fourteen or fifteen, a mere lad, who in crossing Tiger River was ducked by a blunder of his horse. The men laughed and jeered at him very much, at which he got very mad, and swore that boy or no boy, he would kill a man that day or die. He accomplished the former. I remember very well being highly amused at the little fellow charging round a crib after a Tory, cutting and slashing away with his puny arm, till he brought him down.

Waters escaped with 60 men. They were chased for 7 miles in a running fight south down what is now route 56. The chase ended about 3 miles from the Loyalist Fort Williams (Williams's plantation). The Whigs attacked the fort the next day.[509]

★ The next day, Sunday, December 31, 1780, Lieutenant Colonel William Washington (1752–1810) detached Colonel Joseph Hayes (d. 1781) and a small body of troops to capture Williams's Fort, now occupied by Loyalist Colonel Moses Kirkland (1730–1787) after James Williams (1740–1780) was killed at Kings Mountain. Mary Williams and her six children were moved into some outbuildings on other land that Williams owned. Brigadier General Robert Cunningham (1741–1813) joined Kirkland at the plantation after he defeated the Whig militia at Long Cane.

When Colonel Hayes arrived at the gate of the fort, he demanded General Cunningham and Colonel Kirkland to surrender. General Cunningham asked for time to consult with his officers but the Loyalists escaped through the rear of the fort into the woods. Colonel Hayes's men spotted a few of them and killed them, but most escaped. The Whigs then gathered all the supplies they could and destroyed the fort and the mills.

These actions caused General Charles Cornwallis (1738–1805) to send Lieutenant Colonel Banastre Tarleton (1744–1833), "Bloody Ban," to pursue Brigadier General Daniel Morgan (1736–1802). The two clashed at the Cowpens.[510]

Clinton
Hurricane Meeting House (Dec. 30, 1780)

> Hurricane Meeting House was on Hurricane Church Road near the intersection with Double A Trail. Take route U.S. 76 from Clinton; go east for about 3 miles, then turn left onto Hurricane Church Road. The church is on the right about 1.6 miles down the road. The field where the action took place is on the left.

On the way to Hammond's Store, the Whigs captured three stragglers from the Loyalist force near the Hurricane Meeting House on Saturday, December 30, 1780. The prisoners disclosed the location of the main Loyalist force and the number of men at Hammond's Store.[511]

Backcountry (Dec. 1780 or Jan. 1781)

> The Sumter papers mention this incident but don't give a date or location.

A British patrol wounded Lieutenant Colonel James Hawthorne (1750–1809) in late 1780 or early 1781. The musket ball entered under the right breast and exited near the spinal column without injuring his lungs. A party of Crown troops intercepted the small escort taking him to the New Acquisition (York County) settlements to recuperate. The escorts fled, but Captain Thomas Neal, Jr. (d. 1781), his brother in law, remained with the colonel to fight. They drove off the attackers and escaped.

The escorts who had fled reported that Colonel Hawthorne and Thomas Neal, Jr. had been killed, so "there was a great rejoicing when they arrived safe." Shortly after his return, Colonel Hawthorne and Colonel John Lacey (1755–1814) rode to an old deserted warehouse where they found some British soldiers chasing chickens. They raised their rifles and fired at the same time, killing two soldiers. They retreated quickly; but, when his mare fell behind, Hawthorne rode into the brush where he hid until the soldiers left.[512]

Mann's Old Field (Jan. 1781)

The site of Mann's Old Field is unknown but it was probably near Cowpens in the vicinity of Gaffney. The site of William Farr's home was probably about 1.5 miles northwest of Fishdam Ford at the intersection of routes S-44-113 (River Road) and S-44-113 (Woodyard Road) about 1.7 miles northeast of Carlisle, in Union County. His grave is near River Road, about 0.5 miles northeast of this intersection.

Colonel William Farr (1729–1794) took a "squad of Irishmen" and pursued the Crown forces after the battle of Cowpens. He "caught the Tories with their booty in the savage neighborhood near Mann's Old Field" and routed them in a brief skirmish after "killing many of them." He recaptured some stolen property. Some Loyalists took advantage of Farr's absence to occupy his house. When he learned of this, Colonel Farr took several companions and "approached the house cautiously." The Loyalists fled, suspecting a trap. Farr killed a Loyalist with his sword as the man tried to come out the door. The men then pursued the Loyalists and killed several more.[513]

Gaffney, Spartanburg County
"Burr's" (Byces, Byas) Mill (Jan. 15, 1781 middle of July)
Bullock's Ford, Thicketty Creek (June 1780 or mid-July 1780)

Grindal Shoals is located a few miles northeast of Jonesville, where route SC 18 (Union Highway) crosses the Pacolet River on the county line separating Union and Cherokee counties. It was the most noted ford on the Pacolet River during the American War for Independence. Grindal Shoals was a thriving community with grist mills on both sides of the river in the 18th century. "Burr's" Mill was on the north bank of Cowpens Creek about 900 yards south of route U.S. 29 (Old Georgia Highway) and about 0.6 miles west-southwest of the Thicketty Creek Watershed 25 Reservoir.

There are two Bullock's Creek Fords. One is near "Burr's" Mill in Cherokee County west of the Broad River. The other is east of the Broad River in Hickory Grove, Sharon. The first is a branch of Thicketty Creek located in Cherokee County. It is near where Thicketty Creek and Bullock's Creek meet about 15 miles northeast of Union in Gaffney. This is where Lieutenant Alexander Chesney's militiamen defeated a band of Whigs attempting to cross the ford. The other is the site of the battle of the Stallions, discussed above p. 17. The date of the action near "Burr's" mill is given as both June 1780 and mid-July 1780.[514]

Brigadier General Daniel Morgan (1736–1802) moved his 200 South Carolina and Georgia Continentals, and 140 North Carolina volunteers northward toward the Broad River on Sunday, January 14, 1781, where he arrived the following day. On the road to "Burr's" Mill, Captain George Gresham and some South Carolina militiamen surprised a small advanced party of Lieutenant Colonel Banastre Tarleton's (1744–1833) Legion and took two prisoners. They also captured a slave and two horses in the same or a related encounter.

Bullock's Ford, Thicketty Creek (June 1780) see **Union County and vicinity** (June 1780) p. 15.

Chesnee
Dugan's Plantation, Newberry County (Indian Creek) (Dec. 14, 1780; Jan. 18, 1781)
Cowpens, Cherokee County (Jan. 17, 1781)

Cowpens National Battlefield (see Photo SC-48) (website: **www.nps.gov/cowp/index.htm**) is 9 miles northwest of Gaffney and 18 miles northeast of Spartanburg, 0.2 miles east of the junction of state routes SC 11 and SC 110 (Battleground Road).

Sites of major action are marked by exhibits along a 1.2-mile walking trail and a 3-mile automobile tour road. The visitor center exhibits a lighted map tracing troop movements during the battle as well as oil paintings, woodcarvings, and weapons. It also shows a multi-media presentation, "Cowpens—A Battle Remembered." Standing at the northwestern end of the battlefield facing south, visitors can view the field of battle as Colonel Daniel Morgan saw it from his command post. The first line of militiamen was placed at the foot of rising ground with the Georgians on the left and the North Carolinians on the right. The men were lying down to conceal

SC-48. Cowpens battlefield

> themselves and Hayes's regiment stood atop the rise to draw the British. Colonel Andrew Pickens's 300 to 1,000 militiamen formed the second line about 150 yards in front of the Continentals in a low area largely hidden by the final rise more than 100 yards in front of them. Colonel John Eager Howard's 290 Continentals and an equal or greater number of others, similarly equipped with bayonets, held the third line about 15 yards behind the crest of the rising ground to hide them from view. A valley behind the third line concealed the reserve, Colonel William Washington's mounted troops.
>
> Hillhouse plantation was on the east side of Blanton Road which is about 6 miles south of Sharon and about 0.5 miles north of route SC 322 (West McConnells Highway|Highway 322) about 1.5 miles east of its intersection with SC 97.
>
> Major James Dugan's plantation was 4 miles north-northwest of exit 72 on I-26. It was about 400 yards east of where Beth Eden Road crosses Gilders Creek.

Colonel Joseph Hayes (d. 1781) and a party of 40 or 50 militiamen under captains Christopher Casey, James Ewing (ca. 1720–ca. 1800) and Harris of his own regiment and Captain Thomas Blasingame of Colonel Thomas Brandon's (1741–1802) regiment attacked about 25 Loyalist militiamen under Major Moses Buffington (d. 1782) at Major James Dugan's plantation, on Thursday, December 14, 1780. Major Buffington had not posted any sentries. The Whigs wounded Major Buffington and three of his men and took seven or eight prisoners. Buffington was listed as mortally wounded, but he didn't die until two years later. This action is commonly called Indian Creek, but it took place at Dugan's plantation which is on Gilder's Creek, a branch of Indian Creek.[515]

★ After the Battle of Kings Mountain on Saturday, October 7, 1780, General Charles Cornwallis (1738–1805) chose to remain in South Carolina. Major General Nathanael Greene (1742–1786), commissioned to reorganize the Continental forces, sent Colonel Daniel Morgan (1736–1802) to divert Cornwallis's attention from the bulk of the Continental forces. Morgan threatened Ninety Six, where there was a British fort, so Cornwallis dispatched Lieutenant Colonel Banastre Tarleton (1744–1833) to stop him.

When Tarleton caught up with Morgan on Wednesday, January 17, 1781, after marching most of the night on bad roads and through deep fords, he was west of Kings Mountain at a place called the "cow pens" because it was used as a spot to tend to breeding cattle. It was an open, sparsely forested area 6 miles from the Broad River. (This was the same location where the frontiersmen gathered to prepare for the Battle of Kings Mountain.) Morgan chose this site to make his stand less by design than by necessity, for he had intended to get across the Broad River. When he learned that Tarleton was only 10 miles away, he decided to prepare for battle rather than be surprised halfway across the river. Nevertheless, on ground seemingly better suited to the action of Regulars, Morgan achieved a little tactical masterpiece, making the most effective use of his heterogeneous force. Although both sides seemed pretty equal, with about 1,100 men each, Tarleton had about three times as many trained Regulars as Morgan and a cavalry of 300. However, Tarleton's reconnaissance was 24 hours old and he was unaware that 1,000 backcountry militiamen arrived to reinforce Morgan the night before the battle.

Selecting rising ground as the center of his position, Morgan placed his Maryland and Delaware Continentals on it, deliberately leaving his flanks open. It seems as if Morgan deliberately picked a place where his men couldn't run or hide and would have to fight. About 150 yards in front of the main line, he posted about 450 militia riflemen from the Carolinas, Georgia, and Virginia in two lines, instructing the first line to fire two volleys and then fall back on the second, the combined line to fire until the British pressed them, then to fall back to the rear of the Continentals and re-form as a reserve. This specific assignment lessened the possibility that the militia would break and run and lead the Continentals to panic.

Behind the militiamen, on a long ridge of rising ground, Morgan posted his regular troops (about 450 men), the Maryland, Delaware, and Virginia Continentals, commanded by Lieutenant Colonel John Eager Howard (1752–1827). In the valley behind the high ground (between the visitor center and the 1856 monument which marks the location of the Continental line), he placed Lieutenant Colonel William Washington's (1752–1810) cavalry (about 180 men, of whom 80 were Continentals), ready to charge the attacking enemy at the critical moment. All the men were rested, well prepared, and ready for the fight.

Tarleton could only see about 200 of Colonel Joseph Hayes's (d. 1781) militiamen standing atop the rise and thought that was all that opposed him. He ordered his soldiers to drop all equipment, except muskets and ammunition, and to attack immediately, expecting to drive the militiamen back into the river. His force slightly outnumbered Morgan's. He put his light infantry on the right, his Legion's infantry in the center, the 7th Regiment on the left, and 50 dragoons on each flank. He left 200 of his cavalry in reserve with the 1st Battalion of the 71st Highlanders. The British infantry advanced about 7 AM. When they got to within about 40 yards, the militiamen, sheltered behind the trees, took careful aim at the officers and sergeants and fired their first volley. They fired a second volley and withdrew. Taking the retreat of the first two lines to be the beginning of a rout, Tarleton's Highlanders rushed headlong into the steady fire of the Continentals on the hill, who outnumbered the Highlanders at least five to one.

Colonel Howard gave the order to "refuse the flank." The company on his far right attempted to comply by turning 90 degrees to the right to protect his flank against the 71st's fire. Immediately after firing a volley, they received a volley that threw them into confusion. The company marched to the rear, reloading their weapons. Morgan galloped up from the rear, attempting to re-form the company, reportedly shouting at them "Form! Form! my brave fellows. Give them one more brisk fire and the day is ours! Old Morgan was never beaten yet!" When the Continentals received a bayonet charge from the 71st, Morgan gave the order to wheel and fire, routing the British.

Tarleton ordered the 17th light dragoons after the retreating militiamen, but William Washington's fresh cavalry emerged, almost immediately, from behind the hill to strike Tarleton's right flank. Washington's cavalry now outnumbered Tarleton's dragoons by almost two to one because Tarleton had divided his force, keeping 200 dragoons in reserve. Washington forced Tarleton's Legion back, giving the militiamen time to re-form and charge out from behind the hill to hit the British left.

Tarleton and a few other officers with some 40 men of the 17th light dragoons made a last desperate charge to save the guns, but they were too late. Two hundred of Tarleton's dragoons refused to attack. The Continental cavalry chased them off the field. The British surrendered after suffering heavy losses—about 75% of Tarleton's command: 300 killed and wounded and 525 prisoners of war, two 3-pounders, two regimental flags, 800 muskets, 35 wagons of stores, 100 horses, and 60 slaves. The Continentals only lost 12 lives and about 58 wounded. The backcountry militiamen, more than half of Morgan's force, left after the battle, taking their dead and wounded with them, leaving them unaccounted for in Morgan's casualty count. Tarleton managed to escape with only a small force of cavalry he had left in reserve. The battle, which lasted about an hour, was on a small scale, and with certain significant differences, a repetition of the classic double envelopment of the Romans by a Carthaginian army under Hannibal at Cannae in 216 B.C.—an event of which Morgan, no reader of books, probably had no knowledge. The Battle of Cowpens wrecked Tarleton's feared Legion and ended his reputation of invincibility.[516]

★ Despite his victory at Parker's Ferry, Brigadier General Francis Marion (1732–1795) was still in a precarious position. General Charles Cornwallis (1738–1805) was in the field with a much larger army and could be nearby. Cornwallis and Lieutenant Colonel Banastre Tarleton (1744–1833) were heading to Kings Mountain to cut off Brigadier General Daniel Morgan's (1736–1802) retreat from Cowpens Mountain.

However, Cornwallis may have feared an attack on his right flank from the army of Major General Nathanael Greene (1742–1786) and Brigadier General Isaac Huger (1743–1797). Only a few miles from Camden, Cornwallis waited a week, until General Alexander Leslie (1740–1794) had crossed the Wateree River on his way to join him. Instead of being at Cowpens on the day of the battle, Cornwallis was 60 miles to the southeast at Hillhouse plantation in York County. Even so, he was a threat to Morgan.

Tarleton's fleeing cavalry brought Cornwallis news of the battle five or six hours afterward. If Cornwallis marched light and quickly, he might be able to intercept Morgan's column which was encumbered with prisoners that numbered nearly two-thirds of Morgan's force.

Cornwallis and his army had camped at Turkey Creek which was about the same distance as from Ramsour's Mills, the route which Morgan had to travel from Cowpens to escape to the north. Both roads met at Ramsour's Mills. However, Cornwallis delayed his departure from Turkey Creek until January 19th, and thereby let his prey escape.[517]

★ Major James Dugan (d. 1781) took a British officer's sword during the battle of Cowpens (Wednesday, January 17, 1781) and brought it to his nearby plantation. Loyalists raided his house that night and killed him, Robert Dugan (d. 1781) and two neighbors "by the most savage and deliberate use of their swords . . . literally hewed to pieces."[518]

Newberry County
Watkins (Feb. 1781)

> This engagement occurred in Newberry County.

Lieutenant Colonel Benjamin Roebuck (1755–1788) and his militiamen encountered a party of Loyalist militiamen of equal size in Newberry County around the end of February and engaged them. The skirmish lasted until dark, when both sides ceased firing. They resumed fighting in the morning and the Whigs eventually prevailed.

Georgia's Royal Governor James Wright (1714–1785) wrote that, around the same time, "a party of 60 to 70 rebels came over Savannah River from the Long Cane settlements and assassinated eleven persons in their houses and some in their beds, and those all picked out from amongst the most zealous loyal subjects and no others were ever meddled with."

Colonel James Grierson (d.1781), a Loyalist, also wrote of the incident:

> A party of rebels, from 200 to 250 under the command of Shelby from over the mountains and others, had come into the ceded lands and down towards Augusta and Wrightsborough and assassinated upwards of 40 people whose names are mentioned, these also picked men and such as they thought were most firm in their

loyalty and obedience; and they came so suddenly on the inhabitants that they had not the least notice or time to collect or be on their guard, and the unheard of cruelty of the rebels was so shocking that the generality of the people took to the swamps for shelter against these worse than savages, who say they will murder every loyal subject in the province.[519]

Laurens County
Williams's Fort (Mudlick, Battle of Mudlick Creek, near Fort Williams, Roebuck's Defeat) (March 2, 1781; ca. July 1781)

> Williams's plantation, also known as Mudlick and Mount Pleasant, was probably 5.5 miles due east of Cross Hill, near Mud Lick Creek. From Cross Hill, take route SC 560 east for about 5.25 miles, then turn right (south) onto Mountville Road (S-30-38) and go about 1 mile to the locked gate. This is the closest public access to the site.

Loyalists rebuilt the fort on Mudlick Creek that was destroyed in December 1780 when Brigadier General Daniel Morgan (1736–1802) departed the area. Colonel Benjamin Roebuck's (1755–1788) 150 militiamen were ordered to destroy the fort again. They skirmished with British Regulars and Loyalists from Fort Williams at Mudlick on March 2, 1781. As they had no artillery, they tried to lure the garrison out of the fort. As the Loyalists outnumbered the Whigs, Lieutenant Colonel Henry White (1740–1787) sent a band of mounted riflemen to lure the Loyalists out of the fort into an ambush. The plan succeeded. The fort's occupants rushed out to attack them, confident of an easy victory. White's horsemen fell back and drew the Loyalists into the ambush.

Captain Joseph McJunkin (1755–1846) wrote, "The enemy no sooner saw the militia retreating than they commenced a hot pursuit, confident of an easy victory. Their first onset was a furious one, but was in some measure checked by Colonel White and his riflemen. As soon as the 'green coat cavalry' made their appearance Colonel White leveled his rifle at one of the officers in front and felled him to the ground."

The battlefield changed hands several times in the hotly contested engagement. After an hour, the Loyalists began to retreat and then fled to the fort in a panic. Both sides lost a "great number" of casualties. While the Whigs suffered fewer casualties, they lost Colonel White, who was badly wounded and Captain Robert Thomas (d. 1781) and several other soldiers killed. Colonel Roebuck was wounded in the shoulder and captured, so this action is sometimes referred to as Roebuck's Defeat.[520]

★ Sometime after the siege of Ninety Six, possibly around July 1781, Major Thomas Young (1764–1848) and Colonel Thomas Brandon (1741–1802) went on a scouting mission to Mudlick. They spotted two spies and pursued them. Colonel Brandon sent Major Jolly [possibly Joseph Jolly (ca. 1718–1788)] to seize a ford on their flank to prevent any Loyalists from flanking them. Young's Loyalist cousin, William Young (1730/35–1787), on the other side of the river "hailed us and inquired who commanded. A good deal was said to keep us engaged. Young waved his sword to me several times and holloed [hollered] to me to go away; a moment after we were fired upon by a party who crept up the creek through the bushes. A shot went under Jolly's horse's belly, and another shaved my horse's forelegs. We returned the fire, but did no damage, save a putting a ball through Young's horse's nose. We then retreated, under the hope that they would pursue us, but they did not."[521]

Beattie's Mill, McCormick County (near Ninety Six) (March 21, 1781)
Little River
Dunlap's Defeat (March 21, 23, or 24, 1781)
Pratt's Mill, Abbeville County (Oct. 3, 1781)

> The location of Jane Beattie's Mill was on the Bold Branch about 6.5 miles due north-northwest of Troy in the Sumter National Forest. It was about 400 yards north of where route SC 28 crosses the Bold Branch about 0.5 miles northeast of its intersection with route S-33-38. A mill stone from the mill is on Bold Branch about 340 yards further north on the right.
>
> Joseph Pratt's grist mill was located on the Little River about 8 miles northwest of Abbeville. The site is on route SC 184 (South Main Street) about 3.25 miles west-southwest of the town of Due West where a bridge crosses over the Little River. Pratt's Mill was anchored to a big flat rock. The only such rock for miles along the river is under the bridge. There's a historical marker on the right (west) of the bridge. It shows the date of the battle as October 30, 1781 but most historians use the date of October 3, 1781.

When Brigadier General Andrew Pickens (1739–1817) returned to South Carolina after a period in North Carolina with Major General Nathanael Greene (1742–1786), Colonel Elijah Clarke (1733–1799), who had recovered from the wounds he received at Long Cane the previous December, joined him. Together, they headed to Ninety Six and Augusta, Georgia. Pickens learned that Major James Dunlap (d. 1781) had left Ninety Six with 75 British dragoons on a foraging expedition. Pickens immediately sent Clarke and Lieutenant Colonel James McCall (1741–1781) to attack him.

Clarke and McCall found Dunlap and 180 men encamped at Beattie's mill (thought to be the present Martin's Mill in modern Abbeville County) on Little River on Wednesday, March 21, 1781. They sent a party to seize a bridge which Dunlap would have to cross to retreat. Clarke led the main body to attack Dunlap. They caught him by surprise, driving off the dragoons and surrounding the infantry. Dunlap and his men sought refuge in the mill and some outhouses. However, these structures were too open to serve as defense against Colonel Clarke's riflemen who kept up a withering fire. Dunlap resisted for several hours but surrendered after being wounded and losing 34 of his men killed and others wounded.

Clarke captured 42 prisoners, including the wounded, and sent them to Watauga, in what is now East Tennessee. Dunlap died the next night. The British claimed that he was murdered by the guard after he had surrendered. Major General Nathanael Greene, in a letter to Colonel Nesbit Balfour (1743–1832) regarding the execution of Colonel Isaac Hayne (1745–1781), noted that General Pickens "offered a handsome reward for the murderer." Pickens's report to Greene said that "a set of men chiefly unknown except one Cobb, an over Mountain Man forced the Guard and shot him." Pickens provided the same information to Colonel John Harris Cruger (1738–1807), the commander at Ninety Six, saying that his men regarded the murder "with horror and detestation." He also noted that "the many barbarous massacres committed by those calling themselves officers on our people after their capture" may have been partly the cause. Dunlap's successor was commissioned on March 28 which may have been the same day Dunlap died. Pickens had no casualties.

Colonel Cruger left Ninety Six with 500 troops on March 31 in an attempt to establish fortifications on the Fair Lawn River but Pickens and Clarke presented too great a threat; so Cruger returned to Ninety Six.[522]

★ The roles were reversed at Pratt's Mill on Wednesday, October 3, 1781 when Major William "Bloody Bill" Cunningham (d. 1787) and a large body of Loyalists and Cherokees surprised a group of 30 Whigs stationed at the mill. Cunningham chased them into the woods and burned the mill. He wounded Captain John Norwood (1751–1826) and captured him and the 30 horses belonging to his men.[523]

Horner's (or Horn's) Creek or Corner, Edgefield County
(April 3, 1781)

Hammond's Mill, Aiken County (April 3, 1781)

> The nearest road access to the Horn's Creek site is the Horn's Creek Baptist Church at the junction of Old Stage Road and Yarborough Road about 5 miles south of Edgefield. The creek is about a mile west of the church. There are roads that appear to get closer to the Horn's Creek site, but they are private roads for the Cup's Hill Hunting Lodge and all access roads have locked gates. There's a historical marker near the church.
>
> Hammond's Mill was located at the falls of the Savannah River in North Augusta about 1.5 miles southeast of where route I-20 crosses the river. From route SC 230 (West Martintown Road), take Hammond Drive to its end. Turn right onto Medie Avenue, then turn left onto Cypress Drive and turn right at River Oak Drive. The site is beyond the end of River Oak Drive across the creek. There is much new home construction in this area and new streets are being added.

Colonel Samuel Hammond (1757–1842) and Colonel Le Roy Hammond (1728–1789) joined Brigadier General Andrew Pickens (1739–1817) in arousing the people in the Ninety Six District against the Loyalists after Pickens returned from North Carolina. Colonel Samuel Hammond and Major James Jackson (1757–1806), of Georgia, were both sent to Georgia on a similar mission in April 1781. They passed through the Ninety Six District and arrived on the Savannah River near Pace's Ferry, about 24 miles northwest of Augusta in what is now Edgefield County. Captain Thomas Kee (Key) (1750–1821) of Colonel Le Roy Hammond's regiment joined them with a number of men.

The following day, Tuesday, April 3, 1781, Captain Kee left to attack a band of Loyalists gathered at the residence of a Captain John Clarke (d. 1781) on Horner's Creek, a branch of Stevens's Creek, in what is now Edgefield County. Kee's men killed Clarke and took his entire company prisoners. Kee paroled all the prisoners and then marched to Colonel Le Roy Hammond's mill on the Savannah River. The mill had been captured and made into a Loyalist fort. Kee attacked the post, destroyed the mill, and captured all the provisions.[524]

Other accounts say Captain Clarke was shot in the leg but managed to escape to a bluff about one mile from the ford where his mother applied salve to his wound and dressed it. However, the Loyalists followed his trail of blood and captured him. He was mounted on a skinny horse with a protruding backbone and his legs tied together under the horse. He was brought to the jail at Ninety Six, more than 40 miles away. He contracted smallpox there, but recovered. Nine other prisoners were not so lucky and died from the disease.[525]

Newberry County
Bush River (May 1, 1781)

> This action probably occurred in the Revolutionary era town of Bush River, now Kinnards, in the western part of present-day Newberry County. The town was located about 1.7 miles west of the Bush River. The site of the engagement may have been along Bush River Road (S-36-56) east of its junction with Floyd Road|Garys Lane (S-36-64). The cemetery of the old Bush River Church is on the right just past the church. There's a historical marker for the church nearby.

Colonel John Thomas, Jr. (1751–1819) and a detachment from Brigadier General Thomas Sumter's (1734–1832) force surprised a party of Loyalists at Bush River on Tuesday, May 1, 1781. They killed three and captured 12 Loyalists and took four wagons and several slaves.[526]

Aiken County
Beech Island (May 15, 1781; May 24, 1781)

> Beech Island is on the Savannah River about 8 miles southeast of Augusta, Georgia. The present town of Beech Island in Aiken County, South Carolina is just east of a horseshoe bend of the Savannah River. The action known as the Battle of Beech Island probably occurred in Georgia on that horseshoe bend.

See also Georgia, Beech Island in the next volume, *The Guide to the American Revolutionary War in the Deep South and on the Frontier.*

As Colonel Elijah Clarke (1733–1799) prepared for the siege of Augusta, Georgia, he sent the horses to Beech Island with a 6-man guard. Colonel Thomas Brown (1750–1825) learned of this and sent a detachment of Regulars, militiamen and Native Americans to capture them. Clarke ordered Captain Moses Shelby (1760–1828) and his Over Mountain Men along with Major Patrick Carr and his Georgia militiamen to pursue the raiders traveling down the river in canoes. However, they were too late. The raiders killed the guards, took the horses, and headed back to Augusta. Shelby and Carr waited in a thicket to attack the raiders on their return around Tuesday, May 15, 1781. The Whigs routed the Crown forces and killed about half of them. They recovered the horses without loss about a week before the Whig victory at Fort Galphin on May 21, 1781.

★ Lieutenant Colonel Henry "Light-Horse Harry" Lee's (1756–1818) troops marched for three days after the fall of Fort Granby (May 15, 1781) to intercept the annual presents from the King to the local Creeks and Cherokees. Those presents consisted of firearms, powder and shot to help the Native Americans obtain food and to keep them fighting on the side of the British. They were to be stored at Fort Galphin, 12 miles from Augusta, Georgia which Colonel Elijah Clarke (1733–1799) was preparing to besiege. His men ambushed the British flotilla containing the presents before Lee arrived, but the Loyalist guards from Augusta kept Clarke's men at a distance during a running battle. They wounded six of Clarke's men and brought their boats safely to Fort Galphin.[527]

★ A company of South Carolina militiamen deserted and proceeded down the Savannah River, guided by a man named Rutherford, on Thursday, May 24, 1781. At sunrise, they encountered a horse guard of Congressional troops camped on the South Carolina side of the Savannah River, just opposite Beech Island. The horsemen tried unsuccessfully to stop the fleeing deserters, some of whom fought back and killed several dragoons. Captain Tarleton Brown (1757–1845) heard the alarm and mounted his men quickly to cut off the deserters, but they escaped to the other side of the Savannah.[528]

Backcountry (June 1781; July 1781)

> This event took place west of the Congaree and Santee Rivers and is only mentioned in Brigadier General Thomas Sumter's (1734–1832) dispatches.

Lieutenant Colonel Richard Hampton (1752–1792) defeated Major John Coffin's (1756–1838) party of 50 Loyalist militiamen in the South Carolina Backcountry in June 1781. He killed some of the Loyalists and took others prisoner. The rest escaped into a swamp.[529]

★ Major William "Bloody Bill" Cunningham (d. 1787) raided Whig settlements in the South Carolina backcountry in the middle of July 1781. Major Fields Purdue, of Brigadier General Andrew Pickens's (1739–1817) militia, killed five of Cunningham's militiamen and chased him back north. Purdue also recaptured the stolen slaves and horses.[530]

Near Vaughanville, Newberry County
Caldwell's house (Captain John Caldwell killed) (Nov. 18, 1781)

> Captain John Caldwell's (d. 1781) house was about 1 mile west of where SC 56 crosses Mills Creek near Vaughanville in Newberry County.

After Loyalist militia Major William "Bloody Bill" Cunningham's (d. 1787) massacre at Clouds Creek (Lexington County) (see p. 109), he rode to Captain John Caldwell's house which was only about 3.5 miles from Peach Hill, Brigadier General Robert Cunningham's (1741–1813) house. Cunningham had served under Caldwell in the South Carolina militia before he became disenchanted with the Whigs and changed sides. When Cunningham arrived at the gate, he greeted Caldwell who walked out to meet Cunningham. As Caldwell knew Cunningham, he did not fear him. However, Cunningham drew his pistol and killed Caldwell in front of his wife who fainted when her husband fell. Cunningham ordered the house set on fire before he left and crossed to the south side of the Saluda River and proceeded up the Cherokee Path.[531]

See **Hayes Station** p. 304.

Greenwood County
Swancey's Ferry (ca. Nov. 20, 1781)

> The site Swancey's Ferry is under Lake Greenwood about 7 miles north of Ninety Six. The closest land approach is reached by routes U.S. 221 and SC 72 northeast from Greenwood across the lake bridge and turning right (southeast) onto Whitten Road (S-30-147). Go about 0.75 miles, then turn right (southwest) onto route S-30-408 and go to its end. The site of the skirmish was probably near route U.S. 221 (Greenwood Highway) between routes S-30-151 (Lake Forest Road) and S-30-147 (Whitten Road) on the eastern side of Lake Greenwood.

Loyalist Major William "Bloody Bill" Cunningham (d. 1787) skirmished with a party of Whigs about 1.25 miles from Swancey's Ferry about Tuesday, November 20, 1781. They killed Captain Samuel Moore.[532]

Moore
Moore's Plantation, Spartanburg County (Nov. 1781)

> Charles Moore's plantation has been restored as the Walnut Grove Plantation about 1 mile southeast of route I-26 exit 28 at the junction of Harrison Grove Road (S-42-196) and Otts Shoals Road (S-42-458) in Roebuck. Take route U.S. 221 east from route I-26 exit 28. Proceed about 200 yards and turn right onto Harrison Grove Road (S-42-196). There are historical markers on the right. Go to Otts Shoals Road, turn right and go about 0.4 miles to get to the plantation. The two men shot in the yard were buried there in what became the family cemetery.

Major William "Bloody Bill" Cunningham (d. 1787) visited Charles Moore's plantation in November 1781 and killed Captain Steadman (d. 1781) while he was lying sick in bed. Local legend says that Steadman was recuperating from a fever at the home of his fiancée's parents. He was rendered immobile within a bundling bag and the two soldiers accompanying him were bedded down in a nearby barn. Cunningham personally shot Steadman when the Loyalists attacked the house. The two soldiers in the barn tried to run away, but the Loyalists shot them down in front of the house.[533]

Clinton
Near Joanna, Laurens County
Hayes Station (Nov. 19, 1781)

> Hayes Station is about 9.6 miles south of Clinton. To get there, take Jacobs Highway (SC 56) south for about 8.3 miles to Williams Road. Proceed about 1 mile down Williams Road. From Cross Hill take route S-30-659 (Puckett Ferry Road) east for 5.2 miles. Turn north onto route S-30-38 (Jefferson Davis Road) for 1.6 miles, and turn right (east) on route S-30-46 (Old Milton Road). Proceed for 1 mile. Go over the bridge, then left onto Williams Road. Proceed about 1 mile down Williams Road.
> A monument for the Hayes Station Massacre is on route SC 56 at the intersection of Jacobs Highway (SC 56) and route SC 560.

After the Clouds Creek Massacre (see p. 109) in November 1781, Colonel Joseph Hayes (d. 1781) and 40 Whig soldiers garrisoned a small post previously known as Edge Hill and now called Hayes Station. Hayes had just returned from a scouting expedition that found no evidence of Major William "Bloody Bill" Cunningham (d. 1787) or his men, so when he received a communiqué ordering him to abandon his post because of Cunningham's activities, he decided to disregard the order and notified a nearby post in case he might need help.

A short while later, about 10 AM on Monday, November 19, 1781, some of Cunningham's men arrived at Hayes Station and warned the occupants that if they fired, they would all be killed. Almost immediately after receiving the message, a Whig rifle killed one of the Loyalists.

"Bloody Bill" arrived and sent a courier under a flag of truce to propose the surrender of Hayes Station with no further bloodshed. If the occupants refused, any resistance would be met with indiscriminate slaughter.

Because of Bloody Bill's reputation for lack of integrity and Colonel Hayes's confidence that reinforcements would arrive in time to help, Hayes refused to surrender. After a gunfight that lasted several hours, Cunningham's men threw flaming ramrods wrapped with tow dipped in pitch onto the wooden roof of the outpost. This set the building on fire, and the flames spread quickly. Colonel Hayes led his coughing and choking soldiers out of the smoke-filled fort, with their hands in the air.

Bloody Bill hanged Hayes and one of his men on the pole of a fodder stack. But the pole holding the rope gave way before the men died. As the two men gasped for air, Cunningham finished them with his sword. When someone told Bloody Bill that one of the prisoners, Captain Daniel Williams (d. 1781), had taken part in whipping Cunningham's brother to death, Bloody Bill impaled the suspect with his sword and then allowed his men to execute the rest of the prisoners, as they wished, about sunset. Cunningham justified himself by alleging cruelties by Hayes to women and children. Total casualties were 19 dead. Cunningham had one man killed and five wounded.

Angry Whigs pursued Cunningham and his men. Bloody Bill rode his horse to death in his escape to Charleston. According to legend, the horse received a funeral with full military honors.[534]

Pine Wood House, Edgefield County and White Hall, Greenwood County (Dec. 1781; Dec. 5, 1781)

> Pine Wood House was a tavern near the crossroads of routes U.S. 25 (Augusta Road), routes SC 121 (Pine House Road) and SC 19 (Augusta Road) in Trenton.
> White Hall was located where route U.S. 221 crosses Whitehall Road (S-24-156) about 8.5 miles due south-southwest of Greenwood. The site is in the eastern quarter of this junction.

Loyalist Major William "Bloody Bill" Cunningham (d. 1787) and Colonel Hezekiah Williams went their separate ways on Sunday, December 2, 1781, 20 miles north of Orangeburg. Major Cunningham then split his force into two groups. One headed into the mountains to Cherokee territory. The other group returned safely to Charleston.

Colonel Williams detached Captain John Crawford (1750–1816) to harass the settlers in the Long Cane area. Crawford murdered George Foreman (d. 1781) and his two sons near the Pine Wood House and continued marching north toward Martintown. When he got within 4 miles of the town, he proceeded to White Hall, Colonel Andrew Williamson's (ca. 1730–1786) plantation, on Wednesday, December 5, 1781. Brigadier General Andrew Pickens (1739–1817) had fortified the plantation house into a military post. Crawford attacked the garrison and destroyed all the defenses.[535]

McCord Creek, Abbeville County (Dec. 7, 1781)

> Route SC 72 crosses McCord Creek about 3 miles east of Abbeville. The old road bed east of McCord's Creek is the most likely ambush site because the sides of the road are highest in this area, minimizing room to maneuver the wagons.

Captain John Crawford (1750–1816) rode to Brigadier General Andrew Pickens's (1739–1817) blockhouse on Friday morning, December 7, 1781 and surprised a convoy of wagons guarded by Captain Moses Liddell (1755–1802). Captain Crawford's Loyalists killed several of the guards and drove off the rest in a brief skirmish. They then burned the entire wagon train and took the wagoners prisoner. They escaped into Cherokee territory. Crawford delivered his prisoners to the Cherokees who tortured most of them to death. One of the prisoners, John Pickens (d. 1781), General Andrew

Pickens's brother, was singled out for special torture. General Pickens avenged his death in March 1782 by attacking the whole Cherokee nation.[536]

See **Cherokee Villages** p. 267.

Farrow's Station, Spartanburg County (March 31, 1782)
Bryant's Mills, Spartanburg County

> Farrow's Station was the home of Landon Farrow (1759–1799) who was being held prisoner by the British in Charleston. It was located on the north side of the Enoree River, between the Edisto and Tyger rivers, within sight of Musgrove Mill and was one of the Whig militia outposts of the Spartan Regiment.
>
> The site of Farrow's Station is on route S-42-10 (Horseshoe Falls Road) about 0.75 miles due northwest of the Musgrove mill. To get there from the intersection of route SC 56 and Avenger Road, continue north on route SC 56 about 283 yards, then make a hard left turn onto Horseshoe Falls Road. Proceed about 1.15 miles. Old house foundations have been found in the area on the left about 140 yards on top of the hill. The house had Revolutionary War era artifacts around it.

A band of Loyalists surprised Lieutenant Thomas Farrow (1755–1843), Landon Farrow's (1759–1799) brother, and a small party of men at Farrow's station at sundown on Saturday, March 31, 1782. They surrounded the house and posted sentries to prevent any reinforcements from being summoned. The Whigs barricaded the doors and carried on a gun battle until about midnight, killing at least one Loyalist. The Loyalists made an unsuccessful attempt to burn the house. Seeing that the standoff would continue, both sides held a parley.

The Loyalists agreed to leave if Farrow would supply them with arms and ammunition. Outnumbered and surrounded, Farrow had no choice but to comply. During the transfer of the weapons an argument began over whether the pistols should be handed out butt first or barrel first. Farrow's sister-in-law ended the argument by carrying the weapons out and delivering them. The Loyalists then departed but Farrow mustered men from the Spartan Regiment and pursued them. Farrow's men overtook the Loyalists at Bryant's mills and defeated them. Farrow was severely wounded and it took him three months to recuperate.[537]

Pauline
Bryant's Mill, Spartanburg County (April 1, 1782)

> Bryant's Mill was located along the Tyger River west of route SC 56. Nobody knows the exact location of the mill but there are three likely possibilities. The most likely site is about 100 yards north of the intersection of routes S-42-203 (Grace Chapel Road) and S-42-270 (Wofford Road). The creek has a greater fall here that could have been used for Bryant's mill if it was an undershot mill.
>
> The second site is about 0.75 miles north on the Motley Branch, about 50 yards north of its junction with the Tyger River. It seems to have a river ford nearby, just to the east, and the mouth of the creek is wider as though a mill may have been there. It is the only site on the south side of the river, closest to the road and the ford which the Loyalists probably travelled from Farrow's Station. They rode at night and probably stopped at the mill for a meal before crossing the ford and continuing

> north. The darkness would have slowed their progress. Farrow and his men had the advantage of daylight and could have quickly overtaken the Loyalists at the mill.
>
> The third site is about 350 yards to the east. There is a creek here with a modern reservoir that may have been the location of Bryant's millpond.

The day after the attack on Farrow's Station, South Carolina Whig militia Lieutenant Thomas Farrow (1755–1843) and a party of men from the Spartan Regiment overtook the Loyalist raiding party at Bryant's mill on the Tyger River. They may have stopped at the mill for a meal before crossing the ford and continuing north at night to defeat the Loyalists. Farrow was severely wounded and was unable to resume his command for several months.[538]

Notes

Abbreviation

NDAR: United States. Naval History Division. *Naval Documents of the American Revolution.* William Bell Clark, editor; with a foreword by President John F. Kennedy and an introd. by Ernest McNeill Eller. Washington: Naval History. Division, Dept. of the Navy: For sale by the Supt. of Docs., U.S. G.P.O., 1964–.

Preface

1. Desmarais, Norman. *Battlegrounds of Freedom: A Historical Guide to the Battlefields of the War of American Independence.* Ithaca, NY: Busca, 2005.

2. Heitman, Francis B. *Historical Register of Officers of the Continental Army during the War of the Revolution, April 1775 to December 1783.* Washington, DC.: The Rare Book Shop Publishing Company, 1914; Baltimore: Genealogical Publishing Company, 1967.

3. Peckham, Howard Henry. *The Toll of Independence: Engagements & Battle Casualties of the American Revolution.* Chicago: University of Chicago Press, 1974.

4. Boatner, Mark Mayo. *Encyclopedia of the American Revolution.* 3d ed. New York: McKay, 1980.

5. Boatner, Mark Mayo. *Landmarks of the American Revolution: A Guide to Locating and Knowing What Happened at the Sites of Independence.* Stackpole Books: Harrisburg, PA, 1973; 2nd ed. – Library of Military History. Detroit: Charles Scribner's Sons, 2007.

6. Selesky Harold E., editor in chief. *Encyclopedia of the American Revolution*, 2nd ed. Detroit: Charles Scribner's Sons, 2007.

7. Fremont-Barnes, Gregory, Richard Alan Ryerson, eds. *The Encyclopedia of the American Revolutionary War: A Political, Social, and Military History.* Santa Barbara, CA: ABC-CLIO, 2006.

8. Anderson, Fred. *A People's Army: Massachusetts Soldiers and Society in the Seven Years' War.* Chapel Hill, NC. 1984. pp. 84–85, 129.

9. Waller, George M. *The American Revolution in the West.* Chicago: Nelson Hall, 1976. pp. 30–31.

10. Adams, Charles F., ed. *The Works of John Adams.* Boston: Charles C. Little and James Brown, 1850. vol. 10 p. 110.

11. Adams, Charles F., ed. *The Works of John Adams.* Boston: Charles C. Little and James Brown, 1850, vol. 10 pp. 192–93.

12. Raphael, Ray. *A People's History of the American Revolution: How Common People Shaped the Fight for Independence.* New York: New Press, 2001. pp. 145, 342.

South Carolina

1. National Archives and Records Administration. Bentley Outlaw pension application R7833. Parker, John C. *Parker's Guide to the Revolutionary War in South Carolina: battles, skirmishes and murders.* Patrick, SC: Hem Branch Publishing, 2009. p. 135.

2. National Archives and Records Administration. Bentley Outlaw pension application R7833. Parker, John C. *Parker's Guide to the Revolutionary War in South Carolina: battles, skirmishes and murders.* Patrick, SC: Hem Branch Publishing, 2009. p. 135.

3. Gregg, Alexander. *History of the old Cheraws; containing an account of the aborigines of the Pedee, the first white settlements, their subsequent progress, civil changes, the struggle of the revolution, and growth of the country afterward, extending from about A. D. 1730 to 1810, with notices of families and sketches of individuals.* New York, Richardson, 1867; Spartanburg, SC: Reprint Co., 1965. p. 333. Parker, John C. *Parker's Guide to the Revolutionary War in South Carolina: battles, skirmishes and murders.* Patrick, SC: Hem Branch Publishing, 2009. p. 188.

4. National Archives and Records Administration. Nathaniel Jones pension application W7918. Parker, John C. *Parker's Guide to the Revolutionary War in South Carolina: battles, skirmishes and murders.* Patrick, SC: Hem Branch Publishing, 2009. p. 136.

5. Parker, John C. *Parker's Guide to the Revolutionary War in South Carolina: battles, skirmishes and murders.* Patrick, SC: Hem Branch Publishing, 2009. p. 186.

6. Collins, James. *A Revolutionary Soldier.* Felician Democrat, 1859. pp. 35–38. General Richard Winn's Notes–1780. *The South Carolina Historical and Genealogical Magazine* XLIII:4 (October 1942) pp. 202–204. National Archives and Records Administration. Samuel Walker Pension application S3448. National Archives and Records Administration. Hugh Gaston Pension Application S10729. Lipscomb, Terry W. *South Carolina Revolutionary Battles Part Three, Names in South Carolina.* XXII (Winter 1975). South Carolina Historical Society, 1975. p. 33. Hayes, John T. *The Saddlebag Almanac.* VI (Jan. 1998) p. 84. Hill, William. *Col. William Hill's Memoirs of the Revolution*, edited by A. S. Sally, Columbia, SC, 1921. Draper, Lyman. Thomas Sumter Papers, Draper Manuscript Collection, State Historical Society of Wisconsin. 9VV159; 10VV41, 11VV509–519, 14VV59–60. Ellet, E. F. (Elizabeth Fries). *The*

Women of the American Revolution. New York, Baker and Scribner, 1848. III: 177, 291–292. O'Kelley, Patrick. *Nothing but Blood and Slaughter*. Booklocker.com, 2004. 2: 169–172. Parker, John C. *Parker's Guide to the Revolutionary War in South Carolina: battles, skirmishes and murders*. Patrick, SC: Hem Branch Publishing, 2009. p. 184.

7. Greene, Nathanael. *The Papers of General Nathanael Greene*. Richard K. Showman, ed. Chapel Hill: the University of North Carolina Press, published for the Rhode Island Historical Society. c1976–2006. 8:149. Parker, John C. *Parker's Guide to the Revolutionary War in South Carolina: battles, skirmishes and murders*. Patrick, SC: Hem Branch Publishing, 2009. p. 184.

8. Letter of Robert Brownfield in James, William Dobein. *A Sketch of the Life of Brig. Gen. Francis Marion, and a History of his Brigade, from its Rise in June 1780, until Disbanded in December, 1782*. Charleston, SC: Gould and Riley, 1821. Appendix.

8a. Scotti, Anthony Jr. *Brutal Virtue: the Myth and Reality of Banastre Tarleton*. Bowie, MD: Heritage Books, 2002. p. 173.

9. *Encyclopedia of the American Revolution*. Harold E. Selesky, editor in chief. 2nd Ed. Detroit: Charles Scribner's Sons, 2007. II: 1245–1246. *The Encyclopedia of the American Revolutionary War: a political, social, and military history*. Gregory Fremont-Barnes, Richard Alan Ryerson, editors. Santa Barbara, CA: ABC-CLIO, 2006 IV: 1333–1334. Morrill, Dan L. *Southern Campaigns of the American Revolution*. Baltimore: the Nautical & Aviation Publishing Company of America [nd]. Pancake, John S. *This Destructive War: the British Campaign in the Carolinas*. Tuscaloosa: University of Alabama Press, 1985. Ripley, Warren. *Battleground: South Carolina in the Revolution*. Charleston, SC: Evening Post, 1983. Scotti, Anthony J. *Brutal Virtue: the myth and reality of Banastre Tarleton*. Westminster, MD: Heritage Books, 2002. Ward, Christopher. *The War of the Revolution*. New York: Macmillan, 1952. Tarleton, Banastre. *A History of the Campaigns of 1780 and 1781 in the Southern Provinces of North America*. London: T. Cadell, 1787; [sl]: the New York Times & Arno Press, 1968. pp. 28–31, 83–84. Stedman, C. (Charles). *the History of the Origin, Progress, and Termination of the American War*. (Eyewitness Accounts of the American Revolution). [New York]: New York Times ; Arno Press, c1969. 2: 193. Parker, John C. *Parker's Guide to the Revolutionary War in South Carolina: battles, skirmishes and murders*. Patrick, SC: Hem Branch Publishing, 2009. p. 245. Scoggins, Michael C.; Edgar, Walter. *The Day It Rained Militia: Huck's Defeat and the Revolution in the South Carolina Backcountry, May–July 1780*. Charleston: The History Press, c2005. pp. 44–46.

10. Extract of a letter from North-Carolina, dated Camp, near 12 Mile Creek, October 14, 1780. *The Pennsylvania Packet or the General Advertiser*. X: 697 (Jan. 9, 1781), p. 3. Extract of a letter from an officer in the Southern army, dated Camp, near the Waxaws, October 31. *The Pennsylvania Packet or the General Advertiser*. X: 697 (Jan. 9, 1781), p. 3.

11. Extract of a letter from an officer in the Southern army, dated Camp, near the Waxaws, October 31. *The Pennsylvania Packet or the General Advertiser*. X: 697 (Jan. 9, 1781), p. 3.

12. Parker, John C. *Parker's Guide to the Revolutionary War in South Carolina: battles, skirmishes and murders*. Patrick, SC: Hem Branch Publishing, 2009. p. 244.

13. Garden, Alexander. *Anecdotes of the American Revolution, Illustrative of the Talents and Virtues of the Heroes and Patriots who Acted the Most Conspicuous Parts Therein*. Second series. Charleston, S. C.: A.E. Miller, 1828. pp. 424–425. Draper, Lyman. Thomas Sumter Papers, Draper Manuscript Collection, State Historical Society of Wisconsin. 4VV51–53, 56–58; 9VV261–269. O'Kelley, Patrick. *Nothing but Blood and Slaughter*. Booklocker.com, 2004. 2: 173; 3: 107–8. Parker, John C. *Parker's Guide to the Revolutionary War in South Carolina: battles, skirmishes and murders*. Patrick, SC: Hem Branch Publishing, 2009. p. 123–125.

14. Scoggins, Michael C. Alexander's Old Field, or the Battle of Beckhamville. *Southern Campaigns of the American Revolution*. 2:6 (June 2005) p. 6. http://www.southerncampaign.org/newsletter/v2n6.pdf. Corlew, Jane Wade. Memoir. in Pettus, Louise. The Wade Family in the Revolution. http://www.rootsweb.ancestry.com/~sclancas/records/bio_wadefamily.htm. Wright, Annie Julia Mims "Mrs W. R. Wright". *A Record of the Descendants of Isaac Ross and Jean Brown and the Allied Families of Alexander, Conger, Harris, Hill, King, Killingworth, Mackey, Moores, Sims, Wade, etc.* Jackson, MS: Consumers Stationery and Printing Co., 1911. p. 165.

15. Lossing, Benson John. *The Pictorial Field-book of the Revolution; or, Illustrations, by pen and pencil, of the history, biography, scenery, relics, and traditions of the War for Independence*. New York, Harper & Brothers [1860]. Lipscomb, Terry W. *South Carolina Revolutionary Battles Part Three, Names in South Carolina*. Volume XXII. Winter 1975. South Carolina Historical Society, 1975. p. 33. Hayes, John T. *The Saddlebag Almanac*. VI (Jan. 1998) pp. 33, 83–84. Draper, Lyman. Thomas Sumter Papers, Draper Manuscript Collection, State Historical Society of Wisconsin. 5VV150; 9VV12, 15, 19 37, 177; 9VV159; 9VV215–217; 10VV235; 14VV436–443, 452–460. John Craig. "the War in York and Chester." *Chester Standard*. (Chester, SC) March 16, 1854. O'Kelley, Patrick. *Nothing but Blood and Slaughter*. Booklocker.com, 2004. 2: 167–169. National Archives and Records Administration. Hugh McClure Pension Application W21789. National Archives and Records Administration. William McGarity Pension Application R6713. Daniel G. Stinson. Communication. *Chester Reporter*. (Chester, SC). May 29, 1873. John Craig. The War in York and Chester. *Chester Standard*. (Chester, SC). March 16, 1865. Gaston, Joseph. *A Reminiscence of the Revolution*. The Southern Presbyterian (Columbia, SC) May 22, 1873. Ellet, E. F. (Elizabeth Fries). *The Women of the American Revolution*. New York, Baker and Scribner, 1848. III: 132, 159–160, 176–177, 217. Scoggins, Michael C.; Edgar, Walter. *The Day It Rained Militia: Huck's Defeat and the Revolution in the South Carolina Backcountry, May–July 1780*. Charleston: The History Press, c2005. p. 57.

16. Southern Studies Program. *Figures of the Revolution in South Carolina, An Anthology*. Spartanburg, Anderson, Beaufort, Aiken, Florence, Georgetown. Columbia: University of South Carolina, 1976. pp. 103–104, 208. British National Archives. Cornwallis Papers, Class 30, Vol. 11, 2 pp. 158–159. Draper, Lyman. Thomas Sumter Papers, Draper Manuscript Collection, State Historical Society of Wisconsin. 4VV16. Ellett. 217–219, 225–226. O'Kelley, Patrick. *Nothing but Blood and Slaughter*. Booklocker.com, 2004. 2: 173–174. www.carolana.com/SC/Revolution/

revolution_fishing_creek_church.html. Parker, John C. *Parker's Guide to the Revolutionary War in South Carolina: battles, skirmishes and murders*. Patrick, SC: Hem Branch Publishing, 2009. p. 127, 133.

17. Draper, Lyman. Draper Manuscript Collection, State Historical Society of Wisconsin. 9VV72, 9VV215–216. Ellet, E. F. (Elizabeth Fries). *The Women of the American Revolution*. New York, Baker and Scribner, 1848. III: 127. Scoggins, Michael C.; Edgar, Walter. *The Day It Rained Militia: Huck's Defeat and the Revolution in the South Carolina Backcountry, May–July 1780*. Charleston: The History Press, c2005. p. 55.

18. Chesney, Alexander. *The Journal of Alexander Chesney, a South Carolina Loyalist in the Revolution and After*, edited by E. A. Jones. Columbus, Ohio: Ohio State University, 1921. *The Ohio State University Bulletin*. 26:4 (October 30, 1921) p. 10 n72. Moss, Bobby Gilmer. *Journal of Captain Alexander Chesney, Adjutant to Major Patrick Ferguson*. [s.l.]: Scotia-Hibernia Press, 2002. p. 18 n125.

19. Saye, James Hodge. *Memoirs of Major Joseph McJunkin, Revolutionary Patriot*. [sl]: A Press, Inc., 1977. p. 13.

20. Deed of sale recorded April 1770, in Brent H. Holcomb. *Tryon County North Carolina Minutes of the Court of Pleas and Quarter Sessions 1769–1779*. Columbia: SCMAR, 1994. p. 27. Michael C. Scoggins. The Battles of Stallions' Plantation and Bigger's Ferry. *Southern Campaigns of the American Revolution*. 2:10 p. 10. (www.southerncampaigns.com).

21. Davis, Robert Scott, Jr. *The Battle of Kettle Creek*. State of Georgia Department of Natural Resources, Office of Planning and Research, Historical Preservation Section, 1974. pp. 32–33. Southern Studies Program. *Figures of the Revolution in South Carolina, An Anthology*. Spartanburg, Anderson, Beaufort, Aiken, Florence, Georgetown. Columbia: University of South Carolina, 1976. pp. 129–130. Draper, Lyman. *Kings Mountain and its Heroes: History of the Battle of King's Mountain, October 7th, 1780, and the Events Which Led To It*. The Overmountain Press, 1996. p. 127. O'Kelley, Patrick. *Nothing but Blood and Slaughter*. Booklocker.com, 2004. 1: 239–240. Parker, John C. *Parker's Guide to the Revolutionary War in South Carolina: battles, skirmishes and murders*. Patrick, SC: Hem Branch Publishing, 2009. pp. 335, 337, 376.

22. Young, Thomas. Memoir of a Revolutionary Patriot of South Carolina. *The Orion* 3 (Oct. 1843), pp. 84–88 et seq. Lipscomb, Terry W. *South Carolina Revolutionary Battles Part Three, Names in South Carolina*. XXII (Winter 1975). South Carolina Historical Society, 1975. p. 35. Draper, Lyman. Thomas Sumter Papers, Draper Manuscript Collection, State Historical Society of Wisconsin. 11VV316–321, 14VV77–79, 136; 23VV168; 23VV204. Lambert, Robert Stansbury. *South Carolina Loyalists in the American Revolution*. Columbia, SC: University of South Carolina Press, c1987. p. 206. O'Kelley, Patrick. *Nothing but Blood and Slaughter*. Booklocker.com, 2004. 2: 164–165.

23. Chesney, Alexander. *The Journal of Alexander Chesney, a South Carolina Loyalist in the Revolution and After*, edited by E. A. Jones. Columbus, Ohio: Ohio State University, 1921. pp. 5–6. Hill, William. *Colonel William Hill's Memoirs of the Revolution*, edited by A. S. Sally, Columbia, SC, 1921. Saye, James Hodge. *Memoirs of Major Joseph McJunkin, Revolutionary Patriot*. [sl]: A Press, Inc., 1977. (First printed in the Richmond, VA *Watchman and Observer* in 1847) p. 13. O'Kelley, Patrick. *Nothing but Blood and Slaughter*. Booklocker.com, 2004. 2: 178–179.

24. Young, Thomas. Memoir of a Revolutionary Patriot of South Carolina. *The Orion*. 3 (Oct. 1843), pp. 84–88 et seq.

25. Saye, James Hodge. *Memoirs of Major Joseph McJunkin, Revolutionary Patriot*. [sl]: A Press, Inc., 1977. (First printed in the Richmond, VA *Watchman and Observer* in 1847) p. 13. Young, Thomas. Memoir of a Revolutionary Patriot of South Carolina. *The Orion*. 3 (Oct. 1843), pp. 84–88 et seq. Lipscomb, Terry W. *South Carolina Revolutionary Battles Part Three, Names in South Carolina*. XXII (Winter 1975). South Carolina Historical Society, 1975. p. 33. Hayes, John T. *The Saddlebag Almanac*. VI (Jan. 1998) p. 35. Draper, Lyman. Thomas Sumter Papers, Draper Manuscript Collection, State Historical Society of Wisconsin. 11VV411; 14VV177–179; 9VV28–42. O'Kelley, Patrick. *Nothing but Blood and Slaughter*. Booklocker.com, 2004. 2: 179–80; 198–199. Parker, John C. *Parker's Guide to the Revolutionary War in South Carolina: battles, skirmishes and murders*. Patrick, SC: Hem Branch Publishing, 2009. pp. 358, 376, 379.

26. British National Archives. Cornwallis Papers, Class 30, Vol. 11/2/250–251. Draper, Lyman. Thomas Sumter Papers, Draper Manuscript Collection, State Historical Society of Wisconsin. 4VV120. O'Kelley, Patrick. *Nothing but Blood and Slaughter*. Booklocker.com, 2004. 2: 189. Parker, John C. *Parker's Guide to the Revolutionary War in South Carolina: battles, skirmishes and murders*. Patrick, SC: Hem Branch Publishing, 2009. p. 376.

27. Parker, John C. *Parker's Guide to the Revolutionary War in South Carolina: battles, skirmishes and murders*. Patrick, SC: Hem Branch Publishing, 2009. p. 333.

28. Draper, Lyman. *Kings Mountain and its Heroes: History of the Battle of King's Mountain, October 7th, 1780, and the Events Which Led To It*. The Overmountain Press, 1996. pp. 135–138. Draper, Lyman. Thomas Sumter Papers, Draper Manuscript Collection, State Historical Society of Wisconsin. 16VV402–405. O'Kelley, Patrick. *Nothing but Blood and Slaughter*. Booklocker.com, 2004. 2: 218–19.

29. Parker, John C. *Parker's Guide to the Revolutionary War in South Carolina: battles, skirmishes and murders*. Patrick, SC: Hem Branch Publishing, 2009. p. 364.

30. Chesney, Alexander. *The Journal of Alexander Chesney, a South Carolina Loyalist in the Revolution and After*. edited by E. A. Jones. Columbus, Ohio: Ohio State University, 1921. p. 7. O'Kelley, Patrick. *Nothing but Blood and Slaughter*. Booklocker.com, 2004. 2: 293.

31. Chesney, Alexander. *The Journal of Alexander Chesney, a South Carolina Loyalist in the Revolution and After*. edited by E. A. Jones. Columbus, Ohio: Ohio State University, 1921. O'Kelley, Patrick. *Nothing but Blood and Slaughter*. Booklocker.com, 2004. 2: 360–61. Parker, John C. *Parker's Guide to the Revolutionary War in South Carolina: battles, skirmishes and murders*. Patrick, SC: Hem Branch Publishing, 2009. pp. 335, 354.

32. Lipscomb, Terry W. *South Carolina Revolutionary Battles Part Ten, Names in South Carolina*. XXX (Winter 1983). South Carolina Historical Society, 1983. p. 13. O'Kelley, Patrick. *Nothing but Blood and Slaughter*. Booklocker

.com, 2004. 2: 387. Parker, John C. *Parker's Guide to the Revolutionary War in South Carolina: battles, skirmishes and murders*. Patrick, SC: Hem Branch Publishing, 2009. p. 293.

33. Draper, Lyman. Thomas Sumter Papers, Draper Manuscript Collection, State Historical Society of Wisconsin. O'Kelley, Patrick. *Nothing but Blood and Slaughter*. Booklocker.com, 2004. 3: 101.

34. Saye, James Hodge. *Memoirs of Major Joseph McJunkin, Revolutionary Patriot*. [sl]: A Press, Inc., 1977. (First printed in the Richmond, VA *Watchman and Observer* in 1847). O'Kelley, Patrick. *Nothing but Blood and Slaughter*. Booklocker.com, 2004. 3: 101–2. Parker, John C. *Parker's Guide to the Revolutionary War in South Carolina: battles, skirmishes and murders*. Patrick, SC: Hem Branch Publishing, 2009. p. 359.

35. Saye, James Hodge. *Memoirs of Major Joseph McJunkin, Revolutionary Patriot*. [sl]: A Press, Inc., 1977. (First printed in the Richmond, VA Watchman and Observer in 1847). Draper, Lyman. Thomas Sumter Papers, Draper Manuscript Collection, State Historical Society of Wisconsin. O'Kelley, Patrick. *Nothing but Blood and Slaughter*. Booklocker.com, 2004. 3: 106–7.

36. Lipscomb, Terry W. *South Carolina Revolutionary Battles: Part Ten. Names in South Carolina*. XXX (Winter 1983). South Carolina Historical Society, 1983. p. 14. O'Kelley, Patrick. *Nothing but Blood and Slaughter*. Booklocker.com, 2004. 3: 224. Parker, John C. *Parker's Guide to the Revolutionary War in South Carolina: battles, skirmishes and murders*. Patrick, SC: Hem Branch Publishing, 2009. p. 361.

37. Landrum, J. B. O. (John Belton O'Neall). *Colonial and Revolutionary History of Upper South Carolina; embracing for the most part the primitive and colonial history of the territory comprising the original county of Spartanburg*. Greenville, SC, Shannon, printers, 1897. [Spartanburg, SC, Reprint Co., 1959] pp. 354–355. Lipscomb, Terry W. *South Carolina Revolutionary Battles: Part Ten. Names in South Carolina*. XXX (Winter 1983). South Carolina Historical Society, 1983. pp. 13–14. The Diary of Anthony Allaire says that they camped on Sugar Creek at Blasingame's.

38. Ellet, Elizabeth F. *Domestic History of the American Revolution*. New York: Charles Scribner, 1859. pp. 177–181. O'Kelley, Patrick. *Nothing but Blood and Slaughter*. Booklocker.com, 2004. 2: 175. Parker, John C. *Parker's Guide to the Revolutionary War in South Carolina: battles, skirmishes and murders*. Patrick, SC: Hem Branch Publishing, 2009. pp. 124–125, 239.

39. Davie, William Richardson. *The Revolutionary War Sketches of William R. Davie*. Blackwell Pierce Robinson. Raleigh: North Carolina Dept. of Cultural Resources, Division of Archives and History, 1976. pp. 8–10. Kirkland, Thomas J. and Kennedy, Robert M. *Historic Camden*. State Company, 1905. p. 263. Schenck, David. *North Carolina 1780–81*. Raleigh: Edwards and Broughton, Publishers, 1889. pp. 64–66. Lipscomb, Terry W. *South Carolina Revolutionary Battles Part Three, Names in South Carolina*. XXII (Winter 1975). South Carolina Historical Society, 1975. p. 33. Hayes, John T. *The Saddlebag Almanac*. VI (Jan. 1998) pp. 35–36. O'Kelley, Patrick. *Nothing but Blood and Slaughter*. Booklocker.com, 2004. 2: 207–208. Parker, John C. *Parker's Guide to the Revolutionary War in South Carolina: battles, skirmishes and murders*. Patrick, SC: Hem Branch Publishing, 2009. pp. 239, 241, 246.

40. Scoggins, Michael C.; Edgar, Walter. *The Day It Rained Militia: Huck's Defeat and the Revolution in the South Carolina Backcountry, May–July 1780*. Charleston: The History Press, c2005.

41. General Richard Winn's Notes–1780. *The South Carolina Historical and Genealogical Magazine*. XLIII: 4 (October 1942) p. 209. Draper, Lyman. Thomas Sumter Papers, Draper Manuscript Collection, State Historical Society of Wisconsin. O'Kelley, Patrick. *Nothing but Blood and Slaughter*. Booklocker.com, 2004. 2: 220–221. Parker, John C. *Parker's Guide to the Revolutionary War in South Carolina: battles, skirmishes and murders*. Patrick, SC: Hem Branch Publishing, 2009. p. 123.

42. Clark. Murtie June. *Loyalists in the Southern Campaign of the Revolutionary War*. Baltimore: Genealogical Publishing Company, Inc., 1981. 1: 361–362. Moultrie, William. *Memoirs of the American Revolution so far as it related to the States of North and South Carolina and Georgia*. New York, 1802; (Eyewitness Accounts of the American Revolution). [New York]: New York Times, [1968]. 2: 220. Schenck, David. *North Carolina 1780–'81. Being a History of the Invasion of the Carolinas by the British Army under Lord Cornwallis in 1780–'81*. Raleigh, NC: Edwards & Broughton, 1889. pp. 66–67. Robinson, Blackwell P. *The Revolutionary War Sketches of William R. Davie*. Raleigh: North Carolina Department of Cultural Resources, Division of Archives and History, 1976. pp. 11–12. Commager, Henry S. and Richard B. Morris, eds. *The Spirit of '76: the Story of the American Revolution as Told by Participants*. Bicentennial edition. New York: Harper and Row, 1976. p. 1170. Hayes. *Saddlebag Almanac*. VII (January 1999), pp. 6–7. Draper, Lyman. Thomas Sumter Papers, Draper Manuscript Collection, State Historical Society of Wisconsin. 5VV166-167, 7VV42. O'Kelley, Patrick. *Nothing but Blood and Slaughter*. Booklocker.com, 2004. 2: 217–218.

43. Collins. James. *A Revolutionary Soldier*. Felician Democrat, 1859. p. 25. Lipscomb, Terry W. *South Carolina Revolutionary Battles: Part Three. Names in South Carolina*. XXII (Winter 1975). South Carolina Historical Society, 1975. p. 33. Hayes, John T. *The Saddlebag Almanac*. VI (Jan. 1998) pp. 33, 187–88. Lambert, Robert Stansbury. *South Carolina Loyalists in the American Revolution*. Columbia: University of South Carolina, 1987. pp. 119, 128. British National Archives. Cornwallis Papers. Class 30, Vol. 11/2/158–159, 162–163, 171–172. Gaston, Joseph. A Reminiscence of the Revolution. *The Southern Presbyterian* (Columbia SCO May 22, 1873. Hill, Daniel Harvey. *Col. William Hill and the campaign of 1780*. [N.p., 1919] p. 8. Hill, William. *Col. William Hill's Memoirs of the Revolution*, edited by A. S. Sally, Columbia, SC: Printed for the Historical commission of South Carolina by the State Co., 1921. pp. 8, 10. Tarleton, Banastre. *A History of the Campaigns of 1780 and 1781 in the Southern Provinces of North America*, London, 1787; (Eyewitness Accounts of the American Revolution). [New York] New York Times [1968] p. 117. Saye, James Hodge. *Memoirs of Major Joseph McJunkin, Revolutionary Patriot*. [sl]: A Press, Inc., 1977. (First printed in the Richmond, VA *Watchman and Observer* in 1847). Draper, Lyman. Thomas Sumter Papers, Draper Manuscript Collection, State Historical Society of Wisconsin. 9VV10, 12–13, 28–29; 11VV329-332; 16VV49-50; 17VV70-71. O'Kelley, Patrick. *Nothing but Blood and Slaughter*. Booklocker.com, 2004. 2: 175–178. Michael C. Scoggins. Alexander's Old Field, or the Battle of Beckhamville. *Southern Campaigns of the American Revolution* 2:6 p. 6. www.southerncampaigns.org. Parker, John C. *Parker's Guide to the Revolutionary War in South Carolina: battles,*

skirmishes and murders. Patrick, SC: Hem Branch Publishing, 2009. p. 380. Scoggins, Michael C.; Edgar, Walter. *The Day It Rained Militia: Huck's Defeat and the Revolution in the South Carolina Backcountry, May–July 1780.* Charleston: The History Press, c2005. pp. 80–83.

44. Parker, John C. *Parker's Guide to the Revolutionary War in South Carolina: battles, skirmishes and murders.* Patrick, SC: Hem Branch Publishing, 2009. p. 348.

45. Draper, Lyman. Thomas Sumter Papers, Draper Manuscript Collection, State Historical Society of Wisconsin. O'Kelley, Patrick. *Nothing but Blood and Slaughter.* Booklocker.com, 2004. 3: 299. Parker, John C. *Parker's Guide to the Revolutionary War in South Carolina: battles, skirmishes and murders.* Patrick, SC: Hem Branch Publishing, 2009. p. 350.

46. Moore, M. A. *The life of Gen. Edward Lacey: with a list of battles and skirmishes in South Carolina, during the revolutionary war.* Spartanburg, SC: Douglass, Evins & Co., 1859. p. 8.

47. *Encyclopedia of the American Revolution.* Harold E. Selesky, editor in chief. 2nd ed. Detroit: Charles Scribner's Sons, 2007. II:1276. *The Encyclopedia of the American Revolutionary War: a political, social, and military history.* Gregory Fremont-Barnes, Richard Alan Ryerson, editors. Santa Barbara, CA: ABC-CLIO, 2006. IV: 1366. Draper, Lyman. Draper Manuscript Collection, State Historical Society of Wisconsin. 9VV13–14, 9VV206, 15VV355. Ripley, Warren. *Battleground: South Carolina in the Revolution.* Charleston, SC: Evening Post, 1983. Lieutenant Colonel Turnbull to Lord Rawdon. July 12, 1780. British National Archives. 30/11/2/285–286. Parker, John C. *Parker's Guide to the Revolutionary War in South Carolina: battles, skirmishes and murders.* Patrick, SC: Hem Branch Publishing, 2009. p. 378. Scoggins, Michael C.; Edgar, Walter. *The Day It Rained Militia: Huck's Defeat and the Revolution in the South Carolina Backcountry, May–July 1780.* Charleston: The History Press, c2005. pp. 112–118. Extract of a letter dated at Hillsborough, North Carolina, July 22, 1780. *The Norwich Packet and the Weekly Advertiser.* 363 (Sept. 14, 1780) p. 2.

48. Southern Studies Program. *Figures of the Revolution in South Carolina, An Anthology.* Spartanburg, Anderson, Beaufort, Aiken, Florence, Georgetown. Columbia: University of South Carolina, 1976. pp. 303–304. Tarleton, Banastre. *A History of the Campaigns of 1780 and 1781 in the Southern Provinces of North America,* London, 1787; (Eyewitness Accounts of the American Revolution). [New York] New York Times [1968]. p. 98. *The Pennsylvania Gazette.* Aug. 30, 1780. British National Archives. Cornwallis Papers, Class 30, Vol. 11 p. 2. Lipscomb, Terry W. *South Carolina Revolutionary Battles: Part Three. Names in South Carolina.* XXII (Winter 1975). South Carolina Historical Society, 1975. p. 37. Hayes. *Saddlebag Almanac.* VII (Jan. 1999) pp. 4–6. Lambert, Robert Stansbury. *South Carolina Loyalists in the American Revolution.* Columbia: University of South Carolina, 1987. pp. 116–117. *A List of all the officers of the Army: viz. the general and field officers: the officers of the several troops, regiments, independent companies, and garrisons: with an alphabetical index to the whole. Also, a list of the officers of the Royal Regiment of Artillery, the Corps of Engineers, the Irish Artillery and Engineers, and of the Marine Forces: the officers on half pay; and a succession of colonels. : To which are likewise added the officers of the militia forces, and of the fencible and provincial regiments in Great Britain.* [London, England?]: War-Office, 1780. pp. 145. O'Kelley, Patrick. *Nothing but Blood and Slaughter.* Booklocker.com, 2004. 2: 208–209. Parker, John C. *Parker's Guide to the Revolutionary War in South Carolina: battles, skirmishes and murders.* Patrick, SC: Hem Branch Publishing, 2009. pp. 283–284.

49. Gregg, Alexander. *History of the old Cheraws; containing an account of the aborigines of the Pedee, the first white settlements, their subsequent progress, civil changes, the struggle of the revolution, and the growth of the country afterward, extending from about A. D. 1730 to 1810, with notices of families and sketches of individuals.* by the Right Rev. Alexander Gregg. Columbia, S. C.: the State Company, 1905. p. 352. Thomas, J. A. W. (John Alexander William). *A History of Marlboro County: with traditions and sketches of numerous families.* Atlanta, GA: Foote & Davies Co., 1897. p. 105. Parker, John C. *Parker's Guide to the Revolutionary War in South Carolina: battles, skirmishes and murders.* Patrick, SC: Hem Branch Publishing, 2009. pp. 283–284.

50. Caruthers, E. W. (Eli Washington). *Interesting Revolutionary Incidents and Sketches of Character, Chiefly in the "Old North State."* Philadelphia: Hayes & Zell (King & Baird), 1856. pp. 273–281. Fowler, Tom. *Carolina journeys: exploring the trails of the Carolinas—both real and imagined.* Boone, NC: Parkway Publishers, 2004. p. 126. Fanning, David; Savary, A. W. *The adventures of David Fanning in the American Revolutionary War.* Ottawa, Canada: Golden Dog Press, 1983? p. 57. Gregg, Alexander. *History of the old Cheraws; containing an account of the aborigines of the Pedee, the first white settlements, their subsequent progress, civil changes, the struggle of the revolution, and the growth of the country afterward, extending from about A. D. 1730 to 1810, with notices of families and sketches of individuals.* by the Right Rev. Alexander Gregg. Columbia, S. C.: the State Company, 1905. p. 383. Parker, John C. *Parker's Guide to the Revolutionary War in South Carolina: battles, skirmishes and murders.* Patrick, SC: Hem Branch Publishing, 2009. p. 187.

51. Lawrence, James Walton. *Hogback Country.* The News Leader, 1982. p. 41. Draper, Lyman. *Kings Mountain and its Heroes: History of the Battle of King's Mountain, October 7th, 1780, and the events which led to it.* The Overmountain Press, 1996. pp. 87–89, 423. White, Katherine Keogh. *The King's Mountain Men, the story of the Battle with Sketches of the American Soldiers who took part.* Baltimore: Genealogical Publishing Company, 1966. p. 178. Schenck, David. *North Carolina 1780–'81, Being a History of the Invasion of the Carolinas by the British Army under Lord Cornwallis in 1780–'81.* Edwards & Broughton, Publishers, 1889. pp. 76–77. Johnson, Uzal. *Memo of Occurrence during the Campaign of 1780.* South Carolina Historical Society, Military Manuscripts. p. 59. Hayes, John T. *The Saddlebag Almanac.* VII (Jan. 1999) p. 4. O'Kelley, Patrick. *Nothing but Blood and Slaughter.* Booklocker.com, 2004. 2: 209–210. Parker, John C. *Parker's Guide to the Revolutionary War in South Carolina: battles, skirmishes and murders.* Patrick, SC: Hem Branch Publishing, 2009. p. 187. Smith, Gordon Burns. *Morningstars of Liberty: the Revolutionary War in Georgia, 1775–1783.* Milledgeville, GA: Boyd Publishing, 2006. I: 207. Johnson, Uzal. *Memo of Occurrence During the Campaign of 1780.* South Carolina Historical Society, Military Manuscripts. p. 51. Draper, Lyman. *Kings Mountain and its Heroes: History of the Battle of King's Mountain, October 7th, 1780, and the Events Which Led To It.* Johnson City, TN: the Overmountain Press, 1996. pp. 87–88. Scoggins, Michael C.; Edgar, Walter. *The Day It Rained*

Militia: Huck's Defeat and the Revolution in the South Carolina Backcountry, May–July 1780. Charleston: The History Press, c2005. p. 141.

52. Draper, Lyman. Thomas Sumter Papers, Draper Manuscript Collection, State Historical Society of Wisconsin. 4VV51–53, 56–58. O'Kelley, Patrick. *Nothing but Blood and Slaughter.* Booklocker.com, 2004. 2: 172. Parker, John C. *Parker's Guide to the Revolutionary War in South Carolina: battles, skirmishes and murders.* Patrick, SC: Hem Branch Publishing, 2009. pp. 124–126.

53. O'Kelley, Patrick. *Nothing but Blood and Slaughter.* Booklocker.com, 2004. 3: 397–400. Parker, John C. *Parker's Guide to the Revolutionary War in South Carolina: battles, skirmishes and murders.* Patrick, SC: Hem Branch Publishing, 2009. p. 295.

54. *Encyclopedia of the American Revolution.* Harold E. Selesky, editor in chief. 2nd ed. Detroit: Charles Scribner's Sons, 2007. II: 997. *The Encyclopedia of the American Revolutionary War: a political, social, and military history.* Gregory Fremont-Barnes, Richard Alan Ryerson, editors. Santa Barbara, CA: ABC-CLIO, 2006. III: 1084–1085. Bass, Robert. *Gamecock: the life and campaigns of General Thomas Sumter.* Orangeburg, SC: Sandlapper, 2000. Ripley, Warren. *Battleground: South Carolina in the Revolution.* Charleston, SC: Evening Post, 1983. Robinson, Blackwell P. *The Revolutionary War Sketches of William R. Davie.* Raleigh: North Carolina Department of Cultural Resources, Division of Archives and History, 1976. Tarleton, Banastre. *A History of the Campaigns of 1780 and 1781 in the Southern Provinces of North America.* London: T. Cadell, 1787; [sl]: the New York Times & Arno Press, 1968. pp. 93–94. Thomas, Sam. *The Dye is Cast: the Scots-Irish and Revolution in the Carolina Back Country.* Columbia, SC: the Palmetto Conservation Foundation, 1994. pp. 23–35. General Richard Winn's Notes–1780. *The South Carolina Historical and Genealogical Magazine.* XLIII:4 (October 1942) pp. 207–209. White, Katherine Keogh. *The Kings Mountain Men; the story of the battle, with sketches of the American soldiers who took part.* Baltimore, Genealogical Pub. Co., 1966, 1924. pp. 198, 226, 229. Clark. Murtie June. *Loyalists in the Southern Campaign of the Revolutionary War.* Baltimore: Genealogical Publishing Company, Inc., 1981. III: 177–218. Moultrie, William. *Memoirs of the American Revolution so far as it related to the States of North and South Carolina and Georgia.* New York, 1802; (Eyewitness accounts of the American Revolution). [New York]: New York Times, [1968]. II: 219–220. Moss, Bobby Gilmer. *Roster of South Carolina Patriots in the American Revolution.* Baltimore: Genealogical Pub. Co., 1983. pp. 5, 427, 1006. Robinson, Blackwell P. *The Revolutionary War Sketches of William R. Davie.* Raleigh: North Carolina Department of Cultural Resources, Division of Archives and History, 1976. pp. 11–12. Clark, Walter, et al., editors. *The State Records of North Carolina.* Winston and Goldsboro: Various publishers, 1895–1907. Volumes XIV—1779–'80 pp. 540–543. Vol. XIX—1782–'84 with Supplement–1771–'82. Nash Brothers, 1901. pp. 985–989. Hill, William. *Col. William Hill's Memoirs of the Revolution,* edited by A. S. Sally, Columbia, SC: Printed for the Historical commission of South Carolina by the State Co., 1921. Draper, Lyman. Thomas Sumter Papers, Draper Manuscript Collection, State Historical Society of Wisconsin. 9VV62–63, 101; 11VV457–458; 14VV260–261, 436–443. O'Kelley, Patrick. *Nothing but Blood and Slaughter.* Booklocker.com, 2004. 2: 216. Parker, John C. *Parker's Guide to the Revolutionary War in South Carolina: battles, skirmishes and murders.* Patrick, SC: Hem Branch Publishing, 2009. p. 181.

55. General Richard Winn's Notes–1780. *The South Carolina Historical and Genealogical Magazine.* XLIII: 4 (October 1942) p. 209. Draper, Lyman. Thomas Sumter Papers, Draper Manuscript Collection, State Historical Society of Wisconsin. O'Kelley, Patrick. *Nothing But Blood and Slaughter.* Booklocker.com, 2004. 2: 220–221. Parker, John C. *Parker's Guide to the Revolutionary War in South Carolina: battles, skirmishes and murders.* Patrick, SC: Hem Branch Publishing, 2009. p. 123.

56. Parker, John C. *Parker's Guide to the Revolutionary War in South Carolina: battles, skirmishes and murders.* Patrick, SC: Hem Branch Publishing, 2009. p. 351.

57. Parker, John C. *Parker's Guide to the Revolutionary War in South Carolina: battles, skirmishes and murders.* Patrick, SC: Hem Branch Publishing, 2009. p. 352.

58. Lambert, Robert Stansbury. *South Carolina Loyalists in the American Revolution.* Columbia: University of South Carolina, 1987. p. 115. Bass, Robert Duncan. *Swamp Fox: the life and campaigns of General Francis Marion.* Orangeburg, SC: Sandlapper, 1989. p. 105. O'Kelley, Patrick. *Nothing But Blood and Slaughter.* Booklocker.com, 2004. 2: 349. Parker, John C. *Parker's Guide to the Revolutionary War in South Carolina: battles, skirmishes and murders.* Patrick, SC: Hem Branch Publishing, 2009. p. 233.

59. Davies, K.G. *Documents of the American Revolution 1770–1783.* (Colonial Office Series) Shannon: Irish University Press 1972, 1981. 18: 140–141. Kirkland, Thomas J. and Kennedy, Robert M. *Historic Camden.* State Company, 1905. pp. 143–149. Tarleton, Banastre. *A History of the Campaigns of 1780 and 1781 in the Southern Provinces of North America,* London, 1787; (Eyewitness Accounts of the American Revolution). [New York] New York Times [1968]. p. 99. National Archives and Records Administration. Pension Applications RG 15, Microcopy 804. James, William Dobein. *A Sketch of the Life of Brig. General Francis Marion, and a History of his Brigade, from its Rise in June 1780, until Disbanded in December, 1782.* Charleston, SC: Gould and Riley, 1821. p. 17. Clark, Walter. *The State Records of North Carolina XIV–1779–'80.* Winston, 1896. pp. 584–585. Batt, Richard John. *The Maryland Continentals, 1780–1781.* Tulane University dissertation, 1974. pp. 24–25, 28–33. Davis, Robert Scott, Jr. Thomas Pinckney and the Last Campaign of Horatio Gates. *South Carolina Historical Magazine.* 86:2 (April 1985) pp. 76–79. Miller, A. E. *Sketches of the Life and Correspondence of Nathanael Greene.* Charleston, SC, 1922. I: 488, 493. Aspinall, A., ed. *The Correspondence of George, Prince of Wales, 1770–1812.* Oxford University Press. 4: 192–197. O'Kelley, Patrick. *Nothing But Blood and Slaughter.* Booklocker.com, 2004. 2: 236–243.

60. Gibbes, Robert Wilson. *Documentary History of the American Revolution.* New York: D. Appleton & Co., 1855 (3 vols: 1764–1776, 1776–1782, 1781–1782). reprinted New York Times & Arno Press, 1971. III: 28.

61. Extract of a letter from General Marion, dated April 21st, 1781. *The Connecticut Gazette and the Universal Intelligencer.* XVIII: 919, p 1. Parker, John C. *Parker's Guide to the Revolutionary War in South Carolina: battles, skirmishes and murders.* Patrick, SC: Hem Branch Publishing, 2009. pp. 230, 260.

62. Parker, John C. *Parker's Guide to the Revolutionary War in South Carolina: battles, skirmishes and murders.* Patrick, SC: Hem Branch Publishing, 2009. pp. 190, 274.

63. Chesney, Alexander. *The Journal of Alexander Chesney, a South Carolina Loyalist in the Revolution and After*, edited by E. A. Jones. Columbus, Ohio: Ohio State University, 1921. O'Kelley, Patrick. *Nothing But Blood and Slaughter.* Booklocker.com, 2004. 2: 46.

64. Saye, James Hodge. *Memoirs of Major Joseph McJunkin, Revolutionary Patriot.* [sl]: A Press, Inc., 1977. (First printed in the Richmond, VA *Watchman and Observer* in 1847) pp. 39–40. O'Kelley, Patrick. *Nothing But Blood and Slaughter.* Booklocker.com, 2004. 2: 320–321. Parker, John C. *Parker's Guide to the Revolutionary War in South Carolina: battles, skirmishes and murders.* Patrick, SC: Hem Branch Publishing, 2009. p. 363.

65. Norfleet, Phil. Biographical Sketch of Lieutenant-Colonel John Mayfield the Loyalist, of Browns Creek. http://sc_tories.tripod.com/john_mayfield.htm. Draper, Lyman. Thomas Sumter Papers, Draper Manuscript Collection, State Historical Society of Wisconsin. Parker, John C. *Parker's Guide to the Revolutionary War in South Carolina: battles, skirmishes and murders.* Patrick, SC: Hem Branch Publishing, 2009. p. 362.

66. Kirkland, Thomas J. and Kennedy, Robert M. *Historic Camden.* Columbia, SC: State Company, 1905. pp. 140–144. O'Kelley, Patrick. *Nothing but Blood and Slaughter.* Booklocker.com, 2004. 2: 161–162.

67. Ramsay, David. *The History of the Revolution of South Carolina.* Trenton, NJ: Isaac Collins, 1785. I: 141–142. James, William Dobein. *A Sketch of the Life of Brig. Gen. Francis Marion, and a History of his Brigade, from its Rise in June 1780, until Disbanded in December, 1782.* Charleston, SC: Gould and Riley, 1821. pp. 40–41. Kirkland, Thomas J. and Kennedy, Robert M. *Historic Camden.* Columbia, SC: State Company, 1905. pp. 139–141. Simms, William Gilmore. *The Life of Francis Marion.* New York: H.G. Langley, 1844. O'Kelley, Patrick. *Nothing but Blood and Slaughter.* Booklocker.com, 2004. 2: 161. Scoggins, Michael C.; Edgar, Walter. *The Day It Rained Militia: Huck's Defeat and the Revolution in the South Carolina Backcountry, May–July 1780.* Charleston: The History Press, c2005. pp. 225–226.

68. White, Katherine Keogh. *The King's Mountain Men, the story of the Battle with Sketches of the American Soldiers who took part.* Baltimore: Genealogical Publishing Company, 1966. p. 198. Kirkland, Thomas J. and Kennedy, Robert M. *Historic Camden.* Columbia, SC: State Company, 1905. p. 153. Lawrence, James Walton. *Hogback Country.* The News Leader, 1982. p. 105. *The Pennsylvania Gazette.* Sept. 13, 1780. Clark, Walter. *The State Records of North Carolina XIV–1779–'80.* Winston, 1896. pp. 540–543. Batt, Richard John. *The Maryland Continentals, 1780–1781.* Tulane University Dissertation, 1974. p. 41. Davis, Robert Scott, Jr. Thomas Pinckney and the Last Campaign of Horatio Gates. *South Carolina Historical Magazine.* 86:2 (April 1985) p. 78. Senf, Johann Christian. Extract from a Journal Concerning the Action of the 16th of August 1780 between Major General Gates and Gen. Lord Cornwallis. Library of Congress. Manuscript Division. Hayes, John T. *The Saddlebag Almanac.* VII (Jan. 1999) pp. 54–55. Miller, A.E. *Sketches of the Life and Correspondence of Nathaniel Greene.* Charleston, SC. I: 494. Stevens, John Austin. The Southern Campaign, 1780, Gates at Camden. *Magazine of American History.* V: 4 (October 1880) pp. 265–266. Draper, Lyman. Thomas Sumter Papers, Draper Manuscript Collection, State Historical Society of Wisconsin. 1VV189, 5VV262, 7VV27–28. O'Kelley, Patrick. *Nothing but Blood and Slaughter.* Booklocker.com, 2004. 2: 243–245.

69. Dudley, Guilford. A Sketch of the Military Services Performed by Guilford Dudley, Then of the Town of Halifax, North Carolina, During the Revolutionary War. *Literary Messenger.* 1845 Part II p. 146; Part III pp. 231–235.

70. Davies, K.G. *Documents of the American Revolution 1770–1783.* (Colonial Office Series) Shannon: Irish University Press 1972, 1981. 18: 149–150. Carrington, Henry B. *Battles of the American Revolution, 1775–1781, Historical and Military Criticism, with Topographic Illustrations.* A.S. Barnes & Co. 1876. p. 515. Seymour, William. *A Journal of the Southern Expedition, 1780–1783.* Wilmington: the Historical Society of Delaware, 1896. p. 5. Kirkland, Thomas J. and Kennedy, Robert M. *Historic Camden.* State Company, 1905. pp. 143–159. Tarleton, Banastre. *A History of the Campaigns of 1780 and 1781 in the Southern Provinces of North America*, London, 1787; (Eyewitness Accounts of the American Revolution). [New York] New York Times [1968]. pp. 99–110, 143. British National Archives. Cornwallis Papers, Vol. 103 folio 2. National Archives and Records Administration. Pension Applications. RG 15, Microcopy 804. *The Pennsylvania Gazette.* Sept. 13, 1780. James, William Dobein. *A Sketch of the Life of Brig. Gen. Francis Marion, and a History of his Brigade, from its Rise in June 1780, until Disbanded in December, 1782.* Charleston, SC: Gould and Riley, 1821. p. 17. Clark, Walter. *The State Records of North Carolina XIV–1779–'80.* Winston, 1896. pp. 584–585. Landers, H.L. *The Battle of Camden, South Carolina, August 16, 1780.* Washington, DC: United States Government Printing Office, 1929. pp. 41–42. Batt, Richard John. *The Maryland Continentals, 1780–1781.* Tulane University Dissertation, 1974. pp. 24–25, 28–33. Davis, Robert Scott, Jr. Thomas Pinckney and the Last Campaign of Horatio Gates. *South Carolina Historical Magazine.* 86:2 (April 1985) pp. 78–81, 86–88. Hayes, John T. *The Saddlebag Almanac.* VII (Jan. 1999) pp. 43–53. *A List of all the officers of the Army: viz. the general and field officers; the officers of the several troops, regiments, independent companies, and garrisons: with an alphabetical index to the whole. Also, a list of the officers of the Royal Regiment of Artillery, the Corps of Engineers, the Irish Artillery and Engineers, and of the Marine Forces: the officers on half pay; and a succession of colonels. To which are likewise added the officers of the militia forces, and of the fencible and provincial regiments in Great Britain.* [London, England?]: War-Office, 1780. p. 86. Maas, John. *"That Unhappy Affair" Horatio Gates and the Battle of Camden, August 16, 1781.* The Kershaw County Historical Society, 2000. p. 34. Dudley, Guilford. A Sketch of the Military Services Performed by Guilford Dudley, Then of the Town of Halifax, North Carolina, During the Revolutionary War. *Literary Messenger*, 1845. Part II pp. 146–146; Part III pp. 231–235. Johnson, William. *Sketches of the Life and Correspondence of Nathanael Greene, Major General of the Armies of the United States in the War of the Revolution.* Charleston, SC: W. E. Miller, 1822. 1: 494. Stedman, Charles. *The History of the Origin, Progress and Termination of the American War.* London: printed for the author, 1794. II: 205–207. Aspinall, A., ed. *The Correspondence of George, Prince of Wales,*

1770–1812. Oxford University Press. pp. 192–197. O'Kelley, Patrick. *Nothing But Blood and Slaughter.* Booklocker. com, 2004. 2: 247–256.

71. *Encyclopedia of the American Revolution.* Harold E. Selesky, editor in chief. 2nd Ed. Detroit: Charles Scribner's Sons, 2007. I: 146–154. *The Encyclopedia of the American Revolutionary War: a political, social, and military history.* Gregory Fremont-Barnes, Richard Alan Ryerson, editors. Santa Barbara, CA: ABC-CLIO, 2006. I: 172–176. Bass, Robert Duncan. *The Green Dragoon: the lives of Banastre Tarleton and Mary Robinson.* New York: Holt, 1957. Buchanan, John. *The Road to Guilford Courthouse.* New York: John Wiley and Sons, Inc., 1997. Fischer, Sydney George. *The Struggle for American Independence.* Philadelphia: Lippincott Company, 1908. Fortescue, Sir John William. *A History of the British Army.* 2nd ed. London: Macmillan and Company, 1911. Johnson, William. *Sketches of the Life and Correspondence of Nathanael Greene, Major General of the Armies of the United States in the War of the Revolution.* Charleston, SC: W. E. Miller, 1822 vol. 1. Landers, Lieutenant Colonel H. L. *"the Battle of Camden"* House Document No. 12. Seventy-first Congress, First Session. Washington, DC: Government Printing Office, 1929. Lumpkin, Henry. *From Savannah to Yorktown: the American Revolution in the South.* New York: Paragon, 1981. McCrady, Edward. *History of South Carolina in the Revolution, 1775–1780.* New York: Paladin Press, 1969 (reprint of 1901 ed.). Morrill, Dan L. *Southern Campaigns of the American Revolution.* Baltimore: the Nautical & Aviation Publishing Company of America, 1993. Pancake, John S. *This Destructive War: the British Campaign in the Carolinas.* Tuscaloosa: University of Alabama Press, 1985. Pinckney, General Thomas. "General Gates's Southern Campaign." *Historical Magazine.* X: 8 (1866) pp. 244–253. Raab, James W. *Spain, Britain, and the American Revolution in Florida, 1763–1783.* Jefferson, NC and London: McFarland & Company, Inc., 2008. p. 123. Sheer, George F. and Hugh F. Rankin. *Rebels and Redcoats.* Cleveland, OH: World Publishing, 1957. Tarleton, Banastre. *A History of the Campaigns of 1780 and 1781 in the Southern Provinces of North America.* London: T. Cadell, 1787; [sl]: the New York Times & Arno Press, 1968. Trevelyan, George Otto. *The American Revolution.* London: Longmans, Green and Co., 1904–1914. Ward, Christopher. *The War of the Revolution.* New York: Macmillan, 1952. pp. 722–730. Wickwire, Franklin, and Mary Wickwire. *Cornwallis: the American Adventure.* Boston: Houghton Mifflin, 1970. Parker, John C. *Parker's Guide to the Revolutionary War in South Carolina: battles, skirmishes and murders.* Patrick, SC: Hem Branch Publishing, 2009. p. 236–237. Smith, Gordon Burns. *Morningstars of Liberty: the Revolutionary War in Georgia, 1775–1783.* Milledgeville, GA: Boyd Publishing, 2006. 1: 243–244.

71a. *Encyclopedia of the American Revolution.* Harold E. Selesky, editor in chief. 2nd Ed. Detroit: Charles Scribner's Sons, 2007. II: 1008. *The Encyclopedia of the American Revolutionary War: a political, social, and military history.* Gregory Fremont-Barnes, Richard Alan Ryerson, editors. Santa Barbara, CA: ABC-CLIO, 2006. IV: 1099. Haller, Stephen E. *William Washington: Cavalryman of the Revolution.* Bowie, MD: Heritage Press, 2001. Morrill, Dan L. *Southern Campaigns of the American Revolution.* Baltimore: the Nautical & Aviation Publishing Company of America [nd]. Tarleton, Banastre. *A History of the Campaigns of 1780 and 1781 in the Southern Provinces of North America.* London: T. Cadell, 1787; [sl]: the New York Times & Arno Press, 1968. Parker, John C. *Parker's Guide to the Revolutionary War in South Carolina: battles, skirmishes and murders.* Patrick, SC: Hem Branch Publishing, 2009. p. 238.

72. Kirkland, Thomas J. and Kennedy, Robert M. *Historic Camden.* State Company, 1905. pp. 252–254, 402. Lambert, Robert Stansbury. *South Carolina Loyalists in the American Revolution.* Columbia: University of South Carolina, 1987. pp. 201–202. Mathis, Samuel. *The Battle of Hobkirk's Hill.* Columbia, SC: South Carolina Archives. O'Kelley, Patrick. *Nothing But Blood and Slaughter.* Booklocker.com, 2004. 3: 192–93. Parker, John C. *Parker's Guide to the Revolutionary War in South Carolina: battles, skirmishes and murders.* Patrick, SC: Hem Branch Publishing, 2009. p. 231.

73. Kirkland, Thomas J. and Kennedy, Robert M. *Historic Camden.* State Company, 1905. pp. 18, 204–205, 221–223. Seymour, William. Journal of the Southern Expedition, 1780–1783. *Papers of the Historical Society of Delaware.* XV. Wilmington: the Historical Society of Delaware, 1896. p. 24. Kirkwood, Robert. "The Journal and Orderly Book of Captain Robert Kirkwood of the Delaware Regiment of the Continental Line." *Papers of the Historical Society of Delaware.* vol. 56, 1910, p. 16. Ward, Christopher L. *The Delaware Continentals.* Historical Society of Delaware, 1941. p. 426. Pancake, John S. *This Destructive War: the British Campaign in the Carolinas.* Tuscaloosa: University of Alabama Press, 1985. p. 195. Batt, Richard John. *The Maryland Continentals, 1780–1781.* Tulane University Dissertation, 1974. p. 154. *A List of all the officers of the Army: viz. the general and field officers; the officers of the several troops, regiments, independent companies, and garrisons: with an alphabetical index to the whole. Also, a list of the officers of the Royal Regiment of Artillery, the Corps of Engineers, the Irish Artillery and Engineers, and of the Marine Forces: the officers on half pay; and a succession of colonels. To which are likewise added the officers of the militia forces, and of the fencible and provincial regiments in Great Britain.* [London, England?]: War-Office, 1780. pp. 137. Draper, Lyman. Thomas Sumter Papers, Draper Manuscript Collection, State Historical Society of Wisconsin. 7VV581. O'Kelley, Patrick. *Nothing But Blood and Slaughter.* Booklocker.com, 2004. 3: 193–95.

74. Kirkland, Thomas J. and Kennedy, Robert M. *Historic Camden.* State Company, 1905. pp. 18, 204–205, 221–223. Seymour, William. Journal of the Southern Expedition, 1780–1783. *Papers of the Historical Society of Delaware.* XV. Wilmington: the Historical Society of Delaware, 1896. p. 24. Kirkwood, Robert. "The Journal and Orderly Book of Captain Robert Kirkwood of the Delaware Regiment of the Continental Line," *Papers of the Historical Society of Delaware.* 56, 1910, pp. 1–277. Ward, Christopher L. *The Delaware Continentals.* Historical Society of Delaware, 1941. p. 426. Pancake, John S. *This Destructive War: the British Campaign in the Carolinas.* Tuscaloosa: University of Alabama Press, 1985. p. 195. Batt, Richard John. *The Maryland Continentals, 1780–1781.* Tulane University Dissertation, 1974. p. 154. *A List of all the officers of the Army: viz. the general and field officers; the officers of the several troops, regiments, independent companies, and garrisons: with an alphabetical index to the whole. Also, a list of the officers of the Royal Regiment of Artillery, the Corps of Engineers, the Irish Artillery and Engineers, and of the Marine Forces: the officers on half pay; and a succession of colonels. To which are likewise added the officers of the militia forces, and of the fencible and provincial regiments in Great Britain.* [London, England?]: War-Office, 1780. pp. 137. Draper, Lyman. Thomas Sumter Papers, Draper Manuscript Collection, State Historical Society of Wisconsin. 7VV581. O'Kelley, Patrick. *Nothing But*

Blood and Slaughter. Booklocker.com, 2004. 3: 195–96. Parker, John C. *Parker's Guide to the Revolutionary War in South Carolina: battles, skirmishes and murders.* Patrick, SC: Hem Branch Publishing, 2009. p. 232.

75. Seymour, William. Journal of the Southern Expedition, 1780–1783. *Papers of the Historical Society of Delaware.* XV. Wilmington: the Historical Society of Delaware, 1896. p. 24. O'Kelley, Patrick. *Nothing But Blood and Slaughter.* Booklocker.com, 2004. 3: 196.

76. Lambert, Robert Stansbury. *South Carolina Loyalists in the American Revolution.* Columbia: University of South Carolina, 1987. p. 202. O'Kelley, Patrick. *Nothing But Blood and Slaughter.* Booklocker.com, 2004. 3: 197.

77. *Encyclopedia of the American Revolution.* Harold E. Selesky, editor in chief. 2nd ed. Detroit: Charles Scribner's Sons, 2007. I: 508–511. *The Encyclopedia of the American Revolutionary War: a political, social, and military history.* Gregory Fremont-Barnes, Richard Alan Ryerson, editors. Santa Barbara, CA: ABC-CLIO, 2006. II: 596–600. Greene, Nathanael. Letter "to Samuel Huntington, President of the Continental Congress, 27 April 1781." In *the Papers of General Nathanael Greene.* Edited by Dennis M. Conrad. Chapel Hill: University of North Carolina Press, 1995. Vol. 8. Howard, John Eager. "Letter to [John Marshall, 1804] Bayard Collection, MS 109, box 4, file 2. Maryland Historical Society, Baltimore, MD. Lee, Henry. *Memoirs of the War in the Southern Department of the United States,* New York: University Publishing Co., 1869. Williams, Otho H. Letter "to Elie Williams, 27 April 1781" *American Monthly.* 4:48 (Feb. 1875) pp. 99–104. Alden, John Richard. *The South in the Revolution, 1763–1789.* Baton Rouge: Louisiana State University Press, 1957. McCrady, Edward. *History of South Carolina in the Revolution, 1775–1780.* New York: Paladin Press, 1969 (reprint of 1901 ed.). Pancake, John S. *This Destructive War: the British Campaign in the Carolinas.* Tuscaloosa: University of Alabama Press, 1985. Tarleton, Banastre. *A History of the Campaigns of 1780 and 1781 in the Southern Provinces of North America.* London: T. Cadell, 1787; [sl]: the New York Times & Arno Press, 1968. Thayer, Theodore. *Nathanael Greene: Strategist of the Revolution.* New York: Twayne, 1960. Ward, Christopher. *The War of the Revolution.* New York: Macmillan, 1952. pp. 731–736. Parker, John C. *Parker's Guide to the Revolutionary War in South Carolina: battles, skirmishes and murders.* Patrick, SC: Hem Branch Publishing, 2009. p. 234–235. Smith, Gordon Burns. *Morningstars of Liberty: the Revolutionary War in Georgia, 1775–1783.* Milledgeville, GA: Boyd Publishing, 2006. 1: 243–244.

78. *Southern Presbyterian Review.* 8 (1855) pp. 144–146. Parker, John C. *Parker's Guide to the Revolutionary War in South Carolina: battles, skirmishes and murders.* Patrick, SC: Hem Branch Publishing, 2009. p. 368–370.

79. James, William Dobein. *A Sketch of the Life of Brig. Gen. Francis Marion, and a History of his Brigade, from its Rise in June 1780, until Disbanded in December, 1782.* Charleston, SC: Gould and Riley, 1821. jollyroger.com/library/LifeofFrancisMarionbyJamesebook.html.

80. Balfour to Cornwallis. Nov. 24, 29, 30 and Dec. 4, 1780. Cornwallis Papers, British National Archives. 30/11/4. Rogers, George C. *The history of Georgetown County, South Carolina.* Columbia: University of South Carolina Press 1970. p. 132. Bass, Robert D. (Robert Duncan). *Swamp Fox; the life and campaigns of General Francis Marion.* New York, Holt [c1959]. pp. 96–99.

81. Parker, John C. *Parker's Guide to the Revolutionary War in South Carolina: battles, skirmishes and murders.* Patrick, SC: Hem Branch Publishing, 2009. p. 371.

82. Southern Studies Program. *Figures of the Revolution in South Carolina, An Anthology.* Spartanburg, Anderson, Beaufort, Aiken, Florence, Georgetown. Columbia: University of South Carolina, 1976. p. 347. Simms, William Gilmore. *The Life of Francis Marion.* New York, 1844. pp. 77–78. O'Kelley, Patrick. *Nothing But Blood and Slaughter.* Booklocker.com, 2004. 2: 302. Parker, John C. *Parker's Guide to the Revolutionary War in South Carolina: battles, skirmishes and murders.* Patrick, SC: Hem Branch Publishing, 2009. p. 213.

83. *The Encyclopedia of the American Revolutionary War: a political, social, and military history.* Gregory Fremont-Barnes, Richard Alan Ryerson, editors. Santa Barbara, CA: ABC-CLIO, 2006. 1:104–105. *Encyclopedia of the American Revolution.* Harold E. Selesky, editor in chief. 2nd ed. Detroit: Charles Scribner's Sons, 2007. 1:79. Writers' Program of the Work Projects Administration in the State of South Carolina. *South Carolina a guide to the Palmetto state,* compiled by workers of the Writers' Program of the Work Projects Administration in the State of South Carolina. Sponsored by Burnet R. Maybank, governor of South Carolina. New York: Oxford University Press, 1946, c1941. p. 408.

84. Parker, John C. *Parker's Guide to the Revolutionary War in South Carolina: battles, skirmishes and murders.* Patrick, SC: Hem Branch Publishing, 2009. p. 140.

85. Simms, William Gilmore. *The Life of Francis Marion.* New York, 1844. pp. 100–101. Bass, Robert Duncan. *Swamp Fox: the life and campaigns of General Francis Marion.* Orangeburg, SC: Sandlapper, 1989. pp. 105–107. O'Kelley, Patrick. *Nothing But Blood and Slaughter.* Booklocker.com, 2004. 2: 377–78.

86. Southern Studies Program. *Figures of the Revolution in South Carolina, An Anthology.* Spartanburg, Anderson, Beaufort, Aiken, Florence, Georgetown. Columbia: University of South Carolina, 1976. pp. 329–330. Simms, William Gilmore. *The Life of Francis Marion.* New York, 1844. pp. 125–126. Moultrie, William. *Memoirs of the American Revolution so far as it related to the States of North and South Carolina and Georgia.* New York, 1802; (Eyewitness Accounts of the American Revolution). [New York] New York Times [1968]. p. 226. Bass, Robert Duncan. *Swamp Fox: the life and campaigns of General Francis Marion.* Orangeburg, SC: Sandlapper, 1989. pp. 148–153. James, William Dobein. *A Sketch of the Life of Brig. General Francis Marion, and a History of his Brigade, from its Rise in June 1780, until Disbanded in December, 1782.* Charleston, SC: Gould and Riley, 1821. pp. 31–33. www.worldwideschool.org/library/books/hst/biography/ASketchoftheLifeofBrigGenFrancisMarion/chap3.html. Hayes, John T. *The Saddlebag Almanac.* IX (Jan. 2001) pp. 61–62. O'Kelley, Patrick. *Nothing But Blood and Slaughter.* Booklocker.com, 2004. 3: 129–30. Lipscomb, Terry W. South Carolina Revolutionary Battles: Part Four. *Names in South Carolina.* XXIII (Winter 1976). South Carolina Historical Society, 1976. p. 34. Parker, John C. *Parker's Guide to the Revolutionary War in South Carolina: battles, skirmishes and murders.* Patrick, SC: Hem Branch Publishing, 2009. pp. 141, 206, 208. 371, 372.

87. Parker, John C. *Parker's Guide to the Revolutionary War in South Carolina: battles, skirmishes and murders.* Patrick, SC: Hem Branch Publishing, 2009. p. 208.

88. *Encyclopedia of the American Revolution.* Harold E. Selesky, editor in chief. 2nd ed. Detroit: Charles Scribner's Sons, 2007. I: 74. *The Encyclopedia of the American Revolutionary War: a political, social, and military history.* Gregory Fremont-Barnes, Richard Alan Ryerson, editors. Santa Barbara, CA: ABC-CLIO, 2006. I: 100. Bass, Robert Duncan. *Swamp Fox: the life and campaigns of General Francis Marion.* Orangeburg, SC: Sandlapper, 1989. Ward, Christopher. *The War of the Revolution.* New York: Macmillan, 1952. Parker, John C. *Parker's Guide to the Revolutionary War in South Carolina: battles, skirmishes and murders.* Patrick, SC: Hem Branch Publishing, 2009. p. 210–211. www.patriotresource.com/people/marion/page3.html.

89. Simms, William Gilmore. *The Life of Francis Marion.* New York, 1844. p. 78. British National Archives. Cornwallis Papers, Class 30, Vol. 11 p. 3. Lambert, Robert Stansbury. *South Carolina Loyalists in the American Revolution.* Columbia: University of South Carolina, 1987. p. 115. Bass, Robert Duncan. *Swamp Fox: the life and campaigns of General Francis Marion.* Orangeburg, SC: Sandlapper, 1989. pp. 55–58. James, William Dobein. *A Sketch of the Life of Brig. Gen. Francis Marion, and a History of his Brigade, from its Rise in June 1780, until Disbanded in December, 1782.* Charleston, SC: Gould and Riley, 1821. p. 18. O'Kelley, Patrick. *Nothing But Blood and Slaughter.* Booklocker.com, 2004. 2: 308–9. Parker, John C. *Parker's Guide to the Revolutionary War in South Carolina: battles, skirmishes and murders.* Patrick, SC: Hem Branch Publishing, 2009. p. 366–367.

90. Sabine, Lorenzo. *Biographical Sketches of Loyalists of the American Revolution.* Baltimore, 1994 I: 569, II: 58. Tarleton, Banastre. *A History of the Campaigns of 1780 and 1781 in the Southern Provinces of North America.* London: T. Cadell, 1787; [sl]: the New York Times & Arno Press, 1968. 171–173. Simms, William Gilmore. *The Life of Francis Marion.* New York, 1844. pp. 84–85. Bass, Robert Duncan. *Swamp Fox: the life and campaigns of General Francis Marion.* Orangeburg, SC: Sandlapper, 1989. pp. 78–84. James, William Dobein. *A Sketch of the Life of Brig. Gen. Francis Marion, and a History of his Brigade, from its Rise in June 1780, until Disbanded in December, 1782.* Charleston, SC: Gould and Riley, 1821. pp. 19–20. O'Kelley, Patrick. *Nothing But Blood and Slaughter.* Booklocker.com, 2004. 2: 353–54.

91. McCrady, Edward. *History of South Carolina in the Revolution, 1775–1780.* New York: Paladin Press, 1969 (reprint of 1901 ed.) p. 748. James, William Dobein. *A Sketch of the Life of Brig. Gen. Francis Marion, and a History of his Brigade, from its Rise in June 1780, until Disbanded in December, 1782.* Charleston, SC: Gould and Riley, 1821. p. 58. Ramsay, David. *the History of the Revolution of South-Carolina from a British Province to an Independent State.* Trenton: Collins, 1900–1983? 2:188–189. Bass, Robert D. *The Green Dragoon: the lives of Banastre Tarleton and Mary Robinson Bass.* New York: Holt, 1957. p. 105. Parker, John C. *Parker's Guide to the Revolutionary War in South Carolina: battles, skirmishes and murders.* Patrick, SC: Hem Branch Publishing, 2009. p. 158.

92. Parker, John C. *Parker's Guide to the Revolutionary War in South Carolina: battles, skirmishes and murders.* Patrick, SC: Hem Branch Publishing, 2009. p. 159.

93. National Archives and Records Administration. Matthew McClurkin (McCluskin) pension application S32403. Archibald De Bow Murphey, William Henry Hoyt, William Alexander Graham. *The Papers of Archibald D. Murphey:* 1914. 1: 189. Parker, John C. *Parker's Guide to the Revolutionary War in South Carolina: battles, skirmishes and murders.* Patrick, SC: Hem Branch Publishing, 2009. p. 381.

94. Parker, John C. *Parker's Guide to the Revolutionary War in South Carolina: battles, skirmishes and murders.* Patrick, SC: Hem Branch Publishing, 2009. p. 162.

95. Gregg, Alexander. *History of the old Cheraws; containing an account of the aborigines of the Pedee, the first white settlements, their subsequent progress, civil changes, the struggle of the revolution, and growth of the country afterward, extending from about A. D. 1730 to 1810, with notices of families and sketches of individuals.* New York, Richardson, 1867; Spartanburg, SC: Reprint Co., 1965. p. 394. Stokes, Durward T. *The History of Dillon County, South Carolina.* Columbia: University of South Carolina Press, 1978. p. 43. Parker, John C. *Parker's Guide to the Revolutionary War in South Carolina: battles, skirmishes and murders.* Patrick, SC: Hem Branch Publishing, 2009. p. 162.

96. *Encyclopedia of the American Revolution.* Harold E. Selesky, editor in chief. 2nd ed. Detroit: Charles Scribner's Sons, 2007. I: 582–588. *The Encyclopedia of the American Revolutionary War: a political, social, and military history.* Gregory Fremont-Barnes, Richard Alan Ryerson, editors. Santa Barbara, CA: ABC-CLIO, 2006. I: 667–671. Alderman, Pat. *Our Heroic Hour at King's Mountain.* Johnson City, TN: Overmountain Press, 1990. Clinton, Henry. *The American Rebellion: Sir Henry Clinton's Narrative of His Campaigns, 1775–1782, with an appendix of original documents.* Edited by William B. Willcox. New Haven: Yale University Press, 1954. Cox, William E. *Battle of King's Mountain Participants, October 7, 1780.* Fort Washington, PA: Eastern National Park and Monument Association, 1972. DeMond, Robert O. *The Loyalists in North Carolina during the Revolution.* Durham, NC: Duke University Press, 1940. Draper, Lyman C. *King's Mountain and its Heroes: History of the Battle of King's Mountain.* Johnson City, TN: Overmountain Press, 1996. Dykeman, Wilma. *The Battle of King's Mountain, 1780: with fire and sword.* Washington, DC: National Park Service, 1978. Edgar, Walter B. *Partisans and Redcoats: the Southern Conflict that Turned the Tide of the American Revolution.* New York: William Morrow of Harper/Collins, 2001. Gordon, John W. *South Carolina and the American Revolution: a battlefield history.* Columbia: University of South Carolina Press, 2003. Hoffman, Ronald, et. Al. eds. *An Uncivil War: the Southern Backcountry during the American Revolution.* Charlottesville: University Press of Virginia, 1985. Lee, Henry. *Memoirs of the War in the Southern Department of the United States,* New York: University Publishing Co., 1869. Palmer. Dave R. *This Destructive War: the British Campaign in the Carolinas, 1780–1781.* Tuscaloosa: University of Alabama Press, 1985. Ward, Christopher. *The War of the Revolution.* New York: Macmillan, 1952. Weigley, Russell F. *The Partisan War: the South Carolina Campaign of 1780–1782.* Columbia: University of South Carolina Press, 1970. Parker, John C. *Parker's Guide to the Revolutionary War in South Carolina: battles, skirmishes and murders.* Patrick, SC: Hem Branch Publishing, 2009. p. 374. Smith, Gordon Burns. *Morningstars of Liberty: the Revolutionary War in Georgia, 1775–1783.* Milledgeville, GA: Boyd Publishing, 2006. 1: 219–220.

97. Stokes, Durward T. *The History of Dillon County, South Carolina*. Columbia: University of South Carolina Press, 1978. p. 39. Parker, John C. *Parker's Guide to the Revolutionary War in South Carolina: battles, skirmishes and murders*. Patrick, SC: Hem Branch Publishing, 2009. p. 163.

98. Parker, John C. *Parker's Guide to the Revolutionary War in South Carolina: battles, skirmishes and murders*. Patrick, SC: Hem Branch Publishing, 2009. p. 142.

99. *Encyclopedia of the American Revolution*. Harold E. Selesky, editor in chief. 2nd ed. Detroit: Charles Scribner's Sons, 2007. I:361. *The Encyclopedia of the American Revolutionary War: a political, social, and military history*. Gregory Fremont-Barnes, Richard Alan Ryerson, editors. Santa Barbara, CA: ABC-CLIO, 2006. II: 406–407. Bass, Robert. *Gamecock: the life and campaigns of General Thomas Sumter*. Orangeburg, SC: Sandlapper, 2000. Commager, Henry Steele. *The Spirit of Seventy Six*. New York, Harper & Row [1967]. Ripley, Warren. *Battleground: South Carolina in the Revolution*. Charleston, SC: Evening Post, 1983. Ward, Christopher. *The War of the Revolution*. New York: Macmillan, 1952. Parker, John C. *Parker's Guide to the Revolutionary War in South Carolina: battles, skirmishes and murders*. Patrick, SC: Hem Branch Publishing, 2009. p. 131.

100. Ellet, E. F. (Elizabeth Fries). *The Women of the American Revolution*. New York, Baker and Scribner, 1848. III:185–186. Scoggins, Michael C.; Edgar, Walter. *The Day It Rained Militia: Huck's Defeat and the Revolution in the South Carolina Backcountry, May–July 1780*. Charleston: The History Press, c2005. p. 132.

101. Draper, Lyman. Thomas Sumter Papers, Draper Manuscript Collection, State Historical Society of Wisconsin. 4VV12–13. O'Kelley, Patrick. *Nothing But Blood and Slaughter*. Booklocker.com, 2004. 2: 374–75.

102. Draper, Lyman. Thomas Sumter Papers, Draper Manuscript Collection, State Historical Society of Wisconsin. O'Kelley, Patrick. *Nothing But Blood and Slaughter*. Booklocker.com, 2004. 2: 354–55. Parker, John C. *Parker's Guide to the Revolutionary War in South Carolina: battles, skirmishes and murders*. Patrick, SC: Hem Branch Publishing, 2009. p. 128. Smith, Gordon Burns. *Morningstars of Liberty: the Revolutionary War in Georgia, 1775–1783*. Milledgeville, GA: Boyd Publishing, 2006. I: 221–222.

103. Draper, Lyman. Thomas Sumter Papers, Draper Manuscript Collection, State Historical Society of Wisconsin. O'Kelley, Patrick. *Nothing But Blood and Slaughter*. Booklocker.com, 2004. 2: 388.

104. Bailey, Rev. J.D. *History of Grindal Shoals and Some Early Adjacent Families*. 1990. pp. 75–83. O'Kelley, Patrick. *Nothing But Blood and Slaughter*. Booklocker.com, 2004. 2: 380–381. Parker, John C. *Parker's Guide to the Revolutionary War in South Carolina: battles, skirmishes and murders*. Patrick, SC: Hem Branch Publishing, 2009. p. 118.

105. Saye, James Hodge. *Memoirs of Major Joseph McJunkin, Revolutionary Patriot*. [sl]: A Press, Inc., 1977. pp. 41–42. Parker, John C. *Parker's Guide to the Revolutionary War in South Carolina: battles, skirmishes and murders*. Patrick, SC: Hem Branch Publishing, 2009. p. 132.

106. Draper, Lyman. Thomas Sumter Papers, Draper Manuscript Collection, State Historical Society of Wisconsin. Babits, Lawrence E. *A Devil of a Whipping, the Battle of Cowpens*. University of North Carolina Press, 1998. pp. 134–135. O'Kelley, Patrick. *Nothing But Blood and Slaughter*. Booklocker.com, 2004. 3: 52–3.

107. Draper, Lyman. Thomas Sumter Papers, Draper Manuscript Collection, State Historical Society of Wisconsin. O'Kelley, Patrick. *Nothing But Blood and Slaughter*. Booklocker.com, 2004. 3: 65.

108. Parker, John C. *Parker's Guide to the Revolutionary War in South Carolina: battles, skirmishes and murders*. Patrick, SC: Hem Branch Publishing, 2009. p. 298.

109. Saye, James Hodge. *Memoirs of Major Joseph McJunkin, Revolutionary Patriot*. [sl]: A Press, Inc., 1977. (First printed in the Richmond, VA *Watchman and Observer* in 1847). Draper, Lyman. Thomas Sumter Papers, Draper Manuscript Collection, State Historical Society of Wisconsin. 7VV135, 11VV459. O'Kelley, Patrick. *Nothing But Blood and Slaughter*. Booklocker.com, 2004. 2: 375. Parker, John C. *Parker's Guide to the Revolutionary War in South Carolina: battles, skirmishes and murders*. Patrick, SC: Hem Branch Publishing, 2009. p. 129.

110. Greene, Nathanael. *The Papers of General Nathanael Greene*. Richard K. Showman, ed. Chapel Hill: the University of North Carolina Press, published for the Rhode Island Historical Society. c1976–2006. 8:149. Parker, John C. *Parker's Guide to the Revolutionary War in South Carolina: battles, skirmishes and murders*. Patrick, SC: Hem Branch Publishing, 2009. p. 184.

111. Young, Thomas. Memoir of a Revolutionary Patriot of South Carolina. *The Orion*. 3 (Oct. 1843), pp. 84–88 et seq. Draper, Lyman. Thomas Sumter Papers, Draper Manuscript Collection, State Historical Society of Wisconsin. 14VV177–179. O'Kelley, Patrick. *Nothing But Blood and Slaughter*. Booklocker.com, 2004. 3: 281–82. Parker, John C. *Parker's Guide to the Revolutionary War in South Carolina: battles, skirmishes and murders*. Patrick, SC: Hem Branch Publishing, 2009. p. 129–130.

112. Simms, William Gilmore. *The Life of Francis Marion*. New York, 1844. pp. 120–124. Ervin, Sara Sullivan. *South Carolinians in the Revolution*. Baltimore: Genealogical Publishing Company, Inc., 1971. pp. 67–77. Bass, Robert Duncan. *Swamp Fox: the life and campaigns of General Francis Marion*. Orangeburg, SC: Sandlapper, 1989. pp. 95–99, 107–111. James, William Dobein. *A Sketch of the Life of Brig. Gen. Francis Marion, and a History of his Brigade, from its Rise in June 1780, until Disbanded in December, 1782*. Charleston, SC: Gould and Riley, 1821. pp. 30–31. O'Kelley, Patrick. *Nothing But Blood and Slaughter*. Booklocker.com 2004 2: 384–387. Parker, John C. *Parker's Guide to the Revolutionary War in South Carolina: battles, skirmishes and murders*. Patrick, SC: Hem Branch Publishing, 2009. p. 143–144, 347.

113. McArthur to Haldane (Aid de camp to Lord Cornwallis), Camp at Owens's plantation, 24th December 1780 4(384A). McArthur to Haldane (Aid de camp to Lord Cornwallis), Camp at Owens's plantation, 25th December 1780 4(388). *The Cornwallis Papers: the Campaigns of 1780 and 1781*. 3: 328–329. Refitment at Winnsborough and the winter campaign. *Southern Campaigns of the American Revolution*. 3 (No. 12.3, December 2006) p. 36. National Archives and Records Administration. Sherwood Fort pension application S8499.

114. McArthur to Haldane (Aid de camp to Lord Cornwallis), Camp at Owens's plantation, 24th December 1780 4(384A). McArthur to Haldane (Aid de camp to Lord Cornwallis), Camp at Owens's plantation, 25th December 1780 4(388). *The Cornwallis Papers: the Campaigns of 1780 and 1781*. 3: 328–329. Refitment at Winnsborough and the winter campaign. *Southern Campaigns of the American Revolution*. 3 (No. 12.3, December 2006) p. 36.

115. Kirkpatrick, Melvin E. *A Kirkpatrick genealogy: being an account of the descendants of the family of James Kirkpatrick of South Carolina, ca. 1715–1786*. Bloomington, Minn. (10609 Upton Ave. S., Bloomington): M.E. Kirkpatrick, 1985. Parker, John C. *Parker's Guide to the Revolutionary War in South Carolina: battles, skirmishes and murders*. Patrick, SC: Hem Branch Publishing, 2009. p. 377.

116. Southern Studies Program. *Figures of the Revolution in South Carolina, An Anthology. Spartanburg, Anderson, Beaufort, Aiken, Florence, Georgetown*. Columbia: University of South Carolina, 1976. pp. 287–293. Moultrie, William. *Memoirs of the American Revolution so far as it related to the States of North and South Carolina and Georgia*. New York, 1802; (Eyewitness Accounts of the American Revolution). [New York] New York Times [1968]. II: 340–341. Lee, Henry. *Memoirs of the War in the Southern Department of the United States*. New York: University Publishing Co., 1869. p. 553. James, William Dobein. *A Sketch of the Life of Brig. Gen. Francis Marion, and a History of his Brigade, from its Rise in June 1780, until Disbanded in December, 1782*. Charleston, SC: Gould and Riley, 1821. p. 22. www.worldwideschool.org/library/books/hst/biography/ASketchoftheLifeofBrigGenFrancisMarion/chap2.html. O'Kelley, Patrick. *Nothing But Blood and Slaughter*. Booklocker.com, 2004. 2: 378–79; 3: 213–14. Parker, John C. *Parker's Guide to the Revolutionary War in South Carolina: battles, skirmishes and murders*. Patrick, SC: Hem Branch Publishing, 2009. pp. 164–165, 279–280. Simms, William Gilmore. *The Life of Francis Marion*. New York, 1844. pp. 94–95. Draper, Lyman. Thomas Sumter Papers, Draper Manuscript Collection, State Historical Society of Wisconsin. 3VV58–63.

117. Parker, John C. *Parker's Guide to the Revolutionary War in South Carolina: battles, skirmishes and murders*. Patrick, SC: Hem Branch Publishing, 2009. pp. 279–280.

118. Parker, John C. *Parker's Guide to the Revolutionary War in South Carolina: battles, skirmishes and murders*. Patrick, SC: Hem Branch Publishing, 2009. pp. 279–280.

119. Parker, John C. *Parker's Guide to the Revolutionary War in South Carolina: battles, skirmishes and murders*. Patrick, SC: Hem Branch Publishing, 2009. p. 280.

120. Parker, John C. *Parker's Guide to the Revolutionary War in South Carolina: battles, skirmishes and murders*. Patrick, SC: Hem Branch Publishing, 2009. pp. 279–280.

121. Parker, John C. *Parker's Guide to the Revolutionary War in South Carolina: battles, skirmishes and murders*. Patrick, SC: Hem Branch Publishing, 2009. pp. 279–280, 285.

122. Parker, John C. *Parker's Guide to the Revolutionary War in South Carolina: battles, skirmishes and murders*. Patrick, SC: Hem Branch Publishing, 2009. p. 164–165.

123. Simms, William Gilmore. *The Life of Francis Marion*. New York, 1844. pp. 128–129. Ervin. Sara Sullivan. *South Carolinians in the Revolution*. Baltimore: Genealogical Publishing Company, Inc., 1971. p. 70. Bass, Robert Duncan. *Swamp Fox: the life and campaigns of General Francis Marion*. Orangeburg, SC: Sandlapper, 1989. pp. 156–157. James, William Dobein. *A Sketch of the Life of Brig. General Francis Marion, and a History of his Brigade, from its Rise in June 1780, until Disbanded in December, 1782*. Charleston, SC: Gould and Riley, 1821. pp. 22, 33. Hayes, John T. *The Saddlebag Almanac*. VIII (Jan. 2000) pp. 88–89; IX (Jan. 2001) p. 63. Simcoe, John Graves. *Simcoe's Military Journal. A History of the Operations of a Partisan Corps Called the Queen's Rangers, Commanded by Lieut. Colonel J. G. Simcoe, During the War of the American Revolution*. New-York: Bartlett & Welford, 1844; [New York]: New York Times; Arno Press. (Eyewitness Accounts of the American Revolution). [1968]. pp. 244–246. Draper, Lyman. Thomas Sumter Papers, Draper Manuscript Collection, State Historical Society of Wisconsin. 5VV268. O'Kelley, Patrick. *Nothing But Blood and Slaughter*. Booklocker.com, 2004. 3: 173. Parker, John C. *Parker's Guide to the Revolutionary War in South Carolina: battles, skirmishes and murders*. Patrick, SC: Hem Branch Publishing, 2009. p. 212.

124. Bass, Robert Duncan. *Swamp Fox: the life and campaigns of General Francis Marion*. Orangeburg, SC: Sandlapper, 1989. p. 157–162.

125. Simms, William Gilmore. *The Life of Francis Marion*. New York, 1844. pp. 128–129. Ervin. Sara Sullivan. *South Carolinians in the Revolution*. Baltimore: Genealogical Publishing Company, Inc., 1971. p. 70. Bass, Robert Duncan. *Swamp Fox: the life and campaigns of General Francis Marion*. Orangeburg, SC: Sandlapper, 1989. pp. 156–157. James, William Dobein. *A Sketch of the Life of Brig. General Francis Marion, and a History of his Brigade, from its Rise in June 1780, until Disbanded in December, 1782*. Charleston, SC: Gould and Riley, 1821. pp. 22, 33. Hayes, John T. *The Saddlebag Almanac*. VIII (Jan. 2000) pp. 88–89; IX (Jan. 2001) p. 63. Simcoe, John Graves. *Simcoe's Military Journal. A History of the Operations of a Partisan Corps Called the Queen's Rangers, Commanded by Lieut. Colonel J. G. Simcoe, During the War of the American Revolution*. New-York: Bartlett & Welford, 1844; [New York]: New York Times; Arno Press. (Eyewitness Accounts of the American Revolution). [1968]. pp. 244–246. Draper, Lyman. Thomas Sumter Papers, Draper Manuscript Collection, State Historical Society of Wisconsin. 5VV268. O'Kelley, Patrick. *Nothing But Blood and Slaughter*. Booklocker.com, 2004. 3: 173. Parker, John C. *Parker's Guide to the Revolutionary War in South Carolina: battles, skirmishes and murders*. Patrick, SC: Hem Branch Publishing, 2009. p. 193.

126. Graves, William T.; Reuwer, David P. and Baxley, Charles B. Thomas Sumter Timeline. *Southern Campaigns of the American Revolution*. 2:4 (April 2005) p. 9. www.southerncampaign.org/newsletter/v 2n4.pdf, p. 9. *Encyclopedia of the American Revolution*. Harold E. Selesky, editor in chief. 2nd ed. Detroit: Charles Scribner's Sons, 2007. I: 370. Hayes, John T. *The Saddlebag Almanac*. IX (Jan. 2001) pp. 55–56. Draper, Lyman. Thomas Sumter Papers, Draper Manuscript Collection, State Historical Society of Wisconsin. 10VV111, 11VV526–529, 14VV452–460. O'Kelley, Patrick. *Nothing But Blood and Slaughter*. Booklocker.com, 2004. 3: 86–90.

127. Lipscomb, Terry W. South Carolina Revolutionary Battles: Part Ten. *Names in South Carolina*. XXX (Winter 1983). South Carolina Historical Society, 1983. p. 11. O'Kelley, Patrick. *Nothing But Blood and Slaughter*. Booklocker. com, 2004. 3: 90–91. Parker, John C. *Parker's Guide to the Revolutionary War in South Carolina: battles, skirmishes and murders*. Patrick, SC: Hem Branch Publishing, 2009. p. 268.

128. Hayes, John T. *A Gentleman of Fortune, the Diary of Baylor Hill. First Continental Light Dragoons, 1777–1781*. The Saddlebag Press, 1995. III: 153. Kirkland, Thomas J. and Kennedy, Robert M. *Historic Camden*. State Company, 1905. p. 273. Ervin. Sara Sullivan. *South Carolinians in the Revolution*. Baltimore: Genealogical Publishing Company, Inc., 1971. pp. 81–82. Pancake, John S. *This Destructive War: the British Campaign in the Carolinas*. Tuscaloosa: University of Alabama Press, 1985. p. 199. Draper, Lyman. Thomas Sumter Papers, Draper Manuscript Collection, State Historical Society of Wisconsin. 6VV22–24, 7VV260. battleofcamden.org/sherman.htm, 22 May 1781. Parker, John C. *Parker's Guide to the Revolutionary War in South Carolina: battles, skirmishes and murders*. Patrick, SC: Hem Branch Publishing, 2009. p. 263–264.

129. Lipscomb, Terry W. South Carolina Revolutionary Battles: Part Ten. *Names in South Carolina*. XXX (Winter 1983). South Carolina Historical Society, 1983. p. 11. Draper, Lyman. Thomas Sumter Papers, Draper Manuscript Collection, State Historical Society of Wisconsin. 7VV320–321. O'Kelley, Patrick. *Nothing But Blood and Slaughter*. Booklocker.com, 2004. 3: 269. Parker, John C. *Parker's Guide to the Revolutionary War in South Carolina: battles, skirmishes and murders*. Patrick, SC: Hem Branch Publishing, 2009. p. 270.

130. Hayes, John T. *The Saddlebag Almanac*. X (Jan. 2002) pp. 86–87. Garden, Alexander. *Anecdotes of the American Revolution, Illustrative of the Talents and Virtues of the Heroes and Patriots who Acted the Most Conspicuous Parts Therein*. Second series. Charleston, S. C.: A.E. Miller, 1828. pp. 123–125. Tarleton, Banastre. *A History of the Campaigns of 1780 and 1781 in the Southern Provinces of North America*, London, 1787; (Eyewitness Accounts of the American Revolution). [New York] New York Times [1968]. pp. 514–505. Moultrie, William. *Memoirs of the American Revolution so far as it related to the States of North and South Carolina and Georgia*. New York, 1802; (Eyewitness Accounts of the American Revolution). [New York] New York Times [1968]. II: 290. Lee, Henry. *Memoirs of the War in the Southern Department of the United States*. New York: University Publishing Co., 1869. pp. 381–383. *The Pennsylvania Gazette*. Aug. 15, 1781. Draper, Lyman. Thomas Sumter Papers, Draper Manuscript Collection, State Historical Society of Wisconsin. 11VV524–525. O'Kelley, Patrick. *Nothing But Blood and Slaughter*. Booklocker.com, 2004. 3: 277–78. Parker, John C. *Parker's Guide to the Revolutionary War in South Carolina: battles, skirmishes and murders*. Patrick, SC: Hem Branch Publishing, 2009. p. 265.

131. O'Kelley, Patrick. *Nothing But Blood and Slaughter*. Booklocker.com, 2004. 3: 276. Parker, John C. *Parker's Guide to the Revolutionary War in South Carolina: battles, skirmishes and murders*. Patrick, SC: Hem Branch Publishing, 2009. p. 266.

132. Graves, William T.; Reuwer, David P. and Baxley, Charles B. Thomas Sumter Timeline. *Southern Campaigns of the American Revolution*. 2:4 (April 2005) p. 9. www.southerncampaign.org/newsletter/v 2n4.pdf, p. 9. *Encyclopedia of the American Revolution*. Harold E. Selesky, editor in chief. 2nd ed. Detroit: Charles Scribner's Sons, 2007. I: 370. Hayes, John T. *The Saddlebag Almanac*. IX (Jan. 2001) pp. 55–56. Draper, Lyman. Thomas Sumter Papers, Draper Manuscript Collection, State Historical Society of Wisconsin. 10VV111, 11VV526–529, 14VV452–460. Hayes, John T. *A Gentleman of Fortune, the Diary of Baylor Hill. First Continental Light Dragoons, 1777–1781*. The Saddlebag Press, 1995. III:153. Kirkland, Thomas J. and Kennedy, Robert M. *Historic Camden*. State Company, 1905. p. 273. Ervin. Sara Sullivan. *South Carolinians in the Revolution*. Baltimore: Genealogical Publishing Company, Inc., 1971. pp. 81–82. Pancake, John S. *This Destructive War: the British Campaign in the Carolinas*. Tuscaloosa: University of Alabama Press, 1985. p. 199. Draper, Lyman. Thomas Sumter Papers, Draper Manuscript Collection, State Historical Society of Wisconsin. 6VV22–24, 7VV260. O'Kelley, Patrick. *Nothing But Blood and Slaughter*. Booklocker.com, 2004. 3: 217. battleofcamden.org/sherman.htm, 22 May 1781.

133. Boatner, Mark Mayo. *Landmarks of the American Revolution; A Guide To Locating and Knowing What Happened at the Sites of Independence*. Stackpole Books: [Harrisburg, Pa.], [1973]; 2nd ed. Library of Military History. Detroit: Charles Scribner's Sons, 2007. p. 328.

134. Garden, Alexander. *Anecdotes of the American Revolution, Illustrative of the Talents and Virtues of the Heroes and Patriots who Acted the Most Conspicuous Parts Therein*. Second series. Charleston, S. C.: A.E. Miller, 1828. p. 441. Simms, William Gilmore. *The Life of Francis Marion*. New York, 1844. p. 115. Moultrie, William. *Memoirs of the American Revolution so far as it related to the States of North and South Carolina and Georgia*. New York, 1802; (Eyewitness Accounts of the American Revolution). [New York] New York Times [1968]. II: 262–263. Brown, Tarleton. *Memoirs of Tarleton Brown, a Captain in the Revolutionary Army, Written by Himself*. With a Preface and Notes by Charles I. Bushnell. New York: Privately Printed, 1862. *The Pennsylvania Gazette*. Feb. 28, 1781. Bass, Robert Duncan. *Swamp Fox: the life and campaigns of General Francis Marion*. Orangeburg, SC: Sandlapper, 1989. pp. 137–138. Greene, Nathanael. *The Papers of General Nathanael Greene*. Richard K. Showman, ed. Chapel Hill: The University of North Carolina Press, published for the Rhode Island Historical Society. c1976–2006. p. 226. James, William Dobein. *A Sketch of the Life of Brig. Gen. Francis Marion, and a History of his Brigade, from its Rise in June 1780, until Disbanded in December, 1782*. Charleston, SC: Gould and Riley, 1821. p. 49. University of New Brunswick. Harriet Irving Library. Saunders Family Papers, Correspondence, 1780–1803. O'Kelley, Patrick. *Nothing But Blood and Slaughter*. Booklocker.com, 2004. 3: 64–5. Parker, John C. *Parker's Guide to the Revolutionary War in South Carolina: battles, skirmishes and murders*. Patrick, SC: Hem Branch Publishing, 2009. p. 66.

135. Draper, Lyman. Thomas Sumter Papers, Draper Manuscript Collection, State Historical Society of Wisconsin. 7VV227–228. O'Kelley, Patrick. *Nothing But Blood and Slaughter*. Booklocker.com, 2004. 3: 92. Sumter was using this site as a base when he attacked the British at Big Savannah.

136. Lipscomb, Terry W. South Carolina Revolutionary Battles: Part Five. *Names in South Carolina*. XXIV (Winter 1977). South Carolina Historical Society, 1977. p. 17. Hayes, John T. *The Saddlebag Almanac*. IX (Jan. 2001) pp.

56–57. Draper, Lyman. Thomas Sumter Papers, Draper Manuscript Collection, State Historical Society of Wisconsin. 4VV56–58. O'Kelley, Patrick. *Nothing But Blood and Slaughter*. Booklocker.com, 2004. 3: 93. battleofcamden.org/sherman.htm, February 1781.

137. Boatner, Mark M. *Encyclopedia of the American Revolution*. 3d ed., New York: McKay, 1980. pp. 388–89.

138. Cashin, Edward J. *The King's Ranger. Thomas Brown and the American Revolution on the Southern Frontier*. Athens: University of Georgia Press, 1989. pp. 129–130. Clark. Murtie June. *Loyalists in the Southern Campaign of the Revolutionary War*. Baltimore: Genealogical Publishing Company, Inc., 1981. 3:101, 255–265. Hayes, John T. *The Saddlebag Almanac*. IX (Jan. 2001) pp. 57–58. William L. Clements Library, University of Michigan. Sir Henry Clinton Papers. Vol. 232 folio 21. Draper, Lyman. Thomas Sumter Papers, Draper Manuscript Collection, State Historical Society of Wisconsin. 4VV51–53, 5VV150. O'Kelley, Patrick. *Nothing but Blood and Slaughter*. Booklocker.com, 2004. 3: 102–105.

139. *Encyclopedia of the American Revolution*. Harold E. Selesky, editor in chief. 2nd ed. Detroit: Charles Scribner's Sons, 2007. I: 381–382. *The Encyclopedia of the American Revolutionary War: a political, social, and military history*. Gregory Fremont-Barnes, Richard Alan Ryerson, editors. Santa Barbara, CA: ABC-CLIO, 2006. II: 445. Bass, Robert Duncan. *Swamp Fox: the life and campaigns of General Francis Marion*. Orangeburg, SC: Sandlapper, 1989. Gordon, John W. *South Carolina and the American Revolution: a battlefield history*. Columbia: University of South Carolina Press, 2003. Ripley, Warren. *Battleground: South Carolina in the Revolution*. Charleston, SC: Evening Post, 1983. Russell, David Lee. *The American Revolution in the Southern Colonies*. Jefferson, NC: McFarland, 2000. Ward, Christopher. *The War of the Revolution*. New York: Macmillan, 1952. Weigley, Russell F. *The Partisan War: the South Carolina Campaign of 1780–1782*. Columbia: University of South Carolina Press, 1970.

140. Draper, Lyman. Thomas Sumter Papers, Draper Manuscript Collection, State Historical Society of Wisconsin. O'Kelley, Patrick. *Nothing But Blood and Slaughter*. Booklocker.com, 2004. 3: 268. Parker, John C. *Parker's Guide to the Revolutionary War in South Carolina: battles, skirmishes and murders*. Patrick, SC: Hem Branch Publishing, 2009. p. 64.

141. Tarleton, Banastre. *A History of the Campaigns of 1780 and 1781 in the Southern Provinces of North America*, London, 1787; (Eyewitness Accounts of the American Revolution). [New York] New York Times [1968]. p. 474. Moultrie, William. *Memoirs of the American Revolution so far as it related to the States of North and South Carolina and Georgia*. New York, 1802; (Eyewitness Accounts of the American Revolution). [New York] New York Times [1968]. II: 280. *The Pennsylvania Gazette*. June 13, 1781. Colonel Robert Gray's Observations on the War in Carolina. *South Carolina Historical and Genealogical Magazine*. XI: 3 (July 1910) pp. 154–155. Ervin. Sara Sullivan. *South Carolinians in the Revolution*. Baltimore: Genealogical Publishing Company, Inc., 1971. pp. 80–87. Draper, Lyman. Thomas Sumter Papers, Draper Manuscript Collection, State Historical Society of Wisconsin. 14VV177–179. O'Kelley, Patrick. *Nothing But Blood and Slaughter*. Booklocker.com, 2004. 3: 232–33.

142. Hayes, John T. *The Saddlebag Almanac*. X (Jan. 2002) p. 57. Simms, William Gilmore. *The Life of Francis Marion*. New York, 1844. pp. 148. Lee, Henry. *Memoirs of the War in the Southern Department of the United States*. New York: University Publishing Co., 1869. p. 385–386. Kirkwood, Robert. "The Journal and Orderly Book of Captain Robert Kirkwood of the Delaware Regiment of the Continental Line," *Papers of the Historical Society of Delaware*. 56 (1910) p. 20. Lipscomb, Terry W. South Carolina Revolutionary Battles: Part Six. *Names in South Carolina*. XXV (Winter 1978). South Carolina Historical Society, 1978. pp. 30–31. Ervin. Sara Sullivan. *South Carolinians in the Revolution*. Baltimore: Genealogical Publishing Company, Inc., 1971. pp. 67–77. Lambert, Robert Stansbury. *South Carolina Loyalists in the American Revolution*. University of South Carolina Press, 1987. pp. 110–111. Ward, Christopher L. *The Delaware Continentals*. Historical Society of Delaware, 1941. pp. 455. Batt, Richard John. *The Maryland Continentals, 1780–1781*. Tulane University Dissertation, 1974. pp. 182–183. Chesney, Alexander. *The Journal of Alexander Chesney, a South Carolina Loyalist in the Revolution and After*. edited by E. A. Jones. Columbus, Ohio: Ohio State University, 1921. *A List of all the officers of the Army: viz. the general and field officers; the officers of the several troops, regiments, independent companies, and garrisons: with an alphabetical index to the whole. Also, a list of the officers of the Royal Regiment of Artillery, the Corps of Engineers, the Irish Artillery and Engineers, and of the Marine Forces: the officers on half pay; and a succession of colonels. To which are likewise added the officers of the militia forces, and of the fencible and provincial regiments in Great Britain*. [London, England?]: War-Office, 1780. pp. 167. O'Kelley, Patrick. *Nothing But Blood and Slaughter*. Booklocker.com, 2004. 3: 283–84.

143. Extract of a letter from major-general Greene, dated head-quarters, on the High Hills of Santee, July 17, 1781. *The Pennsylvania Evening Post, and Public Advertiser*. 7:763 (Aug. 14, 1781) 126.

144. Chesney, Alexander. *The Journal of Alexander Chesney, a South Carolina Loyalist in the Revolution and After*, edited by E. A. Jones. Columbus, Ohio: Ohio State University, 1921. p. 12. Letter from William Washington to Nathanael Greene, July 28, 1781, McCord's Ferry. Worcester, MA: American Antiquarian Society. Extract of a letter from major-general Greene, dated head-quarters, on the High Hills of Santee, July 17, 1781. *The Pennsylvania Evening Post, and Public Advertiser*. 7:763 (Aug. 14, 1781) 126. Hayes, John T. *The Saddlebag Almanac*. XI (Jan. 2003), p. 43. Draper, Lyman. Thomas Sumter Papers, Draper Manuscript Collection, State Historical Society of Wisconsin. O'Kelley, Patrick. *Nothing But Blood and Slaughter*. Booklocker.com, 2004. 3: 301.

145. O'Kelley, Patrick. *Nothing But Blood and Slaughter*. Booklocker.com, 2004. 3: 309. Parker, John C. *Parker's Guide to the Revolutionary War in South Carolina: battles, skirmishes and murders*. Patrick, SC: Hem Branch Publishing, 2009. p. 308–309. Kirkwood, Robert. "The Journal and Orderly Book of Captain Robert Kirkwood of the Delaware Regiment of the Continental Line," *Papers, of the Historical Society of Delaware*. 56 (1910), pp. 21, 1–277. Lipscomb, Terry W. South Carolina Revolutionary Battles: Part Seven. *Names in South Carolina* XXVI (Winter 1979). South Carolina Historical Society, 1979. p. 33. Hayes, John T. *The Saddlebag Almanac*. XI (Jan. 2003) pp. 43–44.

146. Hairr, John. *Colonel David Fanning, the Adventures of a Carolina Loyalist*. Averasboro Press, 2000. pp. 106–107. National Archives and Records Administration. Abraham Elledge Pension Application #S10625. Draper,

Lyman. Thomas Sumter Papers, Draper Manuscript Collection, State Historical Society of Wisconsin. 17VV32. O'Kelley, Patrick. *Nothing But Blood and Slaughter.* Booklocker.com, 2004. 3: 315–16.

147. Barefoot, Daniel W. *Touring South Carolina's Revolutionary War Sites.* Winston-Salem: John F. Blair, 1999. p. 227. Parker, John C. *Parker's Guide to the Revolutionary War in South Carolina: battles, skirmishes and murders.* Patrick, SC: Hem Branch Publishing, 2009. p. 310. Lipscomb, Terry W. South Carolina Revolutionary Battles: Part Seven. *Names in South Carolina* XXVI (Winter 1979). South Carolina Historical Society, 1979. p. 36; Part Ten. *Names in South Carolina.* XXX (Winter 1983). South Carolina Historical Society, 1983. pp. 13–14. Southern Studies Program. *Figures of the Revolution in South Carolina, An Anthology. Spartanburg, Anderson, Beaufort, Aiken, Florence, Georgetown.* Columbia: University of South Carolina, 1976. p. 122. O'Kelley, Patrick. *Nothing But Blood and Slaughter.* Booklocker.com, 2004. 3: 384–85.

148. Lipscomb, Terry W. South Carolina Revolutionary Battles: Part Seven. *Names in South Carolina* XXVI (Winter 1979). South Carolina Historical Society, 1979. p. 37. O'Kelley, Patrick. *Nothing But Blood and Slaughter.* Booklocker.com, 2004. 3: 408. Parker, John C. *Parker's Guide to the Revolutionary War in South Carolina: battles, skirmishes and murders.* Patrick, SC: Hem Branch Publishing, 2009. p. 315.

149. Parker, John C. *Parker's Guide to the Revolutionary War in South Carolina: battles, skirmishes and murders.* Patrick, SC: Hem Branch Publishing, 2009. p. 63. Lipscomb, Terry W. South Carolina Revolutionary Battles: Part Ten. *Names in South Carolina.* XXX (Winter 1983). South Carolina Historical Society, 1983. p. 11. O'Kelley, Patrick. *Nothing But Blood and Slaughter.* Booklocker.com, 2004. 4: 47.

150. Lipscomb, Terry W. South Carolina Revolutionary Battles: Part Nine. *Names in South Carolina.* XXVIII (Winter 1981). South Carolina Historical Society, 1981. p. 35. O'Kelley, Patrick. *Nothing But Blood and Slaughter.* Booklocker.com, 2004. 4: 61. Parker, John C. *Parker's Guide to the Revolutionary War in South Carolina: battles, skirmishes and murders.* Patrick, SC: Hem Branch Publishing, 2009. p. 311.

151. Clark. Murtie June. *Loyalists in the Southern Campaign of the Revolutionary War.* Baltimore: Genealogical Publishing Company, Inc., 1981. 1: 214. Thompson to Gen. William Henderson. June 2. Gibbes, Robert Wilson. *Documentary History of the American Revolution.* New York: D. Appleton & Co., 1855 (3 vols: 1764–1776, 1776–1782, 1781–1782). reprinted New York Times & Arno Press, 1971 (3 vols. in 1). 2: 185.

152. Lipscomb, Terry W. South Carolina Revolutionary Battles: Part Nine. *Names in South Carolina.* XXVIII (Winter 1981). South Carolina Historical Society, 1981. p. 35. O'Kelley, Patrick. *Nothing But Blood and Slaughter.* Booklocker.com, 2004. 4: 73. Parker, John C. *Parker's Guide to the Revolutionary War in South Carolina: battles, skirmishes and murders.* Patrick, SC: Hem Branch Publishing, 2009. p. 66.

153. National Archives and Records Administration. Samuel Otterson pension application #S25344.

154. *Encyclopedia of the American Revolution.* Harold E. Selesky, editor in chief. 2nd ed. Detroit: Charles Scribner's Sons, 2007. I: 375–376. *The Encyclopedia of the American Revolutionary War: a political, social, and military history.* Gregory Fremont-Barnes, Richard Alan Ryerson, editors. Santa Barbara, CA: ABC-CLIO, 2006. II: 430–431. Barbour, R.L. *South Carolina's Revolutionary War Battlefields: a Tour Guide.* Pelican Publishing Co: Gretna, 2002. Barefoot, Daniel W. *Touring South Carolina's Revolutionary War Sites.* Winston-Salem: John F. Blair, 1999. Gordon, John W. *South Carolina and the American Revolution: a battlefield history.* Columbia: University of South Carolina Press, 2003. Lee, Henry. *Memoirs of the War in the Southern Department of the United States.* New York: University Publishing Co., 1869. Ward, Christopher. *The War of the Revolution.* New York: Macmillan, 1952. Weigley, Russell F. *The Partisan War: the South Carolina Campaign of 1780–1782.* Columbia: University of South Carolina Press, 1970.

155. Hilborn, Nat & Sam. *Battleground of Freedom: South Carolina in the Revolution.* Columbia, SC: Sandlapper Press, 1970. Parker, John C. *Parker's Guide to the Revolutionary War in South Carolina: battles, skirmishes and murders.* Patrick, SC: Hem Branch Publishing, 2009. p. 147.

156. Simms, William Gilmore. *The Life of Francis Marion.* New York, 1844. p. 125. Bass, Robert Duncan. *Swamp Fox: the life and campaigns of General Francis Marion.* Orangeburg, SC: Sandlapper, 1989. pp. 146–148. O'Kelley, Patrick. *Nothing But Blood and Slaughter.* Booklocker.com, 2004. 3: 126. Parker, John C. *Parker's Guide to the Revolutionary War in South Carolina: battles, skirmishes and murders.* Patrick, SC: Hem Branch Publishing, 2009. p. 372.

157. Lossing, Benson John. *The Pictorial Field-book of the Revolution; or, Illustrations, by pen and pencil, of the history, biography, scenery, relics, and traditions of the War for Independence.* New York, Harper & Brothers [1860] Volume II. Chapter XI. freepages.history.rootsweb.com/~wcarr1/Lossing1/Chap53.html. Simms, William Gilmore. *The Life of Francis Marion.* New York, 1844. p. 128 arthurwendover.com/arthurs/simms/1sfox10.html. Moultrie, William. *Memoirs of the American Revolution so far as it related to the States of North and South Carolina and Georgia.* New York, 1802; (Eyewitness Accounts of the American Revolution). [New York] New York Times [1968]. II: 227–228. Bass, Robert Duncan. *Swamp Fox: the life and campaigns of General Francis Marion.* Orangeburg, SC: Sandlapper, 1989. pp. 153–155. Hayes, John T. *The Saddlebag Almanac.* IX (Jan. 2001) pp. 62–63. O'Kelley, Patrick. *Nothing But Blood and Slaughter.* Booklocker.com, 2004. 3: 172. Parker, John C. *Parker's Guide to the Revolutionary War in South Carolina: battles, skirmishes and murders.* Patrick, SC: Hem Branch Publishing, 2009. p. 206. web.ftc-i.net/~gcsummers/revolution.htm.

158. Parker, John C. *Parker's Guide to the Revolutionary War in South Carolina: battles, skirmishes and murders.* Patrick, SC: Hem Branch Publishing, 2009. p. 182.

159. Parker, John C. *Parker's Guide to the Revolutionary War in South Carolina: battles, skirmishes and murders.* Patrick, SC: Hem Branch Publishing, 2009. p. 190.

160. Simms, William Gilmore. *The Life of Francis Marion.* New York, 1844. pp. 131–132. Clark. Murtie June. *Loyalists in the Southern Campaign of the Revolutionary War.* Baltimore: Genealogical Publishing Company, Inc., 1981. 3: 267–323. Moss, Bobby Gilmer. *Roster of South Carolina Patriots in the American Revolution.* Baltimore: Genealogical

Pub. Co., 1983. p. 514. O'Kelley, Patrick. *Unwaried Patience and Fortitude: Francis Marion's Orderly Book.* Infinity Publishing (PA), 2006. Hayes, John T. *The Saddlebag Almanac.* IX (Jan. 2001) p. 63. James, William Dobein. *A Sketch of the Life of Brig. Gen. Francis Marion, and a History of his Brigade, from its Rise in June 1780, until Disbanded in December, 1782.* Charleston, SC: Gould and Riley, 1821. p. 34. Bass, Robert Duncan. *Swamp Fox: the life and campaigns of General Francis Marion.* Orangeburg, SC: Sandlapper, 1989. pp. 164–168. Lipscomb, Terry W. *South Carolina Revolutionary Battles Part Ten, Names in South Carolina.* XXX (Winter 1983). South Carolina Historical Society, 1983. p. 13. O'Kelley, Patrick. *Nothing But Blood and Slaughter.* Booklocker.com, 2004. 3: 176–180. Parker, John C. *Parker's Guide to the Revolutionary War in South Carolina: battles, skirmishes and murders.* Patrick, SC: Hem Branch Publishing, 2009. p. 190–191.

161. National Archives and Records Administration. Josias Sessions Pension application S18202. Parker, John C. *Parker's Guide to the Revolutionary War in South Carolina: battles, skirmishes and murders.* Patrick, SC: Hem Branch Publishing, 2009. p. 222.

162. Parker, John C. *Parker's Guide to the Revolutionary War in South Carolina: battles, skirmishes and murders.* Patrick, SC: Hem Branch Publishing, 2009. p. 241, 247.

163. J. A. Rhame, in *Social Bulletin* No. 156. Extension Division, (University of South Carolina: Columbia, 1925), p. 52. Parker, John C. *Parker's Guide to the Revolutionary War in South Carolina: battles, skirmishes and murders.* Patrick, SC: Hem Branch Publishing, 2009. p. 261.

164. Parker, John C. *Parker's Guide to the Revolutionary War in South Carolina: battles, skirmishes and murders.* Patrick, SC: Hem Branch Publishing, 2009. p. 285.

165. National Archives and Records Administration. William Caldwell Pension application S2116. Parker, John C. *Parker's Guide to the Revolutionary War in South Carolina: battles, skirmishes and murders.* Patrick, SC: Hem Branch Publishing, 2009. p. 297.

166. Kirkland, Thomas J. and Kennedy, Robert M. *Historic Camden.* State Company, 1905. pp. 268–269. Kirkwood, Robert. "The Journal and Orderly Book of Captain Robert Kirkwood of the Delaware Regiment of the Continental Line," *Papers of the Historical Society of Delaware.* 56 (1910), 1–277. p. 17. Dann, John C. *The Revolution Remembered, Eyewitness Account of the War for Independence.* University of Chicago Press, 1980. pp. 221–224. Moultrie, William. *Memoirs of the American Revolution so far as it related to the States of North and South Carolina and Georgia.* New York, 1802; (Eyewitness Accounts of the American Revolution). [New York] New York Times [1968]. II: 278–279. Fanning, David. *The Narrative of Colonel David Fanning.* Edited with an introduction and notes by Lindley S. Butler. Davidson, NC: Briarpatch Press; Charleston, SC: Tradd Street Press, 1981. pp. 58–59. *The Pennsylvania Gazette.* June 13, 1781. Clark, Walter, et al., editors. *The State Records of North Carolina.* Winston and Goldsboro: Various publishers, 1895–1907. XVII–1781–1785. p. 1060. James, William Dobein. *A Sketch of the Life of Brig. General Francis Marion, and a History of his Brigade, from its Rise in June 1780, until Disbanded in December, 1782.* Charleston, SC: Gould and Riley, 1821. p. 37. Batt, Richard John. *The Maryland Continentals, 1780–1781.* Tulane University Dissertation, 1974. pp. 165–166. *A List of all the officers of the Army: viz. the general and field officers; the officers of the several troops, regiments, independent companies, and garrisons: with an alphabetical index to the whole. Also, a list of the officers of the Royal Regiment of Artillery, the Corps of Engineers, the Irish Artillery and Engineers, and of the Marine Forces: the officers on half pay; and a succession of colonels. To which are likewise added the officers of the militia forces, and of the fencible and provincial regiments in Great Britain.* [London, England?]: War-Office, 1780. pp. 137, 304. O'Kelley, Patrick. *Nothing But Blood and Slaughter.* Booklocker.com, 2004. 3: 224–26. Parker, John C. *Parker's Guide to the Revolutionary War in South Carolina: battles, skirmishes and murders.* Patrick, SC: Hem Branch Publishing, 2009. p. 242.

167. National Archives and Records Administration. Robert Coleman pension application W23858. Gregg, Alexander. *History of the old Cheraws; containing an account of the aborigines of the Pedee, the first white settlements, their subsequent progress, civil changes, the struggle of the revolution, and growth of the country afterward, extending from about A. D. 1730 to 1810, with notices of families and sketches of individuals.* New York, Richardson, 1867; Spartanburg, SC: Reprint Co., 1965. p. 352. Parker, John C. *Parker's Guide to the Revolutionary War in South Carolina: battles, skirmishes and murders.* Patrick, SC: Hem Branch Publishing, 2009. p. 276.

168. Neuffer, Claude. *Names in South Carolina,* Volume I–XII, 1954–1965. State Printing Co., 1967. p. 95. O'Kelley, Patrick. *Nothing But Blood and Slaughter.* Booklocker.com, 2004. 3: 371.

169. Lipscomb, Terry W. South Carolina Revolutionary Battles: Part Seven. *Names in South Carolina* XXVI (Winter 1979). South Carolina Historical Society, 1979. p. 36. O'Kelley, Patrick. *Nothing But Blood and Slaughter.* Booklocker.com, 2004. 3: 389.

170. Southern Studies Program. *Figures of the Revolution in South Carolina, An Anthology. Spartanburg, Anderson, Beaufort, Aiken, Florence, Georgetown.* Columbia: University of South Carolina, 1976. pp. 119–121. Cashin, Edward J. *The King's Ranger. Thomas Brown and the American Revolution on the Southern Frontier.* Athens, University of Georgia Press, 1989. p. 149. Moultrie, William. *Memoirs of the American Revolution so far as it related to the States of North and South Carolina and Georgia.* New York, 1802; (Eyewitness Accounts of the American Revolution). [New York] New York Times [1968]. II: 302–303. Lipscomb, Terry W. South Carolina Revolutionary Battles: Part Seven. *Names in South Carolina* XXVI (Winter 1979). South Carolina Historical Society, 1979. p. 36–37. Lambert, Robert Stansbury. *South Carolina Loyalists in the American Revolution.* Columbia: University of South Carolina, 1987. pp. 208, 218–222. Pancake, John S. *This Destructive War: the British Campaign in the Carolinas.* Tuscaloosa: University of Alabama Press, 1985. p. 88. Draper, Lyman. Thomas Sumter Papers, Draper Manuscript Collection, State Historical Society of Wisconsin. O'Kelley, Patrick. *Nothing But Blood and Slaughter.* Booklocker.com, 2004. 3: 390–91. *Traditions and Reminiscences Chiefly of the American Revolution in the South; Including Biographical Sketches, Incidents and Anecdotes, Few of Which Have Been Published, Particularly of Residents In the Upper Country.* By Joseph Johnson, M.D. of Charleston, S.C. Charleston, SC: Walker & James. 1851. pp. 420–422.

171. Hairr, John. *Colonel David Fanning, the Adventures of a Carolina Loyalist.* Averasboro Press, 2000. pp. 153, 155, 157–161. Caruthers, Eli W. *The Old North State in 1776.* Guilford County Genealogical Society, 1985. pp. 200–201. Clark, Walter. *The State Records of North Carolina.* Winston, 1896. XIX–1782–'84. p. 963. Barefoot, Daniel W. *Touring North Carolina's Revolutionary War Sites.* Winston-Salem: John F. Blair, 1998. p. 141. McGeachy, John, "Revolutionary Reminiscences from the "Cape Fear Sketches," North Carolina State University History Paper, 2001. O'Kelley, Patrick. *Nothing But Blood and Slaughter.* Booklocker.com, 2004. 3: 385. Parker, John C. *Parker's Guide to the Revolutionary War in South Carolina: battles, skirmishes and murders.* Patrick, SC: Hem Branch Publishing, 2009. p. 324.

172. Ripley, Warren. *Battleground: South Carolina in the Revolution.* Charleston, SC: Evening Post, 1983. pp. 194–195. Moss, Bobby Gilmer. *Roster of South Carolina Patriots in the American Revolution.* Baltimore: Genealogical Pub. Co., 1983. p. 13. Lipscomb, Terry W. South Carolina Revolutionary Battles: Part Nine. *Names in South Carolina.* XXVIII (Winter 1981). South Carolina Historical Society, 1981. pp. 38–39. O'Kelley, Patrick. *Nothing But Blood and Slaughter.* Booklocker.com, 2004. 4: 95. Parker, John C. *Parker's Guide to the Revolutionary War in South Carolina: battles, skirmishes and murders.* Patrick, SC: Hem Branch Publishing, 2009. p. 271, 325.

173. Garden, Alexander. *Anecdotes of the American Revolution, Illustrative of the Talents and Virtues of the Heroes and Patriots who Acted the Most Conspicuous Parts Therein. Second series.* Charleston, S. C.: A.E. Miller, 1828. pp. 375–375. Southern Studies Program. *Figures of the Revolution in South Carolina, An Anthology. Spartanburg, Anderson, Beaufort, Aiken, Florence, Georgetown.* Columbia: University of South Carolina, 1976. pp. 232–233, 268–269. National Archives and Records Administration. Abraham Elledge Pension application, #S10625. Lipscomb, Terry W. South Carolina Revolutionary Battles Part Nine. *Names in South Carolina.* XXVIII (Winter 1981). South Carolina Historical Society, 1981. p. 35. O'Kelley, Patrick. *Nothing But Blood and Slaughter.* Booklocker.com, 2004 4: 71–72. Peckham, Howard Henry. *The Toll of Independence: engagements & battle casualties of the American Revolution.* edited by Howard H. Peckham. Chicago: University of Chicago Press, 1974. p. 95. Parker, John C. *Parker's Guide to the Revolutionary War in South Carolina: battles, skirmishes and murders.* Patrick, SC: Hem Branch Publishing, 2009. p. 12.

174. Ripley, Warren. *Battleground: South Carolina in the Revolution.* Charleston, SC: Evening Post, 1983. pp. 237–238. Clark. Murtie June. *Loyalists in the Southern Campaign of the Revolutionary War.* Baltimore: Genealogical Publishing Company, Inc., 1981. 1: 226. Moss, Bobby Gilmer. *Roster of South Carolina Patriots in the American Revolution.* Baltimore: Genealogical Pub. Co., 1983. p. 40, 371. Lipscomb, Terry W. South Carolina Revolutionary Battles: Part Nine. *Names in South Carolina.* XXVIII (Winter 1981). South Carolina Historical Society, 1981. p. 39. O'Kelley, Patrick. *Nothing But Blood and Slaughter.* Booklocker.com, 2004. 4: 96.

175. Parker, John C. *Parker's Guide to the Revolutionary War in South Carolina: battles, skirmishes and murders.* Patrick, SC: Hem Branch Publishing, 2009. p. 220.

176. Gibbes, Robert Wilson. *Documentary History of the American Revolution.* New York: D. Appleton & Co., 1855 (3 vols: 1764–1776, 1776–1782, 1781–1782). reprinted New York Times & Arno Press, 1971. III: 185.

177. O'Kelley, Patrick. *Nothing But Blood and Slaughter.* Booklocker.com, 2004. 4: 73–4. James, William Dobein. *A Sketch of the Life of Brig. General Francis Marion, and a History of his Brigade, from its Rise in June 1780, until Disbanded in December, 1782.* Charleston, SC: Gould and Riley, 1821. Chapter 4. Lipscomb, Terry W. South Carolina Revolutionary Battles: Part Nine. *Names in South Carolina.* XXVIII (Winter 1981). South Carolina Historical Society, 1981. p. 36. Parker, John C. *Parker's Guide to the Revolutionary War in South Carolina: battles, skirmishes and murders.* Patrick, SC: Hem Branch Publishing, 2009. pp. 189, 220, 277.

178. Diary of Captain Barnard Elliott Laurens Collection, South Carolina Historical Society. NDAR 2:102, 114.

179. Diary of Captain Barnard Elliott. Laurens Collection, South Carolina Historical Society. NDAR 2:102, 127. Journal of H.M. Sloop Tamar, Captain Edward Thornbrough, British National Archives, Admiralty 51/968. O'Kelley, Patrick. *Unwaried Patience and Fortitude: Francis Marion's Orderly Book.* Infinity Publishing (PA), 2006. pp. 14–15. Russell, David Lee. *Victory on Sullivan's Island: the British Cape Fear.* Infinity Publishing (PA), 2002. p. 51. Parker, John C. *Parker's Guide to the Revolutionary War in South Carolina: battles, skirmishes and murders.* Patrick, SC: Hem Branch Publishing, 2009. p. 88.

180. *The Pennsylvania Evening Post.* 1: 142 (Dec. 12, 1775), p. 582. *Journal of the South Carolina Provincial Congress.* November 12, 1775. Provincial Congress of South Carolina pp. 74–80. William Henry Drayton to the Georgia Council of Safety, Savannah. Provincial Congress of South Carolina. pp. 83–85. NDAR 2:1002–1003, 1004–1005. Parker, John C. *Parker's Guide to the Revolutionary War in South Carolina: battles, skirmishes and murders.* Patrick, SC: Hem Branch Publishing, 2009. p. 80–81.

181. *The Massachusetts Spy: Or, American Oracle of Liberty.* IX: 429, p. 2. Massey, Gregory D. *A Hero's Life: John Laurens and the American Revolution.* University of South Carolina Press, 1992. pp. 118–120, 134–136. Ripley, Warren. *Battleground: South Carolina in the Revolution.* Charleston, SC: Evening Post, 1983. pp. 24–28. Davies, K.G. *Documents of the American Revolution 1770–1783.* (Colonial Office Series) Shannon: Irish University Press 1972, 1981. 17: 127. Lipscomb, Terry W. South Carolina Revolutionary Battles: Part Two. *Names in South Carolina.* XXI (Winter 1974). South Carolina Historical Society, 1974. p. 23. Moultrie, William. *Memoirs of the American Revolution so far as it related to the States of North and South Carolina and Georgia.* New York, 1802; (Eyewitness Accounts of the American Revolution). [New York] New York Times [1968]. I: 393–404. Lee, Henry. *Memoirs of the War in the Southern Department of the United States.* New York: University Publishing Co., 1869. p. 125. James, William Dobein. *A Sketch of the Life of Brig. General Francis Marion, and a History of his Brigade, from its Rise in June 1780, until Disbanded in December, 1782.* Charleston, SC: Gould and Riley, 1821. p. 8. *A List of all the officers of the Army: viz. the general and field officers; the officers of the several troops, regiments, independent companies, and garrisons: with an alphabetical index to the whole. Also, a list of the officers of the Royal Regiment of Artillery, the Corps of Engineers, the Irish Artillery and Engineers, and of the Marine Forces: the officers on half pay; and a succession of colonels. To which are likewise added the officers of the militia forces, and of the fencible and provincial regiments in Great Britain.* [London,

England?]: War-Office, 1780. p. 302. *The Providence Gazette; and Country Journal.* XVI: 807 p. 2. O'Kelley, Patrick. *Nothing But Blood and Slaughter.* Booklocker.com, 2004. 1: 272–74.

182. Scoggins, Michael C.; Edgar, Walter. *The Day It Rained Militia: Huck's Defeat and the Revolution in the South Carolina Backcountry, May–July 1780.* Charleston: The History Press, c2005. p. 38. Borick, Charles P. *A Gallant Defense: the Siege of Charleston, 1780.* Columbia: University of South Carolina Press, 2003. pp. 27–28. Boatner, Mark M. *Encyclopedia of the American Revolution.* 3d ed., New York: McKay, 1980. pp. 206–207.

183. Parker, John C. *Parker's Guide to the Revolutionary War in South Carolina: battles, skirmishes and murders.* Patrick, SC: Hem Branch Publishing, 2009. p. 89.

184. O'Kelley, Patrick. *Unwaried Patience and Fortitude: Francis Marion's Orderly Book.* Infinity Publishing (PA), 2006. p. 497. Parker, John C. *Parker's Guide to the Revolutionary War in South Carolina: battles, skirmishes and murders.* Patrick, SC: Hem Branch Publishing, 2009. p. 88.

185. Smith, Charles R. *Marines in the Revolution: a history of the Continental Marines in the American Revolution, 1775–1783.* Washington: History and Museums Division, Headquarters, U.S. Marine Corps: For sale by the Supt. of Docs., U.S. Govt. Print. Off., 1975. pp. 247–250. Gruber, Ira D. *John Peebles' American War, the Diary of a Scottish Grenadier, 1776–1782.* Stackpole Books, 1998. pp. 343–344. Ewald, Johann von. *Diary of the American War: a Hessian journal.* translated and edited by Joseph P. Tustin New Haven: Yale University Press, 1979. p. 203. *The Siege of Charleston, with an Account of the Province of South Carolina: Diaries and Letters of Hessian Officers from the Von Jungkenn Papers in the William L. Clements Library.* Translated and Edited by Bernhard A. Uhlendorf. Ann Arbor: University of Michigan Press 1938. p. 195. Bauer, Carl. The 1780 Siege of Charleston as Experienced by a Hessian Officer, Part One. (Journal of the Hochfuerstlichen Grenadier Battalion Platte from 16 February 1776 to 24 May 1784 by the Regimental Quartermaster. Carl Bauer. Edited by George Fenwick Jones. *South Carolina Historical Magazine.* 88:1 (Jan. 1987) pp. 28, 30. Jennison, William, Jr. Extracts from the Journal of William Jennison, Jr., Lieutenant of the Marines in the Continental Navy. By Captain Richard S. Collum, U.S.M.C. *The Pennsylvania Magazine of History and Biography.* 15:1891 pp. 106. O'Kelley, Patrick. *Nothing But Blood and Slaughter.* Booklocker.com, 2004. 2: 32–33.

186. Parker, John C. *Parker's Guide to the Revolutionary War in South Carolina: battles, skirmishes and murders.* Patrick, SC: Hem Branch Publishing, 2009. p. 88.

187. Peckham, Howard Henry. *The Toll of Independence: engagements & battle casualties of the American Revolution.* edited by Howard H. Peckham. Chicago: University of Chicago Press, 1974. p. 70.

188. Parker, John C. *Parker's Guide to the Revolutionary War in South Carolina: battles, skirmishes and murders.* Patrick, SC: Hem Branch Publishing, 2009. p. 88. Haiman, Miecislaus. *Kosciuszko in the American Revolution.* New York, Kosciuszko Foundation and Polish Institute of Arts and Sciences, 1975. p. 132. From Colonel Thaddeus Kosciuszko 10 October, 1782. Greene, Nathanael. *The Papers of General Nathanael Greene.* Richard K. Showman, ed. Chapel Hill: the University of North Carolina Press, published for the Rhode Island Historical Society. c1976–2006. XII: 51. Markland, John. Revolutionary Services of John Markland. *Pennsylvania Magazine of History and Biography.* 9 (1885) pp. 102, 110. Lipscomb, Terry W. South Carolina Revolutionary Battles: Part Nine. *Names in South Carolina.* XXVIII (Winter 1981). South Carolina Historical Society, 1981. p. 39 (NSC XXVIII: 39) Winter 1981 & PJO Vol. 4, p. 97.

189. Garden, Alexander. *Anecdotes of the American Revolution, Illustrative of the Talents and Virtues of the Heroes and Patriots who Acted the Most Conspicuous Parts Therein. Second series.* Charleston, S. C.: A.E. Miller, 1828. pp. 91–93. Hayes, James P. James and related Sea Islands. [S.l.]: Hayes, 1978. pp. 31–32. Moultrie, William. *Memoirs of the American Revolution so far as it related to the States of North and South Carolina and Georgia.* New York, 1802; (Eyewitness accounts of the American Revolution). [New York]: New York Times, [1968]. 2: 343. *Pennsylvania Gazette.* Dec. 11, 1782. British National Archives. , War Office, Class 12, Vol. 247, pp. 493, 509, 513. *A List of all the officers of the Army: viz. the general and field officers; the officers of the several troops, regiments, independent companies, and garrisons: with an alphabetical index to the whole. Also, a list of the officers of the Royal Regiment of Artillery, the Corps of Engineers, the Irish Artillery and Engineers, and of the Marine Forces: the officers on half pay; and a succession of colonels. To which are likewise added the officers of the militia forces, and of the fencible and provincial regiments in Great Britain.* [London, England?]: War-Office, 1780. p. 69. Lipscomb, Terry W. South Carolina Revolutionary Battles: Part Nine. *Names in South Carolina.* XXVIII (Winter 1981). South Carolina Historical Society, 1981. p. 39–40. George Wray Papers. University of Michigan. William Clements Library Vol. 7. O'Kelley, Patrick. *Nothing but Blood and Slaughter.* Booklocker.com, 2004. 4: 97–99. Parker, John C. *Parker's Guide to the Revolutionary War in South Carolina: battles, skirmishes and murders.* Patrick, SC: Hem Branch Publishing, 2009. p. 86.

190. Journal of the HM Sloop *Tamar* Captain Edward Thornbrough. British National Archives. Admiralty 51/968. NDAR, 2:140. Parker, John C. *Parker's Guide to the Revolutionary War in South Carolina: battles, skirmishes and murders.* Patrick, SC: Hem Branch Publishing, 2009. p. 104.

191. Griffiths, John William. *"To Receive them Properly": Charlestown prepares for war, 1775–1776.* M.A. Thesis, University of South Carolina, 1992. pp. 189, 199, 201–202. O'Kelley, Patrick. *Nothing but Blood and Slaughter.* Booklocker.com, 2004. 1: 67–68.

192. Griffiths, John William. *"To Receive them Properly": Charlestown prepares for war, 1775–1776.* M.A. Thesis, University of South Carolina, 1992. pp. 189, 199, 201–202. O'Kelley, Patrick. *Nothing but Blood and Slaughter.* Booklocker.com, 2004. 1: 67–68.

193. Journal of HM Sloop *Tamar,* British National Archives, Admiralty 51/968; NDAR 3:202.

194. Ripley, Warren. *Battleground: South Carolina in the Revolution.* Charleston, SC: Evening Post, 1983. pp. 10–12. Davies, K.G. *Documents of the American Revolution 1770–1783.* (Colonial Office Series) Shannon: Irish

University Press 1972, 1981. XII: 29. Simms, William Gilmore. *The Life of Francis Marion*. New York: H.G. Langley, 1844. p. 37. Moultrie, William. *Memoirs of the American Revolution so far as it related to the States of North and South Carolina and Georgia*. New York, 1802; (Eyewitness accounts of the American Revolution). [New York]: New York Times, [1968]. 1: 112–113. NDAR 3:202. *Pennsylvania Gazette*. Dec. 20, 1775. Coggins, Jack. *Ships and seamen of the American Revolution; vessels, crews, weapons, gear, naval tactics, and actions of the War for Independence*. Written and illustrated by Jack Coggins. [Harrisburg,] Stackpole Books [1969]. p. 20. Lipscomb, Terry W. South Carolina Revolutionary Battles: Part One. *Names in South Carolina*. XX (Winter 1973). South Carolina Historical Society, 1973. pp. 20–21. Griffiths, John William. "To Receive them Properly ": Charlestown prepares for war, 1775–1776*. M.A. Thesis, University of South Carolina, 1992. pp. 201, 206–215. O'Kelley, Patrick. *Nothing but Blood and Slaughter*. Booklocker.com, 2004. 1: 68–70. Parker, John C. *Parker's Guide to the Revolutionary War in South Carolina: battles, skirmishes and murders*. Patrick, SC: Hem Branch Publishing, 2009. p. 104.

195. Peckham, Howard Henry. *The Toll of Independence: engagements & battle casualties of the American Revolution*. edited by Howard H. Peckham. Chicago: University of Chicago Press, 1974. p. 70. Master's Log of the *Cherokee*. British National Archives, Admiralty 52/1662. NDAR 3:667–669.

196. John Well's Account of the British attack on Charleston. *South-Carolina and American General Gazette*, May 31 to Aug. 2, 1776; NDAR 5:781. O'Kelley, Patrick. *Nothing But Blood and Slaughter*. Booklocker.com, 2004. 1: 137–145.

197. Sir Henry Clinton Papers, Clements Library. NDAR, 5:747.

198. Parker, John C. *Parker's Guide to the Revolutionary War in South Carolina: battles, skirmishes and murders*. Patrick, SC: Hem Branch Publishing, 2009. p. 81.

199. *Encyclopedia of the American Revolution*. Harold E. Selesky, editor in chief. 2nd ed. Detroit: Charles Scribner's Sons, 2007. I: 181–186. *The Encyclopedia of the American Revolutionary War: a political, social, and military history*. Gregory Fremont-Barnes, Richard Alan Ryerson, editors. Santa Barbara, CA: ABC-CLIO, 2006. I: 203–203. Clinton, Henry. *The American Rebellion: Sir Henry Clinton's Narrative of His Campaigns, 1775–1782, with an appendix of original documents*. Edited by William B. Willcox. New Haven: Yale University Press, 1954. Clowes, William Laird. *The Royal Navy: a history from the earliest times to 1900*. 7 vols. London: Chatham, 1996. Gardiner, Robert, ed. *Navies and the American Revolution, 1775–1783*. London: Chatham, 1996. Gordon, John W. *South Carolina and the American Revolution: a battlefield history*. Columbia: University of South Carolina Press, 2003. Lipscomb, Terry W. *The Carolina Lowcountry, April 1775–June 1776 and the Battle of Fort Moultrie*. 2nd ed. Columbia: South Carolina Department of Archives and History, 1994. Lumpkin, Henry. *From Savannah to Yorktown: the American Revolution in the South*. New York: Paragon, 1981. Morrill, Dan L. *Southern Campaigns of the American Revolution*. Baltimore: the Nautical & Aviation Publishing Company of America, 1993. Moultrie, William. *Memoirs of the American Revolution so far as it related to the States of North and South Carolina and Georgia*. New York, 1802; (Eyewitness accounts of the American Revolution). [New York]: New York Times, [1968]. NDAR 5. Russell, David Lee. *The American Revolution in the Southern Colonies*. Jefferson, NC: McFarland, 2000. Willcox, William B. *Portrait of a General: Sir Henry Clinton in the War of Independence*. New York: Knopf, 1964. Ward, Christopher. *The War of the Revolution*. New York: Macmillan, 1952. pp. 665–678.

200. Parker, John C. *Parker's Guide to the Revolutionary War in South Carolina: battles, skirmishes and murders*. Patrick, SC: Hem Branch Publishing, 2009. p. 83.

201. *The Siege of Charleston, with an Account of the Province of South Carolina: Diaries and Letters of Hessian Officers from the Von Jungkenn Papers in the William L. Clements Library*. Translated and Edited by Bernhard A. Uhlendorf. Ann Arbor: University of Michigan Press 1938. pp. 51, 53, 241, 243, 383. Parker, John C. *Parker's Guide to the Revolutionary War in South Carolina: battles, skirmishes and murders*. Patrick, SC: Hem Branch Publishing, 2009. p. 82.

202. *The Siege of Charleston, with an Account of the Province of South Carolina: Diaries and Letters of Hessian Officers from the Von Jungkenn Papers in the William L. Clements Library*. Translated and Edited by Bernhard A. Uhlendorf. Ann Arbor: University of Michigan Press 1938. p. 247. Ewald, Johann von. *Diary of the American War: a Hessian journal*. translated and edited by Joseph P. Tustin New Haven: Yale University Press, 1979. p. 228.

203. Parker, John C. *Parker's Guide to the Revolutionary War in South Carolina: battles, skirmishes and murders*. Patrick, SC: Hem Branch Publishing, 2009. p. 109.

204. Peckham, Howard Henry. *The Toll of Independence: engagements & battle casualties of the American Revolution*. edited by Howard H. Peckham. Chicago: University of Chicago Press, 1974. p. 70.

205. Parker, John C. *Parker's Guide to the Revolutionary War in South Carolina: battles, skirmishes and murders*. Patrick, SC: Hem Branch Publishing, 2009. p. 84.

206. For a description of the defenses of Charleston during the siege of 1780, see O'Kelley, Patrick. *Nothing But Blood and Slaughter*. 1: 109–111.

207. Henry Laurens, Philip May Hamer. The papers of Henry Laurens South Carolina Historical Society - 1979- Page 271. Laurens, Henry. The papers of Henry Laurens. Philip M. Hamer, editor. Columbia: Published for the South Carolina Historical Society by the University of South Carolina Press, [1968] 1: 224. Keith Krawczynski. *William Henry Drayton: South Carolina revolutionary patriot*. Baton Rouge: Louisiana State University Press, c2001. 125. Godbold, E. Stanly. *Christopher Gadsden and the American Revolution*. E. Stanly Godbold, Jr., Robert H. Woody. Knoxville: University of Tennessee Press, c1982. p. 133. Parker, John C. *Parker's Guide to the Revolutionary War in South Carolina: battles, skirmishes and murders*. Patrick, SC: Hem Branch Publishing, 2009. p. 107.

208. NDAR 8: 395, 1061.

209. Captain Nicholas Biddle to Robert Morris. *Papers of the Continental Congress, 1774–1789*. Washington: National Archives and Records Service, General Services Administration, 1971. (Letters Addressed to Congress, 1775–89), 78, II, 241–243, NA. NDAR 9:919–920.

210. O'Kelley, Patrick. *Unwaried Patience and Fortitude: Francis Marion's Orderly Book.* Infinity Publishing (PA), 2006. Massey, Gregory D. *A Hero's Life: John Laurens and the American Revolution.* Ph.D. Thesis, University of South Carolina, 1992. pp. 136–137. Davies, K.G. *Documents of the American Revolution 1770–1783.* (Colonial Office Series) Shannon: Irish University Press 1972, 1981. XVII: 127–128. Moultrie, William. *Memoirs of the American Revolution so far as it related to the States of North and South Carolina and Georgia.* New York, 1802; (Eyewitness accounts of the American Revolution). [New York]: New York Times, [1968]. 1:407–416; 423–425. Hayes, John T. *The Saddlebag Almanac.* Fort Lauderdale, Fla.: Saddlebag Press. V: 76, 81–82. *Pennsylvania Gazette.* June 30, 1779. O'Kelley, Patrick. *Nothing but Blood and Slaughter.* Booklocker.com, 2004. 1: 275–76. Parker, John C. *Parker's Guide to the Revolutionary War in South Carolina: battles, skirmishes and murders.* Patrick, SC: Hem Branch Publishing, 2009. p. 70.

211. *The Norwich Packet and the Weekly Advertiser.* 298 (June 22, 1779) p. 2. Extract of a letter from Edenton, North Carolina, dated June 1, 1779. *The Pennsylvania Evening Post.* V: 607 (June 15, 1779), p. 158.

212. *The Siege of Charleston, with an Account of the Province of South Carolina: Diaries and Letters of Hessian Officers from the Von Jungkenn Papers in the William L. Clements Library.* Translated and Edited by Bernhard A. Uhlendorf. Ann Arbor: University of Michigan Press 1938. p. 213.

213. Ewald, Johann von. *Diary of the American War: a Hessian journal.* translated and edited by Joseph P. Tustin New Haven: Yale University Press, 1979. pp. 216–220. Massey, Gregory D. A Hero's Life: John Laurens and the American Revolution. Ph.D. Thesis, University of South Carolina, 1992. pp. 370–372. Burgoyne, Bruce E. *Diaries of Two Anspach Jaegers.* Bowie, MD: Heritage Books, 1997. pp. 123–125, 131. Peebles, John. *John Peebles' American War: the Diary of a Scottish Grenadier, 1776–1782.* edited by Ira D. Gruber. Mechanicsburg, PA: Stackpole Books, 1998. 314–346, 352, 354. Murdoch, Richard Kenneth. *A French Account of the siege of Charleston, 1780.* [s.l.: s.n.] 1966. Reprinted from *South Carolina Historical Magazine,* vol. 67, 1966. pp. 142, 144. Rosengarten, J. G. *The German Allied Troops in the North American War of Independence, 1776–1783.* by Max Von Eelking. Joel Munsell's Son's Publishers, 1893. pp. 189–220. Henry Clinton, Sir; William T Bulger. Sir Henry Clinton's "Journal of the siege of Charleston, 1780." [Charleston, S. C.]: s.n. 1965. The Journal is in the Manuscript Division of the William L. Clements Library. In the *South Carolina Historical Magazine.* 66:3 (July 1965) 147–182. p. 149. Scott, Ruth. Loyalist Anthony Allaire. *Officers Quarterly.* York-Sunbury Historical Society of Fredericton, New Brunswick. Summer 1997. Moultrie, William. *Memoirs of the American Revolution so far as it related to the States of North and South Carolina and Georgia.* New York, 1802; (Eyewitness Accounts of the American Revolution). [New York] New York Times [1968]. II: 62–63, 65. Johnson, Uzal. *Memo of Occurrence During the Campaign of 1780.* South Carolina Historical Society, Military Manuscripts. p. 19. Wallace, Lee A. *The Orderly Book of Captain Benjamin Taliaferro, 2d Virginia Detachment. Charleston, South Carolina, 1780.* Virginia State Library, 1980. pp. 23–24. *The Pennsylvania Gazette.* Aug. 20, 1777. *The Siege of Charleston, with an Account of the Province of South Carolina: Diaries and Letters of Hessian Officers from the Von Jungkenn Papers in the William L. Clements Library.* Translated and Edited by Bernhard A. Uhlendorf. Ann Arbor: University of Michigan Press 1938. pp. 223–227, 381. Bauer, Carl. The 1780 Siege of Charleston as Experienced by a Hessian Officer, Part One. (Journal of the Hochfuerstlichen Grenadier Battalion Platte from 16 February 1776 to 24 May 1784 by the Regimental Quartermaster: Carl Bauer. Edited by George Fenwick Jones. *South Carolina Historical Magazine.* 88:1 (Jan. 1987), Part One p. 33. Clinton, Henry. *The American Rebellion: Sir Henry Clinton's Narrative of His Campaigns, 1775–1782, with an appendix of original documents.* Edited by William B. Willcox. New Haven: Yale University Press, 1954. p. 163. *A List of all the officers of the Army: viz. the general and field officers; the officers of the several troops, regiments, independent companies, and garrisons: with an alphabetical index to the whole. Also, a list of the officers of the Royal Regiment of Artillery, the Corps of Engineers, the Irish Artillery and Engineers, and of the Marine Forces: the officers on half pay; and a succession of colonels. To which are likewise added the officers of the militia forces, and of the fencible and provincial regiments in Great Britain.* [London, England?]: War-Office, 1780. pp. 93, 138, 156. Borick, Carl P. *A Gallant Defense, the Siege of Charleston, 1780.* University of South Carolina Press, 2003. Ellet, Elizabeth F. *The Women of the American Revolution.* New York: Baker and Scribner, 1849. O'Kelley, Patrick. *Nothing But Blood and Slaughter.* Booklocker.com, 2004. 2: 130–34. Tarleton, Banastre. *A History of the Campaigns of 1780 and 1781 in the Southern Provinces of North America.* London, 1787; (Eyewitness accounts of the American Revolution). [New York]: New York Times, [1968]. p. 9. Moultrie, William. *Memoirs of the American Revolution so far as it related to the States of North and South Carolina and Georgia.* New York, 1802; (Eyewitness accounts of the American Revolution). [New York]: New York Times, [1968]. II: 62. Simms, William Gilmore. *South-Carolina in the Revolutionary War: being a reply to certain misrepresentations and mistakes of recent writers in relation to the course and conduct of this state.* by a Southron. Charleston: Walker and James, 1853 (reprinted from the *Southern Quarterly Review,* v. 14, 1848, and v. 22, 1852) p. 104. De Saussure, Wilmot Gibbes. *An Account of the Siege of Charleston, South Carolina, in 1780.* Charleston, News and Courier Book Presses, 1885. Bass, Robert Duncan. *The Green Dragoon: The lives of Banastre Tarleton and Mary Robinson.* New York: Holt, 1957. p. 73. Borick, Carl P. *A Gallant Defense, The Siege of Charleston, 1780.* Columbia: University of South Carolina Press, 2003. pp. 104–106. Wilson, David K. *The Southern Strategy: Britain's conquest of South Carolina and Georgia, 1775–1780.* Columbia: University of South Carolina Press, c2005. p. 206. McCrady, Edward. *History of South Carolina in the Revolution, 1775–1780.* New York: Paladin Press, 1969 (reprint of 1901 ed.) p. 454. Sherman, William Thomas. *Calendar and Record of the Revolutionary War in the South: 1780–1781,* 2003–2006. p. 90. Parker, John C. *Parker's Guide to the Revolutionary War in South Carolina: battles, skirmishes and murders.* Patrick, SC: Hem Branch Publishing, 2009. p. 73.

214. Ewald, Johann von. *Diary of the American War: a Hessian journal.* translated and edited by Joseph P. Tustin New Haven: Yale University Press, 1979. p. 224. *The Siege of Charleston, with an Account of the Province of South Carolina: Diaries and Letters of Hessian Officers from the Von Jungkenn Papers in the William L. Clements Library.* Translated and Edited by Bernhard A. Uhlendorf. Ann Arbor: University of Michigan Press 1938. p. 383.

215. O'Kelley, Patrick. *Nothing but Blood and Slaughter.* Booklocker.com, 2004. 2: 73–80. Massey, Gregory D. A Hero's Life: John Laurens and the American Revolution. Ph.D. Thesis, University of South Carolina, 1992. pp.

155–159; 370–372. Hanger, George. *The Life, Adventures, and Opinions of Col. George Hanger*. George Coleraine; William Combe. London: , J. Debrett, 1801. Clinton, Sir Henry. Papers, (William L. Clements Library, University of Michigan); Volumes 95, 99. Davies, K.G. *Documents of the American Revolution 1770–1783*. (Colonial Office Series) Shannon: Irish University Press 1972, 1981. XX: 173–174. Ewald, Johann von. *Diary of the American War: a Hessian journal*. translated and edited by Joseph P. Tustin New Haven: Yale University Press, 1979. pp. 190, 192, 199, 221–232. Gibbes, Robert Wilson. *Documentary History of the American Revolution*. New York: D. Appleton & Co., 1855 (3 vols: 1764–1776, 1776–1782, 1781–1782). reprinted New York Times & Arno Press, 1971 (3 vols. in 1). 2: 132–135. Burgoyne, Bruce. *Diaries of Two Ansbach Jagers*. Bowie, MD: Heritage Books, 1997. pp. 127–154. Boatner, Mark M. *Encyclopedia of the American Revolution*. 3d ed., New York: McKay, 1980. pp. 21, 213, 404, 686, 952. Southern Studies Program. *Figures of the Revolution in South Carolina, An Anthology*. Spartanburg, Anderson, Beaufort, Aiken, Florence, Georgetown. Columbia: University of South Carolina, 1976. p. 175. Magallon de la Morliere, Louis-Antoine. A French Account of the Siege of Charleston, 1780. *The South Carolina Historical Magazine*. 67: 3 (July 1966), pp. 140–154. Rosengarten, J. G. *The German Allied Troops in the North American War of Independence, 1776–1783*. by Max Von Eelking and, J. G. Rosengarten. Albany: Joel Munsell's Son's Publishers, 1893. pp. 199,289–320, 332–334. Lowell, Edward J. (Edward Jackson). *The Hessians and the other German auxiliaries of Great Britain in the Revolutionary War*. New York: Harper & Bros., 1884. Weinmester, Oscar K. The Hessian Grenadier Battalions in North America, 1776–1783. *Military Collector & Historian*. (Winter 1975). Tarleton, Banastre. *A History of the Campaigns of 1780 and 1781 in the Southern Provinces of North America*. London, 1787; (Eyewitness accounts of the American Revolution). [New York]: New York Times, [1968]. pp. 52–57. Heitman, Francis B. *Historical Register of Officers of the Continental Army during the War of the Revolution, April 1775 to December 1783*. Washington, DC.: the Rare Book Shop Publishing Company, 1914; Baltimore: Genealogical Publishing Company, 1967. pp. 62–131,498,603. Duncan, Francis. *History of the Royal Regiment of Artillery*. London, J. Murray, 1879. Cannon, Robert. *Historical Record of the Seventeenth Regiment of Light Dragoons Lancers*. London: John W. Parker, 1843. pp. 26–27. Journal of the Siege of Charleston. *The South Carolina Historical Magazine*. V: 66 Number 3 (July 1965), pp. 149–182. Lamb, Roger. *An original and authentic journal of occurrences during the late American War*. Eyewitness accounts of the American Revolution. [New York] New York Times, 1968, 1809. pp. 298–301. Peebles, John. *John Peebles' American War: the Diary of a Scottish Grenadier, 1776–1782*. edited by Ira D. Gruber. Mechanicsburg, PA: Stackpole Books, 1998. pp. 314,345–373. Simcoe, John Graves. *Simcoe's Military Journal. A History of the Operations of a Partisan Corps Called The Queen's Rangers, Commanded by Lieut. Col. J. G. Simcoe, During the War of the American Revolution*. New-York: Bartlett & Welford, 1844; [New York]: New York Times; Arno Press. Eyewitness Accounts of the American Revolution. [1968]. pp. 217, 233. Draper, Lyman. *Kings Mountain and its Heroes: History of the Battle of King's Mountain, October 7th, 1780, and the Events Which Led To It*. Johnson City, TN: The Overmountain Press, 1996. pp. 31, 33. Clark, Murtie June. *Loyalists in the Southern Campaign* of the Revolutionary War. Genealogical Publishing Company, Inc., 1981. I:1–48, 255–295, 311–630, II: 436, 453 III: 61–124, 177–213, 267–323, 353. Moultrie, William. *Memoirs of the American Revolution so far as it related to the States of North and South Carolina and Georgia*. New York, 1802; (Eyewitness accounts of the American Revolution). [New York] New York Times, [1968]. II: 50–1 14, 202. Smith, Charles R. *Marines in the Revolution: a history of the Continental Marines in the American Revolution, 1775–1783*. Washington: History and Museums Division, Headquarters, U.S. Marine Corps: For sale by the Supt. of Docs., U.S. Govt. Print. Off., 1975. pp. 246–250. Johnson, Uzal. *Memo of Occurrence During the Campaign of 1780*. South Carolina Historical Society, Military Manuscripts. Wallace, Lee A. *The Orderly Book of Captain Benjamin Taliaferro, 2d Virginia Detachment*. Charleston, South Carolina, 1780. Virginia State Library, 1980. pp. 18–156. Grimke, John Faucheraud. Order Book of John Faucheraud Grimke, August 1778 to May 1780. *The South Carolina Historical and Genealogical Magazine*. XVII: 3 (July 1916) p. 119; XVIII: 2 (April 1917), pp. 78–80, 82; XVIII: 3 (July 1917), pp. 151–152; XVIII: 4 (Oct. 1917), pp. 175–176; XIX: 2 (April 1918), pp. 101–103; XIX: 4 (Oct. 1918), pp. 181–182, 185, 187–188. *Pennsylvania Gazette*. April 5, 1780; April 27, 1780; June 7, 1780. Great Britain, Public Record Office. *Headquarters Papers of the British Army in America*, p. 2482; Colonial Office, Class 5, Volume 99, p. 493. Cornwallis Papers, Class 30, Volume 11, p. 2; Chancery, Class 106, Volume 90, Part 2, Bundle 13. Buchanan, John. *The Road to Guilford Courthouse*. New York: John Wiley and Sons, Inc., 1997. pp. 26–72, 202. Salley, A. S. *Records of the Regiments of the South Carolina Line in the Revolutionary War*. Baltimore: Genealogical Pub. Co., 1977. pp. 9, 14–21, 39, 42–43. Moss, Bobby Gilmer. *Roster of the South Carolina Patriots in the American Revolution*. Baltimore: Genealogical Pub. Co., 1983. pp. 48, 81, 101, 118, 226, 232, 290, 310, 339, 342, 440–441, 537–538, 673, 898, 940. Coggins, Jack. *Ships and Seamen of the American Revolution; vessels, crews, weapons, gear, naval tactics, and actions of the War for Independence*. Written and illustrated by Jack Coggins. [Harrisburg,] Stackpole Books [1969]. pp. 102–103. Ervin. Sara Sullivan. *South Carolinians in the Revolution*. Baltimore: Genealogical Publishing Company, Inc., 1971. pp. 63, 67–77. South Carolina Historical Society. Troop Returns. Jarvis, Stephen; Hayes, John T. *The King's Loyal Horseman, His Narrative. 1775–1783*. Fort Lauderdale, Fla.: The Saddlebag Press, 1996. pp. 42–45. *The Siege of Charleston, with an Account of the Province of South Carolina: Diaries and Letters of Hessian Officers from the Von Jungkenn Papers in the William L. Clements Library*. Translated and Edited by Bernhard A. Uhlendorf. Ann Arbor: University of Michigan Press 1938. pp. 87, 95, 109, 141, 209, 233, 243, 247, 25 I, 253, 263–287, 293, 373, 387–393, 405. Bauer, Carl. The 1780 Siege of Charleston as Experienced by a Hessian Officer, Part One. (Journal of the Hochfuerstlichen Grenadier Battalion Platte from 16 February 1776 to 24 May 1784 by the Regimental Quartermaster: Carl Bauer. Edited by George Fenwick Jones. *South Carolina Historical Magazine*. 88:1 (January 1987) pp. 24, 27, 31–33;. 63–69, 74–75. James, William Dobein. *A Sketch of the Life of Brig. Gen. Francis Marion, and a History of his Brigade, from its Rise in June 1780, until Disbanded in December, 1782*. Charleston, SC: Gould and Riley, 1821. p. 11. Clark, Walter, et al., editors. *The State Records of North Carolina*. Winston and Goldsboro: Various publishers, 1895–1907. XXII, Miscellaneous, p. 1022. Clinton, Sir Henry. *The American Rebellion Sir Henry Clinton's Narrative of His Campaigns, 1775–1782, with An Appendix of Original Documents* edited by William B. Willcox. New Haven: Yale University Press, 1954. pp. 157–172. Crow, Jeffrey J. *The Black Experience in Revolutionary North Carolina*. Raleigh: [North Carolina Dept. of Cultural Resources, Division of Archives and

Notes   329

History], 1977. p. 74. Davis, Robert Scott. Thomas Pinckney and the Last Campaign of Horatio Gates. *South Carolina Historical Magazine*. 86: 2 (April 1985), pp. 83, 98. North Carolina Archives. Troop Returns. Box 4, Box 5, Box 7. Hayes, John T. *The Saddlebag Almanac*. Fort Lauderdale, Fla.: Saddlebag Press. September, 1996. V: 73–75; VI: 2–29, 53–54. Pancake, John S. *This Destructive War: The British Campaign in the Carolinas*. Tuscaloosa: University of Alabama Press, 1985. pp. 56–69. George Wray Papers. William L. Clements Library, University of Michigan. Volume 6. Sir Henry Clinton Papers. William L. Clements Library, University of Michigan. Volume 87, item 9; Volume 91, Item 7; Volume 95, item 27; Volume 103, item 1. McAllister, J. T. *Virginia Militia in the Revolutionary War. Mcallister's Data*. Hot Springs, Va.: McAllister Publishing Co., 1913. p. 16. Sanchez-Saavedera, E.M. *A Guide to Virginia Military Organizations in the American Revolution, 1774–1787*. Richmond, VA: Virginia State Library, 1978. pp. 83–85, 124–125, 177–181. National Archives of Canada. Ward Chipman Papers, MG 23, D I, Series 1, Volume 25, p. 23. *A List of all the officers of the Army: viz. the general and field officers; the officers of the several troops, regiments, independent companies, and garrisons: with an alphabetical index to the whole. Also, a list of the officers of the Royal Regiment of Artillery, the Corps of Engineers, the Irish Artillery and Engineers, and of the Marine Forces: the officers on half pay; and a succession of colonels. To which are likewise added the officers of the militia forces, and of the fencible and provincial regiments in Great Britain*. [London, England?]: War-Office, 1780. pp. 93, 156, 3 11. Chesney, Alexander. *The Journal of Alexander Chesney, a South Carolina Loyalist in the Revolution and After*, edited by E. A. Jones. Columbus, Ohio: Ohio State University, 1921. Borick, Carl P. *A Gallant Defense, The Siege of Charleston, 1780*. Columbia: University of South Carolina Press, 2003. Draper, Lyman. Thomas Sumter Papers, Draper Manuscript Collection, State Historical Society of Wisconsin. 1VV31–36, 39, 43, 49, 51, 10VV68.

216. O'Kelley, Patrick. *Nothing but Blood and Slaughter*. Booklocker.com, 2004. 2: 82–84.

217. *The Siege of Charleston, with an Account of the Province of South Carolina: Diaries and Letters of Hessian Officers from the Von Jungkenn Papers in the William L. Clements Library*. Translated and Edited by Bernhard A. Uhlendorf. Ann Arbor: University of Michigan Press 1938. p. 247. Ewald, Johann von. *Diary of the American War: a Hessian journal*. translated and edited by Joseph P. Tustin New Haven: Yale University Press, 1979. p. 228.

218. Peebles, John. *John Peebles' American War: the Diary of a Scottish Grenadier, 1776–1782*. edited by Ira D. Gruber. Mechanicsburg, PA: Stackpole Books, 1998. p. 360.

219. *The Siege of Charleston, with an Account of the Province of South Carolina: Diaries and Letters of Hessian Officers from the Von Jungkenn Papers in the William L. Clements Library*. Translated and Edited by Bernhard A. Uhlendorf. Ann Arbor: University of Michigan Press 1938. pp. 59, 249, 387.

220. O'Kelley, Patrick. *Nothing but Blood and Slaughter*. Booklocker.com, 2004. 2: 87–89.

220a. O'Kelley, Patrick. *Nothing but Blood and Slaughter*. Booklocker.com, 2004. 2: 92–93.

221. Parker, John C. *Parker's Guide to the Revolutionary War in South Carolina: battles, skirmishes and murders*. Patrick, SC: Hem Branch Publishing, 2009. p. 108.

222. Ewald, Johann von. *Diary of the American War: a Hessian journal*. translated and edited by Joseph P. Tustin New Haven: Yale University Press, 1979. pp. 228–229. *The Siege of Charleston, with an Account of the Province of South Carolina: Diaries and Letters of Hessian Officers from the Von Jungkenn Papers in the William L. Clements Library*. Translated and Edited by Bernhard A. Uhlendorf. Ann Arbor: University of Michigan Press 1938. pp. 65, 67.

223. O'Kelley, Patrick. *Nothing but Blood and Slaughter*. Booklocker.com, 2004. 2: 96–98. Ewald, Johann von. *Diary of the American War: a Hessian journal*. translated and edited by Joseph P. Tustin New Haven: Yale University Press, 1979. p. 233.

224. Ewald, Johann von. *Diary of the American War: a Hessian journal*. translated and edited by Joseph P. Tustin New Haven: Yale University Press, 1979. p. 233.

225. *The Siege of Charleston, with an Account of the Province of South Carolina: Diaries and Letters of Hessian Officers from the Von Jungkenn Papers in the William L. Clements Library*. Translated and Edited by Bernhard A. Uhlendorf. Ann Arbor: University of Michigan Press 1938. Ewald, Johann von. *Diary of the American War: a Hessian journal*. translated and edited by Joseph P. Tustin New Haven: Yale University Press, 1979. p. 233. O'Kelley, Patrick. *Nothing but Blood and Slaughter*. Booklocker.com, 2004. 2: 101.

226. *The Siege of Charleston, with an Account of the Province of South Carolina: Diaries and Letters of Hessian Officers from the Von Jungkenn Papers in the William L. Clements Library*. Translated and Edited by Bernhard A. Uhlendorf. Ann Arbor: University of Michigan Press 1938. pp. 69, 391, 393. Ewald, Johann von. *Diary of the American War: a Hessian journal*. translated and edited by Joseph P. Tustin New Haven: Yale University Press, 1979. p. 233.

227. O'Kelley, Patrick. *Nothing but Blood and Slaughter*. Booklocker.com, 2004. 2: 105.

228. Moultrie, William. *Memoirs of the American Revolution so far as it related to the States of North and South Carolina and Georgia*. New York, 1802; (Eyewitness Accounts of the American Revolution). [New York] New York Times [1968].

229. Tarleton, Banastre. *A History of the Campaigns of 1780 and 1781 in the Southern Provinces of North America*. London, 1787; (Eyewitness Accounts of the American Revolution). [New York]: New York Times, [1968]. p. 22. Borick, Carl P. *A Gallant Defense, The Siege of Charleston, 1780*. Columbia: University of South Carolina Press, 2003. pp. 35–36. 219–220.

230. *Encyclopedia of the American Revolution*. Harold E. Selesky, editor in chief. 2nd ed. Detroit: Charles Scribner's Sons, 2007. I: 186–191. *The Encyclopedia of the American Revolutionary War: a political, social, and military history*. Gregory Fremont-Barnes, Richard Alan Ryerson, editors. Santa Barbara, CA: ABC-CLIO, 2006. I: 205–209. Allaire, Anthony. *Diary of Lieutenant Anthony Allaire*. New York: New York Times and Arno, 1968. Borick, Carl P. *A Gallant Defense, The Siege of Charleston, 1780*. Columbia: University of South Carolina Press, 2003. Clinton, Henry. *The American Rebellion: Sir Henry Clinton's Narrative of His Campaigns, 1775–1782, with an appendix of original*

documents. Edited by William B. Willcox. New Haven: Yale University Press, 1954. Ewald, Johann von. *Diary of the American War: a Hessian journal*. translated and edited by Joseph P. Tustin New Haven: Yale University Press, 1979. pp. 237–240. Gordon, John W. *South Carolina and the American Revolution: a battlefield history*. Columbia: University of South Carolina Press, 2003. Hough, Franklin B. ed. *The Siege of Charleston by the British Fleet and Army under the Command of Admiral Arbuthnot and Sir Henry Clinton which Terminated with the Surrender on the 12th of May, 1780*. Spartanburg, SC: Reprint Company, 1867, 1975. Mattern, David B. *Benjamin Lincoln and the American Revolution*. Columbia: University of South Carolina Press, 1995. Moultrie, William. *Memoirs of the American Revolution so far as it related to the States of North and South Carolina and Georgia*. New York, 1802; (Eyewitness accounts of the American Revolution). [New York]: New York Times, [1968]. Pancake, John S. *This Destructive War: the British Campaign in the Carolinas*. Tuscaloosa: University of Alabama Press, 1985. Peebles, John. *John Peebles' American War: the Diary of a Scottish Grenadier, 1776–1782*. edited by Ira D. Gruber. Mechanicsburg, PA: Stackpole Books, 1998. Russell, Peter. "the Siege of Charleston: Journal of Captain Peter Russell, December 25, 1779 to May 2, 1780. *American Historical Review*. 4:3 (1899) pp. 478–501. *The Siege of Charleston, with an Account of the Province of South Carolina: Diaries and Letters of Hessian Officers from the Von Jungkenn Papers in the William L. Clements Library*. Translated and Edited by Bernhard A. Uhlendorf. Ann Arbor: University of Michigan Press 1938. Tarleton, Banastre. *A History of the Campaigns of 1780 and 1781 in the Southern Provinces of North America*. London: T. Cadell, 1787; [sl]: the New York Times & Arno Press, 1968. Ward, Christopher. *The War of the Revolution*. New York: Macmillan, 1952. pp. 665–678.

230a. Extract of a Letter from General Greene's Camp Dated 25th August, 1781. *New-Jersey Gazette*. IV: 196 (Sept. 26, 1781) p. 3. Gen. Greene's letter to Colonel William Henderson dated August 16, 1781. Greene, Nathanael. *The Papers of General Nathanael Greene*. Richard K. Showman, ed. Chapel Hill: the University of North Carolina Press, published for the Rhode Island Historical Society. c1976–2006. IX: 188–189. Gen. Greene's letter to Thomas McKean, President of the Continental Congress dated August 25, 1781. Greene, Nathanael. *The Papers of General Nathanael Greene*. Richard K. Showman, ed. Chapel Hill: the University of North Carolina Press, published for the Rhode Island Historical Society. c1976–2006. IX: 241–243.

231. *Pennsylvania Gazette*. June 5, 1782; June 12, 1782. O'Kelley, Patrick. *Nothing but Blood and Slaughter*. Booklocker.com, 2004. 4: 55.

232. Brooke, Francis J. *A Family Narrative Being the Reminiscences of a Revolutionary Officer Afterwards Judge of the Court of Appeals Written for the information of his children*. By Francis J. Brooke Richmond, Va.: Macfarlane & Fergusson, 1849; *The Magazine of History with Notes and Queries*. 19:2 (1921) Extra Number 74. p. 98. Garden, Alexander. *Anecdotes of the American Revolution, Illustrative of the Talents and Virtues of the Heroes and Patriots who Acted the Most Conspicuous Parts Therein. Second series*. Charleston, SC: A.E. Miller, 1828. pp. 369–372. Ripley, Warren. *Battleground: South Carolina in the Revolution*. Charleston, SC: Evening Post, 1983. pp. 230–232. Heitman, Francis B. *Historical Register of Officers of the Continental Army during the War of the Revolution, April 1775 to December 1783*. Washington, DC.: The Rare Book Shop Publishing Company, 1914; Baltimore: Genealogical Publishing Company, 1967. pp. 62–89. DeMond, Robert O. *The Loyalists in North Carolina during the Revolution*. Durham, NC: Duke University Press, 1940. pp. 217–239. Clark. Murtie June. *Loyalists in the Southern Campaign of the Revolutionary War*. Baltimore: Genealogical Publishing Company, Inc., 1981. 1:121–123, 138–140, 152, 348–370, 396 3:125–254, 267–323. Moultrie, William. *Memoirs of the American Revolution so far as it related to the States of North and South Carolina and Georgia*. New York, 1802; (Eyewitness accounts of the American Revolution). [New York]: New York Times, [1968]. 2: 358–361. *Pennsylvania Gazette*. Jan. 8, 1783. Bennett, John. Marion—Gadsden Correspondence. *The South Carolina Historical and Genealogical Magazine*. XLI: 1 (Jan. 1940) pp. 48–49. British National Archives. Headquarters Papers of the British Army in America. Folio 2482, 493, 30/55/10277. British National Archives. War Office. Class 12, Vol. 247 pp. 493, 509, 513. Lambert, Robert Stansbury. *South Carolina Loyalists in the American Revolution*. Columbia: University of South Carolina, 1987. pp. 188, 218–222. South Carolina Historical Society. Troop Returns. Robinson, St. John. Southern Loyalists in the Caribbean and Central America. *South Carolina Historical Magazine*. 93: 3&4 (July/Oct. 1992) pp. 211–213. Batt, Richard John. *The Maryland Continentals, 1780–1781*. Tulane University Dissertation, 1974. p. 202. Trussell, John B. B. Jr. *The Pennsylvania Line, Regimental Organizations and Operations, 1776–1783*. Pennsylvania Historical and Museum Commission, 1977. pp. 51, 62, 72, 76, 82, 91, 196–199, 210, 219–220, 227–229. O'Kelley, Patrick. *Nothing but Blood and Slaughter*. Booklocker.com, 2004. 4: 110.

233. Journal of the HM Sloop *Tamar* Captain Edward Thornbrough. British National Archives. Admiralty 51/968. NDAR, 2: 511.

234. Journal of the HM Sloop *Tamar* Captain Edward Thornbrough. British National Archives. Admiralty 51/968. NDAR, 2:1015.

235. Moultrie, William. *Memoirs of the American Revolution so far as it related to the States of North and South Carolina and Georgia*. New York, 1802; (Eyewitness accounts of the American Revolution). [New York]: New York Times, [1968]. 1: 112–113. Griffiths, John William. *"To Receive them Properly ": Charlestown prepares for war, 1775–1776*. M.A. Thesis, University of South Carolina, 1992. pp. 100, 184, 191–192, 209. O'Kelley, Patrick. *Nothing but Blood and Slaughter*. Booklocker.com, 2004. 1: 63–64.

236. Journal of HMS *Sphynx*, Captain Anthony Hunt. British National Archives. Admiralty 51/922. NDAR 5:224.

237. *The Pennsylvania Gazette*. July 30, 1777; July 9, 1777. NDAR, IX: 192–195. O'Kelley, Patrick. *Nothing but Blood and Slaughter*. Booklocker.com, 2004. 1: 180–81.

238. Captain Charles Morgan's Letter of Marque brig *Fair American*. The *Margery* had been taken by the Letter of Marque, Brig *Fair American*, Captain Charles Morgan commanding. Charles-Town, August 28, 1777. Extract of a letter from Mr. John Raven Bedon, dated New Providence, August 2, 1777. *The Pennsylvania Ledger: or the Weekly Advertiser*. XCVIII (Oct. 10, 1777) p. 2. Parker, John C. *Parker's Guide to the Revolutionary War in South Carolina*:

battles, skirmishes and murders. Patrick, SC: Hem Branch Publishing, 2009. p. 93. *The South Carolina and American General Gazette*. Aug. 28, 1777. *Gazette of the State of South Carolina*. Sept. 18, 1777.

239. Parker, John C. *Parker's Guide to the Revolutionary War in South Carolina: battles, skirmishes and murders*. Patrick, SC: Hem Branch Publishing, 2009. p. 215.

240. *The Pennsylvania Gazette*. May 12, 1779. O'Kelley, Patrick. *Nothing But Blood and Slaughter*. Booklocker .com, 2004. 1: 263.

241. Davies, K.G. *Documents of the American Revolution 1770–1783*. (Colonial Office Series) Shannon: Irish University Press 1972, 1981. XX: 173. Smith, Charles R. *Marines in the Revolution: a history of the Continental Marines in the American Revolution, 1775–1783*. Washington: History and Museums Division, Headquarters, U.S. Marine Corps: For sale by the Supt. of Docs., U.S. Govt. Print. Off., 1975. p. 246. Hayes, John T. *The Saddlebag Almanac*. Fort Lauderdale, Fla: Saddlebag Press. VI (Jan. 1998) 3–4. *Pennsylvania Gazette*. March 8, 1780 March 15, 1780. O'Kelley, Patrick. *Nothing but Blood and Slaughter*. Booklocker.com, 2004. 2: 21–23.

242. Parker, John C. *Parker's Guide to the Revolutionary War in South Carolina: battles, skirmishes and murders*. Patrick, SC: Hem Branch Publishing, 2009. p. 107.

243. Parker, John C. *Parker's Guide to the Revolutionary War in South Carolina: battles, skirmishes and murders*. Patrick, SC: Hem Branch Publishing, 2009. p. 107.

244. Parker, John C. *Parker's Guide to the Revolutionary War in South Carolina: battles, skirmishes and murders*. Patrick, SC: Hem Branch Publishing, 2009. p. 82. O'Kelley, Patrick. *Nothing but Blood and Slaughter*. Booklocker .com, 2004. 2: 104.

245. Parker, John C. *Parker's Guide to the Revolutionary War in South Carolina: battles, skirmishes and murders*. Patrick, SC: Hem Branch Publishing, 2009. p. 82.

246. Bass, Robert D. (Robert Duncan). *Ninety Six, the struggle for the South Carolina back country*. Lexington, SC: Sandlapper Store, 1978. pp. 177–178. *The Siege of Charleston, with an Account of the Province of South Carolina: Diaries and Letters of Hessian Officers from the Von Jungkenn Papers in the William L. Clements Library*. Translated and Edited by Bernhard A. Uhlendorf. Ann Arbor: University of Michigan Press 1938. p. 273. Peckham, Howard Henry. *The Toll of Independence: engagements & battle casualties of the American Revolution*. Edited by Howard H. Peckham. Chicago: University of Chicago Press, 1974. Scott, Ruth. Loyalist Anthony Allaire. *Officers Quarterly*. York-Sunbury Historical Society of Fredericton, New Brunswick. Summer 1997. Lee, Henry. *Memoirs of the War in the Southern Department of the United States*. New York: University Publishing Co., 1869. pp. 155–156. Johnson, Uzal. *Memo of Occurrence During the Campaign of 1780*. South Carolina Historical Society, Military Manuscripts. pp. 34–36. Wallace, Lee A. *The Orderly Book of Captain Benjamin Taliaferro, 2d Virginia Detachment, Charleston, South Carolina, 1780*. Virginia State Library, 1980. p. 154. Allaire, Anthony. *Diary of Lieut. Anthony Allaire*. (Eyewitness accounts of the American Revolution). [New York] New York times [1968]. pp. 14–15. Borick, Carl P. *A Gallant Defense, The Siege of Charleston, 1780*. Columbia: University of South Carolina Press, 2003. *A List of all the officers of the Army: viz. the general and field officers; the officers of the several troops, regiments, independent companies, and garrisons: with an alphabetical index to the whole. Also, a list of the officers of the Royal Regiment of Artillery, the Corps of Engineers, the Irish Artillery and Engineers, and of the Marine Forces: the officers on half pay; and a succession of colonels. To which are likewise added the officers of the militia forces, and of the fencible and provincial regiments in Great Britain*. [London, England?]: War-Office, 1780. p. 120. O'Kelley, Patrick. *Nothing But Blood and Slaughter*. Booklocker.com, 2004. 2: 144–146.

247. Parker, John C. *Parker's Guide to the Revolutionary War in South Carolina: battles, skirmishes and murders*. Patrick, SC: Hem Branch Publishing, 2009. p. 82.

248. *The Pennsylvania Gazette*. May 1, 1776. O'Kelley, Patrick. *Nothing But Blood and Slaughter*. Booklocker.com, 2004. 1: 92. Parker, John C. *Parker's Guide to the Revolutionary War in South Carolina: battles, skirmishes and murders*. Patrick, SC: Hem Branch Publishing, 2009. p. 92.

249. Captain Alexander Campbell to Lord William Campbell. Sir Henry Clinton Papers vol. 101, item 45. University of Michigan. William L. Clements Library. British National Archives. Admiralty 51/39. NDAR 5:1172–1175. Narrative of Major General Henry Clinton. Manuscript history of the Revolution by Sir Henry Clinton CL NDAR 5:1309. Gibbes, Robert Wilson. *Documentary History of the American Revolution*. New York: D. Appleton & Co., 1855 (3 vols: 1764–1776, 1776–1782, 1781–1782). reprinted New York Times & Arno Press, 1971. 2:19, 28. Forster, Thompson. *Diary of Thompson Forster, Staff Surgeon to His Majesty's Detached Hospital in North America, October 19th 1775 to October 23rd 1777*. [s.l.: s.n.], 1938. pp. 78, 81–82. *Pennsylvania Gazette*. Aug. 28, 1776; Sept. 11, 1776. Ramsay, David. *Ramsay's History of South Carolina from Its First Settlement in 1670 to the year 1808*. Newberry, SC: W.J. Duffie, 1858. Volume 1. O'Kelley, Patrick. *Nothing But Blood and Slaughter*. Booklocker.com, 2004. 1: 155–157. Parker, John C. *Parker's Guide to the Revolutionary War in South Carolina: battles, skirmishes and murders*. Patrick, SC: Hem Branch Publishing, 2009. p. 112.

250. Journal of H.M. Sloop *Tamar*, Captain Edward Thornbrough, British National Archives, Admiralty 51/968. NDAR 2: 235. Parker, John C. *Parker's Guide to the Revolutionary War in South Carolina: battles, skirmishes and murders*. Patrick, SC: Hem Branch Publishing, 2009. p. 80.

251. Ellet, E. F. (Elizabeth Fries). *The women of the American Revolution*. New York: Baker and Scribner, 1848 1: 211–212. O'Kelley, Patrick. *Nothing But Blood and Slaughter*. Booklocker.com, 2004. 2: 501–502 n. 218.

252. Davies, K.G. *Documents of the American Revolution 1770–1783*. (Colonial Office Series) Shannon: Irish University Press 1972, 1981. 12: 168. *Divers Accounts of the Battle of Sullivan's Island in His Majesty's Province of South Carolina the 28th June 1776*. South Carolina Historical Society, 1976. pp. 4–5. Forster, Thompson. *Diary of Thompson Forster, Staff Surgeon to His Majesty's Detached Hospital in North America, October 19th 1775 to October 23rd 1777*. [s.l.: s.n.], 1938. pp. 54–55. Boatner, Mark M. *Encyclopedia of the American Revolution*. 3d ed., New York: McKay, 1980. p. 924. Moultrie, William. *Memoirs of the American Revolution so far as it related to the States of North and South*

Carolina and Georgia. New York, 1802; (Eyewitness Accounts of the American Revolution). [New York] New York Times [1968]. I: 140–141. Ramsay, David. *Ramsay's History of South Carolina from its First Settlement in 1670 to the year 1808.* Newberry, SC: W. J. Duffie, 1858. vol. 1. *The Pennsylvania Gazette.* July 25, 1778. Griffiths, John William. *"To Receive them Properly ": Charlestown prepares for war, 1775–1776.* M.A. Thesis, University of South Carolina, 1992. pp. 167–168, 245, 254, 324–325. O'Kelley, Patrick. *Nothing But Blood and Slaughter.* Booklocker.com, 2004. 1: 109–111. NDAR 5: 572–573, 781.

253. Parker, John C. *Parker's Guide to the Revolutionary War in South Carolina: battles, skirmishes and murders.* Patrick, SC: Hem Branch Publishing, 2009. p. 93.

254. *The Pennsylvania Gazette.* July 30, 1777. O'Kelley, Patrick. *Nothing But Blood and Slaughter.* Booklocker.com, 2004. 1: 184. Parker, John C. *Parker's Guide to the Revolutionary War in South Carolina: battles, skirmishes and murders.* Patrick, SC: Hem Branch Publishing, 2009. p. 92.

255. Charles-Town, August 28, 1777. Extract of a letter from Mr. John Raven Bedon, dated New Providence, August 2, 1777. *The Pennsylvania Ledger: or the Weekly Advertiser.* XCVIII (October 10, 1777) p. 2. *The South Carolina and American General Gazette.* (Aug. 28, 1777). *The Gazette of the State of South Carolina* (Sept. 8, 1777). Charles-Town (S. Carolina) Sept. 15. *The Maryland Journal and Baltimore Advertiser.* V: 209 (Nov. 4, 1777) p. 1. Parker, John C. *Parker's Guide to the Revolutionary War in South Carolina: battles, skirmishes and murders.* Patrick, SC: Hem Branch Publishing, 2009. p. 92–93.

256. National Archives and Records Administration. Edward Barnwell Pension Application W8352. Ripley, Warren. *Battleground: South Carolina in the Revolution.* Charleston, SC: Evening Post, 1983. p. 234. Lipscomb, Terry W. South Carolina Revolutionary Battles: Part Two. *Names in South Carolina.* XXI (Winter 1974). South Carolina Historical Society, 1974. p. 25. O'Kelley, Patrick. *Nothing But Blood and Slaughter.* Booklocker.com, 2004. 1: 285. Parker, John C. *Parker's Guide to the Revolutionary War in South Carolina: battles, skirmishes and murders.* Patrick, SC: Hem Branch Publishing, 2009. p. 96.

257. Ripley, Warren. *Battleground: South Carolina in the Revolution.* Charleston, SC: Evening Post, 1983. p. 234. Davies, K.G. *Documents of the American Revolution 1770–1783.* (Colonial Office Series) Shannon: Irish University Press 1972, 1981. XVII Transcripts 1779, pp. 141–142. Rosengarten, J.G. *The German Allied Troops in the North American War of Independence, 1776–1783.* by Max Von Eelking. Joel Munsell's Sons Publishers, 1893. pp. 320–323. Davis, Robert Scott, Jr. *Georgians in the Revolution: at Kettle Creek (Wilkes Co.) and Burke County.* Southern Historical Press, Inc., 1986. p. 209. Lipscomb, Terry W. South Carolina Revolutionary Battles: Part Two. *Names in South Carolina.* XXI (Winter 1974). South Carolina Historical Society, 1974. p. 25. *The Siege of Charleston, with an Account of the Province of South Carolina: Diaries and Letters of Hessian Officers from the Von Jungkenn Papers in the William L. Clements Library.* Translated and Edited by Bernhard A. Uhlendorf. Ann Arbor: University of Michigan Press 1938. pp. 186–187. O'Kelley, Patrick. *Nothing But Blood and Slaughter.* Booklocker.com, 2004. 1: 286–87.

258. Moultrie, William. *Memoirs of the American Revolution so far as it related to the States of North and South Carolina and Georgia.* New York, 1802; (Eyewitness Accounts of the American Revolution). [New York] New York Times [1968]. I: 465–467. O'Kelley, Patrick. *Nothing But Blood and Slaughter.* Booklocker.com, 2004. 1: 287–88. *The Independent Ledger, and the American Advertiser.* II: 54 (June 29, 1779), p. 4. Parker, John C. *Parker's Guide to the Revolutionary War in South Carolina: battles, skirmishes and murders.* Patrick, SC: Hem Branch Publishing, 2009. p. 98.

259. Extract of a Letter (dated) Camp at Sommer's plantation 20th June 1779. Laurens Collection. Extract of a Letter from an Officer in Gen Lincoln's Army of the same date. Laurens Collection. Extract of a Letter from an Officer of Rank in So Carolina—22 June 1779. Laurens Collection. *The Massachusetts Spy: Or, American Oracle of Liberty.* IX: 429, p. 2.

260. Ripley, Warren. *Battleground: South Carolina in the Revolution.* Charleston, SC: Evening Post, 1983. pp. 233–234. Moultrie, William. *Memoirs of the American Revolution so far as it related to the States of North and South Carolina and Georgia.* New York, 1802; (Eyewitness Accounts of the American Revolution). [New York] New York Times [1968]. II: 3–5. Lipscomb, Terry W. South Carolina Revolutionary Battles: Part Two. *Names in South Carolina.* XXI (Winter 1974). South Carolina Historical Society, 1974. p. 25. O'Kelley, Patrick. *Nothing But Blood and Slaughter.* Booklocker.com, 2004. 1: 299–300.

261. Ripley, Warren. *Battleground: South Carolina in the Revolution.* Charleston, SC: Evening Post, 1983. pp. 233–234. Moultrie, William. *Memoirs of the American Revolution so far as it related to the States of North and South Carolina and Georgia.* New York, 1802; (Eyewitness Accounts of the American Revolution). [New York] New York Times [1968]. I: 499–505. Lipscomb, Terry W. South Carolina Revolutionary Battles: Part Two. *Names in South Carolina.* XXI (Winter 1974). South Carolina Historical Society, 1974. p. 25. O'Kelley, Patrick. *Nothing But Blood and Slaughter.* Booklocker.com, 2004. 1: 299–300. McCrady, Edward. *History of South Carolina in the Revolution, 1775–1780.* New York: Paladin Press, 1969 (reprint of 1901 ed.). 3: 398. Parker, John C. *Parker's Guide to the Revolutionary War in South Carolina: battles, skirmishes and murders.* Patrick, SC: Hem Branch Publishing, 2009. p. 93.

262. Ewald, Johann von. *Diary of the American War: a Hessian journal.* translated and edited by Joseph P. Tustin New Haven: Yale University Press, 1979. pp. 197–198, 202–203. Burgoyne, Bruce E. *Diaries of Two Anspach Jaegers.* Bowie, MD: Heritage Books, 1997. pp. 108, 113–114. Moultrie, William. *Memoirs of the American Revolution so far as it related to the States of North and South Carolina and Georgia.* New York, 1802; (Eyewitness Accounts of the American Revolution). [New York] New York Times [1968]. II: 50. Wallace, Lee A. T*he Orderly Book of Captain Benjamin Taliaferro, 2d Virginia Detachment, Charleston, South Carolina, 1780.* Virginia State Library, 1980. pp. 14–22. *The Siege of Charleston, with an Account of the Province of South Carolina: Diaries and Letters of Hessian Officers from the Von Jungkenn Papers in the William L. Clements Library.* Translated and Edited by Bernhard A. Uhlendorf. Ann Arbor: University of Michigan Press 1938. pp. 180–183. Bauer, Carl. The 1780 Siege of Charleston as Experienced

by a Hessian Officer, Part One. (Journal of the Hochfuerstlichen Grenadier Battalion Platte from 16 February 1776 to 24 May 1784 by the Regimental Quartermaster: Carl Bauer. Edited by George Fenwick Jones. *South Carolina Historical Magazine.* 88:1 (Jan. 1987) pp. 26–27. Clinton, Sir Henry. *The American Rebellion Sir Henry Clinton's Narrative of His Campaigns, 1775–1782.* with An Appendix of Original Documents edited by William B. Willcox. New Haven: Yale University Press, 1954. p. 157. Hayes, John T. *The Saddlebag Almanac.* VI (Jan. 1998) pp. 10–11, 15–16. O'Kelley, Patrick. *Nothing But Blood and Slaughter.* Booklocker.com, 2004. 2: 29–30.

263. *The Siege of Charleston, with an Account of the Province of South Carolina: Diaries and Letters of Hessian Officers from the Von Jungkenn Papers in the William L. Clements Library.* Translated and Edited by Bernhard A. Uhlendorf. Ann Arbor: University of Michigan Press 1938. p. 193.

264. Ewald, Johann von. *Diary of the American War: a Hessian journal.* translated and edited by Joseph P. Tustin New Haven: Yale University Press, 1979. pp. 197–198, 202–203. Boatner, Mark M. *Encyclopedia of the American Revolution.* 3d ed. New York: McKay, 1980. pp. 356–357. Gruber, Ira D. *John Peebles' American War, the Diary of a Scottish Grenadier, 1776–1782.* Stackpole Books, 1998. p. 314. *The Siege of Charleston, with an Account of the Province of South Carolina: Diaries and Letters of Hessian Officers from the Von Jungkenn Papers in the William L. Clements Library.* Translated and Edited by Bernhard A. Uhlendorf. Ann Arbor: University of Michigan Press 1938. p. 197. Hayes, John T. *The Saddlebag Almanac.* VI (Jan. 1998) pp. 20–21. O'Kelley, Patrick. *Nothing But Blood and Slaughter.* Booklocker.com, 2004. 2: 34.

265. Ewald, Johann von. *Diary of the American War: a Hessian journal.* translated and edited by Joseph P. Tustin New Haven: Yale University Press, 1979. pp. 214–215. Burgoyne, Bruce E. *Diaries of Two Anspach Jaegers.* Bowie, MD: Heritage Books, 1997. pp. 121–122. Tarleton, Banastre. *A History of the Campaigns of 1780 and 1781 in the Southern Provinces of North America.* London, 1787; (Eyewitness Accounts of the American Revolution). [New York] New York Times [1968] pp. 8–9. Cannon. Robert. *Historical Record of the Seventeenth Regiment of Light Dragoons; Lancers: Containing an Account of the Formation of the Regiment in 1759, and of its Subsequent Services to 1841.* London: John W. Parker, 1843. pp. 26–27. Scott, Ruth. Loyalist Anthony Allaire. *Officers Quarterly.* York–Sunbury Historical Society of Fredericton, New Brunswick. Summer 1997. James, William Dobein. *A Sketch of the Life of Brig. General Francis Marion, and a History of his Brigade, from its Rise in June 1780, until Disbanded in December, 1782.* Charleston, SC: Gould and Riley, 1821. p. 56. Lee, Henry. *Memoirs of the War in the Southern Department of the United States.* New York: University Publishing Co., 1869. p. 146. *The Pennsylvania Gazette.* May 3, 1780. *Pennsylvania Packet.* April 25, 1780. Farr, Thomas. Revolutionary Letters. *South Carolina Historical and Genealogical Magazine.* XXXVIII: 1 (Jan. 1937) p. 8. Hayes, John T. *The Saddlebag Almanac.* VI (Jan. 1998) pp. 13, 30, 33; VII p. 58. O'Kelley, Patrick. *Nothing But Blood and Slaughter.* Booklocker.com, 2004l. 2: 129–30. Parker, John C. *Parker's Guide to the Revolutionary War in South Carolina: battles, skirmishes and murders.* Patrick, SC: Hem Branch Publishing, 2009. p. 98.

266. Parker, John C. *Parker's Guide to the Revolutionary War in South Carolina: battles, skirmishes and murders.* Patrick, SC: Hem Branch Publishing, 2009. p. 99.

267. National Archives and Records Administration. Solomon Freer Pension application W8826.

268. Massey, Gregory D. *A Hero's Life: John Laurens and the American Revolution.* Ph.D. Thesis, University of South Carolina, 1992. pp. 202–207. Garden, Alexander. *Anecdotes of the American Revolution, Illustrative of the Talents and Virtues of the Heroes and Patriots who Acted the Most Conspicuous Parts Therein.* Second series. Charleston, S. C.: A.E. Miller, 1828. pp. 362–364. Ripley, Warren. *Battleground: South Carolina in the Revolution.* Charleston, SC: Evening Post, 1983. pp. 211–212. Hayes, Jim. *James and Related Sea Island.* Walker, Evans and Cogswell Co. 1978. pp. 29–30. Simms, William Gilmore. *The Life of Francis Marion.* New York: H. G. Langley, 1844. pp. 170–171. Letters to General Greene and Others. *The South Carolina Historical and Genealogical Magazine.* XVI: 4 (Oct. 1915) pp. 139–140. Rankin, Hugh F. *North Carolina in the American Revolution.* Raleigh: State Department of Archives and History, 1959. pp. 370–371. O'Kelley, Patrick. *Nothing But Blood and Slaughter.* Booklocker.com, 2004. 4: 26–30. Parker, John C. *Parker's Guide to the Revolutionary War in South Carolina: battles, skirmishes and murders.* Patrick, SC: Hem Branch Publishing, 2009. pp. 96, 98–99.

269. Parker, John C. *Parker's Guide to the Revolutionary War in South Carolina: battles, skirmishes and murders.* Patrick, SC: Hem Branch Publishing, 2009. p. 93.

270. Butler, Pierce; Lipscomb, Terry W. *The letters of Pierce Butler, 1790–1794: nation building and enterprise in the new American republic.* Columbia, SC: University of South Carolina Press, 2007.

271. Parker, John C. *Parker's Guide to the Revolutionary War in South Carolina: battles, skirmishes and murders.* Patrick, SC: Hem Branch Publishing, 2009. p. 215.

272. *The Pennsylvania Gazette.* July 21, 1779. Salley, A.S. Jr. The Battle of Stono. *The South Carolina Historical and Genealogical Magazine.* 5 (April, 1904) p. 90–94. O'Kelley, Patrick. *Nothing But Blood and Slaughter.* Booklocker.com, 2004. 1: 299.

273. Philadelphia, Feb. 23, 1781. *The Pennsylvania Evening Post.* VII: 719 (Feb. 23, 1781) p. 33.

274. Moultrie, William. *Memoirs of the American Revolution so far as it related to the States of North and South Carolina and Georgia.* New York, 1802; (Eyewitness Accounts of the American Revolution). [New York] New York Times [1968]. II: 241–242. *The Pennsylvania Gazette.* Sept. 26, 1781. Bass, Robert Duncan. *Swamp Fox: the life and campaigns of General Francis Marion.* Orangeburg, SC: Sandlapper, 1989. pp. 175–177. Lipscomb, Terry W. South Carolina Revolutionary Battles: Part Seven. *Names in South Carolina* XXVI (Winter 1979). South Carolina Historical Society, 1979. p. 33. O'Kelley, Patrick. *Nothing But Blood and Slaughter.* Booklocker.com, 2004. 3: 316.

275. Lipscomb, Terry W. South Carolina Revolutionary Battles: Part Six. *Names in South Carolina.* XXV (Winter 1978). South Carolina Historical Society, 1978. p. 33. O'Kelley, Patrick. *Nothing But Blood and Slaughter.* Booklocker.com, 2004. 3: 284–85.

276. Chesney, Alexander. *The Journal of Alexander Chesney, a South Carolina Loyalist in the Revolution and After,* edited by E. A. Jones. Columbus, Ohio: Ohio State University, 1921. Ewald, Johann von. *Diary of the American War: a Hessian journal.* translated and edited by Joseph P. Tustin New Haven: Yale University Press, 1979. pp. 208–209. Burgoyne, Bruce E. *Diaries of Two Anspach Jaegers.* Heritage Books, 1997. pp. 127–135. *A List of all the officers of the Army: viz. the general and field officers; the officers of the several troops, regiments, independent companies, and garrisons: with an alphabetical index to the whole. Also, a list of the officers of the Royal Regiment of Artillery, the Corps of Engineers, the Irish Artillery and Engineers, and of the Marine Forces: the officers on half pay; and a succession of colonels. To which are likewise added the officers of the militia forces, and of the fencible and provincial regiments in Great Britain.* [London, England?]: War-Office, 1780. pp. 156. Gruber, Ira D. *John Peebles' American War, the Diary of a Scottish Grenadier, 1776–1782.* Stackpole Books, 1998. p. 314. O'Kelley, Patrick. *Nothing But Blood and Slaughter.* Booklocker.com, 2004. 2: 122. Parker, John C. *Parker's Guide to the Revolutionary War in South Carolina: battles, skirmishes and murders.* Patrick, SC: Hem Branch Publishing, 2009. pp. 60, 90, 91.

277. Ewald, Johann von. *Diary of the American War: a Hessian journal.* translated and edited by Joseph P. Tustin New Haven: Yale University Press, 1979. pp. 211–212. Sir Henry Clinton Papers. Vol. 83 item 38 (William L. Clements Library. University of Michigan. *A List of all the officers of the Army: viz. the general and field officers; the officers of the several troops, regiments, independent companies, and garrisons: with an alphabetical index to the whole. Also, a list of the officers of the Royal Regiment of Artillery, the Corps of Engineers, the Irish Artillery and Engineers, and of the Marine Forces: the officers on half pay; and a succession of colonels. To which are likewise added the officers of the militia forces, and of the fencible and provincial regiments in Great Britain.* [London, England?]: War-Office, 1780. p. 86. O'Kelley, Patrick. *Nothing But Blood and Slaughter.* Booklocker.com, 2004. 2: 126–27. Parker, John C. *Parker's Guide to the Revolutionary War in South Carolina: battles, skirmishes and murders.* Patrick, SC: Hem Branch Publishing, 2009. p. 91.

278. *The Pennsylvania Packet or the General Advertiser.* XI: 838 (Jan. 26, 1782) p. 3 says that the reconnoitering party was commanded by Major Coffin of the New York Volunteers and that Garden's plantations was near Cross Creek, 15 miles from Charleston. Davies, K.G. *Documents of the American Revolution 1770–1783.* (Colonial Office Series) Shannon: Irish University Press 1972, 1981. XX: 267–268. Boatner, Mark M. *Encyclopedia of the American Revolution.* 3d ed. New York: McKay, 1980. p. 335. Simms, William Gilmore. *The Life of Francis Marion.* New York, 1844. pp. 166–167. Extract of a letter from an Officer of distinction in the southern army, dated Round-O, December 9. *The Pennsylvania Gazette.* Jan. 30, 1782. Lipscomb, Terry W. South Carolina Revolutionary Battles: Part Eight (with Map). *Names in South Carolina.* XXVII (Winter 1980). South Carolina Historical Society, 1980. p. 16. Ervin. Sara Sullivan. *South Carolinians in the Revolution.* Baltimore: Genealogical Publishing Company, Inc., 1971. pp. 65, 80–87. Pancake, John S. *This Destructive War: the British Campaign in the Carolinas.* Tuscaloosa: University of Alabama Press, 1985. p. 237. Ward, Christopher L. *The Delaware Continentals.* Historical Society of Delaware, 1941. p. 476. Draper, Lyman. Thomas Sumter Papers, Draper Manuscript Collection, State Historical Society of Wisconsin. 7VV579–589. O'Kelley, Patrick. *Nothing But Blood and Slaughter.* Booklocker.com, 2004. 3: 402–403. Parker, John C. *Parker's Guide to the Revolutionary War in South Carolina: battles, skirmishes and murders.* Patrick, SC: Hem Branch Publishing, 2009. pp. 168, 169, 60, 90.

279. Ewald, Johann von. *Diary of the American War: a Hessian journal.* translated and edited by Joseph P. Tustin New Haven: Yale University Press, 1979. p. 214. O'Kelley, Patrick. *Nothing But Blood and Slaughter.* Booklocker.com, 2004. 2: 127–28.

280. Tarleton, Banastre. *A History of the Campaigns of 1780 and 1781 in the Southern Provinces of North America.* London, 1787; (Eyewitness accounts of the American Revolution). [New York]: New York Times, [1968]. p. 9. Moultrie, William. *Memoirs of the American Revolution so far as it related to the States of North and South Carolina and Georgia.* New York, 1802; (Eyewitness accounts of the American Revolution). [New York]: New York Times, [1968]. II: 62. Simms, William Gilmore. *South-Carolina in the Revolutionary War: being a reply to certain misrepresentations and mistakes of recent writers in relation to the course and conduct of this state.* by a Southron. Charleston: Walker and James, 1853 (reprinted from the *Southern Quarterly Review,* v. 14, 1848, and v. 22, 1852) p. 104. De Saussure, Wilmot Gibbes. *An Account of the Siege of Charleston, South Carolina, in 1780.* Charleston, News and Courier Book Presses, 1885. Bass, Robert Duncan. *The Green Dragoon: The lives of Banastre Tarleton and Mary Robinso*n. New York: Holt, 1957. p. 73. Borick, Carl P. *A Gallant Defense, The Siege of Charleston, 1780.* Columbia: University of South Carolina Press, 2003. pp. 104–106. Wilson, David K. *The Southern Strategy: Britain's conquest of South Carolina and Georgia, 1775–1780.* Columbia: University of South Carolina, c2005. p. 206. McCrady, Edward. *History of South Carolina in the Revolution, 1775–1780.* New York: Paladin Press, 1969 (reprint of 1901 ed.) p. 454. Sherman, William Thomas. *Calendar and Record of the Revolutionary War in the South: 1780–1781,* 2003–2006. p. 90. Parker, John C. *Parker's Guide to the Revolutionary War in South Carolina: battles, skirmishes and murders.* Patrick, SC: Hem Branch Publishing, 2009. p. 76.

281. Francis Marion. *The New Jersey Gazette.* IV: 201 (Oct. 31, 1781), p. 1. Rosengarten, J. G. *The German Allied Troops in the North American War of Independence, 1776–1783.* by Max Von Eelking. Joel Munsell's Son's Publishers, 1893. p. 305. Simms, William Gilmore. *The Life of Francis Marion.* New York, 1844. pp. 155–156. *The Pennsylvania Gazette.* Oct. 24, 1781. Bass, Robert Duncan. *Swamp Fox: the life and campaigns of General Francis Marion.* Orangeburg, SC: Sandlapper, 1989. pp. 212–214. Hayes, John T. *Stephen Jarvis, the King's Loyal Horseman, His Narrative. 1775–1783.* The Saddlebag Press, 1996. pp. 74–76, 130–131. James, William Dobein. *A Sketch of the Life of Brig. Gen. Francis Marion, and a History of his Brigade, from its Rise in June 1780, until Disbanded in December, 1782.* Charleston, SC: Gould and Riley, 1821. p. 40. *Royal Georgia Gazette.* Sept. 13, 1781. Hayes, John T. *The Saddlebag Almanac.* XI (Jan. 2003) pp. 21–22, 25–27. Draper, Lyman. Thomas Sumter Papers, Draper Manuscript Collection, State Historical Society of Wisconsin. 7VV431. Jarvis, Stephen, "An American's Experiences in the British Army." *Journal of American History.* 1 (Sept. 1907) 441–64. Ripley, Warren. *Battleground: South Carolina in the Revolution.* Charleston, SC: Evening Post, 1983. pp. 183–185. O'Kelley, Patrick. *Nothing But Blood and Slaughter.*

Booklocker.com, 2004. 3: 280–81, 323–27. Parker, John C. *Parker's Guide to the Revolutionary War in South Carolina: battles, skirmishes and murders*. Patrick, SC: Hem Branch Publishing, 2009. pp. 71–72, 74.

282. James, William Dobein. *A Sketch of the Life of Brig. General Francis Marion, and a History of his Brigade, from its Rise in June 1780, until Disbanded in December, 1782*. Charleston, SC: Gould and Riley, 1821. p. 40. Lipscomb, Terry W. South Carolina Revolutionary Battles: Part Seven. *Names in South Carolina* XXVI (Winter 1979). South Carolina Historical Society, 1979. pp. 33, 40. O'Kelley, Patrick. *Nothing But Blood and Slaughter*. Booklocker.com, 2004. 3: 327–28. Townsend, Leah. *South Carolina Baptists, 1670–1805*. Baltimore, Genealogical Pub. Co., 1974, 1935. pp. 32–36. James, William Dobein. *A Sketch of the Life of Brig. General Francis Marion, and a History of his Brigade, from its Rise in June 1780, until Disbanded in December, 1782*. Charleston, SC: Gould and Riley, 1821. www.carolana.com/SC/Revolution/revolution_ashley_river_church.html. Parker, John C. *Parker's Guide to the Revolutionary War in South Carolina: battles, skirmishes and murders*. Patrick, SC: Hem Branch Publishing, 2009. p. 76, 171.

283. Parker, John C. *Parker's Guide to the Revolutionary War in South Carolina: battles, skirmishes and murders*. Patrick, SC: Hem Branch Publishing, 2009. p. 76.

284. Parker, John C. *Parker's Guide to the Revolutionary War in South Carolina: battles, skirmishes and murders*. Patrick, SC: Hem Branch Publishing, 2009. p. 168.

285. Lipscomb, Terry W. South Carolina Revolutionary Battles: Part Eight (with Map). *Names in South Carolina*. XXVII (Winter 1980). South Carolina Historical Society, 1980. p. 18. O'Kelley, Patrick. *Nothing But Blood and Slaughter*. Booklocker.com, 2004. 4: 30. Parker, John C. *Parker's Guide to the Revolutionary War in South Carolina: battles, skirmishes and murders*. Patrick, SC: Hem Branch Publishing, 2009. p. 168, 169.

286. Garden, Alexander. *Anecdotes of the American Revolution, Illustrative of the Talents and Virtues of the Heroes and Patriots who Acted the Most Conspicuous Parts Therein*. Second series. Charleston, S. C.: A.E. Miller, 1828. pp. 365–368. Ripley, Warren. *Battleground: South Carolina in the Revolution*. Charleston, SC: Evening Post, 1983. p. 237. Seymour, William. Journal of the Southern Expedition, 1780–1783. *Papers of The Historical Society of Delaware*: xv. Wilmington: The Historical Society of Delaware, 1896. p. 35. Simms, William Gilmore. *The Life of Francis Marion*. New York: H.G. Langley, 1844. p. 179. Moultrie, William. *Memoirs of the American Revolution so far as it related to the States of North and South Carolina and Georgia*. New York, 1802; (Eyewitness accounts of the American Revolution). [New York]: New York Times, [1968]. 2: 298. Lee, Henry. *Memoirs of the War in the Southern Department of the United States*. New York: University Publishing Co., 1869. pp. 546–549. *Pennsylvania Gazette*. June 5, 1782. British National Archives. Treasury Office, Class 50, Vol. 2, folio 372. Crow, Jeffrey J. *The Black Experience in Revolutionary North Carolina*. Raleigh: [North Carolina Dept. of Cultural Resources, Division of Archives and History], 1977. p. 78. Pancake, John S. *This Destructive War: The British Campaign in the Carolinas*. Tuscaloosa: University of Alabama Press, 1985. p. 480. Peckham, Howard Henry. *The Toll of Independence: engagements & battle casualties of the American Revolution*. edited by Howard H. Peckham. Chicago: University of Chicago Press, 1974. p. 95. O'Kelley, Patrick. *Nothing But Blood and Slaughter*. Booklocker.com, 2004. 4: 55–58. Parker, John C. *Parker's Guide to the Revolutionary War in South Carolina: battles, skirmishes and murders*. Patrick, SC: Hem Branch Publishing, 2009. p. 169.

287. Seymour, William. Journal of the Southern Expedition, 1780–1783. *Papers of The Historical Society of Delaware*: xv. Wilmington: The Historical Society of Delaware, 1896. p. 41. *Pennsylvania Gazette*. May 15, 1782. Lipscomb, Terry W. South Carolina Revolutionary Battles: Part Nine. *Names in South Carolina*. XXVIII (Winter 1981). South Carolina Historical Society, 1981. p. 35. O'Kelley, Patrick. *Nothing But Blood and Slaughter*. Booklocker.com, 2004. 4: 72–73. Parker, John C. *Parker's Guide to the Revolutionary War in South Carolina: battles, skirmishes and murders*. Patrick, SC: Hem Branch Publishing, 2009. p. 169.

288. From Rivington's New-York City Gazette, New-York, (City) March 13. *The Massachusetts Spy: Or American Oracle of Liberty*. IX: 468 (April 27, 1780), p. 1. Gruber, Ira D. *John Peebles' American War, the Diary of a Scottish Grenadier, 1776–1782*. Stackpole Books, 1998. p. 314. Hayes, John T. *The Saddlebag Almanac*. VI (Jan. 1998) pp. 21–22. Sanchez-Saavedera, E.M. *A Guide to Virginia Military Organizations in the American Revolution, 1774–1787*. Richmond, VA: Virginia State Library, 1978. O'Kelley, Patrick. *Nothing But Blood and Slaughter*. Booklocker.com, 2004. 2: 34–5.

289. Extract of a letter from Charlestown, dated March 13, 1780. *The New Jersey Gazette*. III: 121 (April 19, 1780), p. 3.

290. Ewald, Johann von. *Diary of the American War: a Hessian journal*. translated and edited by Joseph P. Tustin New Haven: Yale University Press, 1979. pp. 210–211. O'Kelley, Patrick. *Nothing But Blood and Slaughter*. Booklocker.com, 2004. 2: 125–26.

291. *The Pennsylvania Gazette*. June 12, 1782. O'Kelley, Patrick. *Nothing But Blood and Slaughter*. Booklocker.com, 2004. 4: 58–59. Parker, John C. *Parker's Guide to the Revolutionary War in South Carolina: battles, skirmishes and murders*. Patrick, SC: Hem Branch Publishing, 2009. p. 86.

292. Parker, John C. *Parker's Guide to the Revolutionary War in South Carolina: battles, skirmishes and murders*. Patrick, SC: Hem Branch Publishing, 2009. p. 45.

293. Parker, John C. *Parker's Guide to the Revolutionary War in South Carolina: battles, skirmishes and murders*. Patrick, SC: Hem Branch Publishing, 2009. p. 45.

294. Philadelphia, Feb. 23, 1781. *The Pennsylvania Evening Post*. VII: 719 (Feb. 23, 1781) p. 33.

295. Parker, John C. *Parker's Guide to the Revolutionary War in South Carolina: battles, skirmishes and murders*. Patrick, SC: Hem Branch Publishing, 2009. p. 45.

296. www.rootsweb.com/~scbchs/Biggin.html.

297. *The Siege of Charleston, with an Account of the Province of South Carolina: Diaries and Letters of Hessian Officers from the Von Jungkenn Papers in the William L. Clements Library*. Translated and Edited by Bernhard A. Uhlendorf.

Ann Arbor: University of Michigan Press 1938. pp. 59, 249, 387. *Encyclopedia of the American Revolution*. Harold E. Selesky, editor in chief. 2nd ed. Detroit: Charles Scribner's Sons, 2007. II: 729–780. *The Encyclopedia of the American Revolutionary War: a political, social, and military history*. Gregory Fremont-Barnes, Richard Alan Ryerson, editors. Santa Barbara, CA: ABC-CLIO, 2006. III: 804–805. Barbour, R. L. *South Carolina's Revolutionary War Battlefields: a Tour Guide*. Pelican Publishing Co: Gretna, 2002. National Archives and Records Administration. Hugh Gaston Pension Application S10729. Johnson, Uzal. *Uzal Johnson, loyalist surgeon: a Revolutionary War diary*. Blacksburg, SC: Scotia Hibernia Press, 2000. pp. 22–23. Pancake, John S. *This Destructive War: the British Campaign in the Carolinas*. Tuscaloosa: University of Alabama Press, 1985. Ripley, Warren. *Battleground: South Carolina in the Revolution*. Charleston, SC: Evening Post, 1983. Tarleton, Banastre. *A History of the Campaigns of 1780 and 1781 in the Southern Provinces of North America*. London, 1787; (Eyewitness Accounts of the American Revolution). [New York]: New York Times, [1968]. pp. 15–17. Ward, Christopher. *The War of the Revolution*. New York: Macmillan, 1952. Parker, John C. *Parker's Guide to the Revolutionary War in South Carolina: battles, skirmishes and murders*. Patrick, SC: Hem Branch Publishing, 2009. pp. 46–47.

298. *The Encyclopedia of the American Revolutionary War: a political, social, and military history*. Gregory Fremont-Barnes, Richard Alan Ryerson, editors. Santa Barbara, CA: ABC-CLIO, 2006. I: 99. Ripley, Warren. *Battleground: South Carolina in the Revolution*. Charleston, SC: Evening Post, 1983. Ward, Christopher. *The War of the Revolution*. New York: Macmillan, 1952. Parker, John C. *Parker's Guide to the Revolutionary War in South Carolina: battles, skirmishes and murders*. Patrick, SC: Hem Branch Publishing, 2009. p. 46.

299. Lee, Henry. *Memoirs of the War in the Southern Department of the United States*. New York: University Publishing Co., 1869. 2: 298–299. *Charleston Gazette*, Jan. 30, 1826. Draper, Lyman. Thomas Sumter Papers, Draper Manuscript Collection, State Historical Society of Wisconsin. Microfilm. 1DD p. 234. Greene, Nathanael. *The Papers of General Nathanael Greene*. Richard K. Showman, ed. – Chapel Hill: The University of North Carolina Press, published for the Rhode Island Historical Society. c1976–2006. 9: 309, 341–342. Orvin, Maxwell Clayton. *Monck's Corner, Berkeley County, South Carolina*. [Charleston?], 1950. O. H. Williams's account in Gibbes, Robert Wilson. *Documentary History of the American Revolution*. New York: D. Appleton & Co., 1855 (3 vols: 1764–1776, 1776–1782, 1781–1782). reprinted New York Times & Arno Press, 1971 (3 vols. in 1). 3: 156. Johnson, William; Archibald Edward Miller; James Barton Longacre; Henry Breintnall Bounetheau; Henry Schenck Tanner. *Sketches of the life and correspondence of Nathanael Greene, major general of the Armies of the United States, in the War of the Revolution*. Charleston, SC: Printed for the author, by A.E. Miller, no. 4, Broad-Street, near the Bay. 1822. II: 232. James, William Dobein. *A Sketch of the Life of Brig. Gen. Francis Marion, and a History of his Brigade, From its Rise in June 1780, until Disbanded in December, 1782*. Charleston, SC: Gould and Riley, 1821. pp. 136. 464. Simms, William Gilmore. *The Life of Francis Marion*. New York: H.G. Langley, 1844. p. 284. Simms, William Gilmore. *The Life of Nathanael Greene, Major-General in the Army of the Revolution*. New York: Derby & Jackson, 1861. p. 307.

300. Parker, John C. *Parker's Guide to the Revolutionary War in South Carolina: battles, skirmishes and murders*. Patrick, SC: Hem Branch Publishing, 2009. p. 47.

301. Brown, Tarleton. *Memoirs of Tarleton Brown, a Captain in the Revolutionary Army, Written by Himself, with a Preface and Notes by Charles I. Bushnell*. New York: Privately Printed, 1862.

302. Garden, Alexander. *Anecdotes of the American Revolution, Illustrative of the Talents and Virtues of the Heroes and Patriots who Acted the Most Conspicuous Parts Therein*. Second series. Charleston, S. C.: A.E. Miller, 1828. p. 441. Simms, William Gilmore. *The Life of Francis Marion*. New York: H.G. Langley, 1844. p. 115. Moultrie, William. *Memoirs of the American Revolution so far as it related to the States of North and South Carolina and Georgia*. New York, 1802; (Eyewitness Accounts of the American Revolution). [New York] New York Times [1968]. II: 262–263. Brown, Tarleton. *Memoirs of Tarleton Brown, a Captain in the Revolutionary Army, Written by Himself, with a Preface and Notes by Charles I. Bushnell*. New York: Privately Printed, 1862. *The Pennsylvania Gazette*. Feb. 28, 1781. Bass, Robert Duncan. *Swamp Fox: the life and campaigns of General Francis Marion*. Orangeburg, SC: Sandlapper, 1989. pp. 137–138. Greene, Nathanael. *The Papers of General Nathanael Greene*. Richard K. Showman, ed. Chapel Hill: the University of North Carolina Press, published for the Rhode Island Historical Society. c1976–2006. p. 226. James, William Dobein. *A Sketch of the Life of Brig. Gen. Francis Marion, and a History of his Brigade, from its Rise in June 1780, until Disbanded in December, 1782*. Charleston, SC: Gould and Riley, 1821. p. 49. University of New Brunswick. Harriet Irving Library. Saunders Family Papers, Correspondence, 1780–1803. O'Kelley, Patrick. *Nothing But Blood and Slaughter*. Booklocker.com, 2004. 3: 64–5. Parker, John C. *Parker's Guide to the Revolutionary War in South Carolina: battles, skirmishes and murders*. Patrick, SC: Hem Branch Publishing, 2009. pp. 50, 317.

303. Parker, John C. *Parker's Guide to the Revolutionary War in South Carolina: battles, skirmishes and murders*. Patrick, SC: Hem Branch Publishing, 2009. p. 52. Leiding, Harriette Kershaw. *Historic Houses of South Carolina*. Philadelphia; London: J. B. Lippincott Company, 1921. p. 65.

304. Parker, John C. *Parker's Guide to the Revolutionary War in South Carolina: battles, skirmishes and murders*. Patrick, SC: Hem Branch Publishing, 2009. p. 51.

305. Gibbes, Robert Wilson. *Documentary History of the American Revolution*. New York: D. Appleton & Co., 1855 (3 vols: 1764–1776, 1776–1782, and 1781–1782). reprinted New York Times & Arno Press, 1971. III: 213.

306. Gibbes, Robert Wilson. *Documentary History of the American Revolution*. New York: D. Appleton & Co., 1855 (3 vols: 1764–1776, 1776–1782, 1781–1782). reprinted New York Times & Arno Press, 1971. III: 215.

307. Simms, William Gilmore. *The Life of Francis Marion*. New York: H.G. Langley, 1844. pp. 165–166. Moultrie, William. *Memoirs of the American Revolution so far as it related to the States of North and South Carolina and Georgia*. New York, 1802; (Eyewitness accounts of the American Revolution). [New York]: New York Times, [1968]. 2: 296. *Pennsylvania Gazette*. Dec. 19, 1781. Griffiths, John William. *"To Receive them Properly": Charlestown prepares for war, 1775–1776*. M.A. Thesis, University of South Carolina, 1992. p. 96. O'Kelley, Patrick. *Nothing But Blood*

and Slaughter. Booklocker.com, 2004. 3: 391–394. Parker, John C. *Parker's Guide to the Revolutionary War in South Carolina: battles, skirmishes and murders.* Patrick, SC: Hem Branch Publishing, 2009. p. 51.

308. Draper, Lyman. Thomas Sumter Papers, Draper Manuscript Collection, State Historical Society of Wisconsin. 15VV150. National Archives and Records Administration. William Brothertin (Brotherton) Pension application S1793. O'Kelley, Patrick. *Nothing But Blood and Slaughter.* Booklocker.com, 2004. 3: 285. Parker, John C. *Parker's Guide to the Revolutionary War in South Carolina: battles, skirmishes and murders.* Patrick, SC: Hem Branch Publishing, 2009. p. 78.

309. Lipscomb, Terry W. South Carolina Revolutionary Battles: Part Eight (with Map). *Names in South Carolina.* XXVII (Winter 1980). South Carolina Historical Society, 1980. p. 18. Hayes, John T. *Stephen Jarvis, the King's Loyal Horseman, His Narrative. 1775–1783.* The Saddlebag Press, 1996. pp. 78, 134. O'Kelley, Patrick. *Nothing But Blood and Slaughter.* Booklocker.com, 2004. 3: 406. Parker, John C. *Parker's Guide to the Revolutionary War in South Carolina: battles, skirmishes and murders.* Patrick, SC: Hem Branch Publishing, 2009. p. 90.

310. Lee, Henry. *Memoirs of the War in the Southern Department of the United States.* New York: University Publishing Co., 1869. pp. 537–538. *The Pennsylvania Gazette.* March 13, 1782. Hayes, John T. *Stephen Jarvis, the King's Loyal Horseman, His Narrative. 1775–1783.* The Saddlebag Press, 1996. pp. 78, 134–135. Jarvis, Stephen, "An American's Experiences in the British Army," *Journal of American History.* 1 (Sept. 1907) pp. 441–64. O'Kelley, Patrick. *Nothing But Blood and Slaughter.* Booklocker.com, 2004. 3: 407–408. Parker, John C. *Parker's Guide to the Revolutionary War in South Carolina: battles, skirmishes and murders.* Patrick, SC: Hem Branch Publishing, 2009. p. 60.

311. Garden, Alexander. *Anecdotes of the American Revolution, Illustrative of the Talents and Virtues of the Heroes and Patriots who Acted the Most Conspicuous Parts Therein. Second series.* Charleston, S. C.: A.E. Miller, 1828. p. 369. O'Kelley, Patrick. *Nothing But Blood and Slaughter.* Booklocker.com, 2004. 4: 100. Parker, John C. *Parker's Guide to the Revolutionary War in South Carolina: battles, skirmishes and murders.* Patrick, SC: Hem Branch Publishing, 2009. p. 61.

312. Boatner, Mark M. *Encyclopedia of the American Revolution.* 3d ed., New York: McKay, 1980. p. 482. Moultrie, William. *Memoirs of the American Revolution so far as it related to the States of North and South Carolina and Georgia.* New York, 1802; (Eyewitness Accounts of the American Revolution). [New York] New York Times [1968]. II: 290. Lee, Henry. *Memoirs of the War in the Southern Department of the United States.* New York: University Publishing Co., 1869. p. 387. *New York Gazette and the Weekly Mercury.* Aug. 6, 1781; *The Pennsylvania Gazette.* Aug. 8, 1781; Aug. 15, 1781; Sept. 5, 1781. *The Connecticut Gazette.* Aug. 17, 1781. *The Royal Gazette.* July 18, 1781. Ervin, Sara Sullivan. *South Carolinians in the Revolution.* Baltimore: Genealogical Publishing Company, Inc., 1971. pp. 65, 80–87. Draper, Lyman. Thomas Sumter Papers, Draper Manuscript Collection, State Historical Society of Wisconsin. 7VV422, 427 15VV150. O'Kelley, Patrick. *Nothing But Blood and Slaughter.* Booklocker.com, 2004. 3: 286–88. Extract of a letter from Major-General Greene to the President of Congress, dated Head-Quarters, High Hills of Santee, July 26, 1781. *New Jersey Gazette.* 4: 194 (Sept. 12, 1781) p. 2; *Connecticut Journal.* 725 (Sept. 20, 1781) p. 1. Parker, John C. *Parker's Guide to the Revolutionary War in South Carolina: battles, skirmishes and murders.* Patrick, SC: Hem Branch Publishing, 2009. p. 75.

313. *The Boston Evening-Post and the General Advertiser.* I: XXXII (May 25, 1782), p. 3. *The New Jersey Gazette.* V: 230 (May 22, 1782), p. 2. Parker, John C. *Parker's Guide to the Revolutionary War in South Carolina: battles, skirmishes and murders.* Patrick, SC: Hem Branch Publishing, 2009. p. 79. Ripley, Warren. *Battleground: South Carolina in the Revolution.* Charleston, SC: Evening Post, 1983. p. 237. Moultrie, William. *Memoirs of the American Revolution so far as it related to the States of North and South Carolina and Georgia.* New York, 1802; (Eyewitness accounts of the American Revolution). [New York]: New York Times, [1968]. II: 297. Lee, Henry. *Memoirs of the War in the Southern Department of the United States.* New York: University Publishing Co., 1869. pp. 546–547. Garden, Alexander. *Anecdotes of the American Revolution, Illustrative of the Talents and Virtues of the Heroes and Patriots who Acted the Most Conspicuous Parts Therein. Second series.* Charleston, S. C.: A.E. Miller, 1828. pp. 378–379. *The Pennsylvania Gazette.* May 15, 1782. O'Kelley, Patrick. *Nothing But Blood and Slaughter.* Booklocker.com, 2004. 4: 45–46.

314. *The Boston Evening-Post and the General Advertiser.* I: XXXII (May 25, 1782), p. 3. *The New Jersey Gazette.* V: 230 (May 22, 1782), p. 2. Parker, John C. *Parker's Guide to the Revolutionary War in South Carolina: battles, skirmishes and murders.* Patrick, SC: Hem Branch Publishing, 2009. p. 79. Ripley, Warren. *Battleground: South Carolina in the Revolution.* Charleston, SC: Evening Post, 1983. p. 237. Moultrie, William. *Memoirs of the American Revolution so far as it related to the States of North and South Carolina and Georgia.* New York, 1802; (Eyewitness accounts of the American Revolution). [New York]: New York Times, [1968]. II: 297. Lee, Henry. *Memoirs of the War in the Southern Department of the United States.* New York: University Publishing Co., 1869. pp. 546–547. Garden, Alexander. *Anecdotes of the American Revolution, Illustrative of the Talents and Virtues of the Heroes and Patriots who Acted the Most Conspicuous Parts Therein. Second series.* Charleston, S. C.: A.E. Miller, 1828. pp. 378–379. *The Pennsylvania Gazette.* May 15, 1782. O'Kelley, Patrick. *Nothing But Blood and Slaughter.* Booklocker.com, 2004. 4: 45–46.

315. Parker, John C. *Parker's Guide to the Revolutionary War in South Carolina: battles, skirmishes and murders.* Patrick, SC: Hem Branch Publishing, 2009. p. 75.

316. Lipscomb, Terry W. South Carolina Revolutionary Battles: Part Nine. *Names in South Carolina.* XXVIII (Winter 1981). South Carolina Historical Society, 1981. p. 39.

317. National Archives and Records Administration. John China pension application S46593. National Archives and Records Administration. Thomas Broughton pension application W897. Lipscomb, Terry W. South Carolina Revolutionary Battles: Part Ten. *Names in South Carolina.* XXX (Winter 1983). South Carolina Historical Society, 1983. (MS H–2–2), pp. 31–32. McCrady, Edward. *History of South Carolina in the Revolution, 1775–1780.* New York: Paladin Press, 1969 (reprint of 1901 ed.) pp. 487ff. www.carolana.com/SC/Revolution/revolution_wappetaw_church.html. Clement, Christopher Ohm and Grunden, Ramona M. "Where the Wappetaw Independent Congregational

Church Stood.". Archaeological Testing at 38CH1682, Charleston County, SC" (1998). Research Manuscript Series. Book 201. scholarcommons.sc.edu/archanth_books/201.

318. National Archives and Records Administration. Solomon Freer Pension application W8826. Parker, John C. *Parker's Guide to the Revolutionary War in South Carolina: battles, skirmishes and murders.* Patrick, SC: Hem Branch Publishing, 2009. p. 97.

319. Peckham, Howard Henry. *The Toll of Independence: engagements & battle casualties of the American Revolution.* edited by Howard H. Peckham. Chicago: University of Chicago Press, 1974. p. 94. Lipscomb, Terry W. South Carolina Revolutionary Battles: Part Nine. *Names in South Carolina.* XXVIII (Winter 1981). South Carolina Historical Society, 1981. p. 33. O'Kelley, Patrick. *Nothing but Blood and Slaughter.* Booklocker.com, 2004. 4: 44.

320. Draper, Lyman. Thomas Sumter Papers, Draper Manuscript Collection, State Historical Society of Wisconsin. 15VV150–152. O'Kelley, Patrick. *Nothing But Blood and Slaughter.* Booklocker.com, 2004. 3: 288–89. Parker, John C. *Parker's Guide to the Revolutionary War in South Carolina: battles, skirmishes and murders.* Patrick, SC: Hem Branch Publishing, 2009. p. 53.

321. Greene Papers, July 15, 1781 William L. Clements Library. *Historical Magazine.* IX (Sept. 1865) p. 283. Gregoire, Anne King. *Thomas Sumter.* Columbia: R.L. Bryan Company, 1931. pp. 174–75. Hayes, John T. *The Saddlebag Almanac.* X (Jan. 2003) pp. 88–92. Simms, William Gilmore. *The Life of Francis Marion.* New York, 1844. pp. 148–149. Moultrie, William. *Memoirs of the American Revolution so far as it related to the States of North and South Carolina and Georgia.* New York, 1802; (Eyewitness Accounts of the American Revolution). [New York] New York Times [1968]. II: 290. Lee, Henry. *Memoirs of the War in the Southern Department of the United States.* New York: University Publishing Co., 1869. p. 388. *The Pennsylvania Gazette.* Aug. 8, 1781. Hayes, John T. *Stephen Jarvis, the King's Loyal Horseman, His Narrative. 1775–1783.* The Saddlebag Press, 1996. pp. 67–73. James, William Dobein. *A Sketch of the Life of Brig. Gen. Francis Marion, and a History of his Brigade, from its Rise in June 1780, until Disbanded in December, 1782.* Charleston, SC: Gould and Riley, 1821. p. 39. Draper, Lyman. Thomas Sumter Papers, Draper Manuscript Collection, State Historical Society of Wisconsin. 7VV432–433. *A List of all the officers of the Army: viz. the general and field officers; the officers of the several troops, regiments, independent companies, and garrisons: with an alphabetical index to the whole. Also, a list of the officers of the Royal Regiment of Artillery, the Corps of Engineers, the Irish Artillery and Engineers, and of the Marine Forces: the officers on half pay; and a succession of colonels. To which are likewise added the officers of the militia forces, and of the fencible and provincial regiments in Great Britain.* [London, England?]: War-Office, 1780. p. 89. O'Kelley, Patrick. *Nothing But Blood and Slaughter.* Booklocker.com, 2004. 3: 289–91.

322. Extract of a letter from Major-General Greene to the President of Congress, dated Head-Quarters, High Hills of Santee, July 26, 1781. *New Jersey Gazette.* 4:194 (Sept. 12, 1781) p. 2; *Connecticut Journal.* 725 (Sept. 20, 1781) p. 1. Rankin, Hugh F. *Francis Marion: the Swamp Fox.* New York: Thomas Y. Crowell Company, 1973. pp. 226–27. Hayes, John T. *The Saddlebag Almanac.* X (Jan. 2003) pp. 93–94. Garden, Alexander. *Anecdotes of the American Revolution, Illustrative of the Talents and Virtues of the Heroes and Patriots who Acted the Most Conspicuous Parts Therein. Second series.* Charleston, S. C.: A.E. Miller, 1828. pp. 134–135. Simms, William Gilmore. *The Life of Francis Marion.* New York, 1844. pp. 149–152. Moultrie, William. *Memoirs of the American Revolution so far as it related to the States of North and South Carolina and Georgia.* New York, 1802; (Eyewitness Accounts of the American Revolution). [New York] New York Times [1968]. II: 290–291. Lee, Henry. *Memoirs of the War in the Southern Department of the United States.* New York: University Publishing Co., 1869. p. 389–394. *The Pennsylvania Gazette.* Aug. 8, 1781; Aug. 29, 1781; Sept. 25, 1781. Ervin. Sara Sullivan. *South Carolinians in the Revolution.* Baltimore: Genealogical Publishing Company, Inc., 1971. pp. 65–77, 80–84. James, William Dobein. *A Sketch of the Life of Brig. Gen. Francis Marion, and a History of his Brigade, from its Rise in June 1780, until Disbanded in December, 1782.* Charleston, SC: Gould and Riley, 1821. pp. 39–40. Draper, Lyman. Thomas Sumter Papers, Draper Manuscript Collection, State Historical Society of Wisconsin. 7VV340, 412–418, 423–433, 501–504; 10VV91, 184; 15VV133. *A List of all the officers of the Army: viz. the general and field officers; the officers of the several troops, regiments, independent companies, and garrisons: with an alphabetical index to the whole. Also, a list of the officers of the Royal Regiment of Artillery, the Corps of Engineers, the Irish Artillery and Engineers, and of the Marine Forces: the officers on half pay; and a succession of colonels. To which are likewise added the officers of the militia forces, and of the fencible and provincial regiments in Great Britain.* [London, England?]: War-Office, 1780. p. 89. O'Kelley, Patrick. *Nothing But Blood and Slaughter.* Booklocker.com, 2004. 3: 295–99. Parker, John C. *Parker's Guide to the Revolutionary War in South Carolina: battles, skirmishes and murders.* Patrick, SC: Hem Branch Publishing, 2009. p. 48.

323. *The Royal Gazette.* Sept. 5, 1781. Robert Mills's map of Charleston District (1825); Ocean Bay quadrangle topographic map (1943). Lipscomb, Terry W. South Carolina Revolutionary Battles: Part Ten. *Names in South Carolina.* XXX (Winter 1983). South Carolina Historical Society, 1983. pp. 30–31. www.carolana.com/SC/Revolution/revolution_wells_plantation.html. Parker, John C. *Parker's Guide to the Revolutionary War in South Carolina: battles, skirmishes and murders.* Patrick, SC: Hem Branch Publishing, 2009. p. 54.

324. Bass Robert D. *Swamp Fox: the Life and Campaigns of General Francis Marion.* [s.l] Henry Holt and Company, 1959. p. 238. Copy of a Letter from Brigadier General Marion to His Excellency Governor Mathews. Wathoo, St. John's August 30, 1782. *The New-York Gazetteer or Northern Intelligencer.* I: 21 (Oct. 21, 1782) p. 3.

325. Barefoot, Daniel W. *Touring South Carolina's Revolutionary War Sites.* Winston-Salem: John F. Blair, 1999. pp. 34, 38–39. Parker, John C. *Parker's Guide to the Revolutionary War in South Carolina: battles, skirmishes and murders.* Patrick, SC: Hem Branch Publishing, 2009. p. 49.

326. Ripley, Warren. *Battleground: South Carolina in the Revolution.* Charleston, SC: Evening Post, 1983. p. 238. Simms, William Gilmore. *The Life of Francis Marion.* New York: H.G. Langley, 1844. p. 186. British National Archives. Treasury Office, Class 50, Vol. 2, folio 372. British National Archives. Audit Office, Class 13, Vol. 130, folio 293. Lipscomb, Terry W. South Carolina Revolutionary Battles: Part Nine. *Names in South Carolina.* XXVIII (Winter

1981). South Carolina Historical Society, 1981. p. 36. James, William Dobein. *A Sketch of the Life of Brig. Gen. Francis Marion, and a History of his Brigade, from its Rise in June 1780, until Disbanded in December, 1782*. Charleston, SC: Gould and Riley, 1821. p. 54. Crow, Jeffrey J. *The Black Experience in Revolutionary North Carolina*. Raleigh: [North Carolina Dept. of Cultural Resources, Division of Archives and History], 1977. p. 78. O'Kelley, Patrick. *Nothing But Blood and Slaughter*. Booklocker.com, 2004. 4: 81. Parker, John C. *Parker's Guide to the Revolutionary War in South Carolina: battles, skirmishes and murders*. Patrick, SC: Hem Branch Publishing, 2009. pp. 111, 112.

327. Sir James Wright (1714–1785), Governor of Georgia, to Lord Dartmouth July 8 and 10, 1775. Collections of the Georgia Historical Society, III: 191, 192, 194. NDAR 1: 845, 856. Governor Patrick Tonyn To Lord Dartmouth July 21, 1775. British National Archives, Colonial Office, Class 5/555, LC Transcript. NDAR 1: 949. Parker, John C. *Parker's Guide to the Revolutionary War in South Carolina: battles, skirmishes and murders*. Patrick, SC: Hem Branch Publishing, 2009. p. 25.

328. Peckham, Howard Henry. *The Toll of Independence: engagements & battle casualties of the American Revolution*. edited by Howard H. Peckham. Chicago: University of Chicago Press, 1974. p. 64. www.carolana.com/SC/Revolution/revolution_ashs_point.html.

329. Parker, John C. *Parker's Guide to the Revolutionary War in South Carolina: battles, skirmishes and murders*. Patrick, SC: Hem Branch Publishing, 2009. p. 38. *A Revolutionary Story of Intrigue: Hilton Head Island, SC*. Article and photos by B. Schepers www.uelac.org/../2010-02-28-Rev-Story-of-Intrigue-BSchepers.pdf.

330. North Carolina Office of Archives & History, the Colonial Records Project, 1776. Extract of a letter from the camp near Cape Fear, North-Carolina, May 16. *Caledonian Mercury* (Edinburgh). July 29, 1776. NDAR 4: 1321. Parker, John C. *Parker's Guide to the Revolutionary War in South Carolina: battles, skirmishes and murders*. Patrick, SC: Hem Branch Publishing, 2009. p. 83.

331. Allen, Gardner Weld. *A Naval History of the American Revolution, 1856–1944*. Boston; New York: Houghton Mifflin Company, 1913. 1: 323. Smith, D. E. Huger. Commodore Alexander Gillon and the Frigate South Carolina. *The South Carolina Historical Magazine*. IX: 4 (Oct. 1908) p. 193. *Gazette of the State of South Carolina*. June 24, 1778. Parker, John C. *Parker's Guide to the Revolutionary War in South Carolina: battles, skirmishes and murders*. Patrick, SC: Hem Branch Publishing, 2009. p. 83.

332. Parker, John C. *Parker's Guide to the Revolutionary War in South Carolina: battles, skirmishes and murders*. Patrick, SC: Hem Branch Publishing, 2009. p. 84.

333. Parker, John C. *Parker's Guide to the Revolutionary War in South Carolina: battles, skirmishes and murders*. Patrick, SC: Hem Branch Publishing, 2009. p. 84.

334. Parker, John C. *Parker's Guide to the Revolutionary War in South Carolina: battles, skirmishes and murders*. Patrick, SC: Hem Branch Publishing, 2009. p. 84, 216.

335. Parker, John C. *Parker's Guide to the Revolutionary War in South Carolina: battles, skirmishes and murders*. Patrick, SC: Hem Branch Publishing, 2009. p. 84.

336. *The Pennsylvania Gazette*. Jan. 27, 1779. Griffiths, John William. *"To Receive them Properly ": Charlestown prepares for war, 1775–1776*. M.A. Thesis, University of South Carolina, 1992. pp. 250–251. O'Kelley, Patrick. *Nothing But Blood and Slaughter*. Booklocker.com, 2004. 1: 211. Parker, John C. *Parker's Guide to the Revolutionary War in South Carolina: battles, skirmishes and murders*. Patrick, SC: Hem Branch Publishing, 2009. p. 94.

337. Parker, John C. *Parker's Guide to the Revolutionary War in South Carolina: battles, skirmishes and murders*. Patrick, SC: Hem Branch Publishing, 2009. p. 94.

338. Southern Studies Program. *Figures of the Revolution in South Carolina, An Anthology. Spartanburg, Anderson, Beaufort, Aiken, Florence, Georgetown*. Columbia: University of South Carolina, 1976. p. 181. Lipscomb, Terry W. South Carolina Revolutionary Battles: Part Nine. *Names in South Carolina*. XXVIII (Winter 1981). South Carolina Historical Society, 1981. pp. 37–38. O'Kelley, Patrick. *Nothing But Blood and Slaughter*. Booklocker.com, 2004. 4: 88–89. Parker, John C. *Parker's Guide to the Revolutionary War in South Carolina: battles, skirmishes and murders*. Patrick, SC: Hem Branch Publishing, 2009. p. 95.

339. *The Pennsylvania Gazette*. Jan. 27, 1779. O'Kelley, Patrick. *Nothing But Blood and Slaughter*. Booklocker.com, 2004. 1: 211. Parker, John C. *Parker's Guide to the Revolutionary War in South Carolina: battles, skirmishes and murders*. Patrick, SC: Hem Branch Publishing, 2009. p. 26.

340. Davies, K.G. *Documents of the American Revolution 1770–1783*. (Colonial Office Series) Shannon: Irish University Press 1972, 1981. 17: 65–67. Butler, Lewis. *The Annals of the King's Royal Rifle Corps; Volume 1. "the Royal Americans."* London: John Murray, 1913. pp. 311–314. Moultrie, William. *Memoirs of the American Revolution so far as it related to the States of North and South Carolina and Georgia*. New York, 1802; (Eyewitness Accounts of the American Revolution). [New York] New York Times [1968]. I: 303–304. O'Kelley, Patrick. *Nothing But Blood and Slaughter*. Booklocker.com, 2004. 1: 233–34. Parker, John C. *Parker's Guide to the Revolutionary War in South Carolina: battles, skirmishes and murders*. Patrick, SC: Hem Branch Publishing, 2009. p. 27.

341. Ripley, Warren. *Battleground: South Carolina in the Revolution*. Charleston, SC: Evening Post, 1983. pp. 21–23. Heitman, Francis B. *Historical Register of Officers of the Continental Army during the War of the Revolution, April 1775 to December 1783*. Washington, DC.: the Rare Book Shop Publishing Company, 1914; Baltimore: Genealogical Publishing Company, 1967. p. 124. Butler, Lewis. *The Annals of the King's Royal Rifle Corps; Volume 1. "the Royal Americans."* London: John Murray, 1913. pp. 312–318. Moultrie, William. *Memoirs of the American Revolution so far as it related to the States of North and South Carolina and Georgia*. New York, 1802; (Eyewitness Accounts of the American Revolution). [New York] New York Times [1968]. I: 291–297, 312—313. Lee, Henry. *Memoirs of the War in the Southern Department of the United States*. New York: University Publishing Co., 1869. p. 123. *The Pennsylvania Gazette*. March 17, 1779. British National Archives. Colonial Office Class 5, Vol. 98 pp. 307–313. *A List of all the officers of the Army: viz. the general and field officers; the officers of the several troops, regiments, independent companies, and*

garrisons: with an alphabetical index to the whole. Also, a list of the officers of the Royal Regiment of Artillery, the Corps of Engineers, the Irish Artillery and Engineers, and of the Marine Forces: the officers on half pay; and a succession of colonels. To which are likewise added the officers of the militia forces, and of the fencible and provincial regiments in Great Britain. [London, England?]: War-Office, 1780. pp. 86, 133. Lipscomb, Terry W. South Carolina Revolutionary Battles: Part Two. *Names in South Carolina.* XXI (Winter 1974). South Carolina Historical Society, 1974. p. 23. Ervin. Sara Sullivan. *South Carolinians in the Revolution.* Baltimore: Genealogical Publishing Company, Inc., 1971. p. 63. James, William Dobein. *A Sketch of the Life of Brig. General Francis Marion, and a History of his Brigade, from its Rise in June 1780, until Disbanded in December, 1782.* Charleston, SC: Gould and Riley, 1821. p. 8. Hayes, John T. *The Saddlebag Almanac.* V (Jan. 1997) p. 76. Coakley, Robert W. and Conn, Stetson. *The War of the American Revolution.* Center of Military History, United States Army, 1975. pp. 115–116. O'Kelley, Patrick. *Nothing But Blood and Slaughter.* Booklocker.com, 2004. 1: 235–238. Smith, Gordon Burns. *Morningstars of Liberty: the Revolutionary War in Georgia, 1775–1783.* Milledgeville, GA: Boyd Publishing, 2006. I: 141.

342. Parker, John C. *Parker's Guide to the Revolutionary War in South Carolina: battles, skirmishes and murders.* Patrick, SC: Hem Branch Publishing, 2009. p. 28.

343. Parker, John C. *Parker's Guide to the Revolutionary War in South Carolina: battles, skirmishes and murders.* Patrick, SC: Hem Branch Publishing, 2009. p. 27.

344. Moultrie, William. *Memoirs of the American Revolution so far as it related to the States of North and South Carolina and Georgia.* New York, 1802; (Eyewitness Accounts of the American Revolution). [New York] New York Times [1968]. II: 12, 15–16. *The Pennsylvania Gazette.* Sept. 15, 1779. Charlestown, July 28. *Connecticut Journal.* 621 (Sept. 22, 1779) p. 2. www.carolana.com/SC/Revolution/revolution_hunting_island.html. Parker, John C. *Parker's Guide to the Revolutionary War in South Carolina: battles, skirmishes and murders.* Patrick, SC: Hem Branch Publishing, 2009. p. 29. O'Kelley, Patrick. *Nothing But Blood and Slaughter.* Booklocker.com, 2004. 1: 303–304.

345. Davies, K.G. *Documents of the American Revolution 1770–1783.* (Colonial Office Series) Shannon: Irish University Press 1972, 1981. 20: 174. Moss, Bobby Gilmer. *Roster of South Carolina Patriots in the American Revolution.* Baltimore: Genealogical Pub. Co., 1983. p. 48. Lipscomb, Terry W. South Carolina Revolutionary Battles: Part Nine. *Names in South Carolina.* XXVIII (Winter 1981). South Carolina Historical Society, 1981. p. 33. O'Kelley, Patrick. *Nothing But Blood and Slaughter.* Booklocker.com, 2004. 4: 39. Parker, John C. *Parker's Guide to the Revolutionary War in South Carolina: battles, skirmishes and murders.* Patrick, SC: Hem Branch Publishing, 2009. pp. 32, 40, 41, 42.

346. Parker, John C. *Parker's Guide to the Revolutionary War in South Carolina: battles, skirmishes and murders.* Patrick, SC: Hem Branch Publishing, 2009. p. 43. Seymour, William. Journal of the Southern Expedition, 1780–1783. *Papers of the Historical Society of Delaware.* XV. Wilmington: The Historical Society of Delaware, 1896.

347. Campbell, Colin, ed. *Journal of an Expedition against the Rebels in Georgia in North America under the Orders of Archibald Campbell, Esquire, Lieutenant Colonel of His Majesty's 71st Regiment, 1778.* Darien, GA: Ahantilly, 1981. pp. 16, 106. O'Kelley, Patrick. *Nothing But Blood and Slaughter.* Booklocker.com, 2004. 1:222.

348. *Charleston Royal Gazette.* Aug. 25, 1781; Aug. 29, 1781. Parker, John C. *Parker's Guide to the Revolutionary War in South Carolina: battles, skirmishes and murders.* Patrick, SC: Hem Branch Publishing, 2009. p. 36.

349. Peckham, Howard Henry. *The Toll of Independence: engagements & battle casualties of the American Revolution.* edited by Howard H. Peckham. Chicago: University of Chicago Press, 1974. p. 94. Ripley, Warren. *Battleground: South Carolina in the Revolution.* Charleston, SC: Evening Post, 1983. p. 237. Clark. Murtie June. *Loyalists in the Southern Campaign of the Revolutionary War.* Baltimore: Genealogical Publishing Company, Inc., 1981. I: 492. Moss, Bobby Gilmer. *Roster of South Carolina Patriots in the American Revolution.* Baltimore: Genealogical Pub. Co., 1983. p. 48. O'Kelley, Patrick. *Nothing But Blood and Slaughter.* Booklocker.com, 2004. 4: 34–35. Parker, John C. *Parker's Guide to the Revolutionary War in South Carolina: battles, skirmishes and murders.* Patrick, SC: Hem Branch Publishing, 2009. p. 39.

350. Hurley, Suzanne Cameron Linder. *Anglican Churches in Colonial South Carolina: their history and architecture.* Charleston, SC: Wyrick & Co., 2000. Carson, Martha Bray. *History of Old Sheldon Church.* Parker, John C. *Parker's Guide to the Revolutionary War in South Carolina: battles, skirmishes and murders.* Patrick, SC: Hem Branch Publishing, 2009. p. 30, 39.

351. *The New Jersey Gazette.* IV: 201 (Oct. 31, 1781), p. 1.

352. Copy of a letter from Brigadier-General Marion, to his Excellency Governor Mathews. Watboo, St. John's, August 30. *Royal Gazette.* 631 (Oct. 12, 1782), p. 3. Hilborn, Nat & Sam. *Battleground of Freedom: South Carolina in the Revolution.* Columbia, SC: Sandlapper Press, 1970. p. 219. Parker, John C. *Parker's Guide to the Revolutionary War in South Carolina: battles, skirmishes and murders.* Patrick, SC: Hem Branch Publishing, 2009. p. 156.

353. Parker, John C. *Parker's Guide to the Revolutionary War in South Carolina: battles, skirmishes and murders.* Patrick, SC: Hem Branch Publishing, 2009. p. 215.

354. *The Pennsylvania Gazette.* March 31, 1779; April 21, 1779. O'Kelley, Patrick. *Nothing But Blood and Slaughter.* Booklocker.com, 2004 1: 252.

355. Parker, John C. *Parker's Guide to the Revolutionary War in South Carolina: battles, skirmishes and murders.* Patrick, SC: Hem Branch Publishing, 2009. p. 216.

356. James, William Dobein. *A Sketch of the Life of Brig. Gen. Francis Marion, and a History of his Brigade, from its Rise in June 1780, until Disbanded in December, 1782.* Charleston, SC: Gould and Riley, 1821. www.historycarper.com/resources/fmarion/chap2.htm.

357. Parker, John C. *Parker's Guide to the Revolutionary War in South Carolina: battles, skirmishes and murders.* Patrick, SC: Hem Branch Publishing, 2009. p. 216.

358. Southern Studies Program. *Figures of the Revolution in South Carolina, An Anthology.* Spartanburg, Anderson, Beaufort, Aiken, Florence, Georgetown. Columbia: University of South Carolina, 1976. p. 272. Simms, William Gilmore. *The Life of Francis Marion.* New York, 1844. pp. 90–93. Bass, Robert Duncan. *Swamp Fox: the life and campaigns of General Francis Marion.* Orangeburg, SC: Sandlapper, 1989. pp. 87–92. James, William Dobein. *A Sketch of the Life of Brig. Gen. Francis Marion, and a History of his Brigade, from its Rise in June 1780, until Disbanded in December, 1782.* Charleston, SC: Gould and Riley, 1821. p. 21. O'Kelley, Patrick. *Nothing But Blood and Slaughter.* Booklocker.com, 2004. 2: 362–363. Peckham, Howard Henry. *The Toll of Independence: engagements & battle casualties of the American Revolution.* edited by Howard H. Peckham. Chicago: University of Chicago Press, 1974. p. 77. Lt. Col. Francis Marion to Brig. Gen. Henry Harrington. Blackmingo, 17 Novr, 1780.

359. Lockey, Joseph B. "the Florida Banditti 1783." *Florida Historical Quarterly.* 24 (1945) p. 97. Ward, Harry M. *The War for Independence and the Transformation of American Society.* London: UCL Press, 1999. p. 78.

360. Simcoe, John Graves. *Simcoe's Military Journal. A History of the Operations of a Partisan Corps Called the Queen's Rangers, Commanded by Lieut. Colonel J. G. Simcoe, During the War of the American Revolution.* New-York: Bartlett & Welford, 1844; [New York]: New York Times; Arno Press. Eyewitness Accounts of the American Revolution. [1968]. pp. 241–242. British National Archives. Cornwallis Papers, Class 30, Vol. 11 p. 83 folio 63–64. Bass, Robert Duncan. *Swamp Fox: the life and campaigns of General Francis Marion.* Orangeburg, SC: Sandlapper, 1989. pp. 132, 135–137. James, William Dobein. *A Sketch of the Life of Brig. Gen. Francis Marion, and a History of his Brigade, from its Rise in June 1780, until Disbanded in December, 1782.* Charleston, SC: Gould and Riley, 1821. p. 29. O'Kelley, Patrick. *Nothing But Blood and Slaughter.* Booklocker.com, 2004. 2: 389–90.

361. Salley, Alexander S. Horry's Notes to Weems's Life of Marion. *The South Carolina Historical Magazine.* LX: 3. (July 1959) p. 121. Simcoe, John Graves. *Simcoe's Military Journal. A History of the Operations of a Partisan Corps Called the Queen's Rangers, Commanded by Lieut. Colonel J. G. Simcoe, During the War of the American Revolution.* New-York: Bartlett & Welford, 1844; [New York]: New York Times; Arno Press. Eyewitness Accounts of the American Revolution. [1968]. pp. 243–244. Simms, William Gilmore. *The Life of Francis Marion.* New York, 1844. pp. 90–92. Bass, Robert Duncan. *Swamp Fox: the life and campaigns of General Francis Marion.* Orangeburg, SC: Sandlapper, 1989. pp. 120–123. James, William Dobein. *A Sketch of the Life of Brig. Gen. Francis Marion, and a History of his Brigade, from its Rise in June 1780, until Disbanded in December, 1782.* Charleston, SC: Gould and Riley, 1821. pp. 29–30. O'Kelley, Patrick. *Nothing But Blood and Slaughter.* Booklocker.com, 2004. 2: 391–92. Parker, John C. *Parker's Guide to the Revolutionary War in South Carolina: battles, skirmishes and murders.* Patrick, SC: Hem Branch Publishing, 2009. p. 207.

362. Peckham, Howard Henry. *The Toll of Independence: engagements & battle casualties of the American Revolution.* edited by Howard H. Peckham. Chicago: University of Chicago Press, 1974. p. 78.

363. Marion to Greene. Dec. 28, 1780 Greene, Nathanael. *The Papers of General Nathanael Greene.* Richard K. Showman, ed. Chapel Hill: the University of North Carolina Press, published for the Rhode Island Historical Society. c1976–2006. 7: 13. Bass, Robert Duncan. *Swamp Fox: the life and campaigns of General Francis Marion.* Orangeburg, SC: Sandlapper, 1989. Rogers, George C. *The history of Georgetown County, South Carolina.* Columbia: University of South Carolina Press 1970. p. 135. Parker, John C. *Parker's Guide to the Revolutionary War in South Carolina: battles, skirmishes and murders.* Patrick, SC: Hem Branch Publishing, 2009. p. 207.

364. Simcoe, John Graves. *Simcoe's Military Journal. A History of the Operations of a Partisan Corps Called the Queen's Rangers, Commanded by Lieut. Colonel J. G. Simcoe, During the War of the American Revolution.* New-York: Bartlett & Welford, 1844; [New York]: New York Times; Arno Press.–Eyewitness Accounts of the American Revolution. [1968]. pp. 242–243. Bass, Robert Duncan. *Swamp Fox: the life and campaigns of General Francis Marion.* Orangeburg, SC: Sandlapper, 1989. pp. 123–124. Hayes, John T. *The Saddlebag Almanac.* VII (Jan. 1999), p. 99; VIII (Jan. 2000), pp. 86–87. O'Kelley, Patrick. *Nothing But Blood and Slaughter.* Booklocker.com, 2004. 3: 21–2. Parker, John C. *Parker's Guide to the Revolutionary War in South Carolina: battles, skirmishes and murders.* Patrick, SC: Hem Branch Publishing, 2009. p. 214.

365. Philadelphia, Feb. 23, 1781. *The Pennsylvania Evening Post.* VII: 719 (Feb. 23, 1781) p. 33. Simms, William Gilmore. *The Life of Francis Marion.* New York, 1844. pp. 113–115. Moultrie, William. *Memoirs of the American Revolution so far as it related to the States of North and South Carolina and Georgia.* New York, 1802; (Eyewitness Accounts of the American Revolution). [New York] New York Times [1968]. II: 230–231. British National Archives. Cornwallis Papers, Class 30, Vol. 103 folio 2. Ervin. Sara Sullivan. *South Carolinians in the Revolution.* Baltimore: Genealogical Publishing Company, Inc., 1971. pp. 67–77. Greene, Nathanael. *The Papers of General Nathanael Greene.* Richard K. Showman, ed. Chapel Hill: the University of North Carolina Press, published for the Rhode Island Historical Society. c1976–2006. 7: 197–198. Hayes, John T. *The Saddlebag Almanac.* VIII (Jan. 2000) pp. 42, 87. O'Kelley, Patrick. *Nothing But Blood and Slaughter.* Booklocker.com, 2004. 3: 59–61. Parker, John C. *Parker's Guide to the Revolutionary War in South Carolina: battles, skirmishes and murders.* Patrick, SC: Hem Branch Publishing, 2009. p. 203.

366. Nase, Henry. Diary of Henry Nase, King's American Regiment. Nase Family Papers. The New Brunswick Museum. Department of Canadian History, Archives Division. Southern Studies Program. *Figures of the Revolution in South Carolina, An Anthology.* Spartanburg, Anderson, Beaufort, Aiken, Florence, Georgetown. Columbia: University of South Carolina, 1976. p. 333. Simms, William Gilmore. *The Life of Francis Marion.* New York, 1844. p. 117. James, William Dobein. *A Sketch of the Life of Brig. Gen. Francis Marion, and a History of his Brigade, from its Rise in June 1780, until Disbanded in December, 1782.* Charleston, SC: Gould and Riley, 1821. p. 29. O'Kelley, Patrick. *Nothing But Blood and Slaughter.* Booklocker.com, 2004. 3: 85–6. Balfour to Clinton, Feb. 24, 1781. Cornwallis Papers, British National Archives. 30/11/109. James places this episode in January. James, William Dobein. *A Sketch of the Life of Brig. Gen. Francis Marion, and a History of his Brigade, from its Rise in June 1780, until Disbanded in December, 1782.* Charleston, SC: Gould and Riley, 1821. p. 93. Rogers, George C. *The History of Georgetown County, South Carolina.*

Columbia: University of South Carolina Press 1970. p. 138. Parker, John C. *Parker's Guide to the Revolutionary War in South Carolina: battles, skirmishes and murders.* Patrick, SC: Hem Branch Publishing, 2009. p. 212.

367. Simcoe, John Graves. *Simcoe's Military Journal. A History of the Operations of a Partisan Corps Called the Queen's Rangers, Commanded by Lieut. Colonel J. G. Simcoe, During the War of the American Revolution.* New-York: Bartlett & Welford, 1844; [New York]: New York Times; Arno Press. Eyewitness Accounts of the American Revolution. [1968]. pp. 242–243. Hayes, John T. *The Saddlebag Almanac.* VIII (Jan. 2000) pp. 87–88. O'Kelley, Patrick. *Nothing But Blood and Slaughter.* Booklocker.com, 2004. 3: 91. www.rsar.org/military/sherm162.pdf. Parker, John C. *Parker's Guide to the Revolutionary War in South Carolina: battles, skirmishes and murders.* Patrick, SC: Hem Branch Publishing, 2009. pp. 204, 221.

368. Moultrie, William. *Memoirs of the American Revolution so far as it related to the States of North and South Carolina and Georgia.* New York, 1802; (Eyewitness Accounts of the American Revolution). [New York] New York Times [1968]. II: 281. Simms, William Gilmore. *The Life of Francis Marion.* New York, 1844. p. 146. Lossing, Benson John. *The Pictorial Field-book of the Revolution; or, Illustrations, by pen and pencil, of the history, biography, scenery, relics, and traditions of the War for Independence.* New York, Harper & Brothers [1860]. *The Pennsylvania Gazette.* July 18, 1781. O'Kelley, Patrick. *Nothing But Blood and Slaughter.* Booklocker.com, 2004. 3: 267–68.

369. Washington, George. *The Diary of George Washington, from 1789 to 1791; embracing the opening of the first Congress, and his tours through New England, Long Island, and the Southern States. Together with his Journal of a tour to the Ohio, in 1753.* Edited by Benson J. Lossing. Richmond: Press of the Historical Society, 1861. (April 30, 1791) 4: 179–180.

370. Greene, Nathanael. *The Papers of General Nathanael Greene.* Richard K. Showman, ed. Chapel Hill: the University of North Carolina Press, published for the Rhode Island Historical Society. c1976–2006. 9: 102. McCrady, Edward. *History of South Carolina in the Revolution, 1775–1780.* New York: Paladin Press, 1969 (reprint of 1901 ed.) p. 429. *Encyclopedia of the American Revolution.* Harold E. Selesky, editor in chief. 2nd Ed. Detroit: Charles Scribner's Sons, 2007. 1: 415.

371. Moultrie, William. *Memoirs of the American Revolution so far as it related to the States of North and South Carolina and Georgia.* New York, 1802; (Eyewitness Accounts of the American Revolution). [New York] New York Times [1968]. II: 281. Lipscomb, Terry W. South Carolina Revolutionary Battles: Part Seven. *Names in South Carolina* XXVI (Winter 1979). South Carolina Historical Society, 1979. p. 33. James, William Dobein. *A Sketch of the Life of Brig. Gen. Francis Marion, and a History of his Brigade, from its Rise in June 1780, until Disbanded in December, 1782.* Charleston, SC: Gould and Riley, 1821. p. 44. O'Kelley, Patrick. *Nothing But Blood and Slaughter.* Booklocker.com, 2004. 3: 307–308. Parker, John C. *Parker's Guide to the Revolutionary War in South Carolina: battles, skirmishes and murders.* Patrick, SC: Hem Branch Publishing, 2009. p. 204.

372. James, William Dobein. *A Sketch of the Life of Brig. Gen. Francis Marion, and a History of his Brigade, from its Rise in June 1780, until Disbanded in December, 1782.* Charleston, SC: Gould and Riley, 1821. p. 81. Parker, John C. *Parker's Guide to the Revolutionary War in South Carolina: battles, skirmishes and murders.* Patrick, SC: Hem Branch Publishing, 2009. p. 209.

373. Simcoe, John Graves. *Simcoe's Military Journal. A History of the Operations of a Partisan Corps Called the Queen's Rangers, Commanded by Lieut. Colonel J. G. Simcoe, During the War of the American Revolution.* New-York: Bartlett & Welford, 1844; [New York]: New York Times; Arno Press.–Eyewitness Accounts of the American Revolution. [1968]. pp. 246–247. Hayes, John T. *The Saddlebag Almanac.* VIII (Jan. 2000), p. 90. O'Kelley, Patrick. *Nothing But Blood and Slaughter.* Booklocker.com, 2004. 3: 176. www.carolana.com/SC/Revolution/revolution_black_river.html. McCrady, Edward. *History of South Carolina in the Revolution, 1775–1780.* New York: Paladin Press, 1969 (reprint of 1901 ed.) p. 171. James, William Dobein. *A Sketch of the Life of Brig. Gen. Francis Marion, and a History of his Brigade, from its Rise in June 1780, until Disbanded in December, 1782.* Charleston, SC: Gould and Riley, 1821. Parker, John C. *Parker's Guide to the Revolutionary War in South Carolina: battles, skirmishes and murders.* Patrick, SC: Hem Branch Publishing, 2009. p. 208.

374. Peckham, Howard Henry. *The Toll of Independence: engagements & battle casualties of the American Revolution.* edited by Howard H. Peckham. Chicago: University of Chicago Press, 1974. p. 93.

375. National Archives and Records Administration. James Ownbey (Owenby) Pension application W3712.

376. Migliazzo, Arlin C. *To Make This Land Our Own: community, identity, and cultural adaptation in Purrysburg Township, South Carolina, 1732–1865.* Columbia: University of South Carolina Press, 2007. p. 268. Parker, John C. *Parker's Guide to the Revolutionary War in South Carolina: battles, skirmishes and murders.* Patrick, SC: Hem Branch Publishing, 2009. p. 226. Smith, Gordon Burns. *Morningstars of Liberty: the Revolutionary War in Georgia, 1775–1783.* Milledgeville, GA: Boyd Publishing, 2006. I: 147–148.

377. Lincoln Papers. South Carolina Archives. Moultrie, William. *Memoirs of the American Revolution so far as it related to the States of North and South Carolina and Georgia.* New York, 1802; (Eyewitness Accounts of the American Revolution). [New York] New York Times [1968]. I: 379–382, 387–388. Heitman, Francis B. *Historical Register of Officers of the Continental Army during the War of the Revolution, April 1775. to December 1783.* Washington, DC. 1914; Baltimore: Genealogical Publishing Company, 1967. pp. 74–89. Moss, Bobby Gilmer. *Roster of South Carolina Patriots in the American Revolution.* Baltimore: Genealogical Pub. Co., 1983. p. 423. O'Kelley, Patrick. *Nothing But Blood and Slaughter.* Booklocker.com, 2004. 1: 270–71. Parker, John C. *Parker's Guide to the Revolutionary War in South Carolina: battles, skirmishes and murders.* Patrick, SC: Hem Branch Publishing, 2009. p. 226, 227. Smith, Gordon Burns. *Morningstars of Liberty: the Revolutionary War in Georgia, 1775–1783.* Milledgeville, GA: Boyd Publishing, 2006. I: 153–154.

378. Peckham, Howard Henry. *The Toll of Independence: engagements & battle casualties of the American Revolution.* edited by Howard H. Peckham. Chicago: University of Chicago Press, 1974. p. 62.

Notes **343**

379. Jones, Charles Colcock, Jr. *The History of Georgia*. Boston: Houghton, Mifflin and Company, 1883. II: 363–364. Peckham, Howard Henry. *The Toll of Independence: engagements & battle casualties of the American Revolution*. edited by Howard H. Peckham. Chicago: University of Chicago Press, 1974. p. 63.

380. Parker, John C. *Parker's Guide to the Revolutionary War in South Carolina: battles, skirmishes and murders*. Patrick, SC: Hem Branch Publishing, 2009. p. 226.

381. Southern Studies Program. *Figures of the Revolution in South Carolina, An Anthology*. Spartanburg, Anderson, Beaufort, Aiken, Florence, Georgetown. Columbia: University of South Carolina, 1976. pp. 35–36. Salley, Alexander S. Horry's Notes to Weems's Life of Marion. *The South Carolina Historical Magazine*. LX: 3. (July 1959) p. 120. *The (Charleston) Gazette of the State of South-Carolina*. 21 April 1779. Simms, William Gilmore. *The Life of Francis Marion*. New York, 1844. pp. 45–47. Moultrie, William. *Memoirs of the American Revolution so far as it related to the States of North and South Carolina and Georgia*. New York, 1802; (Eyewitness Accounts of the American Revolution). [New York] New York Times [1968]. I: 379–382, 387–388. O'Kelley, Patrick. *Nothing But Blood and Slaughter*. Booklocker.com, 2004. 1: 269–270.

382. Southern Studies Program. *Figures of the Revolution in South Carolina, An Anthology*. Spartanburg, Anderson, Beaufort, Aiken, Florence, Georgetown. Columbia: University of South Carolina, 1976. p. 36. *The Pennsylvania Gazette*. Sept. 15, 1779. O'Kelley, Patrick. *Nothing But Blood and Slaughter*. Booklocker.com, 2004. 1: 306.

383. Johnson, Uzal. *Memo of Occurrence During the Campaign of 1780*. South Carolina Historical Society, Military Manuscripts. p. 4. Hayes, John T. *The Saddlebag Almanac*. V (Jan. 1997), pp. 73–75; VI:10–13. Allaire, Anthony. *Diary of Lieut. Anthony Allaire*. (Eyewitness Accounts of the American Revolution). [New York] New York Times [1968]. O'Kelley, Patrick. *Nothing But Blood and Slaughter*. Booklocker.com, 2004. 2: 121–22.

384. Parker, John C. *Parker's Guide to the Revolutionary War in South Carolina: battles, skirmishes and murders*. Patrick, SC: Hem Branch Publishing, 2009. p. 228.

385. Olson, Gary D. and Dr. David Ramsay. Lieutenant Colonel Thomas Brown: Patriot Historian and Loyalist Critic. *The South Carolina Historical Magazine*. 77:4 (Oct. 1776) pp. 260–262. Brown, Tarleton. *Memoirs of Tarleton Brown, a Captain in the Revolutionary Army, Written by Himself, with a Preface and Notes by Charles I. Bushnell*. New York: Privately Printed, 1862. Lipscomb, Terry W. South Carolina Revolutionary Battles: Part Ten. *Names in South Carolina*. XXX (Winter 1983). South Carolina Historical Society, 1983. p. 10. O'Kelley, Patrick. *Nothing But Blood and Slaughter*. Booklocker.com, 2004. 3: 54–5. Parker, John C. *Parker's Guide to the Revolutionary War in South Carolina: battles, skirmishes and murders*. Patrick, SC: Hem Branch Publishing, 2009. p. 15.

386. McCall, Hugh. *The History of Georgia, Containing Brief Sketches of the Most Remarkable Events up to the Present Day, 1784*. Savannah: Seymour & Williams, 1811; Atlanta, Cherokee Pub. Co., 1969, 1909. p. 513. Cashin, Edward J. *The King's Ranger. Thomas Brown and the American Revolution on the Southern Frontier*. Athens: University of Georgia Press, 1989. p. 126. Brown, Tarleton. *Memoirs of Tarleton Brown, a Captain in the Revolutionary Army, Written by Himself, with a Preface and Notes by Charles I. Bushnell*. New York: Privately Printed, 1862. sciway3.net/clark/revolutionarywar/tbrownmemoirs.htm. Lipscomb, Terry W. South Carolina Revolutionary Battles: Part Ten. *Names in South Carolina*. XXX (Winter 1983). South Carolina Historical Society, 1983. p. 10. O'Kelley, Patrick. *Nothing But Blood and Slaughter*. Booklocker.com, 2004. 3: 56–7. Parker, John C. *Parker's Guide to the Revolutionary War in South Carolina: battles, skirmishes and murders*. Patrick, SC: Hem Branch Publishing, 2009. p. 16. Smith, Gordon Burns. *Morningstars of Liberty: the Revolutionary War in Georgia, 1775–1783*. Milledgeville, GA: Boyd Publishing, 2006. I: 227–228.

387. Parker, John C. *Parker's Guide to the Revolutionary War in South Carolina: battles, skirmishes and murders*. Patrick, SC: Hem Branch Publishing, 2009. p. 224.

388. *The Massachusetts Spy: Or, American Oracle of Liberty*. IX: 429, p. 2. Massey, Gregory D. *A Hero's Life: John Laurens and the American Revolution*. Ph.D. Thesis, University of South Carolina, 1992. pp. 118–120, 134–136. Ripley, Warren. *Battleground: South Carolina in the Revolution*. Charleston, SC: Evening Post, 1983. pp. 24–28. Davies, K.G. *Documents of the American Revolution 1770–1783*. (Colonial Office Series) Shannon: Irish University Press 1972, 1981. 12: 127. Lipscomb, Terry W. South Carolina Revolutionary Battles: Part Two. *Names in South Carolina*. XXI (Winter 1974). South Carolina Historical Society, 1974. p. 23. Moultrie, William. *Memoirs of the American Revolution so far as it related to the States of North and South Carolina and Georgia*. New York, 1802; (Eyewitness Accounts of the American Revolution). [New York] New York Times [1968]. I: 393–404. Lee, Henry. *Memoirs of the War in the Southern Department of the United States*. New York: University Publishing Co., 1869. p. 125. James, William Dobein. *A Sketch of the Life of Brig. General Francis Marion, and a History of his Brigade, from its Rise in June 1780, until Disbanded in December, 1782*. Charleston, SC: Gould and Riley, 1821. p. 8. *A List of all the officers of the Army: viz. the general and field officers; the officers of the several troops, regiments, independent companies, and garrisons: with an alphabetical index to the whole. Also, a list of the officers of the Royal Regiment of Artillery, the Corps of Engineers, the Irish Artillery and Engineers, and of the Marine Forces: the officers on half pay; and a succession of colonels. To which are likewise added the officers of the militia forces, and of the fencible and provincial regiments in Great Britain*. [London, England?]: War-Office, 1780. p. 302. *The Providence Gazette; and Country Journal*. XVI: 807, p. 2. O'Kelley, Patrick. *Nothing But Blood and Slaughter*. Booklocker.com, 2004. 1: 272–74.

389. Parker, John C. *Parker's Guide to the Revolutionary War in South Carolina: battles, skirmishes and murders*. Patrick, SC: Hem Branch Publishing, 2009. p. 225.

390. Tarleton, Banastre. *A History of the Campaigns of 1780 and 1781 in the Southern Provinces of North America*, London, 1787; (Eyewitness Accounts of the American Revolution). [New York] New York Times [1968]. pp. 7–8.

391. Tarleton, Banastre. *A History of the Campaigns of 1780 and 1781 in the Southern Provinces of North America*, London, 1787; (Eyewitness Accounts of the American Revolution). [New York] New York Times [1968]. pp. 7–8. Scott, Ruth. Loyalist Anthony Allaire. *Officers Quarterly*. York-Sunbury Historical Society of Fredericton, New

Brunswick. Summer, 1997. Johnson, Uzal. *Memo of Occurrence During the Campaign of 1780*. South Carolina Historical Society, Military Manuscripts. pp. 5–6. Stryker, William Scudder. *The New Jersey Volunteers in the Revolutionary War*. Trenton, 1887. pp. 9, 57. Hough, Franklin Benjamin, ed. *The siege of Charleston by the British fleet and army, under the command of Admiral Arbuthnot and Sir Henry Clinton, which terminated with the surrender of that place on the 12th of May, 1780*. Albany, J. Munsell, 1867. Spartanburg, SC: Reprint Company, 1975. pp. 157–159. Lipscomb, Terry W. South Carolina Revolutionary Battles: Part Two. *Names in South Carolina*. XXI (Winter 1974). South Carolina Historical Society, 1974. p. 25. Part Ten. *Names in South Carolina*. XXX (Winter 1983). South Carolina Historical Society, 1983. pp. 25–26. Hayes, John T. *The Saddlebag Almanac*. VI (Jan. 1998) pp. 10–12, 28. O'Kelley, Patrick. *Nothing But Blood and Slaughter*. Booklocker.com, 2004. 2: 123. Parker, John C. *Parker's Guide to the Revolutionary War in South Carolina: battles, skirmishes and murders*. Patrick, SC: Hem Branch Publishing, 2009. p. 218. Smith, Gordon Burns. *Morningstars of Liberty: the Revolutionary War in Georgia, 1775–1783*. Milledgeville, GA: Boyd Publishing, 2006. I: 204.

392. Allaire, Anthony. *Diary of Lieut. Anthony Allaire*. (Eyewitness Accounts of the American Revolution). [New York] New York Times [1968]. Johnson, Uzal. *Memo of Occurrence During the Campaign of 1780*. South Carolina Historical Society, Military Manuscripts. pp. 8–11. Johnson, Uzal, 1757?–1827 *Captured at Kings Mountain: the journal of Uzal Johnson, a loyalist surgeon*. edited by Wade S. Kolb III and Robert M. Weir; with the assistance of Anne H. Weir. Columbia : University of South Carolina Press, c2011. p. 5. Tarleton, Banastre. *A History of the Campaigns of 1780 and 1781 in the Southern Provinces of North America*. London, 1787; (Eyewitness Accounts of the American Revolution). [New York] New York Times [1968]. pp. 7–8. Cannon. Robert. *Historical Record of the Seventeenth Regiment of Light Dragoons; Lancers: Containing an Account of the Formation of the Regiment in 1759, and of its Subsequent Services to 1841*. London: John W. Parker, 1843. pp. 26–27. Hayes, John T. *The Saddlebag Almanac*. VI (Jan. 1998), pp. 10–12, 28. James, William Dobein. *A Sketch of the Life of Brig. General Francis Marion, and a History of his Brigade, from its Rise in June 1780, until Disbanded in December, 1782*. Charleston, SC: Gould and Riley, 1821. p. 56. Scott, Ruth. Loyalist Anthony Allaire. *Officers Quarterly*. York-Sunbury Historical Society of Fredericton, New Brunswick. Summer 1997. Lipscomb, Terry W. South Carolina Revolutionary Battles: Part Two. *Names in South Carolina*. XXI (Winter 1974). South Carolina Historical Society, 1974. pp. 25–26. O'Kelley, Patrick. *Nothing But Blood and Slaughter*. Booklocker.com, 2004. 2: 124–25. Parker, John C. *Parker's Guide to the Revolutionary War in South Carolina: battles, skirmishes and murders*. Patrick, SC: Hem Branch Publishing, 2009. p. 149–150.

393. Cannon. Robert. *Historical Record of the Seventeenth Regiment of Light Dragoons; Lancers: Containing an Account of the Formation of the Regiment in 1759, and of its Subsequent Services to 1841*. London: John W. Parker, 1843. pp. 26–27. Scott, Ruth. Loyalist Anthony Allaire. *Officers Quarterly*. York-Sunbury Historical Society of Fredericton, New Brunswick. Summer 1997. James, William Dobein. *A Sketch of the Life of Brig. Gen. Francis Marion, and a History of his Brigade, from its Rise in June 1780, until Disbanded in December, 1782*. Charleston, SC: Gould and Riley, 1821. p. 56. Johnson, Uzal. *Memo of Occurrence During the Campaign of 1780*. South Carolina Historical Society, Military Manuscripts. p. 15. Hayes, John T. *The Saddlebag Almanac*. VI (Jan. 1998), p. 13. O'Kelley, Patrick. *Nothing But Blood and Slaughter*. Booklocker.com, 2004. 2: 127. Parker, John C. *Parker's Guide to the Revolutionary War in South Carolina: battles, skirmishes and murders*. Patrick, SC: Hem Branch Publishing, 2009. p. 102.

394. Tarleton, Banastre. *A History of the Campaigns of 1780 and 1781 in the Southern Provinces of North America*, London, 1787; (Eyewitness Accounts of the American Revolution). [New York] New York Times [1968]. pp. 19–20. Parker, John C. *Parker's Guide to the Revolutionary War in South Carolina: battles, skirmishes and murders*. Patrick, SC: Hem Branch Publishing, 2009. p. 57.

395. Allaire, Anthony. *Diary of Lieut. Anthony Allaire*. (Eyewitness Accounts of the American Revolution). [New York] New York Times [1968]. Babits, Lawrence E. *A Devil of a Whipping, the Battle of Cowpens*. Chapel Hill, NC: University of North Carolina Press, 1998. James, William Dobein. *A Sketch of the Life of Brig. Gen. Francis Marion, and a History of his Brigade, from its Rise in June 1780, until Disbanded in December, 1782*. Charleston, SC: Gould and Riley, 1821. Lossing, Benson John. *The Pictorial Field-book of the Revolution; or, Illustrations, by pen and pencil, of the history, biography, scenery, relics, and traditions of the War for Independence*. New York, Harper & Brothers [1860]. Tarleton, Banastre. *A History of the Campaigns of 1780 and 1781 in the Southern Provinces of North America*. London, 1787; (Eyewitness Accounts of the American Revolution). [New York]: New York Times, [1968]. Parker, John C. *Parker's Guide to the Revolutionary War in South Carolina: battles, skirmishes and murders*. Patrick, SC: Hem Branch Publishing, 2009. p. 58.

396. McCrady, Edward. *History of South Carolina in the Revolution, 1775–1780*. New York: Paladin Press, 1969 (reprint of 1901 ed.). chapter 12. Parker, John C. *Parker's Guide to the Revolutionary War in South Carolina: battles, skirmishes and murders*. Patrick, SC: Hem Branch Publishing, 2009. p. 59.

397. Brown, Tarleton. *Memoirs of Tarleton Brown, a Captain in the Revolutionary Army, Written by Himself, with a Preface and Notes by Charles I. Bushnell*. New York: Privately Printed, 1862. pp. 15–17. Parker, John C. *Parker's Guide to the Revolutionary War in South Carolina: battles, skirmishes and murders*. Patrick, SC: Hem Branch Publishing, 2009. p. 14.

398. Brown, Tarleton. *Memoirs of Tarleton Brown, a Captain in the Revolutionary Army, Written by Himself, with a Preface and Notes by Charles I. Bushnell*. New York: Privately Printed, 1862. p. 31. Parker, John C. *Parker's Guide to the Revolutionary War in South Carolina: battles, skirmishes and murders*. Patrick, SC: Hem Branch Publishing, 2009. p. 14.

399. Parker, John C. *Parker's Guide to the Revolutionary War in South Carolina: battles, skirmishes and murders*. Patrick, SC: Hem Branch Publishing, 2009. p. 9.

400. McCrady, Edward. *History of South Carolina in the Revolution, 1775–1780*. New York: Paladin Press, 1969 (reprint of 1901 ed.). 3:669–700. *The Proceedings of the South Carolina Historical Association*. South Carolina Historical Association. 1945. p. 27. Parker, John C. *Parker's Guide to the Revolutionary War in South Carolina: battles, skirmishes and murders*. Patrick, SC: Hem Branch Publishing, 2009. p. 139.

Notes 345

401. www.carolana.com/SC/Revolution/revolution_nelsons_ferry_2.html. James, William Dobein. *A Sketch of the Life of Brig. General Francis Marion, and a History of his Brigade, from its Rise in June 1780, until Disbanded in December, 1782.* Charleston, SC: Gould and Riley, 1821.

402. *The Pennsylvania Gazette.* Oct. 27, 1779. Hough, Franklin B. *The Siege of Savannah by the Combined American and French Forces under the command of General Lincoln and the Count D'Estaing in the Autumn of 1779.* Albany: J. Munsell, 1866. pp. 102–104, 143–144. Jones, Charles Colcock, Jr. *The siege of Savannah by the fleet of Count d'Estaing in 1779.* [New York]: New York Times [1968]. pp. 23, 61–62. Cowan, Bob. The Siege of Savannah, 1779. *Military Collector and Historian.* XXVII: 2 (Summer 1975) p. 55. O'Kelley, Patrick. *Nothing But Blood and Slaughter.* Booklocker.com, 2004. 1: 311–312.

403. Marx, Robert F. *Shipwrecks in the Americas.* New York: Dover Publications, 1987. Parker, John C. *Parker's Guide to the Revolutionary War in South Carolina: battles, skirmishes and murders.* Patrick, SC: Hem Branch Publishing, 2009. p. 32.

404. *The Royal Georgia Gazette.* Sept. 7, 1780. Spence, E. Lee. *Shipwrecks of South Carolina and Georgia: (includes Spence's list, 1520–1865).* Sullivan's Island, SC (P.O. Drawer V, Sullivan's Island 29482): Sea Research Society, 1984. p. 259. Parker, John C. *Parker's Guide to the Revolutionary War in South Carolina: battles, skirmishes and murders.* Patrick, SC: Hem Branch Publishing, 2009. p. 31.

405. Jones, Charles Colcock, Jr. *The History of Georgia.* Boston: Houghton, Mifflin and Company, 1883. II: 499–501. O'Kelley, Patrick. *Nothing But Blood and Slaughter.* Booklocker.com, 2004. 3: 378–79.

406. Parker, John C. *Parker's Guide to the Revolutionary War in South Carolina: battles, skirmishes and murders.* Patrick, SC: Hem Branch Publishing, 2009. p. 37. Peeples, Robert E. H. *Tales of Ante Bellum Hilton Head Island Families: Hilton Head Island and our family circle.* [S.l.: s.n.], 1970. p. 41. Rowland, Lawrence Sanders; Moore, Alexander; Rogers, George C. *The History of Beaufort County, South Carolina.* Columbia: University of South Carolina Press, 1996–. Vol. 1: 1514–1861 p. 256.

407. Parker, John C. *Parker's Guide to the Revolutionary War in South Carolina: battles, skirmishes and murders.* Patrick, SC: Hem Branch Publishing, 2009. p. 33.

408. Parker, John C. *Parker's Guide to the Revolutionary War in South Carolina: battles, skirmishes and murders.* Patrick, SC: Hem Branch Publishing, 2009. p. 34. Rowland, Lawrence Sanders; Moore, Alexander; Rogers, George C. *The History of Beaufort County, South Carolina.* Columbia: University of South Carolina Press, 1996–. Vol. 1: 1514–1861 p. 239–240.

409. Parker, John C. *Parker's Guide to the Revolutionary War in South Carolina: battles, skirmishes and murders.* Patrick, SC: Hem Branch Publishing, 2009. p. 167.

410. Lieutenant Colonel William Harden to Brig. General Francis Marion. Force Transcripts: Library of Congress. Brown, Tarleton. *Memoirs of Tarleton Brown, a Captain in the Revolutionary Army, Written by Himself, with a Preface and Notes by Charles I. Bushnell.* New York: Privately Printed, 1862. Southern Studies Program. *Figures of the Revolution in South Carolina, An Anthology.* Spartanburg, Anderson, Beaufort, Aiken, Florence, Georgetown. Columbia: University of South Carolina, 1976. pp. 216–217. Commager, Henry S. and Richard B. Morris, eds. *The Spirit of '76: the Story of the American Revolution as Told by Participants.* Bicentennial edition. New York: Harper and Row, 1976. p. 1171. Hayes, John T. *The Saddlebag Almanac.* IX (Jan. 2001), p. 71. O'Kelley, Patrick. *Nothing But Blood and Slaughter.* Booklocker.com, 2004. 3: 181. Parker, John C. *Parker's Guide to the Revolutionary War in South Carolina: battles, skirmishes and murders.* Patrick, SC: Hem Branch Publishing, 2009. p. 167.

411. *The Royal Gazette.* April 11, 1781. Lieutenant Colonel William Harden to Brig. Gen. Francis Marion. Force Transcripts: Library of Congress. Parker, John C. *Parker's Guide to the Revolutionary War in South Carolina: battles, skirmishes and murders.* Patrick, SC: Hem Branch Publishing, 2009. p. 149–150.

412. Parker, John C. *Parker's Guide to the Revolutionary War in South Carolina: battles, skirmishes and murders.* Patrick, SC: Hem Branch Publishing, 2009. p. 149–150.

413. Gibbes, Robert Wilson. *Documentary History of the American Revolution.* New York: D. Appleton & Co., 1855 (3 vols: 1764–1776, 1776–1782, and 1781–1782). reprinted New York Times & Arno Press, 1971. III: 54. Lieutenant Colonel William Harden to Brig. Gen. Francis Marion. Force Transcripts: Library of Congress. Simms, William Gilmore. *The Life of Francis Marion.* New York, 1844. p. 135. Brown, Tarleton. *Memoirs of Tarleton Brown, a Captain in the Revolutionary Army, Written by Himself, with a Preface and Notes by Charles I. Bushnell.* New York: Privately Printed, 1862. Ervin, Sara Sullivan. *South Carolinians in the Revolution.* Baltimore: Genealogical Publishing Company, Inc., 1971. p. 67. Hayes, John T. T*he Saddlebag Almanac.* IX (Jan. 2001), p. 72. O'Kelley, Patrick. *Nothing But Blood and Slaughter.* Booklocker.com, 2004. 3: 184. Parker, John C. *Parker's Guide to the Revolutionary War in South Carolina: battles, skirmishes and murders.* Patrick, SC: Hem Branch Publishing, 2009. p. 35.

414. Parker, John C. *Parker's Guide to the Revolutionary War in South Carolina: battles, skirmishes and murders.* Patrick, SC: Hem Branch Publishing, 2009. p. 167.

415. Jarvis, Stephen, "An American's Experiences in the British Army," *Journal of American History.* 1 (Sept. 1907), pp. 441–64. Hayes, John T. *The Saddlebag Almanac.* X (Jan. 2002) pp. 47–48. Southern Studies Program. *Figures of the Revolution in South Carolina, An Anthology.* Spartanburg, Anderson, Beaufort, Aiken, Florence, Georgetown. Columbia: University of South Carolina, 1976. pp. 299–300. Simcoe, John Graves. *Simcoe's Military Journal. A History of the Operations of a Partisan Corps Called the Queen's Rangers, Commanded by Lieut. Colonel J. G. Simcoe, During the War of the American Revolution.* New-York: Bartlett & Welford, 1844; [New York]: New York Times; Arno Press. Eyewitness Accounts of the American Revolution. [1968]. pp. 246–247. Chesney, Alexander. *The Journal of Alexander Chesney, a South Carolina Loyalist in the Revolution and After.* edited by E. A. Jones. Columbus, Ohio: Ohio State University, 1921. pp. 11–12. Brown, Tarleton. *Memoirs of Tarleton Brown, a Captain in the Revolutionary Army, Written by Himself, with a Preface and Notes by Charles I. Bushnell.* New York: Privately Printed, 1862. O'Kelley, Patrick. *Nothing*

But Blood and Slaughter. Booklocker.com, 2004. 3: 270–72. Parker, John C. *Parker's Guide to the Revolutionary War in South Carolina: battles, skirmishes and murders*. Patrick, SC: Hem Branch Publishing, 2009. p. 153.

416. *Royal Georgia Gazette*. 126 (July 26, 1781), p. 4. *Charlestown Royal Gazette*. (July 10, 1781). Lipscomb, Terry W. South Carolina Revolutionary Battles: Part Seven. *Names in South Carolina* XXVI (Winter 1979). South Carolina Historical Society, 1979. p. 31. O'Kelley, Patrick. *Nothing But Blood and Slaughter*. Booklocker.com, 2004. 3: 281. Parker, John C. *Parker's Guide to the Revolutionary War in South Carolina: battles, skirmishes and murders*. Patrick, SC: Hem Branch Publishing, 2009. p. 154.

417. Letters to General Greene and Others. *The South Carolina Historical and Genealogical Magazine*. XVI: 3 (July 1915); 4 (Oct. 1915) pp. 107–108. Lipscomb, Terry W. South Carolina Revolutionary Battles: Part Seven. *Names in South Carolina* XXVI (Winter 1979). South Carolina Historical Society, 1979. p. 31. O'Kelley, Patrick. *Nothing But Blood and Slaughter*. Booklocker.com, 2004. 3: 311–312. Parker, John C. *Parker's Guide to the Revolutionary War in South Carolina: battles, skirmishes and murders*. Patrick, SC: Hem Branch Publishing, 2009. p. 151.

418. Brown, Tarleton. *Memoirs of Tarleton Brown, a Captain in the Revolutionary Army, Written by Himself, with a Preface and Notes by Charles I. Bushnell*. New York: Privately Printed, 1862. *The Pennsylvania Gazette*. Oct. 3, 1781. O'Kelley, Patrick. *Nothing But Blood and Slaughter*. Booklocker.com, 2004. 3: 310–11. Parker, John C. *Parker's Guide to the Revolutionary War in South Carolina: battles, skirmishes and murders*. Patrick, SC: Hem Branch Publishing, 2009. pp. 312, 313, 316.

419. *Encyclopedia of the American Revolution*. Harold E. Selesky, editor in chief. 2nd ed. Detroit: Charles Scribner's Sons, 2007. I: 343–347. *The Encyclopedia of the American Revolutionary War: a political, social, and military history*. Gregory Fremont-Barnes, Richard Alan Ryerson, editors. Santa Barbara, CA: ABC-CLIO, 2006. II: 391–395. Davies, K.G. *Documents of the American Revolution 1770–1783*. (Colonial Office Series) Shannon: Irish University Press 1972, 1981. XI. Greene, Nathanael. *The Papers of General Nathanael Greene*. Richard K. Showman, ed. Chapel Hill: the University of North Carolina Press, published for the Rhode Island Historical Society. c1976–2006. vol. 9. Higginbotham, Don. *The War of American Independence: Military Attitudes, Policies, and Practice, 1763–1789*. New York: Macmillan, 1971. Lee, Henry. *Memoirs of the War in the Southern Department of the United States*. New York: University Publishing Co., 1869. Mackenzie, Frederick. *The Diary of Frederick Mackenzie*. Cambridge, MA: Harvard University Press, 1930. Royster, Charles. *Light-Horse Harry Lee and the Legacy of the American Revolution*. New York: Knopf, 1981. Symonds, Craig L. *A Battlefield Atlas of the American Revolution*. Mount Pleasant, SC: Nautical and Aviation Publishing Company of America, 1986. Tarleton, Banastre. *A History of the Campaigns of 1780 and 1781 in the Southern Provinces of North America*. London: T. Cadell, 1787; [sl]: the New York Times & Arno Press, 1968. Ward, Christopher. *The War of the Revolution*. New York: Macmillan, 1952. 823–834. Parker, John C. *Parker's Guide to the Revolutionary War in South Carolina: battles, skirmishes and murders*. Patrick, SC: Hem Branch Publishing, 2009. p. 318–319. Smith, Gordon Burns. *Morningstars of Liberty: the Revolutionary War in Georgia, 1775–1783*. Milledgeville, GA: Boyd Publishing, 2006. I: 252–254.

419a. Parker, John C. *Parker's Guide to the Revolutionary War in South Carolina: battles, skirmishes and murders*. Patrick, SC: Hem Branch Publishing, 2009. pp. 168–170.

420. Parker, John C. *Parker's Guide to the Revolutionary War in South Carolina: battles, skirmishes and murders*. Patrick, SC: Hem Branch Publishing, 2009. p. 17.

421. Lipscomb, Terry W. South Carolina Revolutionary Battles: Part Ten. *Names in South Carolina*. XXX (Winter 1983). South Carolina Historical Society, 1983. p. 11. Draper, Lyman. Thomas Sumter Papers, Draper Manuscript Collection, State Historical Society of Wisconsin. 16VV432. O'Kelley, Patrick. *Nothing But Blood and Slaughter*. Booklocker.com, 2004. 3: 371. Parker, John C. *Parker's Guide to the Revolutionary War in South Carolina: battles, skirmishes and murders*. Patrick, SC: Hem Branch Publishing, 2009. p. 20.

422. Caruthers, Eli W. *The Old North State in 1776*. Guilford County Genealogical Society, 1985. pp. 57–58. O'Kelley, Patrick. *Nothing But Blood and Slaughter*. Booklocker.com, 2004. 3: 380. Parker, John C. *Parker's Guide to the Revolutionary War in South Carolina: battles, skirmishes and murders*. Patrick, SC: Hem Branch Publishing, 2009. p. 20.

423. Brown, Tarleton. *Memoirs of Tarleton Brown, a Captain in the Revolutionary Army, Written by Himself, with a Preface and Notes by Charles I. Bushnell*. New York: Privately Printed, 1862. pp. 24–25. Parker, John C. *Parker's Guide to the Revolutionary War in South Carolina: battles, skirmishes and murders*. Patrick, SC: Hem Branch Publishing, 2009. p. 21.

424. Brown, Tarleton. *Memoirs of Tarleton Brown, a Captain in the Revolutionary Army, Written by Himself, with a Preface and Notes by Charles I. Bushnell*. New York: Privately Printed, 1862. p. 27. Parker, John C. *Parker's Guide to the Revolutionary War in South Carolina: battles, skirmishes and murders*. Patrick, SC: Hem Branch Publishing, 2009. p. 21.

425. Lipscomb, Terry W. South Carolina Revolutionary Battles: Part Ten. *Names in South Carolina*. XXX (Winter 1983). South Carolina Historical Society, 1983. pp. 10–11. O'Kelley, Patrick. *Nothing But Blood and Slaughter*. Booklocker.com, 2004. 3: 409. Parker, John C. *Parker's Guide to the Revolutionary War in South Carolina: battles, skirmishes and murders*. Patrick, SC: Hem Branch Publishing, 2009. p. 22.

426. Parker, John C. *Parker's Guide to the Revolutionary War in South Carolina: battles, skirmishes and murders*. Patrick, SC: Hem Branch Publishing, 2009. p. 23.

427. British National Archives. Audit Office, Class 13, Vol. 4 p. 321. O'Kelley, Patrick. *Nothing but Blood and Slaughter*. Booklocker.com, 2004. 4: 99–100. Parker, John C. *Parker's Guide to the Revolutionary War in South Carolina: battles, skirmishes and murders*. Patrick, SC: Hem Branch Publishing, 2009. p. 56.

428. Cashin, Edward J. and Heard Robertson. *Augusta and the American Revolution Events in the Backcountry*. Darien, GA, 1975. pp. 12–13. Davis, Robert Scott, Jr. *Georgia Citizens and Soldiers of the American Revolution*. Southern Historical Press, 1979. p. 161.

429. A Loyalist View of the Drayton-Tennent-Hart Mission to the Upcountry. Edited by James O'Donnell. *The South Carolina Historical Magazine*. 67:1 (Jan. 1966) p. 15. Cashin, Edward J. *The King's Ranger. Thomas Brown and the American Revolution on the Southern Frontier*. Athens: University of Georgia Press, 1989. pp. 27–28, 31–33. O'Kelley, Patrick. *Nothing but Blood and Slaughter*. Booklocker.com, 2004. 1: 39–40. Parker, John C. *Parker's Guide to the Revolutionary War in South Carolina: battles, skirmishes and murders*. Patrick, SC: Hem Branch Publishing, 2009. p. 179. Thomas Browne (sic) to Jonas Browne at Whitby, dated Charles Town, SC, 10 November 1775 in "Thomas Brown and the Sons of Liberty." *Richmond County* History, 28 (Augusta, GA: winter, 1997): 4–10. *A History of the Georgia Loyalists and the Plantation Period In the Turks and Caicos Islands*. Ph.D. dissertation, Middle Tennessee University, 1983. pp. 117–20. Landrum, J. B. O. *Colonial and Revolutionary History of Upper South Carolina: embracing for the most part the primitive and colonial history of the territory comprising the original county of Spartanburg, with a general review of the entire military operations in the upper portions of South Carolina and portions of North Carolina*. Spartanburg, SC: Reprint Co., 1977, 1897. p. 48. Patrick Carr to John Martin, dated Silver Bluff, 22 August 1782, Letters of Patrick Carr, Terror To British Loyalists, To Governors John Martin and Lyman Hall, 1782 and 1783. *Georgia Historical Quarterly*, 1 (December 1917), p. 339. Smith, Gordon Burns. *Morningstars of Liberty: the Revolutionary War in Georgia, 1775–1783*. Milledgeville, GA: Boyd Publishing, 2006. I: 41–42.

430. Peckham, Howard Henry. *The Toll of Independence: engagements & battle casualties of the American Revolution*. edited by Howard H. Peckham. Chicago: University of Chicago Press, 1974. p. 9.

431. Kirkland, Thomas J. and Kennedy, Robert M. *Historic Camden*. State Company, 1905. pp. 111–114. Cashin, Edward J. *The King's Ranger. Thomas Brown and the American Revolution on the Southern Frontier*. Athens: University of Georgia Press, 1989. p. 35. Olson, Gary D. Loyalists and the American Revolution: Thomas Brown and the South Carolina Backcountry, 1775–1776. *The South Carolina Historical Magazine*. 68:4 (Oct. 1967) p. 216. Moultrie, William. *Memoirs of the American Revolution so far as it related to the States of North and South Carolina and Georgia*. New York, 1802; (Eyewitness accounts of the American Revolution). [New York]: New York Times, [1968]. 1: 96–101. Fanning, Nathaniel. *Fanning's Narrative*. (Eyewitness accounts of the American Revolution). [New York]: New York Times [1968, c1912]. pp. 20–23. Cann, Marvin L. "War in the Backcountry: The Siege of Ninety Six, May 22–June 19, 1781." *South Carolina Historical Magazine*. 72 (January 1971) pp. 14–15. O'Kelley, Patrick. *Nothing but Blood and Slaughter*. Booklocker.com, 2004. 1: 51–52. Parker, John C. *Parker's Guide to the Revolutionary War in South Carolina: battles, skirmishes and murders*. Patrick, SC: Hem Branch Publishing, 2009. p. 323.

432. Moultrie, William. *Memoirs of the American Revolution so far as it related to the States of North and South Carolina and Georgia*. New York, 1802; (Eyewitness accounts of the American Revolution). [New York]: New York Times, [1968]. 1: 80. Fanning, Nathaniel. *Fanning's Narrative*. (Eyewitness accounts of the American Revolution). [New York]: New York Times [1968, c1912]. pp. 22–23. Cann, Marvin L. "War in the Backcountry: The Siege of Ninety Six, May 22–June 19, 1781." *South Carolina Historical Magazine*. 72 (January 1971) pp. 9–10. Jones, Lewis P. *The South Carolina Civil War of 1775*. Lexington, SC: Sandlapper Store, 1975. pp. 33–34. Griffiths, John William. *"To Receive them Properly ": Charlestown prepares for war, 1775–1776*. M.A. Thesis, University of South Carolina, 1992. p. 121. www.carolana.com/SC/Revolution/revolution_ninety_six_kirkland.html. O'Kelley, Patrick. *Nothing but Blood and Slaughter*. Booklocker.com, 2004. 1: 36–37.

433. Cancellation notice for a recruitment meeting, distributed by Drayton due to the risk of "civil bloodshed" perpetrated by Loyalist leader Moses Kirkland, District of Ninety Six, South Carolina, 30 August 1775. *"we shall be involved in a civil war in spite of our teeth:" Recruiting Backcountry Settlers to the Patriot Cause, 1775: Reports to the South Carolina Council of Safety, August–September 1775*. National Humanities Center Resource Toolbox Making the Revolution: America, 1763–1791. 30 August 1775. Report to the S. C. Council of Safety by Drayton. at Mr. Hammond's near Augusta. p. 7 1 September 1775. *Report to the S. C. Council of Safety by Tennent*. Long Canes. p. 7. nationalhumanitiescenter.org/pds/makingrev/rebellion/text4/backcountrydraytontennent.pdf. Cann, Marvin L. Prelude to War: the First Battle of Ninety Six: November 19–21, 1775. *The South Carolina Historical Magazine*. 76:4 (Oct. 1975), pp. 197–214. *Encyclopedia of the American Revolution*. Harold E. Selesky, editor in chief. 2nd Ed. Detroit: Charles Scribner's Sons, 2007. 2: 837. Chesney, Alexander. *The Journal of Alexander Chesney, a South Carolina Loyalist in the Revolution and After*, edited by E. A. Jones. Columbus, Ohio: Ohio State University, 1921. p. 69. Ripley, Warren. *Battleground: South Carolina in the Revolution*. Charleston, SC: Evening Post, 1983. pp. 10–12. Gibbes, Robert Wilson. *Documentary History of the American Revolution*. New York: D. Appleton & Co., 1855 (3 vols: 1764–1776, 1776–1782, 1781–1782). reprinted New York Times & Arno Press, 1971 (3 vols. in 1). 1: pp. 172–174. Cashin, Edward J. *The King's Ranger. Thomas Brown and the American Revolution on the Southern Frontier*. Athens: University of Georgia Press, 1989. p. 35. Laurens, Henry. *The Papers of Henry Laurens*. Columbia: Published for the South Carolina Historical Society by the University of South Carolina Press, [1968]. 1: 374–378, 80, 145–146, 149–150, 152. O'Kelley, Patrick. *Nothing but Blood and Slaughter*. Booklocker.com, 2004. 1: 46–48.

434. Parker, John C. *Parker's Guide to the Revolutionary War in South Carolina: battles, skirmishes and murders*. Patrick, SC: Hem Branch Publishing, 2009. p. 200. Smith, Gordon Burns. *Morningstars of Liberty: the Revolutionary War in Georgia, 1775–1783*. Milledgeville, GA: Boyd Publishing, 2006. I: 42–43. Scoggins, Michael C.; Edgar, Walter. *The Day It Rained Militia: Huck's Defeat and the Revolution in the South Carolina Backcountry, May–July 1780*. Charleston: The History Press, c2005. p. 31. *Extracts from the Journals of the Provincial Congress of South Carolina, 1775–1776 South Carolina*. Provincial Congress. Columbia : South Carolina Archives Dept., 1960. 7–8 and 13 November 1775. pp. 99–105, 137–138.

435. Hairr, John. *Colonel David Fanning, The Adventures of a Carolina Loyalist*. Erwin, NC: Averasboro Press, 2000. p. 58. Fanning, Nathaniel. *Fanning's Narrative*. (Eyewitness accounts of the American Revolution). [New York]: New York Times [1968, c1912]. p. 24. O'Kelley, Patrick. *Nothing but Blood and Slaughter*. Booklocker.com, 2004. 1: 109.

436. Parker, John C. *Parker's Guide to the Revolutionary War in South Carolina: battles, skirmishes and murders*. Patrick, SC: Hem Branch Publishing, 2009. p. 200. Smith, Gordon Burns. *Morningstars of Liberty: the Revolutionary*

War in Georgia, 1775–1783. Milledgeville, GA: Boyd Publishing, 2006. I: 252–254. www.carolana.com/SC/Revolution/revolution_battle_of_ninety_six.html.

437. O'Kelley, Patrick. *Nothing But Blood and Slaughter*. Booklocker.com, 2004. 2: 390.

438. Extract of a letter from General Marion, dated April 21st, 1781. *The Connecticut Gazette and the Universal Intelligencer*. XVIII: 919, p. 1. Parker, John C. *Parker's Guide to the Revolutionary War in South Carolina: battles, skirmishes and murders*. Patrick, SC: Hem Branch Publishing, 2009. p. 288.

439. Seymour, William. Journal of the Southern Expedition, 1780–1783. *Papers of the Historical Society of Delaware*: XV. Wilmington: the Historical Society of Delaware, 1896. p. 27. Kirkwood, Robert. The Journal and Orderly Book of Captain Robert Kirkwood of the Delaware Regiment of the Continental Line. *Papers of the Historical Society of Delaware*. 56 (1910) p. 18. Pancake, John S. *This Destructive War: the British Campaign in the Carolinas*. Tuscaloosa: University of Alabama Press, 1985. p. 445. O'Kelley, Patrick. *Nothing But Blood and Slaughter*. Booklocker.com, 2004. 3: 242–43.

440. Kirkwood, Robert. The Journal and Orderly Book of Captain Robert Kirkwood of the Delaware Regiment of the Continental Line. *Papers of the Historical Society of Delaware*. 56 (1910) p. 18. Ward, Christopher L. *The Delaware Continentals*. Historical Society of Delaware, 1941. p. 445. O'Kelley, Patrick. *Nothing But Blood and Slaughter*. Booklocker.com, 2004. 3: 244–245.

441. *The Worcester Magazine*. XVII: 821 (Jan. 1, 1789), p. 1. Hayes, John T. *The Saddlebag Almanac*. X (Jan. 2002) pp. 49–50. Tarleton, Banastre. *A History of the Campaigns of 1780 and 1781 in the Southern Provinces of North America*. London, 1787; (Eyewitness accounts of the American Revolution). [New York]: New York Times, [1968]. pp. 486–487. Dann, John C. *The Revolution Remembered, Eyewitness Account of the War for Independence*. University of Chicago Press, 1980. p. 230. Ervin, Sara Sullivan. *South Carolinians in the Revolution*. Baltimore: Genealogical Publishing Company, Inc., 1971. pp. 83–84. Draper, Lyman. Thomas Sumter Papers, Draper Manuscript Collection, State Historical Society of Wisconsin. O'Kelley, Patrick. *Nothing But Blood and Slaughter*. Booklocker.com, 2004. 3: 275–76. Parker, John C. *Parker's Guide to the Revolutionary War in South Carolina: battles, skirmishes and murders*. Patrick, SC: Hem Branch Publishing, 2009. p. 269.

442. Parker, John C. *Parker's Guide to the Revolutionary War in South Carolina: battles, skirmishes and murders*. Patrick, SC: Hem Branch Publishing, 2009. p. 270.

443. *Continental Journal*. CCLXXXVII (Aug. 23, 1781), p. 2.

444. Tarleton, Banastre. *A History of the Campaigns of 1780 and 1781 in the Southern Provinces of North America*. London, 1787; (Eyewitness Accounts of the American Revolution). [New York] New York Times [1968]. p. 523.

445. Extract of a letter from major-general Greene, dated head-quarters, on the High Hills of Santee, July 17, 1781. *The Pennsylvania Evening Post, and Public Advertiser*. 7:763 (Aug. 14, 1781) p. 126.

446. Johnson, Joseph. *Traditions and Reminiscences, Chiefly of the American Revolution in the South: including biographical sketches, incidents, and anecdotes, few of which have been published, particularly of residents in the upper country*. Charleston, SC: Walker & James, 1851. pp. 497–498. Parker, John C. *Parker's Guide to the Revolutionary War in South Carolina: battles, skirmishes and murders*. Patrick, SC: Hem Branch Publishing, 2009. p. 321–323.

447. Draper, Lyman. Thomas Sumter Papers, Draper Manuscript Collection, State Historical Society of Wisconsin. 17VV32. Lambert, Robert Stansbury. *South Carolina Loyalists in the American Revolution*. Columbia: University of South Carolina, 1987. pp. 218–222. O'Kelley, Patrick. *Nothing But Blood and Slaughter*. Booklocker.com, 2004. 3: 307. Parker, John C. *Parker's Guide to the Revolutionary War in South Carolina: battles, skirmishes and murders*. Patrick, SC: Hem Branch Publishing, 2009. p. 249.

448. *Encyclopedia of the American Revolution*. Harold E. Selesky, editor in chief. 2nd ed. Detroit: Charles Scribner's Sons, 2007. II: 838–840. *The Encyclopedia of the American Revolutionary War: a political, social, and military history*. Gregory Fremont-Barnes, Richard Alan Ryerson, editors. Santa Barbara, CA: ABC-CLIO, 2006. II: 431–434. Bass, Robert Duncan. *Ninety Six: the Struggle for the South Carolina Backcountry*. Lexington, SC: Sandlapper Store, 1978. Cann. Marvin L. War in the Backcountry: the Siege of Ninety Six, May 22–June 19, 1781. *South Carolina Historical Magazine*. 72 (Jan. 1971): 1–14. Lumpkin, Henry. *From Savannah to Yorktown: the American Revolution in the South*. New York: Paragon, 1981. McCrady, Edward. *History of South Carolina in the Revolution, 1775–1780*. New York: Paladin Press, 1969 (reprint of 1901 ed.). Pancake, John S. *This Destructive War: the British Campaign in the Carolinas*. Tuscaloosa: University of Alabama Press, 1985. Nelson, Paul David. Military Genius [Nathanael Greene] at Work: Winning the Revolutionary War in the South. *William and Mary Quarterly*. 58 (2001): 1017–1022. Thayer, Theodore. *Nathanael Greene: Strategist of the American Revolution*. New York: Twayne, 1960. Ward, Christopher. *The War of the Revolution*. New York: Macmillan, 1952. pp. 816–822.

449. National Archives and Records Administration. Samuel Dunlap pension application S3310. National Archives and Records Administration. George Davidson pension application W283. Parker, John C. *Parker's Guide to the Revolutionary War in South Carolina: battles, skirmishes and murders*. Patrick, SC: Hem Branch Publishing, 2009. p. 195.

450. Saye, James Hodge. *Memoirs of Major Joseph McJunkin, Revolutionary Patriot*. [sl]: A Press, Inc., 1977. p. 6.

451. Parker, John C. *Parker's Guide to the Revolutionary War in South Carolina: battles, skirmishes and murders*. Patrick, SC: Hem Branch Publishing, 2009. p. 196.

452. Lawrence, James Walton. *Hogback Country*. The News Leader, 1982. pp. 13–15. O'Kelley, Patrick. *Nothing but Blood and Slaughter*. Booklocker.com, 2004. 1: 102. Landrum, J. B. O (John Belton O'Neall). *Colonial and Revolutionary History of Upper South Carolina: embracing for the most part the primitive and colonial history of the territory comprising the original county of Spartanburg, with a general review of the entire military operations in the upper portions of South Carolina and portions of North Carolina*. Spartanburg, SC: Reprint Co., 1977, 1897. pp. 87, 94–95.

Parker, John C. *Parker's Guide to the Revolutionary War in South Carolina: battles, skirmishes and murders.* Patrick, SC: Hem Branch Publishing, 2009. p. 327.

453. Brown, Douglas Summers. *The Catawba Indians: the people of the river.* Columbia, University of South Carolina Press, 1966. p. 263. Parker, John C. *Parker's Guide to the Revolutionary War in South Carolina: battles, skirmishes and murders.* Patrick, SC: Hem Branch Publishing, 2009. p. 197.

454. Saye, James Hodge. *Memoirs of Major Joseph McJunkin, Revolutionary Patriot.* [sl]: A. Press, Inc., 1977. (First printed in the Richmond, VA Watchman and Observer in 1847) p. 23. Chesney, Alexander. *The Journal of Alexander Chesney, a South Carolina Loyalist in the Revolution and After.* edited by E. A. Jones. Columbus, Ohio: Ohio State University, 1921. Southern Studies Program. *Figures of the Revolution in South Carolina, An Anthology.* Spartanburg, Anderson, Beaufort, Aiken, Florence, Georgetown. Columbia: University of South Carolina, 1976. pp. 174–175. Davis, Robert Scott, Jr. *Georgians in the Revolution: at Kettle Creek (Wilkes Co.) and Burke County.* Southern Historical Press, Inc., 1986. pp. 166–167. Lawrence, James Walton. *Hogback Country.* The News Leader, 1982. pp. 20–25. Draper, Lyman. *Kings Mountain and its Heroes: History of the Battle of King's Mountain, October 7th, 1780, and the Events Which Led To It.* The Overmountain Press, 1996. p. 80. Johnson, Uzal. *Memo of Occurrence During the Campaign of 1780.* South Carolina Historical Society, Military Manuscripts. pp. 54–56. Schenck, David. *North Carolina 1780–81.* Raleigh: Edwards and Broughton, Publishers, 1889. p. 123. Lipscomb, Terry W. South Carolina Revolutionary Battles: Part Three. *Names in South Carolina.* XXII (Winter 1975). South Carolina Historical Society, 1975. p. 35. Pancake, John S. *This Destructive War: the British Campaign in the Carolinas.* Tuscaloosa: University of Alabama Press, 1985. p. 96. Hayes, John T. *The Saddlebag Almanac.* VII (Jan. 1999), pp. 92–94. O'Kelley, Patrick. *Nothing But Blood and Slaughter.* Booklocker.com, 2004. 2: 202. Parker, John C. *Parker's Guide to the Revolutionary War in South Carolina: battles, skirmishes and murders.* Patrick, SC: Hem Branch Publishing, 2009. p. 327, 329. Smith, Gordon Burns. *Morningstars of Liberty: the Revolutionary War in Georgia, 1775–1783.* Milledgeville, GA: Boyd Publishing, 2006. I: 206–207. Allaire, Anthony. *Diary of Lieut. Anthony Allaire.* (Eyewitness accounts of the American Revolution). [New York] New York times [1968]. p. 500. Scoggins, Michael C.; Edgar, Walter. *The Day It Rained Militia: Huck's Defeat and the Revolution in the South Carolina Backcountry, May–July 1780.* Charleston: The History Press, c2005. p. 130.

455. Southern Studies Program. *Figures of the Revolution in South Carolina, An Anthology.* Spartanburg, Anderson, Beaufort, Aiken, Florence, Georgetown. Columbia: University of South Carolina, 1976. pp. 174–175. Lawrence, James Walton. *Hogback Country.* The News Leader, 1982. pp. 23–24. Schenck, David. *North Carolina 1780–81.* Raleigh: Edwards and Broughton, Publishers, 1889. p. 123. Lipscomb, Terry W. South Carolina Revolutionary Battles: Part Three. *Names in South Carolina.* XXII (Winter 1975). South Carolina Historical Society, 1975. p. 35. Hayes, John T. *The Saddlebag Almanac.* VIII (Jan. 2000), p. 95. O'Kelley, Patrick. *Nothing But Blood and Slaughter.* Booklocker.com, 2004. 2: 203. Parker, John C. *Parker's Guide to the Revolutionary War in South Carolina: battles, skirmishes and murders.* Patrick, SC: Hem Branch Publishing, 2009. p. 331.

456. Collins. James. *A Revolutionary Soldier.* Felician Democrat, 1859. pp. 51–54. Chesney, Alexander. *The Journal of Alexander Chesney, a South Carolina Loyalist in the Revolution and After.,* edited by E. A. Jones. Columbus, Ohio: Ohio State University, 1921. pp. 8–10. White, Katherine Keogh. *The King's Mountain Men, the story of the Battle with Sketches of the American Soldiers who took part.* Baltimore: Genealogical Publishing Company, 1966. pp. 3–215, 237, 245, 249–255, 262, 266–267, 271, 273, 275, 277, 283–285, 288–289, 292, 340, 406, 416–424, 456–461, 464–465, 467, 470, 473–476, 481–483. Draper, Lyman. *Kings Mountain and its Heroes: History of the Battle of King's Mountain, October 7th, 1780, and the Events Which Led To It.* The Overmountain Press, 1996. pp. 139–145. Kentucky Archives. Kentucky Pension Accounts. Moultrie, William. *Memoirs of the American Revolution so far as it related to the States of North and South Carolina and Georgia.* New York, 1802; (Eyewitness Accounts of the American Revolution). [New York] New York Times [1968]. II: 242–245. Young, Thomas. Memoir of a Revolutionary Patriot of South Carolina. *The Orion.* 3 (Oct. 1843) pp. 84–88 et seq. Johnson, Uzal. *Memo of Occurrence During the Campaign of 1780.* South Carolina Historical Society, Military Manuscripts. pp. 79–100. National Archives and Records Administration. Mathew Sparks Pension application #S31385. Schenck, David. *North Carolina 1780–'81, Being a History of the Invasion of the Carolinas by the British Army under Lord Cornwallis in 1780–'81.* Edwards & Broughton, Publishers, 1889. pp. 130–177. New York Historical Society. Gates Papers. Reel 12 p. 829. *The Pennsylvania Gazette.* Nov. 15, 1780; Oct. 25, 1780. National Archives and Records Administration. Pension Applications. RG 15 Microcopy 804. Robinson, Blackwell P. *The Revolutionary War Sketches of William R. Davie.* Raleigh: North Carolina Department of Cultural Resources, Division of Archives and History, 1976. p. 35. British National Archives. Cornwallis Papers. Class 30, Vol. 11 p. 3 folio 261–262. Lambert, Robert Stansbury. *South Carolina Loyalists in the American Revolution.* University of South Carolina Press, 1987. pp. 110–111, 144–147, 218–222. Ervin. Sara Sullivan. *South Carolinians in the Revolution.* Baltimore: Genealogical Publishing Company, Inc., 1971. pp. 80–87. MacKenzie, Roderick. *Strictures on Lieutenant Colonel Tarleton's History of the Campaigns of 1780 and 1781 in the Southern Provinces, to Which is Added a Detail of the Siege of Ninety Six, and the Recapture of the Island of New Providence.* London, 1787. pp. 66–67. Commager, Henry S. and Richard B. Morris, eds. *The Spirit of '76: the Story of the American Revolution as Told by Participants.* Bicentennial edition. New York: Harper and Row, 1976. pp. 1142–1143. Pancake, John S. *This Destructive War: the British Campaign in the Carolinas.* Tuscaloosa: University of Alabama Press, 1985. pp. 116–121. *Royal Gazette.* Feb. 24, 1781. Sanchez-Saavedera, E.M. *A Guide to Virginia Military Organizations in the American Revolution, 1774–1787.* Richmond, VA, 1978. pp. 143–144. Hill, William. *Colonel William Hill's Memoirs of the Revolution.* edited by A. S. Sally. Columbia, SC, 1921. Graves, William T. *James Williams: An American Patriot in the Carolina Backcountry.* Writers Club Press, 2002. p. 54. Draper, Lyman. Thomas Sumter Papers, Draper Manuscript Collection, State Historical Society of Wisconsin. 4VV213–215, 9VV28–42, 14VV177–179. Barefoot, Daniel W. *Touring South Carolina's Revolutionary War Sites.* Winston-Salem: John F. Blair, 1999. pp. 217, 242, 245, 252–261, 268–269, 335. O'Kelley, Patrick. *Nothing But Blood and Slaughter.* Booklocker.com, 2004. 3: 380–81. Parker, John C. *Parker's Guide to the Revolutionary War in*

South Carolina: battles, skirmishes and murders. Patrick, SC: Hem Branch Publishing, 2009. p. 329. Smith, Gordon Burns. *Morningstars of Liberty: the Revolutionary War in Georgia, 1775–1783*. Milledgeville, GA: Boyd Publishing, 2006. I: 206–207.

457. Lipscomb, Terry W. South Carolina Revolutionary Battles: Part Ten. *Names in South Carolina*. XXX (Winter 1983). South Carolina Historical Society, 1983. p. 15.

458. Southern Studies Program. *Figures of the Revolution in South Carolina, An Anthology*. Spartanburg, Anderson, Beaufort, Aiken, Florence, Georgetown. Columbia: University of South Carolina, 1976. p. 173. Lawrence, James Walton. *Hogback Country*. The News Leader, 1982. pp. 16–19. O'Kelley, Patrick. *Nothing But Blood and Slaughter*. Booklocker.com, 2004. 1: 113–114. Landrum, J. B. O. (John Belton O'Neall). *Colonial and Revolutionary History of Upper South Carolina: embracing for the most part the primitive and colonial history of the territory comprising the original county of Spartanburg, with a general review of the entire military operations in the upper portions of South Carolina and portions of North Carolina*. Spartanburg, SC: Reprint Co., 1977, 1897.

459. Correspondence with John Parker, author of *Parker's Guide to the Revolutionary War in South Carolina: battles, skirmishes and murders*. Patrick, SC: Hem Branch Publishing, 2009.

460. Parker, John C. *Parker's Guide to the Revolutionary War in South Carolina: battles, skirmishes and murders*. Patrick, SC: Hem Branch Publishing, 2009. p. 251.

461. Griffiths, John William. "To Receive them Properly:" *Charlestown prepares for war, 1775–1776*. M.A. Thesis, University of South Carolina, 1992. pp. 117–118. O'Kelley, Patrick. *Nothing but Blood and Slaughter*. Booklocker. com, 2004. 1: 39.

462. The Cherokee Attack on Captain James McCall's Camp June 26, 1776 from Gordon, John W. *South Carolina and the American Revolution: a battlefield history*. Columbia: University of South Carolina Press, 2003. www.schistory .net/3CLD/Articles/Cherokee.html. Hilborn, Nat & Sam. *Battleground of Freedom: South Carolina in the Revolution*. Columbia, SC: Sandlapper Press, 1970. pp. 59–63.

463. Nichols, John L. Alexander Cameron, British Agent Among the Cherokee, 1764–1781. *South Carolina Historical Magazine*. 97: 2 (April 1996) pp. 95–98, 105. Gibbes, Robert Wilson. *Documentary History of the American Revolution*. New York: D. Appleton & Co., 1855 (3 vols: 1764–1776, 1776–1782, and 1781–1782). reprinted New York Times & Arno Press, 1971. 2:26. Lipscomb, Terry W. South Carolina Revolutionary Battles: Part One. *Names in South Carolina*. XX (Winter 1973). South Carolina Historical Society, 1973. p. 21. Ripley, Warren. *Battleground: South Carolina in the Revolution*. Charleston, SC: Evening Post, 1983. p. 233. Heitman, Francis B. *Historical Register of Officers of the Continental Army during the War of the Revolution, April 1775 to December 1783*. Washington, DC.: the Rare Book Shop Publishing Company, 1914; Baltimore: Genealogical Publishing Company, 1967. p. 89. Moss, Bobby Gilmer. *Roster of South Carolina Patriots in the American Revolution*. Baltimore: Genealogical Pub. Co., 1983. p. 594. O'Kelley, Patrick. *Nothing But Blood and Slaughter*. Booklocker.com, 2004. 1: 113, 148.

464. *The Encyclopedia of the American Revolutionary War: a political, social, and military history*. Gregory Fremont-Barnes, Richard Alan Ryerson, editors. Santa Barbara, CA: ABC-CLIO, 2006. 4: 1365.

465. Salvador was the first person of the Jewish faith to hold public office in South Carolina (member of the First Provincial Congress) and the first Jew to be killed in the Revolution.

466. Charlestown, (South-Carolina) Aug. 14. *Dunlap's Pennsylvania Packet or, the General Advertiser*. V: 256 (September 17, 1776) p. 2. *Maryland Journal*. III: 144 (September 18, 1776) p. 5. *Pennsylvania Journal*. 1762 (September 17, 1776) p. 3. *The Pennsylvania Ledger: or the Virginia, Maryland, Pennsylvania, & New-Jersey Weekly Advertiser*. LXXXVII (September 21, 1776) p. 3. *Dunlap's Maryland Gazette Or The Baltimore General Advertiser*. II: LXXIV (September 24, 1776) p. 2. *The Virginia Gazette*. 1312 (September 27, 1776) p. 2. *Connecticut Journal*. 468 (October 2, 1776) p. 2. *The Essex Journal and New-Hampshire Packet*. III: 144 (October 4, 1776) p. 2. www.carolina .com/SC/Revolution/revolution_seneca_town.html.

467. Ramsey, J. G. M. (James Gettys McGready). *The Annals of Tennessee to the End of the Eighteenth Century; comprising its settlement, the Watauga Association, from 1769 to 1777; a part of North-Carolina, from 1777 to 1784; the state of Franklin, from 1784 to 1788; a part of North-Carolina, from 1788 to 1790; the territory of the U. States, South of the Ohio, from 1790 to 1796; the state of Tennessee, from 1796 to 1800*. Charleston: J. Russell, 1853; [Knoxville, reprinted for the East Tennessee Historical Society, 1967. p. 163. Parker, John C. *Parker's Guide to the Revolutionary War in South Carolina: battles, skirmishes and murders*. Patrick, SC: Hem Branch Publishing, 2009. p. 300.

468. The Cherokee Prayer Initiative historical notes page. web.archive.org/web/20101122170714/ genebrooks .com/cherokeehistory.html. Cherokee Prayer Site Guide www.geocities.ws/gileadintl/atrocity-list.html. Historical Notes on the Cherokee People by Linda Fulmer www.geocities.ws/gileadintl/cherokeehistory.html#VIII.%20 CHEROKEE%20SOURCES.

469. Ripley, Warren. *Battleground: South Carolina in the Revolution*. Charleston, SC: Evening Post, 1983. p. 233. Davis, Robert Scott, Jr. *Georgians in the Revolution: at Kettle Creek (Wilkes Co.) and Burke County*. Southern Historical Press, Inc., 1986. p. 131. Cashin, Edward J. *The King's Ranger. Thomas Brown and the American Revolution on the Southern Frontier*. Athens: University of Georgia Press, 1989. p. 52. Milling, Chapman J. *Red Carolinians*. The University of South Carolina Press, 1969. p. 253. Lipscomb, Terry W. South Carolina Revolutionary Battles: Part One. *Names in South Carolina*. XX (Winter 1973). South Carolina Historical Society, 1973. p. 22. Ervin. Sara Sullivan. *South Carolinians in the Revolution*. Baltimore: Genealogical Publishing Company, Inc., 1971. pp. 67–77. O'Donnell, James H. *Southern Indians in the American Revolution*. University of Tennessee Press, 1971. pp. 43–47. O'Kelley, Patrick. *Nothing But Blood and Slaughter*. Booklocker.com, 2004. 1: 160.

470. Draper, Lyman. Thomas Sumter Papers, Draper Manuscript Collection, State Historical Society of Wisconsin. O'Kelley, Patrick. *Nothing But Blood and Slaughter*. Booklocker.com, 2004. 3: 300.

471. Saye, James Hodge. *Memoirs of Major Joseph McJunkin, Revolutionary Patriot*. [sl]: A Press, Inc., 1977. (First printed in the Richmond, VA Watchman and Observer in 1847) p. 8.

472. Drayton, John. *Memoirs of the American Revolution as Relating to the State of South Carolina*. Charleston: A.E. Miller, 1821; reprinted New York Times & Arno press, 1969. pp. 356–357.

473. Gregoire, Anne King. *Thomas Sumter*. Columbia: R.L. Bryan Company, 1931. p. 55.

474. Gregoire, Anne King. *Thomas Sumter*. Columbia: R.L. Bryan Company, 1931. pp. 54–57. O'Kelley, Patrick. *Nothing but Blood and Slaughter*. Booklocker.com, 2004. 1: 161–163.

475. Parker, John C. *Parker's Guide to the Revolutionary War in South Carolina: battles, skirmishes and murders*. Patrick, SC: Hem Branch Publishing, 2009. pp. 301, 305.

476. Cherokee Prayer Site Guide www.geocities.ws/gileadintl/atrocity-list.html. Historical Notes on the Cherokee People by Linda Fulmer www.geocities.ws/gileadintl/cherokeehistory.html#VIII.%20CHEROKEE%20SOURCES .gaz.jrshelby.com/chauga.htm.

477. Cherokee Prayer Site Guide www.geocities.ws/gileadintl/atrocity-list.html. Historical Notes on the Cherokee People by Linda Fulmer www.geocities.ws/gileadintl/cherokeehistory.html#VIII.%20CHEROKEE%20SOURCES .gaz.jrshelby.com/quacoratchee.htm. National Archives and Records Administration. Pension application of Christopher Casey S16685.

478. *Dunlap's Pennsylvania Packet or, the General Advertiser*. V: 256 (Sept. 17, 1776) p. 2. *Maryland Journal*. III: 144 (Sept. 18, 1776) p. 5. *Pennsylvania Journal*. 1762 (Sept. 18, 1776) p. 3. *Pennsylvania Ledger: or the Virginia, Maryland, Pennsylvania, & New-Jersey Weekly Advertiser*. LXXXVII (Sept. 18, 1776) p. 3. *Dunlap's Maryland Gazette Or the Baltimore General Advertiser*. I: LXXIV (Sept. 24, 1776) p. 2. *Virginia Gazette*. 1312 (Sept. 27, 1776) p. 2. *Connecticut Journal*. 468 (Oct. 2, 1776) p. 2. *The Essex Journal And New-Hampshire Packet*. III: 144 (Oct. 4, 1776) p. 2.

479. Ashe, Samuel A'Court. *History of North Carolina*. Greensboro: Charles L. Van Noppen, 1925. I: 553.

480. Garden, Alexander. *Anecdotes of the American Revolution, Illustrative of the Talents and Virtues of the Heroes and Patriots who Acted the Most Conspicuous Parts Therein. Second series*. Charleston, S. C.: A.E. Miller, 1828. pp. 374–375. Ripley, Warren. *Battleground: South Carolina in the Revolution*. Charleston, SC: Evening Post, 1983. p. 237. Moss, Bobby Gilmer. *Roster of South Carolina Patriots in the American Revolution*. Baltimore: Genealogical Pub. Co., 1983. pp. 86, 91, 667. O'Kelley, Patrick. *Nothing But Blood and Slaughter*. Booklocker.com, 2004. 4: 38–3.

481. Moultrie, William. *Memoirs of the American Revolution so far as it related to the States of North and South Carolina and Georgia*. New York, 1802; (Eyewitness accounts of the American Revolution). [New York]: New York Times, [1968]. 2: 320. Moss, Bobby Gilmer. *Roster of South Carolina Patriots in the American Revolution*. Baltimore: Genealogical Pub. Co., 1983. pp. 86, 91. Draper, Lyman. Thomas Sumter Papers, Draper Manuscript Collection, State Historical Society of Wisconsin. 1VV107. O'Kelley, Patrick. *Nothing But Blood and Slaughter*. Booklocker.com, 2004. 4: 89–93.

482. Hairr, John. *Colonel David Fanning, the Adventures of a Carolina Loyalist*. Averasboro Press, 2000. pp. 40–41. O'Kelley, Patrick. *Nothing But Blood and Slaughter*. Booklocker.com, 2004. 1: 186.

483. Lipscomb, Terry W. South Carolina Revolutionary Battles: Part Seven. *Names in South Carolina* XXVI (Winter 1979). South Carolina Historical Society, 1979. p. 35. O'Kelley, Patrick. *Nothing But Blood and Slaughter*. Booklocker.com, 2004. 3: 332. National Archives and Records Administration. Thomas Arnold pension application W5640. Parker, John C. *Parker's Guide to the Revolutionary War in South Carolina: battles, skirmishes and murders*. Patrick, SC: Hem Branch Publishing, 2009. p. 252.

484. Lipscomb, Terry W. South Carolina Revolutionary Battles: Part Seven. *Names in South Carolina* XXVI (Winter 1979). South Carolina Historical Society, 1979. p. 35. Parker, John C. *Parker's Guide to the Revolutionary War in South Carolina: battles, skirmishes and murders*. Patrick, SC: Hem Branch Publishing, 2009. p. 175.

484a. Parker, John C. Parker's guide to the Revolutionary War in South Carolina: battles, skirmishes and murders. Patrick, S.C.: Hem Branch Publishing, 2009. p. 178.

485. Peckham, Howard Henry. *The Toll of Independence: engagements & battle casualties of the American Revolution*. edited by Howard H. Peckham. Chicago: University of Chicago Press, 1974. p. 57. Parker, John C. *Parker's Guide to the Revolutionary War in South Carolina: battles, skirmishes and murders*. Patrick, SC: Hem Branch Publishing, 2009. p. 178.

486. Lipscomb, Terry W. South Carolina Revolutionary Battles: Part Ten. *Names in South Carolina*. XXX (Winter 1983). South Carolina Historical Society, 1983. p. 12. O'Kelley, Patrick. *Nothing But Blood and Slaughter*. Booklocker .com, 2004. 3: 274. Parker, John C. *Parker's Guide to the Revolutionary War in South Carolina: battles, skirmishes and murders*. Patrick, SC: Hem Branch Publishing, 2009. pp. 174, 175.

487. Lipscomb, Terry W. South Carolina Revolutionary Battles: Part Seven. *Names in South Carolina* XXVI (Winter 1979). South Carolina Historical Society, 1979. p. 35. Draper, Lyman. Thomas Sumter Papers, Draper Manuscript Collection, State Historical Society of Wisconsin. 17VV36–37. O'Kelley, Patrick. *Nothing But Blood and Slaughter*. Booklocker.com, 2004. 3: 332–33.

488. Lipscomb, Terry W. South Carolina Revolutionary Battles: Part Seven. *Names in South Carolina* XXVI (Winter 1979). South Carolina Historical Society, 1979. p. 35. O'Kelley, Patrick. *Nothing But Blood and Slaughter*. Booklocker.com, 2004. 3: 372–73. *The New Jersey Gazette*. IV: 201 (Oct. 31, 1781) p. 1. Parker, John C. *Parker's Guide to the Revolutionary War in South Carolina: battles, skirmishes and murders*. Patrick, SC: Hem Branch Publishing, 2009. p. 178.

489. Parker, John C. *Parker's Guide to the Revolutionary War in South Carolina: battles, skirmishes and murders*. Patrick, SC: Hem Branch Publishing, 2009. p. 2.

490. Boatner, Mark Mayo, *Landmarks of the American Revolution: A Guide to Locating and Knowing What Happened at the Sites of Independence*. Harrisburg, Pa.: Stackpole Books, 1992, p. 79. Davis, Robert Scott, Jr. *The Battle of Kettle Creek*. State of Georgia Department of Natural Resources, Office of Planning and Research, Historical Preservation Section, 1974, p. 34–36. Davis, Robert Scott, Jr. *Georgia Citizens and Soldiers of the American Revolution*. Southern Historical Press, 1979. pp. 160–161. Davis, Robert Scott, Jr. *Georgians in the Revolution: at Kettle Creek (Wilkes Co.) and Burke County*. Southern Historical Press, Inc., 1986. p. 126. McCall, Hugh. *The History of Georgia, containing brief sketches of the most remarkable events up to the present day, 1784*. Savannah: Seymour & Williams, 1811; Atlanta, Cherokee Pub. Co., 1969, 1909. p. 394. National Archives and Records Administration. Pension applications of John Verner (S.C.S 7793), John Harris (S.C.S 21808), Francis Carlisle (S.C.W 10576), Patrick Cain (S.C.S 1185), and Thomas Hamilton (S.S.S 30470). Smith, Gordon Burns. *Morningstars of Liberty: the Revolutionary War in Georgia, 1775–1783*. Milledgeville, GA: Boyd Publishing, 2006. I: 142. O'Kelley, Patrick. *Nothing But Blood and Slaughter*. Booklocker.com, 2004. 1: 244. Petigru, James Louis; Carson, James Petigru. *Life, Letters and Speeches of James Louis Petigru, the Union man of South Carolina*. [Edited] by James Petigru Carson, etc. [With portraits.]. Washington: W.H. Lowdermilk & Co., 1920. p. 3. National Archives and Records Administration. Mordecai Millar (Miller) pension application S16972. National Archives and Records Administration. John Long pension application W5026. Jones, Charles Colcock, Jr. *The History of Georgia*. Boston: Houghton, Mifflin and Company, 1883. p. 338. www.carolana.com/SC/Revolution/revolution_cherokee_ford.html.

491. National Archives and Records Administration. Matthew Brown pension application of, S3213S, dated September 5, 1832. Parker, John C. *Parker's Guide to the Revolutionary War in South Carolina: battles, skirmishes and murders*. Patrick, SC: Hem Branch Publishing, 2009. p. 250.

492. Parker, John C. *Parker's Guide to the Revolutionary War in South Carolina: battles, skirmishes and murders*. Patrick, SC: Hem Branch Publishing, 2009. p. 250.

493. Caldwell, William W. *David Caldwell, 1705–1781, and his descendants in the United States of America*. Parkdale, AR (Box 55, Parkdale 71661): J. Caldwell Files, 1987. Howe, George. *History of the Presbyterian Church in South Carolina*. Columbia, Duffie & Chapman, 1870. 2: 389. National Archives and Records Administration. Adam J. Files Pension application #S13026. Parker, John C. *Parker's Guide to the Revolutionary War in South Carolina: battles, skirmishes and murders*. Patrick, SC: Hem Branch Publishing, 2009. p. 6.

494. Parker, John C. *Parker's Guide to the Revolutionary War in South Carolina: battles, skirmishes and murders*. Patrick, SC: Hem Branch Publishing, 2009. p. 338.

495. Parker, John C. *Parker's Guide to the Revolutionary War in South Carolina: battles, skirmishes and murders*. Patrick, SC: Hem Branch Publishing, 2009. p. 360.

496. Draper, Lyman. *Kings Mountain and its Heroes: History of the Battle of King's Mountain, October 7th, 1780, And the Events Which Led To It*. Johnson City, TN: The Overmountain Press, 1996. pp. 85–86. Lipscomb, Terry W. South Carolina Revolutionary Battles: Part Ten. *Names in South Carolina*. XXX (Winter 1983). South Carolina Historical Society, 1983. p. 14. O'Kelley, Patrick. *Nothing But Blood and Slaughter*. Booklocker.com, 2004. 2: 189–90.

497. Saye, James Hodge. *Memoirs of Major Joseph McJunkin, Revolutionary Patriot*. [sl]: A Press, Inc., 1977. pp. 23–26. Davis, Robert Scott, Jr. *Georgians in the Revolution: at Kettle Creek (Wilkes Co.) and Burke County*. Southern Historical Press, Inc., 1986. p. 128. Draper, Lyman. *Kings Mountain and its Heroes: History of the Battle of King's Mountain, October 7th, 1780, and the Events Which Led To It*. The Overmountain Press, 1996. pp. 91–93, 423. White, Katherine Keogh. *The King's Mountain Men, the story of the Battle with Sketches of the American Soldiers who took part*. Baltimore: Genealogical Publishing Company, 1966. pp. 108–109, 158, 220–221. Cashin, Edward J. *The King's Ranger. Thomas Brown and the American Revolution on the Southern Frontier*. Athens: University of Georgia Press, 1989. p. 113. Schenck, David. *North Carolina 1780–'81, Being a History of the Invasion of the Carolinas by the British Army under Lord Cornwallis in 1780–'81*. Edwards & Broughton, Publishers, 1889. pp. 77–78. Lambert, Robert Stansbury. *South Carolina Loyalists in the American Revolution*. Columbia: University of South Carolina, 1987. pp. 110–111. Chesney, Alexander. *The Journal of Alexander Chesney, a South Carolina Loyalist in the Revolution and After*, edited by E. A. Jones. Columbus, Ohio: Ohio State University, 1921. Draper, Lyman. Thomas Sumter Papers, Draper Manuscript Collection, State Historical Society of Wisconsin. 16VV402-405. Ellet, Elizabeth F. *The Women of the American Revolution*. New York: Baker and Scribner, 1849. Heitman, Francis B. *Historical Register of Officers of the Continental Army during the War of the Revolution, April 1775. to December 1783*. Washington, DC. 1914; Baltimore: Genealogical Publishing Company, 1967. p. 449. O'Kelley, Patrick. *Nothing But Blood and Slaughter*. Booklocker.com, 2004. 2: 235–236. Parker, John C. *Parker's Guide to the Revolutionary War in South Carolina: battles, skirmishes and murders*. Patrick, SC: Hem Branch Publishing, 2009. p. 336–339. Smith, Gordon Burns. *Morningstars of Liberty: the Revolutionary War in Georgia, 1775–1783*. Milledgeville, GA: Boyd Publishing, 2006. I: 207–208.

498. Parker, John C. *Parker's Guide to the Revolutionary War in South Carolina: battles, skirmishes and murders*. Patrick, SC: Hem Branch Publishing, 2009. p. 292.

499. John Earle Bomar to Dr. John Belton O'Neall Landrum. letter dated March 18, 1894 relating the tradition told to him by his grandmother, who died in 1837. Parker, John C. *Parker's Guide to the Revolutionary War in South Carolina: battles, skirmishes and murders*. Patrick, SC: Hem Branch Publishing, 2009. p. 340–341.

500. Barefoot, Daniel W. *Touring South Carolina's Revolutionary War Sites*. Winston-Salem: John F. Blair, 1999. pp. 177–178. O'Kelley, Patrick. *Nothing But Blood and Slaughter*. Booklocker.com, 2004. 3: 400–401. Parker, John C. *Parker's Guide to the Revolutionary War in South Carolina: battles, skirmishes and murders*. Patrick, SC: Hem Branch Publishing, 2009. pp. 292, 342, 360.

501. Parker, John C. *Parker's Guide to the Revolutionary War in South Carolina: battles, skirmishes and murders*. Patrick, SC: Hem Branch Publishing, 2009. pp. 338, 343–344.

502. Saye, James Hodge. *Memoirs of Major Joseph McJunkin, Revolutionary Patriot.* [sl]: A Press, Inc., 1977. (First printed in the Richmond, VA Watchman and Observer in 1847) p. 15. Buchanan, John. *The Road to Guilford Courthouse.* New York: John Wiley and Sons, Inc., 1997. *The Encyclopedia of the American Revolutionary War: a political, social, and military history.* Gregory Fremont-Barnes, Richard Alan Ryerson, editors. Santa Barbara, CA: ABC-CLIO, 2006 III: 341-342. Draper, Lyman. *Kings Mountain and its Heroes: History of the Battle of King's Mountain, October 7th, 1780, And the Events Which Led To It.* Johnson City, TN: The Overmountain Press, 1996. pp. 104-115. Ward, Christopher. *The War of the Revolution.* New York: Macmillan, 1952. Parker, John C. *Parker's Guide to the Revolutionary War in South Carolina: battles, skirmishes and murders.* Patrick, SC: Hem Branch Publishing, 2009. p. 258. Smith, Gordon Burns. *Morningstars of Liberty: the Revolutionary War in Georgia, 1775-1783.* Milledgeville, GA: Boyd Publishing, 2006. I: 210-211.

503. *Encyclopedia of the American Revolution.* Harold E. Selesky, editor in chief. 2nd ed. Detroit: Charles Scribner's Sons, 2007. I: 74-76. *The Encyclopedia of the American Revolutionary War: a political, social, and military history.* Gregory Fremont-Barnes, Richard Alan Ryerson, editors. Santa Barbara, CA: ABC-CLIO, 2006. I:100-102. Bass, Robert. *Gamecock: the life and campaigns of General Thomas Sumter.* Orangeburg, SC: Sandlapper, 2000. Fortescue, Sir John William. *The War of Independence: the British Army in North America, 1775-1783.* Mechanicsburg, PA: Stackpole Books, 2001. Gordon, John W. *South Carolina and the American Revolution: a battlefield history.* Columbia: University of South Carolina Press, 2003. Gregorie, Anne K. *Thomas Sumter.* Sumter, SC: Gamecock City Printing, 2000. Lumpkin, Henry. *From Savannah to Yorktown: the American Revolution in the South.* New York: Paragon, 1981. Ward, Christopher. *The War of the Revolution.* New York: Macmillan, 1952. Weigley, Russell F. *The Partisan War: the South Carolina Campaign of 1780-1782.* Columbia: University of South Carolina Press, 1970. Parker, John C. *Parker's Guide to the Revolutionary War in South Carolina: battles, skirmishes and murders.* Patrick, SC: Hem Branch Publishing, 2009. pp. 355-356. Smith, Gordon Burns. *Morningstars of Liberty: the Revolutionary War in Georgia, 1775-1783.* Milledgeville, GA: Boyd Publishing, 2006. I: 222-224.

504. Johnson, Joseph. *Traditions and Reminiscences Chiefly of the American Revolution in the South,* Charleston, S. C.: Walker & James, 1851. p. 530. Lipscomb, Terry W. South Carolina Revolutionary Battles: Part Ten. *Names in South Carolina.* XXX (Winter 1983). South Carolina Historical Society, 1983. p. 12. Hayes, John T. *The Saddlebag Almanac.* VIII (Jan. 2000), p. 35. O'Kelley, Patrick. *Nothing But Blood and Slaughter.* Booklocker.com, 2004. 2: 373-74. Parker, John C. *Parker's Guide to the Revolutionary War in South Carolina: battles, skirmishes and murders.* Patrick, SC: Hem Branch Publishing, 2009. p. 3.

505. National Archives and Records Administration. James Young pension application R11977.

506. *Ruddimon's Weekly Mercury* (Edinburgh, Scotland). Feb. 28, 1781. Extract of a letter from Lt. Col. John Harris Cruger to Lt. Gen. Charles Lord Cornwallis, dated 15 December 1780 from Ninety Six. *Cornwallis Papers* 3: 282-283. Davis, Robert Scott, Jr. *Georgians in the Revolution: at Kettle Creek (Wilkes Co.) and Burke County.* Southern Historical Press, Inc., 1986. p. 128. Tarleton, Banastre. *A History of the Campaigns of 1780 and 1781 in the Southern Provinces of North America.* London: T. Cadell, 1787; [sl]: the New York Times & Arno Press, 1968. p. 183. British National Archives. Cornwallis Papers, Class 30, Vol. 103 pp. 335-336. Hayes, John T. *The Saddlebag Almanac.* VIII (Jan. 2000), pp. 36-37. O'Kelley, Patrick. *Nothing But Blood and Slaughter.* Booklocker.com, 2004 2: 382-383. Parker, John C. *Parker's Guide to the Revolutionary War in South Carolina: battles, skirmishes and murders.* Patrick, SC: Hem Branch Publishing, 2009. pp. 289-290. Smith, Gordon Burns. *Morningstars of Liberty: the Revolutionary War in Georgia, 1775-1783.* Milledgeville, GA: Boyd Publishing, 2006. I: 225.

507. O'Kelley, Patrick. *Nothing But Blood and Slaughter.* Booklocker.com, 2004. 2: 382-383. Sargent, Mildred Crow. *William Few, A Founding Father: A Biographical Perspective of Early American History.* New York: Vantage Press, 2004. Peckham, Howard Henry. *The Toll of Independence: engagements & battle casualties of the American Revolution.* edited by Howard H. Peckham. Chicago: University of Chicago Press, 1974. p. 78.

508. Boatner, Mark M. *Encyclopedia of the American Revolution.* 3d ed. New York: McKay, 1980. p. 866. Pancake, John S. *This Destructive War: the British Campaign in the Carolinas.* Tuscaloosa: University of Alabama Press, 1985. p. 85. Hayes, John T. *The Saddlebag Almanac.* VIII (Jan. 2000), pp. 197-98. Draper, Lyman. Thomas Sumter Papers, Draper Manuscript Collection, State Historical Society of Wisconsin. 16VV361. O'Kelley, Patrick. *Nothing But Blood and Slaughter.* Booklocker.com, 2004. 3: 22.

509. Bearss, Edwin C. *Battle of Cowpens.* Johnson City, TN: The Overmountain Press, 1996. pp. 3-4. Seymour, William. Journal of the Southern Expedition, 1780-1783. *Papers of the Historical Society of Delaware:* XV. Wilmington: The Historical Society of Delaware, 1896. p. 11. White, Katherine Keogh. *The King's Mountain Men, the story of the Battle with Sketches of the American Soldiers who took part.* Baltimore: Genealogical Publishing Company, 1966. p. 185. Moultrie, William. *Memoirs of the American Revolution so far as it related to the States of North and South Carolina and Georgia.* New York, 1802; (Eyewitness Accounts of the American Revolution). [New York] New York Times [1968]. II: 252-253. Young, Thomas. Memoir of a Revolutionary Patriot of South Carolina. *The Orion.* 3 (Oct. 1843), pp. 84-88 et seq. National Archives and Records Administration. Pension Applications. RG 15, Microcopy 804. Batt, Richard John. *The Maryland Continentals, 1780-1781.* Tulane University Dissertation, 1974. p. 72. Saye, James Hodge. *Memoirs of Major Joseph McJunkin, Revolutionary Patriot.* [sl]: A Press, Inc., 1977. (First printed in the Richmond, VA Watchman and Observer in 1847). O'Kelley, Patrick. *Nothing But Blood and Slaughter.* Booklocker. com, 2004. 2: 393-396. Parker, John C. *Parker's Guide to the Revolutionary War in South Carolina: battles, skirmishes and murders.* Patrick, SC: Hem Branch Publishing, 2009. p. 255. Smith, Gordon Burns. *Morningstars of Liberty: the Revolutionary War in Georgia, 1775-1783.* Milledgeville, GA: Boyd Publishing, 2006. I: 226-227.

510. Garden, Alexander. *Anecdotes of the American Revolution, Illustrative of the Talents and Virtues of the Heroes and Patriots who Acted the Most Conspicuous Parts Therein.* Second series. Charleston, S. C.: A.E. Miller, 1828. pp. 441-442. Boatner, Mark M. *Encyclopedia of the American Revolution.* 3d ed., New York: McKay, 1980. pp. 481-482. Lambert, Robert Stansbury. *South Carolina Loyalists in the American Revolution.* Columbia: University

of South Carolina, 1987. p. 207. Ward, Christopher L. *The Delaware Continentals*. Historical Society of Delaware, 1941. p. 371. Hayes, John T. *The Saddlebag Almanac*. Fort Lauderdale, Fla.: Saddlebag Press. VIII (Jan. 2000) pp. 39–40. Graves, William T. *James Williams: An American Patriot in the Carolina Backcountry*. Writers Club Press, 2002. p. 55. Draper, Lyman. Thomas Sumter Papers, Draper Manuscript Collection, State Historical Society of Wisconsin. O'Kelley, Patrick. *Nothing But Blood and Slaughter*. Booklocker.com, 2004. 2: 393–394. Parker, John C. *Parker's Guide to the Revolutionary War in South Carolina: battles, skirmishes and murders*. Patrick, SC: Hem Branch Publishing, 2009. p. 253.

511. Young, Thomas. Memoir of a Revolutionary Patriot of South Carolina. *The Orion*. 3 (Oct. 1843): 84–88; (Nov. 1843): 100–105. Parker, John C. *Parker's Guide to the Revolutionary War in South Carolina: battles, skirmishes and murders*. Patrick, SC: Hem Branch Publishing, 2009. p. 256.

512. Draper, Lyman. Thomas Sumter Papers, Draper Manuscript Collection, State Historical Society of Wisconsin. O'Kelley, Patrick. *Nothing But Blood and Slaughter*. Booklocker.com, 2004. 3: 22–23.

513. Draper, Lyman. Thomas Sumter Papers, Draper Manuscript Collection, State Historical Society of Wisconsin. O'Kelley, Patrick. *Nothing But Blood and Slaughter*. Booklocker.com, 2004. 3: 53. Communications with Patricia Forster and Jack Parker, June 1, 2012.

514. Chesney, Alexander. *The Journal of Alexander Chesney, a South Carolina Loyalist in the Revolution and After*, edited by E. A. Jones. Columbus, Ohio: Ohio State University, 1921. *The Ohio State University Bulletin* 26:4 (October 30, 1921) p. 10 n72. Moss, Bobby Gilmer. *Journal of Captain Alexander Chesney, Adjutant to Major Patrick Ferguson*. [s.l.]: Scotia-Hibernia Press, 2002. p. 18 n125.

515. Parker, John C. *Parker's Guide to the Revolutionary War in South Carolina: battles, skirmishes and murders*. Patrick, SC: Hem Branch Publishing, 2009. p. 293.

516. *Encyclopedia of the American Revolution*. Harold E. Selesky, editor in chief. 2nd ed. Detroit: Charles Scribner's Sons, 2007. I: 278–284. *The Encyclopedia of the American Revolutionary War: a political, social, and military history*. Gregory Fremont-Barnes, Richard Alan Ryerson, editors. Santa Barbara, CA: ABC-CLIO, 2006. I: 305–310. Babits, Lawrence E. *A Devil of a Whipping: the Battle of Cowpens*. Chapel Hill: University of North Carolina Press, 1998. Bass, Robert Duncan. T*he Green Dragoon: the lives of Banastre Tarleton and Mary Robinson*. New York: Holt, 1957. Buchanan, John. *The Road to Guilford Courthouse*. New York: John Wiley and Sons, Inc., 1997. Fleming, Thomas J. *Cowpens "Downright Fighting" the story of Cowpens*. Washington, DC: National Park Service, 1988. Fortescue, Sir John William. *A History of the British Army*. 2nd ed. London: Macmillan and Company, 1911. Graham, James. *The Life of General Daniel Morgan*. Bloomingburg, NY: Zebroski Historical Services, 1993. Haller, Stephen E. *William Washington: Cavalryman of the Revolution*. Bowie, MD: Heritage Press, 2001. Higginbotham, Don. *Revolutionary Rifleman*. Chapel Hill: University of North Carolina Press, 1961. Lee, Henry. *Memoirs of the War in the Southern Department of the United States*, New York: University Publishing Co., 1869. Tarleton, Banastre. *A History of the Campaigns of 1780 and 1781 in the Southern Provinces of North America*. London: T. Cadell, 1787; [sl]: the New York Times & Arno Press, 1968. Ward, Christopher. *The War of the Revolution*. New York: Macmillan, 1952. pp. 755–762. Parker, John C. *Parker's Guide to the Revolutionary War in South Carolina: battles, skirmishes and murders*. Patrick, SC: Hem Branch Publishing, 2009. pp. 119–121. Smith, Gordon Burns. *Morningstars of Liberty: the Revolutionary War in Georgia, 1775–1783*. Milledgeville, GA: Boyd Publishing, 2006. I: 231–233.

517. Ward, Christopher. *The War of the Revolution*. New York: Macmillan, 1952. pp. 763–64.

518. Babits, Lawrence E. *A Devil of a Whipping, the Battle of Cowpens*. University of North Carolina Press, 1998. pp. 138, 203. O'Kelley, Patrick. *Nothing But Blood and Slaughter*. Booklocker.com, 2004. 3: 53–4.

519. Davies, K.G. *Documents of the American Revolution 1770–1783*. (Colonial Office Series) Shannon: Irish University Press 1972, 1981. 20: 117–118. Lipscomb, Terry W. South Carolina Revolutionary Battles: Part Ten. *Names in South Carolina*. XXX (Winter 1983). South Carolina Historical Society, 1983. p. 10. O'Kelley, Patrick. *Nothing But Blood and Slaughter*. Booklocker.com, 2004. 3: 100–101. Parker, John C. *Parker's Guide to the Revolutionary War in South Carolina: battles, skirmishes and murders*. Patrick, SC: Hem Branch Publishing, 2009. p. 296.

520. Draper, Lyman. *Kings Mountain and its Heroes: History of the Battle of King's Mountain, October 7th, 1780, and the Events Which Led To It*. The Overmountain Press, 1996. p. 470. Lipscomb, Terry W. South Carolina Revolutionary Battles: Part Ten. *Names in South Carolina*. XXX (Winter 1983). South Carolina Historical Society, 1983. p. 13. Saye, James Hodge. *Memoirs of Major Joseph McJunkin, Revolutionary Patriot*. [sl]: A Press, Inc., 1977. (First printed in the Richmond, VA *Watchman and Observer* in 1847). Draper, Lyman. Thomas Sumter Papers, Draper Manuscript Collection, State Historical Society of Wisconsin. O'Kelley, Patrick. *Nothing But Blood and Slaughter*. Booklocker.com, 2004. 3: 105–6. Parker, John C. *Parker's Guide to the Revolutionary War in South Carolina: battles, skirmishes and murders*. Patrick, SC: Hem Branch Publishing, 2009. p. 253.

521. Young, Thomas. Memoir of a Revolutionary Patriot of South Carolina. *The Orion*. 3 (Oct. 1843), pp. 100–105.

522. Draper, Lyman. *Kings Mountain and its Heroes: History of the Battle of King's Mountain, October 7th, 1780, and the Events Which Led To It*. The Overmountain Press, 1996. pp. 163–164. Letters to General Greene and Others. *The South Carolina Historical and Genealogical Magazine*. XVI: 3 (July 1915) pp. 101–102. Extract of a letter from General Marion, dated April 21st, 1781. *The Connecticut Gazette and the Universal Intelligencer*. XVIII: 919, p. 1. Moultrie, William. *Memoirs of the American Revolution so far as it related to the States of North and South Carolina and Georgia*. New York, 1802; (Eyewitness Accounts of the American Revolution). [New York] New York Times [1968]. II: 336–337. Schenck, David. *North Carolina 1780–81*. Raleigh: Edwards and Broughton, Publishers, 1889. p. 129. Lambert, Robert Stansbury. *South Carolina Loyalists in the American Revolution*. University of South Carolina Press, 1987. p. 169. Pancake, John S. *This Destructive War: the British Campaign in the Carolinas*. Tuscaloosa: University of Alabama Press, 1985. pp. 190–181. Hayes, John T. *The Saddlebag Almanac*. VIII (Jan. 2000) pp. 98–99; IX (Jan.

2001), p. 65. Draper, Lyman. Thomas Sumter Papers, Draper Manuscript Collection, State Historical Society of Wisconsin. 1VV209–211. Extract of a letter from General Marion, dated April 21st, 1781. *The Connecticut Gazette and the Universal Intelligencer.* XVIII: 919, p. 1. O'Kelley, Patrick. *Nothing But Blood and Slaughter.* Booklocker. com, 2004. 3: 162–164. Parker, John C. *Parker's Guide to the Revolutionary War in South Carolina: battles, skirmishes and murders.* Patrick, SC: Hem Branch Publishing, 2009. p. 288. Smith, Gordon Burns. *Morningstars of Liberty: the Revolutionary War in Georgia, 1775–1783.* Milledgeville, GA: Boyd Publishing, 2006. I: 241–242.

523. Lipscomb, Terry W. South Carolina Revolutionary Battles Part Ten, Names in South Carolina. XXX (Winter 1983). South Carolina Historical Society, 1983. p. 35. Lambert, Robert Stansbury. *South Carolina Loyalists in the American Revolution.* University of South Carolina Press, 1987. 218–222. O'Kelley, Patrick. *Nothing But Blood and Slaughter.* Booklocker.com, 2004. 3: 371. Parker, John C. *Parker's Guide to the Revolutionary War in South Carolina: battles, skirmishes and murders.* Patrick, SC: Hem Branch Publishing, 2009. p. 4.

524. Lipscomb, Terry W. South Carolina Revolutionary Battles: Part Ten. *Names in South Carolina.* XXX (Winter 1983). South Carolina Historical Society, 1983. pp. 11–12. O'Kelley, Patrick. *Nothing But Blood and Slaughter.* Booklocker.com, 2004. 3: 180. Parker, John C. *Parker's Guide to the Revolutionary War in South Carolina: battles, skirmishes and murders.* Patrick, SC: Hem Branch Publishing, 2009. pp. 8, 176. Johnson, Joseph. *Traditions and Reminiscences Chiefly of the American Revolution in the South,* Charleston, S. C.: Walker & James, 1851. pp. 477, 514. National Archives and Records Administration. Pension application of Samuel Hammond,. For the correct spelling of the commander's name, see the Audited Account of Thomas Key (AA4264), South Carolina Archives.

525. screwarguide.com/updates/292A.pdf.

526. Draper, Lyman. Thomas Sumter Papers, Draper Manuscript Collection, State Historical Society of Wisconsin. 7VV260. O'Kelley, Patrick. *Nothing But Blood and Slaughter.* Booklocker.com, 2004. 3: 217. Parker, John C. *Parker's Guide to the Revolutionary War in South Carolina: battles, skirmishes and murders.* Patrick, SC: Hem Branch Publishing, 2009. p. 294.

527. Simms, William Gilmore. *The Life of Francis Marion.* New York: H.G. Langley, 1844. p. 136. Lee, Henry. *Memoirs of the War in the Southern Department of the United States.* New York: University Publishing Co., 1869. pp. 354–355. Brown, Tarleton. *Memoirs of Tarleton Brown, a Captain in the Revolutionary Army, Written by Himself, with a Preface and Notes by Charles I. Bushnell.* New York: Privately Printed, 1862. Lipscomb, Terry W. South Carolina Revolutionary Battles: Part Six. *Names in South Carolina.* XXV (Winter 1978). South Carolina Historical Society, 1978. pp. 29, 33. Ervin. Sara Sullivan. *South Carolinians in the Revolution.* Baltimore: Genealogical Publishing Company, Inc., 1971. p. 67. O'Kelley, Patrick. *Nothing But Blood and Slaughter.* Booklocker.com, 2004. 3: 238–39. Parker, John C. *Parker's Guide to the Revolutionary War in South Carolina: battles, skirmishes and murders.* Patrick, SC: Hem Branch Publishing, 2009. p. 10.

528. Brown, Tarleton. *Memoirs of Tarleton Brown, a Captain in the Revolutionary Army, Written by Himself, with a Preface and Notes by Charles I. Bushnell.* New York: Privately Printed, 1862. O'Kelley, Patrick. *Nothing But Blood and Slaughter.* Booklocker.com, 2004. 3: 262. Parker, John C. *Parker's Guide to the Revolutionary War in South Carolina: battles, skirmishes and murders.* Patrick, SC: Hem Branch Publishing, 2009. p. 11.

529. Lipscomb, Terry W. South Carolina Revolutionary Battles: Part Ten. *Names in South Carolina.* XXX (Winter 1983). South Carolina Historical Society, 1983. p. 11. Draper, Lyman. Thomas Sumter Papers, Draper Manuscript Collection, State Historical Society of Wisconsin. 7VV321. O'Kelley, Patrick. *Nothing But Blood and Slaughter.* Booklocker.com, 2004. 3: 274.

530. Lipscomb, Terry W. South Carolina Revolutionary Battles: Part Seven. *Names in South Carolina* XXVI (Winter 1979). South Carolina Historical Society, 1979. p. 35. O'Kelley, Patrick. *Nothing But Blood and Slaughter.* Booklocker.com, 2004. 3: 299.

531. O'Kelley, Patrick. *Nothing But Blood and Slaughter.* Booklocker.com, 2004. 3: 397–400. Parker, John C. *Parker's Guide to the Revolutionary War in South Carolina: battles, skirmishes and murders.* Patrick, SC: Hem Branch Publishing, 2009. p. 295.

532. Parker, John C. *Parker's Guide to the Revolutionary War in South Carolina: battles, skirmishes and murders.* Patrick, SC: Hem Branch Publishing, 2009. p. 199.

533. Lipscomb, Terry W. South Carolina Revolutionary Battles: Part Seven. *Names in South Carolina* XXVI (Winter 1979). South Carolina Historical Society, 1979. pp. 13–14. Southern Studies Program. *Figures of the Revolution in South Carolina, An Anthology. Spartanburg, Anderson, Beaufort, Aiken, Florence, Georgetown.* Columbia: University of South Carolina, 1976. pp. 122. O'Kelley, Patrick. *Nothing But Blood and Slaughter.* Booklocker.com, 2004. 3: 387. Parker, John C. *Parker's Guide to the Revolutionary War in South Carolina: battles, skirmishes and murders.* Patrick, SC: Hem Branch Publishing, 2009. p. 334.

534. Wyman, Frank and Goldsmith, Joe. Commemorating the Massacre at Hayes Station and the Little River Regiment. *Southern Campaigns of the American Revolution.* 11:3 (www.southerncampaigns.org). O'Kelley, Patrick. *Nothing But Blood and Slaughter.* Booklocker.com, 2004. 3: 397–400. Parker, John C. *Parker's Guide to the Revolutionary War in South Carolina: battles, skirmishes and murders.* Patrick, SC: Hem Branch Publishing, 2009. p. 254.

535. Lipscomb, Terry W. South Carolina Revolutionary Battles: Part Seven. *Names in South Carolina* XXVI (Winter 1979). South Carolina Historical Society, 1979. p. 37. O'Kelley, Patrick. *Nothing But Blood and Slaughter.* Booklocker.com, 2004. 3: 404. Parker, John C. *Parker's Guide to the Revolutionary War in South Carolina: battles, skirmishes and murders.* Patrick, SC: Hem Branch Publishing, 2009. pp. 177, 201.

536. Lipscomb, Terry W. South Carolina Revolutionary Battles: Part Seven. *Names in South Carolina* XXVI (Winter 1979). South Carolina Historical Society, 1979. p. 37. O'Kelley, Patrick. *Nothing But Blood and Slaughter.* Booklocker.com, 2004. 3: 405. Parker, John C. *Parker's Guide to the Revolutionary War in South Carolina: battles, skirmishes and murders.* Patrick, SC: Hem Branch Publishing, 2009. p. 5.

537. Lipscomb, Terry W. South Carolina Revolutionary Battles: Part Seven. *Names in South Carolina* XXVI (Winter 1979). South Carolina Historical Society, 1979. pp. 14–15. Moss, Bobby Gilmer. *Roster of South Carolina Patriots in the American Revolution*. Baltimore: Genealogical Pub. Co., 1983. p. 305. O'Kelley, Patrick. *Nothing But Blood and Slaughter*. Booklocker.com, 2004. 4: 47–48. Parker, John C. *Parker's Guide to the Revolutionary War in South Carolina: battles, skirmishes and murders*. Patrick, SC: Hem Branch Publishing, 2009. p. 354.

538. Parker, John C. *Parker's Guide to the Revolutionary War in South Carolina: battles, skirmishes and murders*. Patrick, SC: Hem Branch Publishing, 2009. p. 336.

Glossary

1. *Oxford English Dictionary.*

Glossary

Abatis: Sharpened branches pointing out from a fortification at an angle toward the enemy to slow or disrupt an assault.

Accoutrement: Piece of military equipment carried by soldiers in addition to their standard uniform and weapons.

Bar shot: A double shot consisting of two half cannon balls joined by an iron bar, used in sea-warfare to damage masts and rigging. (See Photo SC-25.)

Bastion: A fortification with a projecting part of a wall to protect the main walls of the fortification. (See Photo SC-15.)

Battalion: The basic organizational unit of a military force, generally 500 to 800 men. Most regiments consisted of a single battalion which was composed of ten companies.

Bateau: A light flat-bottomed riverboat with sharply tapering stern and bow.

Battery: Two or more similar artillery pieces that function as a single tactical unit; a prepared position for artillery; an army artillery unit corresponding to a company in an infantry regiment. (See Photo SC-31.)

Bayonet: A long, slender blade that can be attached to the end of a musket and used for stabbing. (See Photo SC-19.)

Best bower: The large anchor (about 4,000 pounds) on the starboard side of the bow of a vessel. The other is called the small-bower. Also the cable attached to this anchor. (See Photo SC-24.)

Blunderbuss: A short musket with a large bore and wide muzzle capable of holding a number of musket or pistol balls, used to fire shot with a scattering effect at close range. It is very effective for clearing a narrow passage, door of a house or staircase, or in boarding a ship. (See Photo SC-44.)

Bomb: An iron shell, or hollow ball, filled with gunpowder. It has a large touch-hole for a slow-burning fuse which is held in place by pieces of wood and fastened with a cement made of quicklime, ashes, brick dust, and steel filings worked together with glutinous water. A bomb is shot from a mortar mounted on a carriage. It is fired in a high arc over fortifications and often detonates in the air, raining metal fragments with high velocity on the fort's occupants. (See Photos SC-25 and SC-26.)

Bombproof: A structure built strong enough to protect the inhabitants from exploding bombs and shells.

Brig: A small two-masted sailing vessel with square-rigged sails on both masts.

Brigade: A military unit consisting of about 800 men.

Broadside: 1. The firing of all guns on one side of a vessel as nearly simultaneously as possible. 2. A large piece of paper printed on one side for advertisements or public notices.

Canister or **Cannister shot:** A kind of case-shot consisting of a number of small iron balls packed in sawdust in a cylindrical tin or canvas case. They were packed in four tiers between iron plates. (See Photo SC-25.)

Carronade: A short, stubby piece of artillery, usually of large caliber, having a chamber for the powder like a mortar. It is chiefly used on shipboard.

Chain shot: A kind of shot formed of two balls, or half-balls, connected by a chain, chiefly used in naval warfare to destroy masts, rigging, and sails. (See Photo SC-25.)

Chandeliers: Large and strong wooden frames used instead of a parapet. Fascines are piled on top of each other against it to cover workmen digging trenches. Sometimes they are only strong planks with two pieces of wood perpendicular to hold the fascines.

Chevaux-de-frise: Obstacles consisting of horizontal poles with projecting spikes to block a passageway. They were used on land and modified to block rivers to enemy ships.

Cohorn or **coehorn:** A short, small-barreled mortar for throwing grenades.

Company: The smallest military unit of the army consisting of about 45 to 110 men commanded by a captain, a lieutenant, and an ensign, and sometimes by a second lieutenant. A company usually has two sergeants, three or four corporals and two drums.

Crown forces: The allied forces supporting King George III. They consisted primarily of the British army, Hessian mercenaries, Loyalists, and Native Americans.

Cutter: 1. A single-masted sailing vessel similar to a sloop but having its mast positioned further aft. 2. A ship's boat, usually equipped with both sails and oars. In the eighteenth century, the terms sloop and cutter seem to have been used almost interchangeably.

Demilune: Fortification similar to a bastion but shaped as a crescent or half-moon rather than as an arrow.

Dragoon: A soldier who rode on horseback like cavalry. Dragoons generally fought dismounted in the 17th and 18th centuries.

Earthworks: A fortification made of earth. (See Photos SC-31 and SC-32.)

Embrasure: A slanted opening in the wall or parapet of a fortification designed for the defender to fire through it on attackers. (See Photo SC-31.)

Envelopment: An assault directed against an enemy's flank. An attack against two flanks is a double envelopment.

Espontoon: See **Spontoon**.

Fascine: A long bundle of sticks tied together, used in building earthworks and in strengthening ramparts.

Fraise: Sharpened stakes built into the exterior wall of a fortification to deter attackers..

Gabion: A cylindrical basket made of wicker and filled with earth for use in building fortifications.

Galley: A long boat propelled by oars. These boats had a shallow draft and were particularly useful in rivers, lakes, and other shallow bodies of water.

General engagement: An encounter, conflict, or battle in which the majority of a force is involved.

Grape shot: A number of small iron balls tied together to resemble a cluster of grapes. When fired simultaneously from a cannon, the balls separate into multiple projectiles. The shot usually consisted of nine balls placed between two iron plates. (See Photos SC-17 and SC-25.)

Grenadier: A soldier armed with grenades; a specially selected foot soldier in an elite unit selected on the basis of exceptional height and ability. (See Photos SC-14 and SC-30.)

Gun: A cannon. Guns were referred to by the size of the shot they fired. A 3-pounder fired a 3-pound ball, a 6-pounder fired a 6-pound ball. (See Photos SC-32, SC-36, and SC-40.)

Gundalow: An open, flat bottomed vessel about 53 feet long, 15 feet wide, and almost four feet deep in the center. It is equipped with both sails and oars, designed to carry heavy loads, usually armed with one gun at the bow and two mid-ship.

Hessian: A German soldier who fought with the British army. Most of the German soldiers came from the principality of Hesse-Cassel, hence the name. Other German states that sent soldiers include Brunswick, Hesse-Hanau, Waldeck, Ansbach-Bayreuth, and Anhalt-Zerbst. (See Photo SC-30.)

Howitzer: A cannon with a short barrel and a bore diameter greater than 30 mm and a maximum elevation of 60 degrees, used for firing shells at a high angle of elevation to reach a target behind cover or in a trench.

Hussars or **Huzzars:** Horse soldiers resembling Hungarian horsemen. They usually wore furred bonnets adorned with a cock's feather, a doublet with a pair of breeches, to which their stockings are fastened, and boots. They were armed with a saber, carbines, and pistols.

Jaeger: A hunter and gamekeeper who fought with the Hessians for the British army. They wore green uniforms, carried rifles, and were expert marksmen.

Jollyboat: A sailing vessel's small boat, such as a dinghy, usually carried on the stern. "A clincher-built ship's boat, smaller than a cutter, with a bluff bow and very wide transom, usually hoisted at the stern of the vessel, and used chiefly as a hack-boat for small work."[1]

Langrage: A particular kind of shot, formed of bolts, nails, bars, or other pieces of iron tied together, and forming a sort of cylinder, which corresponds with the bore of the cannon.

Letter of marque: A license granted by a monarch authorizing a subject to take reprisals on the subjects of a hostile state for alleged injuries. Later: Legal authority to fit out an armed vessel and use it in the capture of enemy merchant shipping and to commit acts which would otherwise have constituted piracy. See also **Privateer**.

Light infantry: Foot soldiers who carried lightweight weapons and minimal field equipment.

Loophole: Aperture or slot in defenses through which the barrels of small arms or cannon can be directed at an outside enemy. (See Photo SC-5.)

Loyalist: An American who supported the British during the American Revolution; also called Tory.

Magazine: A structure to store weapons, ammunition, explosives, and other military equipment or supplies.

Man-of-war: A warship. (See Photo SC-24.)

Glossary 359

Matross: A private in an artillery unit who needed no specialized skills. Matrosses usually hauled cannon and positioned them. They assisted in the loading, firing, and sponging the guns.

Militia: Civilians who are part-time soldiers who take military training and can serve full-time for short periods during emergencies.

Minuteman: Member of a special militia unit, called a Minute Company. A minuteman pledged to be ready to fight at a minute's notice.

Mortar: A cannon with a relatively short and wide barrel, used for firing shells in a high arc over a short distance, particularly behind enemy defenses. They were not mounted on wheeled carriages. (See Photo SC-26.)

Musket: A firearm with a long barrel, large caliber, and smooth bore. It was used between the 16th and 18th centuries, before rifling was invented. (See Photo SC-19.)

Open order: A troop formation in which the distance between the individuals is greater than in close order (which is shoulder to shoulder). Also called extended order. (See Photo SC-7.)

Parapet: Earthen or stone defensive platform on the wall of a fort.

Parley: A talk or negotiation, under a truce, between opposing military forces.

Parole: A promise given by a prisoner of war, either not to escape, or not to take up arms again as a condition of release. Individuals on parole can remain at home and conduct their normal occupations. Breaking parole makes one subject to immediate arrest and often execution. From the French *parole* which means one's word of honor.

Pettiauger or **pettyauger:** 1. A long, narrow canoe hollowed from the trunk of a single tree or from the trunks of two trees fastened together. 2. An open flat-bottomed schooner-rigged vessel or two-masted sailing barge, of a type used in North America and the Caribbean. (See Photo SC-23.)

Pinnace: 1. A small light vessel, usually having two schooner-rigged (originally square-rigged) masts, often in attendance on a larger vessel and used as a tender or scout, to carry messages, etc. 2. A small boat, originally rowed with eight oars, later with sixteen, forming part of the equipment of a warship or other large vessel. It could also be navigated with a sail.

Polacre: A three-masted vessel with square-rigged sails and pole masts without tops and crosstrees.

Portage: An overland route used to transport a boat or its cargo from one waterway to another; the act of carrying a boat or its cargo from one waterway to another.

Privateer: An armed vessel owned and crewed by private individuals and holding a government commission known as a letter of marque authorizing the capture of merchant shipping belonging to an enemy nation. See **Letter of marque.**

Rampart: An earthen fortification made of an embankment and often topped by a low protective wall.

Ravelin: A small outwork fortification shaped like an arrowhead or a V that points outward in front of a larger defense work to protect the sally port or entrance.

Redoubt: A temporary fortification built to defend a prominent position such as a hilltop. (See Photo SC-32.)

Regiment: A permanent military unit usually consisting of two or three companies. British regiments generally consisted of ten companies, one of which was grenadiers. Some German regiments consisted of 2,000 men.

Regular: Belonging to or constituting a full-time professional military or police force as opposed to, for example, the reserves or militia.

Ropewalk: A long, narrow building where rope is made.

Round shot: Spherical ball of cast-iron or steel for firing from smooth-bore cannon, a cannon ball. The shots were referred to by the weight of the ball: a 9-pound shot weighed 9 pounds; a 12-pound shot weighed 12 pounds. Round shot was used principally to batter fortifications. The balls could be heated ("hot shot") and fired at the hulls of ships or buildings to set them on fire. The largest balls (32- and 64-pounders) were sometimes called "big shot." (See Photo SC-25.)

Sapper: A soldier who specializes in making entrenchments and tunnels for siege operations.

Schooner: A fast sailing ship with at least two masts and with fore and aft sails on all lower masts.

Scow: A flat-bottomed sailboat with a rectangular hull.

Sedan chair: A chair or windowed cabin suitable for a single occupant. It is borne on poles or wooden rails that pass through brackets on the sides of the chair. The two or more porters who bear the chair are called "chairmen."

Shell: An explosive projectile fired from a large-bore gun such as a howitzer or mortar. See also **Bomb, Howitzer,** and **Mortar.** (See Photo SC-25.)

Ship of the line: A large warship with sufficient armament to enter combat with similar vessels in the line of battle. A ship of the line carried 60 to 100 guns. (See Photo SC-24.)

Shot: A bullet or projectile fired from a weapon. See also: **Bar shot, Canister shot, Chain shot, Grape shot, Round shot, Sliding bar shot, Star shot.** (See Photo SC-25.)

Sliding bar shot: A projectile similar to a bar shot. A sliding bar shot has two interlocked bars that extend almost double the length of a bar shot, thereby increasing the potential damage to a ship's rigging and sails. (See Photo SC-25.)

Sloop: A small single-masted sailing vessel with sails rigged fore-and-aft and guns on only one deck. In the 18th century, the terms sloop and cutter seem to have been used almost interchangeably.

Sloop of war: A three-masted, square-rigged naval vessel with all her guns mounted on a single uncovered main deck.

Snow: A small sailing-vessel resembling a brig, carrying a main and fore mast and a supplementary trysail mast close behind the mainmast; formerly employed as a warship.

Sons of Liberty: Patriots who belonged to secret organizations to oppose British attempts at taxation after 1765. They often resorted to violence and coercion to achieve their purposes.

Spike [a gun]: To destroy a cannon by hammering a long spike into the touch hole or vent, thereby rendering it useless.

Spontoon: A type of half-pike or halberd carried by infantry officers in the 18th century (from about 1740). (See Photo SC-21.)

Stand of arms: A complete set of arms (musket, bayonet, cartridge box, and belt) for one soldier.

Star shot: A kind of chain-shot. (See Photo SC-25.)

Tory: A Loyalist, also called Refugee and Cow-Boy. The Whigs usually used the term in a derogatory manner.

Trunnions: Two pieces of metal sticking out of the sides of an artillery piece. They serve to hold the artillery piece on the carriage and allow it to be raised or lowered. The trunnions are generally as long as the diameter of the cannonball and have the same diameter. (See Photo SC-40.)

Whig: Somebody who supported independence from Great Britain during the American Revolution. The name comes from the British liberal political party that favored reforms and opposed many of the policies of the King and Parliament related to the American War for Independence.

Index

10 Mile House, 184
13 Mile House, 156, 159
15 Mile House, 184
1st Continental light dragoons, 162
1st Maryland Regiment, 50, 51, 54
1st Regiment, 119
1st South Carolina Regiment, 116, 146, 150, 205
1st Virginia Detachment, 146
2nd Battalion of light infantry, 167
2nd Maryland, 51
2nd South Carolina Regiment, 118, 125, 135, 136, 146, 150, 151, 155, 159, 173
3rd Foot Guards (Scots Guards), 101
3rd North Carolina Light Infantry, 147
3rd Regiment of Continental Light Dragoons, 168, 174, 292
3rd South Carolina Rangers, 271
3rd South Carolina Regiment, 136, 137, 140, 275
3rd Virginia, 209, 231
4th South Carolina Artillery, 118
4th South Carolina Regiment, 143
4th Virginia Regiment, 54, 209
5th Maryland Regiment, 54, 47
5th South Carolina Regiment, 135, 222, 225
5th Virginia Regiment, 54
6th South Carolina Regiment, 19, 221
7th Regiment of Foot, 121, 140, 168, 297
16th Regiment, 143
17th Regiment, 209
17th Light Dragoons, 297
19th Regiment of Foot, 180, 186, 189, 190, 193
23rd Regiment of Foot, 39, 46, 49, 121, 131, 140, 162, 176
33d Regiment of Foot, 39, 46, 49, 122, 131, 139, 140, 147, 167, 168, 179, 198
37th Light Infantry, 142
42nd Regiment (Highlanders), 122, 140, 147
60th (Royal American) Regiment, 159, 202
63rd Regiment of Foot, 63, 71, 95, 289
64th Regiment, 55, 57, 77, 78, 88, 95, 208, 209, 235, 244
71st Regiment (Highlanders), 32, 39, 47, 75, 78, 144, 146, 160, 168, 205, 224, 240
84th Regiment of Foot, 163, 183, 224

Abatis, 33, 34, 52, 86, 101, 141, 160, 162, 176, 186, 226, 240
Abbeville County, 110, 279, 281, 289, 300, 305
Abercorn, Georgia, 221
Abercromby's light infantry, 167
Actaeon (or *Acteon*) (HMS), 130, 144
Adder (galley), 205, 207
Aeolus (*Eolus*), 131
African American dragoons, 193
African Americans, 73, 91, 112, 126, 151, 160, 202, 242, 273, 281
Aiken County, 113, 233, 253, 301, 302
Alexander Captain, 155, 157
Alexander's Old Field, 11, 13
Allaire, Anthony, 68
Allen, Isaac, 255, 291
Allendale County, 222, 232, 243
Alligator, 98

Alligator (galley), 185, 186, 187
Allison Creek, 27, 28
Allston, John, 125
Alston, William, 212, 215
Alston's plantation, 210, 212, 214, 215, 216, 218
Ambush, 32, 41, 58, 59, 63, 88, 90, 92, 94, 95, 109, 113, 121, 122, 125, 135, 136–138, 162, 170, 171, 176, 185, 193, 202, 209, 215, 217, 223, 225, 236–239, 243, 254, 272, 273, 286, 287, 299, 305
Amelia Township, 92, 94, 100
American Volunteers (Loyalists), 66, 153, 154, 228, 262, 263, 284
Amis's Mill, 80
Ammunition, 7, 15, 22, 27, 28, 59, 71, 84, 85, 90, 95, 96, 102, 113, 120, 121, 131, 134, 140, 142, 148, 161, 163, 171, 173, 174, 179, 192–194, 204, 215, 234, 251, 252, 258, 260, 261, 264, 276, 297, 306
Amusette, 137, 167
Ancrum's Plantation, 86, 90
Anderson County, 275, 281
Anderson, Archibald, 80
Anderson, David, 261
Anderson, Robert, 70, 233, 273, 279
Anderson's mill, 110
Andrews, Israel, 198
Andrews, John, 237
Angelina (schooner), 151
Anspach jaeger, 144
Anthony, Hezekiah, 161, 162
Antioch, 37, 43, 44
Appalachian Mountains, 271
Arbuthnot (British brig), 198
Arbuthnot, Marriot, 121, 131, 143, 145, 153
Ardesoif, John Plummer, 213
Argo (Pennsylvania privateer sloop/brig), 198
Armand, Charles (Charles-Armand Tuffin, Marquis de la Rouerie), 39, 48, 50
Armand's Legion, 48–50
Armstrong, John, 49
Armstrong, James, 168, 185, 233
Armstrong, William, 191
Armstrong's Skirmish, 166, 167
Arnold, Benedict, 169
Arnold, Thomas, 277
Articles of Association, 251
Articles of Capitulation, 169
Artillery, 97, 100, 101, 108, 118–120, 122, 138, 139, 141–143, 146, 147, 153, 162, 165, 167, 169, 173, 192, 193, 202–204, 209, 213, 217, 225, 226, 234, 244, 256, 299
Ash's Point, 196
Ashburn, Thomas, 198
Ashe, John, 125, 202
Ashe's plantation, 123, 125
Ashepoo, 208, 225
Ashepoo River, 237
Ashley, William, 162
Ashley Ferry, 160, 167, 168, 185, 225, 226
Ashley River, 100, 116, 118, 131, 135, 136, 138–142, 158, 160, 166–169, 171–173, 175, 176, 179, 185–188, 208
Ashley River Baptist Church, 165, 168, 171
Atkins, Christopher, 130

Augusta, Georgia, 47, 52, 55, 88, 92, 135, 201, 223, 224, 233, 246, 249, 254–256, 277, 279, 280, 300, 302
Austin, George, 199
Avant's Ferry, 210, 213, 220
Awendaw, 195
Awendaw Bridge, 230

Back River, 226
Backcountry, 1, 65, 266, 293, 303
Backcountry militia, 200
Bacon's Bridge, 100, 163, 168, 173, 175, 225
Balfour (British row galley), 205, 208
Balfour, Nesbit, 57, 170, 218, 219, 235, 238, 300
Ball, Elias, 231
Ball, John Coming, 62
Ball's Plantation, 230, 231
Ballingall, Robert, 240, 241
Bamberg County, 247
Barfield, Jesse, 5, 58, 70, 109, 215
Barnwell County, 110, 246, 247
Barnwell, Edward, 226
Barnwell, John, 199, 205, 207, 226
Barnwell, Robert, 158, 159, 207
Barr Crossing, 86
Barriedale, John, 137, 138
Barton, John, 239
Barton's Post, 238, 239
Baskin, James, 271
Baskin, William, 279
Baskins, Hugh, 281
Baskins, William, 281
Bass, Moses, 109
Bass's Mill, 80, 108, 109
Bastion, 118, 119, 128, 141, 172
Bates, William "Bloody Bill", 264
Batesburg, 109
Baxter, John, 114, 215, 216, 220
Baylor, George, 209
Bayonet charge, 10, 66, 192, 291
Bayonet counterattack, 138
Bayonet, 51, 161, 181, 192, 204, 216, 217, 228, 244, 263, 296
Bear Bluff, 106
Bear Island, 235, 237
Bear Swamp, 68, 70, 106
Bear Swamp Baptist Church, 68
Beattie, Jane, 300
Beattie's Mill, 255, 300
Beaufort, 10, 160, 161, 199–201, 203–207, 210, 226–228, 236, 237
Beaufort (brig), 162
Beaufort Company, 156, 158
Beaufort County, 196, 200, 206, 207, 227, 238
Beaufort Loyalist militia, 207
Beaufort Museum, 200
Beaufort River, 200
Beaver Creek, 23–25, 97, 106, 107
Beaver Creek Ford, 23, 25
Beaver, Arthur, 147
Beaverdam Creek, 16, 264
Beckham's Old Field, 11, 13
Beckhamville, 11
Beding's Fields, 32
Bee, Thomas, 229
Bee's Plantation, 229
Beech Island, 302
Belle Isle plantation, 36, 213
Belleville, 91, 93, 94, 101

Belleville Plantation, 91, 93–95, 101
Bell's Branch, 38
Bellona (brig), 162
Benbow's Ferry, 70
Bennett, William, 193
Bennington, Vermont/New York, 68
Benton, Lemuel, 5, 61, 220
Berkeley County, 166, 177, 181, 182, 189, 194, 195, 230, 248
Berkeley County Museum, 182
Bermuda, 153
Best, Henry, 233
Bethabara, 68
Bethea, "Sweat Swamp" John, 65
Bethea, "Sweat Swamp" William, 65
Bethesda Presbyterian Church, 44
Betsey (schooner), 158
Biddle, Nicholas, 134
Big Branch, 107
Big Browns Creek, 42
Big Gate, 235, 237
Big Glades, 93
Big House, 246
Big Lick, 109, 111
Big Pine Tree Creek, 38, 45
Big Savannah, 91–94
Big Stevens Creek Baptist Church, 278
Big Warrior (Tustanagee Thlucco), 265
Bigger's Ferry, 64
Biggin Bridge, 177–180, 189, 190, 193
Biggin Church, 177–180, 186, 189, 190
Biggin Creek, 186
Birch's Mill see Burch's Mill
Bishopville, 37, 38
Black Creek, 3, 5, 64, 241
Black Dragoons, 195
Black Lake, 114
Black Mingo, 62, 214
Black Mingo Creek (swamp), 61, 62
Black Pioneer Troop, 195
Black River Road, 210, 213
Black River Swamp, 210, 213, 220
Black River, 40, 56, 57–61, 70, 84, 102, 103, 213, 214, 220
Black Swamp, 220–225
Blacksmith, 24
Blackstock, 35
Blackstock, William, 288
Blackstock's Plantation, 75, 286, 288
Blackville, 247
Blair, 6
Blakeley's plantation, 61, 104
Blasingame, Thomas, 18, 22, 23, 296
Blasingame's house, 16
Bledsoe, Bartley, 111
Blenheim, 31
Blewford, Major, 99
Blitchington, 247
Blockhouse, 73, 81, 255, 261, 277, 279, 280, 281, 305
Blonde, 131
Bloody Point, 196
Bloody Savannah, 28, 29
Bloody Scout, 71, 110, 112
Blue Savannah, 58, 234
Blunderbuss, 147, 279
B'nai B'rith Klutznick Exhibit Hall, 268
Bohicket Creek, 156, 175
Boiling Springs, 282

Index

Boitard, Marshal, 221
Bold Branch, 300
Boreas, 158
Borough House, 29
Bostick, Chesley, 251
Boston (Continental Navy frigate), 121, 122, 139, 140, 152, 198
Boston, 157
Boutard, Captain, 161
Bowen, Lieutenant, 151
Bowling Green, 114, 115
Bowman, John, 138
Boyce, John, 71, 110, 281, 283, 284
Boyd, John, 279
Boyd, Samuel, 158
Boyd, St. Lawrence, 167
Boykin, Samuel, 275
Brabrant plantation, 194
Bradley, James, 37
Bradley, Matthew, 37
Bradley, Samuel, 46, 53
Bradley, Thomas, 37
Brandon, Thomas, 17–20, 22, 75, 76, 79, 296, 299
Brandon's Camp, 15, 20
Brandon's Defeat, 15
Brandywine, Pennsylvania, 68
Brass Town, 267, 270, 275
Brasstown Creek, 270
Bratton, William, 7, 9, 28, 29, 94, 95
Brattonsville, 29
Breach Inlet, 123, 124, 128
Breastwork, 141, 144, 176, 287
Breitenbach, Lieutenant, 202
Brereton, William, 208
Bricole (South Carolina frigate), 121
Brier Creek, 222, 223, 232
Brierly's Ferry, 74, 78, 79
Bristol (HMS), 130, 155, 157
Britigney, Marquis de, 161
British Army, 33, 84, 174, 194, 222, 225, 255, 259
British grenadier, 143, 144, 168
British Legion, 48, 64, 65, 131, 153, 163, 179, 228
British light infantry, 143, 162
Britton's Ferry, 57
Britton's Neck, 41, 114
Broad River, 6, 16, 17, 19, 33, 42, 71–75, 78, 88, 135, 200–203, 210, 249, 263, 294–296
Brockington, John, 60, 64
Brockington's plantation, 64
Brookgreen, 212, 216
Brookgreen Creek, 212
Brotherton, William, 184
Brown "Plundering Sam", 16, 21
Brown, Charity, 21
Brown, Colonel, 182, 223, 224
Brown, Tarleton, 182, 232, 233, 238–240, 246, 303
Brown, Thomas, 5, 68, 222–224, 234, 236, 249, 251, 254, 302
Browne, Thomas Alexander, 233
Brownfield, Robert, 10
Brown's Creek, 21, 23, 42, 43
Brown's Mill, 81, 82, 107
Brownsville Baptist Church, 107
Brownsville Church, 107
Bruce, Donald, 92
Bruere, George, 204
Brune (British frigate), 130
Bryan's Station, 115
Bryant's Mill, 306, 307

Buchanan, John, 8
Buckhead, 101
Buckhead Creek, 101
Buckingham Landing, 235, 237, 238
Bucks County Light Dragoons, 153
Buckshot, 34, 170, 204, 214, 215, 289
Buffalo Creek, 17
Buffington, Moses, 22, 296
Buford, Abraham, 7, 10, 12, 13, 24, 29, 45, 68, 231
Buford's Defeat, 9
Bull Creek Swamp, 110
Bull Head, 189, 193
Bull Pen, 80, 81
Bull Swamp, 92, 100
Bull Swamp Creek, 92
Bull, Fenwick, 151
Bull, Stephen, 203
Bull, William, Jr., 134, 163, 202
Bull, William, Sr., 206
Bull's Creek, 218
Bull's Inlet, 150, 152
Bull's plantation, 200, 201, 202
Bullock Creek Presbyterian Church, 79
Bullock's Creek, 16, 17, 19, 21, 72, 254
Bullock's Creek Ford, 294
Bullock's Ford, 15, 294
Bullock's Meeting House, 19
Bundling bag, 304
Bunker Hill, 128
Burch's (Birch's) Mill, 114, 115
Burdell's plantation, 180
Burgess Creek, 270
Burgoyne, John, 68
"Burr's" (Byces, Byas) Mill, 16, 19, 294, 295
Bush River, 292, 302
Bush River Church, 302
Butler, James, 21, 110–112
Butler, Jeffery, 105
Butler, John, 159
Butler, Thomas, 112
Butler, William, 110, 112
Buzzard's Island, 235, 236
Byce's Mill or Byas's Mill see "Burr's" (Byces, Byas) Mill,
Bynum, John, 266

Cain, Patrick, 247
Cainhoy, 131, 177, 194
Cainhoy Tavern, 177
Calderwood, Lieutenant, 203
Calderwood, William, 200
Caldwell, John, 35, 303
Caldwell's House, 110, 303
Calhoun County, 91, 92, 94, 96, 100
Calibogue (or Callibogie) Sound, 135, 237
Calk Brothers, 93
Calk, James, 88, 96
Calk, William, 96
Camden Battlefield site, 45
Camden, 1, 7, 10–13, 15, 21, 23, 24, 26, 31, 36, 37–41, 43, 44, 46, 47, 50–53, 55, 57, 59, 65, 68, 74, 76, 78, 85, 88, 94, 96, 97, 101–104, 106–108, 181, 233, 235, 244, 287, 298
Cameron, Alexander, 271, 272, 275
Camp, John Massey, 255
Campbell, David, 63
Campbell, Niel, 149
Campbell, Alexander, 155
Campbell, Archibald, 171, 194, 201
Campbell, Charles, 29

Campbell, David, 63
Campbell, George, 215–217
Campbell, James (also referred to as Campaign or Campen), 147
Campbell, John, 78, 166
Campbell, Robert, 221
Campbell, William, 116, 119, 124, 151
Camping Creek, 108
Canada, 149
Cane Brake, 98, 259
Cane Creek, 258, 269, 290
Canister, 146
Cannae, 298
Cannon, 32, 52, 57, 88–90, 96, 97, 104, 119–122, 130, 131, 137, 139, 141, 144, 145–149, 159, 160, 162, 163, 165, 176, 177, 179, 199, 203, 226, 237, 244, 249
Cannonade, 120, 131, 147
Canoe, 84, 115, 151, 155, 302
Cantey, John, 102
Cantey, Joseph, 102
Cantey's Plantation, 102, 218
Cape Fear, 151
Cape Fear River, 125, 198
Cape Hatteras, 153
Cape Romain, 150, 153, 198
Capers Creek, 200, 201, 205
Capers, George Sinclair, 195
Capitulation see surrender
Carey's Fort, 43, 47
Caribbean, 149
Carlisle, 71, 294
Carnes, Patrick, 217, 233
Carolina, 118
Carolina militia, 231
Carr, Patrick, 291, 302
Carrington, George, 99, 191
Carr's Fort (Georgia), 279
Carter, John, 114
Carter's House, 109, 111
Carter's Old Field, 109, 111
Cary, James, 44
Case, Christopher, 22
Casey, Christopher, 285, 296
Casey, Levi, 76
Cashua, 107
Cashua Ferry, 107, 109
Cashway Ferry, 107
Cassells, James, 57
Caswell, Richard, 39, 48, 288
Catawba Ford, 14
Catawba River, 9, 19, 24, 35, 36, 52, 64–66, 74
Catawbas, 14, 222, 229, 274, 275
Catfish Swamp, 80
Cavalry, 10, 11, 43, 46, 50, 54, 61, 62, 73, 89, 98, 108, 113, 121, 122, 141, 160, 161, 171, 173, 180, 181, 194, 214, 216, 225, 226, 230, 231, 244, 245, 256, 257, 287, 296, 297 see also dragoons
Cave, John, 233
Caw Caw Swamp, 243
Cayce, 86, 100
Cayce House, 86
Cayce Museum, 86
Cayce, John, 86
Cedar Creek, 286
Cedar Shoals, 12, 280
Cedar Springs, 90, 262, 281, 283–285
Ceres (HMS), 235, 236
Chace or Chase, John, 198

Champlin, Samuel, 198
Chaney, Baley [Baily], 243, 246, 247
Chapman, Joseph, 152
Chappel, James, 90
Chappell, Hicks, 94
Charles Town Artillery, 119, 120, 143
Charles Town Militia, 135, 254
Charleston, 1, 7–10, 19, 29, 31, 33, 36, 39, 43, 46–48, 55, 59, 77, 78, 85, 89, 90, 92–94, 98–102, 110, 113, 115, 116, 120–126, 128, 130–136, 138–140, 143–145, 148–154, 156–159, 161–174, 176, 177, 179, 180, 183–190, 193, 194, 196, 198–202, 205, 207, 208, 210, 213, 214, 217–219, 222–225, 227–229, 231, 232, 235, 238–240, 244, 245, 248, 252–254, 256–259, 261, 271, 287, 292, 305, 306
Charleston Bar, 130, 134, 150–152, 165
Charleston County, 123, 156, 165, 166, 175, 176, 185, 187, 189, 195, 198, 199, 229, 230
Charleston Harbor, 116, 118, 123, 125, 128, 150, 152–154, 157, 198, 254, 271
Charleston Lighthouse, 157
Charleston Neck, 135, 145, 159
Charleston Road, 165, 166, 251, 253
Charleton, Thomas, 251, 252
Charlotte Sophia of Mecklenburg-Strelitz, 249
Charlotte, North Carolina, 20, 24, 39, 50, 51, 64, 66, 100, 249, 257
Charming Peggy (brig), 134
Chatham (HMS), 165
Chatham, SC, 156
Chatooga, 275
Chattahoochee River, 276
Chauga, 267, 270, 275
Chauga River, 270
Chehaw, 208, 209
Chehaw Neck, 209, 210
Chehaw Point, 207, 209
Chehohee, 267, 275
Chehokee, 267, 275
Cheohee, 267, 270, 275
Cheowee, 267, 271, 275
Cheowie, 267, 275
Cheraw, 32, 33, 63, 75, 78, 79
Cherokee (HM Sloop), 118, 120, 125, 126, 155
Cherokee, 16, 71, 112, 134, 229, 234, 251, 252, 261, 263–266, 267, 270–276, 280, 281, 301, 302, 305, 306
Cherokee Campaign, 249, 266, 275
Cherokee County, 16, 19, 33, 66, 72, 294, 295
Cherokee Falls, 72
Cherokee Ford, 33–35, 263, 279, 280
Cherokee Indian Town, 267
Cherokee lands, 259–261, 271
Cherokee Path, 35, 303
Cherokee settlements, 277
Cherokee territory, 272, 276, 305
Cherokee Town, 267
Cherokee Villages, 267, 268
Cherokee wars, 270
Cheshire, Tenison, 114
Chesnee, 295
Chesney, Alexander, 16, 19, 21, 42, 98, 241, 262, 294
Chester, 8, 14, 17, 71, 72, 74, 75
Chester County, 8, 11, 12, 14, 17, 23, 36, 72, 74, 75
Chester Courthouse, 72
Chester District, 71, 72
Chester militiamen, 74
Chesterfield County, 3, 5, 78
Chicamaugas, 264, 271

Index

Chinnery, St. John, 151
Choate, Georgia, 272
Chovin's plantation, 103
Chowan Creek, 201
Christ Church, 125
Christ Church Parish, 195
Christmas, 79, 217, 255, 292
Church Creek, 166, 167
Clarendon County, 56, 58, 70, 76, 91, 102, 234
Clark, Alured, 162
Clark, George Rogers, 255
Clark Hill Reservoir, 249
Clark's Creek, 82
Clark's Ford, 281, 282, 284
Clarke, Elijah, 34, 233, 276, 283, 284, 287, 289–292, 300, 302
Clarke, John, 218, 301
Clemson University, 268
Clemson, 268, 271
Clermont, 43, 45
Clinton, Henry, 1, 10, 47, 66, 116, 121, 126, 128, 133, 136–138, 140–142, 144, 145, 147, 148, 154, 162, 169, 179, 227, 271
Clinton, James, 17
Clinton County, 292
Clitherall, James, 243
Clouds Creek, 35, 109, 110, 112, 303
Clouds Creek Massacre, 111, 304
Clover, 64
Clyo, Georgia, 222
Coates, John, 178, 180, 186, 189–191
Cobb, 300
Cochran's Magazine, 133, 134
Cochrane, Charles, 228
Cockades, 41
Cockspur Island, 196
Coehorns, 143, 215
Coffin Land, 165
Coffin, John, 8, 11, 75, 77, 168, 174, 185, 194, 257, 303
Coleman, Charles, 7
Coleman, Richard, 26
Coleman, Samuel, 36
Colleton, John, 182, 193, 194
Colleton, Peter, 182
Colleton City, 238
Colleton County, 165, 227, 228, 238, 240
Colleton County Company, 158, 228
Colleton County Regiment, 169, 241
Colleton House, 182, 183
Colleton's plantation, 193
Collins, James Potter, 7
Collins, Mr., 246, 247
Columbia, 2, 8, 86, 87, 94, 256, 278
Combahee (Salkehatchie) River, 238
Combahee Bluff, 209
Combahee Ferry, 205, 207, 209, 210
Combahee River, 206, 227
Comet (row galley), 143, 154, 221
Comet (schooner tender), 151
Communication trench, 139, 143
Conch Creek, 57
Concord, Massachusetts, 116
Confederacy (Continental Navy frigate), 198
Congaree, 88, 149, 182, 258
Congaree militiamen, 114
Congaree River, 76, 86, 87, 94, 97, 99, 101, 235, 251, 303
Congarees, 23, 76

Congress (galley), 199, 220, 221
Congress (Pennsylvania privateer), 198
Congressional forces, 96, 99, 140, 141, 193, 225, 245, 273, 287
Congressional troops, 97, 139, 144, 228, 302
Connaway, William, 99
Connecticut, 35, 198
Continental Army, 1, 21, 33, 52, 68, 93, 97, 138, 149, 163, 173, 190, 196, 202, 247, 256, 284
Continental Congress, 130, 272
Continental light dragoons, 176, 223, 228
Continental light infantry, 160
Continental line, 143
Continental Navy, 121
Continental troops, 12, 201, 272, 296
Continentals, 48, 50, 51, 54, 55, 78, 96, 98, 121, 126, 128, 130, 133, 136, 139–143, 147–149, 153, 160, 164, 167, 173, 183, 184, 191, 202–205, 209, 223, 226, 231, 234, 235, 244, 245, 256–259, 295–297
Conway, 106, 216
Conyers, Daniel, 102, 166
Cooke, William, 34
Cooper, George, 171
Cooper, John, 239, 242
Cooper, Richard, 96
Cooper, Robert, 71
Cooper, Samuel, 170
Cooper, William, 95
Cooper River, 55, 118, 125, 131, 136, 138–140, 143, 146, 154, 179, 181, 182, 189, 193, 232
Coosaw Island, 206
Coosaw River, 200
Coosawhatchie, 224, 225
Coosawhatchie Bridge, 221, 228
Coosawhatchie River, 224, 225
Coosawhatchie Swamp, 224
Corn-acre Creek, 272
Corner Creek, 275
Cornwallis, Charles, 1, 8, 10, 29, 31, 38, 43, 45–47, 50, 52, 54, 62, 64, 66, 74, 75–79, 133, 137, 140, 146, 162, 163, 173, 183, 194, 208, 217, 231, 245, 255, 292, 293, 296, 298
Corruthers, Mr., 281
Cotter, Moses, 251, 252
Cotton, James, 278
Council of Safety, 125, 172, 249, 251, 254
Council, Henry, 3
Court-martial, 59, 68, 175
Courtney, 82
Cowens Ford, 249
Cowpens, 22, 73, 74, 75, 217, 283, 284, 293, 294, 295, 298
Cowpens Creek, 294
Cowpens Mountain, 298
Cowpens National Battlefield, 295
Craig, James Henry, 163, 164
Craig, John, 11
Crane, Charles, 22
Crawford, John, 305
Crawford, Robert, 11
Crawford, Thomas, 11
Creech, Richard, 291
Creeks, 234, 271, 302
Croft State Park, 16
Crookshanks, John, 217
Cross Anchor, 286
Cross Hill, 299
Cross Roads, 72, 188
Crown dragoons, 24

Crown forces, 14, 24, 31, 32, 39, 41, 55, 64, 70, 76, 78, 85, 92, 97–99, 121, 131, 133, 135, 136, 138–140, 142, 146–148, 153, 158, 159, 161, 163, 174, 177, 185–187, 190, 194, 205, 208, 215, 216, 221, 226, 232, 233, 240, 241, 245, 255, 258, 261, 266, 287, 291, 292, 294
Crown troops, 57, 72, 74, 104, 141, 144, 161, 163, 209, 217, 223, 225, 229, 235, 294
Cruger, John Harris, 98, 233, 244, 253, 255–258, 291, 292, 300
Cryer, James, 217
Culbertson, Josiah, 18, 21
Cumberland Gap, 271
Cummings Point, 126, 140, 155
Cunningham, John, 255, 292
Cunningham, Joseph, 112
Cunningham, Patrick, 251, 254, 255, 259
Cunningham, Robert, 35, 99, 100, 254, 293, 303
Cunningham, William "Bloody Bill", 18, 23, 35, 71, 99, 100, 110–113, 247, 255, 258, 273, 276–278, 282, 284, 285, 301, 304, 305
Curacao, 151
Cusack, Adam, 64
Cypress Swamp, 168, 171

Dabb, Joseph, 82
Daniel, Oliver, 198
Daniel Island, 193
Dansey, William, 122
Daphne (HMS), 151, 152
Darlington County, 64
Daufuskie Island, 196, 198, 236
Daughters of the American Revolution, 24, 29, 43, 55, 101, 210, 244, 260, 261, 268
Dauzey, 198
Davant, Charles, 196, 235–237
Davie, William Richardson, 9, 11, 24, 25, 52, 160
Davis, 113, 304
Davis, William Ransom, 219
Dawkins, 90, 91
Dawkins, George, 175
de Grasse, François Joseph Paul Comte, 244, 258
de Kalb, Johann Baron, 44, 47, 50
De Lancey's Regiment, 94
DeLancey's Brigade, 255, 287
De Peyster, Abraham, 68, 154, 228, 263
De Peyster, James, 84, 218
De Peyster's (or De Peister's) Capture, 82
Dean Swamp, 113, 114
Dean, Captain, 213
Dean, John, 39
Dean's Swamp Creek, 253
Declaration of Independence, 133, 188, 202, 203, 208
Deer, John, 80
Defiance (brig), 198
Defiance (sloop), 198
Defiance (South Carolina schooner), 120
Delany, Thomas, 3
Delaware Continentals, 48, 50, 53, 164, 235, 256, 296, 297
Delaware light infantry, 256
Delaware Regiment, 51, 175, 205, 208
Delaware, 198
Delawares, 271
d'Estaing, Jean-Baptiste-Charles-Henri-Hector, 136
Deveaux (also spelled DeVeaux), Andrew, Jr. 205, 207, 226, 240
Dewee's Island, 154
Dewee's Tavern, 185, 187

Dewey's (Dewee's) Inlet, 154
DeWitt's Corner, 275
Dickson, Joseph, 283
Dill, Philip, 149
Dill's Bluff, 116, 118, 122
Dillon, 65
Dillon County, 65, 68, 70, 80, 82, 106, 108, 109
Dinkins, Samuel, 46
Dirty Creek, 277
Dispatch (Brigantine), 206
Dixon, Major, 11
Doharty, James, 237
Dollard's Tavern, 62
Dorchester, 90, 98, 165, 168, 171, 172, 173, 174, 175, 177, 238, 245
Dorchester, Massachusetts, 171
Dorchester County, 168, 171, 238, 240
Dorchester Road, 165, 168, 172, 244, 245
Dougherty, Captain, 202
Douglas, Charles, 165
Downes, William, 43, 45, 52
Downs, Jonathan, 266
Dowse, Dr., 183
Doyle, John, 41, 85, 92, 98, 103, 183
Doyle, Welbore Ellis, 41, 52, 85, 88, 103–105, 107, 257
Dragging Canoe, 264
Dragoons, 10, 11, 24, 25, 41, 46, 52, 64, 65, 71, 74, 88, 90, 98, 99, 104, 108, 122, 162, 166–168, 170, 179, 185, 194, 195, 225, 231, 233, 234, 239, 240, 242, 258, 263, 278, 283, 284, 291, 292, 300, 303 see also cavalry
Draper, Lyman Copeland, 11, 22, 90, 241
Drayton Hall, 167, 169
Drayton, John, 274
Drayton, William Henry, 125, 167, 254, 272
Drayton's Plantation, 166–168
Dreher Plantation, 86
Dreher, Godfrey, 87, 90
Dreher's mill, 90
Drew, Thomas Haynes, 49
Drowning Creek, 80
Du Bose, Peter, 38
Du Bose's Crossing, 38
Du Coin, Sergeant, 187
Dubose Ferry, 37
Dudley, 50
Dudley, Guilford, 48
Due West, 275, 300
Dugan, James, 296, 298
Dugan, Robert, 298
Dugan, Thomas, 16, 22
Dugan's Plantation, 295, 296, 298
Duncan's Creek, 281, 282, 285
Dundas, Thomas, , 167
Dunlap, James, 255, 262, 263, 273, 284, 292, 300
Dunlap's Defeat, 300
Dunmore, John Murray, 4th Earl of, 126
Duplin County, 80
Duprees and Lippees ferry, 144
Durant, Henry, 56
Dutch Fork, 6
Dutchman's Creek, 104
Dysentery, 48

Eadytown, 248
Eagle, (*Ranger*'s tender), 153
Earle, Baylis, 23, 261
Earle, John, 261

Index

Earle's Ford, 260–262, 265
Earle's Fort, 16, 23, 260, 261, 264
Earle's Plantation, 23, 260
Earlesville, 260
Earthworks, 93, 141, 153, 162, 255
East Fork, 74
Edge Hill, 304
Edgefield, 28, 113, 277, 278, 301
Edgefield County, 110, 249, 258, 277, 278, 301, 305
Edgefield plantation, 28
Edisto Island, 161, 199, 200, 204, 206
Edisto Island Volunteer Company, 199
Edisto River, 91, 92, 97, 100, 113, 165, 169, 199, 227, 229, 237, 238, 241, 243, 247, 253, 306
Eggleston, Joseph, 90, 180, 191, 233, 258
Eggleston's capture, 87
Elder, Robert, 22
Ellet, Elizabeth, 156, 159
Elliott, Barnard, 118–120
Ellison's Fort, 280
Elphinstone (British brig), 198
Embrasures, 139, 144
Empress of Russia, 236
Engineer, 78, 122, 135, 138, 141, 145, 146, 165, 187, 256
Enoree River, 16, 21, 22, 258, 282, 284, 286, 287, 306
Ervin, Hugh, 85
Ervin, John, 166
Esseneca, 267, 272, 273
Estatoe, 267, 270, 273
Estatoy, 273
Eustash, 275
Eustaste, 267, 271, 275
Eustustie, 267, 275
Eutaw Springs, 165, 180, 181, 243, 244, 245, 284
Eutawville, 234, 243
Evans Creek, 71, 284
Eveleigh's plantation, 156, 161
Ewald, Johann von, 137, 139, 143, 148, 162, 167, 176
Ewing, James, 296
Experiment (HMS), 130, 235, 236
Experiment (privateer), 152

Fair American (South Carolina privateer brig), 158, 198
Fair Bluff, North Carolina, 80
Fair Forest, 21, 23, 292
Fair Forest Spring, 260
Fair Forest Swamp, 189
Fair Lawn, 23, 177, 180, 182, 183, 193, 194
Fair Lawn River, 301
Fair Spring, 171, 173, 175
Fairfield County, 6, 8, 35, 75, 79, 104
Fairforest Creek, 16–18, 22, 23, 282
Fanning, David, 33
Fanning, Edward, 75
Farr, Thomas, 176
Farr, William, 294
Farrow, Landon, 306
Farrow, Thomas, 306, 307
Farrow's Station, 306, 307
Farr's plantation, 95
Featherstone (Featherson, Fetherston or Fetherstone), John, 13, 15
Featherstone (Featherson, Fetherston or Fetherstone), Richard, 15
Fenwick, Edward, 238–240
Fenwick, Thomas, 158
Fenwick Hall, 156, 164, 165
Fenwick's Point, 141

Ferguson, James, 21, 30, 262
Ferguson, John, 126, 130
Ferguson, Moses, 27
Ferguson, Patrick, 33, 66, 154, 228, 284, 288
Ferguson's Plantation, 175, 176, 225
Fergusons Swamp, 180
Few, Benjamin, 289–292
Fickling, Joseph, 199
Field pieces, 32, 36, 88, 96, 102, 128, 135, 138, 159–161
Fields Point, 209
Files, Adam, 281
Finlay, John, 200, 203
First Continental Congress, 133, 188, 208
Fish Dam, 71
Fish Dam Engagement, 74
Fish Dam Ford, 42, 71, 72, 75, 294
Fish Ponds, 208
Fishing Creek, 12, 14, 15, 17, 35, 36, 51
Fishing Creek Church, 14, 30, 46
Five-Fathom Hole, 131
Flag of truce, 10, 20, 37, 75, 77, 85, 95, 171, 174, 242, 304
Flat Rock, 23
Flatboats, 61
Fleming, Robert, 21
Flenniken or Flennekin or Flanagan, Samuel, 25
Fletchall, Thomas, 251, 253, 254
Florence, 37, 38, 58, 109
Florence County, 3, 5, 31, 41, 82, 104, 105, 114
Florida, 277
Floyd, Abraham, 27, 31
Floyd, Matthew, 21, 27, 30
Folly Island, 156, 165
Forage, 3, 36, 61, 90, 105, 158, 165, 167, 171, 194, 199, 200, 208–210, 216, 220, 223, 231, 247, 257, 291, 300
Ford, Mary, 242
Ford, Tobias, 242
Ford's Bridge, 263
Ford's Horseshoe plantation, 240–242
Foreman, George, 305
Forks of Edisto, 91, 112, 243, 258, 278
Forlorn hope, 118, 192
Fort Anderson, 33, 34
Fort Balfour, 97, 238–240
Fort Carey, 43, 44
Fort Charlotte, 249, 254
Fort Cornwallis, 234
Fort Dorchester, 170–173, 186, 244
Fort Dreadnought, 233
Fort Galphin, 233, 234, 302
Fort Granby, 1, 55, 86–88, 90, 91, 95, 233, 256, 302
Fort Grierson, 234
Fort Independence, 279
Fort Johnson, 116, 118–122, 126, 128, 131, 138, 141, 144, 150, 151, 155, 159, 176
Fort Lindley (Lyndley) (Rayborn, Raeburns, Rabun's, Rabon or Creek), 263, 266, 272, 277
Fort Lyttleton, 135, 200–202, 204, 237
Fort Motte, 1, 55, 88, 89, 92–94, 96, 97, 101, 256
Fort Moultrie, 116, 123, 124, 128, 131, 136, 140, 141, 146, 148, 150, 153, 154, 159, 179, 271
Fort Prince, 260–264
Fort Prince George, 252, 268
Fort Rutledge, 268, 273
Fort Saltketcher, 238
Fort Sullivan, 116, 118, 123, 128, 130, 134, 140, 150, 154

Fort Sumter, 116
Fort Sumter National Monument, 123, 155
Fort Thicketty, 33
Fort Upton, 59
Fort Watson, 1, 40, 41, 53, 54, 85, 91, 93, 95, 96, 101, 102, 234
Fort Williams, 293, 299
Fortifications, 35, 53, 92, 93, 116, 128, 153, 161, 172, 213, 218, 233, 249, 256
Fortune, Pompey, 8
Fortune Springs Garden, 9
Foster, George, 171
Fountain Inn, 280
Four Columns Mansion, 260
Four Holes, 240
Four Holes Creek, 186
Four Holes Swamp, 238, 239
Four Mile Branch (Four Mile Creek), 92, 99
Francis, Colonel, 38, 105, 135
Francis Marion National Forest, 165, 177, 189
Francis Marion Park, 210
Francis Marion State Forest, 230
François (privateer), 134
Franks, Theobald, 241
Fraser James, 287
Fraser, Simon, 242, 243
Fraser, Thomas, 23, 40, 170, 190, 193, 224, 242
Freer, John, 188
Freer, Solomon, 188
French and Indian War, 172, 271
French Quarter Creek, 194
French, 138, 151, 161, 211, 221, 236, 268
Friday's or Fridig's Ferry, 86, 88, 235, 257, 258
Frigate, 121, 130, 131, 134, 136, 150, 154, 199, 235
Frisbie, Paul, 159, 161
Frost, Jonathan, 21
Fuller Swamp Creek, 240
Fuller, William, 122
Fuller's (Benjamin) House Plantation, 168, 169, 171
Futhey, John, 220

Gadsden, Christopher, 116
Gadsden's Wharf, 118, 140
Gadsden's regiment, 116
Gaffney, 16, 33, 34, 294, 295
Gage, Thomas, 126
Gaillard, Mr., 248
Gaillard's Island, 98
Gaither, Richard, 13
Gaither's Old Field, 11, 13
Galatea (frigate), 134, 157
Gales, Kit, 46
Galley, 57, 154, 159, 161, 164, 165, 176, 186, 187, 205, 219–221, 236, 237
Galphin, George, 233
Ganey or Gainey, Micajah, 41, 58, 80, 114, 115, 216
Gapway Swamp, 214, 216
Garden, Alexander, 184, 185
Garden, John, 26, 27, 36
Garden's Plantation, 168, 184, 185
Gardiner, Valentine, 121, 201, 202
Gardiner's or Gardner, 237
Garnett, 222
Garth, George, 235
Gaston, John, 12–14
Gaston, Joseph, 13
Gates, Horatio, 1, 15, 38, 45, 47, 50, 51, 53, 59, 78, 214, 287
Geiger, Emily, 90

General Clinton, 151
General Lincoln (brig), 153
General's Island, 60
George (transport), 136
George III, 27, 55, 78, 213, 249
Georges Creek, 247
Georgetown, 3, 5, 10, 32, 55–58, 61, 62, 70, 78, 82, 84, 85, 102–104, 114, 181, 198, 210–220, 256
Georgetown Artillery Company, 213
Georgetown Bar, 210, 212
Georgetown Bay, 84
Georgetown County, 56–58, 82, 103, 210
Georgetown harbor, 213
Georgia, 1, 5, 11, 19, 27, 54, 58, 70, 96, 100, 153, 196, 202, 207, 222, 224, 233–235, 243, 245, 246, 249, 251, 262, 270, 275, 276, 279, 280, 283, 288, 296, 301, 302
Georgia Continentals, 223, 295
Georgia Legionnaires, 149
Georgia Loyalist Dragoons, 135
Georgia Loyalist militiamen, 292
Georgia Loyalists, 223, 229, 232, 291
Georgia militia, 34, 275, 276, 289, 290, 292, 302
Georgia Navy, 221
Georgia Packet, 118
Germain (HMS), 131
Gibbes Farm, 156
Gibbes, Robert Reeve, 159, 163
Gibbes, Sarah Reeve, 159
Gibbes, William, 164
Gibbes's (John) Plantation, 136, 138, 166, 167
Gibbes's (Robert) Plantation, 156, 163
Gibbes's (William) Plantation, 156, 161, 162, 164
Gibbs, Zacharias, 262
Gibson's Meeting House, 6, 7
Giesendanner, Henry, 97, 99
Gilbert, 68, 252, 253
Gilders Creek, 16, 296
Giles, William, 22
Gillam, Captain, 79
Gillespie, James, 32
Gillon, Alexander, 93, 198
Gillon's Retreat, plantation, 93
Girard, Georgia, 245
Gist, Mordecai, 205, 208–210
Givham's Ferry, 238
Glasgow Packet (transport brig), 155
Goddard's plantation, 82
Godfrey's Savannah, 208, 225
Goings, Mike, 81
Golden Grove Creek, 259
Golden Rule (British transport), 198
Goldesbrough, Thomas, 236
Goodwyn, William, 114
Goose Creek, 168, 171, 173, 175, 184, 185
Goose Creek Bridge, 184, 186
Gordon, Roger, 105
Gornell, George, 174
Gose, Manning, 75
Goucher Creek, 19, 34
Governor Tonyn's Revenge, 198
Gowen, John, 264
Gowen's Fort, 260–264
Gowen's Old Fort, 261, 262, 273
Gowensville, 260
Graham, Colin, 204, 229
Graham, William, 284
Granby, 86
Grannies Quarter Creek, 44

Index **369**

Granny's Quarter, 39
Grant, Alexander, 140
Granville County Loyalist militia, 205
Grape shot, 54, 103, 104, 122, 124, 142–145, 155, 204, 237, 244
Graves, John, 155
Gray, Robert, 218
Gray's Hill, 200
Great Branch, 253
Great Cane Brake, 259, 260
Great Falls, 14, 24, 35, 36
Great Savannah, 40, 58, 234
Great Swamp, 221
Greeleyville, 102
Green Pond, 165
Green Spring, 15, 17, 21, 282, 285
Green Swamp, 43, 44
Greene, Nathanael, 1, 8, 46, 51–53, 75, 78, 80, 85, 90, 91, 93, 96–100, 108, 114, 149, 164, 166, 170, 173, 174, 180, 181, 183, 186, 190, 193, 200, 208, 215, 217, 218, 233, 234, 244, 253, 256–258, 296, 298, 300
Greenland Swamp, 248
Greenville, 16
Greenville County, 259–261, 266, 275, 289
Greenwich (HM Sloop), 221
Greenwood County, 251, 252, 255, 303, 305
Greer, 261, 264
Gregg, James, 33
Gregg, Robert, 31, 33
Grenadier Battalion von Graff, 122
Grenadiers, 84, 118–120, 138, 145, 147, 244
Gresham, George, 295
Grey, Captain, 104
Grierson, James, 298
Grimke, John Faucheraud, 143
Grindal Shoals, 292, 294
Guerrillas, 11
Guilford Courthouse, 33, 54
Gum Swamp, 43, 44, 48

Hacker, Hoysted, 153
Haddrell's Point, 123–126, 131, 150, 153, 154, 177
Hale, William, 71
Half-Moon Battery, 154
Halfway Creek, 93
Halfway Creek Swamp, 253
Halfway House, 200, 203
Halfway Swamp, 76, 77, 82
Halifax, Nova Scotia, 126
Hall William, Captain, 162
Ham Creek, 3
Hamilton, James, 164
Hamilton, John (1720–1790), 196
Hamilton, John (d. 1817), 160
Hamilton, Paul, 239
Hamilton, Robert, 251
Hamilton's Ford, 72
Hamilton's landing place, 144
Hammond, LeRoy, 254, 272, 278, 301
Hammond, Samuel, 181, 278, 289, 301
Hammond's Mill, 301
Hammond's Plantation, 166, 167
Hammond's Store, 10, 292, 293
Hamond, Andrew Snape, 131
Hampton, 90
Hampton, Andrew, 34, 263
Hampton, Anthony, 262, 263, 265, 266
Hampton, Edward, 23, 71, 110, 263, 265, 273, 274

Hampton, Henry, 7, 11, 88, 186, 191, 273
Hampton, John, 7
Hampton, Noah, 262
Hampton, Preston, 265, 266
Hampton, Richard, 86, 90–92, 100, 257, 303
Hampton, Wade, 86, 88, 90, 91, 94, 173, 182, 184, 186, 189
Hampton County, 3, 227
Hampton house, 265, 266
Hampton Massacre, 260, 264, 265
Hampton's cavalry, 186
Hampton's Store, 86
Hampton's Surprise, 99
Handy, Levin, 233
Hanger, George, 64
Hanging Rock, 1, 10, 15, 18, 23–27, 36, 39, 40, 74
Hannibal, 298
Hannon, Edwin, 261
Hannon, John, 261
Hannon, Winnie, 261
Hardeeville, 220
Harden, Charles, 170
Harden, William, 99, 149, 169, 170, 199, 222–224, 238–240, 242, 247
Hargis, William, 144
Harlee's Bridge, 65
Harrington, Henry William, 140
Harris, Colonel, 135
Harrison, Elizabeth (Hampton), 265
Harrison, James, 265
Harrison, John, 38, 41, 85, 96, 102
Harrison, Robert, 37, 38
Harrison, Samuel, 38
Hartley's Creek, 109, 110
Hartstone, Joachim, 221
Hartzog, George, 247
Hartzog, Tobias, 247
Harvey, Thomas, 278
Hasty Point, 82
Hasty Point plantation, 84
Hathaway, Elkanah, 151
Hawthorne, James, 35, 95, 293
Hayes, Joseph, 22, 23, 246, 293, 296, 297, 304
Hayes Mill Pond, 246
Hayes Station, 35, 110, 304
Hayes Station Massacre, 304
Hayne, Isaac, 166, 169, 170, 242, 300
Heath Springs, 23, 24, 106
Height, Colonel, 261
Height's Blockhouse, 260, 261
Hellhole Creek, 109, 110
Hem Branch, 3
Hemingway, 57, 62
Hempstead Hill, 138
Henderson, James, 134
Henderson, John, 160
Henderson, William, 145, 200, 221
Henry, William, 32
Hermitage Mill, 43, 52
Hessian grenadiers, 122, 139, 140, 142, 143, 146, 168
Hessian light infantrymen, 137
Hessian Regiment von Benning, 176
Hessians, 121, 136, 139, 141–144, 146, 159, 160, 205
Hetty, 124, 151
Hewlett, Thomas, 26, 203
Heyward, Thomas, 202
Heyward, Thomas, Jr., 119
Hickory Grove, 16, 294
Hicks, George, 65

High Hills of Santee, 29, 40, 63, 98, 170
Highlanders, 50, 128, 155, 158, 160, 162, 225, 240, 297
Hightower River, 275
Hill, Robert, 28
Hill, William, 27, 28, 30
Hillhouse plantation, 296, 298
Hill's Iron Works, 27
Hillsborough, North Carolina, 7, 47, 51, 288
Hilton Head, 235–238
Hilton Head Island, 196, 202, 235, 236
Hinrichs, Johann, 141, 143, 145, 146, 168
Historic Brattonsville, 29
Historic Camden Revolutionary War site, 43
Hobcaw Magazine, 132–134, 150
Hobkirk Hill, 43, 46, 51, 53, 54, 108, 256
Hog Island, 120, 150, 153
Hog Island Creek, 120, 125, 150
Hoil's Old Place, 289
Holker (privateer brig), 198
Hollingsworth Mill, 42, 259
Holmes, James, 255
Holy Cross Church, 28
Hopkins, David, 72
Hopkins Place, 72
Horn's Creek, 301
Horn's Creek Baptist Church, 301
Horner's Creek or Corner, 301
Hornet, 158, 221
Hornwork, 133, 140, 141, 144, 147
Horry, Elias, 230
Horry, Hugh, 62, 85, 105, 208, 235
Horry, Peter, 3, 59, 61, 97, 102–104, 190, 195, 214–216, 218, 230, 231
Horry County, 106, 114, 216
Horse Creek, 258
Horse Neck, 241
Horse Savannah, 168, 169, 242
Horseshoe Creek, 154
Hot shot, 140–142
House, Christian, 100
Houseman, Henry, 13
Howard, John Eager, 296, 297
Howard, Oliver Otis, 206
Howard, Thomas, 265
Howard's Gap, 264, 265
Howe, John, 236
Howe, Richard, 130
Howe, Robert, 202
Howe, William, 126
Howell, John, 236
Howitzer, 103, 121, 139–143, 191, 192, 202, 203, 209
Howland, Captain, 152
Huck, Christian, 14, 21, 27, 29
Huck's Defeat, 29
Hudson, Charles, 153
Huger, 161, 189, 194
Huger, Benjamin, 226
Huger, Daniel, 162, 204
Huger, Isaac, 141, 159, 160, 175, 179, 298
Huger's bridge, 231
Hughes, Benjamin, 111
Hughes, Captain, 19
Hughes, Isaac, 76
Hulin's (Hulon's) Mill, 80, 109
Hunt, Anthony, 151
Hunter, Andrew, 33
Hunting Island, 200, 201, 205, 206

Hunting-shirts, 13
Huntington Beach State Park, 212
Hunts Bluff, 31
Hurricane Meeting House, 293
Hussars, 179
Hutchinson Island, 205, 206, 226
Hyrne, Edmund, 137, 138
Hyrne's plantation, 208

Independent Troop of Black Dragoons, 175
Indian Campaign, 266
Indian Creek, 16, 22, 253, 295, 296
Indian Massacre Grave, 290
Indian Villages, 267
Indiantown, 85, 216
Indiantown Presbyterian Church, 62, 63
Indigo, 1, 118, 202, 214
Infantry, 10, 11, 47, 50, 58, 64, 88, 89, 105, 122, 135, 153, 167, 168, 180, 183, 190, 192, 194, 208, 209, 225, 233, 244, 262, 289
Ingles, 242, 243
Inman, Joshua, 291
Inman, Shadrack, 286, 287
Innes, Alexander, 262, 263, 287
Inness (Innis), James, 190
Irby's Mills, 32
Iron works, 28
Iroquois, 271
Irvine, Major, 217
Irwin, John, 149
Island Ford, 21
Islandton, 227
Isle of Palms, 128, 154
Iva, 281
Izard, Ralph, 175

Jack, Samuel, 275
Jack's Creek, 63, 70
Jackson, 3, 5, 9, 11, 26, 143, 213, 233
Jackson, Andrew, 9, 11, 26
Jackson, Captain, 143, 154
Jackson, James, 149, 301
Jackson, Robert, 26
Jackson, Stephen, 5
Jackson, Steven, 3
Jacksonboro Bridge, 225
Jacksonboro County, 227
Jacksonboro, 164, 165, 227–229, 231, 232, 237
Jaegers, 137, 138, 143, 145–147, 162, 167, 168, 176
Jamaica, 134, 157, 158
James' Creek, 285
James Island, 116, 118, 121, 122, 143, 144, 150, 155, 156, 158, 160, 162, 164, 165, 176, 187
James Island Company, 147
James, John, 55
James, John, Jr., 63
James, John, Sr., 41, 56, 58, 60, 62, 63, 77
James, Robert, 115
Jameson, John, 162
Jamestown, 230
Jamieson, David, 231
Jarvis, Stephen, 170, 185, 241
Jasper, William, 222, 223
Jasper County, 220, 224, 226
Jefferies Creek (Jeffries, Jeffers's Creek), 3, 41, 114
Jefferson, 5
Jenkin's Cross Roads, 72
Jimmies Creek, 285
Joanna, 304

Index

Jocassee, 267, 270, 273
John Town, 113
Johns Island, 136, 156–158, 160, 161, 164, 179, 188, 199
Johnson, Jimmy, 74
Johnson, Uzal, 68
Johnson's Swamp, 61
Johnsonville, 41, 82, 105
Johnston, Peter, 11
Johnston, William, 33, 283
Jolly, John, 22
Jolly, Joseph, 299
Jolly, Major, 76, 299
Jones, John, 262
Jones, Joseph, 80, 81, 114
Jones, Thomas, 284
Jonesville, 294
Juniper Spring, 252, 253, 257

Kean, Roger, 198
Kee (Key), Thomas, 301
Keith, George Keith Elphinstone, viscount, 162
Keithfield, 94, 181, 182
Keithfield Plantation, 181
Kellett, Joseph, 280
Kellett's Blockhouse, 280, 281
Kelsall or Kelsell, William, 149, 240
Kelsey Creek, 15, 18, 281
Kelty, John, 174
Kemp, Lieutenant, 223
Kenan, James, 80
Keneshaw's Creek, 38
Kennedy, Thomas, 20
Kennedy, William, 20
Kennedy Tavern, 157
Keowee, 252, 267, 268, 270, 273
Keowee River, 252, 272, 273
Kerr, Samuel, 291
Kershaw, James, 86
Kershaw, Joseph, 43, 45, 86
Kershaw County, 23, 24, 38, 43, 46, 108
Kershaw's Creek, 38, 41
Kettle Creek, 280
Kiawah Island, 156, 159
Kienen, Ludwig (or Lewis Kenan), 168, 185
Kilgore, Benjamin, 280
King's American Regiment, 218
Kings Mountain, 9, 22, 33, 35, 43, 59, 65, 66, 68, 183, 284, 293, 296, 298
Kings Mountain National Military Park, 66
Kings Mountain State Park, 66
King's Rangers, 223, 251
Kingstree, 36, 37, 55–57, 60–63, 70, 104, 214, 215
Kingstree Regiment, 181
Kinnards, 302
Kirkland, Moses, 253, 254, 293
Kirkpatrick, James, 79
Kirkwood, Robert H., 53, 98, 256
Kitfield Plantation, 181
Knox, James, 71
Knyphausen, Wilhelm von, 136
Kolb, Abel, 33, 80, 81
Kolb, Sarah, 81
Kosciusko, Thaddeus, 78, 122, 187, 256
Kowatch or Kovats, Michael de, 135
Kuykendall, Peter, 17

Lacey, Edward, 199
Lacey, Edward, Jr., 30, 72, 94, 190, 200

Lacey, Edward, Sr., 30
Lacey, John, 294
Lacey, Reuben, 30
Ladson, James, 228, 229
Ladson, Thomas, 163
Lady William (schooner), 128
Ladys (or Ladies) Island, 200, 206
Lafayette, Marie Jean Paul Joseph du Motier Marquis de, 9, 44, 211
Lafayette Park, 211
Lake Greenwood, 303
Lake Hartwell, 267, 268, 270
Lake Isaquenna, 271
Lake Keowee, 268
Lake Marion, 92, 98, 101, 165, 234, 244, 248
Lake Moultrie, 181
Lake Murray, 289
Lake Saranac, 282
Lake Strom Thurmond, 249
Lake View, 68
Lake Wateree, 108
Lake Wylie, 27, 64
Lancaster, 9, 12
Lancaster County, 9, 23, 106
Land, John, 11, 12, 24
Landrum, 260, 261
Lang, Captain, 24, 291
Langham, Elias, 47
Latta, 80
Laurel Bay, 202
Laurens, Henry, 251
Laurens, John, 136, 146, 164, 171, 175, 186, 187, 208, 209, 224
Laurens County, 22, 110, 252, 255, 258, 266, 277, 280, 292, 299, 304
Lawson, John, 23, 285
Lawson, Mr., 282
Lawson's Fork, 281, 283, 285
Lawson's Fork Creek, 282, 284, 289
Leacraft or Leacroft, John, 149, 196, 237
Leacraft or Leacroft, William, 237
Lean, Osburn, 80
Lechmere, Nicholas, 240
Lee (galley), 220, 221
Lee, Charles, 128, 272
Lee, Henry "Light–Horse Harry", 52–54, 79, 88, 90, 96–99, 101, 164, 168, 173, 175, 179, 180, 185, 186, 188, 190, 191, 208, 217, 233, 256, 258, 302
Lee County, 37, 38, 107
Lee Creek, 74
Lee's Legion, 79, 86, 90, 96, 175, 185, 186, 191, 208, 233, 258
Lee's Tavern, 110
Leesville, 87, 109, 253
Legion infantry, 164
Legionnaires, 135, 162, 171, 229
Leighton's House, 17
Lemprière's Point, 146, 150, 153
Lenud's (Lanneau's) Ferry, 56, 214, 230
Leonard, David, 15
Leslie, Alexander, 100, 137, 141, 149, 162, 164, 167, 168, 194, 208, 298
Lewis, James, 214
Lewisfield Plantation, 182
Lexington, 35, 86, 87, 109, 116, 257
Lexington, Massachusetts, 134
Lexington County, 35, 86, 90, 109, 110, 252, 257, 258, 303
Liberty (Georgia schooner), 196

Liberty Boys, 251
Lick Creek, 109
Liddell, Moses, 289, 305
Light dragoons, 153, 228
Light Infantry, 39, 48, 95, 96, 108, 118, 136–138, 143, 146, 147, 160, 167, 168, 225, 229, 244
Lighthouse Island, 122
Liles, James, 18
Lincoln, Benjamin, 47, 135, 136, 141, 142, 144, 146–148, 153, 158–160, 162, 201, 202, 205, 220–222, 224, 225, 232
Lindsay (Lindsey), John, 108, 291
Linning, John, 176
Lisle, John, 266
Lisles's Ford, 79
Little, James, 279
Little Allison Creek, 27
Little Bermuda, 236
Little Carpenter (British), 206
Little Creek, 74
Little Eastatoe Creek, 270
Little Landing, 182
Little Lynches Creek, 38
Little River, 6, 7, 21, 272, 273, 300
Little River Regiment, 277
Little Thicketty Creek, 19
Live Oak (schooner), 152
Lively (frigate), 235
Lively (Philadelphia privateer), 157
Livingston, Henry B., 90
Livingston, Robert, 95
Log Creek, 277
Log Town, 40, 43, 45, 53
Logan, George, 62
London Creek Branch, 72
London, 132
Long, Joshua, 106
Long Bluff, 64, 81
Long Branch Creek, 167
Long Cane, 278, 289–293, 298, 300, 305
Long Cane militia, 252
Long Island, 128, 130, 154, 155
Long Swamp Creek, Georgia, 275
Loose square, 96
Lord George Germain (armed brig), 202, 204
Lord North (privateer sloop), 154
Lorick's Ferry, 109, 112
Love, James, 19, 20
Love, William, 20
Love's Ford, 72, 73, 75
Love's Plantation, 15, 16
Loves Creek, 16
Low country, 1
Lowe, Major, 138
Lower Bridge, 55–58, 60, 61, 102, 103
Lower Fort, 213
Lower Settlements, 267
Lower Three Runs Creek, 246
Lowndes Grove, 136, 166, 167
Lowry's Bridge, 70
Loyalist dragoons, 28, 41, 77, 102, 193
Loyalist militiamen, 5, 28, 30, 32, 42, 47, 58, 59, 79, 80, 100, 223, 234, 253, 254, 256, 259, 262–264, 279, 296, 298, 303
Loyalist sharpshooters, 54
Loyalist South Carolina Rangers, 180
Loyalists, 3, 5, 7–9, 11, 13–15, 18, 20–23, 26, 27, 30, 32, 33, 36, 37, 41, 50, 52, 54, 58, 59, 61, 62, 64–66, 70, 71, 73, 75, 76, 79, 80, 88, 99, 101, 105–107, 110–112, 114, 115, 130, 136, 147, 149, 154, 158, 160, 171, 174–176, 186, 191, 205, 208, 216, 218, 222, 224, 232, 237, 239, 240, 242–247, 249, 253–255, 258–260, 262, 263, 265, 266, 271, 272, 275, 276, 278–281, 283–285, 288, 291, 298, 299, 302, 304, 306, 307
Lumber River, 80
Lynchburg, 107
Lynches Creek, 37, 39, 41, 82, 84, 85, 106, 214
Lynches River, 37, 38, 40, 57, 104, 105, 106
Lynches River Massacre, 104
Lyndley's (Lindley's) Fort, 272 see also Fort Lindley
Lyon (British), 131
Lyon, Captain, 134

Mackays Creek, 235, 236
MacLaine, Murdock, 183
MacNeil, Hector, 80
Maddox, 20
Maham Tower, 88, 96
Maham, Hezekiah, 96, 162, 175, 177, 180, 183, 188, 190, 231, 240
Maitland, John, 158, 160, 224
Maitland, Richard, 196
Malmedy, Bernard François Lellorquis Marquis de, 153, 177
Manchester State Forest, 76
Manigault's Ferry, 91, 92, 94, 100, 181
Manning, 70, 101, 102
Mann's Old Field, 294
Mansen, Peter, 214
Manson, Captain, 219
Mantelets, 139
Maple's Mill, 5
March, Captain, 175, 195
Margaret and Martha (transport), 202
Margery (schooner), 158
Marines, 130
Marion, Francis, 1, 3, 11, 23, 33, 36, 38, 40, 41, 47, 52–63, 70, 77, 79, 80, 82, 84, 85, 94, 96–98, 101, 102, 104, 105, 107, 114, 115, 116, 118, 125, 149, 159, 163, 166, 170, 171, 173, 174, 177, 179–181, 183, 188, 191, 193, 195, 208, 210, 213,–218, 220, 231, 235, 238, 241, 244, 248, 256, 298
Marion, Gabriel, 212, 215
Marion County, 58, 108, 114, 115
Marjoribanks, John, 244, 245
Markland, John, 122, 187
Marlboro County, 31, 65, 70, 78, 80, 107
Mars Bluff, 115
Marsh Creek, 108, 109
Marsh Island, 120
Martin, Alexander, 114
Martin, Edward, 29
Martin, Josiah, 151
Martin, William, 23, 24
Martin's Mill, 300
Martinangel (also spelled Martinangle or Martinangele), Phillip, 196, 236
Martintown, 305
Maryland Continentals, 47, 48, 80, 122, 149, 164, 173, 174, 205, 235, 296
Maryland militiamen, 78
Mason, General, 160
Mason's Ferry, 64
Mathew's Bluff, 222
Mathew's Ferry, 156, 157, 162
Mathews, John, 158
Mathews's Plantation, 156, 158

Index

Matrosses, 143, 209
Matthew, Captain, 121
Matthews (Matthewes), John, 114
Maxwell, Andrew, 86, 88
Maxwell, Arthur, 236
Maybank, Joseph, 125
Mayesville, 37
Mayfield, John, 42, 43
Mayson, James, 249, 252, 254, 255
McArthur, Archibald, 31, 75, 78, 79, 180
McBee, 3
McCall, James, 271, 272, 289, 291, 292, 300
McCallum's Ferry, 37, 41, 85
McClellanville, 230
McClure, Hugh, 13
McClure, James, 29
McClure, John, 7, 9, 13, 29, 30
McClure, Mary Gaston, 30
McConnells, 29
McCopin, Alexander, 279
McCord Creek, 305
McCord's Creek
McCord's Ferry, 91, 93, 94, 99, 110, 166
McCormick County, 249, 255, 290, 300
McCottry or McCottrey, William Robert, 57, 60, 85, 105
McCottry's riflemen, 57, 60, 61, 85, 105
McCoy, James, 291
McCoy, Ranald, 224
McCree, Mr., 11
McCumber, George, 236
McDaniels, Thomas, 15
McDonald, Adam, 231
McDonald, Aeneas, 52, 162
McDonald, Alexander, 61
McDonald, Archibald, 57
McDonald, Sergeant, 216
McDougall, Duncan, 155
McDowell, Charles, 34, 262, 263, 288
McDowell, Joseph "Quaker Meadows", Jr., 263
McDowell's Camp, 35, 260, 262
McGarity, William, 13
McGill's Plantation, 62, 63
McGirth, Daniel, 223, 233, 243, 245, 246
McGowan's (McGowin's) blockhouse, 279
McIlwain's Creek, 263
McIntosh General, 138
McIntosh, Alexander, 64, 135, 222
McIntosh, Lachlan, 140, 224
McJunkin, Daniel, 18, 75
McJunkin, Joseph, 17, 19, 22, 75, 263, 288, 299
McKay, James, 96, 223, 243
McKay, Rannal, 224
McKenzie, Lieutenant, 221
McKown's Mill, 72, 73
McLaughlin, Thomas, 242
McLeroth, Robert, 57, 77, 88, 95
McNeil, John, 158
McNicoll, Captain, 155
McPherson, Charles, 94
McPherson, Isaac, 228
McPherson's plantation, 3, 227, 228
McPhersonville, 227
McWhartry, John, 91
Meador's Plantation, 15
Meador's plantation, 17, 21
Mecan, Thomas, 176
Mecklenburg, North Carolina, 31
Melrose House, 77
Melton, John, 214, 242

Mepkin plantation, 232
Merritt, Thomas, 215, 216, 241
Metts Crossroads, 91, 93, 100
Middle Branch, 31, 33
Middleton (Mydelton), Charles, 90, 257
Middleton Place, 188, 208
Middleton Plantation, 167, 188
Middleton, Arthur, 188, 208
Middleton, Henry, 188, 208
Middleton, Hugh, 278
Middleton's (Mydelton's) Ambuscade, 252
Middleton's Defeat, 252, 253
Mile-end, 205
Militiamen, 3, 7, 11, 13, 14, 18, 20–22, 26–28, 30, 32, 36, 47, 50, 53–55, 71, 90, 95, 97, 98, 100, 107, 112–114, 120, 125, 147–149, 154, 159, 166, 173, 177, 179, 193, 202, 204, 213–216, 221, 223, 229, 232, 233, 236, 240, 244, 248, 254, 257, 265, 271, 272, 276–278, 284, 287, 288, 292, 294–298, 302, 303
Miller Sam, 30
Miller, John, 279
Miller, Jonathan, 5
Milligan, Jacob, 124, 130, 221
Mills, Ambrose, 262
Mills, John, 30, 74
Mills, Robert, 44
Mills, William Henry, 32
Milton, 304
Mine Creek, 251, 253
Mingo, 59, 195
Mingo, Lieutenant, 195
Mississippi River, 157
Mobley, 8, 75
Mobley's Meeting House, 6, 12
Moccasins, 13, 275
Modoc, 278
Mohawks, 271
Molasses Creek, 133
Molloy, Lieutenant, 157
Moncks Corner, 36, 55, 76, 96, 98, 141, 168, 177–182, 186, 189–191, 230, 235, 248, 257
Moncks Corner Road, 177
Moncrieff, James, 135, 138, 140
Montford, Joseph, 147
Monticello Reservoir, 74, 79
Moore, 18, 33, 34, 71, 73, 76, 112, 233, 303, 304
Moore, Charles, 304
Moore, James, 99
Moore, John, 18, 283
Moore, Major, 112
Moore, Patrick, 33, 283
Moore, Samuel, 303
Moore, Tom, 76
Moore's Defeat, 93, 99
Moore's Mill, 71
Moore's Plantation, 304
Moore's Surprise, 91
Morgan, Charles, 158
Morgan, Daniel, 52, 73–75, 78, 283, 292, 293, 295, 296, 298, 299
Morgan, Francis, 152, 157
Morrall (Murrell), Daniel, 106
Morris Island, 155
Morrow, William, 273
Mortars, 135, 142–144, 146
Moss Creek, 235, 236
Moss Island Creek, 205
Motley Branch, 306
Motley, Mr., 264

Motte, Isaac, 118
Motte, Rebecca Brewton, 101, 134
Moultrie, Thomas, 146
Moultrie, William, 118, 125, 128, 135, 143–145, 148, 149, 151, 160, 161, 174, 178, 199, 200, 202, 222, 224, 225
Mount Carmel, 249
Mount Croghan, 5
Mount Hope Swamp, 60, 101–103
Mount Pleasant, 124, 125, 133, 134, 147, 148, 150, 153, 155, 187, 195, 292, 299
Mount Willing, 109, 110, 112
Mountain Rest, 264
Mouzon, William Henry, 56, 62
Mouzon's House, 55, 56
Mowat, Henry, 118
The Muck, 156, 168
Muddy Creek, 81
Muddy Spring, 86, 88
Mudlick Creek, 292, 299
Murphey, Colonel, 65
Murphy, Malachi, 81, 109
Murphy, Maurice, 65
Murphy's Defeat, 3
Murray, Patrick, 204
Murray's Ferry, 36, 57, 102, 103, 235
Muse, Daniel, 12
Musgrove, Edward Gordon, 286
Musgrove Mill State Historic Site, 286
Musgrove Mill, 16, 21, 286, 288, 306
Musgrove's plantation, 287
Mutiny, 98, 174

Nairne, John, 32
Naked Creek, 109
Nantahala Gorge Recreation Site, 271
Nantahala National Forest, 271
Nation Ford, 14
Native American rangers, 125
Native Americans, 10, 86, 125, 126, 160, 196, 221–223, 225, 234, 259, 266, 268, 271, 281, 302
Neal, Andrew, 26
Neal, Andrew, Jr., 21, 27
Neal, Andrew, Sr., 21, 42
Neal, Thomas, Colonel, 30
Neal, Thomas, Jr., 294
Neal, Thomas. Sr., 254
Neck stock, 284
Neel, Thomas, 275
Nelson's Ferry, 41, 61, 85, 89, 92, 95, 102, 193, 234, 235, 244
New Acquisition (York County), 21, 71
New Acquisition (York County) Militia, 21, 27, 35
New Acquisition (York County) settlements, 294
New Cut, 122, 156, 158, 164
New Jersey Continentals, 231
New Jersey Volunteers, 255, 287
New Providence, 52, 236
New Richmond, 249, 251
New York City, 208
New York Loyalists, 85, 255
New York Volunteers, 21, 26, 30, 35, 88, 104, 153, 174, 185, 229
New York, 10, 47, 121, 134, 136, 144, 158, 235
Newberry County, 16, 74, 108, 109, 112, 281, 282, 285, 295, 298, 302, 303
Newberry militiamen, 73
Newport, Rhode Island, 136
Newton, John, 222

Newtown, 122
Neyle, Philip, 144
Ninety Six, 1, 8, 10, 14, 19, 22, 39, 47, 52, 68, 74, 88, 90, 92, 97, 98, 100, 169, 181, 218, 233, 234, 244, 249, 251–260, 262, 266, 270, 277, 278, 283, 288–292, 296, 299–301, 303
Ninety Six District, 289, 301
Ninety Six National Historic Site, 253
Nolichucky River, 275
North Carolina, 3, 9, 10, 19–21, 24, 27, 33, 37, 47, 48, 52, 59, 63, 66, 74, 80, 114, 128, 136, 152, 275, 283, 300
North Carolina border, 262
North Carolina horsemen, 160
North Carolina light infantry, 49, 224
North Carolina Line, 147, 176
North Carolina Loyalists, 68, 160
North Carolina militia, 5, 47, 48, 50, 80, 108, 115, 140, 148, 153, 159, 233, 259
North Carolina regiments, 148
North Carolina volunteers, 295
North Pacolet River, 262
Norwood, John, 301
Notre Dame (brigantine), 176
Notre Dame (South Carolina brig), 162, 213
Notre Dame (British), 122
Nuckolls, John, 72, 73

O'Neal or O'Neale, Ferdinand, 175, 191, 233
Oath of allegiance, 6, 13, 14, 19, 21, 27, 37, 147, 169, 213, 214, 233
Oconee, 267, 269, 273
Oconee County, 267, 270, 275, 276
Oconee Creek, 267, 270, 271
Oconee Station, 270
Oconee Station State Historic Site, 269
Oconore, 267, 271, 275
Oconore (Oconoree) Creek, 271
O'Dell's Ford, 22
Odom, Benjamin, 247
Ogeechee River, 243
Ogier, Lewis (Louis), 205
Ogilvie's plantation, 229
Olar, 247
Old Dorchester State Park, 172
Old Exchange and Provost Dungeon, 132
Old Iron Works, 281–283, 285
Old Man Palmer Killed, 252
Old Race Track, 132, 134–136
Oldfield, 114
Oliphant, David, 125
Oliphant's Mill, 52
O'Neal's Mill, 110
Oohey River, 116
Orangeburg, 55, 88, 91–93, 97–100, 114, 193, 238, 243, 245, 246, 253, 256, 258, 305
Orangeburg County, 91, 92, 110, 234, 243, 253
Ostatoy, 275
O'Sullivan, Florence, 123
Otranto, 184
Otterson, Samuel, 72–74
Otterson's Fort, 72
Outer Banks, 136, 152
Overhill Cherokees, 275
Owen's plantation, 79
Owenby (Ownby or Ownbey), James, 220
Ox Swamp, 61, 70
Oxford, 31
Oyster Bank, 128

Index

Pace's Ferry, 301
Pacolet River, 17, 34, 73, 78, 261, 265, 282, 292, 294
Palliser, 118, 125
Palmer, Mr., 257
Palmer, Turpentine John, 178
Palmetto, 128, 130
Pamplico, 3
Parker, John, 184, 185
Parker, Peter, 126, 128, 130, 155, 271
Parker, Richard, 146
Parker's Ferry, 165, 170, 171, 241, 298
Parker's Old Field, 43, 44, 48
Parley, 111, 306
Parole, 14, 46, 64, 148, 166, 169, 183, 186, 187, 283, 292
Parris Island, 205
Parson's plantation, 241, 242
Parsons, Captain Major, 264
Patterson, Thomas, 227
Patterson's Bridge, 238, 239
Pattison, James, 169, 223, 227, 229
Patton, Matthew, 18
Pauline, 306
Pawley's Bridge, 5
Peace & Harmony (Brig), 210, 213
Peace Treaty of 1763, 271
Peaceful Retreat Plantation, 156, 159, 163
Peach Hill, 35, 303
Peach Orchard Fight, 281, 283, 285
Pearis, Richard, 277
Pee Dee, 38, 41, 79, 106, 177, 210, 217
Pee Dee River, 3, 31, 32, 41, 52, 57–59, 62, 65, 78, 80, 82, 84, 107, 109, 114, 115, 166, 211, 213, 215, 217, 218
Pee Dee Swamp, 57, 58
Peebles, John, 142
Peggy (Charleston, SC, privateer schooner), 214
Peggy (Loyalist privateer schooner), 219
Pelzer, 259
Pendarvis, Richard, 237
Pendleton, Henry, 174
Pendleton, Philip, 174
Pennsylvania Continentals, 164, 174, 187
The Pens, 212, 215
Perseus (frigate), 157
Pest House, 123, 124
Peters Creek, 253
Peters, Sergeant, 174, 175
Pettiauger, 126
Pettit, Charles, 25
Peyre's plantation, 98
Philadelphia, 196
Phillipa (armed schooner), 196
Phillips, John, 35
Pickens County, 266, 267, 271, 275
Pickens, Andrew, 1, 11, 14, 23, 52, 97, 100, 112, 113, 233, 244, 256, 270, 273–276, 279, 280, 292, 296, 300, 301, 303, 305
Pickens, John, 305
Pickens, Joseph William, 274, 279
Pickering, Francis, 155
Piedmont, 289
Pinckney, Charles Cotesworth, 116, 125, 146, 205
Pinckney, Eliza Lucas, 116
Pinckney, Thomas, 116, 118
Pine Log Bridge, 64
Pinewood House, 110, 305
Plantation, 1, 6, 7, 15, 25, 56, 61, 63, 105, 110, 167, 192, 198, 202, 208, 213, 218, 220, 260

Pledger's Mill, 81
Plowden, Edward, 37, 56
Plowden, William, 37, 56
Plummer, Daniel, 22
Pocotaligo Bridge., 202, 225, 238
Pocotaligo Road, 227, 238, 239, 240
Poinsett State Park, 76
Polk, William, 25, 255
Polk County, 264, 266
Polk County, North Carolina, 260
Polk Swamp, 31, 33
Polly (privateer sloop), 151, 157
Polly (merchant vessel), 150
Pomaria, 74
Pon Pon, 227, 229 see also Edisto
Pon Pon Chapel, 165, 229
Ponder, Colonel, 106
Popple, Lieutenant, 151
Port, Frances, 41
Port, Thomas, 41
Port's Ferry, 41, 62
Port Royal, 135, 149, 202, 228, 235
Port Royal Ferry, 200, 205, 210
Port Royal Harbor, 200, 201
Port Royal Island, 200–202, 204, 227, 237
Port Royal River, 196
Porterfield, 50
Porterfield, Charles, 48, 49
Portholes, 34
Postell, James, 94, 181, 182, 216
Postell, John, 82, 84, 181, 216, 217
Potomac River, 198
Powder Magazine, 43, 133, 134, 144
Pratt, Joseph, 300
Pratt's Mill, 300, 301
Prevost, Augustine, 121, 135, 158, 163, 201, 202, 204, 222, 224, 235
Prevost, James Mark, 158, 159, 161, 200
Prince George County Militia Regiment, 125
Prince George Parish Church, Winyah, 211, 213
Prince of Wales American Regiment, 26, 27, 36, 46, 88, 193
Prince William Parish Church, 206
Prince's Fort, 262
Prosper (Carolina frigate), 130, 150
Prosperity, 108
Providence (sloop), 121, 122, 139, 140, 152, 153
Provincial Congress, 32, 41, 120, 125, 251, 254, 259
Pulaski, Casimir, 121, 135, 159–162, 225
Pulaski's Legion, 50, 121, 135, 159, 162
Puncheon, 158
Purdue, Fields, 303
Purysburg, 202, 220–222
Pyle's Massacre, 10
Pyne (Payne, Paine), James, 161

Quacoratchee, 267, 270, 275
Quaker cannons, 88
Quaker, 46
Quarter House Tavern, 134, 173, 179, 185–187
Queen of France (frigate), 136, 152, 153
Queen's Rangers, 61, 179, 208, 215, 216–218, 220, 241
Quinby Bridge, 189–191, 194
Quinby Creek, 189

Rabon Creek, 266, 280
Raccoon Company, 125
Radcliffe, Captain, 111, 112

Raiford, Robert, 70
Raleigh, 131
Ramsour's Mill (North Carolina), 21, 283, 298
Randolph (Continental Navy frigate), 134
Ranger (Continental Navy brigantine), 121, 139, 140, 153, 198
Ranger (sloop), 152
Rantowles, 157
Rantowles (Rentowle) Bridge, 156
Rantowles Creek, 157
Ratcliffs or Radcliff's Bridge, 38, 40
Rattlesnake, 59
Rattlesnake (South Carolina Navy schooner), 159, 163
Ravenel, 157
Ravenel, Daniel, 180
Ravenel's plantation, 180
Rawdon, Francis, 14, 24, 27, 39, 40, 48, 53, 54, 64, 68, 85, 88–90, 94–97, 101, 104, 108, 169, 233, 244, 256–258, 278
Rebellion Road, 119, 120, 124, 125, 150, 154
Red Bank Creek, 253
Red Bluff Point, 222
Red Hill, 238, 239
Redoubt, 46, 53, 55, 57, 97, 108, 118, 121, 122, 135, 137–139, 141, 142, 160, 165, 182, 183, 244, 253, 256, 257
Reedy River, 259, 277
Regiment Von Bose, 158
Regulars, 50, 62, 77, 85, 88, 96, 122, 162, 166, 208, 214, 223, 224, 234, 244, 263, 289, 291, 296, 299, 302
Reid or Reed, Davie, 19
Reid, John, 186
Renown (frigate), 131, 154
Rhems, 61, 62
Rhodes (Whig privateer), 131
Rice Museum, 210, 211
Rice, 1, 98,147, 174, 205, 208, 217, 218, 219, 226, 236
Ricepatch Creek, 227
Richard B. Russell Lake, 279
Richard B. Russell Reservoir, 279
Richardson, Richard, 63, 70
Richardson, Richard, Jr., 177, 194, 252, 254, 259, 260, 266
Richardson, Richard, Sr., 63, 254
Richardson's plantation, 70
Richbourgh's Mill, 70
Richland County, 41, 86, 91
Richmond (or *Richard*) (British armed transport), 198
Richmond, 131
Ridge Spring, 253
Ridgeway, John, Jr., 277
Ridgeway's Fort, 277
Ridley, Captain, 151
Rifle, 13, 20, 21, 23, 40, 57, 60, 68, 88, 111, 113, 143, 144, 190, 193, 241, 251, 256, 289, 299, 304
Riflemen, 27, 60, 61, 65, 66, 88, 103, 104, 125, 126, 128, 136, 137, 143, 145, 167, 183, 192, 204, 225, 283, 284, 287, 294, 296, 299, 300
Rimini, 76
Ring Fight, 267, 270, 271
Ritchie, William, 255
Robert, Captain, 279
Roberts, James, 243
Roberts, John, 37
Roberts, Jonathan, 234
Robertson, Charles, 34
Robins, James, 185

Robinson, John, 106
Robinson, Joseph, 255
Rochester's Ferry, 226
Rocky Creek, 13, 15, 23, 26, 35, 36
Rocky Creek Congregation, 23, 24
Rocky Mount, 1, 10, 14, 15, 18, 21, 24–27, 29, 35–37, 74
Rocky Mount Regiment, 31
Rocky River, 279, 281
Rodney (brig), 198
Roebuck (HMS), 131
Roebuck, Benjamin, 16, 22, 298, 299
Roebuck's Defeat, 299
Roger's (or Rogiard's) Plantation, 277, 278
Rogers, Captain, 213
Rogers Cemetery, 107
Rogers Creek, 82
Rogers Mill, 82
Romulus, 131
Ross, Francis, 261
Rossville, 12, 13
Rothmaler, Job, 125
Round Mountain, 264–266
Round O, 164, 173, 174, 241
Round O Company, 162, 229
Roupelles Ferry, 202
Rouse's Ferry, 65
Row galley, 140, 143, 147, 159, 162
Rowe, Michael Christopher, 93, 99
Rowe's Plantation, 91, 93, 99, 110, 112
Royal Americans, 159
Royal Artillery, 47, 139
Royal Fusiliers, 77
Royal Highland Emigrants, 154, 155
Royal Navy, 55, 116, 125, 134, 136, 150, 153, 157, 213
Royal North Carolina militia, 100
Royal North Carolina Regiment, 46, 63
Rudolph, Michael, 164, 175, 186, 217, 233, 234
Rugeley, Henry, 45, 52, 107
Rugeley's Fort, 43, 45
Rugeley's Mill, 40, 43–45
Rumph, Jacob, 99
Rush's Mill, 247
Russell, Captain, 139
Rutherford, Griffith, 273, 275
Rutledge Shoals, 289
Rutledge, Edward, 203
Rutledge, John, 18, 45, 92, 128, 135, 141, 169, 225, 273
Rutledge's Ford, 289
Ryan, Captain, 99
Ryan, James, 258

Sadler, David, 95
Sadler, Mrs., 265
Sadler, William, 19, 20
Sagittair (French man-of-war), 236
Saint Andrews, 166
Saint Andrews Creek, 166, 167
Saint Andrews Episcopal Church, 166–168
Saint Helena Island, 201, 205, 206
Saint Matthews, 91–94, 96
Salem Black River community, 56
Salem Black River Presbyterian Church, 37
Salem, 59, 214, 268, 270
Salisbury, 53
Salisbury district, 98
Salkehatchie bridge, 209

Index

Salkehatchie Presbyterian Church, 227
Salkehatchie River, 114, 229, 240
Salkehatchie River, 227
Salley, 113
Sally (sloop), 199, 201
Sally (transport), 206
Salley's Cowpens, 243
Salter, Tom, 76
Saltketcher (Salkehatchie or Salkahatchie) River, 227
Saltketcher Bridge, 227, 238, 239
Saltketcher Ferry, 228
Saltketcher River, 225, 227
Saltketcher Swamp, 227, 229
Saluda, 251, 253, 254
Saluda, North Carolina, 265
Saluda County, 109, 110, 251, 289
Saluda Mountain, 264
Saluda River, 35, 47, 90, 108–110, 112, 113, 252, 253, 256–258, 277, 289, 291, 303
Salvador, Francis (Daniel Jezurun Rodriguez), 268, 272, 273
Sampit, 61, 103, 218
Sampit Bridge, 61, 102–105
Sanders, Adam, 144
Sanders, William, 136, 162, 229
Sandwich (armed ship), 131
Sandwich (HMS), 122
Sandy Point, 154
Sandy (Run) River, 8, 75, 76
Santee, 8, 29, 36, 40, 41, 47, 56, 57, 60, 61, 63, 70, 76, 85, 91, 93, 95, 98, 102, 166, 182, 193, 194, 231, 235
Santee River, 8, 36, 47, 56, 57, 60, 70, 76, 87, 89, 92–95, 98, 101, 102, 144, 152, 165, 166, 230–232, 234, 235, 241, 303
Santee Swamp, 36
Saratoga, 47
Saunder's (Saunders) Creek, 43, 44, 48, 50
Saunders, John, 61, 85, 217, 218, 220, 241
Savage, John, 254, 255
Savage (British), 198, 199
Savage's Plantation, 166, 167, 255
Savannah, Georgia, 10, 55, 130, 136, 159, 161, 179, 201, 202, 206, 223, 226, 227, 235, 238, 255, 258
Savannah River, 47, 58, 196, 202, 205, 206, 220–222, 224, 232, 233, 237, 243, 249, 276, 278, 279, 281, 298, 301, 302
Sawney's Creek, 108
Scalp, 15, 185, 221, 264, 268, 272, 281
Scorpion (HM sloop of war), 118, 124, 125, 150, 151
Scotch-Irish, 9
Scott, John, 62, 104
Scourge (British galley), 205, 207, 221
Seabrook, 200
Screven, Benjamin, 177
Seabrook Island, 121
Second Continental Congress, 128
Selacoa, 276
Seneca, 266–268, 271, 272
Seneca County, 267
Seneca River, 267, 272
Sessions, Josias, 106
Seven Years War, 172, 271
Severn, 134
Sevier, John, 34
Seymour, William, 53, 175, 205
Shanklin, Thomas, 279
Sharon, 79, 294
Sharp, James, 100

Sharp, William, 22
Sharp's Skirmish, 92, 94
Shark (British row galley), 205, 208
Shaw Air Force Base, 28
Shawnee, 271
Shelby Colonel, 288
Shelby, Isaac, 34, 183, 284, 287
Shelby, Moses, 22, 302
Sheldon, 206, 207
Sheldon Church, 206, 207
Sheldon plantation, 207
Shem Creek, 124, 150
Shepherd's Ferry, 61, 62
Sherman, William Tecumseh, 206
Shiloh Church, 260, 263
Shirer's (or Sherer's) Ferry, 6
Shoemake, 82
Shubrick, Richard, 119
Shubrick, Thomas, 192, 225
Shubrick's Plantation, 189, 191
Shutes Folly, 136
Shutes Folly Island, 150, 154
Siege, 46, 88, 94, 96–98, 101, 134–136, 138, 140, 148, 159, 169, 218, 223, 225, 227, 233, 244, 256–258, 270, 299, 302
Silk Hope plantation, 194
Silver Bluff, 233
Simcoe, John Graves, 179
Simmons Island, 121
Simpson, John, 7, 14
Simpson, Thomas, 122, 139, 140, 153
Simpsonville, 259
Singleton, John, 29, 263
Singleton's Mill, 76, 77
Sinkler, Dorothy, 63
Skull Creek, 236
Skyuka, 265, 266
Slaughter Field, 110, 247
Slaves, 3, 7, 18, 30, 63, 124–126, 140, 141, 149, 161, 187, 202, 204, 205, 215, 217, 219, 223, 236, 242, 248, 253, 275, 276, 297, 302, 303
Smallpox, 38, 77, 78, 96, 169, 292, 301
Smallwood, William, 51
Smedley, Samuel, 198
Smith Esaw, [Esau], 21
Smith, Aaron, 272, 273
Smith, Ballard, 187
Smith, Captain, 209, 222
Smith, Eliphalet, 130
Smith, Lieutenant, 187
Smith, William, 122
Snider House, 132, 149
Snipers, 27, 54, 143, 146, 147, 204, 229
Snipes, William Clay, 241, 242
Snipes's Horseshoe plantation, 240–242
Snoddy, John, 110, 283, 285
Snow Campaign, 255, 259, 260
Snow Hill, 254
Snow Island, 41, 80, 82, 84, 85, 102, 104, 105, 215–217, 235
Snow, James, 82
Snow, William, 82
Snowden, 65
Socastee Swamp, 216
Society Hill, 64, 81
Soconee, 273
Solebay (British frigate), 199
South Carolina cavalry, 167, 168
South Carolina coast, 198, 202

South Carolina Continentals, 148, 295
South Carolina Deaf and Blind School, 282
South Carolina dragoons, 162, 170, 175, 186, 190, 239
South Carolina frontier, 270, 271
South Carolina Loyalist militia, 107, 109
South Carolina Loyalist mounted dragoons, 239
South Carolina militia, 29, 35, 53, 61, 64, 65, 79, 88, 99, 100, 102, 115, 128, 158, 159, 163, 177, 193, 196, 199, 200, 203, 204, 222, 227, 228, 232, 237, 244, 275, 279, 289, 295, 302, 303
South Carolina Militia (Loyalist), 193
South Carolina militia (Whig), 56, 64, 307
South Carolina Navy, 93, 162, 198
South Carolina Provincial Congress see Provincial Congress
South Carolina Rangers, 38, 63, 96, 186
South Carolina Royalists, 40, 90, 173, 175, 185, 191, 241–243, 287
South Carolina Senate, 254
South Carolina Whigs, 232
South Carolina, western, 264
South Edisto Inlet, 199
Southport, 281, 282
Sparks, Daniel, 33, 82
Sparks, Harry, 33
Spartan Regiment, 306, 307
Spartanburg, 17, 18, 33, 261, 262, 281, 282, 285, 295
Spartanburg County, 15–17, 71, 110, 260, 261, 262, 264, 265, 281, 286, 294, 304, 306
Spencer's Inlet, 154
Sphynx (HMS), 130, 151
Spike's Mill, 3
Spontoon, 122
Spring Grove, 175, 225
Spring Grove Creek, 76
Spy, 56, 72, 88, 242, 248, 299
St. Andrews Church, 166–168
St. Andrews Creek, 167
St. Augustine, Florida, 151, 153, 166, 198, 199, 205, 206, 213, 237, 249
St. Clair, Arthur, 164, 174
St. David's Episcopal Church, 78
St. Eustatia, 134, 151, 157
St. George parish Church, 172
St. Helena, 135
St. Helena Episcopal Church, 206
St. Helena Island, 201, 205, 206
St. Helena Sound, 206
St. Helena Volunteer Militia Company, 158, 205, 207
St. James (privateer brig), 151
St. John's Berkeley Church, 178, 186
St. John's Baptist Church, 102
St. Lawrence (schooner), 155
St. Mark's Church, 29
St. Stephen's Parish, 98
St. Thomas Parish, 188
Stalling, Sterling or Stallings, John, 17
Stallion's (probably Sterling or Stalling), 15, 17
Stallion's plantation, 17
Stand of arms, 183
Stan's Bridge, 176
Stanyarne's Plantation, 156, 161
State House Armory, 133, 134
Statesville, 21
Steadman, Captain, 304
Steedham, Adam, 18, 20
Steel Creek, 246

Sterling or Stalling, John, 20
Stevens, Edward, 51
Stevens Creek, 277, 278, 301
Stewart, Alexander, 90, 97, 173, 180, 183, 244, 257, 258
Stinson, Daniel, 12, 74
Stirling, Charles, 198
Stirrup Branch, 38
Stock plantation, 209
Stockade, 46, 94, 96, 101, 233, 234, 253, 255, 266, 268
Stockade Fort, 255
Stone, Benjamin, 201
Stone, Lieutenant, 221
Stone's Ferry, 233, 243, 245
Stoneboro, 24, 106
Stones landing, 118
Stoney Landing, 245
Stono Ferry, 156–158, 161, 162, 166
Stono Inlet, 154, 156–158, 160
Stono River, 116, 118, 121, 138, 156–159, 161–164, 167, 176, 205, 207
Stratton, Lieutenant, 155
Strawberry Ferry, 189, 191, 193, 231
Strong, Janet, 14
Strong, William, 13, 14, 26, 30, 36, 46
Stuart, John, 271
Stutter, 59, 70
Sugar Creek, 18, 23
Sugar Town, 267, 270, 273
Sullivan's Island, 119, 123, 124, 126, 131
Summerton, 70, 91, 93
Summerville, 171, 208, 238
Sumner, Jethro, 98, 160, 244
Sumter, SC, 28, 37
Sumter, Thomas, 1, 8, 11, 14, 15, 19, 25, 26, 29, 30, 31, 33, 35, 36, 38,–40, 47, 51, 52, 55, 63, 64, 70–72, 75, 85, 86, 88, 90, 92, 94–99, 101, 108, 173, 179, 184, 186, 190, 191, 218, 219, 221, 233, 234, 241, 256, 257, 259, 274, 283, 288, 289, 302, 303
Sumter County, 28, 37, 56, 76
Sumter National Forest, 277, 282, 300
Sumter's plantation, 234
Sumter's Rounds, 86
Supply Lines, 1
Surrender, 7, 9, 10, 19, 20, 32, 34, 35, 43, 47, 52, 58, 68, 71, 74, 78, 81, 85, 88–90, 94, 96, 99, 101, 106, 107, 111, 142, 145, 148, 149, 158, 160, 164, 169, 179, 183, 186, 203, 209, 213, 217, 218, 229, 239, 240, 276, 279, 285, 293, 304
Sutton, William, 157
Sutton's Tavern, 43, 44
Swamp, 1, 31, 33, 36, 43, 44, 48, 57–63, 65, 68, 70, 76, 77, 80, 82, 92, 96, 100–104, 106, 110, 113, 114, 168, 171, 180, 189, 210, 212–214, 216, 220–225, 227, 229, 238–240, 243, 248, 253, 275
Swallow (packet), 120
Swancey's Ferry, 110, 303
"Sweat Swamp", 65
Sweet Potatoes, 85
Swift Creek, 77
Swinney, James, 100
Swivel Gun, 28, 150, 152, 186, 215, 255, 279
Sycamore Shoals, 66
Syren, 130

Tabby, 141, 172
Takwashua, 267, 275
Talbird, Thomas, 237

Index

Tamar (HM Sloop), 116, 118–120, 124–126, 150, 155, 254
Tamassee, 267, 269–271, 273, 275
Tarleton, Banastre, 10, 13, 15, 26, 29, 37, 38, 45, 46, 48, 50, 56, 63, 68, 70, 73–76, 98, 131, 141, 163, 179, 214, 227–231, 234, 257, 283, 288, 293, 295, 296, 298
Tarleton's Legion, 48, 51, 71,163, 231, 295, 297, 298
Tarrar Spring, 109, 110
Tart, Enos, 82
Tart's Mill, 81
Tawse (Taws or Tawes), Thomas, 135
Taylor, Colonel, 191
Taylor, Major, 273
Taylor, Thomas, 11, 47, 88, 192
Tearcoat or Tarcote Swamp, 58, 59, 63, 214
Tennent, William, 254
Tennessee, 66, 275
Ternant, Jean-Baptiste, 138
Terrapin, Chief, 276
Terrill, Lieutenant, 221
Thicketty Creek, 15–17, 19, 73, 294
Thicketty Fort, 33, 34
Thicketty Mountain, 33
Third South Carolina Regiment, 255
Thomas, Captain, 62
Thomas, Colonel, 223
Thomas, Hilliard, 110, 281, 283, 285
Thomas, Jane Black, 18, 283
Thomas, John, 16
Thomas, John, Jr., 14, 18, 262, 283, 302
Thomas, John, Sr., 14, 18, 255, 283
Thomas, Robert, 299
Thomas, Tristram, 32
Thomas, William, 18, 275
Thomas and Stafford, 151
Thompson, Abner, 264
Thompson, Andrew, 16, 21
Thompson, Benjamin, 182, 231
Thompson, Charles, 158
Thompson, Elisha, 264
Thompson, Israel, 198
Thompson Creek, 5
Thompson's Fort, 264
Thompson Memorial Bridge, 123
Thomson Park, 123
Thomson, William "Danger", 94, 128, 254, 259
Thomson, William, 100, 101, 254
Thomson's (Thompson) Plantation, 91, 93, 94, 182
Thornbrough, Edward, 124, 126, 150, 155
Three Creeks, 31, 33
Three Runs, 278
Three Runs Baptist Church, 246
Threwitts, Ned, 82
Thunder (HM Bomb Brig), 130
Thunderer (British galley), 221
Tierce, 158, 202
Tillman Hall, 268
Tobacco, 88, 152
Tockorachee, 267, 275
Tollemache, John, 125, 151
Tomahawk, 224, 252, 265, 281
Tomassy, 267, 273, 275
Topton, 271
Torriano, George, 57, 61
Tory Camps, 92
Towles, Oliver, 112
Town Creek, 139, 140
Trapier, Paul, 213

Treaty of Long Island of Holston, 275
Treaty of Ninety Six, 254
Treaty of Paris, 149
Trenton, 305
Treutlen, John Adam, 100
Treville, John Francis de, 202, 203
Troy, 278, 290, 291, 300
True Britain, 134, 135
Trunnions, 218
Trusler, William, 186
Tryon, Captain, 162
Tryon, North Carolina, 260
Tuck, John, 46
Tuckasegee Ford, 19
Tuft Mr., 264
Tufts, Simon, 120
Tugaloo, 275
Tugaloo River, 267, 270, 273
Tuger (galley), 236
Tulifiny Bridge, 225
Tulifiny Hill, 225
Tulifiny River, 225
Turkey Creek, 21, 79, 277, 278, 298
Turkey Hill, 98, 243
Turnbull, George, 21, 24, 27, 29, 35, 63
Turncoat Swamp, 58
Turner House Massacre, 109
Turner, Stirling, 99, 110, 112
Tutt, Benjamin, 273
Twelve Mile Creek (River), 90, 253, 289
Twitty's Mill, 106, 107
Two Oaks Plantation, 235, 237
Two Sisters Ferry, 220–223
Tybee Bar, 196
Tybee Lighthouse, 153
Tybee, Georgia, 236
Tydiman's Plantation, 230, 232
Tyger (Tiger) River, 15, 16, 21, 72, 75, 79, 262, 264, 285, 286, 288, 306, 307
Tynes, Samuel, 57, 59, 63

Unicoi (Blue Ridge) Mountains, 275
Unicorn, 152
Union, 157
Union, 16–18, 72, 294
Union County, 15, 17, 42, 71, 110, 281, 284, 286, 292, 294
Union District, 19
Upcountry, 66
Upcountry Militia, 135
Upper District Loyalist Militia, 27
Ustanali, 267, 271, 276

Vanderhorst Plantation, 195
Vanns Creek, 279
Vardell, Sergeant, 113
Vaudant's Old Field, 87, 90
Vaughanville, 303
Vengeance (British privateer snow), 213
Venture, Thomas, 134
Vernier, Pierre-Jean François, 121, 168
Videau's Bridge, 194
Vigilant (British privateer), 235
Vigilant (HMS), 205, 235, 236
Vince, Joseph, 243, 245, 246
Vince's Fort, 246, 247, 278
Vindictive (British galley), 221
Virginia Continentals, 148, 173, 245, 297
Virginia Infantry Regiment, 231

Virginia Militiamen, 48–50, 78, 160
Virginia, 131
Virginia, 52, 66, 128, 233, 272, 275, 296
Volant (South Carolina sloop), 198
Volunteer (South Carolina privateer schooner), 130
Volunteers of Ireland, 39, 41, 46, 64, 85, 88, 98, 105, 146, 187
von Graff see Grenadier Battalion von Graff
von Trumbach Regiment, 158
von Wurmb, Ludwig Johann Adolph, 139

Waccamaw Neck, 210, 213, 216, 217
Waccamaw River, 106, 210, 213, 216, 218
Wadboo, 94, 181, 189, 191, 193
Wadboo Bridge, 181, 189, 190, 194
Wadboo plantation, 194
Wadboo River, 191
Wadboo Swamp, 189
Wade, George, 15
Wade, Joe, 13
Wadmalaw Island, 199
Wadmalaw River, 175
Wagener, 253
Wagons, 7, 15, 25, 39, 42, 47, 51, 53, 61, 64, 89, 90, 94–96, 99, 100, 148, 149, 166, 173, 179–182, 191, 193, 194, 251, 258, 262, 266, 291, 297, 302, 305
Wahab's (Wauchope's) plantation, 9
Walhalla, 269–271
Walhalla Reservoir, 269
Walker, 119, 126
Walker, Samuel, 7
Wallace, 78
Wallace, James, 236
Wallace Baptist Church, 78
Wallace Creek, 157
Wallace's Road, 116
Walnut Grove Plantation, 71, 110, 284, 304
Walterboro, 239, 240
Wambaw Bridge, 232
Wambaw Creek, 230–232
Wando, 189
Wando River, 131, 144, 177, 187, 193
Wannamaker Catfish Ponds, 243
Wantoot, 180
Wappetaw Bridge, 187
Wappetaw Church, 195
Wappetaw Meeting House, 153, 187, 188, 193
Wappoo Canal, 143, 176
Wappoo Creek, 118, 176
Wappoo Cut, 122, 161, 176
Wappoo River, 175
Warachy, 267, 275
Ward, 253
Ward, Dexy, 96
Ware Shoals, 277
Washington, George, 43, 47, 86, 133, 136, 141, 174, 179, 209, 219, 227
Washington, William, 37, 52–54, 74, 98, 108, 163, 166, 168, 173, 179, 181, 230, 231, 245, 256, 283, 292, 293, 296, 297
Washington's (William) cavalry, 54, 256
Watauga, North Carolina, 288
Watauga, East Tennessee, 300
Wateree, 91
Wateree Ferry, 43, 44, 108
Wateree Ford, 44
Wateree River, 15, 38, 44, 47, 65, 76, 101, 108, 244, 298
Waters, Philemon, 88, 97

Waters, Thomas, 275, 276, 292
Watkins, 298
Watson, John Watson Tadwell, 3, 41, 52, 53, 57, 60, 70, 85, 95, 101, 102, 104, 108
Watson, Michael, 113
Watts, John, 92, 98
Waugh, David, 186
Waxhaw Creek, 25
Waxhaw River, 50
Waxhaws, 7–14, 26, 40, 41, 45, 46, 68, 75, 106
Waxhaws Church (Meeting House), 9, 11
Waxhaws Presbyterian Church, 9
Wayne "Mad Anthony", 149, 207, 226
Weaver's Old Field, 87
Webb, Hendley, 111
Webster, James, 162, 167, 179
Welch Fusiliers, 39
Wellford, 260
Wells's Plantation, 189, 193
Wemyss, James, 38, 55, 56, 59, 62–64, 71, 75, 78
Wesley, John, 165, 229
West Florida militia, 277
West Indies, 134, 151, 165, 236
West's Old Field, 252, 253
Whale Branch, 237
Whig Hill, 72, 73
Whigs, 3, 5, 7, 9, 11, 13, 15, 19, 21, 29, 30, 31, 33–35, 37, 42, 43, 55, 56, 61, 64, 73, 74, 80, 99, 106, 109, 110, 112, 114, 116, 132, 134, 145, 159, 163, 185, 196, 198, 205, 221, 228, 233, 236, 246, 254, 255, 258, 259, 261, 266, 278, 284, 288, 291, 293, 294, 303, 304
Whipple, Abraham, 152, 153
White Hall (Whitehall), 195, 305
White Meeting House, 243–245
White, Anthony Walters, 230, 231
White, Henry, 299
White, John, 221
White's Bridge, 210, 211, 214, 216
White's Mill, 28
White's (Wright's) Plantation, 210, 211, 215
Whites Creek, 211
Whitmire, 16, 22, 72, 282, 283
Wiboo Swamp, 60, 101, 102, 104
Wiggin's Hill, 222, 238
Wiggin's (Wiggan's) Plantation, 222, 223
Wilkes County, Georgia, 279
Wilkes County (Georgia) militiamen, 279
Wilkins, Benjamin, 203
William (sloop), 198
William, Captain, 57, 63, 90, 113, 222
Williams, Colonel, 112
Williams, Daniel, 305
Williams, Hezekiah, 99, 110, 112, 243, 246, 247, 277, 278, 305
Williams, James, 254, 266, 287, 293
Williams, Mary, 293
Williams, Otho Holland, 51, 173
Williams's Fort, 22, 292, 299
Williams's Plantation, 292, 293
Williamsburg, 41, 56
Williamsburg County, 55, 56, 58, 60, 62, 70, 102
Williamsburg County Courthouse, 55
Williamsburg County Museum, 55
Williamsburg Township, 62
Williamson, Andrew, 14, 135, 169, 242, 252, 254, 255, 266, 272, 273, 275, 305
Williamson, James, 29
Williamson's Plantation, 17, 29, 30, 305

Index **381**

Willow Grove, 107
Willtown, 62
Wilmington, North Carolina, 164, 188
Wilmot, William, 122
Wilson, James, 63
Wilson, John, 57, 61, 215, 216, 218, 220
Wilson, Robert, 75
Wilson's Creek, 281
Windy Hill Creek, 247
Winea plantation, 213
Winn, Richard, 6, 7, 26, 36
Winnsboro, 8, 9, 68, 71, 75, 77, 78, 104, 292
Winston-Salem, 2
Winyah Bar, 214
Winyah Bay, 210, 212, 213
Winyah Harbor, 218
Winyah Harbor Bar, 219
Withers, John, 126
Withers, William, 125
Witherspoon, Gavin, 56, 57, 61, 193
Witherspoon, Robert, 55, 56
Witherspoon's Ferry, 85, 104–106, 214
Witherspoon's Plantation, 56, 57, 60
Wofford, Benjamin, 285
Wofford, William, 18
Wofford's Iron Works, 21, 42, 110, 281–283, 285
Wood, Adam, 246
Wood, James, 110, 281, 282, 285
Wood, John, 281, 282, 285
Wood, William, 264
Wood's Fort, 261, 264, 265

Woodford, William, 140
Woodyard Swamp, 63, 70
Woolford, Thomas, 47
Wragg's Ferry, 210, 220
Wright, James, 226, 298
Wright, John, 186
Wright, Major, 229
Wright's Plantation, 226
Wright's Bluff, 91, 93, 95
Wylie, James, 13
Wylly, Alexander, 223
Wyly (Wiley, Wylie Wylley or Wyllie), Samuel, 46
Wyly, John, 46

Yamasee, 220
Yamassee County, 227
Yankee Doodle Dandy, 13
Yarborough, Lewis, 12
Yauhannah Bridge, 114
Yemassee Bluff, 221
Yemassee, 206, 220, 221, 227, 241
York, 65
York County, 15, 27, 28, 64–66, 79, 298
York District, 19, 35
Yorktown, Virginia, 163, 164, 173, 183, 208, 231, 245
Young, Thomas, 18–20, 76, 97, 292, 299
Young, William, 299
Young, William, Sr., 256, 285

Zion Hill Church, 285

Other titles in the
BATTLEGROUNDS OF FREEDOM series
by Norman Desmarais

Battlegrounds of Freedom: A Historical Guide to the Battlefields of the War of American Independence. 2005. This fascinating travelogue invites readers to re-enact each battle with maps and photos, well-written text, abundant notation of websites, and many other useful references. This work covers Maine to Georgia as well as western territories, listing all the major battles and many minor ones. 262 pages, 19 maps, 109 photos. Paperback. 0-9666196-7-6. $26.95.

The Guide to the American Revolutionary War in Canada and New England: Battles, Raids, and Skirmishes. 2009. Follow along as the author retraces every encounter of the Revolutionary War in Canada and New England along geographical lines. 262 pages, 8 maps, 49 photos. Paperback. 978-1-934934-01-2. $21.95.

The Guide to the American Revolutionary War in New York: Battles, Raids, and Skirmishes. 2010. Follow along as the author retraces every encounter of the Revolutionary War in New York along geographical lines. 284 pages, 4 maps, 37 photos. Paperback. 978-1-934934-02-9. $22.95.

The Guide to the American Revolutionary War in New Jersey: Battles, Raids, and Skirmishes. 2011. Follow along as the author retraces every encounter of the Revolutionary War in New Jersey along geographical lines. 286 pages, 3 maps, 44 photos. Paperback. 978-1-934934-04-3. $22.95.

The Guide to the American Revolutionary War in Pennsylvania, Delaware, Maryland, Virginia, and North Carolina: Battles, Raids, and Skirmishes. 2011. Follow along as the author retraces every encounter of the Revolutionary War in Pennsylvania and several South Atlantic states along geographical lines. 356 pages, 7 maps, 62 photos. Paperback. 978-1-934934-05-0. $29.95.

All titles available at www.buscainc.com or from book vendors everywhere

CPSIA information can be obtained
at www.ICGtesting.com
Printed in the USA
BVHW081535190821
614526BV00002B/70

9 781934 934067